CHARLES I AND THE PEOPLE OF ENGLAND

David Cressy was born in England and educated at Cambridge, but built his career in the United States. He has taught at colleges and universities in California, Ohio, and New Mexico, and has won numerous fellowships and awards. His work is driven by curiosity about the relationships of central and local authority, elite and popular culture, official and unofficial religion, and ordinary men and women, a curiosity that ranges from kinship to book-burning, from cross-dressing to Gypsies. When not engaged in historical research he may be found exploring the deserts and beaches of the American West.

Praise for *Charles I and the People of England*

A *Financial Times* Book of the Year 2015

'A brilliantly evocative account of the life and times of Charles I, as seen primarily from the perspective of the millions of ordinary English men and women who lived under his rule. Drawing on an impressive array of archival and printed sources, Cressy is able to recreate the concerns and reactions of those usually hidden from history to provide a fresh perspective on the shortcomings of the Caroline regime and the origins of the English revolution.'

Tim Harris, author of *Rebellion: Britain's First Stuart Kings*

'Cressy's eye for vivid detail . . . remains undimmed . . . readable and highly engaging'

Journal of British Studies

'This is a rich account, brimming with details culled from a huge range of original sources'

Noel Malcolm, *The Daily Telegraph*

'David Cressy's lively new study . . . leaves aside the elite narrative of this troubled reign and focuses instead on the beliefs, expectations, actions, and reactions of the vast majority of the King's subjects.'

R. C. Richardson, *Times Higher Education*

'The sort of book written on the basis of a lifetime's exploration of the sources . . . it is never less than fascinating'

Church Times

'Cressy writes evocatively, giving fluent snapshots of individual reactions to particular issues or events . . . illuminating aspects of what it was like for people of various sorts to live in these turbulent times.'

Michael Braddick, *Times Literary Supplement*

'An outstanding contribution . . . Highly recommended.'

R. Fritze, *CHOICE*

CHARLES I AND THE PEOPLE OF ENGLAND

DAVID CRESSY

OXFORD
UNIVERSITY PRESS

Great Clarendon Street, Oxford, OX2 6DP,
United Kingdom

Oxford University Press is a department of the University of Oxford.
It furthers the University's objective of excellence in research, scholarship,
and education by publishing worldwide. Oxford is a registered trade mark of
Oxford University Press in the UK and in certain other countries

First published 2015
First published in paperback 2018

Impression: 1

Published in the United States of America by Oxford University Press
198 Madison Avenue, New York, NY 10016, United States of America

British Library Cataloguing in Publication Data
Data available

Library of Congress Cataloging in Publication Data
Data available

ISBN 978–0–19–870829–2 (Hbk.)
ISBN 978–0–19–870830–8 (Pbk.)

Printed in Great Britain by
Clays Ltd, St Ives plc

Contents

Preface

As always, I am beholden to the many scholars who have shaped and sustained my work. Special thanks are due to Tim Breen, Tom Cogswell, John Craig, Barbara Donagan, Lori Anne Ferrell, Chris Haigh, Tim Harris, Steve Hindle, Mark Kishlansky, Chris Kyle, John Morrill, Jason Peacey, the late Kevin Sharpe, Alison Wall, and Michelle Wolfe, though we do not always agree. Valerie Cressy saved me from myriad errors; any remaining are mine alone.

I am grateful to the National Endowment for the Humanities for a full-year fellowship in 2011, to the Huntington Library for its ambience as well as its collections, and to the Ohio State University for research support over several years. The work would have taken even longer without access to State Papers Online.

All dates are given 'old style', with the year taken to begin 1 January. All works cited were published in London unless otherwise indicated. England's monetary system made twelve pennies (abbreviated '*d.*' for *denarii*) one shilling, and twenty shillings (abbreviated '*s.*' for *solidi*) one pound (indicated '£' for *librae*). Standard abbreviations include:

APC	*Acts of the Privy Council*
BL	British Library
CSPD	*Calendar of State Papers, Domestic*
HMC	Historical Manuscripts Commission
ODNB	*Oxford Dictionary of National Biography*
TNA	The National Archives, Kew

List of Figures

Prologue

Lucy Martin's Message

Lucy Martin, the wife of a London tailor, wanted to meet the king. She wanted a private audience with Charles I to warn him of dangers facing his kingdom, and also to unburden herself of deeply troubling personal sins. Lucy Martin approached her monarch with the visionary conviction of a prophet and the ingenuity of a London housewife. She imagined herself as a dutiful subject bearing an urgent message, but she also wanted the king to serve as her confessor. She was evidently moved by notions of love and obligation, and the reciprocity of duties between the king and his people.

Not surprisingly, Lucy found King Charles to be screened and protected by layers of courtiers, councillors, and guards. She was not to know that Charles I was especially prickly about his regal dignity, nor that his style of kingship made him more than ordinarily remote. But anyone could have told her that kings did not normally commune with common subjects.

Failing to find a conventional avenue of access, Lucy Martin committed her message to paper. (She was one of the minority of metropolitan women who knew how to write, in her case with a strong but idiosyncratic script.) On Palm Sunday, 2 April 1626, she joined the crowd of citizens who were traditionally admitted to the Lenten sermons at court, and positioned herself in the public area on the terrace above the outdoor preaching place at Whitehall. Judging her moment, as the king and courtiers proceeded to their seats, she wrapped her letter around a stone and lobbed it towards King Charles. It landed in the royal pew, to much surprise and consternation.[1] Flattened out, and preserved in The National Archives, the missive (almost a missile!) reveals Lucy Martin as an unpublished female author with trouble on her mind.[2]

In her letter to King Charles, Lucy Martin prayed for God 'to look down with the eyes of mercy, pity and compassion on us all, for our sins do stink worse nor [i.e. than] Sodom and Gomorrah, city, court and country'. This put her in the tradition of moralists and reformers who railed against drunkenness and swearing, venality and irreligion. She prayed that God would 'bless our king and make him as wise as Solomon, as holy as David, for thy Christ Jesus sake, make him like that good king Joshua'. These words bore close resemblance to official prayers at Charles's coronation two months earlier, that the new king be 'armed with the fortitude of Joshua, exalted with the humility of David, [and] beautified with the wisdom of Solomon'.[3] As successors to the people of Israel, the people of England prayed for a king with the character of an Old Testament godly monarch.

Lucy's letter then took a dangerous turn by referring to King Charles's French catholic wife, Henrietta Maria. 'I pray God bless our queen and convert her to God, or confound her, that she do not bring a greater plague on us all.' It is probably just as well that these words did not reach the king, who at that time had been married less than a year. Londoners knew that the queen had not joined her husband at his recent coronation because she could not abide protestant worship, and they would know that the ceremony had been postponed to avoid the city's worst outbreak of bubonic plague in living memory. Religious leaders almost universally attributed the plague to the wrath of God, some muttering furiously about 'the sin of Achan' and divine displeasure at harbouring 'the accursed thing'. It took little effort to associate the queen and her catholic retinue with religious contamination.[4]

Lucy Martin then moved on to her personal troubles, her private moral and religious distress, and the urgency of her need for a royal audience.

> I pray God to be merciful to me for presuming to sin. I am really possessed with an ill spirit. I pray God to take it out of me, for I know I shall never be well till our good king let me speak with him. In my fall and prayer I prayed God that he would send some sign, that the rulers might believe me, and when I was at my good sister's house in Great Marlow, as I was at prayer alone, my good God did put it in my heart that I should go to the rulers. Then I cried and said, oh God, thou knowest how oft I have been with them, and they will not believe me.

It sounds as if the thrown letter was not Lucy Martin's first attempt to reach the monarch, only the most spectacular. Her claim of never being well until she spoke with the king suggests a chronic affliction that could only be remedied by royal thaumaturgy, like touching for the king's evil.[5]

The letter next turned to providential marvels that seemingly authorized Lucy's mission. God, she continued,

> did put it in my heart that I should tell you, that he sent the blazing star; and when the rulers would not believe me, God hath sent two tides in three hours; and last year when I came to the city there was the six brightest stars that ever I saw, long before the rest did appear; for as sure as our God is in heaven you must look for a greater nor ever was seen in our time. Therefore for God's sake as you tender your salvation, good king, give me leave to speak with you this sabbath; for by God's help I will not go out of the court till you throw me out; by God's help I must tell you how this great judgment may be turned away.

Blazing stars or comets were thought to be warnings of coming distress, while wondrous sightings in the waters and the sky were seen as portents and prognostications. Much of Europe took note of *three* blazing stars in 1618, the opening year of the Thirty Years War, and another apparent comet had been sighted in 1625. *A New Almanacke or Prognostication* for 1626 observed that seven years had passed 'since the great blazing star'.[6] By associating herself with prodigious phenomena—astral, fluvial, or meteorological—Lucy Martin claimed membership in a venerable prophetic tradition. She emerges as a humble and obscure counterpart to the celebrated Dame Eleanor Davies ('never soe mad a ladie') whose prophetic writings and utterances berated the Caroline court.[7]

She ended her remarkable letter with enigmatic words of confession, referring to her personal 'fall' and her subsequent pursuit of mystical and medical relief.

> In Wood Street at the sign of the Mermaid was my fall, and now hath been these many years the sign of the Rose and Crown, and I have sealed it for North East and South West and for myself with six ounces at one time of my own blood let from my heart. I hope God will behold me Christ's righteousness and holiness. By me your obedient true servant till death, Lucy Martin.

These were opaque and troubling remarks, that would be elaborated in subsequent examinations.

Rather than securing a private meeting with the king of England, Lucy Martin's message brought her only trouble. She was immediately surrounded by guards and taken for questioning. Her audacious and heart-wrenching text brought her not an audience with King Charles but two weeks of confinement and examination before Sir Thomas Wilson and bishop Richard Neile of Durham, both senior justices of the peace.[8]

Under examination, Lucy Martin acknowledged that she wrote the letter 'all of her own hand, and of her own inditing'. 'Being asked whether . . . she did ever show this paper to anybody before she showed it to the king, or acquainted anybody with the contents thereof, she answered no.' She had no accomplice, no co-conspirator, no conniving counsellor or husband directing her outrage. Officials could be relieved that Lucy Martin was no plotter or assassin, though she had evidently committed sedition. By delivering her letter in so unorthodox a manner she had in effect published it and was therefore liable for the consequences. Shown the scandalous sentences about the queen, 'she confesseth that she did both indite and write those words; which she now acknowledgeth she did for want of wit and grace, and is heartily sorry for it, and asketh God, the king, and the queen forgiveness'.

Naturally enough, the examiners asked Lucy Martin 'what that great message is, or what that great business is that she hath to deliver to the king'. Her answer suggests a wavering of purpose, or at least some disjuncture between the national mission of a prophetess and the personal needs of a deeply disturbed woman. Rather than revealing her message, which remained secret, she spoke of her own moral torment. She told the magistrates that she aimed

> to procure her one of the guard to go with her to the places in Wood Street at the sign of the Mermaid, and in the Old Bailey, and in Westminster, where some years past she played the harlot with one Henry Merry, then a yeoman of the guard to Queen Elizabeth, that in those places she might ask God forgiveness for those sins.

Protestant England had long since abolished the sacrament of confession, but Lucy Martin seems to have yearned for its psychic consolation. The sins she wanted to confess to the king stretched back a quarter of a century or more. (Henry Merry remains unidentified, but an Edward Merry was involved in victualling and supply for Elizabeth I, and Sir Thomas Merry became clerk controller of the household under James I.)

Asked to elucidate her reference to sealing north-east and south-west, and about the blood from her heart vein,

> she saith she did miswrite it, for she meant north and east and south and west, for she did five several times cause herself to be let blood (as she thought at the heart vein) with Dr Wilson's advice, and at five several times in several years she carried her said blood in a pot to the sign of the now Rose and Crown in Wood Street which formerly had been the Mermaid, and casting her said blood at the said sign cried... woe be to the time that I went into the doors of this house, where first I committed that folly with Merry.

The ritual libation of specially gathered blood at key places in cardinal directions hints at semi-magical practices designed to cure illness, counteract evil, or offset error. Perhaps the scattering of bodily fluid, painfully obtained, would extinguish the stain of bodily sin. It is extremely rare to hear this related in the first person. Dr Wilson remains unidentified, but an orthodox pastor would have counselled faith in the blood of Christ, rather than a sanguinary pilgrimage around the inns of London.[9]

Anxious, as were many in Charles I's England, about the fate of protestantism and the loss of God's favour, Lucy Martin exhibited a muddle of national, personal, and particular concerns. Several decades had passed since she 'played the harlot' with yeoman Merry, but London, the court, and her own heart seemed still to be stained with sin. Her private remorse for errors of the flesh was amplified by anxiety about the sins of the kingdom, especially its toleration of a practising catholic queen.

A Privy Council warrant dated 15 April 1626 completes Lucy Martin's story, or at least relates the end of this particular episode. The government evidently decided that she posed no threat to state security, and was only a minor offender against royal and patriarchal authority. Women, of course, were supposed to be silent, chaste, and obedient, and Lucy was none of these. Commoners, men or women, had no business with state affairs, since *arcana imperii* were the preserve of princes, yet she ostentatiously violated this taboo. For writing and presenting to the king 'many foolish and idle lines, some of them being scandalous against the queen's majesty', Lucy Martin was sentenced to be 'well corrected with the whip' at Bridewell (the prison for vagrants, prostitutes, and petty offenders), and then set at liberty. Accordingly four days later she was punished at Bridewell 'according to the warrant', with the same shameful lashes that were inflicted on bawds and whores. She was then delivered back to her husband, the tailor John Martin, about whom we know nothing.[10] Lucy Martin apparently returned to her artisan home humiliated, her writing unrewarded, her mission unfulfilled, her demons unassuaged, and her matronly reputation severely damaged.

Thereafter she disappears from the record. The outdoor Preaching Place at Whitehall, the scene of Lucy Martin's attempt to share her message, soon fell into disuse as court culture changed, and by 1638 had been replaced by a masquing house.

Lucy Martin's story, like many told in this book, does not appear in conventional histories. She is invisible, not only in studies of early Stuart politics, but also in works on women and religion. Yet the episode deserves attention, not just as an arresting anecdote but as a point of entry for exploring the social and religious complexities of the early Stuart era. Lucy Martin was one of more than four million English commoners, the often-ignored subjects of Charles I. Her concerns connected such topics as health and anxiety, sexual transgression and guilt, obedience and outspokenness, the topography of the court and the city, and the dynastic and religious affairs of the kingdom. Her role in the Eastertide events of 1626 illuminates relationships between the crown and the subject, the powerful and lowly, insiders and outsiders, men and women. It invites close analysis of political, religious, cultural, epidemiological, urban, and gendered contexts in the reign of Charles I. It sets the stage for *Charles I and the People of England*.

Introduction

The reign of Charles I, as everybody knows, ended in turmoil, regicide, and revolution. From his accession in 1625 to his execution in 1649, Charles Stuart clung to a vision of sacred kingship, in which subjects owed their monarch obedience, service, and love. How the people regarded their king, and how they performed their duty, have less often been explored. This book examines the personality, politics, and problems of a flawed and complex king in counterpoint with the lives of his subjects. It attends to the religious aspirations and political expectations of a wide variety of men and women as they went about their everyday affairs. Presenting a fresh approach to the tortured relationship between King Charles and his people, and a richer picture of a troubled age, this book has elements of a social history of early Stuart kingship, a political history of popular culture, and a cultural history of English politics in the second quarter of the seventeenth century. Though Charles was also king of Scotland and Ireland, this book deals primarily with England, the most populous and prosperous of the Stuart realms.

The standard story dwells on kings and queens, courtiers and councillors, members of parliament and the elite groups they represented.[1] A number of studies probe beyond the circles of royalty, nobility, gentry, and the university-trained clergy, though rarely to the lower reaches of the social order.[2] The privileged and powerful elite (never more than 1 or 2 per cent of the population) controlled most of the nation's wealth, conducted most of its political and cultural business, and generated most of its documentation. Historians have dubbed them 'the political nation' or 'the people who count', and many of them feature here. But the concerns of ordinary men and women, though obscured, are neither irrelevant nor irretrievable. Even the powerless had opinions. The apparatus of the state extended outwards to parishes and corporations, engaging relatively humble people as constables, officers, wardens, or jurors. Abundant evidence survives in the records of legal processes, ecclesiastical courts, parish administration, correspondence, and the popular press to give commoners of all sorts their voice.

An Incomplete Narrative

The familiar narrative of Charles I's reign can be told in a few paragraphs. Born in Scotland in 1600, but raised at court in England under the shadow of his dashing elder brother, Charles Stuart became heir to three thrones when Henry, Prince of Wales, died in 1612. In 1623, accompanied by his father's favourite, the Duke of Buckingham, Prince Charles undertook a perilous journey to Madrid to woo the Spanish catholic Infanta, but returned home spurned and angry and ready for war. Succeeding as king in March 1625, Charles took the French catholic Henrietta Maria as his queen. Charles maintained Buckingham in power, despite opposition in parliament, and compounded the conflict with Spain by opening hostilities with France. The years 1625 to 1629 were occupied with war, with paying for war, and with the politics of finance and the constitution. Parliamentary opposition to the 'forced loan', the billeting of troops, and the power of the Duke of Buckingham culminated in the Petition of Right, a guarantee of liberties that Charles reluctantly approved. The assassination of Buckingham in August 1628 left Charles bereft of his closest advisor.

The opening years of Charles's reign saw a tilt in ecclesiastical policy in favour of the 'high church', 'ceremonialist', or 'Arminian' faction. These were churchmen who rejected the Calvinist doctrine of predestination, and whose practice celebrated ceremony and 'the beauty of holiness'. Central to this tendency, and most rewarded by the king, was William Laud, who rose from bishop of St David's to become a royal councillor, bishop of Bath and Wells, bishop of London, and, as soon as the vacancy occurred in 1633, archbishop of Canterbury. Charles and Laud in tandem instituted a policy of liturgical order and episcopal discipline, requiring strict adherence to the canons and the Book of Common Prayer. Sparks flew with the imposition of the king's Book of Sports in 1633, permitting festive recreation on the Sabbath, and with the programme in the 1630s to relocate communion tables as railed east-set altars at which communicants were required to kneel. Puritans who wanted further reformation of the church to remove 'popish' elements were forced on the defensive, and some despaired that protestantism was in peril.

When parliament ended in dissension in 1629, Charles determined to rule without it, exercising his prerogative powers. No parliament sat from 1629 to 1640, in which time the king raised funds by various expedients, most notoriously the extension and exploitation of Ship Money, a levy on property intended for naval and coastal defence. Ship Money yielded substantial revenue from 1635 to 1639, but provoked complaints that it was an illegal form of taxation. A closely watched and closely determined lawsuit in 1637 found in favour of the king, but left many payers seething with resentment.

Charles kept his kingdoms out of European wars throughout the 1630s, at a time of savage conflict on the Continent, and presided over a harmonious and cultivated court. Henrietta Maria bore him heirs and offspring, including Charles in 1630, Mary in 1631, and James in 1633. These were 'halycon days' for the king's supporters, rich with patronage, preferments, and prosperity. Disruption followed the ill-advised imposition of a ceremonialist prayer book on Scotland and the revolt of Scottish covenanters against policies emanating from London. Military campaigns to quell the Scottish revolt stretched royal finances and led to the recall of a short-lived parliament from April to May 1640. Military failure that year, when a Scottish army occupied north-east England, necessitated another parliament in November, this one determined on reform that became revolution.

Almost bankrupt and friendless, King Charles sacrificed his deputy in Ireland, the Earl of Strafford, allowed Archbishop Laud to be imprisoned, and watched his prerogative authority unravel. Parliament reversed the financial and religious policies of the 1630s, and punished their principal proponents. The king's attempt to seize the initiative backfired, amid fears that he favoured Roman Catholicism and arbitrary rule. The crisis escalated when Charles and his family fled London in January 1642, and further intensified when the king was denied entry to his fortress and garrison at Hull. Positions hardened in the spring and summer of 1642, assisted by unprecedented outpourings of the newly liberated press. A Catholic uprising in Ireland prompted parliament to claim control of the armed forces, and the king responded to their Militia Ordinance with his own attempt to raise troops, the feudal Commission of Array. Civil war lasted from 1642 to 1646, with another outbreak in 1648, both ending in defeat for the king. Parliament's control of London and most ports, and its alliance with Presbyterian

Scotland, proved stronger than the king's claims to legitimacy. Failure to break the post-war impasse, when the king would not yield his powers, led to a purge of parliament and the king's trial for treason. His execution in January 1649 brought his reign to an end, but initiated his afterlife as a royal martyr.

What's Missing?

Missing from this is consideration of the more than four million people, the king's English subjects, who had lives to live in the second quarter of the seventeenth century. Their views of the crown, their relationship to power, have had little sustained attention. The king's people, from the highest to the lowest, had a stake in the kingdom, a role in the commonwealth, and stories, aspirations, and activities worth recording. The state encountered them as worshippers and parishioners, petitioners and projectors, taxpayers, impressed men, cannon-fodder, and followers of public affairs. They also led gendered lives in families and communities that only occasionally entered history.

Missing too is appreciation of the material and meteorological conditions of early Stuart England, as the kingdom weathered the strains of economic distress and global cooling. The most acute discomforts of Europe's 'little ice age' coincided with the reign of Charles I, and the consequences of this deserve consideration. The narrative is incomplete without reference to social and economic inequalities and the fortunes of agriculture and industry. American colonies opened for settlement in the reign of Charles I, and a small proportion of his people became emigrants and settlers. Trade, piracy, adventure, and the imagination linked the people of England to an ever-widening world.

Political historians have exposed the intrigues of Whitehall and Westminster, but rarely look beyond the governing elite. Social historians have written with sophistication on the 'mutualities and obligations' governing early modern society, including parishioners and local office-holders, but their analysis does not normally extend to the crown. Skilled archival research has exposed webs of neighbourhood and kinship, and the stresses of community, parochial, and domestic affairs, but the strains of loyalty and subjecthood have yet to be examined. This book ventures a wider-ranging account of the life and times of Charles I and his people. Attuned to fresh voices and rooted in original research, it illuminates the lives of the monarch, his subjects, and their complex interactions. *Charles I and the People of England* tells an old story with fresh material, and reconnects the social, political, cultural, and religious histories of the early Stuart era. This is a populated history, rich in stories, incidents, and expressions. The chapters are organized as follows.

Chapter 1. The Commonwealth of England

This chapter surveys the social, material, and cultural landscapes of early Stuart England. It contrasts the complacency of elite political culture, which saw Caroline England as ancient, settled, and secure, a land of law and peace, blessed by God, the happiest state with the best of all monarchs, with the underside of poverty and dissent. Only the most apprehensive observers would see cracks in the edifice, the strains and tensions that would bring Charles I and his kingdom to ruin. The chapter includes discussion of some of these strains, especially economic disparities, social resentments, and the exclusion of voices from the national conversation. Whereas patriots championed the English people as 'free men, free-born, native subjects, natural citizens', with 'honourable parts and endowments', others derided 'the common multitude' as vulgar, fickle, ignorant, 'a many-headed monster, which hath neither head for brains, nor brains for government'. This chapter reveals the energy and agency of parts of that multitude. It also explores connections between English lives and the wider world in a period of worsening weather.

Chapter 2. The Oath of a King

This chapter reconstructs the coronation of Charles I through the eyes of contemporary observers, bishops, courtiers, gatecrashers, and the king himself, to examine the ritual performance, prayers, and promises on which the regime was based. It weighs the damage caused by postponements owing to plague, the absence of the queen, and alterations in the wording of the order of service. The oath that the young king swore in 1626 came back to haunt him in the crisis of the 1640s, when royal authority was under attack. Royalists and parliamentarians disagreed whether King Charles had broken or upheld his oath, and whether that oath obligated him to God, to the church, to parliament, or to the people.

Chapter 3. Sacred Kingship and Dutiful Subjection

This chapter uses prayers, sermons, speeches, political declarations, and King Charles's own words to examine contemporary understandings of the majesty of kingship. It reviews the roles, duties, privileges, and prerogatives of the crown, and the tensions between the theory of sacred kingship and the view that royal magistracy served the needs and safety of the people. The councillor Sir Thomas Wentworth declared that 'the authority of the king is the keystone which closeth up the arch of order and government, which containeth each part in relation to the whole, and which, once shaken, infirmed, all the frame falls together in a confused heap of foundation and battlement'. This chapter examines how that authority was constituted, and how it began to fall apart. Charles himself asserted on several occasions that 'the love of our people' was among his 'greatest riches', but he took few pains to nourish that treasure. 'The people must honour, obey, and support their king,' insisted William Laud, but not all the king's subjects fulfilled their duties with alacrity. The forced loan, Ship Money, purveyance, and the furnishing of horses for transport and saltpeter for gunpowder tested the reciprocity on which kingship was founded. The 'dangerous words' of popular sedition point to gaps between the views of England's governors and those of some of the people they governed.

Chapter 4. Unprosperous Wars

Charles I reigned amid a European war that raged for thirty years. During the first five years of his rule Charles involved England on the fringes of this war, with naval and military campaigns against both Spain and France. At the core of the war, for the English, was the problem of the Palatinate, a German territory contested between catholics and protestants, whose refugee princess was Charles's sister Elizabeth. Royal honour and the protestant cause helped drive foreign policy, and both drove popular conversation. Taking England to war required the mobilization of men and money, with considerable disturbance to everyday life. This chapter examines the social consequences of military conflict, when thousands of families were uprooted, soldiers and mariners went unpaid, and property-owners resisted the fiscal demands of the state. Wherever possible it presents the views and experiences of ordinary men and women who were caught up in military procurement, recruitment, deployment, and the billeting of troops and seamen. A short discussion reviews military readiness in the 1630s, before the fresh disruptions of the wars with Scotland.

Chapter 5. An Accessible Monarch?

Historians have variously characterized Charles I as a king who 'systematically distanced himself from his subjects' and 'arguably the most widely travelled and accessible English monarch of the early modern era'. In the hope of reconciling these opinions, this chapter examines the material and social settings of kingship, both settled and peripatetic. It plots the king's travels, and examines his interactions with his subjects during progresses and hunting trips and while based at Whitehall and other royal palaces. It reveals a king protective of his dignity and honour, exposed more to his people's gaze than to their aspirations. Access was limited to any king who lived in a bubble, but King Charles's predilections made him even more remote.

Chapter 6. Importunate Petitioners

Though petitioning the king was part of 'the birthright of an Englishman', encounters with royal power could be bruising and frustrating. King Charles himself recognized his duty to hear petitions from faithful subjects and to redress their wrongs. Courtiers, ministers, lawyers, and officials served as intermediaries, so that royal audiences with common subjects were rare. But that did not stop hundreds of petitioners each year from presenting their requests, though few with the vehemence and ingenuity of Lucy Martin. The hopes, fears, desires, or ambitions of petitioners hinged on the willingness of the king to hear them. Among them were Henry Butts, the vice-chancellor of Cambridge, who waited weeks on the fringes of the court to present a university petition and got as far as being allowed to kiss the king's hand; John Spencer, a melancholic puritan, who tried several times to address King Charles on the sanctity of the Sabbath and the service book for Scotland,

and who was held overnight in prison for his troubles; and the townsmen of Norwich who sought 'to present their petition unto his majesty in the behalf of some irregular ministers who would be counted conformable', thereby causing 'a great combustion'. Examples of disorderly or importunate petitioning expose the urgency some subjects felt, and the difficulties they encountered when trying to approach the king to open his eyes.

Chapter 7. The King's Religion and the People's Church

Ecclesiastical law obliged parishioners throughout England to pray for their king, who was Supreme Governor of the sole established national church. The king's coat of arms hung in chancels, and clerics reminded congregations of their duties to the monarch. Preachers urged everyone to 'Fear God, Honour the King', but some feared that King Charles was in thrall to 'popery'. Charles I was in fact an avowed protestant, but some people doubted the robustness of his commitment to the Reformation. Married to a catholic, in a court notorious for conversions to Rome, Charles promoted a ceremonialist anti-Calvinist version of protestantism, which favoured episcopal discipline, 'the beauty of holiness', and the reconfiguration of services around communion tables railed as east-set altars. Puritans, for whom the Reformation was not yet complete, reacted defensively and in some cases moved towards separatism. Relating parish disputes to government policy, and exposing the frustrations of conformity and the drama of dissent, this chapter examines the cultural politics of religion from the 1620s to the 1640s. It introduces scores of parishioners whose devotional practice caused problems, as well as some who were profanely indifferent. Court records connect the circumstances, words, beliefs, and actions of previously unrecognized layfolk with the policies and preferences of the Caroline regime.

Chapter 8. The King's Declaration and the People's Sports

Following the example of James I, but without the pragmatism or finesse of that monarch, King Charles issued his 'Declaration of Lawful Sports' in

1633. It was done, he said, 'for the service of God, and for suppressing of any humours that oppose truth, and for the ease, comfort, and recreation of our well-deserving people'. But instead of promoting harmony it led to bitter, polarizing, and unnecessary division. The Declaration authorized 'honest recreations' such as dancing and athletics, and allowed parishioners to engage in them on Sundays after church. It sided with proponents of a 'merry England' who valued 'good fellowship' and traditional festive sports. It clashed, however, with devout protestant views on the sanctity of the Sabbath. Opponents argued that the king's Declaration encouraged sinners in their 'wicked and evil courses', and exposed the people of England to God's 'avenging justice, both general, national, and personal'. Ministers who refused to read the Declaration faced suspension, and parishioners argued whether 'ringing a peal or two, dancing, playing at football, barley-break, and other recreations on the Sunday' were more pleasing to God than the devil. This chapter examines the cultural wars of the 1630s that pitted royal authority against godly conscience and politicized the practices of popular recreation.

Chapter 9. Sacred Kingship Eclipsed

The Scottish crisis that began in 1637, and the resulting wars with the Covenanters, brought Caroline England to ruin. It led to the revolution of 1640–2, in which royal authority foundered, press censorship ended, the church split apart, and parliament dismantled the royal prerogative. The civil wars that followed saw a massive mobilization of energies on all sides. In-fighting among the victors, a purge of parliament, and a contentious radical Leveller movement shaped the environment for the trial and execution of Charles I in January 1649. Beginning with the Scottish crisis and its aftermath, this chapter shows how contending sides appealed for popular support, how men and women articulated their allegiance, and how revolutionary events altered relationships to the state, the commonwealth, and the monarch. Linking demotic voices with constitutional theory, it reviews reassertions of divine-right kingship alongside theories that set the people in parity with the king, or even above him. It traces the leap of imagination and emotion that allowed 'his sacred majesty' to be executed in the name of 'the people of England'.

Chapter 10. The Blindness of Charles I

Contemporaries voiced competing opinions of the character, competence, and kingship of Charles I. Though supporters championed him as 'the best of all monarchs', frustrated subjects charged him with deficiencies, even rating him as metaphorically blind. This chapter reviews assessments of Charles I, with further consideration of the consequences of his rule.

I

The Commonwealth of England

Elite political culture saw Caroline England as ancient, settled, and secure, a land of peace and order blessed by God, the happiest of states with the best of all monarchs. Officially, at least, the king's loving subjects knew their place and knew their duty, protected by the crown, the gospel, and the law. Only the most apprehensive observers would see cracks in the edifice, the strains and tensions that would bring Charles I and his kingdoms to ruin. The royal and clerical establishments cherished harmony and consensus, and upheld values of order, uniformity, and discipline. The crown and the church embraced the community of the realm, but strains exposed the limits of state power. Economic disparities exacerbated social inequities, and untrammelled discourse generated competing visions of the commonwealth. Religious disagreements undermined the godly order and heightened stresses within the Church of England. Deference to rank and authority sometimes eroded in the face of local social and political pressures.

The following survey of the social landscape sets the scene for later discussions of kingship, governance, subjecthood, and religion. It shows how some of the contemporaries of Charles I experienced their environment, and how they handled their obligations. The social topography was more variegated than is often imagined, and the shadows were darker than expected. Cultural stresses did not necessarily lead to fractures, but they exposed fragilities within the fabric of the realm. Ideally, the king and his people went 'orderly and cheerfully . . . together . . . the hearts of each drawing nearer to other, and all to God',[1] but social and political experience strained these reciprocities.

At the time of his accession King Charles ruled some four and three-quarter million subjects in England and Wales and perhaps two million more in Scotland and Ireland.[2] His royal authority encompassed 'all in Great Britain, even from Dan to Beersheba, from Berwick to Dover, from Edinburgh to the utmost Orkneys', and from coast to coast in Ireland. It also extended to recently claimed territory in America.[3] The king's subjects were male and female, clerical and lay, devout and profane, according to gendered, professional, and religious criteria. The people of England included rich and poor, young and old, hale and halt, and could be divided between nobles and commoners, town dwellers and countryfolk, subsidy-payers and the tax-exempt, the rulers and the ruled. Binary classifications like these are easy to apply, but they mask a host of variables and complications with moral and material shadings. The king and his advisors frequently differentiated his majesty's 'well-affected subjects' from 'factious and refractory spirits', distinguishing the 'better sort' from the 'worser sort' of people. Commentators appealed to 'persons of quality' against 'the meaner sort' of the 'rude' and 'vulgar' multitude. The social spectrum ranged from court nobility to the vagrant poor, including cantankerous commoners who proclaimed themselves 'as good a man as any'.

England was also affected by developments beyond its bounds, in the rest of the British Isles, across the Channel, across the Atlantic, and around the world. Commercial expansion brought wealth to leading sectors, but the vicissitudes of the global economy also created slumps and misery. Contemporaries knew that their land was periodically stricken by plague and other diseases, but they did not know that their climate was changing, or that they lived through some of the coldest and stormiest episodes of 'the little ice age'. The challenges of the social environment form the principal themes of this chapter.

A Blessèd Realm

A profound sense of satisfaction moved many of King Charles's leading subjects. They catalogued their privileges and benefits, even as some seemed to be slipping away. 'What nation under heaven hath not envied and wondered at our blessings?' asked Joseph Hall in a sermon before the king in 1626, citing 'our long peace, our full plenty, our wholesome laws, our easeful government, with a world of these common favours'.[4] One imagines the king and courtiers nodding comfortably in agreement.

Views like these abounded in the period of the personal rule, when writers and preachers saw their age as a golden era. Writing in 1630 Richard Brathwaite celebrated 'this flourishing land... whose halcyon days have attained the prerogative of peace, which most parts of Christendom are at this day deprived of'.[5] (The halcyon was the mythical bird of classical antiquity that flourished in conditions of tranquillity and peace.) Viscount Dorchester reported from London that year that 'here all is quiet in the accustomed manner of a well-ordered government under a prudent, just and religious prince'.[6] Bishop William Laud declared before the king in 1631 that 'there is no nation under heaven so happy, if it did but know and understand its own happiness'.[7]

It became a nostrum of sermons, speeches, and letters that England enjoyed special providential favours. Preaching at the Northamptonshire assizes in 1635, Edward Reynolds celebrated 'that long uninterrupted and most blessed tranquillity which these our kingdoms have, to the envy and astonishment of other nations, long enjoyed'.[8] The country was blessed with 'a rich commonwealth, a rich people', the London writer George Garrard reminded Lord Wentworth, and remarked on 'God's infinite mercy to our nation'.[9] The courtier George Goring took comfort in 'the wisdom of the whole body who live so happily and plentifully under this gracious happy government'.[10] Another correspondent wrote approvingly of England's 'calmness', where 'all business goes undisturbedly on'.[11] It became a commonplace of national self-congratulation that, 'amidst the distraction of foreign nations, we only have sat under the shadow of our vines, and drank the wines of our own vintage', as if Charles I governed the land of Canaan rather than a rainy British archipelago.[12] Courtiers, clerics and poets commended not just the international peace that distinguished England from its war-torn neighbours, but also the harmony and order of its social fabric and the godliness of its church and king. The poet Thomas Carew was one of many to reflect on England's 'halcyon days'.[13]

These views persisted into the crisis of the 1640s, but were beginning to be tinged with nostalgia. 'Never did this or any nation enjoy more blessings and happiness than hath been by all his majesty's subjects enjoyed ever since his majesty's access to the crown, nor did this kingdom ever so flourish in trade and commerce as at this present, or partake of more peace and plenty in all kinds whatsoever,' boasted Lord Keeper Sir John Finch in May 1640.[14] King Charles governed 'so flourishing a kingdom, of which the whole world grew jealous daily', Sir Thomas Peyton reminded Henry Oxinden.[15]

Dozens of leaders of both church and state spoke similarly, mentally deflecting the kingdom's mounting problems. The author of *Englands Doxologie* reminded readers in 1641 that 'there is no nation under heaven that hath received more temporal and spiritual favours from almighty God than this kingdom of England . . . We have fullness in our granaries, peace within our walls, and plenty within our palaces . . . And for spiritual mercies, no people under the sun ever went before us.'[16] 'Never hath any kingdom or country been blessed with so flourishing an estate, and such a blessed condition,' declared the bishop of Durham Thomas Morton, as civil war threatened in 1642: 'If ever any state hath enjoyed peace, security and liberty, it hath been that of England,' with its king and church committed to 'uniformity, sincerity and truth'.[17]

The memory of the 1630s as a period of tranquillity and comfort grew even rosier in the later years of civil war and revolution. The royalist Edward Symmons recalled those halcyon days of Charles I,

> wherein the church and faith of Christ did flourish in such high lustre and glory, wherein the subjects of this kingdom, of all ranks and degrees, did more abound in wealth and riches . . . Was there ever so much feasting and plenty of food among all sorts of people? So many good garments and clothes worn by men and women of all degrees? . . . Were ever the protestant subjects of the kingdom more frequently taught, or better fed? Did they ever in any nation under the sun enjoy more peace and happiness than they did all the time of his reign, until this unhappy parliament turned all things upside down?[18]

Aristocrats and Gentlemen

Early Stuart England inherited an antique social topography, with categories and concepts honed in an earlier era. The Tudor formulations of Sir Thomas Smith, archaic even in their own time, still shaped understanding of the social order. The *nobilitas major* of titled aristocrats held sway above the *nobilitas minor* of knights, esquires, and gentlemen. Yeomen, citizens, and burgesses formed a middling group with property and money intermixed. Below them, in massed but muddled ranks, stood the 'fourth sort or class' of artificers and shopkeepers, husbandmen and labourers, dismissively referred to as 'rascals' of mean account who did not rule. 'The rascability of the popular' were of little interest to contemporary social analysts, although their labour formed the backbone of the kingdom's wealth.[19]

The early Stuart economy was more vigorous and more varied than customary classifications admitted. Growing occupational diversity and an expanding urban population made England's social structure more dynamic and more complex than ever. Addressing this development, without fully grasping its measure, the educational theorist John Dury counted 'three sorts of people' in Caroline England. The nobles and gentlemen at the top of society were distinguished by their 'largeness of possessions', and naturally enjoyed 'a preeminence in honour above others of the vulgar sort'. These men constituted the governing elite, who were especially suited for 'public charges in peace and war'. Next in rank came men of Dury's own class, 'the learned for increase of science and training up of others', who might loosely be identified with the professions. Third, with fewer gifts and advantages, though no less value to the commonwealth, came 'the vulgar, for trades and servile work'.[20] This was a functional division between governors, ministers, and workers, which was no more sophisticated than the threefold medieval classification of those who fight (the feudal aristocracy), those who pray (the clergy), and those who work (the peasantry and everyone else).

The *nobilitas major* comprised just 122 English peers in 1633, though Caroline creations made their numbers higher than under Queen Elizabeth or King James. Another 300 men had courtesy titles as sons of nobles, baronets, or members of the Scottish or Irish peerage. Ninety-six lay peers of the realm sat by right in parliament in 1625, a number that grew to 124 by November 1640. These were the men King Charles cultivated, as courtiers, office-holders, and honourable companions. It was to these great lords that the king turned in September 1640 when he summoned a baronial assembly at York. The landed income of the titled nobility ranged from £1,500 to £6,000 a year, though heavy expenses and encumbrances drove some of them into debt.[21]

Aristocratic rank accorded social precedence and courtly privileges, and the prestige and influence of this elite fraction grew under Charles I. No person below the degree of baron was allowed to enter the king's quarters at court unless he was a member of the Privy Council, a Gentleman of the Bedchamber, or a servant.[22] Titled aristocrats dominated the Council, joined by rising gentlemen ennobled for their service. Privy Council registers between May 1629 and May 1630 reveal the attendance of sixteen earls, eight viscounts, and four other lords, as well as seven knights and three bishops.[23] Only twelve of these Councillors were born to the nobility,

Figure 1. King Charles and the Lords in Parliament, 1628. *The Manner of the sitting of the Lords spirituall and temporall, as peeres of the realme in the higher house of Parliament* (1628), broadsheet.

the rest rising through government employment as officers and clients of the king.

Principles of hierarchy and patriarchy still governed the social order, and the elite demanded deference from inferiors; but myriad social encounters agitated this antiquated system. The unspoken rules of dominance and subordination were subject to disturbance and negotiation.[24] Social sway flowed normally from rank and position, land and money, but was also mediated by lines of patronage, reputation, and personal prestige. Distinctions of title, name, and status coincided only roughly with distributions of wealth and power. A lord could have less cash in hand than a knight, and a gentleman, a mere 'Mr' with good investments, could command greater resources than some of his aristocratic superiors. Some rich gentlemen preferred not to accept the knighthoods to which their wealth entitled them, and 'fines for distraint of knighthood'—incurred when landowners worth £40 a year failed to secure knighthoods at King Charles's coronation—became a festering grievance. Over 9,000 esquires and gentlemen paid fines to escape that honour, bringing the crown a revenue exceeding a parliamentary subsidy.[25] Socially ambitious gentlemen, on the other hand, sought aristocratic titles—promotion to the baronage and above—as marks of esteem and favour. A revived Court of Chivalry in the 1630s allowed noblemen and gentlemen to parade their birth and lineage, and to protect their honour from slights. 'The privileges of generous blood are more to be cared for than heretofore, since his majesty has appointed the Lord Marshall to keep his court, and judiciously to punish such as offer injury to gentlemen in any kind,' explained the ever-busy heralds in August 1634.[26]

The gentry and their noble superiors fill the pages of cultural and political history, just as they dominated the high culture and politics of their times. County grandees, sheriffs, justices, and most members of parliament were drawn from these gilded ranks. Ordinary commoners knew them as landlords, magistrates, and powerfully privileged neighbours. The gentry and aristocracy socialized with each other, inter-married, quarrelled, and competed for influence and reward. These were 'the people who count', in conservative views of the Caroline polity,[27] though attempts to enumerate them pose problems. It is hard to gauge reliable numbers, but there cannot have been more than a few thousand significant families among a gentry total of less than 25,000. One plausible estimate for the early 1630s suggests as many as 1,500 to 1,800 knights, with an annual average income around £800; 7,000 to 9,000 esquires, on roughly £500 a year; and 10,000 to 14,000 mere gentlemen, with landed income averaging £150. Even the most generous estimate pegs the gentry and their superiors at less than 2 per cent of the English population.[28] Much of the social history of the early modern era can be read as a struggle by this class to maintain their status against others who would undermine them, either from above or from below.

Classic Elizabethan theory identified gentlemen by their breeding, demeanour, and landed wealth, and above all by their freedom from having to work. A gentleman, one contemporary explained, 'hath a fortune to maintain himself... without the assistance of an art or occupation'.[29] Leisured independence, sustained by rent or fortune, allowed a gentleman to devote himself to honourable activity and service. The leaders of Caroline society took pride in their gentility as 'men of place and power', distinct from 'the vulgar common sort of men'.[30] Income from rent had been rising for several decades by the 1630s, thereby further enriching the landed class ahead of the rise in prices.[31] Younger sons, however, barred from inheritance, could be downwardly mobile unless they turned their advantages in fresh directions.

A gentleman was expected to be educated, perhaps as far as the university and the Inns of Court, though he did not necessarily emerge with a degree. He would learn a modicum of history, letters, and law, flavoured with Latin classics, and would know how to carry himself with probity and restraint. An English gentleman was supposed to be a paragon of virtue and moderation, able to speak his mind 'in a smooth and graceful manner',[32] although these qualifications were not formally tested. His social rank would make him eligible for military command. Reports of military operations (written, of course, by fellow officers) distinguished the bravery of 'our gentry' from the cowardice and dishonour of 'common soldiers', even when their leadership was wanting.[33] On public occasions a gentleman commonly carried a sword, as much a fashion accessory and mark of status as a weapon.[34] It would raise suspicion if servants, artisans, or common labourers were seen with swords, and justices of the peace (gentlemen, of course) could arrest them and take away their blades.[35] A basic sword cost 7*s.* 6*d.* in 1638, and 2*s.* more for a girdle and hanger, though a gentleman might pay many times that amount for engraving and decoration.[36]

A gentleman was expected to look the part, dressed to display his rank. Socially ambitious gentlemen paid expensive attention to their appearance, wearing clothes that announced their position in society. This was why Sir John Coke spent over £39 on tailoring in 1625, including £3 8*s.* 1*d.* for a satin suit with hanging sleeves.[37] Surviving accounts show John Moreton, the feckless son of a Cheshire squire, owing £4 19*s.* 11*d.* in 1633 for a tailored suit and cloak.[38] The young Paul Bayning, son of a viscount, spent even more lavishly while ostensibly studying at Oxford. Like many fellow-commoners, he spent more on shoes and gloves than on books. Bayning's tailors' bill in September 1633 was over £6, in November £23, and £48 the following March. Going a-courting in 1634, he arrayed himself with £23 worth of gold and silver buttons and almost £13 worth of silk.[39]

A gentleman's hat could be his crowning glory, its band and dressing a sign of breeding and taste. John Willoughby at Oxford paid 12*s.* for a hat and another 8*d.* for dressing it in 1630.[40] Paul Bayning spent 15s. in 1633 on facing his hat with satin.[41] Expenditures of several shillings for accessorizing a hat were not uncommon,[42] though few matched the extravagance of the Earl of Salisbury, whose new black beaver in 1630 cost £2 18s.[43] Commoners were supposed to doff their own hats to these worthy peacocks.

Gentle followers of the court could only be amazed by the extravagant display of the high aristocracy.[44] In 1625 the Duke of Buckingham sported clothes as 'rich as invention can frame', including a suit of purple satin, embroidered with orient pearls, 'the value whereof will be twenty thousand pounds'. It could be argued that these were professionally appropriate accoutrements for someone so essential to the state.[45] The king himself was displayed like a potentate, spending £9,884 16*s.* 6*d.* on robes between Lady Day and Michaelmas 1627, more than £2,300 over the budgeted allowance. His purchases included more than 500 pairs of shoes.[46] On one occasion that summer, noted William Laud, 'the king lost a jewel in hunting of £1000 value'.[47] Aristocratic followers ran up debts to keep pace, like Lord Dungarvon, the son of the Earl of Cork, who spent £700 on clothes and £270 on jewels while making an impression at court in 1635.[48]

These sums can be put in perspective by noting that a servant could be fully attired for 6*s.* 8*d.*,[49] a soldier outfitted with cassock, shirt, shoes, hose, stockings, and cap for 4*s.*[50] Cheap 'clouted shoes and russet coat' defined a working countryman.[51] When the tanner John Clements died at Bristol in the 1630s, with an inventoried wealth of just £55, he had only one pound's worth of wearing apparel. The butcher Richard Maskal died worth £3 17*s.* 4*d.*, with ten shillings worth of clothing. The total probate valuation of the card-maker John Jordan was £10 6*s.* 3*d.*, including 'all the wearing apparel of the deceased' worth just 2*s.*[52] The travelling tinker Nicholas Leigh who died in Leicestershire in 1632 had apparel worth 6*s.* 8*d.*, 'a blanket to cover him and his wife in the night time' worth 8*d.*, and not much else, though a friend kept £4 'in readiness for his relief as he should chance to have need'.[53]

Gentlemen also dined differently from the masses, with greater variety and refinement of food and drink.[54] Household accounts reveal the reckoning. A gentleman's kitchen might furnish turkeys, geese, ducklings, partridges, larks, quail and pigeon, crab and lobster, oysters, and fish of all sorts, as well as conies (rabbits), veal, pork, mutton, and beef. Those with parks or hunting privileges would enjoy roast venison, exchanging gifts of a buck or half a buck with kindred or patrons. Meals would feature a wide range of grains and staples, wheat, barley, rye, oats, rice, peas, beans, and flour for bread. A gentleman's cook would use sugar, raisins, currants, nutmeg, cloves, mace, saffron, cinnamon, and ginger to flavour food, as well as potherbs and salt. Preserved quinces and green apricots, damsons, plums, gooseberries, and cherries might be supplemented by oranges and lemons. Imported lemons circulated as gifts among some gentry families, as when Lady Elizabeth Gorges sent four lemons to her daughter, which she had received in turn from a Mrs Popley. On one occasion the kitchen at Redgrave Hall, Suffolk, took in eleven and a quarter pounds of old Dutch cheese, four pounds of Genoa capers, three pounds of Genoa anchovies, and a pottle of small olives, as though they were making pizza. To drink, besides beer, small and large, a gentleman's table might offer claret or canary wine, sack, and aqua vitae.[55] The most exotic and expensive items were reserved for special occasions, but even at routine meals a gentleman could expect to eat as well as he dressed. To spend 8*s*.–10*s*. shillings on an individual dinner while travelling was not exceptional.[56] Merchants and yeoman might aspire to these provisions, but little of this abundance appeared lower down the social scale, except at guild and borough feasts.

A workman's diet, by contrast, was hard fare, heavy with bread, beer, and cheese. Rabbit, bacon, chicken, or mutton would be added as available, with what could be grown at home or foraged nearby. An alehouse dinner of 'good and wholesome meat' for a countryman attending a muster in 1625 was supposed to cost no more than 8*d*.[57] A soldier could be fed on 4*d*. a day, a vagrant for 2*d*. or less. Military recruits in the late 1620s ate butter, biscuit, and cheese with beer, and oatmeal, rice, beef, pork, and fish if they were lucky.[58] Another glimpse of social differentials comes from London's Fleet prison, where inmates (mostly debtors) dined according to their social status; in 1638 the authorities allowed 33*s*. 4*d*. a week for a lord, 18*s*. 6*d*. for a knight, 10*s*. for a gentleman, and 5*s*. for a yeoman, while the humblest prisoners made do with scraps.[59] Detailed physiological studies are not available, but it seems likely that the gentry were taller, plumper, and generally better nourished than their social inferiors, as they were into the twentieth century.[60]

Ordinary People

'The common sort' constituted everyone below the gentry, perhaps 98 per cent of the English population. Their households were headed by merchants and tradesmen, artisans and shopkeepers, yeomen, husbandmen, labourers, and the vagrant poor. A few were wealthy, some prosperous, many comfortable, and too many struggling, marginal, or mired in poverty. Household incomes varied enormously, with some families phenomenally rich, but most got by on £10 a year or less. All were affected by rising prices

Figure 2. Diggers of England. William Lawson, *A New Orchard and Garden* (1626), title page.

and widening disparities in an economy subject to irregular stresses. All were supposed to know their place. It was a sign of restless discontent, preached John Swan, if 'labourers strive to be as good as their masters, farmers despise yeomen, yeomen would be gentlemen, artisans in our very country towns and villages would be citizens; gentlemen and citizens though of ordinary rank do not always delight to keep within the compass of their tether'.[61]

Recent research shows that gentlemen who served as witnesses before ecclesiastical courts in the reign of Charles I had an average net worth of £95. Yeomen were rising in wealth, with a mean net value of £74. The mean worth of craftsmen and tradesmen was £16 (with carpenters and clothworkers worth more than £17, and tailors and shoemakers worth less than £10). Husbandmen were generally poorer, worth on average £15. Labourers, the largest and most impoverished group of Charles I's subjects, could barely command £2.[62] These figures may be compared with cruder measures of probated wealth over the entire seventeenth century, showing gentlemen worth £329 at death, yeomen £195, husbandmen £80, and labourers £28. The cultural marker of literacy closely followed these socio-economic indicators.[63]

The professional men of the church, medicine, education, and the law were technically commoners, though often connected to the gentry by kinship, education, and service.[64] The clerical estate comprised some 12,000 men, of whom just over 9,000 served as rectors, vicars, or curates to parish congregations. There were also hundreds more private chaplains, unbeneficed clergy, place seekers, and hopeful ordinands, as well as clerics associated with Oxford and Cambridge colleges and cathedral chapters. Not surprisingly, they varied in their theological orientation, churchmanship, and moral and personal characteristics, as well as resources and income.[65] Lay people experienced them as teachers and pastors, as leaders of local communities, but also as agents of a hierarchical church and a centralized state. Rectors collected great tithes on agricultural produce, while vicars drew stipends and had some claim on minor tithes from animal husbandry. The shifting spiral of price increases favoured rectors over vicars, though most ministers augmented their incomes with fees for baptisms, weddings, funerals, and special services.

Some incumbents were comfortably wealthy, others dormouse poor. The average rectory in the West Midlands was worth £78 a year on the eve of the civil war, the average vicarage £42, but many had additional sources of income.[66] The rector of Petworth, Sussex, commanded a living worth more than £600 a year, on top of his income from fees and tithes.[67] Nicholas Andrews, the pluralist rector of Guildford who was also vicar of Godalming, Surrey, pulled in £320 a year from his livings, £100 a year from his 'temporal means', and another £60 a year as a prebendary of Salisbury. Add in fees and tithes, and Andrews easily outmatched many gentlemen with an income exceeding £500 a year.[68] The vicar of Warseley, Huntingdonshire, John Pocklington, had a benefice worth £50 a year, and allowed his curate an annual stipend of £20. But he was also rector of Yelden, Bedfordshire, and from 1637 a royal chaplain, so he too could aspire to the style of a gentleman.[69] Some ecclesiastical livings were seriously under-resourced, yielding less than £12 a year.[70]

Lawyers and doctors lived on fees, which varied with talent and demand. An income of several hundred pounds a year was not impossible, though most were comparable to the upper ranks of clergymen.[71] Schoolmasters earned as little as £10 or as much as £80 a year.[72] In 1627 the richly endowed Charterhouse paid the master of the hospital £50 a year, the schoolmaster £30, and the assistant master or usher £15, but these salaries too could be supplemented by 'allowances' for food and firing, and fees from pupils and parents.[73]

Most officials under the crown lived not on salaries but on fees and perquisites, and some grew rich in the process. Few gained places without patronage, and most had gentle, clerical, or mercantile connections. Among minor servants of the state, a footman in royal service earned £40 a year in 1632.[74] Members of the king's elite horse guards drew £50.[75] Common soldiers were allowed 8*d.* a day (perhaps £10 or £12 a year), but their pay was often in arrears. The gentleman captain of the garrison at Scilly, by contrast, earned 10*s.* a day in 1627, his lieutenant 4*s.* (equivalent to £182 10*s.* and £73 a year).[76]

Detailed figures are scarce for the middling sorts of people, so we have to rely on indirect indicators. Yeomen, 'in the temperate zone between greatness and want', might accrue £40 to £100 a year from their profits. Husbandmen, who farmed leased or rented land at a lower level, would be lucky to clear £15.[77] Yeomen who were commercial producers did very well in this era of rising prices, whereas many small farmers and husbandmen lived closer to subsistence. Cloth workers depended on national and foreign markets, and suffered cruelly when trading collapsed, as it did in 1629. Essex weavers earned from 2*s.* to 4*s.* a week in the 1630s, but nothing if the clothiers could not shift their product.[78] Wage rates generally failed to stay abreast of inflation, so that the standard of living of many artisans and craftsmen was worse in the 1630s than in previous generations.[79]

People in the bottom half of the population often relied on makeshift, with occasional or seasonal employment supplemented by payments in kind of food, drink, apparel, or accommodation. Access to a patch of ground or woodland could make the difference between subsistence and destitution. Customary rights were under pressure, pitting richer villagers against their poorer neighbours.[80] Wage labour was often piecework, paid by the job or by the yard rather than a standard sum based on time. Most workers were paid by the task, 'for carrying sand . . . for digging earth . . . for carrying loads', and so on.[81] Skilled and strong men would be principal breadwinners, but children and women augmented household budgets. An average workman's wage was in the region of 1*s.* a day, depending upon the demand for labour, the individual's skill, and the duration of the job. The skilled farm workers on Thomas Cawton's estate in Essex earned from £10 to £12 a year in the early 1630s, whereas ordinary agricultural labourers rarely brought in more than £9 a year.[82]

Figure 3. Tradesmen of London. *These Trades-men are Preachers in and about the City of London* (1647), broadsheet.

The Welsh landowner Sir John Wynn paid 'wages by day 12*d.* a piece' for men to drive his cattle in 1626.[83] The Earl of Huntingdon's steward paid 1*s.* 2*d.* 'to goodman Wilkinson for two days work digging in the orchard' in August 1638.[84] The Exeter merchant John Hayne offered 14*d.* and 16*d.* a day to experienced labourers, and 12*d.* to a boy.[85] Other accounts from the 1630s show workmen in the salt manufactures earning 2*s.* a day,[86] and a shepherd in Gloucestershire on 3*s.* a week.[87] Churchwardens' accounts preserve a multitude of disbursements for labour, including 22*d.* a day for three days' work with molten lead to 'the plumber and his man' at Salisbury in 1630.[88] At Crediton, Devon, in 1632 the churchwardens paid a workman 1*s.* 2*d.* a day to whiten the chancel.[89]

Women's wages were always substantially lower. The Yorkshire farmer Henry Best paid 8*d.* a day to men and 6*d.* a day to women for harvesting peas in 1641, but only 3*d.* for women engaged to spread manure.[90] The Bayning household paid 3*s.* 6*d.* for 'the woman in the kitchen for seven days' in 1633 and 4*s.* 8*d.* 'to a woman labourer fourteen days' (4*d.* a day) in 1634.[91] Occasional work in Sir Henry Oxinden's kitchens brought goodwife Ladd 3*s.* 6*d.* for seven days (6*d.* a day) at Christmas 1634, 2*s.* to her girl for six days to help her, and 1*s.* 6*d.* for boys to turn the spit.[92] A skilled nurse employed by a gentle household could command 44*s.* a quarter, or £8 16*s.* a year, but demand for her services would not be constant.[93]

Domestic servants and servants in husbandry were commonly hired by the year, and might enjoy other perquisites besides relative security. The Yorkshire farmer Henry Best hired servants in husbandry at varying rates from £1 6*s.* to £3 a year. One of the best paid, Robert Gibson, was 'to have £3 wages and an old hat'. William Wallis, hired in 1631, received £1 19*s.* 'and a pair of old stockings'. Their master would take care of their board and lodging.[94] Sir Humphrey Mildmay hired a servant in 1633 with 'wages' of £4 a year, but also provided a cloak and accommodation.[95] Viscount Bayning paid his horse-keeper £10 a year in 1634, a goodly amount but only a fraction of his lordship's expenditure on horses.[96] The Wiltshire patrician Sir Edward Gorges found a horseman who was 'careful and diligent' but also came cheap, 'for that he is so ragged a poor fellow, the less money will satisfy him'.[97]

Commerce required a cash economy, eased by credit, with informal transactions involving barter. It paid to be literate, as the Cheshire yeoman Richard Higginson discovered in January 1642. He complained to the quarter sessions that Edward Leadbetter owed him 27*s.*, and that he had 'notes' for the payment thereof. He was cheated of his money, so Higginson claimed, when one of Leadbetter's friends took the notes to read, 'and knowing this examinate could not read, delivered him two other papers which did neither concern this examinate nor the business'. Richard Higginson was immersed in a world of cash and paper transactions, like most yeomen who farmed for the market, but his illiteracy let him down. He belonged to that substantial third of mid-Stuart yeomen judged illiterate because they could not write their names, and he signed his testimony with a cross.[98] Illiteracy among husbandmen was much higher, perhaps 75 per cent, and among labourers 85 per cent. It varied among tradesmen and craftsmen, as might be expected, so that practitioners of clean, indoor, and profitable occupations could mostly read and write, while those in poorer, rougher, outdoor employment could not. Evidence from East Anglia, then the most dynamic of English regions, shows 10 per cent or lower illiteracy among grocers, haberdashers, and merchants, 35–45 per cent among maltsters, brewers, weavers, and glovers, and as many as 80–90 per cent of bricklayers, shepherds, and thatchers unable to write their names. Signature illiteracy was roughly 65 per cent among English men and 85 per cent among women on the eve of the civil war.[99]

An Ordered Society

To its apologists and beneficiaries the hierarchical arrangement of society appeared natural and God-given, as well as customary and convenient. The social order, like the power of kings, was an aspect of 'the powers that be' that were 'ordained of God'.[100] Hierarchy and order were abiding principles, explained the Cambridgeshire minister John Swan, for even heaven had its ranks of 'archangels, angels, principalities, powers, dominions, thrones, cherubims and seraphims', which mirrored the hierarchies of the church and state. Just as 'the body natural' was composed of 'members and ligaments, of which some are more honourable than other', so in the body politic 'the wise, the noble, the mighty, must govern the foolish, ignorant and weak, suppress the stubborn, and bridle the obstinate. For thus doth order maintain the brittle fabric of the world from ruin.' There should be no closing of the gap of comforts and conditions, for 'kings and princes must not live like peasants; neither may peasants live like princes'.[101]

It was a commonplace of Caroline preaching that authority and deference followed status and wealth. Disparity was proper and perdurable, a levelling parity absurd. Preaching before the Devon assizes in 1630, Thomas Foster denounced the notion of 'parity of persons' as 'impious, absurd, and ridiculous', as preposterous as parity of 'possessions, vocations, labours, deserts... Men of place would never abide to be ranked with basest peasants, nor these of best deserts to share alike with unworthiest drones,' for that would lead to 'an anabaptistical anarchy'.[102] The Oxford preacher John Randol likewise postulated the 'absurdity' of 'servants riding on horseback and princes walking beneath on foot'. It was too preposterous, 'a vanity for slaves to be seen above their betters'.[103] The 'affectation of parity', concurred John Swan, was one of the 'poisonsome humours of headstrong schismatics', for 'one man of judgment is better by far than a numerous multitude of the common sort'.[104]

Preaching at Canterbury in 1632, Francis Rogers explained that 'this difference of man and man is not . . . in respect of our matter, for we are all made of the same earth; but it is in regard of the use and service of men in a civil state, for parity breedeth confusion both in church and commonwealth.' Those men of birth, wealth and virtue who served the king as nobles, counsellors, and magistrates were naturally more valuable than the mass of 'base born' subjects.[105] In his sermon to the Lincoln assizes in 1637, the royal chaplain Thomas Hurste poured further scorn on the notion 'that one man should be as good as another'. To think such a thing, he declared, was to go against God, who had instituted 'the just power of one man over another'. It was 'upon the firm basis of divine institution that some should ride on horse-back, while other walk on foot', and that 'inferiors . . . owe suit, service and homage to their superiors'. People should know this instinctively, as a matter of conscience, but in case they forgot, Hurste reminded his hearers, the state had 'jailers and fetters, halters and gibbets, axes and scaffolds, fire and faggots . . . either [to] find or [to] force obedience'.[106]

The soft power of culture and indoctrination buttressed this hard apparatus of power and command. Local versions of the social hierarchy were displayed at quarter sessions and assizes, and at every church service where seats were distributed according to rank, wealth, and gender. At Puddletown, Dorset, for example, the pews were reassigned in 1635 to men and women 'according to their several ranks and degrees', from lords of the manor and 'chief parishioners' to poor 'under-tenants or cottagers'. At St Michael's, Chester, in 1639 the bishop reminded communicants to go up to the altar 'in rank according to their quality and condition, and then return to their seats', so that even the body of Christ was socially mediated.[107] Standard instructional catechisms asked, 'what is the duty of inferiors?' and answered, 'they must be subject, reverent and thankful to their superiors, bearing with their wants, and covering them with love'.[108] Social cohesion involved sanctified mutualities in which everyone knew their place.[109]

Individuals within this hierarchical framework were identified by their status or occupation (esquire, gentleman, yeoman, husbandman, blacksmith, weaver, and a hundred more descriptions and designations), but collectively they were grouped according to their moral, social, or political 'worth'. Government officials regularly differentiated 'the better sort' from 'the worser sort' of subject. They reserved approbation for people who cooperated with crown policy, and heaped contempt on others who were 'ill disposed', 'refractory', or 'malignant'. Normally these estimations mirrored social and economic rank, as when the Privy Council distinguished 'the better and richer sort of the inhabitants' from 'persons of the meaner and poorer sort'.[110]

The language of 'sorts' was ubiquitous.[111] Considering candidates for village office in 1631, James Prescot told Sir Thomas Temple, 'I was careful to make choice of the better sort of men'. Temple in turn sought 'help of labourers of the better sort' to work on landscaping his estate.[112] At Emneth, Cambridgeshire, in 1638 the churchwardens reported 'the better sort do receive [communion] three times in the year', whereas some of the 'poorer sort' failed even to communicate at Easter.[113] Civic officials in London differentiated 'the better sort of citizens', who were orderly and respectful, from 'the meaner sort of people', who were prone to 'disorders'. When King Charles returned to his deeply divided capital in November 1641, his supporters differentiated 'the better and main sort', who were 'loyal and affectionate' towards him, from 'the meaner sort of people' who they blamed for 'tumults and disorders'.[114] 'The better sort' recognized the obligations of subjecthood, and earned approbation, while the 'worser' or 'meaner' sort violated the implicit contract and short-shrifted their duties to God.

Other usage ranged 'persons of honour' against 'mean and contemptible persons', 'sufficient men' against 'the vulgar', or the king's 'good and loving subjects' against 'lewd and malicious persons' or 'unquiet and restless spirits'.[115] Reports in 1637 said that 'the light common people' showed sympathy for the seditious libellers Burton, Bastwick, and Prynne, whereas 'the better sort' sided with the government.[116] The Buckinghamshire cleric Robert Sibthorpe contrasted 'the best of my parishioners', who shared his Laudian agenda, with the 'insolent clowns' who supported the puritan 'faction'.[117] William Sclater, a prebend of Exeter, differentiated 'a true subject' from 'the more ignorant vulgar'.[118] Even the London puritan William Gouge distinguished the 'men of place and power' from those 'timorous, weak, and feeble persons' who comprised 'the vulgar, common sort of men'.[119] The language was vague but divisive, separating 'credible persons of good worth' from those who were 'unfit', 'infamous', and 'disordered'.[120]

Many of the preachers and politicians who insisted on the superiority of their own sort poured scorn on the people below them. The view was widespread among the gentry that 'the common people are naturally of a loose disposition'.[121] Faced with reports of economic hardship in 1631, the Council declared itself 'not easily credulous of light reports nor apt to take impression from the vain speeches or ejaculations of some mean and contemptible persons' who happened to be hungry.[122] Other authorities expressed disdain for 'men of mean and middle quality', and remarked on the unworthiness of 'the common multitude'.[123] A masque presented to the court in 1627 included performers 'with divers open-mouthed dogs' heads, representing the people's barking'.[124]

King Charles's tutor, Robert Dallington, taught him that 'the inconstant multitude is naturally desirous of novelty... and ever in dislike with the present times'. The multitude, he explained, was 'this many-headed monster, which hath neither head for brains, nor brains for government', who needed the wise and firm direction of royal government.[125] 'Such a floating thing is the vulgar,' declared Sir Henry Wotton in 1627, with reference to 'acclamations' and 'imprecations' for the Duke of Buckingham.[126] 'Avaunt you giddy-headed multitude,' cries Buckingham himself in one of the libels that represented his voice.[127] Commentators condemned the ignorance, inconstancy, and perversity of the vulgar mob, whose fickleness they likened to jackdaws 'flying in the air uncertain where to take stand'.[128]

The people, preached Thomas Hurste in 1637, were restless, rash, giddy, discontented, and envious. Without magisterial authority to guide them, he said, the 'people are like a riotous rout in war... as sheep without a shepherd, or a body without a head'.[129] To Henry King, dean of Rochester, 'the people are as an inundation of water, like the waves for number and for noise, and would resemble the wild disorder of a wrought sea... did not the king in his authority limit their incessant motion'. Without the power of the crown to restrain them, he warned, the people might break out in a 'tumultuous parity' with disastrous consequences.[130]

Other preachers railed similarly against the whisperings of 'the rude vulgar',[131] and 'the frothy agitations of unquiet heads'.[132] The East Anglian cleric John Yates was scathing of the 'multitude, whose very wisdom... is to be despised'.[133] His Cambridgeshire colleague John Swan would have no truck with 'the humours of the common multitude' or the judgement 'of the common sort, whose very wisdom is but as a light feather in matters of this nature, as being too far above their reach'.[134] The assize preacher Thomas Trescot expressed disdain for 'the more simple and untutored vulgar' who made up 'the ragged regiment, a company of rude illiterate rascals that know not the law'.[135]

Thomas Morton of Durham preached similarly in 1639 against 'the tumultuousness of the people' and 'the madness of the people' who resisted royal authority by favouring the Scots.[136] When King Charles introduced the new church canons the following year he warned against the 'brain-sick jealousies' of 'the weaker sort, who are prone to be misled by crafty seducers'.[137] 'There is no trust to be put in the common people, they have neither constancy nor gratitude... nor continue in their love to anyone,' complained Viscount Conway in May 1640.[138] Rhetorically as well as socially, the distance between governors and governed was growing. It was 'the giddy people', especially 'mechanicks of all sorts', who drove King Charles from his capital, declared one royalist partisan a few years later.[139] It was 'ignorant men' like 'cobblers and tradesmen' with 'upstart opinions' who dishonoured God and ruined the nation, claimed another.[140] Even the cynical Marchamount Nedham, who had courted popularity as a parliamentary journalist, railed in 1648 against 'the rascal multitude... the profane vulgar, that are as mutable as the air, and never content with their present condition'.[141] Dispirited royalists found themselves wishing not that the kingdom had a different king, but that the king had a better people.[142]

Weak Women

The social order was a gendered order, which subordinated half the king's people to male domination. Female identity was partially subsumed within the status and authority of fathers, husbands, and brothers, though the patriarchal system did not prevent some women from acting independently. Feminist scholarship has shown how easy it is to collect contemporary statements in support of misogyny, but also examples of female agency and initiative. Recent work has shown that women sought informal spiritual authority in some communities, and that households could be arenas of gendered struggle.[143] Rather than dwelling on victims and exceptions, it helps to think of the gendered domain as a zone of negotiation involving language, personality, roles, and ranks, a zone that included masculinity as well as womanhood and the contests of sexuality.

It was widely believed, and supported by Scripture, that women were lighter, weaker-willed, and less rational than men. 'Women are more easily seduced than men, and have their judgements first and soonest poisoned,' declared John Elborow at a visitation sermon in Essex in 1637. They were ensnared by their 'credulous simplicity' to embrace nonconformity and error. Biblical examples from Genesis to the Epistles showed women to be 'weak' and 'wilful', and churchmen could only hope that 'our female zealots would not so busily intermeddle with church matters . . . in our Church of England'.[144] Vicar Elborow's strident misogyny reveals his anxiety that women, at least some of them, were not as docile and deferential as patriarchal ideology expected. Few went so far as John Seiman of Welbourne, Norfolk, who was admonished by church officials in 1627 'for saying women have no souls'.[145]

Upholding a system of order based on 'due observation of time, place, person, sex, condition, gifts, abilities, and the like', the Exeter preacher Henry Paynter marked as disorderly and 'preposterous' any 'church-destroying confusion' caused by 'women not keeping their station in a decorum becoming their sex'. Paynter, like many conservative contemporaries, feared 'a certain petulancy of forward behaviour appearing in the weaker vessel . . . to the prejudice of the sovereignty and royalty of the man'. Female subordination, he believed, was ordained by God, so that forwardness among women was not just rebellion but sin. The key texts came from the epistles of St Paul, refracted through generations of clerical interpretation.[146]

In the secular arena of village and urban life, women could be each other's worst enemies. Social historians have exposed the rich language of insult, with gendered invective in the mouths of both men and women. It would be defamatory to call a neighbour 'a hot-tailed whore', because this impugned her chastity and honour. It was likewise actionable to label her 'an idle housewife', because this disparaged her credit and good standing. But such words were as likely to be spoken by a woman as a man.[147] In 1626 the Oxford widow Mary Bolt defamed Avis Saunders, the wife of Robert Saunders, by saying she 'was a whore and an arrant whore, and that all her children were bastards'.[148] This was a matter for the authorities, not only because goodwife Saunders was aggrieved, but because altercations of this sort exposed the fragilities of the social system. The gendered order, like the rest of the social fabric, required constant maintenance and repair, though the risk of unravelling was exaggerated.

Wanderers

The underside of early modern England was occupied by 'jugglers, cony-catchers, Gypsies, rogues, base gamesters, lying mountebanks, vile bawds, and most damned cozeners',[149] as well as impoverished wayfarers, 'vagranting, idling, and shifting from place to place'.[150] 'Beggars, tinkers, bedlam men and all sorts of people' joined these people on the margins.[151] Their demography is impossible to determine, but they probably numbered in the thousands. These too were King Charles's subjects, though they belonged to no county or parish. Some had slipped into vagrancy through accident or hardship, some were veterans of military service, while others were criminals, adventurers, or mildly deranged. Popular culture tended to vilify the wandering poor, while officialdom sought their correction. Their disorderly living and gross dependency was an affront to the sensibilities of respectable Christians. In the words of the Oxfordshire minister John Randol, preaching in 1631, they were 'a dishonour to the king, confusion to the kingdom, the off-scouring both of men and beasts, and the very scum of all the land'. Unchurched, unemployed, and unable to give a good account of themselves, these wanderers, Randol charged, 'offer scorn and abuse both to God and man'.[152]

Moralists conventionally distinguished between 'God's poor', who had suffered misfortune, and 'the Devil's poor', who were 'idle devourers' and 'miscreants'.[153] The principle guiding social policy was that 'the truly poor and impotent should be relieved, those of able bodies should be set on work and employed in honest labours, and the sturdy, idle and dangerous rogues and vagabonds should be repressed and punished'.[154] Echoing the Elizabethan 'Homilies', the London minister Thomas Barnes insisted that 'idleness is permitted to none; employment, the devil's disquieter, is required of all'.[155]

Fortunately for settled society, there were statutes in place for dealing with the destitute and disorderly, placing the principal burden on parish authorities. Local constables and overseers were supposed to set the poor to work, secure whipping for those who were unwilling, and send them back to settle in their parish of origin.[156] No new legislation was necessary, but Charles I's government sought energetic compliance with existing laws. Ramping up the pressure in 1629, the Council demanded 'the apprehension, punishment and suppression of rogues, idle persons, and sturdy beggars', and required sheriffs and magistrates to report on their efforts.[157] In Derbyshire they set their sights on 'suspect persons, rogues, both sturdy beggars and begging vagrants, some whereof pretend to be petty chapmen, hucksters and higglers, and others tinkers, and others palmsters, fortune-tellers, Egyptians, and the like', and ordered weekly searches for members of this disorderly horde.[158]

One such wanderer was Joan Price, a single woman found 'shifting from place to place' in the London area in July 1630. Westminster constables found her 'lodging in hay-mows in a field near Tyburn, and sometimes in outhouses upon the back boards in Petty France and Long Ditch, and many times scraping trenchers at tents and other places for scraps'. Under examination she 'could give no good account how she lived', though it appears that she foraged on the margins of the city. The justices committed her 'to be set to labour' in the house of correction in Tothill Fields, and then to be sent to her birthplace at Tewkesbury with a certificate or pass.[159] Scores more like her were processed through London's Bridewell, along with beggars, prostitutes, and petty criminals.[160]

Viscount Dorchester noted with satisfaction in April 1631 that 'here in England the laws against vagrancy have been revived and made operative', but a new threat to order was emerging from Ireland.[161] The acute period of dearth, poor harvests, and economic dislocation between 1629 and 1631, the harshest social conditions in a generation, coincided with an unwelcome wave of immigration. Authorities in Essex complained in March 1629 that 'our country is now very full and much troubled with a multiplicity of Irish men, women and children beggars, of whom we cannot learn at what port or haven they were landed, or the cause of their landing'.[162] Inhabitants of Pembrokeshire, South Wales, were similarly 'much infested with the continual concourse of Irish beggars', but believed that 'multitudes' came ashore in night-time landings in the coves around Milford Haven.[163] More Irish beggars moved from Ulster to Scotland, and may have travelled south into England. Desperately poor Irish travellers, some following military recruits, added to the pressure on English parishes, and efforts to remove them had only limited effect. The problem was new, but apparently irreversible.[164]

The underclass would remain so long as poverty continued (in other words, for ever), though some policy advisors thought the problem could be exported. A plan to raise volunteers for overseas military service was encouraged in 1631, in the king's name, because it promised to 'disburden' the kingdom 'of so many unnecessary men that want employment'.[165] The fledgling colonies in Virginia and the Caribbean also seemed promising dumping grounds for England's surplus population, though few emigrants in Charles I's reign went to the New World in chains.

A somewhat more reputable body of wanderers were the travelling actors who performed stage plays and puppet plays in houses and inns as far apart as

Cornwall and Nottingham. Some were associated with London companies, and could exhibit licences from the master of the revels, but others had questionable legitimacy. One such group apprehended in Oxfordshire in May 1632 had played 'up and down the country these two years' across the English Midlands. One member, Drew Turner, claimed to have been with the company only twelve months, and said 'he doth nothing but drive the horse and beat the drum'.[166] Enemies of the theatre had long excoriated the deception, immorality, and disorder associated with players and play-going. They could take no comfort from the disgraced clergyman James Smith who declared in 1633 'that he loved the company of players above all, and that he thought there might be as much good many times done by a man hearing a play as in hearing a sermon'.[167]

A Balance Disturbed

When the propertied elite of early Stuart England thought about their society, they often imagined it fragmenting, unless people like themselves maintained their sway. They listened for denials of deference and signs of disorder that would seem to confirm their worst fears: the arch of order threatening to tumble, the social body suffering distemper, or the chain of being seemingly ready to snap. Magistrates, ministers, officers, and gentlemen took especial exception to affronts and challenges that threatened their assumptions of authority and power. It did not take a riot or commotion to destabilize the social hierarchy, for damage could be done by scandalous words or insulting gestures. Some gentlemen took offence when 'a base and scurvy fellow' gave them harsh looks, gnashed their teeth, or spat nuts in their direction.[168] It was God's plan to plant 'an awful reverence towards authority in the minds of all men', preached Edward Reynolds in 1635, but the 'many machinations of Satan' led weaker members to 'a repining and calumniating tongue'.[169] Society was sustained 'by the reverent awe and respect which the people and subjects give to the magistrates', preached John Gauden, for otherwise men risked 'degenerating to wolves and tigers'.[170]

The king and his counsellors were adamant that only people of their own understanding and status should concern themselves with state affairs. *Arcana imperii*, the secrets of state, belonged only to an inner circle. 'The scum of the commons, the tags and rags of the people, base mechanicks, men of little knowledge, less honesty, and no discretion at all,' had no business with public matters, preached Michael Wigmore in 1633.[171] The king's affairs were not to be judged 'by goodman the cobbler, by master the mercer, by clouted shoes and russet coats', declared Francis Rogers the same year.[172] 'It is an ambitious ignorance for men to meddle in what they understand not,' especially in 'matters of state', warned the dean of Salisbury, John Bowle.[173] It was not for 'every ignorant illiterate artisan, mechanick high-shoes' to speak on matters of church and state, wrote the Essex minister John Elborow.[174] 'Study to be quiet, and do your own business,' urged Thomas Warmstry in 1641. 'Study to be quiet,' repeated the London minister Ephraim Udall, 'meddle not in things that belong not to your calling'.[175]

Kings, by their nature and position, knew better than 'we inferior people', explained the Leicestershire minister Anthony Cade, 'for we live as it were in low valleys and plains, and see not far about us; but princes sit as on tops of hills, and see both into former ages, what was done then, and into foreign countries, what is done now, how all things are and have been carried, with the reasons, circumstances, and events of all'. Advised and assisted by 'the gravest, wisest, learnedest divines and other choice counsellors of greatest experience', monarchs like King Charles 'set down orders fittest for their times and countries, which we common people should not rashly censure, but willingly submit unto'.[176]

Sir Robert Phelips (if he is the author) joined this discussion in 'A discourse by way of a dialogue between a counsellor of state and a country gentleman', in which the gentleman disavows any 'desire of observing matters above my reach, nor a needless curiosity to busy myself in those things which concern me not'. The counsellor reminds him that, 'though matters of state concern you not in the consultative or directive part, yet in the effect of such consultations the most remote and retired subject hath his interest'.[177] State policies and affairs affected everyone, though they were shaped behind screens and veils.

Unfortunately for the Caroline regime, too few people found this conservative ideology persuasive. Despite the repeated insistence of courtiers and governors that ordinary subjects had no business with *arcana imperii*, the evidence is overwhelming that people of all sorts were hungry for news and information, and eager to share opinions on matters of high concern. They met and talked in 'taverns, ordinaries, inns, bowling-greens and alleys, alehouses, tobacco-shops, highways and water passages', and every place of social interaction.[178] Attempts to silence this discourse and to muzzle the multitude were doomed to failure. The national conversation ranged uncontrollably beyond the elite 'political nation', and rumour, news, and opinion spread everywhere. 'The buzzing multitude' talked of parliaments and the absence of parliament.[179] Alehouse chatter turned from affairs of the neighbourhood to affairs of the king and queen. Charles I's subjects knew the rudiments of the national political narrative, where the king travelled, and what he was doing. Part of this conversation was self-policing, as participants knew that certain words or topics would cause them trouble. Witnesses recalled themselves saying 'have care . . . take heed what you say . . . these are hanging words', as they attempted to steer discussion back to safer ground. Only the most reckless, or most determined, pressed on towards sedition and treason.[180]

People were supposed to know their place, to accept their lot, and to behave accordingly, not just to the king but toward all their betters. It was rebellious transgression, preached Thomas Fuller in 1626, if 'we scornfully cast the cords of superiority from us, and break the bonds of all subjection in sunder'.[181] It was therefore a shock to observers when a humble commoner demeaned a superior. It was socially transgressive for someone of lower social status to claim to be as good as his betters. It was not just a breach of the peace but a blow to hierarchy and order when a husbandman used 'vilifying and disgraceful speeches' against a gentleman, and called him to his face 'a paltry rascal and a false rascal many times together',[182] or when a Smithfield miller's wife was heard 'very much abusing one Mrs Coles, a gentlewoman of good quality, threatening to slit her nose and break her face'.[183] The army captain John Urry was outraged in 1628 when a fellow soldier called him 'base clown, base jack, and puppy'.[184] The Duchy of Lancaster brought action in 1629 when a tenant in Dorset 'did revile and upbraid' steward Ellis Swayne, esquire, saying 'that he sat there with his cap on his head, but he would bring him where he should have cap in hand'.[185] It became a Star Chamber matter in 1639 when 'a gentleman of good family' suffered 'opprobrious language, as calling him base beggarly bastard'.[186] Popular memory stored the medieval levelling verse 'When Adam delved and Eve span, who was then the gentleman?' and was capable of evoking it in confrontational circumstances.

Demeaning words were in fact common, for surly commoners could not always bite their tongues. Social and legal mechanisms sought to sustain the system, but neither deference nor civility could survive angry altercations. Archbishop Laud remarked in 1639 on 'the disease of the time, which he styled now epidemical', because 'the perverseness and malice of men was inveterate against men in authority'.[187] Socially scandalous expressions were sometimes cited in court, or reported to magistrates, as evidence of transgression. When John Leech of Bettisfield, Flintshire, spoke ill of a gentleman, for example, authorities at the Great Sessions reminded him 'that it was a sauciness for any to meddle with his betters'.[188] When the husbandman Thomas Andrews used 'evil and foul words' that provoked 'not only his equals and inferiors, but also his superiors' into quarrels, the Sussex quarter sessions sanctioned him as 'a very troublesome and contentious person' who threatened to make his betters 'buckle unto him'.[189] 'Frothy agitations' of the 'rude vulgar' broke out throughout Charles I's reign, confirming the king's opinion that the people were weak and unreliable. A few more examples will illustrate the vehemence and vocabulary of unruly demotic expression.

In 1632 the Staffordshire quarter sessions heard that the coal miner Thomas Baggely told his employer John Floyd: 'Sirrah, I have heretofore called thee master, but I care not for thee now of a straw, or words to that effect.' The word 'sirrah' was especially insulting, used condescendingly as a sign of disrespect.[190] Also in 1632, the Cambridge victualler John Jermy tangled with university proctors at Stourbridge fair. Accusing them of cheating him 'of six or seven dozen larks' supplied for a university feast, Jermy threatened one that 'he would lay him over the face', and threatened to set the others 'by the heels and make them down on their knees'. These were offensive 'words of disgrace and contempt', but they were made more memorable by Jermy's vaunt 'that he was a better man than they, and that he had given money to maintain better than they'. This was a spat of town against gown, tradesman against cleric, and a collision of different schemes of worth. The university, of course, sided with the proctors, and the offender was sanctioned before its court.[191] In 1633 the Council heard similar complaints against an innkeeper of Stamford 'for using scornful and reviling speeches against all sorts of persons from the highest to the lowest, sparing none, neither, lords, bishops or others'.[192] Hierarchy was imperilled when such people spoke their minds.

Minor clashes over apparently insignificant matters could destabilize relationships of subjecthood and authority, rank and status. Disputes involving money could turn ordinary dealings into tests of social cohesion. Confrontations became disruptive, and could drift towards sedition, when subordinates broke the rules. State authorities became involved when

Christopher Neville, the constable of Alresford, Hampshire, 'made a pish' at a royal warrant, and refused assistance to a royal messenger.[193] It was a matter for the Privy Council when Anthony Spittle, the postmaster at Basingstoke, gave his superior officers 'very ill language' and let it be known that 'he cared not what they could do . . . not so much for his wife's turd, and . . . that he cared no more for them than for one hair of his arse'.[194] A Cambridge man likewise undermined the rules of hierarchy by telling a local magistrate to 'kiss mine arse'.[195]

Yorkshiremen seem to have been especially contemptuous of established authority, at least so the records suggest. One Yorkshire labourer declared, 'I care not for the constable or the king', and a neighbouring blacksmith embellished this by saying, 'the devil go with the king and all the proud pack of them, what care I?'[196] Not content with ignoring rules against dealing in plague-infected goods, the Yorkshire yeoman Robert Bossall threatened the magistrate who arrested him in 1626 by saying: 'I will set such a black bitch on his arse as he never had in his life, and I have no bullets but I will shoot beans in his arse.'[197] Another Yorkshire yeoman contemptuously declared in 1639, 'I care not a fart for Sir Francis Wortley's warrants', and yet another announced of the same worshipful magistrate: 'I worship him with my arse.'[198]

Reports of disorderly and socially disruptive words were so abundant that one risks being swamped by them. In 1630 Daniel White, a husbandman from Berkshire, defamed John Sambach of Oxford as 'a rogue, a base rogue, a knave, an arrant knave, and a very knave'.[199] Oxford magistrates recorded exchanges in which an inferior called a superior 'a rascal and a base scoundrel and a scurvy scab',[200] or 'a beggarly knave, a base fellow . . . sirrah, get you away or I'll beat you like a dog'.[201] Elizabeth Furnivall of Church Hulme, Cheshire, broke social and gendered proprieties alike in 1638 when she defamed John Barker with 'words of scandal and disgrace', calling him 'a tinker, a cobbler, a base fellow of condition and quality, a rascal, and such a one as is not fit for the society of honest Christians'.[202]

Some of the most transgressive utterances involved assertions of social and moral parity. The Shropshire magistrate Sir Gilbert Cornwall was shocked when the wife of Thomas Pringle pulled him by the hair and proclaimed that her husband 'was as good a man as the said Sir Gilbert'.[203] The aldermen of Southampton were outraged when the shoemaker John Pratt declared, 'I care not a fart for them, if I were a mile out of town I were as good a man as the best of them', and threatened 'he would call them knaves . . . to their faces'.[204] A Staffordshire blacksmith, John Webster, demeaned his gentle-born priest by saying 'he did not care a fart of his arse for him', declaring to his face 'that he was as well bred and born as thou art, and as good a man as thyself, excepting thy cloth'.[205] From 1634 to 1640 the High Court of Chivalry provided a venue for aristocrats who believed their honour was impugned. 'Dost though . . . make comparisons with me?' demanded Sir William Essex, after a lowly tailor 'said he was as good a man as' the baronet.[206] Sir Henry Hungate was similarly affronted when a Suffolk haberdasher's wife said 'that her husband was an honester man than would ever go upon Sir Henry Hungate's legs'.[207] Sir Popham Southcott brought action when a Somerset soap-maker said to his face: 'I am sufficient to answer a better man than thou art.'[208]

Assertions like these disturbed the social order and threatened the hierarchical assumptions on which it was based. It was 'a sad presage of danger to this land, when lower strive to get the upper hand', rhymed the poet bishop of Norwich Richard Corbet.[209] Socially disruptive language had high significance, according to the preacher Robert Mossom, because 'contempt of the magistrate, the king's vicegerent, is contempt of the king . . . so contempt of the king, God's vicegerent, is contempt of God . . . for in the chain of orders one link still depends upon the other'.[210] Levelling words appeared more frequently in the revolution of the 1640s, but they simmered and occasionally erupted during England's halcyon days.

Gentlemen candidates for parliament experienced this upsurge directly in some of the contested elections of 1640. At Sandwich, when the 'voices of the better sort' were overwhelmed by 'the meanest sort of people', the defeated Lord Grandison grumbled that the new members were returned 'by the unruly multitude, sore against our wills'.[211] Sir Edward Dering's agent in Kent complained that the electors of Maidstone were as inclined to listen to 'any cobbler or tinker' as to a gentleman.[212] Stunned by the disrespect shown him at the hustings in Essex, Lord William Maynard told Sir Thomas Barrington that he would have no more to do with 'popular assemblies where fellows without shirts challenge as good a voice as myself'. Some of those 'mean-conditioned' *sans chemises* allegedly threatened that 'they would tear the gentlemen in pieces'.[213]

Refractory Disorders

Three brief episodes display these social energies in action, a decade or more before the world turned upside down. The first concerns local elections at Norwich, the second centres on disturbances in the Gloucestershire forests, and the third involves enclosure riots and 'football play' in the eastern fens. Each exposed the fragilities of social hierarchy beneath the crown's capstone authority. Each contributed to the determination of Whitehall and Westminster to hold the line against truculent popular spirits.

In September 1627 the Privy Council learned of 'a dangerous faction' that threatened good order in the nation's second largest city, Norwich. The mayor and aldermen reported with alarm that 'a great multitude of mechanical men and other citizens of mean quality had combined themselves together' to influence the election of sheriffs. One sheriff at Norwich was customarily chosen by the mayor and alderman and the other 'by the greater number of the citizens', but the candidates were always 'able and sufficient' men from the governing elite. Now, however, the 'faction' proposed the basket-maker John Kettle,

> a man so unworthy of a place of magistracy, so rude and uncivil as he is not fit for common society, a man so addicted to drunkenness as that he hath been often bound to his good behaviour, and yet never reformed but refractory to order, and refusing for the most part to bear all manner of charges to the king or city.

To block this danger the mayor and aldermen supported 'Mr Thomas Atkyn, a chief commoner of the city... whose estate, gravity, and sufficiency is well known and approved'. And Atkyn, a gentleman like the mayor's other choice, was 'one of his majesty's commissioners for the loan'.[214] The shrieval election was unusually polarized, pitting a rabble-rousing tribune against a conservative establishment in a city suffering from high unemployment.

Kettle's campaign unnerved the authorities, and they did all they could to thwart him. He had been a trouble-maker for almost a decade, and often said 'he did owe neither suit nor service to the city'. In 1625, for example, he refused to bear the office of 'feastmaker' and gave 'dilatory and uncivil answers' when called to account. 'Refractory to all government', he wanted to be sheriff, he declared, 'because the commons were made slaves by the magistrates, and that he would endeavour to right it'. Whipping up the mean and mechanical multitude, he made 'many violent and outrageous speeches' against gentlemen 'of good worth, credit and reputation'. He called the outgoing sheriff 'a thief to the king... a rascal, a jack, and a peremptory fellow', and said there was no justice in the city, 'nothing but oppression'. He called the rulers of Norwich 'a company of knaves... worse than devils', and said they made laws 'to oppress the poor commons'. Evoking the memory of the Tudor rebel Robert Kett, whose name prefigured his own, Kettle made social justice the core of his campaign. He promised he 'would lay that open for the citizens that had not been formerly laid open, and that none of the citizens should be oppressed as they have been, and that he would give all his officers new gowns, and would ease the poor of burdens which they had formerly borne'. He even provided beer to his followers, to be drunk after his election.[215]

In the event John Kettle won 176 votes, but his respectable opponent Thomas Atkyn received 10 more. The populists rallied 'in discontented manner' and disputed the result, which is why the mayor and aldermen wrote again to the Council. The Council responded by denouncing Kettle's 'miscarriages' and ordering that future elections be better regulated. It was, they declared, 'a matter that his majesty especially careth for, that orderly government of cities and corporations should be maintained, and that popular and factious humours that trouble the same should be suppressed or punished'. John Kettle's upstart political career was ended, and he presumably returned to his beer and his baskets. Only the class of natural governors would be allowed to govern the kingdom's second city.[216]

More dangerous disturbances broke out in the forest communities of the south-west Midlands, after local gentry sought to enclose land that had formerly been in common. A spate of riots between 1629 and 1631 coincided with a period of acute economic distress, when cloth-workers lost employment, fenmen battled drainers, and countrymen lost customary access to ancient woodland. A major disturbance shook the Forest of Dean, Gloucestershire, in March 1631 when some 500 protesters gathered with fife and drums, pikes and halberds, to pull down recently erected enclosures. Asserting traditional common rights against private privilege and property, the rioters assembled 'in warlike and outrageous manner' to destroy fences, banks, and ditches that parcelled the forest. Local authorities reported 'there was great spoil made in the said forest... by a great company of rude people'.[217]

The danger to established order was exacerbated when Peter Simon, the curate of Newland, counselled the rioters and ventured the opinion 'that setting the king's place and quality aside, we were all equal in respect of manhood unto him'. This was seditious levelling that reduced the distance between man and man, subject and monarch, and it brought the clergyman to scrutiny before his bishop. Faced with sanctions, Simon wisely acknowledged 'that he doth with all his soul detest all anabaptistical and Jesuitical opinions and positions that oppose the authority, power, dignity, preeminency, and safety of princes; and that he doth acknowledge that there is upon kings and princes God's character which maketh their persons sacred as God's anointed'. He further assured the bishop that not a day went by 'in which he will not pray for his sacred majesty, and for the upholding of his royal dignity and preservation of his sacred person'. And as to 'the common condition of humanity', far from espousing erroneous opinions, 'his meaning was, though kings and princes did consist of soul and body as other men, yet the endowment of God's grace and gifts of his holy spirit are greater and more abundant upon princes than inferior persons'. Suitably cowed and repentant, Simon was allowed back to his parish.[218]

Later that spring a comparable 'combustion' broke out in Braydon Forest, Wiltshire, where rioters led by 'the Lady Skimmington, as they call her, with a great number of rebels, are now pulling down and defacing all the enclosures in the forest'. They smashed gates, broke rails, and cut up coppices and hedges, 'so that all things is now in common', reported one distressed property-holder. Similar 'tumultuous assemblies' erupted in Dorset and Somerset, so that much of the south-west seemed to be inflamed. The Council ordered magistrates 'to suppress this insufferable insolency', and warned of 'great disorders in the nature of rebellions' against 'the settled peace and government' of the kingdom. Its actors or perpetrators were 'the inferior sort of people' or 'the rude multitude', mostly men who could not be named.[219]

The disguised, cross-dressed folk figure of 'Lady Skimmington' inspired and encouraged the rioters, and gave cover to their leaders. 'Skimmington's lieutenant' led the destruction of banks and ditches at Frampton on Severn, after neighbours at Slimbridge 'wished that Skimmington and his company would come to them and throw open the new enclosures'. Newly pressed soldiers at Bristol joined in the action after hearing 'what Skimmington had done there and in the Forest of Braydon'.[220] The sheriff of Gloucester, Sir Ralph Dutton, tried hard to capture the culprits, but they mostly melted away. A dawn raid to arrest 'John Williams, called by the name of Skimmington', failed to find anyone at home.[221]

These forest confrontations in the west and south-west coincided with grain riots in southern and south-east England.[222] Food prices spiked after poor and wet harvests, at the same sad time as the cloth industry suffered from the closure of European markets. A bushel of wheat, formerly as cheap as 6*s*., cost as much as 14*s*. in London in 1631.[223] Bad weather, grim politics, social stress, and unemployment conspired to raise anger and sap discipline. Sir Nicholas Coote wrote anxiously to the Earl of Totnes in January 1629 about crowds near Upminster, Essex, who prevented the transportation of loads of rye 'according to his majesty's licence'. Hungry villagers armed with stick and pitchforks, and 'offering money to hire muskets', attacked carts and ferries taking grain towards London, 'swearing they will first provide for themselves'.[224] More reports spread in March 1630 of 'commotions' in Hertfordshire, within 3 miles of the king's lodgings at Theobalds, when a mob 300-strong intercepted the corn that was intended for consumption in the capital. The rioters protested that 'they were in want, and would not suffer their corn to be carried to London and themselves to starve'.[225] Another 'outrage' in January 1631 involved a score of 'seditious and turbulent persons' who 'forcibly surprised' a cart filled with grain near Basingstoke.[226]

In normal circumstances these thieves and rioters would have accepted the authority of landlords and gentlemen, bailiffs and justices, and the arrayed representatives of the governing order. They would not disguise themselves, arm themselves, or take the law into their own hands. But when they were hungry, cold, angry, and drawing courage from each other, more elemental passions prevailed. One state response was to buy up food and distribute it cheaply to families in need. Another was to punish transgressors with a vengeance. Mob actions fuelled elite perception that the commons were indeed unstable, and that rude, tumultuous, and seditious subjects needed more disciplined controls.

Similar challenges to order occurred in the eastern fens, where engineers, entrepreneurs, and contractors had tried for fifty years to drain the wetlands to reclaim land for agricultural profit. Elizabethan and Jacobean governments had often mediated between well-financed projectors and 'men of mean condition' whose customary rights of grazing and foraging were threatened. Activists on all sides appealed to the crown against perceived affronts to law and order, using language designed to win approval and curry favour. The royal balancing role shifted under Charles I as the king himself became a principal undertaker and sided more often with the drainers and enclosers. Acrimonious disputes intensified as King Charles exercised his 'regal power and prerogative . . . to force forward and adverse men to give way to that which is for the public good'.[227]

Resistance to a major drainage project in Lincolnshire in August 1629 degenerated into an armed affray, as hundreds of men and women rose against the workmen, burned their spades and barrows, and threw some of the operatives into the water. Menacingly, they erected a gallows 'to terrify the workmen', called them 'rogues [and] dogs', and threatened to kill any who continued to work. In defiance of authority they 'put those that served the king's process . . . upon them into the stocks'. In retaliation Star Chamber imposed punitive fines on the guilty rioters and upheld the king's right 'for the benefit of his crown and people, for the draining of these fens'. As well as straining and testing royal authority, the episode divided local communities, pitting farmers who made use of common pasturage against labourers who were glad to find work with the projectors.[228]

Another confrontation over drainage in Cambridgeshire in 1638 exposed expectations about the king's role in the dispute. Early in June 1638 some forty to fifty men gathered at Whelpmore Fen, near Littleport in the Isle of Ely, 'to throw down the ditches' and restore access to the commons. As on previous occasions, the rioters came armed with pitchforks and were summoned by bells and horns. Here, however, a new and menacing festive element intervened in the form of massed football players, bent on violence and justice. The game was played across a wide area, inviting the destruction of fences and ditches wherever the ball came to rest. On Tuesday, 5 June, as many as 600 men assembled for 'a football play or camp', which targeted the drainers' workings and diggings. The 'tumultuous action' on this occasion was dampened only by a downpour of rain. The next day roughly 200 men from Ely and Lakenheath joined the 'mutinous' action, 'throwing down the undertakers' ditches, but not hurting any man's person or goods'. Outraged officials invoked royal authority and displayed 'warrants . . . in his majesty's name', but found that many of the rioters 'make light of it and refuse it'. Local justices reported to the Privy Council that 'the people grow desperately careless and nourish bad spirits amongst themselves' as the worst sort of subjects.[229]

One especially obstreperous activist, the Ely labourer Edward Anderson (also known as Edward Powell), who brought the football and started the game, asserted 'that he would not leave his commons until he see the king's own signet and royal assent, and that he would obey God and the king and no man else; for he said, we are all but subjects'. Anderson claimed to have access to the king, and to have informed him of the fenmen's problems, but the only justice he received was a stay in Newgate prison.[230] Protesters against fen drainage in Lincolnshire similarly justified their opposition to the project by saying, 'the king knows not of it', implying that a better-informed monarch would surely have taken their side.[231]

A Wider World

Naval, commercial, colonial, and private ventures took some of Charles I's subjects beyond the bounds of his British dominions. Dreams took them even further. Travellers went to the ends of the earth and shared their observations about foreign lands. Traders tapped into the newest and most ancient routes of commerce, across the Baltic, the Atlantic, the Mediterranean, into Asia and the Indian Ocean. In their boldest imaginings the English would again singe the king of Spain's beard, lead expeditions across the Atlantic, and 'affirm for certain the taking of great Lima in Peru'.[232] At the very beginning of Charles I's reign the Council considered a plan 'to abate the pride and terror of the Spanish pretended empire', and to take new territory in the New World. An aggressive intervention in the West Indies would establish outposts from Hispaniola to Panama, and draw Peru and Mexico 'to defection from Spain and confederacy with us', though little developed along these lines until Oliver Cromwell's 'Western Design' in the 1650s. In the late 1620s the Duke of Buckingham sponsored a search for the Northwest Passage, and Captain Thomas Young spent more than a year in the 1630s searching for 'a navigable passage for ships from the Atlantic ocean to the South Sea'.[233]

English merchants traded all over Europe and as far afield as Greenland and Indonesia, sending back tales of adventures as well as exotic products. There was even talk of the southern continent of *Terra Australis Incognita*, and speculation about the inhabitants of the moon.[234] The national conversation repeatedly turned to such topics, especially when war, piracy, or misadventure stranded English men and women beyond their familiar shores. English merchants trading to Guinea and the Gold Coast in Africa had orders to seek out exotic curiosities: 'an elephant's head with teeth . . . a river horse head of the biggest that can be gotten', and strange birds, fish, shells, fruits, and flowers.[235] Plans were afoot in 1626 to explore the 'river of the Amazons in America'.[236] The Muscovy company and the Greenland traders brought back products of the northern lands, especially whale oil, fish, and fur.[237] Traders to the orient supplied gentlemen's kitchens with culinary spices. Caribbean merchants brought sugar, tobacco, and dye-stuffs such as indigo and cochineal to wealthy consumers. Armchair travellers reviewed the merits of the East and West Indies and debated which 'may prove more profitable unto his majesty and his subjects'.[238]

King Charles's foreign correspondents included 'the Grand Signor, the King of Persia, the Emperor of Russia, the Great Mogul, and other remote Princes'.[239] The king of Morocco sent him hawks for hunting, Arabian horses for his stables, and lions for the Tower menagerie.[240] Published reports described travels among Turks, Greeks, Egyptians, and Italians, with accounts of the Brahmins of India and the Parsees of Persia.[241] News reached the court in 1634 that certain English women associated with the embassy to Constantinople had been escorted into the Seraglio, and had even bathed with the Sultana 'after the Turkish manner'. Their chastity was assured, one correspondent remarked, because 'the attendants there are all eunuchs'.[242] More unsettling were lurid tales of the 'cruel Turk' whose emperor was 'so bloody a monster that there passes scarce any day that he kills not someone or other with his own hands'.[243]

Closer to home, coastal communities suffered 'great outrages' from Barbary pirates and slavers from North Africa.[244] 'The distressed wives of almost 2,000 poor mariners' petitioned King Charles in 1626 to help relieve their husbands from captivity in Sallee.[245] More 'poor women' petitioned in 1633 on behalf of 'their husbands, sons and friends . . . lately taken and kept in bondage by the Turks and Moors of Algiers and Tunis'.[246] 'A thousand poor women more' sought freedom in 1636 for some 1,500 English seafarers 'in most miserable, lamentable and woeful slavery and captivity'.[247] English women too were enslaved—forty-five in 1636 alone—as passengers on unfortunate ships, or when raiding parties came ashore.[248] Several members of the aristocratic Godolphin family were plucked that summer from their pleasures on the Isles of Scilly.[249] Returned and redeemed captives turned up from time to time in English towns, amid suspicion that they might have 'turned Turk'.[250] The Muslim menace caused a moral panic, and helped justify the imposition of Ship Money for the build-up of the king's fleet.

By the end of the 1630s there were more than 50,000 English men and women in the American colonies of Virginia and Maryland, Massachusetts and Connecticut, Atlantic Bermuda, and such Caribbean islands as St Kitts and Barbados. Commerce, correspondence, kinship, and memory connected them to households and communities across England.[251] Besides these colonists and settlers there were perhaps 10,000 more of King Charles's subjects in foreign military service, several thousand enslaved or imprisoned in North Africa, and an unknown number engaged in foreign trade or travel.[252] The English community in the Netherlands included religious refugees as well as hundreds of artisans and merchants. In principle, the English beyond the seas enjoyed the same privileges as the rest of the king's subjects, and owed their monarch comparable duties. Like English subjects everywhere, they were obliged to recognize the royal prerogative, even if they did not always pay it respect. Though far from home and 'planted in a strange land', said Emmanuel Downing of the New Englanders in 1633, they were never 'so foolishly besotted as to reject the protection of their natural prince'.[253]

The drama of the wider world reached to the heart of the English Midlands, to the Leicestershire village of Ashby de la Zouch, which sits as far from the sea as is possible within the British Isles. Maritime and foreign affairs appeared remote across distant horizons, yet the world beyond the parish impinged on Ashby, as on most English communities. Imported spices reached rich men's table. Flows of travellers and news added exotic information to the local conversation. Legal and economic business connected Ashby to courts and markets in Coventry, Leicester, Derby, and Nottingham, while the Stuart state and the national church tied the parish to Lincoln and London. It helped, perhaps, to have one of England's premier aristocrats, the Earl of Huntingdon, as lord of the manor. The king and court may have come within a dozen miles of Ashby in Charles I's progress in 1634. Though residents of villages like Ashby might claim to 'live in such an obscure nook... that news is very scarce with us', they were from time to time buffeted by the 'outlandish affairs' of continental Europe.[254]

Evidence that global traffic touched local affairs appears in the accounts of overseers of the poor. These officials collected and distributed funds for poor relief, mostly assisting indigent residents, the aged, the unfortunate, and the infirm. They also gave small sums of money to passing poor travellers, enough to tide them over and move them on. Among the recipients of parish assistance at Ashby de la Zouch between 1624 and

1638 (the years when records survive) were wanderers, outsiders, and people in distress, many with exotic experiences and all with stories to tell. They included families 'that came out of Ireland', smaller contingents from Scotland and Wales, and victims of fires as far away as Barnstaple, Devon, who had briefs or certificates to authenticate their losses. Also passing through Ashby were maimed, wandering, or discharged soldiers, including some 'chosen when they went into Germany' and others 'that had the seal of the king of Bohemia', 'two poor women that lost their husbands and all their goods to shipwreck', other sufferers from maritime disasters, 'an English merchant that brought a certificate from the mayor of Southampton and was robbed by pirates', and 'a man that had his tongue cut forth by the Turks'. The overseers gave these travellers as little at twopence or as much as a shilling, depending on their deserts, and others in Ashby no doubt asked them, 'what news?'[255] Though Leicestershire was not a leading county for emigration to the New World, villagers within a day's ride of Ashby had friends and kinsfolk in New England who hung on their messages or looked for their return.[256]

The material and imaginative horizons of these Midland villagers expanded to all the seas around Britain, to Atlantic and colonial networks, the Islamic Mediterranean, and the Europe of the Thirty Years War. Printed texts, manuscript letters, oral accounts, and rumour further populated those horizons with names and stories. The colonial enterprise, the affairs of Christendom, and trade from the Baltic to the Caribbean left few communities untouched. Royal policy and proclamations affected pockets and purposes, as the kingdom prepared for foreign threats and switched between peace and war. Nowhere in England was exempt from contributing manpower and money for the king's necessities; nowhere was so remote that 'outlandish' matters could not penetrate, nor residents take part in the wider national conversation. If they paid or resisted Ship Money, or pondered its necessity, the inhabitants of Ashby de la Zouch played their part in the commonwealth of England. Charles I's subjects everywhere could reflect on their place in God's scheme and the terms of their relationship with their king.

A Cold Country

Meteorological observers in Charles I's England made special mention of the extremity and misery of the weather. Nobody kept detailed or measured observations, but dozens of diarists and letter-writers made note of conditions they found 'harsh', 'foul', 'unseasonable', or 'extreme'. The Essex diarist Sir Humphrey Mildmay often recorded the weather as 'sad', a condition recognizable to anyone who has lived in southern England.[257] Richard Napier's notebooks, kept with reference to his practice of medicine and astrology, usually record the first snow of the year in November or December, and the last in March or April, marking a longer winter than in modern times.[258] Neither Napier nor his Buckinghamshire neighbours knew that they lived in the trough of 'the little ice age', a period of global cooling at its worst in the seventeenth century.[259]

Then as now, the British Isles were washed by westerly streams of Atlantic air, interspersed with periods of continental high pressure. Countrymen knew that 'an east wind blows no good', and might bring sleet or snow. The normal cycle of the seasons delivered warm summers and cool winters, ideally interspersed with mild springs and autumns, with sufficient moisture all year round. The patterns of agriculture depended upon reliable weather, with soft rain for nourishing the ground and dry spells for harvest. Animals sickened with too much rain, and sodden crops could not be gathered. Flooded or frozen rivers became unnavigable, while washed-out roads and bridges hindered movements of people and goods. An army could not march in the mud, nor could courtiers go hunting. Colder, wetter, and more violent conditions limited growing periods, reduced crop yields, raised prices, and impeded the transport of food and supplies. Adverse weather sapped morale and quickened 'epidemical distempers'.[260] Climate severity spawned crises worldwide.[261] No individual could be blamed, though moralists of the late 1630s thought the 'unseasonable weather in the last and some former years' was a sign of 'God's punishment upon us' for England's sins.[262] The official prayer 'for fair weather' in the *The Book of Common Prayer* acknowledged that 'our iniquities have worthily deserved this plague of rain and waters', explicitly linking the moral and meteorological domains.[263] Most people, as always, endured and grumbled, and tried to get on with their affairs.

A changing climate produced volatile conditions that people experienced as 'unseasonable'. There was no clear trend or pattern, but the chronicle of contemporary comments and observations reveals a drama in the sky and on the ground that paralleled the better-known history of the reign of Charles I. Though comparable reports of weather extremes might be gleaned from earlier decades in the early modern era, no such compilation yet exists.

A brief recitation of the Caroline record contributes new material to climate history and casts fresh light on conditions in the 1620s and the 1630s.

Charles I's reign opened with frigid downpours. The solemn 'show' planned for the transportation of the body of the late King James from Hertfordshire to London on 9 April 1625 'was marred by foul weather, so that there was nothing to be seen', complained the court observer John Chamberlain.[264] The Countess of Huntingdon advised Sir John Davies that she would have written sooner, 'but the waters were so high a messenger on foot could not pass'.[265] Her husband the earl excused himself from attending parliament in June because 'the waters have been so great I could not pass with my coach'.[266] The members of parliament who made it to Westminster that summer prayed for relief from 'unseasonable weather' as well as the killing pestilence. 'The heavens are black over us, and the clouds drop leanness,' observed the special prayer that asked for 'more seasonable weather to give the fruits of the earth their season'.[267]

Congregations nationwide implored God 'for the stoppage of the plague and of the ceaseless rain, which for a month past has fallen to the detriment of all kinds of crops'.[268] Conditions were so appalling, Francis Nethersole reported in July, that men stood to their ankles in water while trying to make hay.[269] The extremes of 'foul weather' that brought 'much rain [and] great flood' to inland areas tested ships at sea and made it impossible for mariners to go from ship to shore.[270]

In August 1625 Owen Wynn noted, some travellers were 'well nigh drowned' in the swollen rivers of Wales.[271] More 'foul weather' in October delayed the Duke of Buckingham's rendezvous with King Charles at Plymouth.[272] It 'rained exceedingly' in October, and the first snow in southern England fell that year on 11 November.[273] Writing from Plymouth that month, Sir James Bagg explained delays in official letters by reference to the unseasonal weather: 'The violent extremity of an unknown snow falling in our country the 16th hath not given passage to these till this instant. The snow hath been the death of many people and the loss of many sheep and cattle, and within the memory of man never covered so thick the face of Devon.'[274] 'This frosty weather... is not [fit] to travel, though fit to stir in,' wrote Viscount Mandeville in Huntingdonshire.[275] At least it was not so bad as continental European, where English veterans of foreign wars were 'crippled with the cold', and some lost their feet in 'the extreme fierce cold of the last winter'.[276] The only good to come of this 'sharp corrosive frost and a hard winter', thought John Holles, was that it might bring an end to the plague.[277]

Frigid conditions continued in January 1626, when Sir Lewis Watson blamed 'this cold morning, both of frost and snow', for not paying a visit.[278] Another wet summer followed, with storms on 12 June 1626 which gave Londoners 'such an extreme thunder, lightning and rain, as the like hath seldom been seen, and much hurt done thereby'. Some thought the Duke of Buckingham's magus John Lambe had conjured up a waterspout. Part of the church of St Andrew Holborne washed away, and a dozen coffins were uncovered. Corpses at Bishopsgate were 'taken out of their graves by the violence of the water', and swam up and down the streets. Thames-side observers saw an extraordinary whirlwind that 'raised the water above the height of a man for about sixty yards in length or breadth', and ripped a limb from a cherry tree at York House. One city chronicler recorded 'a tempest whirling and ghoulish ... it was very fearful, everybody took it as a sign against the Duke [of Buckingham]'.[279] By December the weather turned frigid again, when one of Lord Scudamore's correspondents wrote from London: 'I cannot hold the pen in my hand any longer for very cold, and yet by a fire.' A few weeks later he remarked that the New Year began 'as coldly as ever England did'.[280] An ornithological observer recorded: 'all the last winter there was seen no wrens, which was thought to be ominous.'[281]

At the beginning of April 1627 the Oxford diarist Thomas Crosfield recorded, 'cold sickly weather: snow mutable'.[282] Rain fell at Oxford upon St Swithin's day (15 July), a well-known prognosticator of forty more wet days in store.[283] On the Isle of Wight Sir John Oglander experienced an exceptionally cold summer, with 'great fall of rain in August' followed by a late and poor harvest.[284] In Dorset too the summer of 1627 was 'very full of rain' and the autumn 'full of great storms of wind'. 'An extraordinary great tempest' in November 'blew down many houses and great trees' and caused dozens of ships to founder.[285] Several of the ships that had served at the Isle of Rhé were driven ashore at Plymouth in the 'great storm' that November.[286]

The year 1628 began with 'a wondrous sore wind ... overturning many buildings, barns and other', wrote John Rous in Suffolk. Adverse weather continued 'this spring and summer, even until mid July, wondrous cold and wet, with many frosts'.[287] Viscount Conway complained in early August 1628 that 'the foul weather yesterday stopped my hunting'.[288]

The bad weather of 1629 caused inconvenience to many and distress to millions. Travel in the west in March was hampered by 'days of unseasonable weather'.[289] 'I am sorry the weather proved so ill as to hinder your coming hither,' wrote Sir John Rous to a Buckinghamshire neighbour.[290]

Richard Napier noted on 18 April 1629 that 'it rained extremely most part of the day and all night, and caused so wonderful and great flood as had not been seen of forty years'.[291] By autumn the economic consequences of bad weather became apparent. The grain riots of 1629 were driven by scarcity and dearth. This was 'a pitiful scarce year of fodder, little straw and bad, nothing plentiful', wrote Thomas Wyatt of Ducklington, Oxfordshire.[292] The incumbent of Santon Downham, Suffolk, remarked at Michaelmas that a 'wonderful store of rain' had fallen, 'so that fences be drowned, firing and stover lost . . . corn riseth in price'.[293] Lady Elizabeth Masham told her mother in September that 'the wet weather hath hindered my coming to you, it making our harvest the longer'.[294] The first snow of the winter came early on 27 October 1629.[295] The Isle of Wight escaped severe frost, but the islander Sir John Oglander wrote that 'the winter of 1629 was one of the wettest that ever I knew. It rained almost every other day from Michaelmas till Lady Day' 1630. The ground was sodden, crops rotted, stock sickened, and the following year's wheat could not be sown.[296] 'This sad weather', in Sir William Masham's opinion, was the consequence of England's sin.[297]

January 1630 opened with 'weather as it is extraordinary, so is it feared will breed much sickness'.[298] That winter, noted William Laud, 'was extreme wet', though with 'scarce one week of frost'.[299] The wild January weather included 'a very great wind . . . and on the next night extraordinary fierce meteors . . . which makes the common sort, who are not acquainted with the work of nature, to talk much', reported a correspondent of Viscount Scudamore.[300] Lady Judith Barrington complained in April 1630 of 'this cold weather I think freezing actions as well as spoiling all our hopes of store of plums'.[301] In May 1630 James Harrison wrote of 'the unseasonableness of the weather and unfitness of the ways for travel'.[302]

Some people attributed the recurrence of plague in 1630 to the 'excessive rains' in 'the unseasonableness of the last winter'.[303] More obviously, the wet weather affected the grain crop and hindered the harvest, one of the worst on record, leading to a spike in food prices.[304] Wheat that sold for 7*s.* 4*d.* a bushel in London in October 1630 cost 9*s.* by November. Oatmeal prices shot up from 6*s.* 8*d.* a bushel to 8*s.* in the same short period.[305] In Dorset William Whiteway noted, 'harvest corn began to grow very dear . . . malting was restrained'. Grain prices rose from 6*s.* and 7*s.* a bushel to as much as 10*s.*, 'and in the north country far dearer, by means of the last wet winter'.[306] A rash of grain riots pitted officials and providers against local consumers of scarce food.[307] There was 'a pitiful scarce poor early harvest . . . snow much in some places', wrote a dispirited Thomas Wyatt.[308] His Oxfordshire neighbour John Randol may have had this year's weather in mind when he observed that 'the cataracts of heaven are let loose: dry *Aries* into watery *Pisces* changed . . . these are more than signs that the king of kings is highly displeased with us'. Preaching at Burford, Randol listed God's chastisements: by war and famine, 'by spongy clouds and by tempestuous hail, by scorching summers and snowy winters, he may impoverish us how and when he please'.[309]

Respite from the cold occurred in January 1631, when a London correspondent remarked on 'the weather having been extraordinary warm for winter'.[310] It was the most 'extreme wet and warm January that ever was known in memory', according to William Laud.[311] The summer of 1631 was dry and hot, allowing some recovery of grain crops,[312] but on 18 October Thomas Crosfield noted 'St Luke's day, a tempest of snow and cold'.[313]

The year 1632 opened dramatically with 'a mighty tempest . . . with thunder and lightning' on the south coast.[314] Midsummer that year was 'the coldest June clean through that was ever felt in my memory', with more cold weather in July, according to bishop Laud.[315] Heavy rains spoiled the late summer hay harvest.[316] There was 'much wet' leading to 'an extraordinary backward harvest', wrote Thomas Wyatt.[317] Lady Joan Coke informed her husband in October 1632, 'we have had a great deal of rain which makes great floods'.[318]

More 'unseasonable weather' followed in the winter and spring of 1633. A correspondent in London complained in January that 'the weather hath been so unseasonable and the air so darkened with much rain, which is now turned to snow, that scarce be called or numbered among days'. The weather was so bad, he continued, that it 'hath kept me from going abroad to do any business or hear any news'.[319] On 18 April Thomas Wyatt recorded in Oxfordshire, 'the ground was covered white with snow'.[320] Thomas Knyvett commented in London in May on 'the ill disposition of the weather, which hath been extreme wet and cold here ever since I came'.[321] The king's state entry into York that month was almost eclipsed by 'extreme wind and rain . . . all day long'.[322] On 17 July, however, Sir Humphrey Mildmay noted, 'the day was a hot one'.[323] Laud recorded 'rainy weather continuing' from mid-September to mid-November 1633, 'which made a marvelous ill seed time'.[324] The worst that could be said of November in Essex was that it was 'cold and misty'.[325]

If England's weather appeared warmer and more stable for a while, the benign interlude was brief.[326] The New Year opened with 'an extraordinary great snow' and a frost so hard that the Thames was frozen.[327] ''Tis so foul weather that I cannot go abroad,' wrote George Garrard from London on 9 January 1634.[328] 'Frosty weather' continued for much of the month.[329] In February 'an extraordinary great wind' ripped off part of the roof of Cranbourne House, Dorset, and shook loose structural timbers.[330] By March, however, it was 'very fine', then 'sad and lowering', with 'cold winds'.[331] Spring rain brought floods to Nottinghamshire, where John Holles wrote in April that 'the weather hath been so extreme as the nurse could not get hither for waters'.[332] The end of October saw 'fair and happy weather' in Essex, 'but inclined to rain, for all which blessed be God'.[333] Archbishop Laud noted 'the driest and fairest time' in London that autumn, 'save three days frost'. Frost began in earnest as winter set in, with 'the Thames almost frozen' again from 10 to 17 December.[334]

The year 1635 opened with 'great frost and hard weather' as the harshest winter in memory continued. Several times that January Sir Humphrey Mildmay recorded 'a sore day of frost and snow' in Essex, or 'a sad hard weather for frost and snow'.[335] William Whiteway in Dorset recorded 'an extreme hard winter with much frost, snow, hail, cold, rain . . . Many drowned in snow.' He noted that the Thames in London had frozen 'and men went and rode over it', adding, 'the ink did freeze in my pen while I did write'.[336] The River Thames froze on 5 January 1635, and remained frozen until 3 February.[337] The Court of High Commission had to reschedule its meeting at Lambeth on 29 January 'in regard the passage on the Thames was frozen up, whereby neither commissioners nor parties could have safe access'.[338] The poet William Baker marked the occasion with an ode in Latin, 'Descriptio brumae et intensissimi Januario mense frigoris, quo Thamesis omnino congelata fuit.'[339] The 'great frost' allowed young men of Walton-on-Thames to cross the ice for merriment at 'a house of disorder'.[340] Further north, the Trent in Lincolnshire was frozen so hard that young men of Gainsborough played football on the ice.[341] Commissioners sent to examine witnesses in Staffordshire in January 1635 could not complete their journey because 'the weather was so extreme by reason of the falling snow and strong winds'.[342]

Correspondents recorded 'very deep driving snow' in January 1635, followed by more the next month. On one day in February, 'it snew all the afternoon from three o'clock until afternoon the next day, which weather hath made his majesty to lay aside his Newmarket journey for this winter'.[343] 'The ways and weather are so bad,' complained the Countess of Sunderland, after a February thaw turned to ice again.[344] It snowed in Essex on 22 February, followed by 'bitter weather of snow and frost all the day' next.[345] 'We have had exceeding bad weather ever since Christmas,' wrote the Wiltshire gentleman John Nicholas on 23 February 1635, 'the ground is now covered with snow and our sheep live by hay only, I never knew a harder time ... a great number of sheep will die. I cannot remember a harder winter. The frost and snow keeps us from ploughing, so that I fear we shall be very backward in sowing. God's will be done.'[346]

Writing to the court from Leicestershire on 3 March 1635, Lord Henry Hastings excused his remissness in fulfilling purveyance requirements 'in regard of the sharpness of the weather and rising of the waters ... and since that time the snow and floods have been so extreme that until this very few days we could not stir scarce a mile from our houses but with danger'.[347] 'We have had a very cold season here for this latter part of winter,' wrote the Londoner George Garrard, 'the snowy and frosty weather' again diverting the king and queen from travel.[348] 'Sore weather' continued through the rest of March, with notable wind and rain.[349] Conditions at Nottingham were so severe that 'in regard of the uncertainty of the weather and the coldness of the season' the customary festivities at St Anne's well were postponed from Easter Monday (30 March) to Monday in Whitsun week (18 May).[350] 'We yet scarce know what time of the year it is, so very cold is the weather,' complained a correspondent in Norfolk that May.[351] A late snowfall at Whitsun further disrupted royal travel.[352] The summer was dry, but the 'extreme thunder and lightning' in August was more violent than Archbishop Laud could remember, 'the lightning so thick, bright and frequent'. In November Laud noted 'the greatest tide that hath been seen', inundating his Thames-side stables and cloisters at Lambeth.[353] An unusual phenomenon at the beginning of December, Laud observed, was 'many elm leaves yet upon the trees, which few men have seen'.[354]

The weather seemed out of joint to the assize judges at Worcester in Lent 1636, when they had to hire extra cloths 'to keep the seats dry in respect of abundance of rain'.[355] April and May, however, were mostly 'dry and hot', increasing the likelihood of plague.[356] The summer drought stretched into September, 'causing the greatest suffering to everything and making the miserable weakness of the country people general', according to the Venetian ambassador in London. 'Everyone declares that there is no memory of such a misfortune in England.'[357] Storms returned in the autumn, with 'a very sore wind' in November 1636 that 'overturned many mills, split and sunk two barges and drowned the men' in East Anglia.[358] A year later people were still discussing 'the great windy night that blew down so many houses, barns and trees in all parts of the kingdom'.[359] Sir Humphrey Mildmay recorded 3 November as 'a very wet and windy day, my house being foul and wet'.[360] Archbishop Laud, much given to superlatives, called it 'the most extreme wind that ever I heard'.[361] That same week the courtier Earl of Holland fell unwell 'by reason of a very wet journey to and from Windsor'.[362] The year ended with 'the extremity of this cold and tempestuous weather', which aggravated 'the miserable condition of our poor mariners' off the southern coasts.[363]

The Oxfordshire diarist Thomas Wyatt noted 1637 as 'a very unkindly year' for weather, 'a most hard dear scarce year of corn and all provisions, a cutting hungry year'.[364] Sir Humphrey Mildmay recorded changeable conditions, hot, cold, wet, and dry, but nothing exceptional.[365] Tempests in January ravaged Cambridge with 'a violent wind',[366] and Essex experienced 'a wonderful snowy and stormy night'.[367] 'A great tempest of thunder and rain' struck Oxford in February,[368] and parts of East Anglia received a hard frost.[369] Most of the spring was 'very dry' in southern England, with a 'cold easterly wind'. By July, however, George Garrard could record a 'good store of rain of late'.[370] The Northamptonshire diarist recorded 'much unseasonable rain' in August,[371] and the weather was so wet and 'extreme' that the king's hunting was ruined.[372] Archbishop Laud noted that the weather was 'very rainy' in August, with 'extreme and unnatural hot winter weather' in November.[373] The year ended with 'great snow and very sharp weather' in December.[374]

Courtiers endured another frigid spell in January 1638, when 'the coldness of the weather' depleted audiences for the Twelfth Night masques.[375] 'The sharpness of the weather is such as I cannot bear it,' wrote Lady Brilliana Harley in Herefordshire.[376] In February once again it was 'foul, windy, and no ways fair'.[377] The minister William Morton remarked on the 'extremity' of conditions as he rode to Cambridge that month when 'the weather proved extreme bitter'.[378] It was 'very rainy' again in May, and excessively wet in August, when 'extreme rain' spoiled the waters of Harrogate spa.[379] It was wet and tempestuous again in the autumn, when 'the watermen called it Queen Mother weather', commenting on Marie de Medici's visit to London. 'I was never upon the water in the like storm,'

Laud wrote of this 'most extreme tempest upon the Thames'.[380] It was 'lamentable wet weather... extreme rainy', wrote Robert Woodford in Northamptonshire.[381] Amid 'mighty thundering', a freak ball of lightning struck the church at Widdecombe, Devon, that October, prompting parishioners to 'behold the works of the Lord, what desolations he hath made in the earth'. The violence in the atmosphere was another of God's 'terrible warning pieces', and a sign of his 'judgements and terrible remonstrances'.[382] The 'great wind' that autumn caused deaths from falling chimneys, carried water out of rivers, and made it hard for riders to sit on horseback.[383]

More damaging storms marked the arrival of 1639. January saw 'a most grievous tempest of wind, thunder, lightning and rain'.[384] There was 'a great storm, rain, hail, snow, and great thundering and lightning, but the Lord graciously preserved me', wrote Woodford.[385] A correspondent of the Earl of Cork reported 'an extreme tempest' in mid-January, 'with thunder and lightning, which hath done much harm, and especially to two churches in Surrey near London, and to one at Gravesend'.[386] Thomas Smith told Sir John Pennington that 'the last great lightning has done a world of mischief all over England', striking people with 'a panic fear'.[387] Early in March 'the coldness of the season' induced 'a multitude' at Exeter cathedral to 'put on their hats', so they said, 'without the least thought or intention of irreverence or disrespect' either to the place or the proclamation regarding Scotland that was read on that occasion.[388]

Meterorological conditions reduced the effectiveness of the king's fighting forces, sent north that year to confront the rebellious Scots. An observer reported in June 1639 that 'many of them by reason of ill weather and hard travelling are sick and have died'.[389] Another found the troops at the border ill-equipped for days of 'rain and cold'.[390] The summer in southern England was meanwhile 'calm and pleasant', going on 'clear and very hot', before the dry spell broke at the end of July and more heavy rain followed. August in Essex was windy, rainy, 'very foul' according to Sir Humphrey Mildmay, with calm and clear intervals giving way to 'sad and most unseasonable weather'.[391] The year drew to a close with snow as early as 27 November, and rain so bad that Mildmay thought is 'very like to flood'.[392] On 27 December 1639 southern England suffered a wind so severe that boats were smashed, chimneys toppled, and one of the pinnacles at Croydon fell through the roof of the church. It was, said archbishop Laud, 'the greatest wind that ever I heard blow'.[393] It was a tempestuous end to a decade of violent weather. Snow, frost, storms, and inundations made the revolutionary decade that followed no better.[394]

Social disorders were remediable, social leaders thought, by applications of discipline; hierarchy might be maintained by harping upon it and reminding people of their obligations. Nobody, however, could control the weather. Pessimists among the subjects of Charles I feared that God had withdrawn his blessings. Freezes, storms, and floods, as well as plagues, fires, and famine, were among the handiworks of the Lord, to be interpreted as judgments as well as hardships.[395] Even in halcyon days the times were out of joint.

2

The Oath of a King

Thursday, 2 February 1626, was a day of bright beginnings for Charles Stuart and his kingdom. It was Candlemas in the old religious calendar, the feast of the Purification of the Blessed Virgin Mary, which was still enjoined to be 'kept holy and solemnly of every man, as in time past hath been accustomed'. Though many protestants ignored the holiday, and puritans denounced it as a popish remnant, ceremonial enthusiasts celebrated Candlemas devoutly as a festival of lights. The day testified to Christ's 'true incarnation, by the purification of her that brought him into the world', a day of Christian beginnings.[1] Charles and his advisors chose Candlemas for one of the foundational events of his kingship, his coronation in the ancient hall and abbey church of Westminster. It was the day when he swore to uphold the laws and customs of the people and kings of England.

This chapter reconstructs the coronation of Charles I through the eyes of contemporary observers, bishops, courtiers, gatecrashers, and the king himself, to examine the ritual performance, prayers, and promises on which the regime was based. It weighs the damage caused by postponements owing to plague, the absence of the queen, and alterations in the wording of the order of service. The oath that the young king swore at his coronation in 1626 came back to haunt him in the crisis of the 1640s, when royal authority was under attack. Royalists and parliamentarians disagreed whether King Charles had broken or upheld his oath, and whether that oath obligated him to God, to the church, to parliament, or to the people.

A Royal Ritual

Though Charles became king at the instant of James I's passing—'the king is dead, long live the king'—the ritual fulfilment of his regality came only with the formal ceremony of oath-taking, anointing, and crowning. King Charles had been king since midday on 27 March 1625, and by February 1626 he had issued forty proclamations and assented to seven statutes; but a popular belief lingered that without coronation his kingship was incomplete. Local officials heard occasionally from constitutionally confused citizens who said that they would wait until the coronation before accepting the authority of a new monarch because 'he is no king till he be crowned'.[2]

A contrary notion, held by some theorists, was that the coronation constrained royal power. This was a legacy, most likely, of earlier ideas of kingship based on election and consent.[3] At the very beginning of Charles's reign the Venetian ambassador heard 'talk of the possibility of his majesty not being crowned, so as to remain more absolute, avoiding the obligation to swear to the laws and without the discontent of his subjects'. The ambassador reported in May 1625 that some members of parliament looked forward to the coronation, 'as without it they would consider their laws at the discretion of the king and not dependent on the general public authority'.[4] As was often the case, ambassador Pesaro revealed an imperfect grasp of English law and custom, but captured a kernel of truth: the coronation expressed and illuminated obligations between the king and his people, even if it did not create them. In later years controversialists would argue whether the coronation put limits on arbitrary authority by binding the king to consensual oaths, or whether it heightened the sanctity and separateness of monarchy through divine invocation. Parliamentary patriots would claim that the king had sworn promises to his people, though royal apologists would argue that Charles had solidified his compact with God.

The coronation might have happened several months earlier had not the capital been gripped by sickness. One of the worst outbreaks of plague in living memory coincided with the arrival in England of Queen Henrietta Maria, and some protestant zealots thought the events not unconnected.[5] Court observers expected a coronation close to Whitsuntide, and Sir John Davies told the Earl of Huntingdon that 'the king desires that himself and his queen may be crowned together to save a double charge, which saving will be more than an entire subsidy'.[6] Some still looked forward to a ceremony in June 1625, although 'the king intends to enter London by the river because of the plague'.[7] Alas, it was not to be, as the epidemic disrupted public life. James's coronation too had been shadowed by plague, but his entry into London was postponed, not cancelled.

> Gaze London gaze, that surfet'st with a longing,
> To see thy sovereign's coronation day:
> Thy people jocund in a dang'rous thronging,
> Lift up their voice; on their heart-strings play,

the poet Henry Petowe trilled in 1603.[8]

More than 40,000 Londoners died of the plague in the first year of Charles's reign, almost a fifth of the metropolitan population.[9] Even in January 1626 councillors worried 'that the late great and grievous infection of the plague in our said city' left London unprepared to accommodate the state proceedings of a coronation.[10] The economic consequences of the plague combined with the cost of preparing for war left little money for festivities. Although the decision that the royal party should travel from Whitehall to Westminster by water, rather than process through the city and suburbs, was influenced by concern for the participants' health, it also saved 'the charge of £60,000 in scarlet, which the king should otherwise have been at'. Londoners who had begun to devise triumphal arches for the royal entry set those preparations aside. The Lord Chamberlain told the City they were hazards to traffic.[11] 'All the scaffolds and pageants are pulled down that were erected for the king going through London, there will be no show,' wrote a northern correspondent that winter.[12]

Historians who write about the coronation of Charles I usually emphasize what went wrong. Knowing that Charles's reign ended disastrously, in civil war, regicide, and revolution, they tend to interpret glitches and anomalies in its early years as portents of ills to come. The approach is anachronistic and ironic, in the knowledge that the young monarch in white would one day lose his throne. The verdict is mixed, whether opportunities of the day were botched or well managed, with positive or negative consequences. For bishop William Laud, however, and the king he served, the day was perfect: 'nothing was lost, or broke, or disordered.' There was never solemnity performed 'with so little noise, and so great order', was Laud's delighted appraisal.[13] King Charles shone in a doublet and hose of white satin, with ribbons on his shoulders and arms, and trailed a train of purple velvet. Peter Heylyn, Laud's chaplain and biographer, thought it significant that the king appeared in white, the colour of the saints and of virginal innocence, like a bridegroom espousing his kingdom. But this may be tinged with hindsight, recalling Charles's comment as he went to his execution in 1649, 'this is my second marriage-day ... for before night I hope to be espoused to my blessed Jesus'.[14] Lord Keeper Coventry evoked a happier image in his opening speech to parliament on 6 February 1626, 'his majesty having, at his royal coronation, lately solemnized the sacred rites of that blessed marriage between him and his people'.[15]

No pamphlets or commemorative relations were published to memorialize the coronation of Charles I, in contrast to the flood of publications in 1603, so reconstruction relies on scribal accounts and later memoirs. There was, however, a commemorative coronation medal showing the crowned king on one side and an arm with a sword of power on the other, a declaration of martial might.[16]

We are reminded that the coronation was postponed because of plague, and that it was conducted in the absence of cheering crowds and jostling spectators. The king's passage by barge along the Thames, rather than by carriage along the Strand, forfeited the opportunity for king and people to salute each other. It was royal ceremony, an action of 'high state', but 'without the customary royal cavalcade'. The 'riding through London' was 'put off', so the king made no official ceremonial entry. Contemporary observers described this coronation as 'private' or 'privately conducted', though unusually orderly and 'punctual'.[17] Some historians see this as contributing to the image of a reserved and inaccessible monarch who distanced himself from his subjects.[18] Others regard it as a prudent response to difficult conditions of financial and public health. Even Kevin Sharpe, who treats King Charles as a paragon, concedes that it may have been a miscalculation.[19] Mark Kishlansky alone considers it 'another extravagant public festival' that 'not only included all the great nobles and clerics of the kingdom, but attracted gentry and ordinary people as well'.[20] Historians, like historical observers, perhaps see what they want to see.

On the coronation day in 1626 a strong tide in the Thames forced King Charles's barge to overshoot its intended landing at Sir Robert Cotton's stairs at Westminster, where the antiquarian was waiting with the venerable Anglo-Saxon Book of the Evangelists on which the king would swear his oath. Instead the royal party disembarked at the dirtier and less commodious Parliament Stairs, requiring some hasty readjustment of programme and protocol. At least one historian agrees with Sir Simonds D'Ewes, who saw this as a deliberate snub to Cotton, engineered by enemies associated with the Duke of Buckingham, though it might as well be due to poor boatsmanship. D'Ewes in his autobiography later remarked that 'the dashing of the royal barge into the ground was taken to be an evil and ominous presage', although he made no such comment in his contemporary correspondence.[21]

Court watchers, like later historians, noted who was present and who was absent. The *dramatis personae* and order of placement revealed rising and falling fortunes. Most ostentatiously absent was the queen, whose French Oratorian priests held her back from any ceremony they deemed heretical. Draft plans for the service included a double coronation for both king and queen, but Henrietta Maria preferred to watch from a window rather than take part.

Contemporary commentators could not hide their disapproval, nor their concern for the safety of English protestantism. The Norfolk gentleman Thomas Knyvett wrote to his wife that 'the queen refuses to be crowned unless she may be crowned after the French fashion with her priests'. The Dorchester diarist William Whiteway recorded that 'the queen refused to be crowned by any protestant bishop, without dispensation from the pope'. Sir Benjamin Rudyard observed that the queen's catholic church 'holds the sacring to be a spiritual act and therefore allows no such authority to any of our bishops'. The Cambridge gossip Joseph Meade reported that the queen 'stood at a window in the mean time, looking on, and her ladies frisking and dancing in the room'. Henry Manners added the information that this house with the window belonged to Sir Abraham Williams, the agent for the protestant queen of Bohemia.[22] Reflecting on her majesty's absence two and a half centuries later, the influential historian Samuel Rawson Gardiner remarked, somewhat gratuitously, that the empty seat for Henrietta Maria 'must have reminded Charles bitterly of the misery of his home life and of the most conspicuous failure of his political life'.[23] Henrietta Maria was proclaimed queen on 20 June 1625, a week after her arrival in England, but she was never formally crowned queen consort.

Another significant absentee was John Williams, bishop of Lincoln and dean of Westminster, until recently Lord Keeper of the Great Seal, who would normally have presided in the abbey church. Williams, however, had fallen from power, a casualty of court politics, and would have no part in the ceremony. As the seventeenth-century church historian Thomas Fuller put it, he was 'daily descendant in the king's favour'. In January 1626 Williams wrote plaintively to Buckingham offering his 'best service for the preparation to the coronation', but his opening was quickly spurned.[24] Instead the dean's role was given to a deputy, a Buckingham supporter, the fast-rising churchman William Laud. Laud was bishop of the Welsh diocese of St David's and a relatively junior prebendary of Westminster, but he had the ear of the duke and the king. Laud took a major role in preparing the order of service, including the text of the king's coronation oath, a role that would come back to haunt him in 1644 when he was tried and executed for treason.[25]

The substitution of Laud for Williams offered clues to the future of English religious culture, as Calvinists were eclipsed and anti-Calvinists advanced. In the view of the modern historian Thomas Corns: 'Buckingham turned the procession to Westminster Abbey into the occasion for factional feuding; the high profile given to the Arminian Laud in the proceedings ensured that the ceremony itself was an example of division within the church rather than a manifestation of confessional unity.'[26] Not all scholars would take so harsh a view, nor would all agree that Laud was an Arminian, though most would concur that his appointment was significant. Laud carefully prepared 'the ceremonies of the coronation' in close consultation with the king. Standing in for the dean of Westminster, he 'prepared all things ready for that great solemnity. And finding the old crucifix among the *regalia*, he caused it to be placed on the altar, as in former times.' This went unremarked in 1626 (as it had in 1603), but it was cited in Laud's trial eighteen years later as proof of his predilection for popery.[27]

The coronation had roles for a selection of bishops, though not the entire episcopal bench. The presiding prelate was the primate of England, the Archbishop of Canterbury George Abbot, whose star was otherwise fading. Abbot had the misfortune, several years earlier, to kill a gamekeeper in a hunting accident, and this stain of blood undermined his authority. As a moderate Calvinist, he was out of sympathy with the rising Arminians, though the conflict was yet to be critical. Other bishops on duty, all in their richest copes, included Richard Senhouse of Carlisle to preach the sermon, Samuel Harsnet of Norwich to read the Gospel, Theophilus Field of Llandaff to read the Epistle, George Mountaigne of London to carry St Edward's chalice, Lancelot Andrews of Winchester to carry the paten, Richard Neile of Durham and Arthur Lake of Bath and Wells to support the king's person, and Laud of St David's to administer the communion cup. The arch-Arminian John Cosin also had coronation duties, as chaplain to bishop Neile and as the cleric who prompted the choir when to answer.[28]

The nobility were assembled in force, including a score of earls plus eight more made that day, seven viscounts, two dozen barons, and a phalanx of privy councillors, judges, household officers, and fifty-eight newly dubbed knights of the Bath. Especially honoured were the earls of Dorset, Essex, and Kent, each carrying ceremonial swords; the Earl of Montgomery with the consecrated spurs; Sussex carrying the orb of rule; Rutland carrying the sceptre or rod with the dove of clemency; the Marquess of Hamilton with the sword of state; and the Earl of Pembroke (Lord Chamberlain) with the ancient crown of St Edward. A score more earls were absent, including the earls of Bedford, Bristol, Huntingdon, Somerset, and Northumberland.[29]

Huntingdon's excuse for not attending was an artful brush-off. He told the Lord Chamberlain, 'my desire to do his majesty service would silence me for rendering any reason for my not giving my attendance. But truly my lord, I could not in so short a space provide myself fittingly for so royal a time.' Are we to believe that he could not get his kit ready? Apologizing a month later for his failure to attend parliament, the stay-at-home Huntingdon listed as excuses his health, the weather, his debts, his occasions, and the sending of his son to Cambridge.[30] The Earl of Exeter excused his attendance by reference to 'a grievous fit of the gout', but otherwise protested his readiness to do his duty.[31]

The only commoners involved in the coronation, besides heralds, ushers, and musicians, were the Lord Mayor and aldermen of London, gentlemen of the king's bedchamber, gentlemen pensioners, and guards. There was no need to find places for members of the House of Commons, since parliament was not then sitting.

Most prominent, beside the king, was George Villiers, Duke of Buckingham, who had managed to stay favourite to both James I and his son. Buckingham was the highest-ranking nobleman in England, the sole duke among the aristocracy, much deferred to by suppliants though hated behind his back. On the day of the coronation Buckingham's new office of Lord High Constable required him to walk closely in front of the king, carrying the mace, alongside the Earl of Arundel, Earl Marshall of England. As Master of the Horse it was Buckingham's duty to receive and to wear the consecrated spurs.[32]

A much-repeated story tells that as King Charles mounted the stage to his throne of estate in Westminster Hall he was helped by the duke, 'whether he would or not'. (Gardiner has the king stumbling, though the sources do not indicate a mis-step.) Charles was heard to say to Buckingham, with some levity, 'I have as much needs to assist you as you to assist me,' a comment much-parsed for its political significance. The author of this story, Simonds D'Ewes, remarked that 'searching brains might pick much from it'.

It was testimony to Buckingham's power and confidence that in public, on such an occasion, he should lay his hand on the sacred arm of a king.[33]

D'Ewes followed the procession from Westminster Hall to the abbey, and so had 'the happiness to be a spectator' at the coronation. Though not officially invited, D'Ewes 'endeavoured to get into the church', he reports, and 'spying a door guarded by one, and thronged by a few, I went, and with little trouble found an easy entrance'. Though technically a gate-crasher, D'Ewes managed to get close to 'the stage on which stood the royal seat', and left an eye-witness account of the spectacle. (D'Ewes himself was knighted later in 1626 and subsequently became a baronet.)

Formalities began with the archbishop of Canterbury calling upon 'the people' to recognize and acclaim their monarch. 'The people', in this case, included everyone present in Westminster Abbey, including the London elite and the assembled aristocracy. Archbishop Abbot followed his script and said the words: 'Sirs, here I present unto you King Charles the rightful inheritor of the crown of this realm. Wherefore all you that be come this day to do your homage and service and bounden duty, be ye willing to do the same?' Instead of a cheer there fell an awkward silence, until the Earl Marshal, the Earl of Arundel, restored momentum by leading the cry of 'God save King Charles'. Alternative texts, preserved in manuscript, invited 'the people' to have King Charles 'to be your king and become subjects unto him and submit yourselves to his commandments', and to give 'assents to the said coronation, inunction [i.e. anointing], and consecration'. The words implied that 'the people' freely consented to the authority of their monarch, though no one was going to say 'nay'. 'Consent to the coronation' implied consent to the kingship it endorsed, as if there was any choice in the matter.[34]

Bishop Senhouse rose to deliver his sermon on the text from Revelation: 'And I will give thee a crown of life.' The sermon was designed to fortify King Charles 'against tribulations and oppositions for Christ's cause'. No doubt his majesty listened attentively, but some observers thought it more suited to a funeral than a coronation. Others, D'Ewes among them, 'could hear little or nothing'. Peter Heylyn remarked later that it was 'rather thought to put the new king in mind of his death than his duty in government', though only after 1649, when King Charles was depicted with a crown of thorns, would the coronation sermon be thought to have 'something . . . of presage'.[35] Richard Senhouse himself was said to be suffering from 'the black jaundice . . . a disease which hangs the face with mourning',[36] and died three months after the coronation, falling from his horse.

When the sermon was finished the archbishop went up to the king to tender 'the oath usually taken by his predecessors'. Though not the ritual centrepiece of the coronation, and not mentioned at all by D'Ewes, the royal oath was to generate more political controversy than any other aspect of the ceremony. English monarchs had sworn coronation oaths since Saxon times, but the words were subject to periodic revision. By the sixteenth century the oaths were in English, rather than French or Latin, and were adjusted to reflect the Tudor reformation and royal supremacy in matters ecclesiastical.[37] William Laud had led the committee to prepare the text for the coronation of King Charles, and was later charged with altering the oath to enhance the royal prerogative. Variant versions in different manuscripts show minor differences that would be subject to subsequent dispute, though they mostly adhered to the script of 1603.

The archbishop asked the king four questions pertaining to the people, laws, customs, and church of England, to each of which he replied affirmatively. It is worth paying close attention to these engagements because they articulate a theory of kingship that would soon be controversial. King Charles's coronation oath became a fulcrum of contention in the crises of the 1640s.[38]

First:

> Sir, will you grant and keep, and so by your oath confirm, to the people of England, the laws and customs to them granted by the kings of England your lawful and religious predecessors; and namely the laws, customs, and franchises granted to the clergy by the glorious king St Edward your predecessor (according to the laws of God, the true profession of the Gospel established in this kingdom, and agreeable to the prerogatives of the kings thereof, and the ancient customs of this realm)?

To which the king replied: 'I grant and promise to keep them.'

Second: 'Sir, will you keep peace and godly agreement, entirely according to your power, both to God, the holy church, the clergy and people?' Charles: 'I will keep it.'

Third: 'Sir, will you, to your power, cause law, justice and discretion, in mercy and truth, to be executed in all your judgements?' Charles: 'I will.'

Fourth: 'Sir, will you grant to keep and hold the laws and rightful customs which the commonalty of this your kingdom have; and will you defend and uphold them to the honour of God, so much as in you lyeth?' Charles: 'I grant and promise so to do.'

These questions and answers constitute an oath, but not a contract. Though performed before the people (at least an elite fraction of them), the oath was sworn not to them, but to God. King Charles staked his immortal soul on his fealty to these words, which bound him to strict obligations. The obligations, however, like everything else in these utterances, were subject to interpretation. Important phrases were added or subtracted, to make King Charles's oath different from those of his predecessors. Words and clauses were subject to gloss and spin. The phrase in the first question alluding to the laws of God, the true profession of the Gospel, the prerogatives of kings, and the ancient customs of the realm (shown here in parentheses), was an addition not found in all manuscripts. It may have been added by the committee that prepared the order of service, guided by William Laud. The words can be interpreted as a let-out clause, since who knew exactly what those laws, prerogatives, and customs comprehended? A shorter phrase of equal import was omitted in this first question, when the laws, customs, and franchises were 'granted to the clergy', rather than 'to the clergy and to the people', which had been the usage at the coronation of James I.

Missing from the fourth question, about laws 'which the commonalty of this your kingdom have', was the next word 'chosen', which appeared in sixteenth-century versions. This would become an explosive issue in the 1640s, when parliament charged Laud with leaving out the word *elegerit* from the Latin version of the oath which traditionally read '*quas vulgus elegerit*' (which the people choose, will choose, or have chosen). Though one controversialist argued that 'the word *elegerit*, whether it be future or past, it skills not', another observed 'as much difference between the tenses, as between democracy and monarchy'. Laud's enemies forgot to mention that the same form of words was used in English in the coronation of 1603, with neither 'choose' or 'chosen', and that nobody at the time was troubled by the omission.[39]

The king further bound himself to preserve clerical privileges and to uphold episcopal government of the church, 'as every good king in his kingdom ought' to do. He then went to the high altar and, laying his hand on the ancient Bible, swore: 'The things that I have before promised I shall perform and keep, so help me God, and the contents of this book.'

It is likely that only those closest to the king and archbishop heard the words of the oath, but everyone would know that Charles had sworn to them. He was as much a king before the oath as after, with no augmentation or diminution of his authority, but Charles himself had entered a new relationship with majesty, his ancestors, and with God. The words he had sworn had solemn import, and would stiffen him through later crises.[40] Addressing the House of Lords four days after the ceremony in Westminster Abbey, Lord Keeper Sir Thomas Coventry reminded the peers that the king, 'by a most holy oath, vowed the protection of the laws and maintenance of peace both to the church and people', and that, just as 'his majesty has vowed protection to his people', they in turn, and most of the lords in their own persons, 'have protested their allegiance and service to him'.[41]

After the swearing the ceremony still had hours to go, to its climax of anointing and crowning. The 'unction' or application of holy oils was performed behind curtains, away from observation, but the crowning was done in the face of the congregation. D'Ewes, whose perch beside the stage gave a good vantage point, could not see the crucial anointing of the king's 'naked shoulders, arms, hands, and head'; because 'they were *arcana*, a traverse was drawn' to shield King Charles from onlookers. He told Sir Martin Stuteville: 'I dare say boldly few more single persons than there were thousands within the church saw it.' The anecdote gives grist to those who claim that Charles I was unusually protective of royal mysteries, and that he failed to exercise or exploit his charisma.[42] The ritual unction with oil gave symbolic substance to sacred kingship, though theologians argued that the king was already anointed by divine-right succession. That the king had undergone this ceremony allowed powerful application of the biblical injunction, 'touch not mine anointed', which would become a royalist slogan in the 1640s.[43]

The coronation prayers set forth a vision of sanctified kingship, in which the king was radiant with divine blessing. If God was with him, how could he fail? Prayers called on God that King Charles might be 'strengthened with the faith of Abraham, endued with the mildness of Moses, armed with the fortitude of Joshua, exalted with the humility of David, [and] beautified with the wisdom of Solomon'. It was a tall order for a stripling Stuart, but necessary if his reign was to match his father's.[44]

Subsequent stages of the ritual set forth an agenda for idealized chivalric monarchy, though the qualities prayed for were not necessarily those that the oath had promised. Devoted to God and God's cause, the king would undertake the 'defence and protection of churches, widows, orphans, and all the servants of God, against the savage cruelty of pagans and infidels'. He would 'restore the things that are gone to decay, maintain the things that are restored, be avenged of injustice, and confirm the things that are in good order'. He would 'punish the wicked, and protect the just'.[45] The fact that these were platitudes, conventional bromides, hardly mattered to a king who took platitudes extremely seriously.

Though largely absent from the ceremony, 'the people' appeared in important prayers. The bishops prayed that King Charles 'may joyfully receive the estate of supreme government' and 'may happily govern the people committed to his charge'; that he 'may nourish and teach, defend and instruct' God's church and people; and 'that being underpropped with the due obedience, and honoured with the condign love of this his people, he may... ascend up to the throne of his forefathers'. They prayed for 'health in our country, and peace in our kingdom', and asked that the king 'may be amiable and loving to the lords and nobles, and all the faithful subjects of the kingdom, that he may be feared and loved by all men'. The Machiavellian conundrum of whether it were better to be feared than loved would be resolved by a monarch who aspired to be both.[46]

If the king was like a bridegroom, espoused to his nation, his people, like wives or brides, were obliged to love, honour, and obey. Obligations may have been 'interchanged and mutual', as John Milton later suggested, but the reciprocity was by no means evenly matched. As Milton's royalist antagonist Salmasius put it, 'the people swear allegiance to the king, not the king to the people'. To which Milton retorted, 'what a lovely lie!'[47]

Ordinary people could acknowledge the ceremony at Westminster, and perhaps participate vicariously through token celebrations in their parishes. Instructions went out 'that bells shall be rung at every church, and bonfires made in the streets, to show the people's rejoicing on the day of the king's coronation, which is intended to be Candlemas day next, God willing'. The consequent ringing and fire-making alerted the people of England to the ritual transformation of their monarch.[48]

A Contested Oath

The revolutionary crisis of the 1640s renewed attention to the oaths King Charles performed at his coronation. Critics charged that the king had broken his oath to protect his people, and that he had arbitrarily and wrongly misinterpreted its terms. They also claimed that the actual words of the coronation oath had been altered in favour of prerogative power.

Royalists countered that the king indeed kept all promises, and in particular was bound by his oath to uphold the bishops and their government in the church. As one royalist pamphleteer scolded opponents, 'you are offended with his majesty, not because he hath broke his oath, but because he will not break it'. The conflict between king and parliament over

> the defence and maintenance of the laws, customs, and franchises of the people and clergy; and of peace and godly agreement among them; and of law, justice, and mercy; and of the laws and rightful customs of the commonalty; and the preservation and protection of the bishops, their churches and privileges, is the sum of the king's coronation oath. And is not this also the ground of his late quarrel?[49]

The controversy drew attention to the text and meaning of the oath, and to the fundamental questions of law and principle behind it. The coronation oath encapsulated but failed to clarify the ambiguous relationship between the king and people.

King James had written that 'this oath in the coronation is the clearest civil and fundamental law, whereby the king's office is properly defined'.[50] Yet not all his subjects held the oath to be binding. The controversial civil lawyer John Cowell set forth the absolutist notion that, the coronation oath notwithstanding, the king 'may alter or suspend any particular law that seemeth hurtful to the public estate'.[51] Parliamentarians, for the most part, thought otherwise, and held the king to be subject to law. But it was rare to find anyone who imagined that a king was answerable to his people for the terms of his oath.

One who did was Henry Burton, a former royal chaplain who became a relentless critic of the king's religious policies. According to Burton, the king had sworn 'an explicit solemn oath to maintain the ancient laws and liberties of the kingdom, and so to rule and govern all his people according to those laws established'. The people in turn swore 'fealty, allegiance, subjection and obedience to their king, and that according to his just laws'. The coronation oath, by this interpretation, was a contract that, if broken, dissolved the 'indissoluble bond' between the king and his subjects. Burton suggested in 1636 that 'innovations' in religion, approved or allowed by the king, moved England toward a popish tyranny and therefore violated his oath.[52]

Another troubled puritan, Jeremiah Burroughs, in the course of a private conversation in 1638, 'put a case concerning a king that at his coronation should swear to observe the ancient laws and liberties of the kingdom, yet afterward should exercise tyranny upon his people and make no conscience of his oath, whether it were not lawful to refuse obedience unto him, to resist him by force, and to defend ourselves and liberties by arms?' This, of course, was hypothetical, though his conversation partner recognized it to be 'full of danger'.[53] Speaking a few years later in June 1642 the Yorkshireman John Troutbeck declared that 'if the king did not keep the laws and his oath . . . he might be deposed for ought he knew'.[54]

The form of Charles I's coronation oath had not been printed in 1626, nor was it published in the years of his personal rule. In contrast to the Jacobean era, which saw a flowering of post-coronation publications, the Caroline press was mute on this matter. But, as civil war loomed and then raged, and as the revolution proceeded to regicide, several authors offered versions or summaries of the text. Some replicated, or closely approximated, the form of words to which Charles had formally assented. Others printed incomplete extracts, or different oaths altogether. Royalist publications usually included the proviso, 'according to the laws of God, the true profession of the Gospel established in this kingdom, and agreeable to the prerogatives of the kings thereof, and the ancient customs of this realm', whereas parliamentary treatises tended to omit this Laudian emendation.[55]

Parliamentary publications of 1642 referred to 'the oath which *ought* to be taken by the kings of this realm at their coronation' (emphasis added). Several included a text of 'the oath of the kings of England at their coronation'. But rather than the oath tendered to any Tudor or Stuart, they rendered the oath of the Lancastrian Henry IV, in which the king promised to 'keep the church of God, the clergy and people, entirely in peace and concord'; to 'cause equal right and justice in all judgements and discretion, in mercy and truth'; and to 'grant just laws and customs to be kept and protected, and to the honour of God to be strengthened, which the common people shall choose, according to [his] power'.[56] The product of an entirely different political era, this held kings to a very different standard, more as stewards than as rulers of their people. The same brief text appeared in another parliamentary publication in 1646, *King James His Opinion and Iudgement, concerning a Reall King and a Tyrant*, implying that the Lancastrian oath was the proper form for kings to have sworn.[57]

Some critics of royal policy argued that the oath itself had been amended, to usher in a kingship that was arbitrary and extreme. Archbishop Laud's accusers charged him with altering parts of the coronation oath by adding the words 'agreeable to the king's prerogative' and leaving out the clause '*quae populus elegerit*, which the people have chosen, or shall choose' (otherwise '*quas vulgus elegerit*'). These changes, it was claimed, tilted the constitutional balance away from the commonwealth and towards royal autocracy. They were evidence, so his enemies insisted, of Laud's treasonable design 'to subvert the fundamental laws and government of the kingdom', and to advance 'unlimited and absolute power'. Laud, at his trial in 1644, argued that the phrase about the prerogative did no such thing, 'for the king's just and legal prerogative, and the subject's assurance for liberty and property, may stand well together, and have so stood for hundreds of years'. Laud did not deny making the alteration, only that it had any significance. As to the missing clause '*quae populus elegerit*', that was omitted in the coronation of King James too, and was not found in the working texts at Laud's disposal. Downplaying his central role in drafting the order of service, Laud protested: 'I was merely ministerial, both in the preparation and at the coronation itself, supplying the place of the Dean of Westminster.' Neither protestation nor demonstration that the words of King Charles and King James were substantially the same could prevent the view spreading that Laud had doctored the oath.[58] With minor but disputable differences, the words and the ritual of 1626 were modelled on those of 1603. The church historian Thomas Fuller poured scorn on 'that scandalous pamphleteer, who hath written that King Charles was not crowned like other kings; whereas all essentials of his coronation were performed with as much ceremony as ever before'.[59]

Parliamentary propagandists insisted that *elegerit* was in the future tense, and that the king's oath bound him to uphold all bills passed by Lords and Commons 'for the good of the whole kingdom'. This would include assent to the Militia bill, which would strip the king of control of the armed forces, and bills that would eclipse the ecclesiastical rule of bishops. 'The king's oath', declared one pamphlet of 1643, obliged him to grant and permit such laws and customs as the people 'shall choose justly and reasonably'.[60] Expanding this, the leveller John Wildman declared at Putney in 1647 that the oath obliged the king 'to grant such laws as the people shall choose', with no legislative voice of his own.[61] Royalists claimed that '*quas vulgus elegerit*' referred only to laws already in being, and besides, King Charles swore no such words.[62] Both sides invoked the coronation oath and interpreted it to their own ends.

Responding to pressure from the Long Parliament to weaken or abolish episcopacy, King Charles pointed to the oath he had sworn to uphold the government and privileges of the bishops. A royalist pamphlet of 1642 reminded readers that King Charles had sworn 'to protect and defend the bishops and churches under their government', an oath from which he had not in the least 'prevaricated'. The author remarked, somewhat opaquely, that 'since a king at his first coronation can confirm his subjects no other way but by oath for the maintenance of such rights, this royal king hath divers times solemnly protested, the art of man cannot produce a more divine assurance, but by the performance, which must be attended (as I think) by the faith of his good subjects'. The title page of the pamphlet displayed the royal coat of arms and the text from Proverbs: 'A divine sentence is in the lips of the king, his mouth transgresseth not in judgement.' Inside it offered readers the text of 'his majesty's oath taken at his coronation' to support the bishops, though not his pledge to protect the laws and people.[63]

Royalists argued that 'our king ... doth acknowledge it the great business of his coronation oath to protect us'. To which the commonwealth controversialist Henry Parker responded: 'I hope under this word protect, he intends not only to shield us from all kind of evil, but to promote us also to all kind of political happiness ... and I hope he holds himself bound thereunto, not only by his oath but also by his very office, and by the end of his sovereign dignity.' Kings, in Parker's view, were made to serve the people, not people to serve their kings. 'His dignity was erected to preserve the commonalty, the commonalty was not created for his service ... This directs us then to ... the paramount law ... and that is *salus populi*,' the safety of the people.[64] Parker's *Observations* spawned a spate of rebuttals and confutations in which royal apologists reasserted divine-right kingship against the revolutionary claims of parliament.[65]

The ultimate sticking point was that Charles, in the face of his people and clergy, had sworn his solemn commitment to God. It would be sinful, his supporters insisted, for the king to 'forfeit inward to procure outward peace ... to adventure the heavenly to retain an earthly crown'. It would be 'flat perjury' for him to go back on his word.[66] As he told his commissioners considering a treaty at Uxbridge in January 1645: 'I hold myself particularly bound by the oath I took at my coronation, not to alter the government of this church from which I found it.'[67] The king could make no concessions, even if they seemed tactically advantageous or politically astute, because he had pledged his soul at his coronation. To yield to political pressure would impugn his honour on earth and imperil his repose in eternity.

The matter was taken up at length by presbyterian and episcopal controversialists. The parliamentary preacher John Geree set forth *A Case of Conscience Resolved. Wherein it is Cleared, that the King may without impeachment to his Oath, touching the Clergy at Coronation, consent to the Abrogation of Episcopacy*, which provoked a chain of casuistical rebuttal and counter-rebuttal.[68] Geree's main point was that the oath to defend episcopacy was unlawful from the start, 'and so void the first day'. 'If prelacy in the church be an usurpation, contrary to Christ's institution, then to maintain it is a sin, and all bonds to sin are frustrate.' If that was not persuasive, Geree had a second argument, that the king swore

> to maintain the laws while they are laws; but when they are abrogated by a just power in a regular way, they are then wiped out of his charge and oath. So the king by his oath is bound to maintain the rights of the clergy while they continue such. But if any of their rights be abrogated by just power, he stands no longer engaged to that particular... The king's oath is against acting or suffering a tyrannous invasion on laws and rights, not against a parliamentary alteration of either.

Subsequent arguments were primarily about the merits or demerits of episcopacy and the legitimacy of clerical privileges, but they returned repeatedly to the power and validity of royal oaths. The king's oath to maintain the laws was 'made *populo Anglicano*, to the people of England... to the whole realm', so they said, whereas the more contentious oath to support bishops was made to 'a part of his people, *clero Anglicano*'. But neither, in Geree's view, were impediments to change, since 'the king and parliament may cancel any obligation'.[69]

Charges against King Charles at his trial in January 1649 claimed that he had violated 'his trust, oath, and office, being obliged to use the power committed to him for the good and benefit of the people, and for the preservation of their rights and liberties'. The king, of course, denied this, and insisted that he alone stood for 'the true liberty of all my subjects'. Charles I upheld his interpretation of his oath to the end.[70]

Neither the execution of King Charles nor the abolition of monarchy stopped debate about royal oaths. Parliamentary apologists in particular set forth a contractual view of monarchy that they claimed the late king had violated. Writing in November 1649, Henry Burton referred to the 'laws of the land, which as the ligatures do bind, unite, and fasten the head and body, the king and his subjects together; and which both prince and people are bound by mutual covenant and sacred oath to maintain'.[71] John Milton too stressed the mutuality of oaths that bound monarch and subject, and the evils that befell from Charles breaking them. The coronation oath, in this interpretation, indicated the derivation of royal power from the people.[72] Restoration histories mostly revived the view of a king not only innocent but elevated to a martyr's crown, a king who preserved his oath and his honour. The coronation of Charles II in April 1661 was as grand and traditional as possible, and the new king swore 'the usual oath to confirm the laws of the people . . . and to grant the Commons its rightful customs', as if there was never controversy about the wording.[73]

The coronation and its oaths articulated central themes in the political life of the seventeenth century. Observers and analysts, then and now, could parse the words for deep significance, and examine the ceremony for cultural clues. As Sir Simonds D'Ewes remarked, 'searching brains might pick much from it'. The coronation exhibited the majesty of monarchy, and invoked the king's unique relationship with God. It did not explicitly endorse divine-right kingship, but it signalled that the king's authority, his lineage, and his relationship with his people were all suffused with sanctification.

Not quite a job description, the order of coronation set forth the duties of the king. He was to grant and keep the laws and customs of England, to govern with justice and discretion, and to sustain and protect his people, clergy, and church. In particular King Charles swore to uphold episcopal government and ecclesiastical privileges. He was, after all, Defender of the Faith and Supreme Governor of the Church, as well as the font of clerical patronage. The coronation also displayed King Charles as a feudal monarch, receiving the homage of his principal liegemen. The limits of royal power were not specified, but it was apparent that no king governed in isolation.

The coronation also exposed expectations about the people. They would secure protection and guidance from the Lord's anointed, to whom they in their turn would give their 'condign love'. ('Condign' means 'equal in worth or dignity'.) They would serve their monarch in unspecified ways, with obedience and honour. It was implied that 'the people' had somehow agreed to royal government and consented to their subjection, although the only sign of this was the acclamation of 'God save King Charles'. The people were partners to a kind of political marriage, though not necessarily companionate or equally yoked.

The very phrase 'the people' was problematic. Who did it encompass, who did it entail? Various Latin versions of the order for coronation mentioned the *vulgus*, the *populus*, and *plebs*, which were not quite the same thing. The *vulgus* were the ordinary people, the folk, with connotations of a mob or rabble. *Populus* was a politer term, suggesting the multitude, the people of the nation. The *plebs* were simply the common people, the masses, the generality, the crowd. Some parliamentarians of the 1640s conceived themselves as representatives of the *vulgus*, a view that royalists rejected with contempt.[74]

The English texts used by Stuart kings called on 'the people' to witness the coronation. The archbishop began by calling on 'the people' to give their acclamation, and later the king took his oath 'in the sight of all the people'. By one interpretation 'the people' were just members of the present congregation, those assembled in the ornate abbey, but they also represented the community of the realm. One phrase in the oath referred to the 'commonalty' of the kingdom, which implied the entire nation below the nobility. The people, however, were many and varied. Charles I had more than six million subjects (well over four million in England), but barely a thousand were directly involved in his coronation.

3

Sacred Kingship and Dutiful Subjection

This chapter examines how kingly power was constituted in the reign of Charles I, and how it began to unravel. It addresses the assumptions and justifications sustaining early Stuart kingship, and the reciprocities of authority, duty, and subjection. Using prayers, sermons, speeches, and declarations, it reviews commentary on the privileges, prerogatives, and powers of the crown from the opening years of Charles's reign to the revolution. It shows how dominant opinion upheld divine-right theories of sacred kingship, while a complementary stream asserted that royal magistracy served primarily the needs and safety of the people. These views were by no means incompatible, for God's plan encompassed both the crown and the commonweal. They were, however, in tension, with potential for stressful disagreement.[1]

Royal authority touched people's lives in myriad ways, including demands for money, manpower, service, and facilities. It operated through agents and intermediaries, delegates and surrogates, as well as through the king's own voice, hand, and presence. Officers of central and local government exercised the royal writ, and conducted the nation's business 'in the name of the king'. As the jurist Sir Matthew Hale explained, even petty constables and tithing men 'carry in them so much of the king's authority as makes the neglect thereof subject to fine and imprisonment'.[2]

The early Stuart epigrammist John Owen idealized the top-down relationship of king and people:

> All subjects in their manners follow kings,
> What they do—bids, forebearings, forbids things.
> A king's behaviour sways his subjects' lives,
> As the first mover all the fixed stars drives.[3]

The king was indeed the pivot and driver of politics, religion, and high culture, though not everyone behaved as monarchical ideology intended. English rulers expected their subjects to supply their needs, but compliance was not always forthcoming. Local confrontations over loans and benevolences, purveyance, Ship Money, and the needs of royal messengers and functionaries show some of the shortfalls between theory and practice. The crown had high expectations, but did not always get its way. The emphasis here is on the legal, secular, and financial demands of the crown and their impingement on the liberties of the subject, leaving discussion of the politics of warfare and religion to later chapters.

Excellent Tokens

The accession of King Charles on 27 March 1625 was greeted with noise and good cheer, though without the cascade of commendatory verse that had greeted King James in 1603. It was a day for flags to fly, bells to ring, a day of festive fires and celebratory salutes. Accession-day treats at Cambridge included claret and sack, white wine and sugar cakes, while celebratory bonfires burned and the town waits sang.[4] Trumpets sounded and wine flowed at Woodstock when King Charles was proclaimed.[5] The mayor of Leicester read the proclamation on the steps of the Guildhall and at each of the town crosses, before joining in a banquet.[6] At Dorchester the town clerk proclaimed the new king on 30 March, 'after supper, the magistrates assisting'.[7] The Suffolk diarist John Rous recorded of King Charles, 'his coming to the crown was very joyous to the well-affected, but to papists not very welcome'.[8] Sir John Beaumont was among those wishing his majesty 'large honour, happy conquest, boundless wealth, long life, sweet children, [and] unafflicted health'.[9]

The smooth operation of dynastic hereditary principles was a source of satisfaction. England could celebrate the first unchallenged succession of an adult male monarch since Henry VIII. The end of one reign and the beginning of another was an occasion to reflect on the blessings of kingship and government. 'We have lost our great and wise king,' wrote John Philpot soon after the death of King James in 1625, a loss 'to be borne with patience'.[10] 'What a glorious and good king we have lost,' lamented John Finch, who consoled himself by observing that King Charles was 'the true heir of all his princely virtues'.[11] Edward Tilman expressed similar sentiments in a letter to Paul D'Ewes: 'all fears and sorrows are swallowed up in joy of so hopeful a successor. God be blessed we are not left destitute.'[12]

King Charles would emerge quickly from his father's shadow, though he often presented controversial policies as fulfilments of Jacobean designs. The new king lacked James I's intellectual stature, but shared the belief that God sanctified his rule. As the accession proclamation announced, King Charles was 'the true and undoubted heir and successor unto the crown and kingdoms of England, Scotland, France and Ireland'. Hereditary right, dynastic legitimacy, divine providence, law, and custom gave him 'sole and alone power and authority in all causes and over all persons whatsoever' within his royal dominions.[13]

As usual, when a new regime was installed, great changes were expected. 'It is thought by some that there will appear a great change in the carriage of affairs of state in respect of what was in the former king's time,' wrote Joseph Meade to Sir Martin Stuteville.[14] At court, observed the Tuscan agent Amerigo Salvetti, 'everyone turns his eyes to the new sun and with listening ears seeks to penetrate his majesty's intentions'.[15] Place-seekers and office-holders rushed to court to stake their claim or renew their patents. Observers seeking clues to preferments and policies noted which officer, aristocrat, or statesman was allowed to kiss the king's hands. John Chamberlain, for example, observed early in April that the former chief justice, Sir Edward Coke, 'with his gloves on, touched and kissed the king's hand, but whether he be confirmed a councillor or cashiered I cannot yet learn'.[16] Despite expectation of novelty, 'all continues *in statu quo prius*, with very little addition or alteration,' remarked the ever-astute John Chamberlain to Sir Dudley Carleton.[17] Carleton himself would flourish under the new regime, becoming a privy councillor and household officer in 1625, and secretary of state with elevation to the peerage as Viscount Dorchester in 1628.

Commentators described the new king's court as 'more strait and private than in the former time'. The new regime insisted upon 'dignity, respectful demeanour, and regularity' in state affairs.[18] Sir John Davies wrote to the Earl of Huntingdon on 1 April 1625 that 'the young king doth already show many excellent tokens of a stout, a wise, and a frugal prince, and is like to restore the glory of our nation by his wisdom and valour'.[19] Owen Wynn assured his family in Wales that 'the new king is observed to be religious and attends prayers twice daily'.[20] John Chamberlain described King Charles as 'very gracious and affable . . . attentive and devout at prayers and sermons, gracing the preachers and assembly with amiable and cheerful countenance, which gives much satisfaction'. It was a promising start, offering hope 'that the world will every way mend'.[21]

Royal Majesty

Subjection to royal authority placed legal, fiscal, military, religious, and emotional demands on the people of England. Courtiers, councillors, magistrates, and ministers promoted this message, with slightly varying theological and ideological inflections. Everyone was supposed to obey the law, pay their dues, and do their duty to God and the king. Every church service included prayers for his majesty, with special sermons about kingship on anniversary occasions. In exchange for their sovereign's judgement and protection his people were expected to show him love and honour, obedience and fear, and to assist him in his rule. This fundamental reciprocity of relations survived the usual stresses of politics and bound individuals to their monarch, to their country, and to each other. How that reciprocity was to be achieved, however, remained something of a mystery. Promulgated and explained by theory, it was tested in everyday interactions of authority and governance. Theorists promoted normative accounts of the majesty of monarchy and the relationship of king and people, and seemed to be nonplussed when they did not work.

The powers and prerogatives of the crown were never fully catalogued, and this made them sometimes contentious. They existed, wrote one anonymous contemporary, to cover 'cases of sudden and extraordinary accidents and . . . matters so variable and irregular in their nature as are not provided for by law'.[22] The Jacobean Privy Councillor Sir Francis Bacon enumerated the principal prerogative powers in a work published posthumously in 1641. These were mainstream conservative iterations that could prove useful when kingship was under pressure. A king with such powers would affect the lives of millions:

> The king may summon parliaments, dissolve them, prorogue them, and adjourn them at his pleasure. The king may add voices to his parliament . . . give privileges to borough towns . . . call and create barons at his pleasure . . . The king hath an absolute negative voice to all bills that pass the parliament, so as without his royal assent they have a mere nullity . . . The king hath power to

> declare and proclaim war, and to make and conclude peace and truce at his pleasure ... The king hath power to command the bodies of his subjects for the service of his wars ... and to transport them by sea and land at his pleasure ... The king hath power in time of war to execute martial law ... The king may give knighthoods ... The king may alter the valuations of his coin and raise and fall monies at his pleasure ... The king may constrain the person of any of his subjects not to go out of the realm ... The king may forbid the exportation (or importation) of any commodities ... The king may denizen any foreigner.[23]

These were legal rights of the kind that an Attorney General or Lord Chancellor might compile, and they do not begin to account for the king's cultural authority or his powers of patronage as Defender of the Faith and Supreme Governor of the Church of England. Nor do they delineate the claims of the crown upon a subject's property, purse, or person.

Kingship, as James I understood it, entailed obligations as well as authority. There was ruling to be done as well as reigning. The office of a king, James taught his son, was

> to minister judgement and justice to the people ... to establish good laws to his people, and procure obedience to the same ... to procure the peace of the people ... to decide all controversies ... to be the minister of God for the weal of them that do well, and as the minister of God, to take vengeance upon them that do evil ... and finally, as a good pastor, to go out and in before his people ... that through the prince's prosperity the people's peace may be procured.

Ministering, establishing, procuring, and deciding were part of the active work of government. Based on the Bible as well as Scottish practice, James's view of kingship was transferable to the other kingdoms of Great Britain where the monarch ruled, under God, as the guardian and father of his people. A king was obliged by his oath 'to maintain the religion presently professed ... according to the laws whereby it is established', and 'to maintain the whole country, and every state therein, in all their ancient privileges and liberties'.[24]

Like his father, King Charles promised at his coronation to punish the wicked and protect the just, to defend widows, orphans, 'and all the servants of God', and to 'restore the things that are gone to decay ... and confirm the things that are in good order'.[25] The king's guarantee of 'protection and justice' was 'one prime and principal part of his oath', which was examined in more detail in Chapter 2.[26] The king was the nation's benign protector, God's agent, above the political fray. King Charles also considered it his duty as Supreme Governor of the church to quash religious contentions and preserve 'that circle of order' against 'unquiet and restless spirits', so that 'prince and people together through the whole land shall join in one common and solemn devotion'.[27]

In practice it remained a matter of style and taste, as well as judgement, how a king should exercise his kingship. He could govern remotely, through intermediaries, or he could seek engagement and counsel wherever he chose. An unpublished dialogue from the final year of James's reign complimented that king on being 'well acquainted with the art of winning and keeping the people's affections, and prudently foreseeing the evident necessity and benefit thereof'. This came from a time when Prince Charles and the Duke of Buckingham were courting popularity to hasten England into war. It repeated the well-worn wisdom that the love of the people was the king's greatest asset, but implied that that love needed nourishing. A good king, the author suggested, knew the value of his people's love and also the importance of counsel. 'The resolutions of princes ought to be governed with great advice and circumspection, especially such resolutions as embark the common interest and engage the universal state.' The dialogue called for 'some degree of just and favourable yielding of his majesty's part, and the discreet and dutiful obeying and conforming on the part of the subject', to overcome political 'wrangling'. Though couched in flattering terms, it was designed to jostle King James into a policy that he did not approve.[28] Neither James nor his son could abide 'wrangling', both were averse to any 'yielding', and neither thought himself answerable to the counsels of subjects.

As a monarch in his own right, king of three kingdoms, Charles measured himself against his father, his ancestors, and all the kings of history. The king, his counsellors, and commentators kept up a constant discourse on the nature and obligations of kingship, and the relationship between the ruler and his people. Loyal and dutiful expositions of kingship marked the early years of Charles's reign, when the untried young monarch was establishing his rule. They followed him through the 1630s, when praise for royal majesty eased paths to preferment. Royalists of the revolutionary era would reiterate the theory of divine-right kingship when royal authority began to crumble.

Charles I absorbed and promoted an exalted view of the majesty of kingship. Growing up he learned that 'monarchy is the true pattern of divinity', and that 'kings are called gods by the prophetical King David, because they sit upon God's throne in the earth'.[29] Preachers and politicians reinforced the message that 'kings on their thrones' were 'anointed of God, and sovereign rulers of the people'.[30] Both James and Charles grew accustomed to hearing their kingship praised. A battery of biblical injunctions expounded the power and sanctity of royal authority: 'By me kings reign, and princes decree justice' (Proverbs 8:15); 'The king's heart is in the hand of the Lord' (Proverbs 21:1); 'Touch not mine anointed' (1 Chronicles16:22, Psalms 105:15); 'Where the word of a king is, there is power' (Ecclesiastes 8:4); and 'Kings shall be thy nursing fathers, and queens thy nursing mothers' (Isaiah 49:23). The New Testament taught the rudiments of subjection: 'Fear God. Honour the King' (1 Peter 2:17); 'Obey them that have the rule over you, and submit yourselves' (Hebrews 13:17); 'The powers that be are ordained of God' (Romans 13:1). These and similar verses supplied texts for countless sermons extolling kingship and enjoining subjection. For example, the Devonshire cleric John Pyne declared that the privileges of kings were great because 'they are in a great measure like unto God himself'.[31] Standard references to 'our gracious king', 'most gracious and dread sovereign lord', 'his sacred majesty', and 'the king's most excellent majesty', confirmed and normalized these notions.

William Laud, the rising star of the Caroline episcopate, preached enthusiastically on kingship at the beginning of Charles I's reign. 'The king is God's immediate lieutenant upon earth . . . so God and the king stand very near together . . . God's power is in the king . . . The king is the sun . . . the king is the main pillar and stay of the state,' he proclaimed before the king at Whitehall in June 1625. None of these statements was new or controversial, though they had rarely been expressed with such vigour. King James's 25-year-old son, said Laud, was 'another Hezekiah, a wise and religious king', and '*aptata columna* too, a pillar every way fitted to the state he bears'. Since Charles himself was the principal auditor of this sermon, alongside the governing elite, the praise may have been designed to convince all concerned, the king included, that his majesty was fit for service. The rising bishop may also have been hoping to groom the new king for his role as re-shaper of the church along sacerdotal and ceremonialist lines.[32]

Counsellors and commentators used similar architectural, cosmological, and physiological imagery to depict the king as the mainstay of the social structure, the pole and light of the heavens, and the head of the body politic. He was God's lieutenant, the nation's shield, the captain and steersman of the ship of state. The king was 'the very Atlas and pillar under the supreme

CHARLES BY THE GRACE OF GOD,
Kinge of England, Scotland France and
Ireland. defendor of the faith, etc:

Figure 4. Charles by the Grace of God, King. John Jones, *Christus Dei, The Lords Annoynted . . . written in answer to a late printed pamphlet* (Oxford, 1643), facing title page.

majesty of heaven of our church and government', declared the earl of Cork's chaplain Stephen Jerome.[33] 'The king is the general father and lord or master and head of his whole kingdoms and dominions: all his subjects are his children, his servants, and his body politic,' explained the counsellor Sir Julius Caesar.[34] Taking up his appointment as President of the Council in the North, Sir Thomas Wentworth declared in 1628 that 'the authority of a king is the keystone which closeth up the arch of order and government, which contains each part in due relation to the whole, and which, once shaken, infirmed, all the frame falls together in a confused heap of foundation and battlement'.[35] Wentworth's succinct and perceptive assessment expressed the binding force of royal authority and the nightmare consequences of its potential collapse.

Welcoming the new monarch to Canterbury in May 1625, Edward Finch likened the king's position on the throne to the vantage point of a hilltop, best to 'discover valleys'. This was a topographical analogy, akin to seeing kings as heads of bodies or steersmen of the ship of state. Kings sat on high, 'but when they descend from themselves, and grow acquainted with the hearts and affections of their subjects, this is to measure the valleys at hand, and not at distance, and doth at once win the hope of their goodness, and make us in awe of their wisdom'. Finch assured his majesty that his 'humble and faithful subjects' owed him love, honour, obedience, supplies, and service, along with their 'loyal and hearty affections'.[36] The king no doubt liked what he heard, and Finch rose in royal estimation, but it is doubtful whether Charles ever took the advice to 'descend... and grow acquainted'. This was not to praise 'Charles's connection with his people' (in Kevin Sharpe's words), but rather to imagine it.[37] Charles was more a monarch of the throne than the thoroughfare, more inclined to expect his subjects' affection than to seek it.

'The people must honour, obey, and support their king,' charged William Laud in his 1625 sermon. 'The strength of a people is in the honour and renown of their king; his very name is their shield among nations.'[38] Conventional monarchical theory assured King Charles of 'the duty and allegiance that the lieges owe to their king', as he took responsibility for the 'common safety' and 'public defence of the kingdom'.[39] 'God gives us a king, and... he prescribes obedience to our king', preached Isaac Bargrave, so that disobedience was not just an offence but a sin.[40] Though the relationship of king and people was 'reciprocal', wrote Sir Robert Filmer (in an early use of this important word), all power, right, and authority belonged to the crown: 'As kingly power is by the law of God, so it hath no inferior power to limit it.'[41] The repeated recitation of these assertions in the early years of Charles's reign almost suggests a worry lest they prove not to be true.

Courtiers, preachers, and politicians poured praise on the person of King Charles as well as his sacred office. William Laud had thanked God for giving England 'a wise, a stout, a vigilant, and a most provident king', attributes on which a glorious reign could be founded.[42] Others rushed to celebrate his individual excellence as well as the divine plan he embodied. 'There lives not a prince fuller of religion and virtue, God give us grace to be truly thankful for him as we ought,' declared Thomas Wentworth in December 1629.[43] Lord Keeper Coventry commended 'the wisdom and deep judgement of his majesty', who was 'ever studious and careful of the weal of his people'.[44] He was, declared Lord Dungarvon, 'a man of the finest temper... the best example of any prince alive'.[45]

In the period of the personal rule the piety and virtue of his majesty helped consolidate the myth of England's 'halcyon days'. Praising 'imperial Charles, my sovereign king and master', Sir Henry Wotton gave thanks in 1633 that England enjoyed 'the quiet of so just and pious a governor'.[46] 'Blessed be God,' declared Henry Peacham, 'we now live under a most gracious, mild and merciful prince as ever reigned in England, our dear and dread sovereign King Charles'.[47] The flattery was a form of politeness, designed to display and encourage loyalty and admiration.

The exaltation of monarchy extended beyond cliché. Poets and masque-makers imagined their monarch as 'Phoebus, king of heaven', who brought peace and sunshine to 'the little world', and welcomed his as 'Sol'.[48] Preachers too developed this image, making Charles I the sun king long before Louis XIV acquired that epithet. 'The king is the sun. He draws up some vapours, some supply, some support, from us... for if the sun draw up no vapours, it can pour down no rain,' declared William Laud in June 1625.[49] 'A king is like the sun in the firmament, from whom the other stars receive their light,' preached the Cambridgeshire cleric John Swan.[50] He was 'a perfect sun in our zodiac', waxed Henry King.[51] Extravagant imagery likened 'sacred royalty' to 'the sun's glorious light... its refreshing heat... its celestial body... its heavenly orb'.[52] The courtier William Murray observed in 1631 that 'the sunshine of our gracious master's favour' drove affairs at court.[53] Temporarily excluded from royal beneficence in 1634, Sir Thomas Roe reflected that 'the fault is not in the sun that every earth does not feel his influence, but in the medium or interposition of clouds if not of eclipses'.[54]

Congregations throughout England heard preaching on the 'blessings' of royal authority.[55] They heard such sentiments as 'the king is the fountain of government... the beauty of a nation, the light of the commonwealth, the image of God, the pastor of his people, and the best benefactor of his subjects'. These assertions formed the staple of political education, reminding people of their obligations of gratitude. The vigour and vehemence of royalist preaching intensified at the time of the Scottish rebellion when royal authority was called into question, and further quickened on the threshold of civil war. (See Chapter 9.) The king, Henry Valentine assured auditors at St Paul's in March 1639, was the soul and the sun of the commonwealth, 'appointed by God to rule the day'.[56] The king, repeated John Swan the next year, was father of the country, 'the *primum mobile*... God's instrument for thy safe, quiet and civil being'.[57] The royal chaplain Henry King used familiar imagery to assert that 'the king is the state's pilot, and his law the compass'. Without the king, he continued, we are 'sheep without a shepherd, and water without a bank, and a body without an head'. The king was commander of the ship of state, head of the body politic, and the guardian against disorder and chaos.[58] Without the king as 'defender and keeper' of the people's 'civil blessings', preached a Hampshire minister in 1639, 'our lands, our liberties, and our possessions' were all imperilled. 'We should not safely meet and converse together, had we not a gracious king over us to repress our mutual violences.'[59]

In case any parishioner missed the message, the new ecclesiastical canons of May 1640 required every minister, on pain of suspension, to declare four times each year in church that 'the most high and sacred order of kings is of divine right, being the ordinance of God himself', that 'a supreme power is given to this most excellent order by God himself in the Scriptures', and that 'kings should rule and command in their several dominions all persons of what rank or estate soever, whether ecclesiastical or civil, and that they should restrain and punish with the temporal sword all stubborn and wicked doers'. Any questioning of royal authority, any resistance to divinely ordained power, was 'treasonable against God as well as against the king'.[60] (In December 1640 the newly summoned parliament would vote these canons illegal.)

How should subjects behave in the face of such exalted power? The simple answer was to 'fear God, and honour the king'. The subject's duty was to obey, to serve, and to endure.[61] Preachers celebrated the 'joy' of subjection to monarchical rule, and extolled the 'obedience and submission' due to 'our dread sovereign', who demanded 'the greatest industry of obedient loyalty'.[62] The domestic advisor Matthew Griffith reminded readers that 'the king is an earthly God', and urged subjects to 'fear his crown with honour and reverence, fear his sceptre with subjection and obedience'.[63]

Secular communications likewise assured local governors of 'his majesty's princely care of the honour and safety of the state, and general good of his loving subjects', and referred frequently to the king's 'wisdom', 'grace', and 'vigilant and fatherly care'.[64] People could rely on 'his majesty's princely grace and care for the ease of his subjects', the Council insisted, because 'his majesty... keeps perpetual watch over his people and kingdoms'.[65] As father, nurse, and pastor to his people, the king acted always in the common interest and relied on his subjects' affection. A bond, an amity, a mutuality of interest yoked king and people together, at least in theory. From it flowed order, law, justice, peace, and prosperity, to the benefit of both king and kingdom. Everyone gained, declared Sir Thomas Wentworth, from 'those mutual intelligences of love and protection descending, and loyalty ascending... between a king and his people'.[66]

King Charles himself stressed the blessings and benefits of kingship in a 'Declaration' to the county lieutenants at the time of the Scottish war. 'The defence and welfare of our people and kingdom being our principal care... we, in our princely providence, intend nothing but the safety and preservation of our subjects.' The Scottish revolt was an affront to royal honour, and the war threatened national security, so the king's demands in this regard should be met with 'cheerful observance and ready assistance'.[67]

Even the humblest English men and women had a stake in the kingdom and reason to feel grateful for royal authority, so the royal chaplain Roger Mainwaring argued in 1627.

> The poorest creature which lieth by the wall, or goes by the highway-side, is not without sundry and sensible tokens of that sweet and royal care and providence, which extendeth itself to the lowest of his subjects. The way they pass by is the king's highway. The laws which make provision for their relief take their binding force from the supreme will of their liege lord. The bread that feeds their hungry souls, the poor rags which hide their nakedness, all are the fruit and superfluity of that happy plenty and abundance caused by a wise and peaceable government.[68]

Subjects at every level enjoyed the security, peace, and order secured by kingship, and offered honour, love, and service in return. As the Devonshire preacher Thomas Foster reminded the assize magistrates in 1630: 'Christians and countrymen, gentlemen, yeomen and the like who make up the body of the commons: remember you are one another's members, knit together by the sinews of policy, to one monarchical head.'[69]

King Charles referred frequently to his 'loving subjects', and claimed that the love of his people was among his 'greatest riches'.[70] This love, like the grace of God, was not so much earned as supposedly freely given. The king mentioned it most often when asking for money, or when differentiating 'loving subjects' from 'turbulent and ill-affected spirits'.[71] King Charles invoked 'the love of our people' in 1626 when seeking 'a free gift' to meet financial exigencies.[72] He referred again to 'the love and duty of our people' when asking parliament for 'speedy and proportionable supply'. 'We are confident our loving subjects will not desert either us or themselves,' he told the county Lieutenants in 1628, 'but that God's blessing will be upon our mutual accord and endeavours.'[73] And when parliament reluctantly granted taxation it proved, so the Duke of Buckingham assured his master, that King Charles was 'a glorious king', secure in his subjects' affections, 'loved at home and now to be feared abroad'.[74]

The king's 10*s*. gold angel coin (which few of his subjects would ever see or handle) had the Latin inscription (which even fewer could read or understand) '*amor populi praesidium regis*', the love of the people is the king's protection.[75] It was all fluff and flattery, of course, but it fitted the philosophy and served the times: the polity was held together by love, which was supposed to flow in both directions.

Prerogative Power

King Charles's pursuit of war with Spain and France raised contentious questions about the reach of the royal prerogative. The politics of wartime finance subjected constitutional theory to the test of popular opinion. From 1625 to 1629 the crown's need for men and money turned squabbles over taxation and supply into debates on necessity, liberty, and law. Protagonists took extreme positions as they discussed the limits of royal authority and safeguards for the liberties of the subject. Grim observers sensed a growing 'distance between the king and his people' among 'the symptoms and vapours of a diseased time'.[76]

A crucial question was whether the king could command the wealth and property of his subjects. Important traditions of common law, extending back to Magna Carta, assured the people of England that 'the king hath no absolute power over our lands or goods'. The security of private property was central to 'the fundamental laws and liberties of this kingdom'.[77] In England, Sir John Davies insisted, 'the subjects and free men have property in their goods and freehold and inheritance in their lands', for otherwise 'they are villeins and slaves and proprietors of nothing'.[78] Only by vote of parliament could the sheriffs collect money for the king from holders of property, properly assessed.

An alternative viewpoint, gaining strength in court circles, stressed the king's 'full and entire power, preeminence, authority, prerogative and jurisdiction in all cases spiritual and temporal, happening within this realm . . . By ancient prerogative the king hath a natural interest in the person of every subject to serve him in such function as he shall appoint,' including, if necessary, with money.[79] Proponents of this view allowed that in cases of 'eminent danger', such as the kingdom faced between 1625 and 1629, 'the king may raise such sums of money from the subjects as shall in his wisdom be thought fit'. Since 'the commonwealth' enjoyed 'the benefit of government in time of peace', went the theory, it was obligated 'to supply the necessities of the prince in times of danger'.[80] According to the theoretician of patriarchy Sir Robert Filmer, 'it is for the honour, profit and safety of the people to have their king glorious, powerful, and abounding in riches'.[81]

The king alone would be judge of his needs. Since kings of England were not tyrants, they would not arbitrarily seize their subjects' goods, but they might reasonably ask their people for supply. Courtiers expounded the view in September 1625 that it was perfectly normal 'for kings and princes of this realm to make use of their subjects' good affections by borrowing some such competent sums of money, of persons able to lend, as might supply those present occasions for public service'.[82] If the king was willing to expend his own 'earthly fortune for the preservation of the general', then how could his friends and subjects not contribute freely for 'the common defence of the kingdom'?[83] Arguments like these paved the way for the planned 'benevolence' or free gift that would soon mutate into a scheme for a forced loan.[84]

The king's 'principal care and study', he assured local officials, was 'according to our kingly office, to provide for the welfare, peace and safety of our people'. He was therefore hurt to learn in July 1626 of 'a misunderstanding in the people of his majesty's gracious intentions therein'.[85] The troubled condition of Christendom, threats to the protestant religion, and the danger of foreign invasion required a vigorous military response, yet parliament would not adequately fund the war. Now the king in his wisdom saw the needs of the times, and devised a procedure to meet them. This was what the prerogative was for, and people would see it in action. Privy Councillors explained that this project to raise money was 'in no way meant to be by way of subsidy, but merely as a free gift from the subject to the sovereign'. Subjects would freely contribute to the cost of defending the realm in this time of 'common danger and pressing necessity'.[86]

Initial responses to requests for a gift proved unenthusiastic. Prospective payers in various parts of the country acknowledged their readiness to serve the king with their lives, but were unwilling to provide money except 'in a parliamentary way'. In Yorkshire they offered 'good words and humble excuses'.[87] Few donors would part with their money without particular benefit to themselves. By October 1626 the plan for a free gift had become a scheme for a forced loan. The honour and safety of the kingdom were at stake, and the king needed 'a larger and speedier supply than expected'. Men of property would now be asked to 'loan' the king money equivalent to their parliamentary subsidy assessment. Anyone who demurred would face sanctions.[88]

The project was off to a good start in January 1627 when the king commended 'the readiness and forwardness' of commissioners in Huntingdonshire 'in the late service about the loans'. The money had yet to come in, but King Charles 'took great contentment to hear how lovingly and obediently the people showed themselves in contributing towards the public occasions, wherein every particular man hath his interest'. Even 'the poorer sort' could contribute to 'those important causes of state', because they too shared the benefits.[89] The Council reminded prospective payers that 'all the money collected upon these loans, with much more of the king's own treasure, is employed for the defence of the realm, for the succour of his majesty's allies, and for the maintenance of the cause of religion'.[90] From the point of view of the crown, the loan was an 'unavoidable necessity'.[91] 'Necessity', however, was a complex matter, as Sir Edward Coke explained: there could be 'affected necessity, invincible necessity, and improvident necessity', and not all compelled the subject to empty his purse.[92] Views like these made Coke a champion of 'the liberties of the subject' and an ambivalent supporter of the royal prerogative.

Encouraged by bishop Laud to preach on the duty of obedience, several clerics made extravagant claims about 'the special prerogative' of the sovereign and the 'absolute obedience' that subjects owed him. Preaching at the Northamptonshire assizes in February 1627, and following up quickly in print, Robert Sibthorpe argued that subjects owed their king maintenance as well as obedience, and should willingly 'give or render' their wealth to support his necessities. Sibthorpe was especially dismissive of any suggestion that put 'the law above the king, and the people above the law', for that way lay 'tumults and insurrections'.[93] These views were politically inflammatory, thought the Earl of Clare, as they 'fed the palate of absolute power'.[94]

Even more outspoken was Roger Mainwaring, who preached before the king himself in July 1627 that a king's 'sovereign will . . . gives a binding force to all his royal edicts'. Mainwaring told his master that kings were 'inferior to none, to no man, to no multitudes of men, to no angel', so neither royal needs nor commands should be resisted. 'The honour of his sacred majesty . . . the security of his royal person . . . the safety and protection of his majesty's kingdoms' and 'the securing and preserving' of the 'lives, goods, and states' of all subjects required everyone to meet his majesty's 'extreme and urgent' necessity, set forth in the justification for the loan. Mainwaring's sermon too was soon published 'by his majesty's special command', a mark of royal approbation.[95] And he too would face censure in parliament for his 'wicked and malicious intention to seduce and misguide the conscience of the king . . . touching the observation of the laws and customs of this kingdom, and the rights and liberties of subjects'.[96]

By the time Mainwaring's sermon appeared, the loans had brought in £240,000, several times the sum of a subsidy that could be expected from parliament.[97] Nobody gave gladly, but most gentlemen complied with the king's request. 'Servants must do the commands of their masters,' remarked the Earl of Manchester to his brother, who agreed that it was a matter of 'loyalty and duty', however unpleasant, not to deny 'so amicable . . . a desire of my sovereign lord the king'.[98] This was a barbed remark for anyone who recalled the history of the 'amicable grant' that Cardinal Wolsey had sought to obtain for Henry VIII.[99]

Loan commissioners covered the country to settle assessments and secure compliance. Administrators noted payments and listed the names of refusers.[100] The paperwork helped the government to distinguish between the king's 'loving subjects' and so-called 'refractory spirits'.[101] Non-payers were cited and summoned, and some were threatened with military service, or forced to accept troops for billeting.[102] They represented 'the malignant part of this kingdom', Sir George Goring opined to the Duke of Buckingham.[103] The Council feared that prominent refusers 'would infect the rest of the kingdom'. Scores were placed under house arrest, and some brought to prison in London. George Catesby esquire, one of several hundred refusers in Northamptonshire, called the loan 'a flower of the prerogative' and announced with determination: 'I will be master of mine own purse, and will not part with a penny.'[104] Five knights who were committed to prison 'by his majesty's special commandment' appealed to King's Bench for a writ of *habeas corpus* in November 1627, thereby initiating a celebrated legal action. The question of the king's right to obtain money raised the even more contentious issue of whether his prerogative allowed him to imprison someone without showing cause.[105] Fifty-six loan-refusers were among those elected to parliament in 1628.[106]

Legal opinion was divided whether imprisonment by prerogative was a discretionary right of the crown or a violation of the fundamental laws of England. Common lawyers cited Magna Carta and medieval precedents to prove such imprisonment illegal, but other evidence showed that previous kings had the power to imprison offenders without bail. Following a famous trial, which pitted the defence lawyer John Selden against Attorney General Sir Robert Heath, the judges determined that 'the king may commit a subject without showing cause, for a convenient time', if the security of the state required secrecy.[107] The judgment supported the broad interpretation of the royal prerogative, but it would not satisfy partisans of 'the liberties of the subject', who returned to the issue at Westminster.

An accumulation of episodes persuaded some gentlemen that their liberties were in danger. If the king used prerogative powers to raise money for his wars, Sir Robert Phelips worried, it would 'seem by use and practice to create and invest a right of propriety for the king in the goods of his subjects at his own pleasure'. The king could then take whatever he needed, leading to 'an utter destruction of parliaments' and a crushing of law.[108] In such a case, Sir Edward Coke feared, 'the common laws would be overthrown and the judges would have but little to do at the assizes, because the light of the law would be obscured' by arbitrary government.[109] The real danger to liberty lay in the precedent set, not the money exacted, according to a paper found at King's Lynn.[110] The Earl of Clare wrote anxiously to the Earl of Somerset in August 1627 about 'new rules of policy and government' privileging 'not law but will, modernly termed prerogative, not for the good of the subject, as Fortescue and other ancient sages of our law affirm, but for the commodity of the Prince'. 'Prerogative', he told Lord Haughton, 'is the darling of the time' and was never subject to so much scrutiny or abuse.[111]

The crucial question for Christopher Vernon, who supplied London news to Sir Edmund Bacon, was 'whether his majesty hath any dominion over a man's goods'.[112] Absolutists said yes and commonwealth-men said no. The protections of common law, custom, and Magna Carta seemed to limit the reach of the crown, but 'necessity' could dissolve established principles because 'necessity hath no law'. When the bishop of Norwich endorsed the position that 'every free subject of this realm hath a fundamental propriety in his goods, and a fundamental liberty of his person', William Laud added the proviso, 'but deprivable of them upon just cause, and for fiscal'.[113] In cases of necessity, by absolutist principles, the king had command of his people's goods and bodies, and could tax or imprison them at will. Constitutional niceties took second place to the raw necessities of command.

Concerns like these underlay the Petition of Right, a recapitulation of 'divers rights and liberties of the subject' based on medieval precedents and Magna Carta. Parliamentary debate set 'the king's prerogative against the subject's liberties', as if they were inexorably in conflict.[114] Citing 'the great charter of the liberties of England', the Petition reminded King Charles that 'no person should be compelled to make any loans to the king against his will' nor 'be compelled to contribute to any tax, tallage, aid, or other like charge not set by common consent in parliament'. It was adamant that no man should be imprisoned or disposed except 'by the lawful judgement of his peers... by due process of law'. There could be no more forcing of householders to accept soldiers for billeting against their will, or subjecting civilians to martial law.[115]

This was a constitutional rebuke to a king who had listened too much to the likes of Sibthorpe and Mainwaring, and at first he resisted it. An exasperated King Charles complained in May 1628 'that he had suffered his prerogative to have been longer debated than ever any of his predecessors would have admitted'. Assuring the world of his good intentions, he warned the House of Commons not to encroach on 'that sovereignty and prerogative which God hath put into his hands'.[116] At length, however, with reluctance and prevarication, the king accepted the petition on 6 June 1628, and the country celebrated with bonfires, bells, and 'great rejoicing'.[117] Whether King Charles would adhere to it, and whether he thought his prerogative thereby restricted, would be subject to test.

The Petition of Right was more a gesture of defiance than a redefinition of constitutional practice. It had no teeth, no mechanism of enforcement, and the king's reluctant concession—'*Le Roy le veult*'—guaranteed no liberties.[118] During the final rancorous session of parliament in February 1629, when members refused to fund the continuing war, court advisors proceeded as if the prerogative was untrammelled. The king still had responsibility for the security of the realm, and, 'as a father, is bound to defend the common family'. He would have to raise money, with or without parliament, because 'our religion, liberty and lives are brought into eminent danger'. The king was therefore entitled to 'make a proportionable sessment of all men's goods and estates for the safeguard of the commonweal', with or without parliamentary support. This might violate established law and custom, but, the author of this memorandum insisted, 'the highest law of all laws is... the safeguard of the commonweal'.[119] The parliament came to a disorderly close on 2 March 1629, and King Charles determined never to call another.

The prerogative, however, never slept. 'False, scandalous and seditious rumours' circulated in the poisoned political atmosphere of 1629 to the effect that King Charles was bent on arbitrary and tyrannical rule. Some gentlemen circulated a manuscript entitled 'A proposition for his majesty's service to bridle the impertinency of parliaments', which claimed that the king intended to jettison constraints of law and custom and to govern autocratically, backed by military force. Charles, in reality, had no such plans, and was ill-equipped to be a tyrant. This discourse was especially heinous, thought the civil lawyer Nathaniel Brent, 'because it may breed an opinion in ill-affected persons that our gracious sovereign hath these dangerous plots in his head'. The claims were especially scandalous, Attorney General Heath assured King Charles, because he governed 'with so much justice and moderation that all your good subjects do bear that reverence and love to your sacred person as is just and due to so gracious a sovereign'.[120]

Suspicion for circulating this 'pestilent discourse' fell on a high-profile cluster of 'malicious persons', most notably the earls of Bedford, Clare, and Somerset, and the 'patriots' Sir Robert Cotton, John Selden, and Oliver St John. Reports spread in November 1629 that 'many others both of the nobility and gentry will be questioned'. A correspondent of Thomas Hobbes wrote facetiously that Sir Robert Cotton 'may now learn that imprisonment is almost as old as liberty, of which himself may become a very ancient precedent'. Proceedings opened in Star Chamber in May 1630, but were halted as an act of 'mercy' on news of the birth of a prince. The defendants denied authorship of the treatise, which, they claimed, had surfaced several years earlier from the pen of some 'brain-sick' person, perhaps an Englishman living in Italy. The episode was widely reported among gentry networks, and may have left the impression in some quarters that the king was a threat to 'liberty', in others that he was wrongly maligned. Still unresolved were important issues concerning the royal prerogative and the rights of the subject, for which no national forum existed once parliament had been suspended.[121] Access to the press was restricted, through mechanisms of licensing, because the government held that 'the entering and allowing of printing' was 'a just and unquestionable part of prerogative'.[122]

Following the collapse of the parliament in 1629, Attorney General Sir Robert Heath drew up a memorandum for strengthening Charles I's rule. He recommended enhancement of the royal revenue and securing of the narrow seas, equitable proceedings against recusants, and firm 'discountenance' of 'new fangled opinions' in religion. Careful acknowledgement of the Petition of Right would 'assure the subjects of the king's justice', while firm use of the Court of Star Chamber would 'repress those insolencies which shall oppose sovereignty'. What the Attorney General offered was a blueprint for the king's personal rule, in which Heath himself hoped for a central role. With these policies in place, he announced, 'there will be no doubt, but his sacred majesty, as he is already by his good subjects, shall by all be both loved, honoured and feared, and the apparitions of fear and idolatry in the people will be soon dispelled, and his majesty's reign made glorious and crowned with honour and happiness'.[123] For almost a decade it seemed that this might prove to be true.

Ship Money and the Safety of the Kingdom

Underlying the legal and fiscal technicalities of public finance was the fundamental principle, reiterated in the church canons of 1640, that 'tribute, and custom, and aid, and subsidy, and all manner of necessary support and supply, be respectively due to kings from their subjects by the law of God, nature, and nations, for the public defence, care and protection of them'. If kings were to fulfil their function and protect the kingdom, they needed access to the people's purses and pockets 'for the honourable and comfortable support of both'.[124] It was not tyrannical, but essential for the commonwealth, that subjects should pay and kings should not want. Arguments of this nature justified loans, benevolences, and taxation in the 1620s and reappeared in the 1630s in support of Ship Money.[125] The burden fell primarily on the propertied classes who seemed most capable of paying.

Established principles ordained that the government drew primarily on its ordinary income (from crown lands, customs, fees, fines, and feudal dues), and turned to taxation only in extraordinary circumstances. Parliamentary subsidies were designed for special needs, such as preparation for war. The system was cumbersome and inefficient, and rarely yielded sufficient revenue, but it preserved notions of partnership and reciprocity that sustained the liberties of the subject. It was poorly adapted to times of emergency when large sums of money were needed in a hurry. Charles I's wars with Spain and France strained the resources of the state and quickened debate on the powers and prerogatives of the crown. But there could be no denying that the Stuart realms, and Christendom at large, faced pressing dangers. The recruiting and marshalling of soldiers, and the fitting and dispatching of the fleet, demonstrated King Charles's military resolve, but it also exposed his fiscal and managerial inadequacies.

It was harder to argue that the kingdom was in danger when peace was restored with Spain and France.[126] Writers and preachers of the 1630s celebrated England's 'prerogative of peace, which most parts of Christendom are at this day deprived of'. What need of military might in a state of 'blessed tranquility' or 'halcyon days'?[127] The answer was that perils persisted, dangers threatened, and the king had more need of money than ever. There were ragtag pirates to pursue, Dunkirk raiders to counter, and Barbary slavers from North Africa to suppress. The king's subjects suffered when coals from Newcastle were intercepted, English cloth exports plundered, and West Country fishermen whisked into slavery. Nor was foreign invasion unthinkable amid the shifting alliances of the European wars. News of 'great provisions' by the Spaniards set the south coast on edge in August 1632, and 'a panic fear' of a French incursion followed in March 1634.[128] Only King Charles's closest advisors knew the depth of the danger and the urgency of finding funds. Eyeing the wealth of the City of London in 1633, Secretary Windebank opined that 'there is blood enough in the king's subjects, if the right vein be opened'.[129] Fiscal phlebotomy, judiciously performed, could secure the health of the commonwealth.

In the face of foreign peril it was the responsible course of action to fortify the coasts and assert the 'sovereignty of the seas', tasks that only a monarch could undertake. Defects in naval and land forces, exposed by recent conflicts, required costly remedies. The fleet, in particular, would need to be upgraded and expanded. To meet the charge the government revived Ship Money, a demand that counties and communities provide the king with warships or their cash equivalent. Initial writs for assessments and payments went out to the coastal communities in October 1634, and were extended to the rest of England in August 1635. They promised a 'manly' response to the dangers of the times, which would uphold the king's 'honour' while benefiting his subjects. 'The defence of the sea and kingdom . . . which concerneth all men, ought to be supported by all,' declared the first writ. 'His majesty doubteth not of the readiness of all his subjects to contribute hereunto with cheerfulness and alacrity,' said the follow-up instructions to the sheriffs.[130] Technically this was a prerogative action, a demand for service, but it developed into a major unparliamentary tax. Receipts were declared before the Privy Council, not to the Treasury and Exchequer. By 1640 Ship Money had yielded close to £800,000, more than all of Charles's parliamentary subsidies combined, and more than three times as much as the Forced Loan.[131] Its collection provided yet another opportunity for the regime to differentiate 'persons that are refractory' from 'those that were well affected' to the king's service. Only 'the evil affected' would object or default, declared a sheriff in Essex.[132]

Ship Money refocused attention on the powers and prerogatives of the crown, and the obligations and rights of the subject, and reopened the question of the king's ability to command his people's goods and resources. The burden was supposed to fall on men of substance, but complaints arose of assessments on 'poor cottagers and others who have nothing to live on but their daily work'. The most widespread objections were to inequities of assessment, rather than the absence of approval by a parliament. Indeed, the absence of parliament helps to explain the relative quietness of principled opposition.[133]

The cost of Ship Money fell mainly on holders of landed property, but landless persons of great personal wealth (such as merchants) were also to be rated 'according to their worth'.[134] The Privy Council specifically instructed sheriffs not to trouble cottagers and paupers, and a Derbyshire commissioner reported in 1636, 'there is not any poor men that doth pay, so far forth as I do know of'.[135] Officials agreed in 1638 that 'no person be assessed for Ship Money unless they be known to have estates in money or goods, or other means to live, over and above what they get by daily labour'.[136] This still embraced more families than usually paid parliamentary subsidies. Assessments varied from county to county, and even within counties, as local officials rated their neighbours. One assessor in Northamptonshire explained that payments would 'trench deep upon men of the best rank, being best able to bear it, and somewhat ease the poor tillage man and day labourer, being in my poor opinion not fit to be charged'. Not surprisingly, the wealthy complained of being over-rated.[137] Assessments at Exeter in 1639 ranged from 15*s*. for the wealthiest citizens down to some at just 18*d*. Elsewhere assessments were as high as several pounds or as low as a penny.[138] The assessment process caused disputes and delays, but generally filled the king's coffers.[139]

Complaints accompanied every demand for money, and were especially vigorous when the tax appeared to be new. In December 1634 the Council declared the men of Bristol's objections to Ship Money 'idle and frivolous', and told them 'that his majesty expects the duty of obedience to his commands'.[140] Edward Boys of Goodnestone, Kent, was heard to rail against Ship Money in July 1635, saying we 'were taxed so much' and 'if we have such taxes laid upon us we must rebel'. Warned by his minister, 'for the Lord Jesus Christ's sake to forbear such speeches', a somewhat calmer Boys answered, 'did I say so?'[141] When 'divers of the inhabitants' of Somerset were 'much discontented' by Ship Money in January 1637, Sir Thomas Smyth recommended flexibility rather than strict enforcement, for 'otherwise I fear you will find the people rude and addicted unto opposition'.[142] Especially outspoken was the Sussex gentleman Thomas Chaloner, who declared his willingness to lead an army 'to suppress the new levies of money now raised and to punish the inventers'.[143] Some observers attributed the poor attendance of gentry at a royal progress in 1636 to frustrations regarding Ship Money.[144]

Ship Money was authorized 'by his majesty's writ' and collected 'for his majesty's service'. Refractoriness eroded the bond between the king and his people and resistance sometimes bordered on sedition. When Ship Money officials in Somerset exhibited their royal warrants at Ilchester market in June 1635, the constable John Napper declared that 'he cared not a fart for the said warrant... no more than for a straw in the ground'.[145] Hierarchy and order were further compromised in Northamptonshire in April 1637 when women with sticks and stones defied attempts by sheriff's bailiffs to distrain for Ship Money, and again in January 1638 when more 'women, boys and children with pitchforks, and their aprons full of stones', rose 'in rebellion' against local officials, naming the sheriff's men as 'rogues'. One of the stone-throwers was the daughter of a constable who refused to assist the bailiffs. The unpopularity of the levy produced resentment and confrontation in a system that relied on consensus, cooperation, and goodwill.[146]

Failure to pay brought retaliation. When William Fynne of Hambleton was late paying his assessed 20*s*. in October 1635, the sheriff of Rutland ordered the sum to be delivered by Monday next, 'lest you force me to distrain, or return your name to the Lords, and you be a precedent hereafter . . . I pray you refuse me not for I intend to favour you'. In the name of the king, the sheriffs could seize or distrain the goods, corn, or cattle of those who 'neglected to pay, in contempt of his majesty and the law'.[147] Minor office-holders such as tithingmen and petty constables faced counter-intimidation from recalcitrant neighbours when they tried to collect the money. When the Somerset tithingman John More tried to distrain the goods of Richard Burgegood of Stogumber for not paying Ship Money, he reported, the delinquent 'told me if I did dare take any of his goods he would forthwith arrest me; whereupon (he) being a turbulent man and a troublesome person and full of law amongst his neighbours, I being a poor man, upon these and other threatening left him'.[148] Fortunately for the crown, grumbling cooperation was more common than stubborn objection.

To clarify his rights, King Charles submitted key questions to his judges in February 1637:

> Whether, when the good and safety of the kingdom in general is concerned, and the whole kingdom in danger, the king may not by writ under the Great Seal command all subjects at their charge to provide and furnish such number of ships with men, victuals, ammunition, and for such time as he shall think fit, for the defence and safety of the kingdom, and by law compel the doing thereof in case of refusal or refractoriness, and whether in such case the king is not the sole judge both of the danger, and when and how the same is to be prevented and avoided?[149]

Nobody would wish to endanger the kingdom, but some might well question whether the king was 'sole judge' of perceived threats, and whether he could exact contributions solely by exercise of his prerogative under the Great Seal. To counter this view Lord Keeper Coventry advised that 'no man will expect that *arcana regni*, the private reasons of a prince, should either upon this or other occasions be made public . . . The whole kingdom is concerned in point of honour, safety and profit,' as subjects of all sorts benefited from the king's 'dominion of the seas'.[150] Reports of the judges' confirmation of the king's prerogative rights in this regard spread rapidly through gentry circles. Though the matter was supposedly resolved, many of those affected by 'this extraordinary imposition' had grave misgivings.[151]

A major test case developed in the spring of 1638 when the Buckinghamshire landowner John Hampden challenged the legality of the crown's demands. Lawyers on both sides deployed arguments that went to the heart of the matter. Solicitor General Sir Edward Littleton argued that it was the king's part, and his alone, to judge when the realm was in danger. In case of such danger, he said, 'the king may do whatsoever tends to the preservation and preparation of defence of his kingdom'. If that involved building up forces and levying Ship Money, even in violation of customary legal principles, then necessity justified all.[152] The majority of the judges agreed with Littleton that 'the law of necessity' justified extraordinary measures, that the king was sole judge of that necessity, and that the cost of defence 'should be borne by all the subjects of the kingdom' when the safety of the realm was imperilled. It was '*droit royal* to meddle with war and peace, subjects have nothing to do with it,' claimed Littleton. That power was 'absolutely inherent in the king's person', said Attorney General Sir John Bankes.[153]

John Hampden's lawyers did not disagree with this customary and orthodox assessment of the royal prerogative. Oliver St John, who opposed the levying of Ship Money without grant of parliament, nonetheless acknowledged the king as '*pater familias*... commander in chief... the fountain of bounty... the fountain of justice'. Matters of defence were wholly in royal hands, he acknowledged, for '*suprema potestas* is inherent in his majesty, as part of his crown and kingly dignity'. The king indeed was 'sole judge of dangers from foreigners'. Where St John disagreed with the crown lawyers was whether the king had access to 'the subject's goods' without 'parliamentary assistance'. There should be no 'altering of the property of the subjects' goods without their consent', St John argued. Without the assistance of parliament, 'his majesty cannot in many cases communicate either his justice or power unto his subjects'.[154]

Agreeing with St John, though oversimplifying his position, Justice Sir Richard Hutton avowed 'that the king had no lawful power to levy the Ship Money'. Some people applauded this judgment but others were horrified. It encouraged people 'more and more in a stubborn refusal of this duty', complained the Northamptonshire cleric Thomas Harrison, who rashly accused Hutton of treason. In Harrison's view, Hutton's objection to Ship Money sowed sedition between the king and his people and was tantamount to denying the royal supremacy.[155] These arguments 'against the king... have made men more backward', reported a Ship Money official in Nottinghamshire.[156] The seven to five judgment persuaded some people that Hampden, though defeated, had scored a moral victory.

Hampden's case produced a thorough airing of legal precedents and constitutional principles concerning the royal prerogative and the duties of the subject. The conclusion of the judges was widely reported, 'that in a case of necessity his majesty may call unto his subjects for money, and that his majesty is the judge of this necessity'.[157] It was 'all the talk in London at present', reported the Norfolk gentleman Anthony Mingay.[158] Thomas Knyvett took time from his own legal business to attend Hampden's hearing, but 'could not get near the door by two or three yards, the crowd was so great'.[159] Scribal copies of the opinions and ruling spread through gentry networks, and in 1640 were summarized in print.[160]

The case allowed royal judges to assert that the king alone had the power to evaluate foreign dangers, while the people remained voiceless in matters of state. 'Sometimes dangers are fit to be communicated to the people, and sometimes not,' declared Sir Edward Littleton, 'what can the people tell of these things?' It was part of his majesty's 'princely love and affection to his subjects' that he carried this burden, said Sir John Finch. 'The king is the sole judge, both of the danger, and when and how it is to be avoided,' agreed Sir John Bankes. Subjects had no role in discussions of peace or war, although they were expected to contribute blood and treasure for national defence. The collection of Ship Money was vindicated, along with the principle that a king in need had access to his people's goods.[161]

Upholding this view were gentlemen like Sir Thomas Peyton, who wrote in May 1640 that 'the king may use the goods of his subjects, *nolentibus volentibus*, as he may their particular and private persons, for the conservation of the more universal and general good'.[162] Edward Jeffreys, the vicar of Southminster, Essex, went so far as to say 'that the king hath not only power to command all your persons, but also power to take away your goods at his pleasure'.[163] But many men of property resented Ship Money and continued to doubt its legality. Even some of the sheriffs involved in its collection were known in private to 'oppose it much'. Considering nationwide reports of resistance to Ship Money in March 1638, one observer remarked that, if all refusers were arrested and their cattle distrained, 'there will not be found either prisons or pinfolds enough' to receive them.[164] Elizabeth Mace, a widowed householder at Compton Abdale, Gloucestershire, complained of Ship Money at Shrovetide 1638, saying that the payments 'came daily on, one upon another, [so] she should not be able to live'. One of her workmen, the labourer Thomas Welsh, responded, with subject-like alacrity, 'that howsoever payments went, and her ability was, the king must be served', to which another bystander remarked, 'if it be so, that the king must have all, I would the king were dead'.[165]

Ship Money was deeply controversial, notwithstanding the legal judgment and the overall effectiveness of collection. Disagreement did not necessarily translate into refusal to pay, but it gathered resentment against the regime. Historians who minimize the divisiveness of Charles I's reign have downplayed the voices of opposition, which pre-dated Hampden's case and grew louder in the following months.[166] Even some of the king's officers, who were bound 'to promote and advance' the king's service, could be heard 'prating and grumbling much against the Ship Money'. Such was the case of William Walker, a chief constable in Northamptonshire, who was reported for saying in 1638 that 'the Ship Money was an intolerable exaction, burden and oppression laid upon the land'. Walker acknowledged the judges had determined for Ship Money, 'but the best and most honest had not'. If not withdrawn, he feared, 'the Ship Money here in England would cause the like stirs that were now in Scotland'.[167] Two men of Latton, Essex, were among those briefly imprisoned for 'ill language and reviling speeches against the collectors of Ship Money' in May 1638.[168] John Glascocke of Bedfordshire was charged in Star Chamber in March 1639 for 'contemptuous, scandalous and undutiful speeches' against the king and government, saying that 'Ship Money was but counterfeit and not just and of necessity, but for the caterpillars of the court'.[169] Following high levels of compliance in its early years, the Ship Money shortfall rose to 20 per cent in 1638–9, with almost 80 per cent delinquency in 1639–40.[170]

Clerical leadership of the opposition to Ship Money is usually overlooked. It was not a 'puritan' issue but a matter of citizenship when ministers denounced the hated tax. Henry Nowell, the curate of Great Plumstead, Norfolk, was cited before authorities in May 1638 'for uttering contemptuous words' against Ship Money.[171] The court of High Commission proceeded against the Northamptonshire minister Richard Powell, who 'digressed from the text' that year 'to treat of matters and business of state', and urged his parishioners not to pay. Powell's preaching moved from scripture to political theory when he warned his congregation against 'tyrants and tyrannical princes that laid cruel, unjust and tyrannical taxes upon their subjects, saying that when God gives such a king he gives him in his wrath . . . yet we must pity him and pray for him', meaning 'our gracious sovereign lord King Charles'.[172] Also reprimanded by High Commission was pastor Richard Northen of Hainton, Lincolnshire, who taught 'that there was theft in kings and princes in laying more burdens on their subjects than they were able to bear'.[173] In Dorset the parson of Winterbourne, Mr Hobbie, declared that 'he would lose his life rather than suffer his goods to be taken from him', and encouraged parishioners not to pay. Edward Fox, the curate at nearby Anderson, similarly led local resistance.[174]

Opponents of Ship Money, the defeated parties in Hampden's case, had the opportunity to settle the score three years later when the revolutionary House of Commons attacked the royal prerogative. Demanding reversal of the judgment in Hampden's case, Oliver St John argued in January 1641 that 'our birthright, our ancestral right, our condition of continuing free subjects, is lost, that of late there hath been an endeavour to reduce us to the state of villeinage, nay to a lower'. The law, which was intended for the security of the subject, had been perverted into an 'instrument of taking from us all we have'.[175] Parliament declared Ship Money illegal in August 1641, and damned it further in its Grand Remonstrance of December 1641. 'The new and unheard of tax of Ship Money', remonstrators fumed, was part of 'a malignant and pernicious design of subverting the fundamental laws and principles of government', an attack on 'the common birthright of the subject'.[176] Only through the consent of the governed, by vote of their representatives in parliament, would the free people of England open their pockets to their king.

Material Demands

In normal times, not skewed by revolution, the people of England owed myriad obligations to their monarch. Simply being an inhabitant of England, a subject of his majesty, and a member of a parish, entailed duties and responsibilities, many of them backed by royal warrant. If the king's needs required it, his officers could take a subject's horse or cart, make use of his barn or boat, and requisition supplies of foodstuffs, timber, or other goods for the use of the army, the navy, or the court. This was not brute confiscation so much as forced transaction, with compensation more favourable to the crown than the provider. These were established practices, not tyrannical impositions, but they generated widespread resentment. Inherited from the Middle Ages, the prerogative power of purveyance continued throughout Charles I's reign as 'a chronic rather than an acute grievance', and ended only in 1660.[177]

The prerogative power of purveyance required local communities to furnish goods and to transport supplies for the king's use below market rates. It was implemented, so the Grand Remonstrance complained, because the king could not meet the 'ordinary and necessary expenses' of his household 'without the assistance of his people', and it became a source of 'vexation and oppression'.[178] Traditionally the counties and hundreds fulfilled their obligations by providing purveyance in kind or cash composition, and it was mostly treated as a tax.[179] The best estimates suggest that purveyance brought the crown more than £30,000 a year, and closer to £40,000 by the late 1630s.[180]

Local records preserve details of purveyance 'for the service of the great and small provisions of the king's household'.[181] Charged with providing 'two hundred fat wethers [male sheep] for the king's household', the constables of Martinsley hundred, Rutland, collected the cash equivalence in January 1629 so that 'no taking is made of the goods of any of his majesty's subjects'. The parishioners of Hambleton collected £2 14*s.* 5*d.*, and their neighbours at Little Hambleton £2 13*s.* 1½*d.*, 'for the provision of his majesty's household'.[182] Elsewhere government contractors paid 'the king's price' for items that would have fetched more on the open market, or which their owner preferred not to sell. All through the 1630s the government rated wheat at 5*s.* a bushel for purposes of purveyance, whereas wheat prices ranged as high as 10*s.* or 12*s.* a bushel depending on the year, the season, and the location.[183] The king's price for carting was 2*d.* a mile or 4*d.* a load, when anyone else paid two or three times as much.[184] When market prices were high, as they were through most of the 1630s, the court got a bargain while farmers and carriers caught short shrift. A contract from 1635 shows a Westminster butcher 'taking the king's price' of 6*s.* or 7*s.* each for sheep supplied to the court, at a time when mutton cost almost four times that amount.[185]

Not surprisingly, purveyance led to grievances and grumbles. But complaints had more to do with the equity of assessment than with the fundamental legality of the charge. Responding to efforts in Leicestershire to raise the composition for purveyance, the Earl of Huntingdon wrote in September 1625 that 'many gentlemen and others do complain of the disproportionable taxing regarding the quantity and quality of their possessions'.[186] In that month the financially pressed regime in London informed magistrates in Leicestershire that 'his majesty would have the purveyance to be served in specie [i.e. ready money] as in former times'. But they told the authorities in Worcestershire, 'you are now to return to your former course of serving your provisions in kind and not any longer in money'. The city of Worcester duly delivered 150 lambs to the court in 1626, and a score each of fat oxen, fat mutton, and stock cattle in 1627.[187]

These local manifestations of prerogative power could be arbitrary and inconvenient. When a carter in Berkshire was told in December 1625 that 'his cart should serve the king and go to London', he tried to evade this requirement and was punished.[188] Beer brewers in London complained in December 1629 'that their beer and ale is taken from them for the use of his majesty's house, and their dray horses and servants are forced to carry and deliver the same, by the appointment of certain purveyors... and in case they fail, are committed to the custody of the pursuivants'.[189] Property-owners in Essex complained to the Chelmsford assize in July 1631 about

> the taking of hay, oats and straw for his highness's hounds and huntsmen's horses, pigeons and poultry for his majesty's hawks, the oppression of the saltpeter men, peas and beans for the brown baker, carriage of oysters, taking of wood out of yards... the great charge and abuse daily offered by taking of post horses, and billeting of his majesty's servants' horses in our best pastures and meadows in his majesty's hunting and other sporting journeys.[190]

The Lord Steward's department charged in January 1635 that Leicestershire was 'failing' in its provision of 40 oxen and 200 sheep, 'the necessity of the king's service requiring it'.[191] Property owners in Dorset who claimed exemption were rebuffed because 'purveyance is such an inseparable incident of the crown that no grant can exempt from it'.[192]

A small but not forgotten irritant was the right of the crown to take in the name of the king, 'as many greyhounds, both dogs and bitches, as they shall think meet for his majesty's disport and recreation; and to seize and take away all greyhounds, beagles or whippets as may be offensive to his majesty's game and disport'.[193] Some dog-owners may have thought it a privilege to supply hunting animals to the king, and to subordinate their own to his majesty's pleasures, but others may have regarded this prerogative as an unwarranted reach into their private business. A similar provision enabled the king to buy bears and bulls for his games and pastimes at prices that best suited the crown.[194]

The wars of the 1620s and the naval build-up in the 1630s placed heavy demands on purveyance. The king needed ships for his service, as well as workmen, timber, horses, and carts. In September 1627 he requisitioned every boat on the Isle of Wight to transport soldiers.[195] Some ship-owners waited thirteen months for payment when the crown pressed their vessels for voyages to Cadiz and the Isle of Rhé.[196]

The king's contractors were voracious for timber, for construction or repair of ships and buildings, firewood, or charcoal for smelting. Royal commissioners scoured England for suitable trees, which they bought at 'the king's price'. The provision of carriage for his majesty's plank and timber was 'an essential service for the king and kingdom', and any refusal would be met with sanctions.[197] The timber purveyors in Oxfordshire complained in July 1630 about the 'backwardness' of this service, the lack of cooperation from local constables, and threats that endangered their life.[198] A clash between the purveyor William Willoughby and Sir Timothy Terrill, the ranger of Shotover and Stowe woods in Oxfordshire, produced several years of complaint and recrimination. Willoughby claimed that Terrill's men gave him 'scandalous speeches and other evil language' and impeded necessary work 'to the hindrance of his majesty'. Each charged the other with graft and corruption.[199] Facing similar problems in the New Forest, the timber purveyor Thomas Williams found 'many froward and insolent people that will not accept reasonable and fit wages nor perform their work carefully'. In August 1632 he requested 'letters to be written in the king's name' to assist him 'upon all occasions for his majesty's service'.[200] Purveyance was hindered in Dorset and Wiltshire in 1633 because unpaid carters proved unwilling to perform 'his majesty's service'.[201] When purveyors for timber 'and other provisions of his majesty's work, household and service' were charged in 1638 with taking bribes and abusing their power, the Council merely ordered them to keep better records.[202]

Another clash in 1638 began with complaints over pricing but grew into a test of the prerogative powers of the crown. Francis Joyce, the king's purveyor for wood, and John Halley, the yeoman purveyor for the salt store, would pay no more for goods and transport than 'the accustomed price paid by the crown', but some people in Hertfordshire 'absolutely refused to accept of his majesty's prices'. Told that 'the purveyors refused to give a greater price because the king had never exceeded that rate', the high constable Edward Turner answered 'that it had been accustomed to rob on Shooter's Hill, which being applicable to this case, might make the purveyors liable to the gallows'. The purveyors protested that this 'contemptuous behaviour' was 'to dispute the power and right of his majesty's prerogative' and appealed to their patrons at the Board of Green Cloth to bring their adversaries 'to better obedience'. If Hertfordshire succeeded in raising the price, 'it would be a dangerous blow to the prerogative royal' as well as adding to the king's costs. Their goal, these officers claimed, was to maintain 'his majesty's prerogative royal, founded on an ancient accustomed practice, and yet with a careful respect not to commit any excess in the use of his sovereign power'. Each time they mentioned the 'prerogative royal' in this written declaration of proceedings, they inscribed it in oversize letters, so readers would not miss the point.[203]

Complainants on matters of principle typically vilified their opponents, and in this case they represented critics of purveyance as 'factious persons' engaged in 'refractory proceedings'. They identified the constable who compared the purveyors to highway robbers as one who long laboured 'to make an opposition against his majesty's service by dissuading obedience to his majesty's commission'. Though superficially about money and goods, the dispute was really about politics and power. Edward Turner told one of the purveyors 'that he knew him to be but the arrow, but they must deal with him because they could not come to the bow'. If the king was the bow or the bowman, then Turner was guilty of sedition.[204]

Especially provocative of 'insolencies which shall oppose sovereignty' was the crown's demand for transport. The king's 'necessities' obliged his people to provide his servants and messengers with horses, usually with compensation offered or promised. Such was the case in July 1633 when residents close to the Great North Road were required 'to provide twenty of the best sufficient able horses, with good sufficient saddles and bridles and able men for guides . . . to attend his majesty's return from Scotland'.[205] Some subjects were understandably reluctant to give up their mounts, and arguments produced complaints on both sides. Here, too, minor acts of recalcitrance could expand into challenges to royal authority.

In February 1627, for example, backed by a royal warrant, the constables of Portsmouth demanded that the innholder Robert Woodnot turn over the horses in his stable 'in readiness the next morning for the king's service'. Woodnot, however, resisted, removed the animals, menaced the constables, and displayed his refractoriness in 'very abusive speeches'.[206] A similar incident in August 1627 made the royal emissary Sir Henry Hungate apoplectic with rage, when lowly constables at Alresford, Hampshire, 'abused' him by refusing to provide him with a horse. Hungate was bound for Portsmouth with urgent dispatches when he showed his warrant to constable Christopher Neville and demanded his horse. Rather than being awed by this authorization, Neville 'made a pish at it, and said his nag should not go'. The rider's attachment to his property over-rode his obligations to the crown. It took Hungate four hours to find a suitable mount. Reporting the outrage, he demanded that 'these rogues be punished with strictness' for frustrating the king's business.[207] Though this was a trivial incident, it illuminated stresses in the chain of command, and challenges to monarchical power, since constables as well as messengers formed part of the apparatus of the state. It fed Sir Henry Hungate's view, and perhaps the king's, that the people were insolent and unreliable.[208]

As recalcitrant as the constable at Alresford, Anthony Spittle, the postmaster at Basingstoke, refused to provide arms for the king or to serve in the Hampshire trained band. He claimed that his position as postmaster exempted him from military service, and, when the deputy lieutenant Sir Thomas Jervoise said he had no such privilege, Spittle displayed 'contempt of authority' and gave the officers 'very ill language'. Jervoise wanted Spittle punished for his insolent affront, for 'otherwise authority will be drawn into contempt', so he warned Secretary Conway.[209] In September 1627 Anthony Spittle appeared before the Council in London, in the custody of a royal messenger, charged with being 'a defaulter in finding of arms'. Again he stood his ground, insisted on his privilege, and presented certificates from other postmasters to support his claim of exemption. Back home in Basingstoke he bragged to neighbours that 'he cared not what they could do who caused him to be sent for, not so much for his wife's turd, and . . . that he cared no more for them than for one hair of his arse'. Sir Thomas Jervoise reported Spittles's gendered scatological refractoriness, but no more punishment followed.[210]

Ten years later Anthony Spittle himself complained of subjects who would not fulfil their obligations to the king. His warrant as postmaster allowed him to requisition horses for the king's use 'upon extraordinary occasions', but some people in Hampshire 'neglected the service' of his majesty by failing to provide him with mounts. This complaint triggered a counter-complaint, that Spittle 'notoriously abused the county' by exploiting his warrant for 'private gain'. He would sometimes take as many as ten horses a week 'when there is no such service of his majesty for them' and would either hire them out for 'private occasions', or else release them back to their owners for a bribe. Spittle's career reveals stresses in relationships of subjecthood, authority, rank, status, and position, and shows how altercations over minor matters could implicate the honour and authority of the crown.[211]

Clashes of this sort were petty and legion, but they made manifest the tension between individual rights and the royal prerogative. One postmaster in Lincolnshire found himself arrested for felony theft and trespass, 'to the manifest hindrance of his majesty's service', after taking a horse 'for his majesty's service . . . lawfully and by warrant'.[212] Local magistrates in Hertfordshire rebuked another postmaster in 1639 when he tried to requisition a countryman's carthorse. The justices told the postmaster to 'seek out other horses, more fit for the king's service', so he took theirs instead.[213] When the postmaster at Hereford took horses 'for his majesty's affairs', the subsequent dispute with the innkeeper John Rogers involved refusal, insolent speech, and threats of assault.[214]

The records of local government are sprinkled with episodes in which otherwise upstanding subjects were cited as delinquents for failing to perform their legal and public duties. Parish business would have collapsed if more than a minority reneged on their rates and assessments, or obligations of labour, attendance, and service, but reprimands were common. In 1638, for example, the constables of Ely hundred, Cambridgeshire, presented Christopher Wade of Littleport 'for refusing to watch the 3rd of July last, having lawful warning by the watchmen, and further he threatened the watchmen for coming upon his ground to warn him'. They presented John Clearke of Ely 'for refusing to provide a cart to fetch away the corpse from the gallows that was last executed'. They presented Thomas Worton of Denham, blacksmith, for refusing to pay his rate to the constables, and 'abusing the said constables upon demand of his rate.' Others refused orders to work on the roads and bridges, to keep the highways clear of rubbish, or to assist in the hue and cry 'in the name of the king'.[215] In 1639 the Council at York took action against 'refractory persons' who delayed or refused to clean ditches and build earthworks in advance of the king's coming.[216] Behind each minor act of recalcitrance lay a complex set of contested duties that undergirded the monarchical state. The demands of kingship gave material heft to the ideological persuasions of duty and obedience.

It was an axiom of common law that a man's house was his castle, immune to arbitrary search and seizure. Yet royal needs, both material and financial, subjected this privilege to pressure. A Privy Council warrant in December 1636 specifically empowered the monopoly manufacturers of soap to search the city of Westminster, in the king's name, to seize and carry away all illicit materials, 'to break, deface or destroy' equipment used in their manufacture, and to enlist the support of local officers 'in breaking or forcing open the door or house where they cannot otherwise enter'. With magistrates and constables at their side, the soap-searchers had the power to apprehend all offenders who 'shall oppose, impugn or hinder the due and peaceable execution of his majesty's service in this behalf'.[217]

Similar intrusions governed the collection of saltpeter, as the king's officers repeatedly dug in private ground for the raw material to make gunpowder. Sir Edward Coke insisted that 'the king's ministers . . . cannot dig the floor of any mansion houses which serve for the habitation of man'. He repeated in parliament in 1628 his view that the king's men 'cannot dig any house or wall, for it is for the commonwealth to have houses of habitation'.[218] Yet the king's need for munitions, and his responsibility for national security, repeatedly clashed with this principle. The government required up to 300 tons of gunpowder a year, and its main material, saltpeter, came from nitrous earth, mostly extracted from private grounds. Pigeon houses and stables were especially rich sources of saltpeter, but it also came from bedchambers, privies, and even churches. The state demanded entry to these 'mines', and also required countrymen to provide cartage, labour, and sites for processing. The saltpetermen requisitioned barges, carts, and necessary animals and equipment, in the king's name, for 'the king's service', and 'at the king's price'.[219]

The crown regarded access to saltpeter as a prerogative right, and its furnishing akin to purveyance. A royal proclamation at the beginning of King Charles's reign set forth 'orders and constitutions, to be from henceforth inviolably kept and observed, for the better maintaining of the breed and increase of saltpeter, and the true making of gunpowder'. It expressed the king's 'heavy displeasure' at 'contemnors of his majesty's royal commandment', and threatened Star Chamber against any who challenged his prerogative in this regard. The government recognized that saltpeter extraction 'occasioned many complaints' and was 'very offensive to many of our good subjects', but the security of the kingdom required it to proceed.[220] Another proclamation in March 1635 imposed penalties on 'refractory persons' who disobeyed 'our royal commandment, in a matter of so high consequence for the public service and safety of our state and kingdom'.[221] Complaints arose of abuse and intrusion, but Privy Councillors prioritized 'this so necessary and behooveful a service for the safety of the kingdom'.[222]

Saltpetermen armed with the royal warrant claimed the power 'to dig in houses against consent, and to carry without setting down how far', and threatened reprisal against any challenges. Like purveyors, they paid 'the king's price' for carriage, and sometimes not even that.[223] Nicholas Stephens, the Oxfordshire saltpeterman, 'grievously oppressed the people' through 'manifold abuses', but claimed protection through his commission.[224] Thomas Hilliard, with franchises in the West Country, claimed the right to dig for saltpeter wherever he chose, and warned all who opposed him that they risked 'the fearful threat of his majesty's displeasure'.[225]

The saltpetermen were as intrusive as rats, as busy as moles. They put the country to 'an immense charge', claimed Sir Robert Phelips in 1636, and 'under pretence of his majesty's service, require unreasonable things'. Rather than advancing the king's service, he charged, the saltpetermen, 'to ease themselves, endeavour to make his majesty's subjects their slaves'.[226] Landowners with sufficient means bribed the saltpetermen to dig elsewhere, while others endured their depredations. The sabotage of saltpeter tubs in Herefordshire in 1637 was termed an act of 'abuse and contempt of his majesty's service'.[227] Protests occasionally turned violent. A 'mutiny' against the saltpetermen in Hertfordshire in May 1638 involved 'many of his majesty's officers... in danger of being killed'.[228] In Kent in December 1639 men 'malignantly disposed to his majesty's service' beat the saltpeter operatives with cudgels and locked them in the stocks, saying 'the king employed more rogues in his works than any man'.[229] Saltpeter resisters in Surrey said that 'they knew no service that the king had there; but if the king came that way he should have the key'.[230] The king was made virtually present through the seals, warrants, writs, and badges of his officers, and resistance to their authority was tantamount to denial of his. Officials feared that petty recalcitrance would grow into sedition, and their fears may have been well grounded.

Dishonourable Discourse

Finally, overarchingly, subjects owed their king loyalty, allegiance, honour, and respect, which theorists often construed as 'love'. The proper course was to pray for his sacred majesty, and to uphold his 'authority, power, dignity, and preeminence'.[231] The king was a distant figurehead, but if he should pass within gazing distance the expected course for subjects was to kneel in silence or else proclaim 'God save the king!' Even his statue and picture commanded obeisance, 'for any disgrace offered to his majesty's figure is as much as to himself'.[232] Those who were 'negligent' in their observances, or demeaning of his majesty, whether in parliament or in the parishes, were likely to be termed 'refractory', 'recalcitrant', 'malignant', or worse.

Despite the obligations of subjecthood, a sub-current of criticism leaked into the public sphere as doubts arose about particular policies or qualities of the present king. Some critics thought King Charles too easily led, too much in thrall to the Duke of Buckingham or other favourites. A few were emboldened to call him childlike. The Somerset lawyer Hugh Pyne notoriously likened King Charles to a child with an apple, and questioned his fitness to rule.[233] The London schoolmaster Alexander Gill declared King Charles 'a very weak man and fitter to stand in a shop with a white apron before him than to be a king of England'.[234] Others mouthed the verse from Ecclesiastes warning against young monarchs. One preacher at Oxford was committed in 1626 for choosing as his text 'woe be to the land that shall have princes [that are] children'.[235] Politicians close to the court knew that King James referred to his son as 'baby Charles', even when the prince was a grown man.[236] Gentlemen were not supposed to speak of such matters, but humbler commoners could not be counted on to hold their tongues. King Charles himself may have heard traces of popular criticism when he told parliament in 1626: 'I think it is more honour for a king to be invaded and almost destroyed by a foreign enemy than to be despised by his own subjects.'[237]

Kingship was 'sacred', William Laud preached repeatedly, 'and therefore cannot be violated by the hand, tongue, or heart of any man'. It was 'blasphemous iniquity' to murmur against kings, the sin of 'distempered spirits' to revile any monarch. Let no sin 'whet your tongues, or sour your breasts, against the Lord and his anointed'.[238] Fortunately such voices formed a minority, 'the ill filthy breaths of some few ill-affected persons', according to Lord Goring, who assured the Marquess of Hamilton of 'the real devotion of all this people here to our most blessed king'.[239]

There was no substantial criticism of the institution of monarchy, but a corrosive trickle of commentary dishonoured this particular king. In the

1620s some people even looked to be rid of King Charles, in favour of his sister Elizabeth, the exiled 'winter queen' of Bohemia, married to Frederick the Elector Palatine. Wondering what would befall if King Charles were somehow removed, the soldier Thomas Brediman suggested in October 1626 that 'maybe it shall be a free state, for perhaps the Palatine and the Lady Elizabeth shall have it'.[240] In 1628 John Rous recorded 'a secret whispering of some looking towards the Lady Elizabeth', as 'our king's proceedings have caused men's minds to be incensed, to rove and project'. Rous characterized such thoughts as 'merely the conceit of the multitude', but he was moved to pray God to 'heal this breach, discover the cause and ground of all our grievances, and settle thou, as thou seest fit, the hearts of our sovereign and his subjects in love and loyalty together'.[241] Prophets in London that year predicted that King Charles would not live long as king.[242]

Discourse of this nature was more dangerous to the state than grievances against rank and hierarchy. The king and his people were supposed to be married 'in a happy bond of love and unity', preached Phineas Hodson at York, so it was vital to set aside 'jealousy and combustion' whereby 'the prince hath been rent from the people, and the people from the prince'.[243] The dissolution of parliament in March 1629 prompted the Shropshire gentleman Stephen ap Evans to warn that 'the king would lose the hearts of his people . . . and that the end of it would be that he would be hunted out of the land, and that the Palgrave [Charles's kinsman the Elector Palatine, d. 1632] would be crowned in his stead'.[244] A publicly posted manuscript a month or two later warned King Charles 'thou hast lost the hearts of thy subjects' and therefore he was now 'no king'.[245] A mixture of dread and wishful thinking may explain the false news in Cheshire in May 1630 that the king had been taken to the Tower and the Palgrave proclaimed in his place.[246] Seditious dynastic speculation ended when Henrietta Maria gave birth to a prince, but scandalous murmurings against King Charles continued.

A small chorus of malignant and refractory voices formed a background to the years of personal rule.[247] 'Base, vile, impious, malicious and seditious speeches against his majesty' were no less startling for being egregious, outrageous, and exceptional. Reckless and disloyal subjects called King Charles a bastard, a knave, and a fool.[248] A London physician voiced 'vain fancies' against 'sovereignty itself' in 1633 by saying, 'it was all one to be under the king and under the Turk'.[249] Maurice Bawde in Lincolnshire and John Sheppard in Staffordshire were among those declaring that they 'neither cared for the king nor the king's laws'.[250] 'What care I for the king or his commissioners?' asked John Lewis in 1632, adding of the royal warrant: 'I can make as good a one under a hedge and wipe my tail with it.'[251] Claiming that he could make better laws than any king or peer, Robert Redferne of Gloucester observed in 1634 'that the king was no better than another ordinary man'.[252] John Bassett of Stepney, Middlesex, claimed likewise 'that he did not care for the king, and that he was as good a man as the king'.[253] The demand for Ship Money elicited more reckless remarks, like those of Lawrence Hall of Kilsby, Northamptonshire, who announced in 1637 'that he owed the king nothing'.[254] Refusing to pay, the Bedfordshire man John Glascocke declared outrageously that he did not love the king, 'that he had as good blood in him as' King Charles, and that 'he had read kings had been deposed'.[255] The controversial war with Scotland increased the pressure. Asserting that the king's lawmakers were 'ill-conditioned men', a Smithfield victualler said in May 1639 'that one may say anything now, for the king was at York'.[256]

Loyal clerics sought to quieten the flow of seditious chatter, which seemed to increase as the nation's crisis worsened. There was 'such a vein of refractory disposition', alleged one worried Northamptonshire minister in 1639, that some 'speak never so vile against God, the king, and the church'.[257] 'These latter times have produced a generation of vipers . . . who instead of rejoicing in their king rail at him,' preached Henry Valentine in 1639.[258] John Swan concurred that 'God's anointed' should not be 'touched with any virulent tongue'.[259] Those who 'murmur against his commands' or harbour 'disobedient and discontented thoughts' in their hearts 'are as ill subjects to God as to the king', preached Henry King at St Paul's in March 1640.[260] Lessons in obedience and humility had little effect on the king's 'worst sort' of subjects.

Accumulated Frictions

Assertions of divine-right kingship were not new in King Charles's England, nor was routine exercise of the royal prerogative unexpected. English monarchs had long claimed divine approbation, and always demanded the love and service of their subjects. Though early Stuart insistence on the majesty of the crown may seem excessive, the characterization of the monarch as the keystone, the sun, and even a god goes back to

Tudor times and has roots in the Bible. The vehement reiteration of these assertions, however, moved to a higher register in the reign of Charles I. From William Laud's welcome of King Charles as 'God's immediate lieutenant upon earth', to John Swan's praise of the king as 'the *primum mobile* . . . like the sun in the firmament', the people of England heard a chorus of royal adulation. There may have been an element of logomancy in these remarks, as if saying so would make it so. King Charles repeatedly claimed his people's love as his greatest asset, but he made few efforts to cultivate the affection that he perceived as his right.

Monarchical government made extensive use of the royal prerogative, and only rarely was it resisted. Even today the British crown preserves residual prerogative powers that have withstood calls for reform.[261] The prerogative command of armed forces and the conduct of foreign affairs was unquestioned before 1642, although some people wished the king would take different counsel. The prerogative of purveyance stretched back time out of mind, although that did not make it popular. Contention grew in the reign of Charles I as the king used his prerogative to raise money, and parliamentary patriots intensified the rancor of debate. Common lawyers set 'the liberties of the subject' against the prerogatives of the crown, and, although they scored rhetorical points, they lost the verdicts of politics and law. Crown lawyers and judges of the 1620s and 1630s agreed with courtiers and counsellors that such prerogative devices as the forced loan and Ship Money were both legal and unexceptional, and there was no shortage of clerics to support them. They also reasserted the claim that the king could dispense with the law and imprison without trial if the security of the state so required, an assertion repeated more recently in Northern Ireland and at Guantanamo.

Previous royal regimes had sought loans from their subjects, and earlier governments had demanded Ship Money. But the scale and persistence of exactions was new under Charles I. So too was the indictment and vilification of refusers and resisters as 'refractory' malignants. Charles I's government found it hard to distinguish between everyday sluggishness and principled opposition, and too easily labelled people as 'froward . . . factious . . . recalcitrant' and enemies to the king's service. Successive struggles over law and money conditioned the regime to expect trouble, and to label troublemakers as incendiaries. The language of 'sorts' enabled crown officials to demean their opponents as 'the baser sort' of people.[262]

An accumulation of grievances, major and minor, taught half a generation of Englishmen to suspect or mistrust their king, even while ministers and magistrates insisted on obedience and love. Charles I had no inclination towards tyranny, and he lacked the police power necessary for absolute monarchy; his government was necessarily collaborative, although the king controlled the terms of the collaboration. Yet contemporaries noted a changing pattern, a shift of tone and emphasis, whereby absolutist interpretations of the prerogative were privileged, and commonweal protections of the rights of the subject were eclipsed. Pre-revisionist Whig historians of the twentieth century foregrounded constitutional conflict in the early Stuart era as a fundamental motif of public life, and post-revisionist reappraisal suggests that they were not entirely mistaken. The overreach of the crown occasioned principled resistance, but was more commonly accompanied by low-level insolence and lack of cooperation. Widespread grumbling erupted from time to time into violent disorder, though never to a level that could not be contained. Ill-judged or not, refractoriness was no cause of the civil war, but rather a conditioning factor in the Caroline political environment. Only when discrete grievances were framed as a coherent oppositional narrative would the regime of Charles I be in trouble.

4
Unprosperous Wars

Wars of Christendom

Charles I reigned amid a European war that raged for thirty years, from 1618 to 1648. During the first five years of his rule King Charles involved England on the fringes of this war, with naval and military campaigns against both Spain and France. He also offered support to his protestant kinsmen and allies on the Continent. Unfortunately these involvements produced only ignominy and reproach, as English martial prowess proved wanting. The narrative of policy and action is generally well known, but its social repercussions have yet to be fully measured. Nor have the constitutional consequences of recruitment, billeting, and wartime finance been sufficiently explored.[1] This chapter examines the militarization of England between the end of the Jacobean peace in 1625 and the end of campaigning in 1629, with some further reckoning of military affairs in the 1630s. Wherever possible it assesses the impact on ordinary men and women of the policies directed from Whitehall. The king alone could command war and peace, but his subjects, as always, supplied the blood, sweat, and money.

The weapon-wielding arm on the obverse of Charles's coronation medal of 1626 signified his determination to use military force, but it was not clear where that strength would be directed.[2] Both naval and land campaigns were envisaged, as far away as the Caribbean or as near as the narrow seas. King Charles and the Duke of Buckingham wanted to intervene abroad 'for the succour of his majesty's allies, and for the maintenance of the cause of religion', but they also had to prepare for the defence of the kingdom.[3] The scale and purpose of the mobilization varied as circumstances changed.

English interests turned on trade and religion, but the core of the war concerned the Palatinate, a German territory contested between catholics and protestants, whose refugee princess was Charles's sister Elizabeth. Royal honour and the protestant cause helped drive English foreign policy, and both shaped popular conversation. 'The disturbed state of Christendom' and 'the distress and necessity of our dear brother and sister', the deposed Elector Palatine and Princess Elizabeth of Bohemia, persuaded his majesty to gear for war in 1625. The mobilization continued a policy begun in the final year of James's reign, when the duke and the prince took charge. Councillors cited the 'eminent dangers to true religion, to our allies, to our countries, and the trade of our people', of which 'every well-affected subject will be readily sensible'.[4]

Following some indecision about pursuit of an offensive or defensive strategy, and whether England's forces were better deployed in the West Indies or close to home, the Council determined to launch an attack against Spain. On 8 October 1625, half a year after Charles I's accession, a fleet of 82 ships set forth with 6,264 seamen and 9,507 soldiers, most of them recently pressed into service. They went in thirteen royal vessels, twenty-eight leased merchantmen, and forty-one Newcastle colliers engaged for the expedition, all commanded by Edward Cecil, Viscount Wimbledon.[5] It was a considerable administrative achievement to put this armada to sea, but the men on board had little training, and their aptitude was yet to be tested. Officers, men, and equipment all proved deficient.

The expedition to Cadiz was a shambles. One ship, a merchantman pressed out of Ipswich, went down with 175 men before reaching Spanish waters. Another was captured by Sallee pirates. The recently recruited landsmen were treated to an epic storm, in which masts and cannons loosened and bilges filled with water. The expedition's leaders could barely agree on their target, and when they tried to take Cadiz they met heavy bombardment in relentless rain. The one major landing of troops turned to farce when the soldiers liberated a store of wine and became too drunk to proceed. Commanders blamed the poor quality of recruits, who were 'wonderfully unreasonable and insufficient', and thought that 'his majesty's officers for that press deserve little but punishment'. Survivors straggled home in December, shadowed by sickness, misery, and dishonour, and recriminations continued for months. Naval administrators rushed to shift blame for 'this unadvised miscarriage'.[6] The field commander Lord Wimbledon described poor intelligence, divided counsel, neglected orders, inadequate supplies, defective equipment, and difficult weather, but concluded stoically, 'man proposeth, and God determines'.[7]

Opponents in parliament blamed the Duke of Buckingham, and Buckingham blamed subordinates. Sir John Eliot's outrage was almost palpable: 'our honour is ruined, our ships are sunk, our men perished, not by the sword, not by an enemy, not by chance, but... by those we trust'.[8] A scathing libellous ballad on the Cadiz expedition ends:

God bless Charles our King, and everything
That he war-likely takes in hand.
And in his next choice he shall have my voice
For a wiser man to command.[9]

Further recrimination followed revelations that warships that England had loaned to the French for use against Genoa had been employed against the Hugueneots of La Rochelle. Failure to singe the king of Spain's beard, and failure to advance the godly cause was compounded by the ignominy of English equipment being used against fellow protestants by 'the enemies of our religion'.[10] Goaded by complaints that they had abandoned the godly interest, and encouraged by the Huguenot admiral Baron de Soubise, Charles and Buckingham next determined to assist the protestants besieged at La Rochelle. This shift of policy brought England into hostilities with France, while the war with Spain still lingered. Gentry networks reported in March 1627 that 'Captain Pennington is gone to sea with a fleet of ten sail, and a hundred more are making ready to go after them speedily, but where they are bound no one knows but God and the king'.[11] Another formidable fleet was assembled, the royal ships backed once more by impressed commercial vessels. A combined force of 6,710 landsmen and 3,848 mariners set sail for the Bay of Biscay in June 1627.[12] Reinforcements would follow intermittently, including 2,500 men from Ireland.[13]

The Duke of Buckingham took direct command of the operation that tried for three months to take the Isle of Rhé, the gateway to La Rochelle. The plan was to relieve the embattled Huguenots, recover English assets, assert the sovereignty of the seas, and then 'to receive the event from God, in whom we wholly put our trust'.[14] As at Cadiz, the English were disorganized and ill-prepared, outmanœuvered and poorly led. Farce turned to death when the ladders designed to scale the fortress walls proved 5 feet too short. The siege cost lives and equipment, with minimal useful effect. Starving, diseased, dispirited, and eventually overwhelmed, the survivors withdrew in dishonour at the end of October.[15] Buckingham's army numbered nearly 7,000 when it set out for Rhé in June, but fewer than 3,000 soldiers returned to Plymouth and Portsmouth in November.[16]

King Charles's second major military expedition concluded even worse than his first, and the losses from these 'two unprosperous attempts' were felt throughout the country. The stresses, disturbances, and disappointments of war shaped contentious debate about the power and the policies of the crown. Critics steamed about the waste of 'treasure, shipping, munition and honour', and twenty years later still held hold King Charles responsible for 'the sad business of Rochelle and the Isle of Rhé'.[17] Families across England mourned their dead. Diarists recorded 'bad news' and 'evil news' of the duke's failure, which 'made much muttering and caused much suspicion'.[18] 'Rochelle is now become Rachel weeping for her children... Lord lay not this sin to our charge, the blood of so many thousands of our dear brethren,' declared an anonymous libel, which asked of King Charles, 'the lord open thine eyes'.[19] While libellers lambasted Buckingham for yet another national disgrace, the king treated him as a hero, his virtues intact.[20] As usual, all blame for the debacle fell elsewhere. According to Secretary Conway, speaking for the court in November 1627, the duke's report on the Isle of Rhé 'joyed us much to find loss of so small a number, and so little in point of honour, we taking the greatest loss to be in the quality of some half a dozen persons'. Several lists circulated of 'officers slain', but casualties among common soldiers and seamen were uncounted.[21]

In addition to assisting Dutch and Danish allies, and preparing for raids against Spain and France, English forces braced for a possible invasion. Rumour upon rumour had the homeland threatened by foreign enemies. False reports in September 1625 of landings near Harwich jangled nerves from London to East Anglia.[22] Reports in March 1626 fed fears of a second Armada, 'the greatest which Spain ever had, and now ready to put to sea', perhaps with designs on the naval base at Chatham. By June this imagined Spanish fleet had grown to 'two hundred good ships now ready to put out', with advanced squadrons already menacing the Isles of Scilly.[23] July brought more news of 'great and threatening preparations made in Spain and Flanders', which showed that 'the king's enemies have some design upon his dominions'.[24] The Council issued directions to county lieutenants in 1626 'in case the enemy should land', and in 1627 they warned that the kingdom was 'daily threatened' by the preparations and approach of enemy powers. In July 1627 they worried that Dartmouth in Devonshire was exposed to foreign attack.[25] Feeding these fears, a preacher at York warned of 'the pope, the emperor, the king of Spain, France now, and vast Germany... now in a manner racked and raised against us'.[26]

Strategists considered how best to cope should the Spanish invade along western or southern coasts.[27] More intelligence arrived in February 1628 of armies massing on the coast of Brittany 'and other forces ready to invade us'.[28] In December 1628 the Council received warning of 'hostile preparations' said to target the coast of Dorset and the islands of Jersey and Guernsey. The coastline needed watching, beacons to be readied, ships and armies to be manned and prepared.[29] Even during the 1630s, when England was officially at peace, periodic rumours told of menacing foreign forces and imagined enemy landings.[30]

Putting the kingdom on a war footing was expensive as well as complicated. The Privy Council learned in 1626 that 'to maintain a war offensive and defensive' would cost more than a million pounds a year, an estimate repeated by the parliamentarian Ferdinando Fairfax in letters to his father. It cost the government £30,000 a month to support the king of Denmark, £20,000 a month for Count Mansfeld's operations on the Continent, and £9,000 a month for the Dutch States. On top of these commitments were the costs of 'forty ships to guard our coasts, and for the army of ten thousand men to be always in readiness when an invasion may be threatened'. It cost over £400 a month to set forth a single warship of 200 tons manned by 120 men. It cost over £3,000 pounds just to prepare the *Vanguard* for six months' service in 1625, not counting the wages for its 230 mariners and gunners. The cost of putting forth the fleet in 1625 exceeded £170,000, including £65,000 in wages for mariners.[31] Payments fell severely behind, with inadequate provision from parliament and little certainty of continuing financial supply. By December 1627 arrears in the naval accounts exceeded a quarter of a million pounds.[32]

Correspondents referred to the 'sinews of war', the money that made war possible, and the 'habiliments of war', the materiel and equipment that men needed to fight. Both were costly and disruptive. Commentators who quoted Cicero's adage that 'the sinews of war are unlimited money' (*nervi belli pecunia infinita*) may not have fully recognized the scale of the 'military revolution' that has fascinated modern scholars, but they knew in 1625 that 10,000 men were 'now more chargeable than 40,000 were in times past'.[33] Military logistics were cripplingly expensive, and the early Stuart state had limited financial resources. Parliamentary conflicts over subsidies or taxation, and the king's recourse to extraparliamentary initiatives, like forced loans and Ship Money, had their roots in England's posture as a significant armed power.[34]

Men at Arms

The ability to act forcefully and honourably in Europe would depend on the effectiveness of mobilization and the ability of the king and his Council to make use of it. The machinery of naval and military administration was somewhat rusty after two decades of peace, and the competence of commanders was questionable. King Charles needed mariners and landsmen, ships and stores, and huge amounts of money, but his forces also needed organization, experience, talent, and luck.

The new king began his reign by levying troops, and the subsequent recruiting exposed thousands of people to military contractors, provost marshals, and martial discipline. The mobilization of men and resources caused considerable disturbance to everyday life. Subjects had to yield their bodies for impressment, open their homes for billeting, provide horses, carts, and equipment for the king's commissioners, and cover the cost of the kingdom's exigencies. Though these impositions had medieval roots, and were justified by the royal prerogative, their exercise in the reign of Charles I provoked challenges. Thousands of families were uprooted, as 'serviceable' men (and sometimes men not so serviceable) were turned into mariners and soldiers. Many became sick or injured, and most went months unpaid. Communities bore the cost of the coats and conduct of recruits, their initial furnishing of clothes and transport to their rendezvous or depot. Parishes and counties also made provision for returning veterans, especially men 'maimed' or otherwise unable to work. One such pensioner was John Dudley from Middlesex, who was pressed 'to serve his majesty in the late wars in the Isle of Rhé where he lost the use of both his hands and received divers wounds and hurts . . . and thereby became utterly disabled to take any pains or course to get his living'. His care cost the parish of St James Clerkenwell £2 a year.[35]

Property-owners and men of substance supplied most of the 'sinews' to meet the king's 'necessities' through subsidies, loans, and other exactions. Householders coped with the billeting of troops, and suffered sometimes from their depredations. The forced quartering of mariners and soldiers in private houses became a matter of legal contention, and underlay debates in parliament that led to the Petition of Right. So too did the imposition of martial law on civilian populations in military districts.[36] Rather than rallying the nation, King Charles's wars fuelled social, political, and constitutional contention.

Trained bands of citizen soldiers formed the core of England's military readiness. These were local residents who were called out occasionally for musters and drills. In principle, if the trained bands of every county were mobilized, and if each had its complement of men, the king could command an army 94,000 strong.[37] These forces, however, were the least likely to face foreign conflict, and were kept in reserve in case of invasion. Their level of preparation ranged from indifferent to appalling. County troops, by tradition, would not serve beyond county boundaries and were not prepared for a European war. A general muster of all the trained bands, planned for Whitsun week 1625, exposed some of their deficiencies. Too many were 'decayed by age and impotence of body' and were unfit for training and service.[38] Inspectors found the trained bands 'not well exercised', their arms 'defective', and their muster-masters inexperienced and under-paid.[39] A Yorkshire preacher stated part of the problem:

> Of all the men in this kingdom not one of a thousand trained. Of those that are trained, all are not brought into the field. Of those that are brought to the field in actions of greatest importance, a number, it may be half, never come to strike a stroke. Of so many millions in the king's dominions, not many thousands may come to bear the shock and burden of the day... If we cannot equal our adversaries in number and strength of soldiers [he continued], we can but get the odds by our prayers.[40]

The Caroline regime undertook to improve the trained bands and to develop a more reliable militia, though with varied and limited success.[41] County lieutenants entertained 'propositions for musters for the better perfecting of the trained bands of this kingdom', and conducted drills to ensure that men were 'so trained and ordered as is required'.[42] Experienced sergeants with continental experience helped to teach trained bands 'in martial discipline and to handle their muskets and pikes'.[43] The trained bands may indeed have improved as years went on, but they played little part in Charles I's wars. County lieutenants responsible for raising an army in 1625 were specifically instructed that no troops should be taken from the trained bands, 'which you are still to keep entire'.[44] Recruits in Berkshire were supposed to be 'strong and able and sufficient men and fit for service, but none of them to be of the trained bands'.[45] Campaigns would be waged instead by pick-up armies of pressed men, substitute troops, and hastily recruited volunteers.

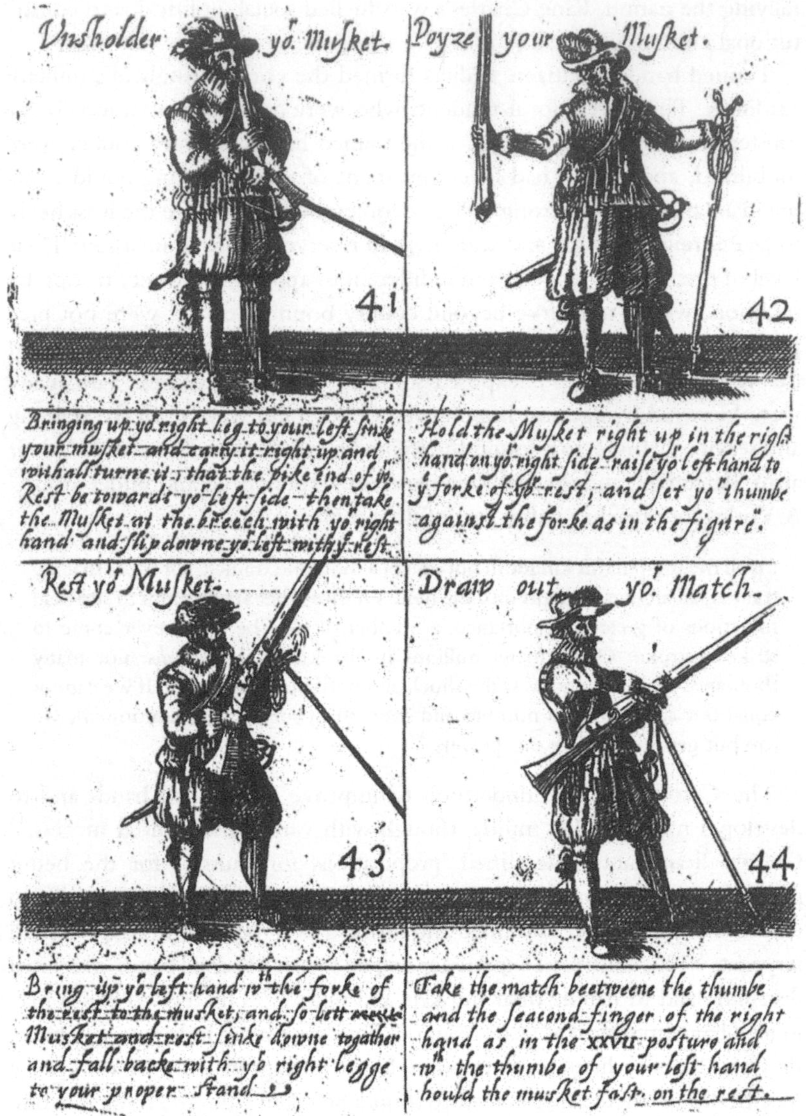

Figure 5. Instructions for Soldiers, 1631. *Instructions for Musters and Armes, and the use thereof* (1631), instructions 41–4.

The mobilization began in autumn 1624, under the direction of the duke and Prince Charles, with a levy of 12,000 men to serve abroad with Count Mansfeld. More would be needed every year. An urgent call went out in April 1625 for 2,000 seamen and 'ten thousand land soldiers' for the expedition to Cadiz. They would come from all parts of King Charles's dominions, and some would be brought back from the Low Countries.[46] 'Common speech' told of 'fifteen thousand land soldiers at least' assembled at Plymouth by June 1625, though this was an overestimate.[47] The evidence points to a total impressment of some 50,000 of the king's subjects over a four-year period, perhaps 4–5 per cent of the adult male population.[48]

The recruits were supposed to be 'able bodied' and of 'years meet for this employment', though sometimes they were found to be 'lame and unfit for his majesty's service'.[49] Local officials had quotas to fill, with the understanding that 'any petty constable failing to bring the men required of him will be himself impressed to serve the king as a soldier'.[50] Deputy lieutenants in county after county were flooded with appeals for exemption, amid complaints of 'conniving, selling, changing or sparing of the most able men'.[51] Constables in Wiltshire faced scrutiny for taking bribes to allow pressed men to be discharged.[52] In London the price of freedom was as high as £3, though 5*s*. could sometimes secure release.[53] Sir Alexander Cave tried to pull rank in Leicestershire to exempt one of his household servants, 'a young fellow not above the age of eighteen or nineteen at the most, whom I entertained to keep my geldings and sometimes to kill hawks' meat'. Favours like this could be granted only if a substitute was found to fill the place.[54] Other tales told of men pressed 'for ill will', denied exemption for 'malice', or sent away as soldiers because they refused the forced loan.[55] The impressments, it was recognized, caused social and economic hardship, distress for families, 'cries of mothers, wives and children', and difficulties with the harvest. The recruiting effort suffered, one deputy lieutenant explained, because 'as soon as there is a fame of levying men for the king a great part of them that it may concern do secretly transport themselves into other counties and places'.[56]

Some recruits proved unfit for service and unamenable to military discipline. The veteran commander Sir John Ogle complained of men 'being pressed very confusedly', and too many unfit 'by reason of age, impotency, sickness, and other infirmities'.[57] Randal Wakefield of Kinderton, Cheshire, was said to be 'a man of untrue, lewd, drunken and ungodly life and conversation', which some might think ideal qualifications for military service. He was 'pressed for a soldier' in the 1625 recruiting drive, but returned without leave, a deserter, and assaulted a female neighbour.[58] Occasionally the criminal courts sent condemned men into military service. These included one Lionel Duckett, 'a notable and notorious thief', whose gang committed robberies in the counties around London, 'with pistols, like Robin Hood and his men'. The Lord Chief Justice Sir Ranulph Crewe protested the robber's reprieve as 'a scandal to the peace of the kingdom', but it was too late, for in September 1626 Duckett was sent as 'a serviceable man' to fight for the king of Denmark.[59] Duckett soon tired of military service and wrote to confederates to 'fetch him out by force, or to fire the prison'. For this he was condemned again, and set on a gibbet at Westminster. Once more he was reprieved, this time by the Duke of Buckingham, who 'hoped he would do good service, and he should bring him back with honour'. King's Bench complained that 'execution is not done on Duckett', but the keeper of the Gatehouse received a warrant to set the criminal at liberty, presumably to serve again overseas.[60]

Every county was assigned its quota of men to be levied for the expedition to Cadiz. Cumberland, for example, was to find 50 foot soldiers, Buckinghamshire 200, Lincolnshire 400, Yorkshire 500, and London 1,000. Most were to march to Plymouth, but 2,000 men from the central counties were redirected to a rendezvous at Hull. Recruiters and pressmen visited nearly every parish, and the roads and lanes became busy with military traffic.[61] Detailed reporting from Northamptonshire reveals the social incidence of this impressment. Of a hundred men sent forth from the eastern division of the county, thirty-six were labourers, fourteen husbandmen, and one a yeoman of slightly higher rank. The rest were tradesman and artisans from various country occupations: six shoemakers, five tailors, five weavers, three butchers, three carpenters, three masons, three shepherds, two bakers, two peddlers, a brewer, a bricklayer, a carter, a currier, a farrier, a fishmonger, a fuller, a glover, a grocer, a hatter, a joiner, a lace-maker, a miller, a musician, a tanner, a tinker, and a smith. By no means the dregs of society but men with trades and addresses, they came from a scatter of small towns and villages, and their lives would never be the same. Some would see the sea for the first time in their lives, and most would soon embark on an ill-planned expedition to fight in southern Spain.[62]

Some of the men sent to Plymouth protested against their impressment. Several cited 'the utter undoing' caused by their separation from dependants, though this won them little sympathy. Several exhibited disabilities that the recruiters had chosen to ignore, such as lame legs or damaged hands. Thomas Coke, a 65-year-old man from Berkshire, suffered from 'the shaking palsy' (perhaps Parkinson's disease). Robert Skinner from Norfolk was 'a very fool' and 'a simple man'. Dozens of men taken in London claimed to have been duped by recruiters. Edward Sterling, in London on legal business for his mother, asked for directions at Temple Bar and ended up a soldier. Peter Markham, a Dutchman with limited English, thought he was being taken to a play. It was a common complaint that men were pressed by the malice of kinsmen or neighbours who stood to gain by their absence. Humphrey Sparrow from Buckinghamshire blamed his misfortune on the 'ill will' of an uncle who disputed his inheritance. Nicholas Palmer from Berkshire cited a butcher who had designs on his house. Some men were simply in the wrong place at the wrong time. Richard Stringer was travelling on business from Cheshire to London when he was pressed at Lichfield 'as he was going to church'. John Harding, a curate from Nottinghamshire, was in London to seek a benefice when the net of impressment fell on him. Equally unfortunate was Hugh Owen Davis, a member of the Worcestershire trained band and a man with a wife and four children, who was pressed for a soldier while in London trying to collect a debt. Hard-luck stories made little impact on the national deployment, but they give a human face to the history.[63]

Once mustered, the men were supposed to march to their rendezvous in an orderly manner 'without damage to the countries through which they pass'.[64] The counties were obliged to pay 'as well for conduct as for coats', to clothe the recruits and send them to their destination, at a usual cost of 4*s.* per coat and 8*d.* a day per soldier, while they made their way to Portsmouth or Plymouth, Harwich or Hull.[65] Refusers were named and punished.[66]

The cost of sending a hundred Northamptonshire men to Plymouth in May 1625 totalled £193 15*s.* 4*d.*, including £4 to an innkeeper to cover 'spoils done him by the soldiers'. Each man received the king's shilling on impressment (though sometimes as little as 4*d.*), and food and clothing for the thirteen-day march. The counties wanted reimbursement not only for the cost of coats and conduct, but also for the work involved in writing warrants, indentures, and reports, but usually they would have to wait.[67]

In principle, the king's men were fed, clothed, housed, and paid for their service. The basic allowance for soldiers was 8*d.* a day, or £12 3*s.* a year. This, however, was a notional sum for estimates and book-keeping. Food and supplies might be charged against it, and the men end up with next to nothing in hand. Billeted at Plymouth in 1625, the soldiers received just 2*s.* 6*d.* a week to cover their victuals, barely 4*d.* a day, with the rest of their allowance held back to pay for their clothes.[68] A schedule of 'entertainment' for the garrison at Scilly in 1627 allowed 12*d.* a day for each sergeant, 10*d.* a day for twelve gunners, and 8*d.* a day for common soldiers, though payment could be months or even years in arrears.[69]

The men recruited for service in Denmark were relatively well treated, at least at the beginning. Each was to receive a cassock, shirt, shoes, hose, stockings, and cap by way of kit, and their daily diet in transit was 'a pottle [half a gallon] of beer, three cakes of biscuit weighing three quarters of a pound, four ounces of butter and six ounces of cheese'.[70] This would just about provide sufficient calories, but it was not sustainably nutritious. The diet for the 135 soldiers aboard the *Talbot* in 1625 was more varied and more generous, including a pound of biscuit, the same pottle of beer, and occasional servings of beef, pork, pease, and fish, with a little butter, cheese, oatmeal, rice, and oil. The *Talbot*'s forty-seven sailors did even better, with beef and pork more often than the landsmen, and an allocation of a full gallon of beer per man each day.[71] Unfortunately, these were caterers' estimates, not actual provisions, and the food was often deficient in both quality and amount.

As many as one in five of the men impressed for service melted away en route to their rendezvous. Report spread in May 1625 that 'a band of Bedfordshire men, they say, have killed their lieutenant or conductor, and are run away and dispersed'.[72] In one of the highest rates of mass desertion, 70 of 150 Norfolk men went missing in April 1627; 34 of 100 soldiers from Hertfordshire likewise 'left in the march', and 21 of 100 Buckinghamshire men also defected.[73] Some of the more enterprising deserters forged passes to allow them to return home.[74] The Council ordered the appointment of provost marshals in the Thames-side counties of Middlesex, Essex, Surrey, and Kent, and instructed justices throughout the kingdom to search among 'loose persons' and vagrants for runaways from the king's service.[75]

Levies, marches, and billeting continued to disturb the civilian population in 1627 and complaints multiplied of insolencies, tumults, and disorders. King Charles committed 3,000 troops to his uncle Christian IV, in addition to the soldiers needed for La Rochelle, but 'voluntaries' were hard to find. The Oxford don Thomas Crosfield observed 'two or three presses of soldiers, both for aiding the king of Denmark and resisting the king of

Spain', in March 1627, and more 'pressing of soldiers by night' in April.[76] As in previous recruiting drives, too many of those who were indentured were aged, diseased, or prone to run away.[77] The men had to be clothed, transported, disciplined, and paid, and not all went quietly or willingly. A mutiny broke out at the transshipment port of Harwich in April 1627 when one veteran of the Danish king's service swore 'he would rather be hanged than serve him again'. Mutinous soldiers took their captains prisoner, and threatened to destroy the ships and throw the officers overboard.

Dozens of troops bound for Denmark melted away into Suffolk and Essex, 'and no hue and cry bringeth any back'. Several contingents got as far as Gravesend, in the Thames estuary, but were stayed there by 'divers women come down in the ships among the soldiers, who will not suffer them to be taken from them' for service overseas.[78] The wars disturbed and stressed the countryside, and subjected coastal towns to burdensome pressures.

Burdensome Billeting

To mobilize and move a large army required organization and facilities that the early Stuart state often lacked. The troops needed to be clothed, fed, housed, and trained before they were ready for deployment. Often they were billeted with private families, whether the householder was willing or not. County funds were supposed to provide compensation at the rate of 3*s.* or 3*s.* 6*d.* a week per man, and somewhat more for officers. Deputy lieutenants promised billeting householders 'that all disbursements in that behalf should be duly satisfied', but payments were up to thirty weeks in arrears.[79] Local officials might reimburse the hosts directly, but, if billeting money passed through the soldiers, the government acknowledged, 'warning must be given to the people not to trust them'.[80] At Plymouth, where several thousand men were billeted in 1625, the government allowed just 2*s.* 6*d.* a head, a little over 4*d.* a day. At that rate, town officials complained, 'we cannot find them meat and drink, so that we have been much troubled by their discontents'.[81]

The three principal complaints against billeting were that reimbursements were late and inadequate, that soldiers behaved like beasts, and that the foisting of soldiers onto the king's subjects was an infringement of their liberty as free men. The billeted soldiers were subject to martial law, but the civilians who housed them also faced military authority.[82] Grievances accumulated as the soldiers prepared to go to war and after the survivors came home. These grumbles and resentments would not bring down the state, but they sapped the 'love' that subjects were supposed to display to their monarch. Critics alleged that the government forced loan resisters to 'lodge and maintain such unruly and unpaid soldiers as were billeted in their towns and villages, for no other service than to punish them'.[83] The discriminatory and punitive use of billeting became apparent in Sussex in 1627, when the Earl of Dorset threatened districts responsible for 'denials and delays' in 'his majesty's service' with further allocation of soldiers, 'so that the difference may appear between the refractory and obedient'.[84] Arbitrary impositions made 'recalcitrant' subjects all the more unhappy.

Billeted soldiers created 'insolencies' and 'disorders' at Southampton and Barnstaple in 1625, and threatened 'mutiny' at Plymouth, though troops at Fareham and Lymington were said to 'contain themselves in order without any show of discontent'. In south Devon it was said to be 'an impossible matter to keep the soldiers in any good order'. Some soldiers augmented their provisions by plunder and theft, at the expense of local civilians. Reports reached London of soldiers who 'commit riots, murders, robberies', 'outrages and thefts', and 'injuries and bloodshed', but these could be sensationalized and exaggerated.[85] The 1,500 Scots billeted on the Isle of Wight in 1627 posed special problems because they were perceived as outlandish redshanks as well as hungry and disorderly soldiers. Leaving 'at least seventy bastards' in their wake was probably par for the course.[86]

The troops who returned from Cadiz, half those who set out, faced winter billets without winter clothing, and limited funding for their maintenance and welfare.[87] Several thousand found quarters around Plymouth with reluctant hosts. Commissioners reported in January 1626 that wealthy householders would not have them, the poor could not support them, and funds for billeting had not arrived. Racked by illness and poverty, by spring the soldiers were too weak and too ill-clothed to be exercised. By April they were ready to mutiny, and some threatened to march on London 'to show their nakedness'.[88] Overwhelmed by the men foisted upon them, hostile communities tried to shut their doors. Others, it was said, 'will yield them lodging, but refuse to give them any meat without money'. The Dorchester chronicler Dennis Bond complained in 1626 of 'soldiers billeted in the county per force upon men'. There was plague at Bridport and Blandford that year, and locals feared, not unreasonably, that an influx of soldiers would spread the infection. The Council hoped to reduce the disorder and alleviate the risk to public health by dispersing the troops over wider geographical areas, but without more money and better management the problem was likely to fester. Discontent mounted all spring, and by summer Plymouth too had the plague.[89]

After the expedition to the Isle of Rhé, returning veterans were reported to have 'run from the colours' and broken from their billets, and to have taken to the highways as vagrants and marauders in bands twenty or more strong. Anxious property-holders feared that 'the meaner sort of people' might 'join with them, to fall into mutiny and rebellion'. 'Diligent watches are therefore to be set upon all the usual roads adjoining the counties where soldiers are billeted.'[90] Rioting soldiers at Exeter attempted to pull down houses, attacked the city gates, broke the gaol, smashed the stocks, and threatened the mayor they 'would make garters of his guts, with other foul abuse'. Others were too weak to protest.[91]

Complaints against billeting climaxed in the aftermath of England's 'two unprosperous attempts', when few soldiers found friendly reception. An incident in Buckinghamshire illuminated the problem and exposed a fundamental clash between military and civilian cultures. A company of soldiers under a Lieutenant Sandelands reached Chesham early in February 1628 and demanded billeting. The householder Richard Bisco refused to accommodate them, prompting the lieutenant to say that 'he would break his head, nay he would take any of his goods that were in his house and sell them, nay he would break open his chests for goods that were therein, and by God's wounds and other oaths, he would cut off his head' and set fire to the house. Terrified by this threat to his life and property, Bisco complained to the justice Sir William Fleetwood, who bound Lieutenant Sandelands to keep the peace. The lieutenant countered that Bisco should be arrested for refusing to billet his men.[92]

The argument then moved to a higher level, between Justice Fleetwood and the army captain John Read. Fleetwood took issue with the very concept of billeting, declaring

> that I had never read the word in any of our laws, and knew not what it meant; but if the meaning were that a man should receive the king's soldier into his house against his will and find him meat and drink without present payment ... I did not know that any of our laws had ordered it to be an offence for any man to refuse to yield thereto, neither had I any authority as a justice of peace to punish it.

Fleetwood committed the inflammatory lieutenant to Aylesbury gaol, but Captain Read declared 'that his majesty's soldiers were not subject to the authority of civilian justices of peace, but to their superior officers'. When Fleetwood insisted on his commission, and commented on the daily 'complaint of threats and menaces to break open men's houses who shall refuse to billet them', the captain responded 'that no justice of peace had to do with any of his soldiers for any default'. Billeting was the precipitant for issues of law and principle that would soon be debated in parliament.[93] The thirty soldiers billeted at Oxford in February 1628 may have been part of this mobilization.[94]

Further problems surfaced in 1628 when the movement of Irish soldiers left a trail of trouble across England. Five companies of Irishmen—perhaps the same men who passed through Chesham—trudged their way east to be shipped to the conflict in Europe. Travelling in cold, wet, and windy conditions, the troops reached East Anglia towards the end of February. Following procedures that were by then normal, the Council instructed the Earl of Arundel, in his role of Lord Lieutenant of Norfolk, to receive and billet the men 'for his majesty's service'. The standard billeting rate of 3*s*. 6*d*. per man per week would be borne by the county 'for the present', to be repaid later when funds became available. Anyone who refused to accommodate the soldiers or to contribute to their charge would be named and proceeded against for 'contempt'. Each company was assigned to a different district, where constables would see to their housing and victualling. A hundred Irishmen were assigned to Harleston, for example, where they would surely overwhelm the community's limited resources.[95]

The Irish troops passed through Thetford without trouble, despite complaints that the assizes the week before had depleted the town of all victuals. As they moved towards Norwich, reports spread of 'intolerable sufferances by the soldiers and dangerous outrages and disorders in the country'. The householders who were expected to accommodate the troops were themselves 'so afflicted with necessity as a great part of them are apt to take any occasion of mutiny and discontentment'. The Irishmen deserted by the dozen and attempted to live off the land, so that the nominal force of 500 numbered only 430 when it reached the gates of Norwich. The city sought to deny them entry on the grounds that the Council warrant applied to the county of Norfolk, whereas Norwich claimed independent jurisdiction. Overriding this technicality, four companies of Irish soldiers marched into the city centre and occupied the market square 'with their drums beaten up and ensigns displayed... armed with pikes and muskets'. They demanded money, food, and shelter, and would not leave without 'carts for carriage of their armour, and horses for their officers to ride upon'. The householders of Norwich pleaded 'great poverty and distress' and pushed the soldiers on to the ports of Lynn and Yarmouth.[96] Eventually, presumably, they reached the Low Countries, where they joined the Thirty Years War. An irony unmentioned in the sources is that many of these Irishmen were most likely catholics, recruited to fight in the protestant cause.[97] The incident would reverberate in parliament a few months later as background to the Petition of Right.

Similar problems arose in Dorset a short while later, when troops assembled for the relief of La Rochelle needed billeting. The deputy lieutenants wrote in March 1628 that 'the richer sort utterly refusing, and the rest being much disabled by the great arrears due for last year's billets, return us peremptory answers that they will no longer undergo the burden'. The upshot was that 'the soldier must either steal or starve', further challenging public order.[98] The villages around Portsmouth too gave out that they were 'already full freight with soldiers', and would receive no more.[99] Householders at Canterbury similarly baulked at billeting soldiers who complained of their food and lodging and refused to go to church.[100] At Wellingborough, Northamptonshire, angry townsmen turned on the soldiers, evicted them from their billets, and called them 'the Duke of Buckingham's rogues'.[101]

Local, legal, and constitutional arguments against billeting crystallized in 1628 in the Petition of Right, which declared illegal, and a 'great grievance and vexation of the people', the quartering of 'great companies of soldiers and mariners' against the inhabitants' wills. Parliamentary orators claimed that billeting produced 'threatenings, beatings, bloodsheds, robberies, or other insolencies', and protested that 'our wives and our daughters have been violated' by soldiers, 'even in the heart and bowels of this kingdom'.[102] King Charles's military apparatus had become a social liability, subverting the values that the king and his counsellors most cherished. Far from enhancing public security or advancing God's cause, the army was responsible for outrage and disorder. The mobilization threatened the social order that it was designed to protect. Repeated complaints of 'tumultuous' behaviour among the troops and their 'unsoldierlike manner of demanding their pay' fuelled resentment and opposition.[103] Though the trouble-makers formed only a minority, and their outrages were exaggerated, they conditioned the environment for political and public debate.

Among 'innumerable mischiefs and grievous vexations' associated with billeting was the worry that townsmen and villagers would be 'corrupted by ill example of the soldiers, and encouraged to idle life'. Social leaders feared that 'great multitudes' of 'the meaner sort' were 'most apt upon this occasion to cast off the reins of government and... fall into mutiny and rebellion'. The forced mixing of soldiers and civilians, they warned the king, could lead to the 'imminent calamity and ruin both of church and state'. Perhaps recalling the recent clash at Norwich, petitioners particularly urged the disbanding of companies of unruly papists.[104]

Critics in parliament linked the three issues of raising of soldiers, billeting of troops, and forcing of loans to help pay for them, to challenge not just the king's policy but his fundamental understanding of constitutional law. The crux of the matter, said Peter Ball in May 1628, was 'whether we have liberty of person and propriety of goods or no'.[105] Billeting was not just 'an unsupportable burden' but an assault on freedom, so several members claimed. It was illegal, said Sir Robert Phelips, to force anyone 'to take men into their houses'. 'There is no law for this,' chimed in George Brown of Taunton, because 'our houses are our castles, and to have such guests put upon us... is a violation of the law'.[106] The House of Commons claimed that 'every free man hath and of right ought to have a full and absolute propriety in his goods and estate, and that therefore billeting or placing of soldiers in the house of any such free man against his will is directly contrary to those laws under which we and our ancestors have been so long and happily governed'.[107] Military exigency clashed with the liberty of the subject and further undermined the arch of good order.

The Petition of Right in May 1628 declared billeting 'against the laws and customs of this realm' and asked the king 'to remove the said soldiers and mariners, and that your people may not be so burdened in time to come'.[108] King Charles reluctantly agreed, saving his prerogative, so that if any king henceforth wished to move and quarter soldiers he would have to find willing hosts, or else house them at market rates in public inns. The winding-down of the wars reduced the need to move soldiers, and billeting became less burdensome. However, the government made it clear, in this regard as in others, that it preferred 'the regard of his majesty's service and obedience due to his commands before the example of refractory and ill-affected persons'.[109] Many of the bills for billeting remained unpaid, and would damage community relations for a decade.[110]

Distressed Mariners

Involuntary impressment also manned the navy, often at the expense of commercial shipping. In April 1625 the Privy Council requested 'that the ablest and sufficientest mariners and sea-faring men be pressed... and not loose and unskillful poor men such as are not fit to be employed, or sent upon so important a service'. The likeliest place to find such 'serviceable men' was in maritime communities, so places like the Cinque Ports, Portsmouth, Plymouth, Hull, and the riverside parishes downstream from London were hard hit by naval impressment. Recruiters had quotas for the 'urgent' provision of thousands of mariners, but officials in the port towns of eastern England apologized, 'the number imposed could not be obtained'.[111] The king's ships needed over 3,000 ordinary seamen, and over twice that number if the country went to war.[112] More mariners were needed in September 1625 'for the defence and security of the kingdom', and this time the burden fell on the southern ports from Dorset to Sussex. Springtime recruiting in 1626 swept the ports of Lancashire and Cheshire. Similar efforts in 1627 targeted Bristol mariners and north Devon.[113]

Unfortunately, but not surprisingly, these efforts failed to find the most suitable and experienced manpower. Those added to the naval rolls in May 1625 included 'tailors, shoemakers, weavers, combers of wool, blacksmiths, turners, tinkers, husbandmen and the like, known by testimony to be pressed rather out of malice than to the care of his majesty's service'.[114] Newly enrolled seamen at Weymouth were 'the poorest and unablest men, more fitting for an hospital than for the king's service'.[115] Some unwilling recruits secured discharge, 'having large families whose maintenance depends on their labour'.[116] Others mutinied or deserted when opportunity arose. Ideal men for his majesty's service might be found among commercial mariners, but few were keen to take the king's money. Experienced sailors were out at sea or good at hiding. The Council responded to reports of men 'disobeying presses and running way from the ships' by empowering officers to wait for incoming vessels and 'provide that the men do not slip away'.[117] A roll-call aboard HMS *Dreadnought* in March 1626 revealed a jumble of accents and experiences among the seamen, with men pressed from London and Kent, Hampshire and Dorset, Devon and Cornwall, Norfolk, Suffolk, Yorkshire, and Ireland.[118]

Mariners on the king's ships in the 1620s were ill served, ill fed, and ill paid. Too many of the ships on which they served were leaky, worm-ridden, and poorly maintained. Sea service in 1626 demonstrated that 'the king's ships are so weakly and imperfectly built that they were not able to endure a storm at sea'. The men lived in nauseous quarters, with inadequate provisions, subsisting on 'rotten bread and stinking beer'. Besides lack of money, the navy suffered from poor leadership, its officers ineffective, and 'inexperienced strangers preferred to be boatswains'. Ordinary seamen were notoriously susceptible to illness, and Captain John Chudleigh aboard the *Rainbow* in June 1625 observed that 'sickness in these voyages doth consume more men than sword or slaughter'.[119] The crown was trying to project naval force without the means to pay for it, and the Duke of Buckingham, as Lord High Admiral, was clearly inadequate to the task. The navy needed a thorough overhaul of its timbers, logistics, manpower, and professionalism, which Ship Money would make possible in the 1630s.[120]

Conditions among the fleet that returned from Cadiz were close to desperate. Their victuals spent, their beer gone, their pay delayed, the mariners were 'discontented and begin to mutiny'. The men aboard the king's ships in the Downs (off Kent) were said to be 'poor, weak and sick', and suffering from scurvy. Some died every day. Some ships lacked crew enough to weigh anchor, and were in no state to oppose a foreign enemy. Veteran sailors were supposed to receive 5*s.* on discharge, if they survived their period of service, but this money too was unforthcoming. Naval paymasters were three months or more in arrears.[121]

Frustrated mariners, many of them 'pressed in remote places' and reluctant from the start, expressed themselves through mutiny and riot. 'Alas, say they, when men have no money, no clothes to wear (much less to pawn), nor victuals to eat, what would you have them do? Starve?'[122] In May 1626 the Privy Council learned that certain disgruntled sailors, along with other 'loose and idle persons', planned 'to meet at the playhouse called the Globe to see a play, as is pretended, but their end is thereby to disguise some routous and riotous action'. The government response was to close the theatres for the day to forestall 'any insolencies or other intentions'.[123] In June came news of 'the tumultuous and disorderly manner of certain mariners and seamen abandoning his majesty's fleet at Portsmouth' and moving en masse towards London. There were said to be 300 in a 'rout', who hoped to represent their case to the king. The Council sent urgent instruction to the deputy lieutenants of Surrey to set 'special watches', to guard 'the frontiers of Hampshire', to bring out the trained bands, to prevent the mutineers from passing Kingston-upon-Thames, and to proceed against offenders by martial law. It was as if a foreign force was advancing on London, instead of unpaid English sailors.[124]

News spread across southern England of 'doubling the watches to prevent mutinies',[125] but the mariners crossed the cordon. Shocked chroniclers and correspondents described disruptions in London caused by sailors agitating for their overdue money. In August, the newswriter John Pory reported, 'some two hundred mariners and sailors came up from Portsmouth for their wages', and 'a pack of sailors to the number of fifty' mobbed the Duke of Buckingham's carriage, 'desiring very stubbornly to have their pay'. The boldest of them took the coach-horses by the head and brought the carriage to a halt. The duke escaped only by giving them 'good words and ten pieces to drink', with promises of pay the next Monday, and then 'beguiled' the mob by taking to the river on his barge.[126] One account claimed that 'seven hundred sailors would have pulled down York House because the duke had not given them their pay', and that they dispersed only when the Lord Treasurer offered to compensate them not with coin but with bullets.[127]

In October 1626 the sailors again thronged Whitehall in strength, 'very rudely demanding money for their wages'. Once again they sought the Duke of Buckingham, the Lord High Admiral and royal favourite, but, failing to find him, 'they revenged their insolent fury' on his empty coach. Two companies of trained bands were called out to protect the court, and the duke was 'fain to set a guard about his house'. Many Londoners witnessed these disturbances, and news of them spread nationally through networks of correspondence.[128] A proclamation in October 1626 took note of 'divers mariners, soldiers and loose people which do in disorderly manner presume to come to his majesty's court, and do flock together in companies which may breed further inconvenience if timely order be not taken to suppress them'. It said nothing about money, but threatened the men with 'his majesty's high indignation' and the penalties of martial law if they did not return to their posts.[129]

The approach of winter did not deter the mutineers, for more 'great troops' of sailors 'tumultuously' demanded money in London at the beginning of December.[130] Sir George Chudleigh warned Secretary Coke that month that the 'seamen grow insolent' for lack of wages. Bartholomew Gifford remarked that 'the mariners still murmur, still unpaid'.[131] Captain

Henry Burton reported in January 1627 that his sailors would not go to sea, would not hoist a sail, and instead shouted, 'home, home, home'.[132]

One London newsletter in February 1627 reported that

> great store of sailors and officers do repair daily to Whitehall for pay; and here are very strong watches set everywhere about the town, and trained soldiers in their arms stand all day in the streets... It is greatly feared (unless the sailors have some satisfaction with pay) this day the prentices and they will join and do much mischief about the city.[133]

Another noted, 'our sailors very earnest for money, and repair to the court in hundreds. They call much on the duke, and threaten boldly on Shrove Tuesday.'[134] Shrove Tuesday (16 February in 1627) was a traditional day of apprentice disturbances, but the potential for urban violence was much greater if augmented by angry sailors. One group at Whitehall dispersed crying 'God save King Charles' when a messenger from the king said they would soon be paid, but reassembled at the Tower a few days later calling for the Duke of Buckingham's head.[135] Even if they were not participants in this disorder, many thousands of Londoners observed and discussed the spectacle.

Emulating their Portsmouth colleagues, mutinous mariners at Harwich set off for London in search of remedy, thereby swelling the disorders. Westminster magistrates charged some of the ringleaders with assembling 'in a tumultuous manner... to the great molestation of his majesty and dishonour of the state'.[136] The king and court expressed puzzlement at 'these commotions', and the trained bands refused to take up arms against the sailors 'in respect that it is against their countrymen'. Sir Henry Herbert, who described this for Lord Scudamore, commented: 'thus you see us in disorder amongst ourselves, and a house at division cannot stand.'[137]

The revolt of the mariners weakened England's military readiness, and fomented the 'disorder' that King Charles most disapproved and feared. The navy was out of hand. It was hard to outfit a squadron or mount an expedition when the principal ports were in turmoil. The sailors were chronically ill paid, distressed, and unmoved by naval discipline. In March 1627, 'in a mutinous and seditious manner', mariners aboard the king's ships at Portsmouth blew a horn to summon the sailors together 'to depart from their ships without leave and to come to London upon pretence of demanding their pay'. The Council sought the ringleaders and hoped to unite them with other mariners already in the Marshalsea prison.[138]

Most of the sailors resumed their duties for the La Rochelle campaign, but once they had returned from Rhé they pursued their grievances, which for many had only multiplied. Commanders placed agitators in the bilboes (iron shackles), but this was not enough to suppress 'insolencies'.[139] Health, morale, and discipline all collapsed, pay was ten months behind, and naval administrators were forced to use untrained soldiers in place of missing seamen who 'daily fall sick and die'. A grim joke that winter was that soon 'the king will have more ships than sailors'.[140]

Despairing of being paid, some veteran mariners turned instead to stealing and embezzling military stores. A proclamation in December 1627 attempted to stop the loss of 'armour, munition, shot, powder, and other habiliments of war' that disappeared from the king's ships.[141] A further proclamation in February 1628 attempted to forbid 'tumultuous assemblies' of mariners. Any more 'outrages or disorders' would be met by military force, and those guilty of 'insolencies' would be deemed 'as rebels to our state'.[142]

It would take more than proclamations, however, to return the sailors to their ships. The mariners wanted their money, but the state expected them to subsist on promises. Some authorities believed that mariners who were fully paid were all the more likely to run away.[143] Others despaired of the tangles of accounting and corruption among paymasters, pursers, and captains.[144] Frustrated seamen were said to have turned brigand, and 'take what they list from those they meet'. John Holles, the Earl of Clare, 'saw them seize upon a drayman and his cart, and take away a hogshead of beer'. He also saw mariners demonstrating again at York House in London, where the Duke of Buckingham's dinner guests sent them packing at sword point. Holles told Lord Vere on 22 February 1628 that 'the king is gone to Newmarket rather to be a little out of the way while the mutinous sailors are in settling'.[145]

The diarist Walter Yonge recorded in March 1628 that the mariners at Plymouth, 'almost ready to set to sea, being unpaid for nine months, and seeing their best victuals sold away, they began to mutiny, in which mutiny there were three slain, and after the tumult was somewhat appeased many of them ran away'.[146] The agitation continued at Portsmouth in August 1628, where the Duke of Buckingham was preparing the fleet yet again.[147] A correspondent described how the duke thought to satisfy the mariners 'by showing some of them the money he had brought, but the rest it seems would not take his word to their fellows, for the next day after that he was come abroad some insolencies was offered to his coach, but as luck would have it there was no hurt done'.[148] Buckingham insisted that he had done more for the mariners than any of his predecessors, and had used all his powers, including money of his own, to make up their shortfall in pay.[149] Few of them believed him.

The matter lay unresolved when the disgruntled John Felton, an unpaid veteran of Cadiz and the Isle of Rhé, plunged his knife into the duke on 23 August 1628. The assassination was followed by mass desertions, as seamen ran away in droves and found 'free passage through the country without any let'.[150] Naval discipline and naval strategy were in shreds. When mariners complained again in 1630 about shortages of pay and victuals, the Council responded, on King Charles's behalf, 'that never prince did more royally provide for the encouragement of seamen than his majesty hath done'.[151] As late as 1633 many officers remained unpaid for their service at Cadiz, Rhé, and La Rochelle in the 1620s.[152]

The Perils of Peace

Charles I withdrew from the European arena in 1630, but the honour and safety of his kingdoms required continuing preparations. There would be no more continental operations on the scale of Cadiz and La Rochelle, though English soldiers were still committed from time to time to assist the Danes, the Swedes, and the Dutch. King Charles authorized a levy of 6,000 men in 1629 'for the distressed case of our dear brother and only sister' in Germany.[153] News went out in February 1631 that 'the king has engaged himself to deliver 10,000 men' to Sweden, though by June the target was reduced to 6,000.[154] In May 1634 another Swedish military commission was given 'liberty to strike up drums for voluntaries', but observers thought it unlikely to raise many troops.[155] Another press in January 1636 sought 1,900 men for the newly expanded navy.[156]

By contrast to recent years the pressure of forced impressment was light, and commentators remarked on England's relative 'quiet... which is God's infinite mercy to our nation'.[157] But reluctant and unsuitable men still found themselves in service. Among them was Henry Arthur, convicted at Winchester for horse theft in 1634, who was sent to serve in the Low Countries.[158] Stephen Pilcher, 'lately pressed for the king's service at sea', was imprisoned in Dover Castle in May 1635 after running away and saying 'he had as leave be hanged at home as be starved in the king's service'.[159]

John Wise, a husbandman of Rettendon, Essex, proved even less amenable to his majesty's service when he said, in May 1636, 'if I were pressed for a soldier the king should be the first that I would aim at'.[160]

Nobody knows how many thousand English men served with the armies of continental Europe. English, Scottish, and Irish troops soldiered abroad in every European theatre from the Baltic to the Mediterranean, perhaps 30,000 or more at peak times. All estimates are elastic and approximate.[161] Service overseas was not necessarily glorious or profitable, but it was, in principle, voluntary. The Imperial and Polish armies paid up to 6*s*. a week, but service was hard and engagements often short. More preferable was indenture with the States of the Netherlands with regular provision of food and clothing, 3*s*. a week year round, and the promise of pay-outs to men who were disabled.[162]

English families followed the fortunes of international protestantism and consumed news of the Thirty Years War, not just because it was stirring or depressing, but because their own loved ones were among the combatants.[163] The fortunes of Gustavus Adolphus might signal the fate of Christendom, but they also presaged news of casualties and survivors. Relaying news of a Swedish defeat in November 1629, John Barrington reported that 'almost all the English officers are dead, some slain, others by famine and pestilence'.[164] The death of Gustavus Adolphus at the battle of Lutzen in November 1632 was widely reported, and sometimes denied, in the news stream of early modern England.[165]

English naval action quickened in the 1630s as the king's ships pursued pirates, Dunkirkers, and Barbary slavers. It was part of his majesty's 'special vigilance, care and providence' that his ships should go forth, 'furnished with men, tackle, munition, victual and other necessaries fit for war', especially 'in these dangerous and warlike times'.[166] 'Christendom is full of war, and there is nothing but rumours of war,' Lord Keeper Coventry told the assize judges in 1635, and these 'doubtful' and dangerous times required a build-up of forces. 'The dominion of the sea', Coventry declared, 'is the best security of the land', and 'the wooden walls are the best walls of this kingdom'. (Classically educated listeners would recognize this echo of the oracle regarding ancient Athens, which some might connect to John Selden's Latin tract, *Mare Clausum*.) The Lord Keeper reminded his audience that 'the causes and occasions and times of war, with the preparations and ordering of them, is proper to the king; and dutiful obedience in such things doth become the subject'. The people should know 'how careful and zealous his majesty is to preserve his honour and the honour of this kingdom' and should pay their Ship Money with 'alacrity and cheerfulness'.[167] The plan in 1635 was to set forth a navy of forty-five ships, manned by seven thousand mariners, at an estimated cost of £218,500.[168] This policy may have strengthened the kingdom, but its political and constitutional costs, addressed in Chapter 3, helped to undermine the regime.

Skilled and energetic administration transformed the rotten and depleted fleet of the 1620s into one of Europe's foremost navies by the end of the 1630s. By 1640 the king's fleet bore almost 1,200 heavy guns, and could indeed claim sovereignty of the seas. Much of its time was spent on routine patrols, firing ceremonial salutes, and forcing foreign ships to dip their ensigns. Foreign peace prevailed, although an anti-French tilt in 1639 fuelled fantasies of a possible English invasion of Normandy.[169] England's contribution to the European conflict that year was limited to the export of a thousand barrels of precious gunpowder as 'favour to the Spaniards'.[170]

When war arrived it came from the north, and demanded an army, not a navy. Charles I's attempt to impose a common prayer book on presbyterian Scotland triggered the covenanter revolt of 1638 and the so-called Bishops' Wars of 1639–40 (discussed in Chapter 9). To crush the Scots and restore his authority, the king required a force of 30,000 men, and managed to raise 20,000 for each of two campaigns.[171] As in the 1620s, the military burden fell mainly on the lower levels of society. The trained bands were reluctant to serve beyond their counties, and many suitable soldiers secured exemptions. Emboldened 'refractaries' refused service, withheld payments, and baulked at military discipline. Pay was scarce, morale low, and the king's standard-bearer, Sir Edmund Verney, observed that he never saw 'so raw, so unskilful, and so unwilling an army brought to fight'.[172] Problems of disorder and desertion were worse than ever, compounded by unease about fighting fellow protestants.

The 'insolencies' of the army of 1640 provided chilling examples of the collapse of deference, the degrading of hierarchy, and the spread of insubordination already presaged in the 1620s.[173] The army spread mayhem as it marched north, and its fighting edge proved ineffective when confronted by the enemy. Better led, better trained, and with superior field intelligence, the Scots crossed the border on 20 August 1640, routed Lord Conway's forces at Newburn a week later, and occupied Newcastle and the north-east of England. It was a crippling defeat for a king who had pledged his honour and his treasure to the rule of both kingdoms.

5

An Accessible Monarch?

The People's Gaze

The king of England was public property, even as he guarded his privacy and privileges. His subjects had an interest in the king's welfare, his actions, and his health, because kingship implicated everyone's security and well-being. Royal policies determined the course of peace or war. Crown appointments and royal patronage ramified across the commonwealth from the national to the local level. The king's religious preferences shaped the culture and practice of the church. His parliaments drew representatives from across the country, and his taxes touched property-holders in their pockets. If the king died, his successor could alter the religion of the nation, involve England more actively in European conflict, and even raise the risk of foreign invasion. Subjects high and low took note of the king's movements as well as his policies, because royal activity affected everyday lives, security, and aspirations.

English monarchs spent much of their time on show, in the rituals of state, the protocols of the court, and the semi-public journeying of progresses. Elite correspondents shared news of the king's doings, his travels, and his health, so subjects could readily learn where the king might be located. The core of government moved with the king, and suppliants and petitioners followed the court in the hope of catching his majesty's attention.

It was no mere gossip, but rather a matter of serious concern, if the king took sick or was injured. Panicked rumour related from time to time that King Charles had actually died.[1] The Cambridge correspondent Joseph Meade informed Sir Martin Stuteville in September 1625 that 'his majesty was sick of the plague, and had a sore, but by the merciful favour of God and the diligence of his surgeons and physicians was now past danger and well recovered'. Meade claimed that this news made him 'stagger in unbelief', and he 'laughed at it as an idle rumour', until reliable informants 'averred it to be true'. His postscript, however, noted that the king was well enough to go hunting, and another correspondent reported confidently that 'the king was never sick'.[2]

Royal illnesses and accidents were worth reporting, not just as marks of the writer's privileged information but as indicators of the work of providence and portents of the nation's future. It was a matter of public concern, not just sympathy for the sufferer, if the king developed smallpox or was injured while hunting. King Charles was 'sore of the smallpox' in December 1632 but otherwise 'well in health', Secretary Nicholas informed Captain Pennington.[3] 'By God's mercy he soon recovered again,' noted William Whiteway of Dorchester.[4] 'The king was wondrous well recovered, and not a mark of smallpox to be seen on his face,' John Flower reassured Viscount Scudamore.[5] It was likewise intelligence to be shared in August 1634 when 'the king had a fall' while following the chase in Sherwood Forest, 'his horse drawing him after him by one of his dogs'.[6] The perils of the road also put the king at risk, it being widely reported in August 1635 that 'the king's coach hath been overturned this progress, his majesty being in it, but he had no hurt'.[7] Gentlemen throughout England held their breath when they heard such news. In an age familiar with the ague, the spleen, the pox, or the stone, and the risk of dying from such ailments, it was imperative to monitor the king's condition. Sir Thomas Stafford wrote to the Earl of Cork in September 1639 to alert him that the king 'is much troubled with a boil on his breech, otherwise extremely well'.[8] Providence seemed to smile on a king who was generally hale of health and untroubled by serious accidents.

A generation ago it was 'common knowledge' that, until the 1640s, 'Charles I systematically distanced himself from his subjects', and that this aloofness 'contributed to the coming of civil war'. Compared to other monarchs he was less visible, less accessible, and less adept at public relations. The king's remoteness, by this account, contributed to his unhappy troubles.[9] Historians wrote of Charles's 'dread of close contact', and his withdrawal 'from his people's gaze', as fatal flaws in his kingship. He was, we were told, 'notorious for his reluctance to deal with petitioners and his attempts to keep them at bay'.[10] A stream of scholars have repeated the assertion that King Charles was 'stiff, proud and prudish', distant and withdrawn.[11]

The Harvard historian Mark Kishlansky has challenged this interpretation, inviting scholars to reconsider the second Stuart monarch. His Charles I 'was by no means insulated from his people' but was rather 'arguably the most widely travelled and accessible English monarch of the early modern era'. Charles I, by this account, was a face-to-face leader who travelled widely around his kingdom. The historiographical 'issue of Charles's isolation', Kishlansky suggests, 'can be settled with an odometer', by tracing the king's progresses and peregrinations.[12]

The matter of Charles I's availability to his subjects is important, not just because it contributes to debate on the origins of the civil war, but because it exposes the dynamics of political interaction, the crucial relationship between the ruler and the ruled. It addresses the performance of kingship, the politics of the public, and the engagement of subjects in the life of their times, which are central themes of this book. By examining both sides of the relationship between king and people, we may illuminate the permeability of the *arcana imperii*, the privileged zone of access and counsel at the heart of the monarchical polity. By exposing tensions between kingly and popular expectations about each other's roles, we may even shed light on the formation of the modern state and the development of the public sphere.

This chapter examines the social environment of early modern kingship, and the layers of screening surrounding Charles I. It looks more closely at the environment of the court and its openness to outsiders. It follows the king on the road to see what might be learned about his interaction with subjects in the course of his travels. Steering between traditional and revisionist positions, it connects King Charles with his kingdom, and shows how some of his subjects witnessed or encountered their monarch.

The Pulse of the Court

The court of Charles I was famous for its dignity and splendour. It served as a setting for sacred kingship in which every ceremony, sermon, royal appearance, or masque served to project and enhance the authority and majesty of the crown. It is well known, and not disputed, that the culture of the Caroline court upheld, modelled, and represented the style and values that King Charles and those close to him most sought to advance. It may even be true, as Kevin Sharpe suggested, that men and women, at least among the elite, looked to the court for models of dress, behaviour, and values.[13] The king had a horror of disorderly proceedings that demeaned his gravity and honour, and was averse to unseemly disruptions. However, the very size, heterogeneity, and unwieldiness of the court made it difficult to survey and control. Alongside its decorous face and royal function was the usual run of jealousies and enmities, as well as occasional disturbances and transgressions. Some of the departments at court had doubled or tripled in size since the parsimonious days of Queen Elizabeth, so that simply feeding the king and his household proved an expensive and cumbersome operation.[14]

The court was a place and an institution, a cultural community and a political environment, a gathering of people and a cluster of facilities. Its members spoke of 'the pulse of the court, whence our temper in all things else moves'.[15] Though reserved and select, the court affected the kingdom beyond. It operated where the king lived, and, since early modern monarchs kept several residences, the personnel, protocols, and offices of the court moved with them. The principal home of the court was at Whitehall, but it shuttled with the king from Theobalds (Hertfordshire) to Windsor (Berkshire), from St James's (London) to Hampton Court (Middlesex). The queen moved in an intersecting arc between Somerset House and her palaces at Greenwich (Kent) and Nonesuch, Oatlands, and Richmond (Surrey).[16] When the king travelled on progress, or even out hunting, key elements of the court formed his retinue and entourage.

The primary court establishment at Whitehall was a maze of buildings, courtyards, galleries, passages, and chambers, designed for the king's privacy and comfort as well as for business and ceremony.[17] It was a working arena for government, a setting for spectacle and entertainment, and a lodging for the king and close associates. Courtiers knew, and newcomers learned, that the Great Hall was generally accessible to anyone appropriately attired, but the inner chambers were progressively private and restricted. High-ranking nobles, councillors, and secretaries attended the king in his bedchamber and inner closet, privy chamber, presence chamber, and in the galleries, courtyards, and passages between them. Great occasions in the Great Hall and Banqueting House featured 'great appearance both of lords and ladies', along with the courtly elite and foreign ambassadors.[18]

Serving the king and court were officers and employees of the royal household, divided between the domains of the Lord Chamberlain, who commanded the state rooms, and the Lord Steward, who ruled the working of the court 'below stairs'. Different officials controlled different areas of access, so that anyone hoping to approach the king should know which paths to tread. The court establishment included gentlemen and grooms of the bedchamber and privy chamber, gentlemen pensioners, gentlemen and yeomen ushers, daily waiters, pages of the back stairs, cup-bearers, carvers, sergeants, and esquires of the body. The payroll covered messengers and musicians, chaplains and physicians, and the staffs of the Jewell House and Wardrobe, as well as hosts of menials and functionaries, kitchen staff, coachmen, stablemen, watermen, falconers, and huntsmen. Queen Henrietta Maria had her own household and chamber, as did each of the princes. More than 2,000 people had positions at court, and many of these had friends or relations who sometimes pressed at its doors. Well-born officers of the chamber, in particular, used their nearness to the sovereign to advance their kinsmen and clients.[19] The promiscuous coming and going of personnel, and occasional rivalries between them, made it possible sometimes to intersect the orbit of the king.

At the very beginning of his reign, in deliberate contrast to the rowdiness of the Jacobean court, King Charles demanded 'dignity, respectful demeanour, and regularity' in state affairs.[20] Observers noted that the court was 'more strait and private than in the former time', and that the new king was 'a friend of state and order'.[21] One of the earliest casualties of this change was the Earl of Anglesey, a younger brother of the Duke of Buckingham, who was banished from the court in April 1625, King Charles saying 'he would have no drunkards of his chamber'.[22] Sir Francis Stuart was banished from court a year later 'for being too bold in his speeches of the Duke', though more for the content than the manner of his conversation.[23]

A proclamation in May 1625 'for restraint of disorderly and unnecessary resort to the court' sought to limit the 'concourse of people of all sorts' who came within the vicinity of the king. The restriction was designed to prevent the spread of plague, but it also signalled a desire to make the court more exclusive; the king, it said, would willingly 'dispense with those public shows of [his people's] zeal, cheerfulness and alacritry' in the interest of safety and decorum.[24]

Plans emerged by March 1629 'to restore the court to the ancient splendour' of an imagined medieval past. This was to be achieved by 'distinguishing of rooms and persons: places of chief respect being frequented with persons of honour and rank, and others with such as were of less quality, every distance and degree being then well known and strictly observed'.[25] It would be difficult for outsiders to navigate such a court, and much less likely that they would encounter the king.

New orders for conduct at court appeared several times in the 1630s. They drew on English precedents, stretching back to the court of Henry VIII, and were also influenced by proceedings at the major courts of Europe, especially Spain and France. Their purpose was to insulate the king from disorderly disruptions and to amplify reverence towards his person, so that 'civility' and 'order ... may spread with more honour through all parts of our kingdoms'. Detailed regulations addressed both the core and the perimeter, subjecting court culture to scrutiny and discipline.[26] Despite these efforts, however, there were occasional signs of slackness, when courtiers let down their guard. Periodic attempts to reform the court underscored the Caroline commitment to seemliness, but they also revealed the difficulty of maintaining decorum. The king with 'great grief observed a general breach of the ancient and laudable orders' of the court and 'resolved to give redress thereunto'.[27]

In charge of routine security, the Knight Marshall was 'to punish and remove vagrant persons, rogues, and all sorts of beggars, idle and loose people', and to prevent them from loitering in the precincts of the court. The teeming life of London pressed up against the gates of Whitehall, and threatened to spill inside. The porters who controlled those gates had orders 'not to permit any straggling or masterless men, any suspicious persons or uncivil, unclean and rude people to come within our court or to haunt or lurk anywhere within our house'. They were to admit no 'profane person or outrageous rioter', none exhibiting drunkenness, rudeness or disorder, and none armed with 'pistols, dags, daggers, cudgels, or other unfit weapons'. Swords, presumably, were permissible, since they were among the accoutrements of a gentleman. Boots and spurs could be worn in the outer precincts of the court, but not in the presence chamber or chapel. The guards and porters were also supposed to deny entrance to anyone 'muffled, masked, or otherwise disguised', who might have dishonest intentions.[28] The porter in Martin Parker's 'merry tale' of *The King, and a Poore Northern Man* looked askance at the suppliant's staff and dog, but eventually let him in.[29]

The court remained an important point of contact between the king and his subjects, especially the most privileged and respectable among them. Recognizing this, the reformed Caroline orders specified that, 'for all that come to our court in civil manner for our service or their own affairs, we require our said porters to receive them with courtesy and make way with all due reverence to men of place and honour'. If visitors penetrated as far as the Chamber of Presence, whether the king was there or not, it was the task of Gentlemen Ushers and Daily Waiters 'to take continual and special notice of all persons' and to expel 'any person not meet or worthy to be therein'.[30]

Repeated several times between 1631 and 1637, these orders specified that no man under the degree of baron was to enter the Inner Closet, unless he was a member of the Privy Council or a gentleman of the bedchamber. Similar restrictions limited approaches to the chairs of state at audiences, masques, dances, and other public occasions, or when the king or queen ate in public, only excepting 'cupbearers, carvers and sewers then waiting'.[31] Another set of 'Orders for the King's Family' instructed Gentlemen Ushers and Daily Waiters to hinder and reveal 'all manner of riots, quarrels, strifes and debates in his majesty's service', and to guard the presence chamber, 'that none be permitted there but persons of quality'.[32]

Anyone with respectable dress and demeanour could gain entry to the outskirts of the court, though penetration to its inner core required rank, status, or special invitation. The palaces had guards and gate-keepers, but some of their zones were semi-public. Access to Whitehall was especially easy when King Charles was not in residence, and visitors could bow to the empty chair of state. The godly steward of Northampton, Robert Woodford, was one who visited Whitehall in1638, escorted by the keeper of the royal apartments, and penetrated as far as 'the king's chamber'. The king, of course, was nowhere to be seen.[33]

Several times a year the court gates opened to admit supplicants for the king's charity or for his healing touch. In 1628, for example, the king, through his almoners, distributed 400 nobles (£133 6*s.* 8*d.*) 'in alms upon Maundy Thursday, Good Friday, and Easter week'.[34] Twice a year, usually at Michaelmas and Easter, carefully vetted and suitably humble suppliants attended the ceremony of 'touching for the king's evil', a ritualized remedy for the glandular disease of scrofula, in which the monarch laid his hand on selected sufferers and gave them each a gold angel worth 10*s*. Between 1629 and 1636 the Exchequer transferred £2,410 to the Mint for 'fine gold' for this purpose.[35]

Touching for the king's evil was an obligation of sacred majesty, a prerogative virtue 'hereditarily descended'.[36] Charles repeatedly declared himself 'as ready and willing as any king or queen of this realm ever was' to relieve the distress of his subjects, so long as 'in this, as in all other things, order is to be observed'.[37] It was not an occasion he relished. Though highly regulated and often postponed, the ceremony sometimes attracted disorderly numbers.

One way of ordering the throng was for the Sergeant Surgeon, who supervised the procedure, to issue tokens for those who were 'approved and allowed'. This only led to a traffic in counterfeit tokens, to the disappointment of those cheated of their angels, 'and the royal presence was disturbed by their outcry'. New tokens, ordered in April 1635, were designed to prevent 'a great abuse committed by dissolute and ill-disposed persons'. Applicants had to bring testimony of their worthiness, and also to certify their freedom from contagious disease. Some who did not immediately spend their angels hung them on ribbons around their necks in hope of prophylactic effect.[38]

At least sixteen proclamations between 1625 and 1639 sought to order, restrain, or limit the ceremony of royal touching. At Easter 1636, with plague threatening the city, the only persons touched were 'such as had some noble man's letter, and it was done privately in the garden'. The strategy in 1637 was 'to prohibit men to repair to the court for healing the king's evil... until such time as it shall please God that the sickness cease, and that such as are to be touched may repair to the court without danger to his majesty's person'.[39] Later in 1637 the Attorney General prepared a proclamation 'for restraint of concourse of people' during court festivities on St George's day. The court would be closed to persons 'not being of quality', and officers and servants not needed for the day's 'solemnity' were warned to stay away. The restrictions were framed as precautions against disease in 'these infectious times', but there was no serious outbreak of plague in London in 1637. The council was concerned to prevent social as well as pestilential contagion by keeping unsuitable persons from court.[40]

On several occasions, most notably during Lent, the court admitted Londoners to hear sermons in the outdoor preaching place at Whitehall. A thousand or more people might jam the terraces and the courtyard around the pulpit, while the king sat comfortably in his covered pew.[41] This was the setting Lucy Martin chose when she launched her paper at the king. The crowd was always watched by guards and pensioners, and security tightened after the Palm Sunday interruption of 1626. Later in the 1630s the terrace and pebbled court to the north of the outdoor pulpit gave way to the newly constructed masquing house, as the court preferred kingly entertainment to public preaching. William Davy reported in March 1638, 'there is a new building now at Whitehall for masques and shows right over against the pulpit in the yard, very near finished'. Though constructed of wood, and designed to be temporary, at £2,500 it 'cost too much money to be pulled down'.[42]

Many members of the aristocracy considered themselves entitled to attend court entertainments. Gate-keepers faced the recurrent problem of controlling access. Those who came to see masques generally required invitations, but there was often some jostling at the door. Yeomen of the Guard had orders 'to keep the doors and to hinder those from coming in that are not fit to come in' for masques or plays.[43] Early in 1633 the gossip George Garrard reported, 'they have found a new way of letting them in by a turning chair [turnstile], besides they let in none but such as have tickets sent them beforehand, so that now the keeping of the door is no trouble'.[44] One who attended 'the queen's pastoral' that January under the new arrangements reported 'that there was a scarcity of spectators and room for many more than were present', as people without tickets stayed away.[45] The Norfolk squire Sir Thomas Knyvett was among those admitted to the masque of *The Temple of Love* at Shrovetide 1635, telling his wife that 'though a country gentleman, yet am I graced with a ticket of her majesty's'.[46]

King Charles went to prayers both morning and evening, usually in the Great Closet, and worshipped diligently on Sundays and holy days in the Chapel Royal. These were predictable movements, when courtiers and visitors might seek to be noticed. Sundays and council days especially saw 'great resort' at court by aristocrats and others who hoped to catch the king's eye.[47] Privileged petitioners might proffer a paper, while appointees and officials would kneel to kiss the king's hand. To limit such interruptions, to maintain order and dignity, and to demonstrate the power of majesty, an escort of axe-bearing Gentlemen Pensioners accompanied the king to and from his devotions. Orders for the Chapel and Closet specified

> that in our going and coming hence, all men keep their ranks orderly and distinctly and not break them with pretence of speaking one with another or for any other occasion whatsoever, but provide both for our honour and their own reputation, that being one of the most eminent and frequent occasions whereby men's ranks in precedency are distinguished and discovered.

On chapel days and other court occasions, noblemen and others were expected to observe 'great distance and respect to our person, and also civility one to another'. The very insistence that courtiers observe these instructions 'in every point... with care and reverence' suggests that sometimes they were remiss.[48]

Major embarrassments were few, compared to the Jacobean scandals, but minor transgressions stained the Caroline court. Gossips talked of sexual misadventures, runaway heiresses, and errant aristocrats, as they did in any era. A minority of courtiers flirted with Catholicism and several went over to Rome. Noblemen were sometimes foolish enough to fight duels and even to commit homicide. Courtiers, like everybody else, could be overcome by anger or by drink. In one drunken episode in 1634 Lord Morley came to court 'in an high distemper of wine, and grossly abused some of the king's servants'. He called Sir George Theobalds 'a base rascal' and 'a dunghill rogue', and threatened to cut his throat, all within sight of 'the chair of state in that room where their majesties were entering'. This was the kind of behaviour that most offended the king, an affront to order and civility. It cost Morley an appearance in Star Chamber, where he was fined and briefly imprisoned.[49]

By the mid-1630s, despite renewed efforts for reform, there were signs of slippage in both the social standards and the physical infrastructure of the court. One writer observed in 1636 that 'Whitehall in most places is so decayed, that it is held unsafe'.[50] One of Lord Scudamore's correspondents remarked in 1637 on 'the concourse of people' in the king's house, and the 'freedom allowed to all comers', though he meant, of course, people like himself.[51] Another observed that year that

> the court is now filled with the families of every mean courtier, dwelling houses are daily erected in every corner of the mews, proper only for stables. The king's servants wait pell-mell without any order, lodge still in court, and feed there, though they be out of their month or quarter. Places are sold at strange rates all the court over, which makes men prey upon the king in the execution of the lowest places.

George Garrard, who relayed this news to Lord Wentworth, shared the opinion that 'all things in court, both above stairs, beneath, and in the stables . . . are out of order, and need great reformation'. Archbishop Laud joined a committee of court lords and officers to set about reform.[52] It was perhaps in this context that the Earl of Holland, Groom of the Stole and Prime Gentleman of the Bed Chamber, claimed authority over the king's intimate apartments and galleries, while the Lord Chamberlain insisted that jurisdiction in the galleries belonged to him.[53] One solution to an over-impacted court was to order people to stay away, but proclamations instructing gentlemen to return to their country estates had little discernible effect.

The King on the Road

We have no convenient compendium of 'the progresses of Charles I', as we do for his two immediate predecessors, but it would not be too difficult to construct one. There are plentiful sources that trace the king's travels. But mobility does not equate to accessibility, and itineraries by themselves tell us little about the monarch's conduct. What counts is not where the king went, but whom he met, what he heard, and how he coped with his people's expectations. An odometer does not do the job.

Like all early modern monarchs, Charles travelled about his kingdom, from palace to palace, between castles, great houses, and hunting lodges. This mobility afforded novelty and entertainment, and allowed the various establishments to recharge their provisions and sanitary arrangements. The king regularly tracked a great arc around London and the Thames Valley, visiting his palaces and lodges on the north side of the river and the queen's residences on the south. Occasionally he travelled further afield, as far as Plymouth or the Isle of Wight, and twice undertook great northern journeys to Scotland. Favourite excursions combined hunting trips with academic junkets at Woodstock and Oxford, or Newmarket and Cambridge. The court followed a seasonal cycle, with summer the time for progresses, but plans were flexible in the face of bad weather and outbreaks of smallpox and plague.[54] Courtiers left behind in London sometimes remarked on the 'dull and dead time here, when both the king and queen are absent and in progress', when 'most people of quality are gone to take the fresh air of the country'.[55] Some countrymen along the route found these royal journeys a nuisance, since prerogatives of purveyance allowed the court to requisition hay, oats, straw, wood and cartage below market prices.[56]

A royal proclamation of May 1625 noted the king's 'great joy and contentment when his loving subjects, out of their loyal and dutiful affections towards him, shall desire to see the persons of himself and his dear consort the queen' as they travelled. It seemed prudent, however, amid the danger of infection, to limit the 'concourse of people' who followed and pestered the court. Nobody was supposed to approach unless they had 'special cause' or specific business. 'And to avoid the great disorder of poor people, who are used to come flocking into the highways and streets where his majesty is to travel, under cover of relief from the almoner', the

Figure 6. King Charles in Procession. Martin Parker, *An Exact Description of the manner how his Maiestie and his Nobles went to the Parliament on Munday, the thirteenth day of Aprill, 1640, to the comfortable expectation of all loyall subiects* (1640), broadsheet.

king's charity would henceforth be distributed through local overseers of the poor.[57]

On the road the king was on show, as his horse or coach passed by. Harbingers and outriders, equerries and attendants, guards and functionaries, maintained safety and decorum. Court officials made strict enquiry 'of all manner of infirmities, or any other casualties, where the king is to pass or lodge'. In London an armed escort rode ahead 'with truncheons in their hands... to keep the street and passage clear from people'. Guards with halberds helped to keep order.[58] Bystanders viewed the entourage from a distance, while carefully screened notables knelt to kiss the royal hand. Church bells rang as the royal party passed by.[59] Like other imperial rulers, past and present, King Charles lived in a bubble, insulated from the people who gazed or cheered. His travel allowed scant unscripted interaction and left little to chance. Nor was any other mode of behaviour expected of an early modern monarch.

The same was true of travel by water, especially along the transit corridor of the Thames. Bystanders could watch, but ordinary rivercraft were edged aside as 'the king and queen in the royal barge, with many other barges of honour, and thousands of boats, passed through London Bridge to Whitehall; infinite numbers, besides these, in wherries, standing in houses, ships, lighters, western barges, and on each side of the shore... all the people shouting amain'.[60] Thames-side observers may have seen the king and queen journeying from Windsor to Hampton Court and thence to Chelsea in September 1628, but this was a private visit to comfort the widowed Duchess of Buckingham.[61] Charles and his courtiers did not go unnoticed, nor unloved, but they were little troubled by contact with ordinary subjects.

Royal progresses were feats of organizational ability. They required transport and lodging for hundreds of officers and staff, from senior members of the household like the Lord Steward, Treasurer, Comptroller and Cofferer to personnel of the Pantry, Cellar, Buttery and Laundry, as well as countless grooms, porters, and clerks. The Ordnance Office alone allocated fifty carts for a major royal progress, and five accompanying wheelwrights to repair them.[62] The king travelled with his surgeon, physician, and apothecary, as well as musicians, messengers, and military attendants. By 1638 the protective screen of horse guards was 100 strong.[63] Privy Councillors, senior officers, courtiers, and 'divers lords and ladies' attended the royal party, thickening the clog on the roads. If the queen or princes joined the progress, their respective households added to the business and bustle. A loose caravan of 2,000–3,000 people might be involved in moving the king from place to place. One household handbook allowed 257 carriages 'for the king and queen's general remove in the times of progress', a number that grew to 406 by the late 1630s.[64] The travel could be exhausting, for monarchs as well as for lesser mortals. Although the king and an intimate group could ride briskly, and post horses along the route sustained a speedy flow of royal letters, the main body moved at the pace of a wagon train, between 12 and 20 miles per day, weather permitting.

In advance of each progress, court officials surveyed the route and arranged for suitable accommodation. Not just the king but his retinue needed to be housed and fed. Household accounts include detailed payments for 'making ready' the private houses and aristocratic palaces that would be needed during the journey. Great houses would be requisitioned for eight to ten days, just for a one-night visit, and the department of Works and Buildings would undertake necessary repairs and alterations. For last-minute adjustments a master mason and a master carpenter accompanied the court on the road, along with their horses, carriages, tools, and locks. Local communities became busy with 'the amending of the highways against his majesty's going by'.[65]

In the first few months of his reign King Charles grew familiar with the roads of southern England. His itinerary avoided places touched by the plague, and people at risk of exposure to disease were supposed to keep 10 miles distance.[66] One early excursion encompassed Canterbury and Dover, another Salisbury, Southampton, and Plymouth. In July 1625 Sir John Davies reported, 'the king is now at Oatlands, being removed from Windsor', and would soon go on to Woodstock and Oxford. Among the gentry homes 'made ready' for the summer progress were Sir Walter Titchbourne's house at Aldershot, Mr Hobby's at Bisham, Sir Thomas Read's at Abingdon, and Mr Dolman's house at Newbury.[67]

Travelling to the West Country in the autumn of 1625, the king stayed with Sir Richard Reynell at Wolborough, Devon, a day's ride from Plymouth, and attended a Sunday service at Wolborough parish church. The congregation was treated to the unusual sight of the king they named in their prayers. Kitchen expenses for the visit exceeded £83, and would have been higher had not local gentlemen contributed bucks, does, and sides of venison.[68] Continuing the royal progress, a correspondent reported, 'the king . . . had most magnificent entertainment one night at Sir Charles Bertlet's house', another at Mr Poulett's, 'of whose nobleness all men talk'.[69] Both hosts were politically ascendant, with ties to the Duke of Buckingham, one becoming a gentleman of the privy chamber, the other soon to be made a baron. King Charles's visit to Somerset, however, was not without controversy. On the night the king stayed with Poulett at Hinton St George a disgruntled neighbour, Hugh Pyne, observed that 'he could have had him at his house, if he would', but that he and 'divers more did refuse to do our duties to him'. King Charles most likely knew nothing of the local rivalry, nor of Pyne's 'dangerous' words to the effect that he was unfit to be king and was like 'a child with an apple', but they blew up later in a landmark case on treasonable and seditious words.[70]

Happier times ensued at Longford Castle, the seat of the Gorges family, where local notables enjoyed 'this long time a great court with us, both of king and queen'. Sir Edward Gorges wrote to Sir Hugh Smyth in November 1625 that he was glad that the royal couple had finally moved on, 'so that now we shall be freed of much trouble and have more leisure to visit and send to one another'.[71] Having the king close by was evidently a responsibility as well as a privilege for select members of the elite.

In June 1627, attended by more than a dozen noblemen, King Charles visited the Isle of Wight, where troops were billeted in readiness for deployment to La Rochelle. Staying on the island for less than six hours, the king reviewed a regiment, made a few knights, and allowed local dignitaries to kiss his hand. The deputy governor Sir John Oglander remarked that 'his majesty neither ate nor drank in our island'. A year later, after the death of the Duke of Buckingham, the king returned for a more leisurely visit, when more intimate contact proved possible. On this occasion, Oglander writes, the king 'took me by the hand and held me a long time riding together, saying he was much bound to us for all our patience and well-usage' during the war. Oglander urged his majesty to find funds for the billeting of soldiers 'and for the fortification of our island', but the king offered only half-promises. 'In Queen Elizabeth's time ... the state was well ordered,' mused Oglander in his commonplace book, but now the Isle of Wight was depressed, '*insula fortunata*, now *infortunata*'.[72]

Normally, wherever the king went, public spaces were well cleared and ordered in advance. Local justices surveyed highways and bridges, and townsmen tidied their shopfronts and streets.[73] The wandering poor were warned away, and officers set 'diligent watch ... in every city, town, village and parish through which his majesty shall pass'.[74] On visits to the two universities the streets were cleared and cleaned 'against the king's coming'.[75] Students at Cambridge were warned against 'rude or immodest exclamations ... nor any other such uncivil or unscholarlike or boyish demeanour' while the royal party was present.[76] At Oxford they were enjoined to 'appear nowhere abroad during the king's being here without their caps ... and particularly that they beware that they wear not any long hair, nor any boots nor double stockings rolled down or hanging loose about their legs, as the manner of some slovens is to do'. Ranks of academic doctors, masters, bachelors, and undergraduates had instructions to 'stand there quietly till the king and his train are past' and to cheer in Latin '*vivat rex*'. Civic officials in their scarlet gowns and velvet tippets, all 'decently apparelled' and 'handsomely and well horsed', offered speeches and gifts of plate.[77]

Woodstock, 10 miles from Oxford, was a favourite summer retreat of the king, where he came to hunt and relax. Local records note when 'the king's gentlemen harbingers ... came to view the state of the town' and ordered the streets cleaned 'against the king's coming'.[78] In 1629, university observers learned, 'the king is to come to Woodstock August 18 and there to stay eight nights'. Although senior members flocked to the court when the king was in their vicinity, the university chancellor ordered 'that no scholars come at Woodstock during the time of his abode there'. Thomas Crosfield of Queen's College commented that King Charles 'is a gracious prince, specially to us that are scholars, to whom upon all occasions and opportunities he is bountiful and loving, and therefore it were a very unwise and unworthy part for us to give him any occasion of disgust or distaste. If any desire to see him they may as he passeth through the town.'[79]

The king and court were at Woodstock again from 17 to 25 August 1631 but 'troubled the country very little', noted Thomas Wyatt the incumbent of nearby Ducklington.[80] During that visit on 23 August King Charles spent part of the morning 'laying his hands on such as came unto him to be cured of the king's evil', then met with university officials in the afternoon to deal with cases of seditious sermons. The king listened to complex legal, procedural, and theological arguments before offering his verdict. He rebuked Thomas Ford, whose sermon questioned 'universal grace', and asked 'how he durst meddle with those points of controversy which in his declaration he had commanded to be forborne?' In another case he called Giles Thorne 'a knave' for suggesting that Dr Christopher Potter was tainted with Pelagianism. The session allowed King Charles to exercise his authority and display his wisdom, prompted by William Laud.[81] The place-seeker Peter Moreton was among the hopeful young men who followed the court that summer 'wherever it hath been . . . almost as far as Winchester'.[82]

The king and court were at Newmarket during Lent 1632, indulging in 'hawking, hunting, coursing, horse-racing and the . . . course of lords and ladies'. On the fringe of this merriment, and eager for news of appointments, Peter Moreton found 'the king as he is very secret and retired'.[83] From Newmarket, 'the theatre of our world', the court then rode to Cambridge for 'the best entertainment of the university'. Select members of the university would see the king in the great hall of Trinity College. His unsmiling response to a dramatic comedy performed in his honour contributed to the tragedy of the vice-chancellor's subsequent suicide.[84] In August the royal party hunted at Windsor. There the Earl of Cork's son Lord Dungarvon kissed the king's hand and believed himself favoured when the king 'withdrew him to the chimney corner' to advise him on matchmaking (on which subject the king had limited expertise).[85] King Charles and his court spent most of the rest of the year at Greenwich, Whitehall, Oatlands, and Hampton Court, and enjoyed a brief summer progress through Surrey and Hampshire.[86]

Longer progresses, with similar protocols, allowed selective opportunities for contact. Bound for Scotland in May 1633, never travelling on Sundays, the court took twenty-three days to cover the 285 miles to Newcastle upon Tyne.[87] Winding through Hertfordshire, Cambridgeshire, Huntingdonshire, Northamptonshire, Lincolnshire, Nottinghamshire, Yorkshire, Durham, and Northumberland, the royal journey became a magnificent procession, with a duke, marquess, ten earls, and scores of knights, chaplains, trumpeters, gentlemen ushers, and yeomen of the guard in attendance. The royal baggage train is said to have included a silver Tudor dining service, that may have been lost in an accident crossing the Firth of Forth.[88] Along the way, as usual, the king acknowledged 'persons of quality and condition . . . who desired the honour of his presence'.[89] Attending Sunday services in country churches, the king 'set a copy to his people how to perform all true humility and religious observations in the house of God'.[90]

A minor detour brought King Charles to the exemplary Christian household of Nicholas Ferrar at Little Gidding, just beyond Huntingdon. With its ornate chapel and deep devotional routine, Little Gidding had the reputation of a protestant nunnery. The women maintained protestant orthodoxy according to the Book of Common Prayer, but watched and prayed before a richly decked altar, much to the king's approval.[91] At Richmond, Yorkshire, he gave money to a woman who had borne quadruplets. King Charles's entertainment by the Earl of Newcastle had 'such an excess of feasting as had never before been known in England'. Correspondents shared the news that 'our king is well, his entertainment great in his journey, the lord of Newcastle most famous for his meat, the bishop of York most famous for his drink'. Other generous hosts included the Earl of Exeter, the Earl of Arundel, and the Earl of Kingston. The many surviving copies of the king's itinerary or 'gists' testify to gentry interest in the movements of the king and court.[92]

It hardly mattered that Charles's formal entry into York in May 1633 was marred by 'extreme wind and rain', for observers found a remarkably approachable monarch, basking in the love of his subjects.[93] According to Henry Jacie, who shared the news with John Winthrop Jr in New England, the king was

> exceeding greatly commended and extolled for his courtesy and affableness and his piety. It was a very rainy day, so that he came to York in a coach, and sent word afore he was sorry he could not so come in that those that desired to see him might all see him, and after forbad those that would keep people from crowding in to see him and come near him, looking still on them with a smiling countenance, and received all the petitions were put up to him.[94]

At Berwick councillors reported the 'good success of our journey', with the king enjoying 'great entertainments . . . in all places of note, and general concourses and acclamations of his people'. Berwick exhibited such 'joy and contentment in his presence' that the memory of King Charles's 'cheerful and daily conversing amongst them' would 'remain in men's hearts to his honour' for ever.[95]

The climax of the journey, and its principal purpose, was King Charles's Scottish coronation at Edinburgh on 18 June. At Holyrood a week later he touched 100 sufferers from the king's evil. The return trip was less sociable, a four-day sprint from the Scottish border to Greenwich, almost 90 miles a day.[96] A similar pace was set on an earlier royal ride from Newmarket, when the king reached London 'in less than five hours, and all the way almost on horseback', with little time for interactions of any sort.[97] This was drive-by kingship, with no loss to royal effectiveness or honour.

London and the Home Counties were glad to have their king back. The Essex diarist Sir Humphrey Mildmay was pleased to record on 17 July 1633 that 'the king's majesty met the queen near Hackney at seven of the clock', and the evening was illuminated by bonfires. Mildmay may have been part of the aristocratic entourage assembled to greet the king as he completed his journey to his capital. Few of the riders would have direct contact with his majesty, but all could bask in the glow of the royal occasion.[98] Church bells rang in the City and Westminster 'at the king's majesty's coming home out of Scotland'.[99]

A more recreational and less ambitious progress later in 1633 traversed the Thames Valley as far as Woodstock, where the king spent another ten nights at the end of August, mostly hunting.[100] The Oxford diarist Thomas Crosfield, who may himself have been part of the welcoming crowd, recorded that 'great multitudes flocked thither to see him'. The court response, to prevent unseemly intrusions, was 'to build a wall about Woodstock park', to spare the king 'disgust or distaste'.[101]

The royal summer progress of 1634 circled through the Midlands as far as north as Nottinghamshire. The planned itinerary originally included York and Pontefract, but the king and queen later 'resolved to go no further than my Lord Newcastle's, where they will stay five or six nights'.[102] The Earl of Huntingdon wrote to his son in May 1634 that 'both their majesties removed upon Monday last from Whitehall to Greenwich, where they stay until near the progress, which is to begin the 14th of July next; the gists, if you have them not already, you shall have them at your coming up' to London.[103]

Learning that the king would pass through their town, the leaders of Leicester organized a frenzy of cleansing and beautification. Instructions went out to every householder to see that 'his pavement before his street door be well and decently paved', and also that each house be painted 'with some decent and convenient colours as by the aldermen of every ward shall be thought meet'. When the king arrived, he would pass through gates freshly decorated with the royal arms, along sparkling streets lined with halberd-bearing guards. The mayor and dignitaries formed ranks in their gowns and best suits to present the royal visitors with bowls of pure gold 'with the king and queen's majesty's pictures on them, with the globe and scepter'. This display of duty cost Leicester more than £144, and citizens faced threats of punishment if they refused to contribute 'towards the defraying of the charges'. No doubt, from the city's point of view, it was money well spent, and also gratified their local Lieutenant and patron, the Earl of Huntingdon.[104]

Measured not by the odometer but by the calendar, the royal journey involved sojourns at fifteen great houses over a period of forty-four days. The longest halts were at Apethorpe, Northamptonshire (the Earl of Westmorland's residence, 17–22 July), Belvoir, Lincolnshire (residence of the Earl of Rutland, 24–28 July), Welbeck, Nottinghamshire (home of the Earl of Newcastle, 29 July–4 August), the city of Nottingham (4–9 August), Tutbury, Staffordshire (a manor of the Duchy of Lancaster, held by the Earl of Shrewsbury, 11–16 August), and Castle Ashby, Northamptonshire (seat of the Earl of Northampton, 19–23 August).[105] By 27 August they were back at Windsor, though by no means stationary or settled, having travelled little more than 200 miles. In September the court made stops at Oatlands, Bagshot, London, and Theobalds, and were expected soon at Hampton Court. The king and queen were at Nonesuch, Surrey, in mid-September when the courtier Henry Jermyn 'was admitted to kiss their majesties' hands'.[106] Shuttling from palace to palace, the king again graced Hampton Court, Windsor, Theobalds, and Whitehall over the next few weeks.[107] Along the way most prominent county gentry paid their compliments, and perhaps gained sight of the masques and entertainments provided for the court. If ambitious petitioners expected more personal contact, they were mostly disappointed.

Summer travels in 1635 took the king and court through Wiltshire, Hampshire, and Berkshire, including stays at Winterbourne, Salisbury, and Lyndhurst, as well as favourite resorts at Windsor, Oatlands, and Woodstock.[108] Reporting plans for the king's progress, to begin in mid-July, George Garrard wrote that 'New Forest is the farthest he will go, if he go so far; but the queen goes not. 'Tis said she is with child.'[109] Correspondents could barely keep pace with the court as summer turned to autumn, tracking the royal family again from Woodstock to Windsor,

Somerset House to Hampton Court, Royston to Whitehall.[110] The king was almost restlessly mobile, though not necessarily more accessible.

Nor did Charles I spurn his capital city. On 24 September 1635 Thomas Davis reported from London, 'the king and prince came hither to see the trained bands . . . He dined at the queen's silkman's in Cheapside, and here he stood to see all the troopers march by; after dinner he returned back to Hampton Court.' The host was Edward Bradbourne, 'the most remarkable silkman of Cheapside', who earned thousands of pounds for furnishing the queen's chambers with luxurious fabric. Observers noted this royal visit, not because it was normal but rather because it was remarkable. 'His majesty vouchsafed . . . to honour the City with his . . . presence, standing two or three hours' at the window at citizen Bradbourne's residence. 'His majesty had a full view' of the military companies, George Garrard reported, but had long departed when a barrel of gunpowder blew up and killed five or six of the city's volunteers.[111] By 4 October the king was expected back at Royston, 'to hunt and hawk until All Hallowtide'.[112]

The king enjoyed Newmarket again in January 1636, and Woodstock and Oxford in April, before setting out for Winchester.[113] Much of the movement that year was designed to keep distance from disease. At short notice in July, for example, 'the king went not to Theobalds . . . by reason of the sickness in those parts, but went instead to Bagshot'.[114] The king and court were away from London for almost ten weeks in the summer of 1636, altering the 'gists' or itinerary to avoid the plague. The northern progress stretched to Nottingham and Derby, by way of great houses at Apethorpe, Belvoir, and Tutbury, with the usual feasting and hunting.[115] On the way home they stayed five more nights at Woodstock, and then were entertained again at Oxford by the chancellor archbishop Laud and the heads of the colleges. One observer commented that 'the archbishop's feast [was] magnificent, but the university plays did not much take the courtiers'. Laud himself remarked in his diary, 'all passed happily'.[116] The general success of the visit may have stemmed in part from the university's order in 1636 that 'it shall not be lawful for any scholar of any degree to go out to meet the king, or to be at or upon the way where the king is to come, upon pain of a month's imprisonment'.[117]

As always, observers saw what they expected. Writing to John Winthrop in Massachusetts, Robert Reyce reported that, in the summer of 1636, 'the king went in progress as I think into Shropshire, where the king was exceeding angry for his bad entertainment'. (Actually the king visited

Staffordshire that year, not Shropshire.) According to Reyce, too few gentleman turned out to greet his majesty, 'and in all the places where the king should lodge the goodman gone, none at home but the wife, with abundance of all sorts of victuals, and servants'. Reyce thought divisive policies explained this snub, for 'here formerly was benevolences and Ship Money denied, which some construed was the cause of every man's general absence'. There was also some danger in the air, for 'during this progress there was one [John] Bumpstead, sometimes a tailor of Melford [Long Melford, Suffolk] then following the Lord Savage... [who] was observed to follow the court, and there apprehended for divers evil words and purposes to the king'.[118] But elsewhere gentlemen showed up as usual for the masques and hunts, dinners and receptions, and vied for the king's attention. On one such occasion Sir John Lenthall invited his kinsman Sir Peter Temple 'to come hither, where there will be this night good company and tomorrow good sport', because 'the king hunts here tomorrow morning'.[119] To mix with the court would be enough for these Buckinghamshire gentlemen, who expected no more than a glimpse of their sovereign.

King Charles's movements in 1637 were again constrained by fear of contagion. Court followers complained that travel plans 'alter every day' on account of the sickness. The royal couple might have taken to the road that spring, but, George Garrard reported in April, 'neither king nor queen yet have thought of stirring' because of the threat of plague. Instead they shuttled between Whitehall, Greenwich, Theobalds, and Oatlands, around greater London, and then planned an abbreviated western progress to the New Forest from August into September.[120] Salisbury was left off the itinerary, 'the town being so infected with the smallpox'.[121] King Charles was evidently accessible to entertainers, however, for Garrard sent to Wentworth 'a ballad made of the wits, sung to the king when he was in the New Forest'.[122] Later that autumn the king and queen went to Woolwich, downstream from Greenwich, to see the launch of the *Sovereign*, 'the goodliest ship that was ever built in England', and then went back to Hampton Court.[123]

The king journeyed less in 1638, mostly along the familiar Thames corridor, from Windsor in the west to Greenwich in the east, with a visit to Newmarket in Lent. In the summer he 'intended a northern progress to Belvoir and farther, but had changed his mind; Woodstock is the farthest place he will go to this year, and thither not until August', George Garrard informed Lord Wentworth.[124] The limited travel may be linked to Henrietta Maria's latest pregnancy, which ended badly in January 1639 with the stillborn Princess Catherine.

Charles went north again the following spring, this time a military monarch to campaign against the rebellious Scots. By way of escort he had 100 horse guards to attend him, along the lines of 'his neighbour princes', for his honour and protection.[125] The progress had more of the trappings of an army than a court, accompanied by an artillery train of fifty heavy guns.[126] Unity was undermined, however, a correspondent of the Earl of Rutland reported, as 'some of the lords have refused to wait on the king'.[127]

King Charles's journey began on 27 March 1639, the anniversary of his accession, and he would be away from London for more than four months.[128] William Laud anticipated that he would find 'a very general offering of their service in almost all men of quality', though he was dubious about 'the common soldiers'.[129] According to Colonel Fleetwood, whose upbeat letter from the north was widely circulated, 'as the king journeyed the common people gave him and his followers most zealous blessing for his and their happy success in their journey'.[130]

Approaching York, after ten days of travel, the royal party was greeted by 'some hundred horse and gentlemen, all in martial habit'. These were 'the *galenteria* of this county, people bravely vested and mounted', observed the courtier Edward Norgate, 'no king Christian can wish better subjects'. The assembly was not spontaneous, however, for the northern notables had been ordered in advance 'to show their duty to his majesty by waiting on him, or sending horse to guard his person'.[131] King Charles was 'sumptuously entertained' in York, and the next day he knighted the recorder and the lord mayor. On Good Friday he touched 200 sufferers from 'the king's evil'.[132] The next few weeks were spent reviewing troops, raising morale, and securing the allegiance and resources of the major nobility, with much kneeling of subjects and kissing of the royal hand. Having engaged the peers to 'oppose all seditions rebellions conspiracies, covenants, conjurations and treasons whatsoever', councillors considered extending the oath 'over all England, so that his majesty might know who were his friends and who his foes'.[133]

King Charles left York on 29 April, and travelled in force via Durham and Newcastle to the limits of his English kingdom west of Berwick upon Tweed.[134] After concluding a peace with the Scots in June, the king set off south, and was home at Whitehall by the beginning of August 1639.[135] The itinerary remained subject to change, for new 'gists' sent to aristocrats showed 'some alteration in the king's return'.[136]

Back in London, 'circled with his royal diadem and the affections of his people', the king rejoiced in the 'great acclamations and joy of his giddy people', according to the diarist John Evelyn.[137] Bells rang out in City parishes again for 'the king's return from Scotland'.[138] Appearance suggested that the king and his people were in harmony, united in common cause for the royal honour and the country's religion, though the 'giddy people' were notoriously capricious. The reality was that the Scots were dominant, English martial might ineffective, and many of the king's English subjects reluctant to judge their northern neighbours traitors.[139]

'Extraordinary' news spread in August 1640 that King Charles was again bound for York to rally the troops, believing that 'his presence would make them more willing to march' against Scotland.[140] Here was the king as warrior, a role he would play more vigorously in the years that followed. Alas, King Charles's army quickly collapsed and allowed the Scots to occupy the region from Newcastle to Durham. He was still 150 miles from the frontier when his forces crumpled. The king's meeting with the peers at York in September 1640 took place beneath the shadow of defeat, and led to the decision to recall parliament. Under enormous military, fiscal, and political pressure, King Charles reached out to his nobles at a great baronial assembly of the kind not seen since the fifteenth century. It was, declared the Earl of Cumberland, 'the most harmonious meeting that ever was between any king of England and his peers: the effects whereof I hope both he and we shall reap this next approaching parliament, and our children's children will be the better for it'.[141] Only hindsight reveals the irony of this assessment, to which one might add *utinam*, if only.

Another court journey in 1641, more a mission than a progress, took King Charles to settle final terms with the Scots. At his homecoming in November, bringing peace to a troubled England, the king had an escort of 500 Londoners on horseback for the last 4 miles of his journey. The sheriffs and aldermen of London staged 'a gallant show' with banners, trumpets, and scarlet liveries, backed by footmen with truncheons. The streets from Bishopsgate to Cheapside were lined by members of city companies, behind railed barriers hung with flags and escutcheons. 'The banks, hedges, highways, streets, stalls and windows were all embroidered with millions of

Figure 7. Citizens greet their Gracious Sovereign, 1641. John Taylor, *Englands Comfort, and Londons Ioy: Expressed in the Royall, Triumphant, and Magnificent Entertainment of our Dread Soveraigne Lord, King Charles, at his blessed and safe returne from Scotland* (1641), 4.

people of all sorts and fashions,' wrote the admiring author John Taylor. 'There was no failings in expressions of love and loyalty by the people,' who drank healths to his majesty from conduits running with sack and claret. King Charles himself almost disappears in Taylor's enthusiastic account, amid the 'brave equipage' of the London guilds and the great turnout of the citizens. Another account lists the order of march through the capital, and reports that 'their majesties and their train passed quietly, without interruption'. People made the customary 'joyful acclamations', and the king and queen thanked them 'reciprocally and heartily... with as great expressions of joy'.[142]

One might not know from these conventional texts that a revolution was rocking the kingdom. London was fraught with tension, its trade disrupted, its social peace disturbed. The Grand Remonstrance had passed a contentious House of Commons on 22 November, only three days before the royal homecoming. Passions ran high, and hope lay thin that King Charles could restore harmony to his kingdom. News was beginning to circulate of the catholic uprising in Ireland, and of more alleged popish plotting. Barely six weeks later the king and his family quit London, fearful for their lives, with none of the usual trappings of a royal journey. His next entry to his capital six years later would be as a prisoner.

Leaving London on 10 January 1642, more like a refugee than a sacred monarch, King Charles embarked on a journey that became a trail of tears. He paused at Hampton Court and Windsor, skirted London to arrive at Greenwich, then rode through Kent to Dover, where he embarked his queen for safety in Holland. By the end of February the king was at Greenwich, then crossed the Thames to travel through Essex to his hunting lodge at Newmarket. All this time the king was poorly attended, though pleased to be joined by his two young sons and their cousin the Palgrave. On 15 March the royal party paused at Cambridge, where some of the king's followers behaved as if they did not have enough to eat. Following a makeshift meal at St John's College, where hungry courtiers crammed food into their pockets, the royal entourage headed north towards Huntingdon, sped on by cries that he return to his parliament and people. One report tells of women throwing stones at the king's departing coach.[143]

One of the few bright spots in the king's dispirited peregrination was his brief sojourn at Little Gidding, Huntingdonshire, where he was entertained by the gentle family of the late Nicholas Ferrar. Charles had been here before in 1633, and had fond memories of the household's pious tranquillity. Word went ahead 'that the king was to pass by that way', so that, when the travellers arrived, they found the Ferrar family and their servants kneeling at the roadside, 'with hands and voices lifted up, crying God save King Charles, God save the king and noble prince'. The king allowed the Ferrars to kiss his hand, in a public display of devotion, then passed an agreeable hour visiting the chapel, examining the 'great book', and nibbling on 'some small banqueting' that the Ferrar women presented on their knees. The 'great book' of Little Gidding was an extra-illustrated Bible or gospel harmony, 'a rare, great and laborious work' with 'several pictures to each page, which did express to the eye what was declared to the ear in the reading of the matter'. The gentlewomen of the household had spent many hours preparing this marvel, which they intended to present to Prince Charles, though the binding was not yet finished. Delighted and uplifted, refreshed in body and spirit, the king reluctantly took his leave. Kneeling again at his departure, the family prayed for the king, that 'holy angels might be his guide, and that he might be preserved from all evil both in soul and body, and that his return might be speedy and safe to his own'. This was a quiet interlude on a troubled journey, which was even more memorable to the hosts than to the monarch.[144]

Eventually, on 19 March 1642, King Charles reached York, accompanied by only thirty-nine gentlemen and seventeen guards. It made stark contrast to the formal royal entries of previous occasions. Over the next few months the king would attempt to repair his fortunes, attracting followers and pledges of support. York became the seat of a thinned-out court and a base for the king's excursions to other northern cities. On 23 April he suffered the humiliation of being denied entry to the stronghold of Hull, after bargaining with Sir John Hotham in the rain. On 3 June he summoned the freeholders of Yorkshire to an assembly on Heworth Moor, and made an enemy of Sir Thomas Fairfax by brushing aside his petition. The attempt to rally support, by one account, produced only 'confused murmur and noise'. While some people shouted 'God bless the king', others prayed to 'unite the king and parliament, and God turn the king's heart'.[145] The king fared better at Lincoln on 13 July, when he was greeted by loyal gentry, clergy, and notables with cries of 'a king, a king' and '*vivat rex*'. At Leicester too, a week later, 'his loving subjects' greeted his majesty with 'joys and shouts', the crowd perhaps swelled by people hoping for peace. One observer noted that 'the people begin to lay their hands on their hearts, and I hope they shall never have cause to lay them on their swords, against conscience or country'.[146] On 22 August King Charles raised his royal standard at Nottingham, in more pouring rain, marking the formal beginning of the Civil War. The king would travel more than ever in the years that followed, driven by the exigencies of war and revolution, as journeys of necessity replaced progresses of pleasure.

6

Importunate Petitioners

Every English ruler received requests, and every monarch fielded petitions. Petitioning the king was a long-established practice, considered a right as well as a privilege. Petitioning, asserted members of parliament in 1628, was the province of 'free and dutiful subjects'.[1] The activity of seeking the king's attention, and the ruler's appropriate response, enacted and displayed the reciprocities of kingship and subjecthood, citizenship and good governance. It invited the monarch to exercise his discretionary prerogative powers on his people's behalf. Henry VIII had announced himself 'prone and ready to hear all his subjects of all degrees resorting with petitions or complaints unto him, and both to grant the same and to see redress made in all things according to justice'.[2] James I, who received hundreds of petitions each year, likewise conceived himself the arbiter of disputes, 'the wiper of the people's tears'.[3] As patriarchal father and nursing mother, the king would offer his people assuagement, judgment, remedy, and reward. Displaying wisdom, extending mercy, and distributing bounty were attributes of the art of governance, and suitors expected the king 'to hear the petitions of [their] faithful subjects, and to redress their wrongs'.[4]

King Charles publicly acknowledged these obligations. Speaking on the king's behalf in March 1626, the Lord Keeper Sir Thomas Coventry assured the House of Commons that 'there was never king more truly loving of his people, not better affected...to hear and answer...just grievances'.[5] Charles himself would later declare 'that all his loving subjects who have any just cause to present, or complain of any grievances or oppressions, may freely address themselves by their humble petitions to his sacred majesty'.[6] Like his predecessors, he recognized his royal duty to accept petitions from his faithful subjects, to adjudicate their causes, and to consider their needs. Courtiers, ministers, lawyers, and officials served as conduits and intermediaries, so that actual royal audiences with commoners were rare. But that did not stop hundreds of petitioners each year from presenting their requests, though few with the vehemence and ingenuity of Lucy Martin. Among them were Henry Butts, the vice-chancellor of Cambridge, who waited weeks on the fringes of the court to present a university petition and got as far as being allowed to kiss the king's hand;[7] John Spencer, a melancholic puritan, who tried several times to address King Charles on the sanctity of the Sabbath and the service book for Scotland, and who was held overnight in the gatehouse for his troubles;[8] and the townsmen of Norwich, who sought 'to present their petition unto his majesty in the behalf of some irregular ministers who would be counted conformable', thereby causing 'a great combustion'.[9] Some people believed that the privilege of petitioning the king was part of 'the birthright of an Englishman', but approaches to majesty could prove bruising.

The Rack of Expectation

Charles I received petitions by the sackful, though there is little scholarship reviewing this business. They arrived through every avenue and agency, furthered by courtiers, officers, and helpful contacts. Two hundred and ten volumes of appearances and 32,000 bundles of pleadings and petitions survive from just one such avenue, the Court of Requests, but historians have shied away from this vast uncalendared archive.[10] Petitions touched every conceivable topic, from medicine to marriage, though most concerned property or debts. Petitioners to the king sought redress or favour, grants or licences, appointments, pensions, legal dispensations, clemency, or pardon. Many came from aristocratic families or former court employees, who wanted their wages or some long-promised reward. Others represented groups or collectives, such as inhabitants of particular towns,[11] workers in particular industries, 'poor mariners and seafaring men',[12] or the wives of sailors captured by the Turks.[13] Place-seeking petitioners hung their hopes 'upon the rack of expectation' and sometimes achieved satisfaction.[14] The fast-rising John Finch recognized the radiance of royal bounty in 1634 when he felt, he said, 'the king's goodness shining upon me', like one emerging from a darkened room, when his hopes for advancement were rewarded.[15]

Most petitioners adhered to the rhetoric of humility in supplication. Their petitions were framed as acts of deference, reproducing relationships of rank and power. Thus: 'Your humble petitioner and most loyal subject most humbly submitteth himself to your majesty's most princely grace, most humbly praying that your petitioner may enjoy the benefit of your majesty's royal grant... in such manner as shall seem best in your princely wisdom. And your petitioner shall according to his bounden duty, daily pray for your majesty's life and happy reign,' fawned Richard Heyrick when he sought the wardenship of Manchester college in 1635.[16] A London gentleman began his petition in 1637: 'To the king's most excellent majesty, in all humble manner complaining, showeth unto your most excellent majesty your highness's loyal, lowly and obedient subject,' and then explained that he had been cheated at dice and now sought royal protection from gambling debts of £32.[17]

A special class of petitioners offered ideas or procedures for the benefit of the kingdom. King Charles had barely taken his throne in 1625 before petitioners offered him schemes 'for enriching his majesty with many millions', plans 'to discover a secret means of rendering cannon useless', and projects to discover *Terra Australis Incognita.* Other petitioners proposed schemes for increasing the speed of ships, guaranteeing supplies of saltpeter, or drying hops and malt 'without the annoyance of smoke'.[18] One petitioner in 1625 received a fourteen-year privilege to develop a substance to preserve ships and rigging from 'hurt by gunpowder or wildfire, or the hulls from hurt by sea-worm or barnacles'. Another in 1627 won favour for 'a method by him invented for the help of memory and grounding of scholars in several languages'.[19] Thomas Russell famously received support for a scheme to make saltpeter for gunpowder from the excrement and urine of Londoners.[20] Successful petitioners in1635 included Hannibal Vivian, who was granted a privilege 'to use an engine for the drawing and drying of waters and raising up of any great weight out of any tin mines', Alexander and Thomas Matthew 'to imprint bills of burials and christenings in and about the cities of London and Westminster', and the keepers of lions and leopards in the Tower of London.[21] There was hardly an enterprise that would not benefit from royal favour, hardly a circumstance not eased by the smile or the signature of a king.[22] Projectors were relentless petitioners, soliciting support for a host of devices, enterprises, and monopolies. 'He begins with a petition to his majesty', but 'can never accomplish the thousand part' of his promises and pretences, said a pamphlet denouncing projectors.[23]

Routine petitions sought grants of honours, licences, offices, pardons, pensions, protections, ratifications, and awards, each a mark of favour to the recipient, each an exercise of the 'prerogative royal'. Former members of the household staff sued for back-wages and annuities. Hopeful careerists sought positions and reversions (to fill future vacancies, when they occurred). Suppliers of goods and services petitioned to be paid. Convicted criminals petitioned to be pardoned for manslaughter, bigamy, or other excusable felonies. Foreign-born merchants requested denizenship. Clergymen, usually royal preachers, petitioned to be non-resident or to hold plural livings. Debtors sought royal protection to prevent their creditors hounding them to prison.[24]

Hundreds of petitioners received royal recognition, grants, or approvals for their desires and projects. These were the lucky ones whose petitioning achieved success. Most of these successful suppliants went through official channels or enjoyed well-connected support, and barely came to the notice of the king. Many received perfunctory review before lawyers or officers of the Court of Requests, who assessed the worthiness or cost of their suit. File upon file survives of dockets, warrants, permissions, and awards to suppliants for royal favour. Hundreds were registered on the patent rolls, and dozens gave rise to proclamations.

The most controversial petitions addressed matters of state and offered warnings or advice, and these were least likely to succeed. Indeed, their authors ran the risk of official displeasure, and might even be punished for their intrusion into *arcana imperii*, the secrets of state. A few intrepid petitioners sought face-to-face parley with King Charles, and attempted to address him directly, but the king was well screened from such disorderly intrusions. Lucy Martin's enterprising effort ended with her being whipped at Bridewell.

Charles I was a busy and conscientious monarch who attended meetings, annotated documents, and signed thousands of papers. Only on hunting days was the king too absorbed in his pleasures to attend to state business, and even then the royal secretaries found ways to gain his attention and place important matters in his path. Sometimes they had to anticipate Charles's moods and decode his reactions. In March 1628, for example, Secretary Conway found the king 'either upon his sports abroad or at tennis', and found time only for the most pressing business. On another occasion in August 1635, while the king was dining in the New Forest, Secretary Nicholas tried to engage the king in discussion of maritime business to do with prizes and letters of marque, a transaction Nicholas described with exasperation: 'His majesty gave him little or no answer, and when at length I perceived in the king no more inclination to the consideration of it, I moved to know whether his majesty would have that business further considered of at his coming to Windsor, to which his majesty said "well," and seemed to incline.'[25]

Perhaps more typical was Sir Robert Heath's successful interception of King Charles in the Privy Lodgings at Whitehall in March 1627, when the king came out of the Stone Chamber and progressed slowly along the Gallery. Heath, the king's Attorney General, was assisting Sir John Heydon, Lieutenant of the Ordnance, who needed the king's signature on papers to do with royal woodlands. 'The king advancing toward the middle of the Gallery, Sir Robert stepped into the king's withdrawing chamber and brought out the king's gilt standish [writing stand].' While Sir John addressed the king and sought confirmation of his contract, Sir Robert placed the standish by the middle window in the Gallery, 'and then put the pen into the king's hand'. Mission accomplished.[26]

If petitioners expected direct contact with his majesty, they were mostly disappointed. Concern for the king's safety and dignity kept them at bay. Though supplicants of all sorts followed the court, they rarely entered the royal presence. Even if they came close enough to witness the king, they had to deal with the guards and ushers whose job it was to keep petitioners

Figure 8. A Petitioner at the Court Gate. Martin Parker, *The King, and a Poore Northerne Man* (1640), sig. A5[v].

from thrusting papers into royal hands. Precautions were in place so that 'no manner of man be so hardy to sue now to put bills nor approach nigh to [the king] during his procession' at court.[27] Most petitions came by way of intermediaries and were handled by specialists, without ever troubling the royal gaze. Most were referred to appropriate offices, though occasionally a batch was brought to the king's attention for review.[28] Successful petitions usually received an endorsement on the document, or a minute to the Signet Office, without the king necessarily being directly involved.[29]

Aristocrats and Intermediaries

Skilled petitioners understood the importance of conduits for their requests, and insinuated themselves with courtiers and senior officials. When a Mr Percy prepared a petition to King Charles in 1626, he asked Viscount St Albans to refer it to Secretary Conway, for him to commend it to his majesty.[30] When Sir John Oglander petitioned the king in 1628 about troops on the Isle of Wight, he went through the 'furtherance' of the Secretary of State, the island governor. His covering letter expressed the 'hope your lordship will be pleased to concede we have endeavoured to keep such a distance as becomes loyal and humble subjects'.[31] Some petitioners feared that the king 'might take it ill' if they went outside this chain of patronage and command.[32] Even the Earl of Falkland, a highly advantaged aristocrat seeking money from his majesty, sent 'the true state of my case with the tenor of my petition' via Secretary Dorchester, 'not otherwise put in form, because I well know his majesty seldom reads them, but trusts to your relation'. Dorchester evidently took up the matter with Treasurer Weston, who indicated that Falkland should wait, with the comment, 'no favours can oblige or satisfy some men'.[33] On another occasion the Lord Treasurer was 'vexed somewhat of late with petitions to the king', and complained that 'men are very bold with me of late' in petitioning for overdue wages.[34] When distressed Essex weavers sought to acquaint his majesty with their 'miseries', they petitioned local justices to appeal to the Council to present their case to the king.[35] The gentle petitioner Sir Henry Clare told Secretary Conway how pleased he was 'that you would yourself exhibit to his majesty my petition left with your honour', and promised to tip Conway 100 marks, 'to be paid out of the first money that shall be collected' if the petition proved successful.[36]

Great nobles had allies and kinsmen to match the complexity of their affairs, and many more resources than ordinary subjects, but they too found that petitioning required patience and perseverance. The Countess of Huntingdon understood the procedure when she took her husband's petition to court in September 1631. The Earl of Huntingdon sought a ruling relating to Leicester Forest and the title to manors, and wanted the king on his side. But, rather then petitioning directly, he involved his wife and a chain of intermediaries. The countess showed the petition to the Lord Treasurer, Lord Weston, who conferred in turn with the Earl of Dorset, who 'said after the court manner he would be ready to do you service'. Discussing this strategy in correspondence with her husband, the countess remarked that 'the way by the Master of Requests is a slow one, wherefore my Lord of Dorset came to me this afternoon and hath taken the old reference to Hampton Court to get the king's hand to it'. That was by no means the end of the matter, for success was not guaranteed. There were still assets to mobilize, wheels to oil, and advocates to press into service. Several months later the business lay unresolved, the countess apologizing 'I am sorry I have lain so long at great charge and at so little purpose.' She was still pressing the petition in July 1632, when she assured her husband that 'your business may suffer for want of money to follow it withal, but if it do it is not my fault'.[37]

Petitioning the king again in 1637, still seeking favour regarding Leicester Forest, the Earl of Huntington approached his cousin the Earl of Manchester, Lord Privy Seal: 'I humbly beseech your lordship's honourable favour and furtherance therein.' He also enlisted another kinsman, the Earl of Pembroke, Lord Chamberlain, in the hope that his majesty might 'grant us a gracious answer'. Huntingdon had made some headway 'at his majesty's being the last summer at Nottingham' on the northern progress of 1636, but he asked now for a word with the Lord Treasurer 'for the perfecting thereof'.[38]

The Earl of Leicester's agent William Hawkins similarly spent weeks on end at court in 'earnest solicitation' of his lordship's business, working through high-placed courtiers, officers, and secretaries to secure payment for Leicester's embassy to France. In October 1636 Hawkins expressed 'little hope that any more will be done in it till the king's return from Newmarket', though a month later he thought it possible that the Earl of Holland would move the king at Hampton Court.[39] The Countess of Leicester, a formidable aristocrat in her own right like the Countess of Huntingdon, pursued her husband's business at court. One attempt early in 1637 failed to gain access to the king, but another, with the queen's assistance, secured an audience, which she described in a letter to Lord Leicester. It provides a rare sample of King Charles's courtly demeanour and small talk:

> In his majesty I found an inclination to show me some kindness, but he could not find the way. At last he told me that he perceived I was too kind to my husband when he was with me which kept me lean, for he thought me much fatter than I use[d] to be. This short speech was worse to me than an absolute silence, for I blushed and was so extremely out of countenance that all the company laughed at me. The other little discourses that passed among us deserve not a repetition.[40]

But at least they met face to face.

Another glimpse of the petitioning process comes from March 1636 when representatives of the city of Chester sought adjustment of their Ship Money assessments. The most enterprising of them, William Edwards, reported that, despite Secretary Windebank's order 'not to read any more petitions', he persuaded the doorkeeper 'to let me in and read my petition upon my knee to my Lord Keeper'. Lord Coventry indicated that he would move his majesty on the following Sunday, when Edwards again returned to court. On this occasion, he related, 'though I was with all others commanded to avoid the room, yet I stayed until the king came in and I proffered another petition to his majesty and besought as afore'.[41]

A minor embarrassment would be an acceptable price if it secured the success of a petition. George Garrard related a remarkable story in May 1638 of someone who gained access to the king but did not recognize him. It concerns the lawyer Thomas Milward,

> an obscure man, formerly of Lincoln's Inn... made Chief Justice of Wales [actually Chester] by my lord Marquis Hamilton's means; being brought to the king, he asked which was the king, it was answered, he who had his hat on. Then he asked whether he must kneel on one or both knees; being on his knee to be knighted, he said, if it please your majesty my name is Thomas, at which his majesty both blushed and laughed, yet knighted him but did not bid him, rise up Sir Thomas.[42]

A similar story appears in 'a merry tale' of a naive but determined countryman who came to court, but failed to identify the king, who had 'cast off his doublet' while bowling.[43]

Better briefed, and guided by a court insider, Dr Henry Butts, vice-chancellor of the University of Cambridge, waited anxiously to present his petition to King Charles. He spent two months at court in 1630, attempting to protect the university's privileges and charters from royal encroachment, while at the same time angling for personal preferment. His first attempt to approach the king at Newmarket proved fruitless, so he moved to London 'to solicit the business'. For more than five weeks, Butts relates, he 'prevailed nothing, but many doubts and scruples in the meantime were raised concerning our petition, as if his majesty might take offence at it because we seemed to limit the king's power, and trench upon his prerogative, which we disavowed, yet were we still deferred'. Eventually, however, with coaching from the Earl of Holland, vice-chancellor Butts made headway. He met Attorney General Heath 'to have the petition revised and transformed', and began to think that his 'long and chargeable attendance' would bear fruit. He was encouraged, he writes, 'because I saw the king took notice of my being there, and ever as he passed by by [*sic*] me smiled on me and nodded his head'. A week later the wait was rewarded when King Charles, on his way to prayer, allowed Butts to kneel before him, 'and gave me his hand, saying, Mr Vice-Chancellor what you desire shall be done... whereupon I gave his majesty most humble thanks and followed him into the Closet to prayers and prayed with him heartily'. This was a triumph, the apogee of courtly connection, though it took a few weeks more to complete the legal and bureaucratic technicalities. Patience and deference brought the petitioner favourable attention, the smile of a king, and Butts appeared to be ascendant. His 'relation' of this episode provides a rare and candid glimpse of the king and court in action.[44]

Subsequent dealings with the crown were less successful for Henry Butts. When plague hit Cambridge later in 1630, the vice-chancellor hoped for praise for his management of the emergency, and a colleague told him he was 'worthy to be taken notice of by our gracious king'. Butts proffered no more petitions, but he 'began to hope for great matters'. His great opportunity came when the king visited Cambridge in March 1632, but unfortunately the entertainment he arranged bombed badly, and the king was not amused. Nor was the Earl of Holland willing to intercede for him again. A despairing Henry Butts declared that 'God had deserted him' and lamented to his wife that 'she knew not what the frown of a king was'. A few days later, on Easter morning, Henry Butts hanged himself in his lodgings.[45]

A Mathematical Petitioner

One more case study illuminates the tactics of petitioning in the pursuit of patronage. Richard Delamain, an ambitious mathematician and deviser of mathematical instruments, agonized about his approach to King Charles. He mobilized his resources, lined up his contacts, and planned his campaign in several stages. In 1634 he prepared a petition 'to present unto the king, for my desired service under the prince, for his highness's instruction'. Delamain imagined himself qualified for appointment as a writing master and teacher of arithmetic to the 4-year old Prince Charles, and enlisted powerful intermediaries as advocates and allies. One such useful contact was the Earl of Bridgewater, whose secretary Mr Martin was married to a 'familiar acquaintance' of Delamain's wife, Sarah. It was not much of a link, but enough for Delamain to solicit Bridgewater to 'stand my friend a little in this business'. Writing to the earl in September 1634, he said that he 'supposed' that the petition 'would have been the better countenanced if it were delivered in the presence of some of the nobility that know me'. He understood 'that it was a far better way, rather by some honourable personage, to be recommended unto the king'. He therefore entreated Bridgewater to write a testimonial, and 'to make me the bearer thereof', to the Lord Chamberlain, the Earl of Pembroke, 'to whom I intend to address myself for moving of the king'. This was just part of Delamain's strategy, for, he explained to Bridgewater, 'I shall make use of my lord of Salisbury to move my Lord Chamberlain by word of mouth, and then withal I will present your lordship's letter', all this by way of prelude to actually tendering a petition.[46]

Anxious job-seeker that he was, Delamain enquired again in October whether Bridgewater had written as requested. By December his plans had matured to the point that the Lord Chamberlain was cognizant of Delamain's ambition, and assured him, noncommittally, 'that what lay in him he should be ready to further'. Delamain also made use of Sir James Paulmore, 'who knows me well', and Dr Mason, Prince Charles's tutor, 'whom I find still affected to me, with loving and friendly expressions, to hasten the thing, for fear that another step in before me'. The stage was set, and Delamain asked Bridgewater again to play his part. 'Now my lord, if I might be presented unto the king at some sermon day, your lordship being present, with the rest of these honourable lords, or as your lordship shall with them advise, it would I doubt not put a period thereto.' As a demonstration of his credentials, Delamain also 'prepared for the king a piece of writing, that his majesty may have a sight of my hand; the subject on which I writ is suitable to an exercise which the king affects, to wit about the practice of great artillery'.[47]

These preparations finally paid off late in 1634 when Delamain was allowed to approach the king, as he described in another letter to Bridgewater. It takes us into the heart of the court, and displays the accessible monarch in action:

> The Tuesday before Christmas, as the king went to the Chapel, I presented to his majesty my tractate of the confutation of some practices used in shooting out of great artillery (formerly signified unto your lordship) in the room next to the Gallery, which the king took, and liking the subject, read in it till he came to the Chapel, afterward gave it to my lord marquess [of Hamilton], at which time my lord of Salisbury acquainted his honour concerning the presentation, and prayed his lordship aid in my behalf therein.

This was a triumph, at considerable social cost, for the king had perused Delamain's paper for a least a few seconds. The petition had yet to bear fruit, and the appointment was not yet decided. Delamain declared to Bridgewater: 'I desire only but that the king might be moved in it,' which would require a further campaign of intervention.[48]

Delamain's petitioning for a court appointment in 1634 was neither his first nor his last attempt to gain royal attention. The records reveal him as a serial petitioner, with dreams of closer contact with his majesty. His account of 'the mathematical ring, showing . . . how to resolve and work all ordinary operations of arithmetic', published in 1631, he made bold to dedicate 'to the high and mighty King Charles king of Great Britain'. He appealed in print to the king's 'most excellent majesty' to extend his 'sacred patronage' and 'accept' the work as a 'pledge in lieu of that dutiful service I owe your sacred majesty'.[49] He backed this up with a campaign of letters and name-dropping, pressing Secretary Dorchester to quicken the process with Attorney General Heath, mentioning a similar entreaty to Endymion Porter, and letting them all know that he 'had a friend, Mr Noy, that would go with me . . . to avoid charge and hasten the bill for the king's hand'.[50] To Delamain's delight, and perhaps his surprise, King Charles acknowledged the gift of the book by indicating through intermediaries that the dedication was acceptable. The author took this as a sign of the king's 'gracious favour', and immediately offered his 'dread sovereign' an expanded account of the 'instrumental projection' of logarithms, casting himself down, so he told the king in print, 'at your sacred feet'.[51] He also presented the king with one of his silver instruments, 'a jewel his majesty much valued', which Charles later gave to his younger son.[52]

It turns out that Delamain was not the mathematical virtuoso that his writings proclaimed and publicized. According to William Oughtred, a Cambridge-trained mathematician and cleric, Delamain was no more than 'a vulgar teacher', the proprietor of a writing school in Drury Lane, who had 'basely and impudently' stolen Oughtred's logarithmic designs. Of artisan origins, he had no more than a grammar-school education, no knowledge of Latin or French, and clothed himself in learning after hearing lectures at London's Gresham College. In a scathing attack, printed in 1632, Oughtred denounced Delamain as 'utterly ignorant', his pamphlet 'worthless', his pretensions fuelled by 'vain-glory', and his knowledge 'only the superficial scum and froth of instrumental tricks and practices'.[53] But this attack failed to drive Delamain into obscurity. Outsiders could view it as a spat between rivals, but Delamain had the ace in his silver instruments, plagiarized or not, which charmed his noble patrons. He was also indefatigable in petitioning the crown and promoting himself among the court nobility.

To build support and to advance his career, Delamain sent copies of his publications to people he thought might help him, and gave select patrons examples of his silver circles and tablets. He presented mechanical spheres to the children in the Earl of Salisbury's household, and secured a temporary assignment as their instructor.[54] He gave a copy of his book *Grammelogia* to Secretary Dorchester, promised to demonstrate his calculating ring, and offered his service in 'the mathematical arts'.[55] The Earl of Bridgewater received a revised copy of *Grammelogia* '*ex dono authoris*' on 29 March 1633. Delamain later sent Bridgewater 'a tablet in silver . . . showing the products, quotients, squares, cubes and roots of numbers, with an inscription of the five geometrical regular bodies', for the use of his lordship's son.[56] He was, however, aiming higher, with hopes of favour from the king.

Earlier in 1633 Delamain had submitted a petition to the king to 'have the sole making of a mathematical instrument extracted from the logarithms and projected in circles for the speedy operating practices, as also the printing of a book called *Grammelogia, or the Mathematical Ring*'. He also asked for 'liberty to teach the use of the said instruments and other parts of the mathematical arts in London and other places in the kingdom, and that he may have the sole making of the said instrumental projections'. This was a typical projector's petition, asking for monopoly rights and royal recognition, and it seems to have achieved success. Granting it cost the crown little. On 4 March 1633 Secretary Windebank referred Delamain's petition to the Solicitor General, to prepare a warrant for the king's signature.[57] There is no indication that the petitioner had direct contact with King Charles on this occasion, although it must have helped that Delamain had previously sent books and instruments to his majesty. These dealings prepared the way and seeded the ground for the more ambitious petitioning of 1634, when Delamain hoped to be made a royal tutor. His later petitions for appointments were unsuccessful, but he did gain commissions for various instruments, dials, and devices.[58]

The petitioning campaign of 1634, in which Delamain marshalled support from Lords Bridgewater, Pembroke, Salisbury, as well as Sir James Paulmore and Dr Mason, failed to win him the appointment he wanted. But failure did not quench his ambition. There would be more projects to float, more petitions to write, more opportunities to pursue. He made more mathematical instruments in silver for the king's 'particular use', and followed the court to present them to his majesty at Whitehall, Greenwich, and Bagshot. On one occasion he petitioned the king for thirty-six pounds of silver, for past and future projects.[59] Another time he petitioned for appointment as an engineer for military works, with suitable recompense, to be 'abled to dedicate his whole life and studies to your majesty's service'. He had, so he claimed, declined invitations to work abroad, reserving himself 'for some happy occasion wherein he might have the honour to be employed in your majesty's service'. He had earlier worked for Sir John Heydon, 'measuring forts and castles' for the Ordnance Office for a fee of £40 per annum, but now he thought himself worth more, and petitioned for a place with £100 annual salary. He was, he reminded the king in 1637, 'long known... unto many of your nobility and gentry, not only to be a professor of the mathematics but especially also versed in the practical part thereof, in arithmetic, geometry, navigation, fortification, etc.', and was still willing to teach mathematics to the prince 'against he come of age'.[60]

It seems likely that Delamain's presentation of his paper, during the king's procession to chapel in Advent 1634, was his closest encounter with royalty. This was a carefully managed and long-prepared supplication by a plausible candidate for an important court appointment. Delamain's subsequent approaches were more routine affairs, which reached no closer than secretaries. The king apparently valued Delamain's instruments, and may have kept one in his bedchamber, but paid little heed to their maker. Perhaps with second thoughts about foreign offers, the arithmetician secured a licence to travel in August 1637, 'to remain abroad during the space of one year'. It was issued to 'Richard Delamain, gentleman', a mark of improved status, and he was permitted to take one servant and £30 in money. His destination was Germany, where he found a place with King Charles's nephew the Prince Elector, who had recently been in England.[61]

Delamain was home again by the time of the first Bishops' War, and helped to survey fortifications in the north. He received pay for this service in December 1639, and also 'for carriage of his majesty's mathematical instruments'.[62] When civil war broke out, he stayed in London and helped to defend the city against the king he had so assiduously sought to serve. After he died in 1645, his widow, Sarah, petitioned parliament for his arrears of pay, from both the king and the state. She styled him 'one of his majesty's engineers for the fortification of the kingdom, and his tutor in mathematical arts'.[63] Delamain would have been pleased to be so remembered, as if his persistent petitioning for court appointment had paid off. King Charles kept a favourite silver calculating ring with him through his troubles, and facing execution in January 1649 bequeathed it to Prince James, the Duke of York. Neither, most likely, knew the name or history of its maker.[64]

Disorderly Petitioning

Polite and deferential approaches had some possibility of success, but disorderly and importunate petitioning was invariably counter-productive. Petitioners who misjudged the mood or the moment were likely to experience rebuff or rebuke. The authors of 'scandalous' and offensive petitions risked censure and even imprisonment. Petitions on behalf of aggrieved subgroups or collectives rarely won favour from the Caroline regime.

One such petition in 1630 led to the imprisonment and ruin of its principal author. Locked in dispute with competitors, and disappointed when Lord Keeper Coventry ruled for other stationers, the printer Bonham Norton and his associates petitioned King Charles for redress. They unwisely implied that Coventry had taken a bribe, and the government retaliated by charging them in Star Chamber with 'preferring a most false and scandalous petition to his majesty'. The petition itself, the government claimed, constituted a publication or utterance that spread 'false tales and rumours concerning his lordship' and tended 'to the dishonour of his majesty'. As the 'author and principal wicked conspirator' behind the petition, Bonham Norton was sentenced to stand in the pillory, to be fined £6,000, and to remain imprisoned at the king's pleasure.[65]

Petitioning also backfired on James and Alice Maxwell, whose appeal to the king alleged that the Lord Keeper had disobeyed royal instructions, infringed the law, and oppressed the subject. This whistle-blowing effort brought the couple to Star Chamber in April 1635, where James Maxwell was fined £3,000 and his wife recommended to be whipped for preferring a 'scandalous petition'. Eventually they received a royal pardon and were sent packing to Scotland, no doubt cured of seeking justice by petition.[66] A similar setback greeted Sir Francis Nethersole, who spent four months in the Tower in 1634 for attempting to advise the king on the matter of the Palatinate. 'Pressing to have had some speech with the king, and being prevented therein,' he was said to have 'intruded too much upon his majesty's person'.[67]

Occasionally petitioners revealed their frustration in attempting to petition the king. William Belou, who claimed to have 'served, toiled and travailed' for the royal family 'the space of thirty-seven years', complained bitterly in 1626 that he had not received his pension. He had twice petitioned King Charles but had been spurned. On one occasion, he says, he 'moved a poor humble petition to the king verbally at Hampton Court', but his majesty 'went away silently, without one word speaking'. Belou complained that the king used him 'worse than a natural fool', worse than a Turk or a dog: 'I can petition no more, for fear I fall a howling when I complain.'[68]

Subjects who sought to address the king discovered the limits of royal accessibility. They faced first the constraints of *arcana imperii*, the idea that ordinary subjects had no business intruding on state affairs. They heard it repeatedly declared 'an ambitious ignorance for men to meddle in what they understand not', or to concern themselves with the business of kings.[69] Would-be suitors also faced the sheer logistical difficulty of penetrating the screen around his majesty. Opportunities might present themselves at court or during progresses, but the king was effectively shielded from importunate commoners. Successful petitioning required patience, politeness, and the use of well-placed intermediaries, so petitions deemed 'scandalous' in their content or their manner of presentation were especially unlikely to succeed.

When disgruntled mariners took advantage of the king's travels in 1630 and 'came in turbulent and unfit manner to complain and importune his majesty' about deficiencies in their pay and victuals, the regime reacted with hostility. Rather than addressing the needs of the seamen or the alleged diversion of money they claimed, the Council moved to punish the 'authors, actors or abettors' of 'so tumultuous and unjust clamours', whereby 'his majesty's own person is in so disorderly a manner pressed upon'.[70] The mariners had sought to present their grievances, but, lacking deference and ignoring channels, they violated the rules of the game.

Similarly rebuffed were the Derbyshire lead miners, angered by leases and exactions, who sought to petition King Charles on his progress in 1634. Led by Raphe Oldfield, a veteran agitator from Litton, and his son-in-law William Bagshawe of Tideswell, 400 Peak District miners congregated to take their case to the king. The miners hoped to find his majesty at Welbeck, where he lodged with the Earl of Newcastle, or perhaps to intercept him at Chesterfield as the progress journeyed south. It is testimony to the visibility of the king that countrymen knew his general whereabouts. On 30 July 1634 Sir John Coke warned Newcastle that 'a great multitude of miners assemble themselves at Baslow with purpose to come tomorrow morning to your house to present a mutinous petition, which is not sufferable in a well-ordered state'. The king authorized Newcastle to assemble the trained bands to suppress the miners' march and to 'imprison the chief authors thereof'. The climax came on 4 August when, despite the arrest of Oldfield and Bagshawe, a 'hurly burly' of miners followed the king to Nottingham but failed to gain an audience. Whatever the justice of their cause, the tumultuous manner of their petitioning prevented its hearing. The leaders remained in gaol until October, when the Countess of Devonshire at Chatsworth secured their release.[71]

Another attempt at collective petitioning failed in 1638, when Cambridgeshire fenmen sought to gain the king's attention while he was hunting at Newmarket during Lent. Protesting the work of the drainers, the labourer Edward Powell persuaded the town crier of Ely to call on neighbours 'to go to the king with a petition about their fens, for the losing of the fens would be the losing of their livelihoods'. He also claimed to have 'ordinary access and speech with the king', saying that on one occasion King Charles 'leaned on his shoulder and wept when he heard his relation'.

Persuaded by this fantasy, about sixty men with cudgels assembled in the market place, ready to march to Newmarket, and refused a justice's request to disperse. Powell told the magistrate John Goodrick: 'I will complain of you to the king, for the king my master bade me tell him of any that hinder me in my petitioning of him, and you now hinder me and the king shall know it.' He warned another justice of the peace 'that if the king did not grant their petition it would cause a great deal of blood to be spilt'. There is no evidence that the fenmen's petition reached the king, through Powell persisted in believing that his majesty would act upon it. Arrested and imprisoned later in 1638, the petitioner was last heard insisting 'he would obey God and the king and no man else, for, he said, we are all but subjects'.[72]

Other collective petitioners who failed in their objectives included the London innkeepers, who 'went to court to petition the king, but were committed to prison for their pains',[73] and the Norwich townsmen who petitioned on behalf of 'irregular ministers'.[74] When sixty parishioners of St Matthew, Friday Street, subscribed a petition for mercy towards Henry Burton, imprisoned for seditious libel, 'two of them brought it, who were committed for their pains'.[75] The authorities repeatedly decried such petitioning as 'turbulent', 'tumultuous', 'mutinous', and 'disorderly'—key words in the Caroline political vocabulary.

Also unsuccessful were the gentry of Yorkshire who petitioned King Charles in an 'unusual' manner in the summer of 1640 against 'the insolency of the soldiers' who had come north to fight the Scots. As the Earl of Strafford told the Yorkshire magistrate Sir Edward Osborne,

> the petition was much misliked of all, as well for the matter as the way of expression, and held to be unusual, in such numbers and such high terms, to go immediately to the king himself, passing by as ciphers not only the Lord Lieutenant but my lords of the Council also, both which we conceive should [have] been first acquainted therewith.[76]

Carrying another Yorkshire petition two years later, also ignoring normal protocol, Sir Thomas Fairfax got as close to King Charles as the pommel of his saddle before being forcefully pushed aside.[77] Scandalous importunity might be expected of mariners and miners, and even of city puritans, but gentlemen were supposed to know better. The organizers of loyal petitions in favour of episcopacy in the early 1640s took pains to declare their own social respectability and the propriety of their proceedings, compared to the insolence and inferiority of their opponents.[78] Many of these mass petitions that preceded the civil war were addressed to parliament, when the 'misfortune' of the times 'made the king in as strait a condition as any of his people'. There was little to be gained from petitioning such a monarch, 'who hath now little in his power to grant them'.[79]

Urgent Messages

A series of ingenious and determined subjects sought ways to penetrate the veil to gain the king's attention. Most of them failed miserably, though few so spectacularly as Lucy Martin with her stone-wrapped scribal message. These were people who took seriously the rhetoric about the king's loving subjects, and believed themselves obliged to give him counsel. Some of them imagined 'the foundations of the earth out of order', and feared that God had turned against England as he formerly spurned the ancient Jews.[80] Others warned of plots against the king. Most wanted King Charles's 'malignant' advisors rooted out, and an end to 'the Achans that trouble our Israel', especially idolatry, Arminianism, and the harbouring of a Catholic queen.[81] Some of these would-be confidants were deeply disturbed individuals, who confused the nation's troubles with their own. They included the Dorset patriot Thomas Jarvis, the Islington beer-brewer Robert Triplet, the veteran soldier Andrew Humfrey, the puritan gentleman John Spencer, the conspiracy-theorist Thomas Harrison, and the Bristol widow Grace Carey. Their names and stories are invisible in most histories of this period, but they too, in their way, were 'people who count'.

Hardly a year went by without some concerned subject warning that 'the king had need look about him', or offering information on impending plots. Several informants attempted to bring their message directly to the king, though with no more success than importunate petitioners. When a Captain Walker heard early in 1626 'that the king should not live to be crowned', he got no further than Secretary Conway, who dismissed the report as wind and noise.[82] When a Captain Tendring learned in 1628 of 'a far more villainous, mischievous, treacherous plot... than the papist powder treason', he sought to report it through the House of Commons.[83] Others told of 'traitorous passages against the king's person and state', [84] rumours that 'the king may be made away',[85] or 'desperate and seditious speeches... against his majesty's sacred person'.[86] None of these claims amounted to much, and King Charles was never in danger, though twice in the 1630s he was menaced by madmen who sought his death. In September 1636 Rochester Carr, the lunatic son of a baronet, 'broke loose' from his keepers in Lincolnshire 'and said in the audience of many people that he would go to the court... only to kill the king, and then he would marry the queen. The people knocked him down for these speeches.'[87] Early the following year a London cobbler, Morris Dunn, startled drinkers at an alehouse by saying: 'I came to kill the king, but he is so fast locked up that I cannot come at him.' Thwarted by royal security, this would-be assassin had spent a spell in Bedlam, though was said to be 'pretty well in his wits ever since'.[88]

In January 1627 Thomas Jarvis of Lyme, Dorset, sought audience with King Charles, 'that your princely wisdom may see the thing that I so earnestly seek after'. He addressed the king by letter, hoping to set up an appointment. Claiming to speak for 'many hundred thousands', and with 'no aim to my own ends or particular gain', Jarvis offered to explain to his majesty what 'causeth God to be angry with us'. Without being specific he claimed, 'there is an offence given... which maketh the whole kingdom to mourn, lament and bewail'. Only face to face with the king would he reveal that 'the remedy is very easy if it please you to hearken unto it, according to your desire... In all humility I do desire to be examined by yourself, or by the Duke in your hearing.' Jarvis stressed his high regard for the king—'such a blessing... as all the outward treasure of the kingdom is not to be compared'—but neither flattery nor zealotry secured him access. The 'offence' which so agitated him was most likely the religion of the queen.[89]

Another well-meaning commoner, the Islington beer-brewer Robert Triplet, attempted to advise the king two years later. In January 1629 Triplet's 'dutiful loyal heart' moved him, like Thomas Jarvis, to write a letter to his 'most gracious sovereign'. The king, he explained, was 'in my esteem like God, who is readier to reward small deserts than to punish great offences... No people in the world hath more cause to give God thanks for a religious wise king than we have.' Nonetheless, there remained 'black clouds... threatening great afflictions if not total destruction to us all' if the protestant religion was not made secure. These clouds included 'the seminary priests and Jesuits which do now much more abound in England... plotters of all dangerous treasons against your state and kingdoms' stirred up by 'that cruel bloody church of Rome', and fear that 'a toleration of that religion' was forthcoming. 'I beseech your highness give me leave to tell you, this fear did cause the hearts of your people to decline as fast from you as from the Duke.'

'I do most humbly beseech your majesty,' implored Triplet, to find

> accord with the great wise general council of your kingdom, the parliament . . . I do most humbly beseech your highness to give me leave to put you in mind . . . there is nothing in this world that can be more dangerous to your sacred majesty for the hindering the blessings of God and the love of your people than your disagreeing with them. Now by your most gracious leave [he continued], I will give your sacred majesty a true and honest reason wherefore I have presumed to trouble your highness so much: I have had a persuasion in my heart that such noble personages that attend your highness daily and do live in great honour and highly in your majesty's favour . . . do not speak so plainly as I have presumed to do, lest they should fall in your highness's displeasure.

The humble brewer, by contrast, desired only 'to serve your sacred majesty with all faithfulness', and cared not 'if my life should be lost for the honour of God, the safety of my king, and the good of my country'. But, having gained the king's attention with such altruistic assertions, Triplet could not miss the opportunity to ask that his son Thomas, an Oxford student, might find preferment.[90]

In case this rambling petition failed to move the king, Robert Triplet followed it with another letter mentioning 'some things that highly concern your majesty to take into your best consideration'. He urged the king 'to discord not with your parliament, for if you do you will lose the hearts both of peers and people'. Next, he did 'most humbly beseech' his majesty to take care 'for the maintaining and preserving of the protestant religion'. Third, he warned that any countenancing of 'the Romish religion' would 'marvelously decline the people's hearts from you'—a prescient if presumptuous prognostication. Then came recommendations for the conversion of the queen to protestantism, for 'none but sound protestants' to serve on the Privy Council, and for the advancement of Sir Edward Coke, 'as good a commonwealth man as any you have in all your kingdoms'. Triplet signed himself, 'your majesty's loyal loving subject', and surely believed he had done good service. The letter never reached its target, however, but was intercepted by William Laud.[91] Similar concerns surfaced in an anonymous libel that circulated a few months later, addressing King Charles as 'king, or rather no king, for thou has lost the hearts of thy subjects', and urging him to account for his rule before it was too late.[92]

Andrew Humfrey, a former soldier from the London suburbs, was another well-intentioned subject who believed that his 'dread sovereign' should listen to him. In July 1633 he addressed a rambling four-page letter to King Charles, signing himself 'your highness's poor but faithful servant, to command in the lord'. The letter related a series of visions and was peppered with references to biblical verses about 'weeping and gnashing of teeth' and God's curse on the man 'whose heart departeth from the lord'. Humfrey tried to deliver it at court on the day following the king's return from Scotland, but without success.[93]

Andrew Humfrey was a prolific visionary who wanted to serve his king. He dreamed of arduous travel amid difficult ways, steep hills, and flooded pits, a veritable slough of despond, through which he was escorted by a mysterious man in grey. In one of these visions his guide showed him the king, 'preparing a place for thee', and explained, 'that is the king that looks upon thee'. In another he told him of 'a man murdered not long since, go tell the king of it'. In a third striking vision Humfrey witnessed 'the queen with the king, hand in hand', and the man in grey instructed him 'to pour wine and pledge a health with the king'. The king looked favourably upon this offer of fellowship and joined him in the pledge, but the queen, significantly, refused the cup, which alluded to holy communion as well as to health-drinking. Humphrey entreated God, 'to remember our noble queen, to be beloved, that it might please him to bring her straight to believe in his holy gospel', and prayed long and hard 'to keep her highness out of hell'.

There is no evidence that this letter reached the king, but the royal secretary Sir John Coke filed it with others of a similar nature that Humfrey had sent in recent years.[94] His visions extended back to the time of his military service in the 1620s, and featured raging bulls, headless bodies, 'the darkening of the sun, and the moon turned into blood' (as in Revelation 6:12). One vision in August 1632 showed Humfrey himself burning at the stake 'for the defence of the gospel'. In September he reported 'a bustling in my ears of altars that shall be set up in the churches of England . . . if not looked to in time, it will bring a leprosy . . . stifle it, lest it grows against the king's will' (this a full year before the development of the Caroline altar policy). Later in September 1633 he saw the late Gustavus Adolphus alive and ready 'to beat down Babylon', ten months after the Swedish king's death at Lützen. Convinced of the significance of these visions, Humfrey was determined to share them with his sovereign. He was especially adamant that the queen 'should forsake her Romish religion'.

One vision showed Humfrey King Charles in a chariot, his face shining like the sun, 'who beckoned with his right hand to me to come to him'. In this dream, though sadly not in reality, the king rewarded Humfrey with money and assured him: 'I should be righted of all my wrongs.' Other visions addressed the material state of the kingdom, warning in August 1632 of 'fearful dearth' to come:

> The mealman, the merchant, and the clown,
> Strives to pull our state down,
> And then they may run clean out of town,
> And buy themselves a velvet gown.

Another vision warned of social upheaval, in which 'Englishmen of the poorest sort of tradesmen, some butchers, smiths, tailors, shoemakers, masons, plasterers, sawyers . . . join hand in hand with the enemy, and say they will not obey no king nor magistrates, they say they will not be starved'.

Andrew Humfrey's visions caused him trouble with his family and with secular and religious authorities. He hoped to tell the king of the 'wrongs that I sustain of my brother, sister and kindred', and also about his treatment, 'more spitefully than the Turks would have done', by officers of the bishop of London. With this in mind, he prayed God 'to preserve our king from all traitors' conspiracies' and to 'guide his majesty's honourable Privy Council in the right way'. Exasperated authorities joined with Humfrey's kinsmen to urge him 'to declare no more visions', but he was unstoppable: 'come life or come death, I will never stay my hand from writing nor my tongue from speaking.' But he never penetrated the royal screen or came close to bringing his message to King Charles. At Laud's instigation, Humfrey spent two nights in prison in March 1633 and several months more in 1634 for his impertinence in 'carrying strange news to the king'.[95]

Even more determined to share her visions was the aristocratic Lady Eleanor Davies (also known as Eleanor Douglas), whose fame as a mad but persistent prophet stretched from the 1620s to the 1640s.[96] In February 1635 Lady Eleanor sent a letter to King Charles to tell him 'that an angel from heaven had told her that the following Sunday all London should be burnt'.[97] Only her rank and connections secured her continuing access to privileged places.

More humble subjects who felt impelled to communicate with his majesty included a poor printer named Green who entered the court at St James in November 1633, 'with a great sword by his side, swearing the king should do him justice'. He was quickly committed to Newgate prison.[98] The Cambridge painter James Priest announced in 1635 that the king was 'overruled by his servants, a company of knaves', and that he could advise him better, but he was too drunk to undertake any action.[99] The Northamptonshire petty chapman John Lewes determined in 1636 'that he would go to the king himself, and that he would have the Council make better laws than have been, only by God's laws', but he made little progress. The cleric Robert Sibthorpe described Lewes as a 'crack-brained' puritan, 'very schismatically affected'.[100] Dozens of reports survive of subjects like these who bragged of their intentions to counsel or confront the king. Most made it no further than the alehouse door, because it was easier to talk than to walk to London.

One such aspirant, the projector Francis Harris, lived in hope of 'favour from the king, that he expected any day to be sent for unto his majesty to speak with him in person', so he bragged in 1638. But Harris's chance of a royal audience was crushed when word leaked out of his talk in the Bowling Green tavern at Westminster, that the king was overruled by archbishop Laud: 'If the king were not a fool it would not be so. But when the land is governed by a fool or a child it must always groan under the burden of oppression.' Instead of discoursing with the king, Harris found himself investigated for seditious speech.[101]

The godly gentleman John Spencer was yet another impassioned subject who tried to tender 'divers petitions of high concernment and great consequence' to his majesty. On one occasion Spencer took exception to the movement of royal wagons on a Sunday, and instructed his sovereign: 'Good King Charles, remember to keep holy the sabbath.' On another he objected to 'the book for recreations' (discussed in Chapter 8) and enjoined, 'good King Charles for evermore let it rest'. Spencer petitioned again in 1639 when the king was going towards Scotland: 'I beseech your highness, give your poor subject leave to entreat you that you would not adventure yourself in the day of battle . . . Let the new Scottish prayer book, and the book for . . . recreation upon the Lord's day, be both thrown over the Scottish bank.' He requested 'that your highness would be graciously pleased to call a parliament' and turn England's armies 'towards the Palatinate, to settle your royal sister in her inheritance . . . Consider what I say and do it, and the lord will bring it to pass.' These were policy interventions, not petitions of grace, and more than once they earned their author a night in prison for disorderly demanding access.[102] Uninhibited by accusations of madness, Spencer had his petitions printed as soon as circumstances allowed (although his printer botched the imprint making '1641' '1461').[103]

The Northamptonshire cleric Thomas Harrison also had advice for his majesty, but found barriers in his path when he tried to penetrate the court. He informed Lord Treasurer Juxon in 1639 that he had 'some things to signify unto his majesty, wherewith I think fitting he should first be made acquainted'. When this approach was rebuffed, he tried again through Secretary Windebank, and was told to summarize his concerns in writing. Harrison, however, wanted nothing less than a private audience with King Charles. 'Knew I any command either divine or human to the contrary,' he explained, 'I should fear the fate of Uzzah for putting his hand to the shaking Ark, a thing which God has expressly prohibited; but if I know none, then I see not wherefore the forwardness of a subject, very loyal and not very foolish . . . should be repressed.' He would rather 'be thought ridiculous', he said, than to hold back a matter that his conscience told him was necessary. Justifying his intrusion into *arcana imperii*, Harrison claimed to have secret information about 'a most horrible conspiracy, plotted here in England, against the king and state'. He sought permission 'to lay myself at your majesty's foot stool' to inform his majesty directly of 'many matters' distressing the kingdom. The king, however, was well screened from such subjects, and Harrison was denied his audience.[104]

More persistent was Grace Cary, the widow of a Bristol brewer, who tried to tell King Charles of her 'strange and wonderful visions, and prophetical revelations, concerning these tragical sinful times'. In 1644 she helped to compile a memoir of her efforts, which circulated in manuscript and was published two years later as *Vox Coeli to England, or, Englands Forewarning from Heaven*. Here she describes how she 'humbly and zealously solicited his majesty, with great travail and expense, to give her an audience, which could not be obtained'. The celebrity aristocratic visionary Eleanor Davis acknowledged Grace Cary as 'a prophetess' in a side-note to her publication *Given to the Elector Prince Charles of the Rhyne* (1648 and 1651).[105]

Widow Cary's career as a petitioner and prophet began at Usk, Monmouthshire, where, immersed in prayer and Bible study, she experienced in 1639 'a most holy rapture'. This followed a period of spiritual temptation, in which she wrestled with 'popish superstition' and may have contemplated conversion to Catholicism. She heard 'hideous shrieks and outcries of the people oppressed', and a voice repeating the incantation, 'treason and death, treason, treason, death, death', which she interpreted as 'a divine and heavenly vision'. Her memoir relates how 'she was in an extraordinary way made sensible of those combustions and disasters which were to befall . . . this sinful nation'. Several more weeks of 'fasting and prayer' brought 'the appearance of glorious shining lights, accompanied with vehement rushing wind', and then the apparition of 'the perfect shape of a king's head and face without a body . . . and the crown was all bloody in the circle round about'. (This, remarkably, was a decade before the Regicide.) In the 'confused clamour' that accompanied this vision, Grace Cary heard 'loud and lamentable cries of God's people persecuted, as she thought, both beyond seas and on this side', including the words 'cruel queen' and 'the greatest bishop in the church of England . . . the enemy of God'.

On hearing these voices, Grace Cary felt impelled to act. 'She was earnestly commanded, by a celestial voice, to notify all these things to the king's majesty.' Frightened and cautious, as a dutiful and guilt-ridden woman, she sought counsel from 'certain godly divines at Bristol'. But 'neither their prayers nor her own could prevail with the Lord to spare her from this service'. She could not disobey 'that heavenly voice . . . though her brethren and kindred, and her own inclination and desire strongly dissuaded her'. God had vouchsafed his vision to a humble messenger, and there was no turning back. She would say, like the woman of Tekoah in 2 Samuel 14: 'I will now speak unto the king; it may be that the king will perform the request of his handmaid.'

Attempting 'to notify all these things to his majesty', Grace Cary travelled to London, where 'she was strongly pushed on within herself to address herself to the court, which was then at Whitehall; whither being come, she earnestly pressed in a petitionary way to present to his majesty the effect of what she had heard and seen'. Like others before her with similar urgent business, Grace Cary found access to his majesty to be restricted. Despite every effort to reach King Charles, she 'soon found herself neglected, and her petition slighted'. She would not give up, however, because she felt 'a strong call from God both inwardly and outwardly to follow the king, whithersoever he went, saying to her, "the king, the king; the king and kingdom is in danger of utter ruin and desolation"'. Grace Cary's message, it seemed, was comparable to that of other visionaries who felt compelled to warn King Charles of impending doom.

Petitioners needed patrons to open doors and help clear hurdles, and Grace Cary found one in the Marquess of Hamilton (spelled 'Hambleton' in this and other contemporary accounts). Hamilton, prime Gentleman of the Bedchamber and Master of the Horse, a nobleman with Scottish royal blood, had close ties to King Charles extending back to their journey into Spain in 1623. Hamilton's young wife Mary, one of the queen's ladies of the bedchamber, had died in 1638, and widow Cary may have given the widower some comfort. As commissioner to the kirk and commander of the army against Scotland in 1639, Hamilton had his plate full, but he evidently agreed to present Grace Cary to King Charles. 'By her importunity,' she writes, and with help from the marquess, 'she was admitted at Richmond to his majesty's presence, who graciously received her petition'. Remarkably, she continues, King Charles indicated 'that he would be pleased to hear her at large declare her errand by word of mouth'.

Grace Cary must have been extraordinarily persuasive and well turned out to achieve such success at court. She had invested everything in this mission, which seemed to be about to bear fruit. She describes a touching tableau in which King Charles held one of her hands and the Marquess of Hamilton the other, when 'the king asked her for her writing; which she having presented, and his majesty slightly viewed over, he demanded if it were her own hand; and she confessing that it was, he then viewed it better. But his majesty being then to take horse, rendered her the said petition, saying, he thought she meant well and was a good woman.' The effect was a condescending brush-off, rather than engagement with the perils of the kingdom, but Grace Cary was not to be deterred. She explained to solicitous courtiers that 'she came to London on her own charges, and had wherewith to serve her occasions, her coming to court having had no other end but the public good of king, church and state, to her great trouble and charge'. Her godly vision still drove her, and 'she was continually pressed by God's hand upon her to follow his majesty from court to court'.

She turned up at York in the autumn of 1640 while King Charles was enmeshed in the Scottish crisis. It was at York on 9 September that an exasperated Charles I cried out to assembled nobles: 'I see ye are all so frighted ye can resolve on nothing.'[106] As *Vox Coeli* recalls, 'there appeared a black cloud over the place where his majesty stood (the Scots had then taken Newcastle)'. Grace Cary would have been a familiar figure on the fringe of court circles, following the king, and there at York 'she enforced her former suit, humbly petitioning him to hear her speak, but without success'. 'Being still urged to solicit his majesty, at last by God's providence [and perhaps more help from Hamilton] she found another opportunity, and falling on her knees before him in the presence chamber, most humbly besought him to hear her relation, which he then utterly refused.' The message remained undelivered, despite all efforts, and God now decided that his handmaiden had done enough and released her to return to London.

In the years that followed, as England was engulfed by greater troubles, Grace Cary revealed what she would have said if King Charles 'had been pleased to give her audience'. She set this forth in her manuscript of 1644, printed in 1646, so it may have been tinged by hindsight. The substance, however, accords with other concerns of the Caroline era. If she could have bearded King Charles, Grace Cary would have urged him, first, 'to apply himself to the finding out of the great plots and treacheries of papists and their confederates, prelates and idol-shepherds, and innovators in religion; wicked and evil counsellors, state-idolizers, or rather self-seekers and [in] novators in the commonwealth', and to suppress 'all idolatry, superstition and profanity, and whatsoever was against sound doctrine, the power of godliness, and the well and liberty of the subjects'. With this in hand she would ask, secondly, 'that God's faithful ministers and servants . . . might have their freedom and liberty'. Thirdly, and audaciously, she would have pressed the king 'with all his might to set himself to use all good means that might be endeavoured for the queen's conversion . . . without which, she was given to understand of the great hazard and trouble, yea, and utter ruin both to king and kingdom'. The message echoes Lucy Martin's of a generation earlier, though without goodwife Martin's sexual disturbance. Grace Cary's turmoil was not over, however, for 'agonies of spirit' redirected her 'to attend the parliament as before she had done the king', petitioning for 'reformation both of church and state' and for constant war against 'idolatry, superstition, profanity, faction, godless-state policy . . . heresy [and] schism'. She was originally reluctant to publish her memoir, so she says, lest 'coming to the view of the meaner sort of vulgar people, by slanderous mouths it might somewhat eclipse the truth hereof', but by 1646 it was on the book stalls and King Charles had become a prisoner.[107]

Warning Libels

A perennial popular fantasy held that the king was misinformed, that his courtiers, wife, and counsellors misled him, and that the world would be better if his highness learned certain truths. It was, then, an act of patriotism, a duty of subjecthood, even a religious obligation, to open the king's eyes. The fantasy continued that the king would reward those who penetrated the screen that surrounded him, and would smile on such bringers of knowledge. The unpaid sailors, who so upset the king in 1630, believed they had to tell him something he did not know. So too did the fenland protesters and individual petitioners who assumed that 'the king knows not of it', for otherwise he would uphold their cause.[108] Similar notions drove critics of the Book of Sports in 1633, who wondered 'if the declaration be his majesty's', and opponents of 'the king's proceedings with Scotland' in 1640 who declared, 'what a shame it was that our king should be so misinformed'.[109]

Determined to counsel the king, but with no forum available through parliament or the press, literate Jeremiahs resorted to 'libels' or anonymous letters. One such writer in 1638 requested a private audience with King Charles:

> Most gracious king, If your majesty will be pleased to hear me speak unto you, I shall within the space of half a quarter of an hour discover the best matter that was ever presented to your highness or any your predecessors, wherein through God's assistance you shall be most happy, and eased of much grievances. I beseech your highness keep it secret, for it is one of the secrets of God, revealed but to very few, and concerneth no other man.

Tantalizing though this was, the anonymous author remained unsummoned, his secret unrevealed.[110]

Another would-be counsellor wrote that

> since the last parliament the kingdom has languished . . . Few of our nobility dare open their mouths . . . The ancient happy government by parliament is altogether despised . . . It is the exchange where all the kingdom's grievances meet, and . . . a sovereign remedy for all enormities: schismatical bishops, corrupt judges, profuse officers, oppression, exacting, projecting, monopolising, and the like, would be easily found and amended. In the general current of our history the state of England has succeeded well when the hearts of the king and subjects have accorded, and the contrary when they have not.

King Charles, this writer continued, 'cannot choose but know these things; but the misfortunes of princes hath ever been to have more flatterers than honest men near them, which hath cost them dear'. The letter was found at Lincoln's Inn in November 1638, and secretary Windebank was urged to 'show it to his majesty'.[111]

A scribal address to King Charles, found in the Crown Inn at Ware, Hertfordshire, in March 1639, purported to represent the king's 'poor yet true and loyal subjects' who feared 'the overthrow of the land'. The writers warned the king against going to war with Scotland, partly because they thought his policies wrong, but also because they feared that the government would be left in the hands of 'wicked men' who would further their 'devilish plot'. (Archbishop Laud was to lead the Council in London while the king was away on campaign.) Already, they claimed, 'God's ordinances are taken away, and our ministers are taken away or their mouths be stopped, and our souls are like to be starved . . . Now we look for our lives and posterity and all to be a prey . . . as soon as your highness is gone to Scotland.' Their only hope was that God would give King Charles 'a discerning spirit' to take this 'danger' into his 'gracious consideration'. The libel went to the heart of *arcana imperii*; it was briefly investigated and then contemptuously ignored.[112]

Yet another rambling letter appeared at court early in 1640, addressed to King Charles directly. Secretary Coke sought in vain to discover the author. The letter urged his majesty: 'Sir, for God's cause and your own, step upon the vantage ground of truth and reason, and there view the present state of affairs.' The anonymous author warned the king of his exposure 'both to present disesteem and to future danger' by neutrality in

> the great work in Germany . . . Your friends grow jealous of you, dare not communicate counsel or designs with you, well knowing to whose view they shall come, and by what affection they shall be both judged and directed . . . Behold your subjects at home, unhappily distracted, full of fear, full of grief, to see you prefer crafty and artificial counsel before that of glory and safety, to see you undervalued abroad, misguided and ill advised at home, to see you reduced to that narrow condition that you are no more fearful to your enemies than comfortable to your friends.

The king was in thrall to evil advisors, the writer continued, 'men addicted to Rome or obliged to Spain', who sustained 'the opinion of the breach between you and your people'.[113]

The letter author continued the prophetic tradition of calling for the blindness of the king to be healed. But the hectoring tone, subversive manner, and disorderly delivery was no way to influence public policy. Nobody talked to King Charles with such candour, except perhaps his wife. If words like these came to the king's attention, they would only confirm his belief that 'turbulent and ill-affected spirits' with 'mischievous' and 'malevolent' designs posed perennial challenges to his rule.[114]

One final messenger was the London ironmonger Henry Walker, an enterprising self-publisher, who used projectile tactics like those of Lucy Martin to communicate with King Charles. In January 1642, amid the turmoil following the attempt to arrest five members of parliament,

> Walker stood watching the king's coming by amongst the drapers in Paul's churchyard, and having one of his pamphlets in his hand meaning to have delivered it to his majesty . . . could not come at him by reason of the press of people, insomuch as Walker (most saucily and impudently) threw it over the folks heads into his majesty's coach.

Based on the verse from Kings, 'to your tents oh Israel', the home-made pamphlet commended the deposition of King Rehoboam. No copy is known to survive.[115] King Charles himself was said to be rattled by 'those many scandalous pamphlets and printed papers which are scattered with such great license', though it remained beneath his 'royal dignity' to take note of them.[116] It was part of the tumult that persuaded him to abandon London.

An Affable King

King Charles insisted on his dignity and distance, but these may have lessened in the forced familiarity of military campaigning. Camp conditions may have weakened normal protocols of access and address. How else can we account for the extraordinary ease with which Sir Thomas Wilford is said to have addressed the king in May 1639?

King Charles had gone north again to campaign against the Scots, and along the way, court writers recorded, 'the common people gave him and his followers most zealous blessing for his and their happy success in their journey'.[117] With the king encamped near Newcastle, a letter in State Papers reports:

> there came to court one Sir Thomas Wilford of Kent, of free speech and courtesy, and vented what came next to hand. He came to the king in his presence and told him, in the hearing of divers of his servants, and myself among the rest, that he was come out of Kent, a long and chargeable journey, and withal told him how many men and horses he had brought him, and said, I pray God send us well to do in this business. But, said he, I like not the beginning. The king asked him why. He replied, because you go the wrong way to work. The king smiled and asked him which was the right way. He answered, if you think to make a war with your own purse you deceive yourself, the only way to prosper is to go back and call a parliament, and so should we have monies enough and do your business handsomely.

This was a remarkable speech of truth to power, but only the beginning.

> The king replied, there were fools in the last parliament. True, said Sir Thomas, but there were wise men too, and if you had let them alone the wise men would have been too hard for the fools. For there was myself for Dover, and shall be again whensover you call a parliament, except your majesty and the Earl of Suffolk hinder, which I think your majesty will not do. The Duke of Lennox stepped up and said, how can you have a parliament, the king being absent? No matter, said Sir Thomas, for the king let him be where he list, we shall do our business well enough without him. At last Sir Thomas turned to the king and said, your wife's father Henry IV is indebted to my father 16,000 pounds for service in the French wars, when the crown stood tottering on his head. The king made answer, I will never pay penny of any of that debt whilst I live. I believe it, said Wilford, for you have no money, nor came I now to demand it. He concluded his discourse with craving pardon for burning his colours. The king demanded him why he did so. He answered, he had trained ten hundred men for his majesty's service, and taught them their lessons so well that sixty of them were worthy to be generals and commanders of armies. But when he saw that the Deputy Lieutenants had sent the king a company of rogues, not good enough to be hanged, he could do no less than sacrifice his colours for anger, to see the king so served. The king said he was sorry to hear that. Sir Thomas answered that he had no reason to be sorry, for, he said, the colours cost you nothing, I paid for them myself.[118]

This report makes Charles I appear open and accessible, capable of banter and accepting of criticism, in casual conversation with an earnest subject in the company of leading advisors. It is hardly the Charles known to history, though history may have got him wrong. It reads more like Jack of Newbury with Henry VIII, more a fantasy of bluff address than a plausible interaction of subject and monarch. Subjects are not known to have spoken so freely with King Charles, even in relaxed conditions. No one, surely, spoke to him of the queen as 'your wife'. Not even the Duke of Buckingham told Charles I to his face that he was deceived or wrong. Given that the report is anonymous, unattributed, and that no Wilford is known from the parliament of 1628–9, we might well exercise caution. Though some historians accept Wilford's conversation with the king as fellow-well-met, and proof of the king's accessibility, others are sceptical and find it somewhat coloured.[119]

There was, however, a Sir Thomas Wilsford (an acceptable alternative spelling) who was a member of parliament for Canterbury in 1625 (though not for Dover in 1629), a Justice of the Peace until 1637, who died at Ileden, Kent, in 1646. We have no evidence of his contribution to the Bishops' Wars, and no corroboration of any meeting with the king, but he certainly existed. He was the son of another Sir Thomas Wilsford, who had fought in France and Flanders under Queen Elizabeth, had accompanied an embassy to France in 1598, and who may well have assisted the future Henry IV. Wilford's tongue caused him trouble in 1624 when, 'transported by choler into words not seemly', he insulted the mayor of Dover. In May 1640, a year after the alleged incident at Newcastle, Sir Thomas Wilsford wrote from his home in Kent to his neighbour Henry Oxinden, advising that soldiers not 'surrender their arms, as they did last year, and so lose them as they did; but if they be wise they will keep them to defend the king and kingdom against foreign enemies and the popish faction which grows too insolent'. He makes one more appearance in the Oxinden letters: when the queen mother, Marie de Medici, was leaving England in 1641, 'she made some stay against Sir Thomas Wilsford's . . . woods where she had some fruit . . . presented to her'.[120] The evidence points to Wilsford's outspokenness, his interest in military matters, and his apparent favour with the French, but questions remain about his moment of intimacy with the king.

Other evidence, however, suggests that campaign conditions loosened court protocols and made King Charles a popular warrior monarch. A newsletter from Newcastle reported in May 1639 that the king planned to march to Berwick, 'lying in the tents with his army all the way'. The enthusiastic courtier Lord Dungarvon wrote on 29 May that 'the king daily visits the camp, where his affability to the soldiers gains their hearts, for he dines among them, and the other day marched eight miles with the foot, and distributed his own dinner among the soldiers . . . He is truly infinitely careful of their accommodation, and grows daily expert in martial discipline.' It may have been the making of him. Less than a week later another correspondent of the Earl of Cork related how just outside Berwick the king 'lies every night in his pavilion, so the gentlemen pensioners watch every night about his tent on horseback'.[121] If everything had turned out differently, like Henry V at Agincourt, we might be recalling 'a little touch of Charlie in the night'.[122]

The Charles I in all these encounters was the subject of his subjects' aspirations. Scores of petitioners and would-be counsellors sought the king's attention and hoped to make him listen. The kingship they imagined was more pastoral than sacred, more accessible than remote, a sad misreading of Caroline style. Their efforts say more about their fears or ambitions than about the actions of the king. But before we dismiss such people as delusional, and return them to obscurity, we should consider both their medium and their message. Few had ill will towards King Charles, and most asserted loyalty and affection. Possessed by visions, intelligence, or insights for the benefit of the kingdom, as well as troubles of their own, they considered themselves dutiful in approaching his majesty and giving him advice. Even the most disorderly petitions had deferential underpinnings. Referring to the nation's sins and God's anger, a catholic queen, a violated sabbath, the neglected Palatinate, rebellious Scotland, and the eclipse of parliament, their talking points matched those of more reputable critics using more conventional modes of address. Gentle and clerical patriots expressed concerns comparable to the visionary petitioners, though usually with more polished exposition. Importunate petitioners also echoed streams of popular opinion expressed in libels and alehouse chatter, the voices of 'the worser sort' of subjects.

As these aspirants to the king's ear discovered, the conduit to the crown was restricted, the perimeter of power well policed. A huge gulf separated King Charles from his common subjects, though perhaps no wider than in other royal regimes. Charles I may have been exceptionally protective of his honour, and more fastidious than most monarchs, but the formalities of access were standard fare. The king, indeed, travelled widely, and made himself available to persons of power, but approaches to his person were necessarily limited. There was, however, a price to pay for dignity and distance. Petitioners opened windows to concerns that a king might profitably consider, but Charles I preferred to keep them closed.

7

The King's Religion and the People's Church

Statute law, church law, canons, and custom demanded that the people of England adhere to uniform religious beliefs and practices. Everyone belonged within the established Church of England, and none was excused its services and rituals. From birth to death, baptism to burial, and throughout the rhythms of the Christian year, the church took charge of belief and spiritual instruction, worship, religious fellowship, and the certainties of salvation. Each parish marked a community, which constituted a congregation, and only deviants, recusants, and transient outsiders lived separate from its embrace. The king was supreme governor of this national church, at the head of a hierarchy from archbishops and bishops to parish clergy and laity. God was in his heaven, but all was not right with the world.

Charles I ruled over a divided religious culture, in which pulpits and parishes marked the embattled front line. The fractures grew deeper as his reign progressed. The protestant Reformation of the sixteenth century was not fully digested, and certainly not settled. While some thought the early Stuart church the best of all churches, others believed that the Reformation had gone too far, or not far enough. Arguments about history, ecclesiology, theology, and churchmanship engaged academic clerics and spilled over among learned laymen. Although the Elizabethan Thirty-Nine Articles set forth core beliefs, within the reformed tradition, contention flared between followers of Calvinism, who held sway under James I, and Arminianism, which gained ascendancy under his successor.[1] Many of the older clergy, especially, espoused Calvin's theology of predestination, and thought of their parishioners as reprobate or elect, damned or saved. Only a minority, they believed, would enter the kingdom of heaven. The Yorkshire puritan John Hansley, for example, said in 1636 that those few parishioners who were 'in the state of salvation' could be enclosed 'in the compass of a ring'.[2] The mostly younger anti-Calvinists and Arminians, by contrast, believed that Christ had died for everyone, and all who were baptized could find salvation.

King Charles disapproved of contentious disputation, but the clerical order was riven with disagreement about the performance of worship, the efficacy of the sacraments, and whether the church of Rome was a true church. A small fraction of Charles I's subjects subscribed to Roman Catholicism, and a few converted to Rome in the ambience of King Charles's catholic queen. Puritans formed a grumpy leavening among both clergy and laity, and an almost invisible minority of religious extremists became sectarian separatists. The king set standards of discipline, piety, and devotion, but not everyone took their religion as seriously as their teachers and preachers intended. Though the crown and the law enjoined uniformity, the people were too unruly to be fully disciplined. This chapter examines religious behaviour as well as religious ideas from the variant perspectives of the Chapel Royal and bishop's palace, the pulpit, the parish, and the pew. It compares the king's view of the English church with the teeming opinions of his subjects. Religion mattered deeply to the people of England, but in different and divisive ways.

A Christian Monarch

Parliamentary statute, the highest law in the land, required everyone to attend their parish church on Sundays and holy days, on pain of fines and other penalties.[3] Contemporaries counted 9,244 parishes in England and Wales,[4] and ecclesiastical law obliged parishioners in each of them to pray for their king, the Defender of the Faith. The royal coat of arms hung in aisles and chancels, in spaces formerly occupied by sacred images, and ministers reminded congregants of their duties to his majesty. Heraldry, invocation, and prayer made the king symbolically present in every parish throughout the kingdom.

According to the governing *Constitutions and Canons Ecclesiastical*, collective prayers for his majesty preceded every sermon, lecture, or homily in church. Preachers were required to pray publicly for the monarch, the royal family, the king's council, the nobility, and the church, so that 'the whole commons of this realm . . . may live . . . in humble obedience to the king, and brotherly charity one to another'.[5] It was the clergy's task, explained the dean of Salisbury in 1629, to 'preach obedience to authority' and to 'pray for all men, but especially for princes, that under them we may lead a godly and quiet life'.[6] Special occasional prayers also focused specifically on King Charles and his family and augmented parishioners' political education on the anniversary of his accession on 27 March, his royal birthday on 19 November, and the anniversary of deliverance from Gunpowder Treason on 5 November—all days of obligatory church attendance. Visitation articles checked that official prayers for the king were properly conducted. Episcopal visitors cited parishes that lacked the required service books, and sanctioned parishioners who worked instead of worshipping on those days.[7] The new ecclesiastical canons of 1640 added punishment for delinquents who failed to recognize the 'blessing' of 'so benign and merciful a sovereign'.[8] The king was the protector of English protestantism, and the people prayed that he was up to the task.

As governor of the Church of England, King Charles had the power to 'visit, repress, redress, reform, order, correct, restrain and amend all such errors, heresies, abuses, offences, contempts and enormities ... to the pleasure of God and peace and unity of the realm'.[9] He appointed bishops and archbishops, and through his prerogative court of High Commission he regulated diocesan and parochial affairs. As Judge William Jones reminded the Oxford assizes in June 1627, 'the king hath absolute authority *tam in spiritualibus quam temporalibus*'.[10] No other monarch in Christendom, beside the pope, has such power in his dominions. Preaching at the Northampton assizes in 1635, Edward Reynolds identified the king as a bulwark against the 'many machinations of Satan'.[11] Few other kings had such responsibilities.

Cuius regio, eius religio ('whose realm, his religion') was a principle promulgated in reformation Germany, but it also applied in practice in early modern England. William Pavey, rector of the Lincolnshire parish of Mareham-le-Fen, taught that 'the people must be of the same religion the king is of, of whatsoever religion it is'.[12] The king set the style and controlled episcopal preferments, so that the tastes and inclinations of the ruler shaped the kingdom's religious culture. By precept and example he offered 'sweet incitements unto all his subjects to follow those most pious steps in which he walks'.[13] It was therefore vital for contemporaries to understand King Charles's personal religion, and also important for historians to gauge its character. We should be better informed than Thomas Shore, a parishioner at Horsted Parva, Sussex, who asked in 1641, when 'prayers for the king's majesty' were introduced, 'of what religion is he? I know not of what religion he is or whether he be of any.'[14]

King Charles was a protestant, reared in a Calvinist-inflected theological environment. But he was wary of puritan enthusiasts, and drawn to ceremonialist advocacy of 'the beauty of holiness'. As a young man he favoured Lancelot Andrewes's preaching on the Christian year, and soon after his accession he commanded the late bishop's sermons to be printed.[15] Charles let it be known at the outset that he 'likes well . . . such ministers as are peaceable, orderly, and conformable to the church government'.[16] It was his desire that his subjects 'demean themselves with all Christian reverence and devout obedience' while fulfilling their religious obligations.[17] The king's opinions hardened in the course of his reign, as he equated puritanism with 'refractoriness', and strict conformity with loyalty and good order. In his preface to the new ecclesiastical canons of 1640 he declared his 'princely inclination to uniformity and peace', to 'the honour of God', and to 'the tranquillity of the kingdom'.[18]

A recurrent fear, from the 1620s to the 1640s, was that Charles might draw England closer to Rome. If the pope was Anti-Christ, as some protestants believed, and Roman Catholicism the church of Babylon, any wavering of protestant watchfulness, any indication of rapprochement with Rome, was a weakening of God's true religion. The nation waited in dread as Prince Charles went to Spain in 1623 to woo the zealous catholic Infanta. What concessions were made, what promises offered, were questions of controversy for several years after. The greatest danger was that Charles himself might succumb to the lure of Catholicism, and ascend the throne with a change of heart. That is why bishops Neile, Andrewes, and Laud secretly cross-questioned Matthew Wren on the latter's return from Spain, asking 'how the Prince's heart stands to the Church of England, that when God brings him to the crown we may know what to hope for'.[19] Charles himself, in a letter supposedly written to Pope Gregory XV, declared himself 'resolved . . . to spare nothing that I have in the world, and to suffer all manner of discommodities, even to the hazarding of my estate and life', on behalf of the religion of Jesus Christ.[20]

In a remarkable 'confession of his faith' dated January 1626, thought by some scholars to be the king's own words, perhaps in his own hand, Charles set forth his religious beliefs for the benefit of European Christendom.[21] 'I am a Catholic Christian,' the writer affirmed, basing his beliefs on the Scriptures, the Apostles', Nicene, and Athanasian creeds, and the works of the early church fathers. 'Whatsoever they held unanimously to be necessary to salvation the first four hundred years after Christ, either I hold with them or I sit down in a modest silence.' There was no sign here of a Calvinist upbringing, but no truck either with Roman Catholicism. This royal 'confession' was never published, so subjects had to trust that their king shared their common theology.

King Charles, if he it is, would honour the memory of the saints, while rejecting the 'fopperies' associated with their worship. He would revere 'the blessed virgin', while considering it blasphemous to pray to her. Surely the mother of God had not 'the leisure in heaven to attend the prayers of every impertinent fellow or interpose in his business . . . towards her son', the busy king of England conjectured. As a protestant the king specifically rejected such 'new fangles' and 'forged doctrine' as purgatory, transubstantiation, the adoration of the sacraments, and the baptizing of bells. He would acknowledge the secular rights of the bishop of Rome, but not his spiritual primacy. King Charles was, without saying so, an upholder of reformed religion. But he wanted 'all Christian princes' to know that he was neither apostate nor heretical, but one whose religion was 'ancient, catholic and apostolical'.[22]

Unlike his father, an amateur theologian, King Charles was not given to religious speculation. Indeed, to the contrary, he thought it sufficient to know what the Scriptures taught 'without digging deeper into the secrets of God'. Disdaining 'them which have stained divinity by a new kind of philosophical dispute', the king declared, ''tis enough for me to call upon God through Jesus Christ'. It was enough to know 'that heaven and hell are the everlasting stations which God hath ordained for men; let us strive to arrive to the one, and shun the other'. This was an untroubled and unreflective Christianity, of the sort that some godly authors thought insufficient.[23] Convinced that people neither knew nor cared about supralapsarian predestination or the complexities of Socinianism, King Charles sought to suppress theological quarrels that distracted from uniform discipline. He frowned on strenuous argument, and would not have the 'high points' of predestination 'meddled withal or debated . . . because it was too high for the people's understanding'. 'His majesty was much displeased' when bishop John Davenant of Salisbury preached before him on the doctrine of predestination in March 1630.[24]

The king's aversion to contentious disputation appears in his proclamation of June 1626 'for the establishing of the peace and quiet of the church'. Here King Charles declares 'his utter dislike to all those who, to show the subtlety of their wits, or to please their own humours, or vent their own passions, do or shall adventure to move any new opinions, not only contrary but differing from the sound and orthodoxal grounds of the true religion, sincerely professed and happily established in the Church of England'. Clerics in particular are admonished not to raise any doubts or maintain any opinions that question official doctrine or discipline. The proclamation responded specifically to the controversy surrounding Richard Montague, whose flamboyant Arminianism raised Calvinist hackles, but it applied as well to hard-line predestinarians. It ended by inviting the king's 'good and loving subjects' to 'bless God for his majesty's pious, religious, wise, just, and gracious government'.[25] Dutiful clerics relayed the message and warned against perplexing the people 'with impertinent disputations' or examining 'those Scriptures that are obscure or dark, of ambiguous and doubtful meaning'.[26] It would have pleased the king to hear Edward Reynolds preach that peace was better than controversy, and discipline superior to pursuit of 'knotty and inextricable questions'.[27]

Charles was neither intellectually nor spiritually sophisticated, but he knew his duty and held to his beliefs. 'It is and always hath been our heart's desire to be found worthy of that title which we account the most glorious in all our crown, Defender of the Faith,' he declared after closing parliament in 1629.[28] Sir Thomas Wentworth wrote fulsomely of his royal master in December that year, 'there lives not a prince fuller of religion and virtue, God give us the grace to be truly thankful for him as we ought'.[29] Almost two decades later, on the eve of the Regicide, royalists cherished the steadfastness of 'the Lord's anointed . . . God's lieutenant', their soon-to-be martyred monarch.[30]

King Charles's religious practice included attendance at prayers twice daily, and participation in all of the Sunday and Holy Day observances of the Church of England. Commentators found him 'attentive and devout'.[31] Court preachers prepared sermons for the royal presence, many of which dwelt on the sacredness of kingship. If William Laud's royal sermons are representative of what King Charles liked to hear, they filled his ears with divine-right theory and reference to the righteousness rulers of Israel. Kings, they reminded him, did God's work on earth.[32]

Clues to the king's religious predilections come from the furnishings of his Chapel Royal and from his ecclesiastical patronage. Charles liked his services to be orderly, dignified, and disciplined, with the same luxurious serenity that he sought in his household and court. Like many of the priests he promoted, King Charles approved of auricular confession.[33] His chapel was richly furnished, as befitted both a royal palace and the house of God. Like the private chapel of any great lord, it was attended by the master's family, his friends and followers, and members of his household. Its clergy could both celebrate and promote 'the beauty of holiness', scrupulously adhering to the rubrics of the prayer book, with standing for the Creed and *Gloria patri*, kneeling for the sacrament, and bowing at the name of Jesus. Privileged visitors might attend the king on his way to service, or follow him into the closet for prayers, and then report what they saw. William Hawkins informed the Earl of Leicester that most of the bishops and clergy 'bowed low towards the altar', and on Palm Sunday 1637 'was hanged up a piece over the altar in the king's chapel, the likest to a crucifix that hath been seen there these forty years'.[34] The puritan Robert Woodford, who visited Whitehall in 1638, reported seeing the 'the four Gospels, the Acts of the Apostles, and the Apocalypse in books all set forth with pictures', which hinted, he feared, at popish idolatry.[35]

Most of the bishops Charles made and promoted were anti-Calvinist disciplinarians with high ceremonial and Arminian leanings. Though they met the king's criteria of being 'peaceable, orderly, and conformable', they could appear to others as uncharitable martinets and liturgical hard-liners.[36] With twenty-six sees to fill in England and Wales, there was room for some variation in theology, spirituality, and efficiency, but the Caroline preferments were more ideologically homogenous than those of the Jacobean era. Episcopal orthodoxy held that the bishops operated *jure divino*—empowered by divine right—making it a marker of puritanism to disagree. The king's remark at Oxford in 1631, 'that if other things were equal in preferments which he bestowed, he should respect those that were unmarried before those that were married', reflects conservative principles.[37] Though the king was orthodox and devout, anxious protestants saw signs that made them worry.

Several leading bishops had long records of prior service to King James, including George Abbot at Canterbury (d. 1633), who had been a bishop since 1609, and John Williams, who held Lincoln from 1621 to 1641. Both men served King Charles under a cloud of royal displeasure. Other Jacobean holdovers included John Thornborough at Worcester (1617–41); John Bridgeman at Chester (1619–52); and John Davenant at Salisbury (1621–41), all old-school Calvinists who adjusted uneasily to a shifting religious culture. Better rewarded by Charles I was Thomas Morton, a moderate

Calvinist but a staunch conformist, a bishop since 1616, who gained Durham in 1632; and the high ceremonialist anti-puritan Richard Neile, first brought to the bench in 1608, who served King James at Rochester, Lichfield, and Lincoln before flourishing under Charles at Durham, Winchester, and York. The unmarried William Laud, who enjoyed Neile's and Buckingham's patronage under James, fared especially well, rising from his first episcopal appointment at St David's in 1621 to become bishop of Bath and Wells in 1626, London in 1628, and then archbishop of Canterbury in 1633. Joseph Hall of Exeter congratulated Laud of London in 1631 for his 'zealous and careful vigilance over that populous world of men'.[38]

The new men, in order of first consecration, included Francis White (Carlisle 1626, Norwich 1629, Ely 1631); Joseph Hall (Exeter 1627, Norwich 1641); Richard Montague (Chichester 1628, Norwich 1638); Walter Curle (Rochester 1628, Bath and Wells 1629, Winchester 1632); Richard Corbet (Oxford 1628, Norwich 1632); Barnaby Potter (Carlisle 1629); John Bowle (Rochester 1630); William Piers (Peterborough 1630, Bath and Wells 1632); John Bancroft (Oxford 1632); George Coke (Bristol 1633, Hereford 1636); Augustine Lindsell (Peterborough 1633, Hereford 1634); William Juxon (London 1633); Francis Dee (Peterborough 1634); Matthew Wren (Hereford 1634, Norwich 1635, Ely 1638); Robert Skinner (Bristol 1637, Oxford 1641); John Warner (Rochester 1638); Brian Duppa (Chichester 1638, Salisbury 1641); and John Towers (Peterborough 1639). Hall and Potter proved moderately sympathetic to Calvinism, Bowle and Coke were undistinguished placemen, and Corbet was lazy; but the rest worked hard to reshape the church along Caroline, Laudian, and Arminian-inflected principles.

The policies and persuasions of Charles I's bishops were crucial in presenting the king's religion to the people. The dominant episcopal style favoured order, ornament, and discipline, and a hard line against nonconformists. In the 1630s they promoted the king's Book of Sports, the railing of communion tables as altars, and the military campaign against Scotland, with varying degrees of zeal and efficiency. With their chancellors and judges, proctors and apparitors, arrayed in spiritual courts, they had the power to suspend ministers from their pulpits, to eject them from their livings, and to subject parishioners to penance and excommunication. The king's prerogative court of High Commission, through which he exercised his supremacy, was never busier, disciplining religious delinquents, both lay and clerical, and correcting nonconformity. Caroline ecclesiastical policies, however controversial, were intended for 'the honour of God', 'the good and quiet of the church', and 'the tranquillity of the kingdom',[39] and King Charles was not entirely to blame if they had the opposite effect.

A Papist in his Heart?

Preachers urged everyone to 'Fear God, Honour the King', but some feared that King Charles was in thrall to 'popery'. Charles I was in fact an avowed protestant, but some people doubted the robustness of his commitment to the Reformation. Married to a catholic, in a court notorious for conversions to Rome, Charles promoted a ceremonialist anti-Calvinist version of protestantism, which favoured episcopal discipline, 'the beauty of holiness', and liturgical accompaniments that could be misconstrued as 'popish'. His advancement of Arminians and ceremonialists, and his evident devotion to his catholic wife, fanned fears that King Charles had succumbed to trickery or flattery, and that he was, perhaps, a papist in his heart. Misperceptions of this sort may not have been widespread, but they gathered momentum in the years preceding the civil war. Simple assertions of steadfastness and orthodoxy did little to assure godly protestants who saw, or misread, the signs of back-sliding.

As we have seen, a stream of loyal subjects sought to warn King Charles of the spiritual dangers facing the kingdom. Distressed petitioners from Lucy Martin to Andrew Humfrey urged his majesty to be wary of God's wrath, to avoid idolatry, and to resist the blandishments of 'that cruel bloody church of Rome'.[40] The desperation of their message was intensified by fear that the king himself was at risk.

King Charles repeatedly asserted his adherence to the protestant faith, and historians overwhelmingly believe him. But rumour persisted that the king was inconstant to his birthright religion and had perhaps even abandoned it. Fears of this nature first surfaced when Charles, as Prince of Wales, visited Spain to court the catholic Infanta. Some claimed, but none could prove, that Charles and his team offered dangerously favourable terms for Roman Catholics in England. Similar rumours recurred when King Charles married Henrietta Maria in 1625. The French catholic queen had catholic attendants, a Roman Catholic chapel, and became associated with a string of courtly converts to Rome. Libellous papers were scattered at Somerset House late in 1637 with the claim that 'half his majesty's Council are of the Romish religion already'.[41] There was even a papal presence at the royal court in the person of Gregorio Panzini, followed by George Con, then Carlo Rossetti. Though Charles was scrupulous in his protestant observances, anxious subjects imagined him succumbing to the blandishments of Babylon. He made too many concessions to recusancy, some protestants feared, and cracked down only intermittently on catholics who refused to attend their parish church.

It was common talk, though never substantiated, 'that the king's majesty had a crucifix in his chamber and did bow to it', that 'the king is a papist', and that 'the king and queen was at mass together'.[42] Rumour spread from York to Yarmouth in 1634 that the king planned 'to grant a general toleration for the papists', although he intended no such thing.[43] Similar canards attached to the king's archbishop, saying Laud 'was turned papist' and was angling for a cardinal's hat.[44]

Worried protestants were not alone in believing that the king was jeopardizing his father's religion. Catholics occasionally claimed that King Charles had secretly embraced their faith. One such was the Shropshire recusant William Pickering, who was questioned in 1635 for bragging that

Figure 9. Archbishop Laud Demonized. *A Prophecie of the Life, Reigne, and Death of William Laud* (1644), title page.

'the king was a papist in his heart' and that 'all protestants were damned heretics and devils'.[45] The Cornish catholic John Trevelyan also predicted 'the utter and speedy ruin of this whole state and church'.[46] Papal agents too were guilty of wishful thinking, reporting that King Charles leaned secretly in their direction.[47]

By 1638 the government thought it necessary to counter the 'horrible and false lies' that 'the king in heart is papist'. Assize judges in every circuit were ordered to 'beat down these scandalous rumours, that all men may know the sincerity of the king's heart'.[48] King Charles himself charged that 'the authors and fomenters of these jealousies . . . would fain have our good subjects imagine that we ourself are perverted, and do worship God in a superstitious way, and that we intend to bring in some alteration of the religion here established'. It was, of course, preposterous, and the king knew better than any the purity of his intentions. Anyone who raised such 'devilish aspersions' would feel the wrath of civil and ecclesiastical justice.[49]

Suspicion that the king was unreliable fed fears of a catholic resurgence backed by foreign invasion. Rumour reported popish armies on the move, recusant gentry amassing weaponry, and armed catholics readying for rebellion. Anxious protestants kept guard at Kettering, Northamptonshire, in April 1639, 'the country being full of the rumour' of a planned popish attack. During Sunday services one man watched from the church tower, while half a dozen heavies 'with swords by their sides and pistols under their cloaks or coats' protected the congregation.[50] By 1640 it was common knowledge, though false information, that 'the king loveth papists better than puritans'.[51] The fear grew viral that King Charles was abandoning protestantism, and that he and his queen were plotting with catholics in Ireland and overseas. A tanner in Somerset lamented in August 1642 'that the king should maintain papists about him against the protestants'.[52] A lecturer in Hertfordshire prayed that month 'that God would give in the king's heart to the cause of Jesus Christ before it was too late'.[53] King Charles did not waver in religion for the rest of his life, but that did not stop some subjects from thinking otherwise.

The King's Catholics

Roman Catholicism had not been an official religion in England since the days of Queen Mary, but an unknown number of families and individuals maintained their 'erroneous opinions' through three generations of legal sanction and social pressure.[54] The estimate that the English catholic community comprised 1 per cent of the general population, 10 per cent of the gentry, and 20 per cent of the nobility seems plausible.[55] Contemporaries claimed almost 1,000 catholic clergy in England, including 500 secular priests, 250 Jesuits, about 100 Benedictines, 30 Franciscans, and 20 Dominicans.[56] Most were English-born but foreign-trained, and conducted their ministry illicitly.

With no churches of their own to attend, and no public priesthood to minister the sacraments, English catholics sought their salvation in secrecy. Their faith had features of a folk religion as well as a counter-reformation mission, with observance of vigils, veneration of the saints, and prayers to the Virgin Mary. Some made obeisance at old sacred sites, such as holy wells, former monasteries, or the image-encrusted Cheapside Cross in London.[57] Their private closets might house relics, paternosters, and imported devotional texts. The catholic lawyer Edward Floyd, for example, possessed a rosary, an *agnus dei*, a friar's girdle, a crucifix, and relics purporting to be 'a piece of our Lady's petticoat and of the cross'.[58] A catholic alehouse-keeper at Bunbury, Cheshire, displayed 'divers pictures and other popish relics, and namely one great crucifix of brass or copper, fairly gilded', in his drinking establishment, and in 1638 regaled customers by praying, 'now God be thanked all things begin to come on well, and in time no doubt will come to good end'.[59] Catholic innkeepers as well as seigneurial families supported networks of believers.[60]

The political fortunes of English catholics generally improved under Charles I, although anti-popery was endemic and recusancy fines cut deep. The moderate Oxford theologian John Prideaux warned in 1634 of 'the great increase of papists within these late years', and seemed to blame Laud, if not the king, for this 'great growth'.[61] Aristocratic converts gained the most attention, but Rome had successes among the common people too. A report from St Giles in the Fields in 1637 alleged that several weak and sick parishioners, including a labourer and a stonecutter, had recently been 'seduced to the Romish religion' with assurances that on death 'their souls are in heaven'.[62] The Venetian ambassador was among those convinced of the resurgence of English Catholicism in the later 1630s, though diocesan returns suggest that in some areas their numbers actually shrank.[63]

Only those catholics identified as blatant refusers of church attendance were labelled recusants. Ingenuity and local connivance allowed others to avoid recusancy fines. At the beginning of King Charles's reign, 'in contemplation of his marriage' with Henrietta Maria, it seemed likely that he might 'grant to his Roman Catholic subjects a cessation of all pains and penalties by reason of their recusancy'.[64] Charles quickly assured protestants to the contrary, promising instead 'stricter courses' against recusants and papists.[65] Episcopal authorities gained assurance in January 1626 of 'his majesty's most princely and pious regard for the true profession and propagation of the gospel, and the severe punishment of all others that do profess and maintain popish religion and superstition'.[66] This remained official policy, though it did not prevent the king from granting pardons and making exceptions. Dozens of high-ranking catholics received royal protection, including Viscount Montagu, who was pardoned in February 1628 for his recusancy, for harbouring popish priests, and for sending his children overseas for a catholic education.[67]

Dealing with recusants in the north of England, Viscount Wentworth hoped 'either to bring them to church, which were most to be desired, or at least to raise out of their estates a good and full revenue, which might enable the king in some measure to be less burdensome to his better subjects'.[68] Wentworth was determined to display his diligence as official receiver of fines and forfeitures under penal laws against recusant catholics, and within four years he raised revenue from recusancy from £2,300 to over £11,000 a year.[69]

Law-abiding English catholics did not threaten state security, despite anxious fears to the contrary, but they formed a continuing affront to principles of uniformity. Catholics could not take the sacraments in a church they considered heretical, though they might use ecclesiastical buildings and precincts for social rituals. Anne Allum, for example, the recusant wife of an Oxford tradesman, acknowledged in 1630 'that she hath always been brought up in the Romish religion', and never came to her parish church 'except when she was married and when she was churched after her delivery of child'.[70] Catholics were officially denied burial in parish churches or churchyards, but local negotiation might find them space in consecrated ground. Diocesan officials in Oxfordshire never determined who interred the catholic Elizabeth Horseman at night in Holton church in 1631, but they recorded the comment of one female parishioner: 'God's blessing on them that buried the dead.'[71] There was less community harmony at Thornton, Yorkshire, in 1634 when friends gave clandestine burial to the body of Ann Hodgson, only for another group of parishioners to dig the recusant up, so that 'the swine tore the sheet off her and had eaten her, if some neighbours had not come and laid her in the coffin again and after buried her'.[72]

The demography of catholic recusancy remains obscure, with urban and artisan as well as rural and aristocratic dimensions. Lists of 'his majesty's erring subjects', sent to the Privy Council by metropolitan magistrates in 1628 and 1629, named a sprinkling of recusant nobles, knights, and gentlemen, court employees, and minor members of the queen's household. The lists included physicians and apothecaries, goldsmiths and embroiderers, and other suppliers of specialist goods and services, along with their wives and families. Recusant tradesmen in London and its environs included lace-weavers and silk-weavers, pewterers and perfumers, but also bricklayers, coachmen, and the occasional baker or cook. These too could be the king's good subjects, but they bore watching because of their potential for trouble.[73] There were many 'of mean condition' among knots of catholics in Somerset, so the bishop of Bath and Wells informed archbishop Laud in 1633, but their numbers were said to be declining.[74]

Ceremonialism and its Discontents

Caroline apologists described the Church of England as 'the envy and admiration of Christendom'.[75] Of all churches, wrote the Arminian controversialist Richard Montague, it was the one most true and pleasing to God, eschewing both the 'popery' that entailed 'tyranny' and the 'puritanism' that led to 'anarchy'.[76] Soundly governed and devoutly attended, according to the ceremonialist John Cosin, the Church of England steered 'the middle way' between 'the superstitiousness and gross errors of the papist', and 'the profane and wild madness of the anabaptist'.[77] The moderate puritan John Brinsley agreed that England possessed a church 'where Christ is plainly and powerfully preached, published, offered, applied in the word and sacraments', balanced between the superstitious adornments of Rome and the bareness of ultra-reformed congregations.[78] Mainstream religious leaders upheld the order and beauty of English worship, but rising tension revealed a religious culture that was scarred and damaged. Irregularities of worship and infringements of discipline were distasteful to a monarch who prized comeliness and decorum in church and state. Caroline episcopal authorities sought conformity and compliance, but parishes generally policed themselves until someone pried or complained. The most common report of churchwardens was *omnia bene*—all well—until puritans pushed the limits or hard-liners came looking for trouble. Diversity prevailed within a tightening framework of uniformity.

Authoritarian clerics demanded strict adherence to the Book of Common Prayer. They were hostile to ministers who ignored or altered the prescribed words or rubrics, or substituted readings that challenged establishment orthodoxy. To the bishops and their backers, the informality that had crept into parish practice was slovenliness that needed correction or nonconformity that warranted punishment. Though James I at Hampton Court had declared himself for 'one doctrine and one discipline, one religion in substance and in ceremony', enforcement had generally been slack. The Jacobean church had privileged 'peace' above 'contentiousness', and authorities often winked at concessions to convenience and custom.[79]

After 1625 the new king oversaw a tilt in religious policy, an alteration of style and tone, as Arminians and ceremonialists extended their authority. English religious culture began to change, especially in the 1630s, as bishops Laud, Neile, Wren, and others conducted energetic visitations. Neither the geography nor the chronology of this change was clear or consistent, since dioceses moved at varying paces, and archdeaconry officials could outmatch or lag behind their bishops. Parishes too could be slow to cooperate, but place after place experienced a new liturgical fastidiousness, backed by disciplinary rigidity.[80] The changes were most apparent, and therefore most controversial, in the policing of gesture, the churching of women, and the apparatus for the celebration of Holy Communion. The renewed ceremonial emphasis, which critics perceived as innovation, or even reversal of the Reformation, was accompanied by large investments in church fabric and ornament in pursuit of 'the beauty of holiness'. It remains a matter of conjecture whether these alterations drew waverers away from Roman Catholicism more than they impelled critics towards puritanism.[81]

As church inspectors demanded 'fit' coverings, 'fair' carpets, 'handsome' communion rails, and 'comely' liturgical equipment, parishes acquired furnishings and fittings not seen since the Reformation.[82] Purchases included multi-hued velvet, scarlet satin, crimson damask, yards of fine Holland, bolts of taffeta, shimmers of silk, and forests of cushions, devotion measured by the yard. Some churches sprouted painted crucifixes, gilded cherubs, and the potent initials IHS, the monogram for Jesus that was also the emblem of the Jesuits. By 1634 Thomas Crosfield of Oxford could reflect that 'more hath been done within this twelve years than many years before' to adorn and beautify churches.[83] These were good times, Robert Skinner preached before the king that year, 'wherein the beauty of holiness . . . seems to revive and flourish'.[84] The process of material renewal had begun earlier but quickened in the 1630s. Laud's acolyte Peter Heylyn crowed in 1637 that England's churches were 'more beautified and adorned than ever since the Reformation'. The king himself deserved credit, he said, for none but 'his sacred majesty' had done so much 'to advance that decency and comeliness in the performance of divine offices'.[85]

Enthusiasts for this decorative frenzy claimed that God expected no less in his house, and that a beautified church should 'beget in our hearts a religious regard and venerable thoughts'.[86] The godly, by contrast, were aghast, though most would have to wait until the collapse of censorship in 1641 to denounce the 'trumperies' of 'idolatry and superstition', the 'gaudiness' of 'profanation', and the 'piebald frippery and ostentation' of spiritual whoredom.[87] Parishioners who thought the re-decking 'idolatrous' had little course besides prayer and intransigence. They could complain, or withhold parish dues, but outright resistance would be deemed an 'insolent carriage . . . in despite and contempt of authority'. So the Earl of Huntingdon informed archbishop Laud in 1634 when parishioners at Loughborough opposed 'the beautifying and decoring' of the church: 'To have his majesty's authority thus confronted, unless these opposers be made examples for their contempt and disobedience, it will make others to be too saucy and presumptuous.'[88]

None reacted so creatively as the half-mad Lady Eleanor Davies, who, finding the cathedral church at Lichfield 'very beautifully set out with hangings of Arras behind the altar, the communion table handsomely railed in, and the table itself set out in the best manner', arrived one communion day in 1636 'with a kettle in one hand and a brush in the other, to sprinkle some of her holy water (as she called that in the kettle) upon these hangings and the bishop's seat, which was only a composition of tar, pitch, sink-puddle water, etc., and such kind of nasty ingredients which she did sprinkle upon the aforesaid things'. Supporters 'said that Lady Davies would better justify that filthy act than those that caused the hangings to be put up' in the first place.[89]

Ecclesiastical disciplinarians could not abide the promiscuous and disorderly diversity they discerned in parish practice. It was 'unseemly', said the Kentish Laudian Edward Boughen, to see 'some few uncovered as they ought, the rest covered most unmannerly; some kneeling at prayers, others sitting or leaning irreligiously; some few standing up at the Creed and the Gospel, and the rest squatting down most unreverently'.[90] It was, he feared, a slippery slope, for 'where disorder is there's confusion, where confusion there's dissention, where dissention there's tumult, and tumult turns to sedition'.[91] The royal chaplain Robert Skinner was similarly horrified by disorderly worship, 'one sitting, another standing, a third kneeling, a fourth walking, a fifth leaning'.[92] The Essex minister Samuel Hoard employed medical imagery in 1638 to liken this nonconformity to 'a gangrene, if it seize and be permitted to settle but on one limb, it speedily runs over and ruins all the body'.[93] The fate of the state might hinge on parishioners kneeling and bowing in unison, as God so clearly intended.[94]

There was no gainsaying the fact that St Paul had instructed the Philippians 'that at the name of Jesus every knee should bow'. But the puritan Anthony Lapthorne argued 'that the same was not meant of our corporeal knees, and that it was sin and idolatry to do it'.[95] The Cheshire minister Samuel Eaton agreed that bowing at the name of Jesus was a superstitious action, and he would not teach it in his parish.[96] Though puritans adhered scrupulously to the word of God, their aversion to 'cringings and bowings' over-rode scriptural literalism in this regard.[97]

Liturgical gestures and postures were as much about power as worship, as their advocates recognized; authority was made manifest in routine genuflection. 'It is not complete worship without a clear demonstration of our subjection,' claimed the royal preacher Robert Skinner.[98] 'The gesture of kneeling at the communion is commanded by the authority of our sovereign lord the king,' insisted Peter Studley of Shrewsbury.[99] Preaching at Oxford, Thomas Lawrence reminded auditors that 'we . . . kneel to show our subjection, and stand to show our obedience', before God or before a king.[100] These were 'gestures and behaviours of humility', explained Foulke Robarts, signs of duty not superstition.[101] Without them, claimed Robert Shelford, God's honour was tarnished, his holy house diminished.[102] If the 'outward rite' of the church required standing, kneeling, crossing, bowing, or uncovering, it was pride and 'contention' to oppose them, preached William Quelch at a visitation in Surrey.[103] 'And not to kneel, when we God's blessings seek, | Doth show we neither lowly are or meek,' trilled the royalist poet John Taylor.[104] One offender, Christopher Ruddy, earned a stay in Newgate when he refused to kneel in St Paul's in 1630.[105]

Archbishop Laud admonished those who sat when they should stand, stood when they should kneel, and failed to bow at the name of Jesus.[106] His visitation in Leicestershire charged John Norris with 'hypocrisy and dissimulation' by applying a 'trick or evasion', so that he might seem to stand at the repetition of the Creed when he was only leaning.[107] The mercer John Blakiston of Newcastle upon Tyne (a future regicide) had learned the same trick of 'leaning in his pew' and 'not kneeling when those prayers are said wherein he is appointed to kneel, not standing when the Creed is read'. The northern court of High Commission prosecuted him in 1636 for this irreverent and disorderly practice, though some of his neighbours found no offence in 'his gesture or deportment of body'.[108] The archdeacon of Northampton likewise proceeded against Elizabeth Perfit of Perbeck 'for not falling down on her knees to pray when she cometh into the church, but very irreverently sitteth on her arse, and will not bow nor make obeisance when the name of Jesus is mentioned'.[109] Durham authorities took action against Damaris Sayre when she said that another woman 'who did bow at the name of Jesus . . . was an idolator'.[110] 'Can ye not stand, ye lazy sows,' cried the ceremonialist John Cosin when some gentlewomen at Durham failed to rise for the Creed.[111]

Harder to evade was the specific provision in the prayer book that participants in Holy Communion should receive the sacrament kneeling. A variety of practices had developed, some standing, some sitting, and others kneeling, in various places in the church, and this diversity too ceremonialists found offensive. The Book of Common Prayer failed to specify *where* people should kneel when they took communion, but during the 1630s it became mandatory in most dioceses to kneel at newly installed rails that guarded tables that had been repositioned as altars. Enforcement caused 'perplexity' to many good Christians who customarily took communion in other places and postures. The Arminian Richard Montague, who became bishop of Norwich in 1638, reported to archbishop Laud that 'they say it is a new, unnecessary, troublesome course, not enjoined by law nor required by canon', which compounded tensions in his diocese.[112]

'The Laudian altar policy' was the most controversial of innovations, and it has continued to trouble historians.[113] The years between 1633 and 1639 saw a revolutionary transformation of the face and demeanour of public worship. Under Queen Elizabeth and King James most parishes followed the loose instructions of the prayer book to place their communion table in the body of the church or chancel, where communicants could approach or gather round to receive the bread and wine. Arrangements had been flexible, and the table moved easily to accommodate varying sacramental practices. Parishioners could ornament their table, position it towards the east, or even enclose it with rails, with no centralized persuasion, policy, or programme.

Under the leadership of bishops Neile, Laud, and Wren and with solid support from King Charles, diocese after diocese implemented new mandatory arrangements. In their most complete form, the tables would be moved to the east end of the chancel, positioned like pre-Reformation altars, and called by that controversial name. Carved wooden rails would separate the altar from the rest of the church, and the sacred ensemble would be approached by a mount of three steps. Decoration of the altar remained optional, but there was pressure to install embroidered frontals and ornamented backcloths, and to furnish the table with candles and upgraded utensils. These changes required considerable expenditure, sometimes recorded in churchwardens' accounts. Though many priests and parishioners embraced these alterations, and most went along with them, a noisy minority protested. Protesters would be considered puritans, 'refractory' to order and discipline, and might be denied access to communion unless they knelt at the rails.

Historians have argued whether the altar policy emanated from the bishops or the court, and whether Neile, Laud, or King Charles himself was its principal author. Most have focused on the formation of policy rather than its implementation and effect. The current consensus finds a community of interest, in which leading ceremonialists attained high office and enlisted a willing king to support their programme. From the point of view of parishioners, it mattered not where the policy originated but how it operated locally. Changes at the parish level were implemented 'by authority', and that authority stretched as high as the crown. As early as September 1632 the visionary Andrew Humfrey had reported 'a bustling in my ears of altars that shall be set up in the churches of England'. He could not imagine that King Charles would permit such a 'leprosy' to develop, and urged Sir John Coke to 'stifle it, lest it grows against the king's will'.[114]

Widespread enforcement of the altar policy began in the northern province towards the end of 1632. An important decision in 1633 approved the railing of the altar at St Gregory-by-St Paul's, London, and allowed the ordinary (the bishop or archbishop) to impose similar arrangements throughout his jurisdiction. The moving and railing of communion tables occurred piecemeal in 1634, with local diocesan approval, to be followed in 1635 by an order from archbishop Laud to standardize the new arrangements throughout the province of Canterbury. There was inevitably some resistance and foot-dragging, but by 1639 the revolution was nigh complete.[115] The new church canons of 1640 confirmed that 'the holy tables should stand in the place where the altars stood' in times of popery, that such tables could properly be called altars, and that they should be 'decently severed with rails' to protect them from profanations. The authors of the canons, to which the king gave full support, expected 'all good and well-affected people' to do 'reverence and obeisance' to these arrangements, though they anticipated resistance from 'the weaker sort, who are prone to be misled by crafty seducers'.[116]

The rearranged altars gave tangible proof to godly activists that their church was moving in the wrong direction. Important reforms of the Reformation were being reversed, and English worship aligned more closely with Rome, not just in doctrine but in furnishing. 'See the practice of these times,' charged Charles Chauncy, the minister of Ware, Hertfordshire, before migrating to New England in 1637; 'they will have priests not ministers, altars not communion tables, sacrifices not sacraments; they will bow and cringe to and before their altars... what is this but the mass itself, for here is all the furniture of it?'[117] The Suffolk gentleman Robert Reyce sent John Winthrop an account of Matthew Wren's visitation of the diocese of Norwich: 'Every communicant is to kneel at the rail now set up in every chancel before the high altar... every woman in her veil goeth to the altar to be churched... they are in many places come to erect curious altars which they adorn with silk and embroidered carpets, in some places with lights, in other places with crucifixes etc.'[118] The controversy reached the theatre in May 1639 when

> the players of the Fortune were fined a thousand pounds for setting up an altar, a basin, and two candlesticks, and bowing down before it upon the stage; and although they allege it was an old play revised, and an altar to the heathen gods, yet it was apparent that this play was revived of purpose in contempt of the ceremonies of the church.[119]

Local resistance flared when priests insisted that none should communicate except at the rails. A minor crisis erupted at Market Harborough, Leicestershire, when 'divers refused to come to the rails, desiring to receive the communion in the accustomed place, which was denied them'.[120] The ceremonialist William Drake at Radwinter, Essex, refused communion to 'at least a hundred' who 'would not come up to the rail, although they all presented themselves kneeling in the chancel or near it'.[121] Forty-five parishioners of St Peter's, Nottingham, refused to kneel at the rails for communion one Sunday in 1638, saying that under the new arrangements they 'could not have it as [they] used to receive it'.[122] Thomas Wolrych, esquire, of Cowling, Suffolk, was excommunicated that year after he refused to communicate at the newly built rails because, he said, he was opposed 'to the alteration of old customs'.[123] Samuel Greygoose, a churchwarden of Epping, Essex, was cited before the diocesan court in 1639 'for attempting to take the communion table out of the rail, saying the rail is an idol'.[124] Seeking harmony but risking further division, the rector of Glooston, Leicestershire, William Sterne, resolved not to give communion 'to any that have spoken against and depraved his majesty's sovereign authority in causes ecclesiastical', explicitly linking central politics with the affairs of the parish.[125]

Puritan Misdemeanours

The puritan movement that grew up with the Church of England from its Elizabethan beginnings had lost its militant momentum by the accession of Charles I. It was fractured, inward-looking, and partly underground.[126] There were few calls fully to rescind the prayer book, few designs for the presbytery to replace bishops. Godly laymen sought spiritual edification and fellowship within their households and communities, while the puritan clerical agenda was mostly confined to such irritants as the surplice, the cross in baptism, and the ring in marriage. The Jacobean 'willingness to wink' allowed mild nonconformists to proceed with minimal harassment. A broad theological consensus around an anglicized Calvinism allowed puritan preachers to rise in the church. These conditions did not survive the 1620s, as puritans came under attack. The Caroline regime pressured some into conformity, and drove a few into exile, but the main effect of King Charles's religious policy was to energize a moribund puritanism.

One of William Laud's first tasks at the accession of King Charles was to draw up a list of churchmen marked with the letters O and P—O for orthodox and P for puritan. The classification was arbitrary and inefficient, but it reflects contemporary concerns with taxonomy and score-keeping.

The new regime could use Laud's information to distinguish the 'better' from the 'worser' sort of ministers, and to distribute rewards to friends and penalties to enemies.[127] The hyper-orthodox Laudian Robert Sibthorpe believed he could smell out 'inward inconformitants, who profess conformity', as well as overt 'puritans' who were especially dangerous to the church.[128] He and his colleagues sent regular reports of 'schismatical puritans' and 'men of mischievous imaginations' to episcopal authorities in London.[129]

Puritans themselves sometimes adopted the language of binary division, identifying themselves as 'the godly' and the rest as the 'profane and dissolute' sort. 'Soul-saving ministers' were 'such as desire to walk by preaching and practice' in the way of God, compared to 'dumb dogs' and time-servers who simply mouthed their way through the Book of Common Prayer.[130] The London artisan Nehemiah Wallington referred to fellow-puritans as 'the holy people of the lord', 'the dear children of the most high God', 'God's saints and servants', and true Christians. Puritan controversialists identified themselves as 'God's people', 'the professors', and 'our tribe', as they relived Old Testament battles.[131] Polarities of this sort increased as puritans grew fearful of a dimming of the light. Taken to extremes, early Stuart puritanism had radical and disruptive potential, but few puritans imagined themselves dangerous to church or state.[132]

There was no Caroline puritan manifesto, no unifying body of principles and beliefs, but many puritans shared the view that the reformations of the sixteenth century had stalled or been compromised. In some minds, the true Reformation in religion lay not in the past but in the future. Such thinkers tended to fear the popish menace, imagined the pope as Antichrist, and braced for invasion or subversion by the enemies of godliness. Some parish puritans identified themselves by their appetite for the word of God, seeking out sermons in other parishes and risking participation in gatherings that the authorities branded 'conventicles'. As they edged towards nonconformity, grating against the prayer book or reacting against Caroline 'innovations', both lay and clerical puritans were increasingly labelled as 'refractory', 'schismatical', and therefore prone to rebellion.

While some parishioners went reluctantly to church, others could not get enough of the word of God. Lay 'professors' met occasionally in private houses to recapitulate sermons, to read the Bible, and to join in prayers and psalms. Sometimes they were joined by godly clerics. Church authorities approved of domestic devotion, but not if it competed with official services.

The slippery slope to separatism might begin in private meetings where parishioners recalled and even questioned the teachings of their ministers. Archbishop Laud made it a priority to root out such irregularities, and action against conventicles quickened in 1634 as he took command of his province.

Laud and his colleagues saw conventicles where others saw only godly gatherings. One of the archbishop's informants at Leicester sent word in 1634 of a suspected conventicle at the house of the mercer Robert Ericke, where friends and neighbours repeated the Sunday sermon and fortified themselves by singing a psalm.[133] The Leicester gentleman John Norris was also investigated for conducting 'private meetings or conventicles' where he recapitulated sermons and spoke scornfully of episcopal authority.[134] A yeomen and four other laymen at Rothwell, Northamptonshire, were called before the High Commission in 1634 for singing psalms, engaging in prayer, and studying scripture and sermons in private houses.[135] Archdeaconry officials in Oxfordshire that year examined participants in prayer at the house of Thomas Jones of Harpsden, where 'they had a Bible before them, and they did there rehearse every man as his memory did serve him some part of the sermon heard that day, and did urge their proofs of Scripture out of the Bible present, and they did sing psalms there'.[136] Heaven forfend they should open those dark and difficult passages that the king wished to keep from discussion.

Legitimate household prayers could become dangerous and disorderly if the doors were open to outsiders. It may have been lawful for John Broxopp of Ormskirk, Lancashire, to summarize sermons to instruct his children and servants 'in the way of godliness', but not to hold night-time meetings with a dozen neighbours in attendance.[137] James Bottomley of the parish of All Saints, Leicester, vehemently protested 'that he had broken none of the king's laws, and that he was questioned only for repeating of sermons in his father's house', but the visitation court excommunicated him until he secured absolution.[138] The Londoner Roger Quatermayne likewise claimed innocence when charged with hosting a conventicle: 'We pray, and we read the scriptures, and as well as we are able find out the meaning of the Holy Ghost therein, and what we understand of the word we impart to our company ... It is nothing but godly conference, which every Christian man is bound to do and perform.'[139] Sceptical of such pleading, a conservative cleric in Wiltshire asserted that 'lay men ought not to meddle with the Scripture'.[140] Conventicles, from this perspective, were nurseries of puritanism and incubators of disorder if laymen were allowed initiatives in religion.

Religious developments under Charles I plunged puritans into pessimism. These years, for the brethren, were the opposite of halcyon days. 'All goes backward... and... God blesses nothing that we take in hand,' muttered anxious members of parliament in 1625.[141] The laments and warnings of distressed petitioners found echoes in the writings of godly correspondents. 'If we look about us we shall see the foundations of the earth out of order,' wrote the Yorkshire minister William Chantrell in September 1628.[142] The Barrington family letters of 1629 include remarks about 'the malice of the insatiated adversary', the need for a refuge in Christ, the sins of 'this lukewarm nation', and the perils of 'these dead declining times'. 'I pray God give us wisdom to prepare for the worst,' wrote Elizabath Masham in February 1629. 'I pray God send us better grounds of comfort... to be armed for the worst that can befall us,' wrote Sir Thomas Barrington in March.[143] Thomas Godfrey of Grantham, Lincolnshire, prayed at this time that 'the Lord shall be so merciful to this sinful land as to suffer good men to make a reformation in the church and commonwealth'.[144] A mood of melancholy accompanied the acrimonious collapse of the parliament, amid the rise of Arminian ceremonialists. Antichrist appeared ascendant in Europe, as 'popery' gained headway at home.

A bleakness of outlook marked godly writings in the 1630s. Richard Saltonstall, Jr, wrote to John Winthrop, Jr, in New England in June 1632 about mounting stresses in the old country: 'all things here do decline very much. The court is jealous of the country, the law is full of oppression and bribery, and the church of superstitions.'[145] The minister Henry Jacie also wrote to New England in 1633 describing the growth of Arminianism and popery, idolatry and superstition. Ecclesiastical disciplinarians were setting communion tables altarwise, genuflecting at the name of Jesus, and observing Wednesday and Friday prayers, ostensibly 'for order and decency and keeping unity in conformity', but effectively allowing God's enemies to advance.[146] The spread of ceremonial practices, the toleration of sports and games on the sabbath, and the prominence of papists at court compounded puritan anxieties. 'Oh lord, look upon us in mercy, it is an evil time and the prudent hold their peace,' the Northamptonshire puritan Robert Woodford confided to his diary in 1637. The times were grim for the godly, who had to endure 'sinful innovations', 'debauched courses', and creeping 'superstition'.[147]

Preaching at Easton, Huntingdonshire, in November 1636, Giles Randall listed the 'many sins which caused the wrath of God to lie heavy upon this nation'. New among them was the 'oppression' of 'the taking of the loan and Ship Money', for 'without restitution there can be no salvation'. Two 'ear witnesses' to this 'seditious' sermon reported Randall's words to a magistrate, initiating a Privy Council investigation.[148] Edward Sparhawk preached similarly at Coggeshall, Essex, in March 1637, despite having been suspended in his home diocese of Norwich. He drew heavily on the lamentations of Jeremiah to associate the rise of ceremonialism with the collection of Ship Money. Sparhawk deplored 'the heavy impositions and cursed adorations newly laid upon Christians', and decried the 'idolatrous mixtures of religion and the treading down of God's people' by the bishop of London's commissary. Robert Aylett reported this outrage to Laud's Dean of the Arches, and fumed that the region was rife with 'rebellious humours'. The vicar of Coggeshall, John Dod, had earlier lamented that 'the new mixture of religion that is commanded in the church' had brought down 'the plague of God'.[149] These were days of darkness, with more tests and troubles in store, though 'the storm may blow over', mused the Leicestershire minister William Morton, who put all his trust in the lord.[150]

The storm struck some puritans in the form of episcopal visitation. Visitation queries asked whether anyone deviated from any rules or rubrics of the Church of England. Bishops did not ask specifically about puritans, who were known by their transgressions, though Richard Montague of Norwich enquired after 'indiscreet zealots of the preciser sort'.[151] The visitors came looking for trouble—with 'nets and sieves to try out all, as bad fish or chaff', according to hostile observers[152]—though churchwardens often overlooked local irregularities.

From the point of view of strict conformity, anyone who jeopardized the 'unity and concord' of the national church deserved punishment, so John Elborow preached at archbishop Laud's visitation in Essex in 1637. Laymen who questioned the authority of the church, or disparaged its ceremonies or discipline, deserved excommunication. Clerics who offended risked degradation and deprivation. Alas, lamented Elborow,

> how is the authority of the church out-faced, how are the canons and constitutions of the same neglected and vilified by every illiterate artisan, mechanick, high-shoes . . . and by too too many ministers too? . . . What lamentable fractions, what scandalous and irreligious libels, what indiscreet and

> satirical pamphlets have lately been dispersed against the governors and government of our church?

After 'fatherly admonitions' and 'gentle persuadings' it was time for the church to flex its muscles and to discipline its members, especially 'our peevish factious schismatical nonconformists'.[153] Episcopal authorities were only too happy to oblige.

Courtesy, commonality, and compromise were among the casualties of the Caroline cultural struggle. The language of religious polemic became increasingly intemperate, as writers berated each other as 'popish innovators' or 'malignant schismatics'. The 1630s saw an erosion of discursive civility, a hardening of hostile debate, and the increased application of disparaging terms. Laud and his colleagues had the gift of seeing mild irregularity as intransigence, moderate nonconformity as sectarianism, and all disagreement as refractoriness or rebellion. Nehemiah Wallington noted how 'our lordly bishops and prelates... hate the dear children of God, showing it by their mocking, taunting, reproaching with scoffs and jeers, and calling them by the names of puritans, schismatical, seditious, factious, trouble-states'.[154] Laudians did indeed deride their opponents as 'precise professors', 'refractory brethren', 'fanatical spirits', and even 'our Jews'.[155] The new church canons of 1640, King Charles believed, would strengthen the hand of his bishops against 'factious people, despisers and depravers of the Book of Common Prayer', commonly known as puritans.[156] Time and circumstance did not allow their implementation, as puritans themselves would soon fragment into Presbyterians and Independents, Baptists of various kinds, and adherents of short-lived radical sects.

God's Ambassadors

One of the few points of concurrence between Laudians and puritans was the need to raise 'maintenance' for God's ministers. Godly and ceremonialist clergy agreed that their cloth and their calling entitled them to higher levels of esteem. Most clerics, by Charles I's time, had gentle connections if not gentle origins, with university degrees that further inscribed their elite status. But their incomes, though variable, were often disproportionately low. Archbishop Laud was determined to increase respect for these mediators between God and mankind, and one way was to improve their social, material, and financial condition.[157] The rising churchmen of the 1630s especially trumpeted 'the sacredness of priesthood' and made high claims for the clerical vocation.[158] They were 'stars in the right hand of Christ', according to the Sussex cleric Richard Bayly.[159] 'Our God will have us reputed as his ambassadors, and as shining stars, yea, as angels,' chorused William Hardwick of Surrey and Francis Rogers of Kent.[160] These sacerdotalist assertions were sometimes overwrought, and evidence suggests that the laity were not all persuaded by them.

Pastoral care, like kingly governance, required a mixture of 'wisdom and courage, zeal and temper, boldness and meekness, power and patience, authority and compassion, reverence and humility, eloquence and plainness, learning and experience', and this could be displayed in the pulpit, at the altar, or on the village green.[161] But character and circumstance tested these qualities, in an era of religious disagreement and social stress. Clerical career patterns took talented and educated professionals, many of them trained in theology and ancient languages, and placed them in country parishes where they pined for scholarly conversation. Their upbringing, education, voice, and profession distinguished the clergy from the bulk of the population, and sometimes caused friction with parishioners. Exasperated ministers lamented their rustication amid the vulgar multitude, as pastors and people talked past each other.

John Street of Stogumber, Somerset, for example, found his parish 'as odious a place to him as hell itself'.[162] George Herbert, the poet parson of Fugglestone with Bemerton, Wiltshire, described his country congregation as 'thick and heavy, and hard to raise to a point of zeal and fervency', and believed himself to be 'both suspected and envied' as an outsider.[163] Even the energetic Richard Baxter was challenged by parishioners of 'heathenish ignorance and wicked obstinacy'.[164] The Lichfield prebendary John Hayward wrote to John Cosin in 1634 about 'the enormities of this country, and the despair of any remedy' in a church and diocese he likened to an Augean stable (a hopeless accumulation of filth). However, he lamented, 'I must be content, though to my great grief, to sit down and . . . live upon the dung of this stable'.[165] The Buckinghamshire minister Nathaniel Gyles sensed in 1635 that he was 'subject to the malevolence of some parishioners'.[166] 'I have to contend with impiety and barbarism,' complained a minister in County Durham,[167] like another cleric in a 'dark corner' of the north who feared that 'his hopes shall be terminated and himself nailed fast'.[168] A manuscript libel from the 1630s satirized the overeducated 'deuteronomical polydoxologist and pantiphilogical linguist' academic who left his 'illiterate semi-pagan auditors' as 'plentifully unedified' as ever.[169]

Angry and frustrated, some ministers turned their pulpits against their parishioners, berating them as 'swinish wretches' and 'currish dogs'.[170] The Somerset minister Roderick Snelling 'publicly railed at his parishioners and called them gypsies and cheating knaves'.[171] The London puritan Stephen Dennison went further and 'reviled some of his parishioners, comparing them to frogs, hogs, dogs and devils, and called them the names of knaves, villains, rascals, queans, she-devils, and pillory whores'.[172] Another minister was suspended in 1634 'for railing against his parishioners and saying in the pulpit, that if whoremongers, drinkers and thieves, rogues and rascals went to heaven, he was sure all or the most part of his parishioners would go thither'.[173]

Like everyone else, the clergy were prey to appetite and subject to temptation; their numbers included sots and sexual predators as well as devoted divines. William Cowper, rector of Gosforth, Cheshire, was allegedly drunk in the pulpit in 1625 when he preached a profane sermon.[174] Another Cheshire minister, George Eccles of Christleton, was so drunk that he fell down in the street.[175] When Thomas Harriman of Durham was called to perform a baptism in 1628, he was so intoxicated 'that he could not stand' and the child died unbaptized.[176] Charges of social misconduct often accompanied citations for liturgical or disciplinary irregularity, though sometimes they were clouded by malicious gossip or neighbourly enmity. John Vernon, the vicar of Cookham, Berkshire, was allegedly another 'frequenter of inns, tippling houses and alehouses', who spent his time 'in wanton, idle and luxurious courses'. He sparred with parishioners over seats in church, gouged them for fees for churchings and burials, and instead of being the parish peacemaker was 'a continual sower of discord and debate betwixt neighbours'. 'Credible report' to the court of High Commission in 1628 told of Vernon's sexual predations, his begetting of bastards, and even soliciting of abortions. Vernon, however, insisted on his 'good name and fame' and his record of charitable and hospitable works. He claimed to be the victim of parish grudges, from people he had put in the stocks or made to perform penance, and from a patron who sought to replace him with another incumbent. Whatever the truth of the matter, in sixty pages of testimony, it is clear that community relations had soured and that this vicar had lost control of his parish.[177]

Some clerics caroused with select parishioners in 'good fellowship', and allowed their homes to be used for disorderly tippling.[178] Though this behaviour may have ingratiated them with 'the vulgar sort', it lost them respect from 'precise' parishioners and from episcopal officials who demanded probity and discipline. Richard Powell, the vicar of Pattishall, Northamptonshire, for example, wore apparel 'not befitting a minister' and 'kept company . . . with carriers, tinkers and other men of base and inferior quality', and was cited before High Commission. William Ward, the parson of Allesley, Warwickshire, was similarly sanctioned in 1638 because he 'sat drinking with cobblers, butchers, tinkers, peddlers and like persons of base condition and conversation' (as did his master Jesus).[179] Ministers disgraced their calling if they embraced the fellowship of the alehouse and socialized too freely with inferiors. Crucial hierarchical principles were imperilled by blurring the boundaries between lay and clerical, vulgar and elite.

John Hubbock, the rector of Nailstone, Leicestershire, took part in Sunday games of football, quoits, and shovelboard, and bought a football and other recreational equipment with his own money.[180] Richard Ruth, the curate of Crosthwaite, Cumberland, likewise enjoyed games of football, and was known to lay violent hands on other players.[181] Clerics like these were among the strongest supporters of King Charles's Declaration of Lawful Sports. Thomas Avery, the vicar of Fleckney, Leicestershire, offended both Laudians and puritans in 1637 when he allowed parishioners to conduct cock fights in the churchyard, and used the communion table to lay out tithe money. He also had a sideline in 'charming of teeth', offering charms and 'mystical words' as remedy against toothache.[182]

In one unhappy case, salaciously detailed in church court records, Thomas Lawton, the minister of Prestbury, Cheshire, had sexual relationships with his wife's sister, and was reportedly spied in 1634 in a barn with Mary Beech, 'his breeches down, betwixt the said Mary's naked thighs, she being reared up to the barn wall'. One witness claimed to have heard Mr Lawton's offer to show Mary the sight of 'a gentleman on horseback' while 'tussling with her in a chair'. It was hard for parishioners to maintain respect for a minister suspected of 'incest, adultery or fornication', even more when Mary Beech gave birth to the minister's child.[183] More scandalous still, beyond the extreme, was the episode in Northamptonshire in 1637 in which the puritan vicar of Pytchley committed incest with his niece, then murdered their bastard, and paid for his crime on the gallows. It showed, wrote the anti-puritan reporter, how 'the precise tribe . . . make no conscience of begetting schisms and disturbing the peace of the church'. But it also reflected ill on the entire clerical profession.[184] Scandalous episodes may have fostered anticlericalism, but they also encouraged calls for a more charitable, more exemplary, and more accommodating parish ministry than zealots of any kind could provide.

God's People

Scholarship on early Stuart religion has focused on clerical, theological, and ecclesiological controversies. Historians who have sought to broaden the conversation have sometimes enquired whether parishioners were more attached to puritanism, ceremonialism, or the familiar routines of the Book of Common Prayer.[185] Much less attention is paid to irregularities and disorders that seemingly lacked ideological moment. Yet profanity and indifference may have been as common among the laity as piety and devotion. Though church and state were concerned to preserve the 'circle of order' against 'unquiet and restless spirits', and church law demanded 'reverence and attention', no one could compel parishioners to worship with decorum.[186]

The people of Caroline England were officially protestant, leaving pagans and atheists to the imagination and Jews and Roman Catholics outside the fold. They could be weak or strong, orthodox or irregular, with varying degrees of preparation, commitment, and devotion. Neighbours and parishioners could be kind or cruel, charitable or hard-hearted, and, by Calvinist standards, elect or reprobate, saved or damned. Judged by contemporaries as 'the better sort' or 'the worser sort', their behaviour provided clues to their soteriological condition. It was an old game, with Elizabethan and medieval antecedents, to rank parishioners by criteria of Christian citizenship against which most mortals fell short.[187]

Richard Baxter, who assisted in parishes at Dudley, Worcestershire, and Bridgenorth, Shropshire, before moving to Kidderminster in 1641, devised a pulpit-eye typology of his congregation in which 'serious professors of religion', always a minority, were closest to the minister's heart. These were dutiful and well-instructed folk, the 'best sort' of parishioners, sometimes labelled less charitably as 'precise' or even 'puritan'. Close behind them came 'some of competent knowledge and exterior performances, and lives so blameless that we can gather from them no certain proof or violent presumption that they are ungodly, or that their profession is not sincere'. Others were 'tractable and of willing minds', though somewhat 'ignorant of the very essentials of Christianity'.

Baxter then characterized his less promising parishioners. 'Some there are that are secret heathens . . . making a scorn of Christ and Moses, and heaven and hell, and scripture and ministers, and all religion . . . And yet for the hiding of their minds, they will hear and urge us to baptize their children, and openly make the most orthodox confessions, and secretly deride it when they have done.' Others 'have tolerable knowledge' but 'live in some notorious, scandalous sins . . . in gross covetousness . . . common drunkenness . . . ordinary swearing, cursing, ribaldry, whoredoms'. Many neglected both 'family duties and the Lord's Day', and made 'bitter scorns at prayer, holy conference, church order and holy living'. These were the parish trouble-makers, who were often cited before ecclesiastical courts.

A substantial number, perhaps the majority, were 'of more tractable dispositions, but really know not what a Christian is'. They attended church and mouthed the catechism, yet remained as ignorant as 'the veriest heathen in America . . . I ask them what Christianity is, the best answer is, that it is serving God as well as we can, or as God will give us leave. So that there is scarce an article of the Creed . . . that they tolerably understand.' The unteachable were joined by the incorrigible: 'Many there be that join this heathenish ignorance and wicked obstinacy together, hating to be instructed . . . They will rail at us bitterly behind our backs if we will not let them have their own will and way about the sacraments and all church affairs.'

Especially troubling were parishioners with overt hostility towards their minister. Some, according to Baxter, 'make it their work to possess people with a hatred of strict professors, and of our churches and administrations'. They take teachings 'contrary to the authors' meanings [and] make them engines to harden others in their impiety and hatred of reformation . . . And thus by misunderstanding some texts of Scripture, and abundant truths of God, they are hardened in ungodliness.'[188] Baxter published this typology in 1658, but it reflected half a lifetime's pastoral experience. Outright atheism was very rare, so it was shocking to hear Robert Butler of Radcliffe on Trent declare in 1640 'that the word of God was not true, neither would he ever believe it'.[189]

Parishioners were supposed to take instruction from their ministers and defer to them as spiritual superiors. Unfortunately, however, there were some who spoke no more honourably of the clergy than of the secular authorities. In 1627, for example, an Essex man declared 'that he would regard his minister as a dog' rather than do reverence to him. Edward Kedgell of Ickburgh, Norfolk, was hauled before his bishop in 1629 'for scandalising the minister with opprobrious speeches . . . saying he would go to the devil [and] wishing to God he would go quickly'. Other ill-mouthed parishioners demeaned their ministers with such words as 'base knave', 'base priest', 'base companion', 'tinkerly parson', and 'wide-mouthed rascal'.[190] Called upon to show respect for the incumbent, Christopher Blithe of Belthorpe, Norfolk, declared in 1634 that 'he did not account such a minister worth a fig or a rush'. His neighbour Thomas Adcocke of Rising bid another minister 'a turd in his teeth' instead of performing penance.[191] A parishioner at Brislington, Somerset, said he respected his minister 'no more than the meanest boy in the belfry'.[192] Another at Chenies, Buckinghamshire, addressed the parson demeaningly as 'sirrah', and told him: 'I am as good a man as yourself.'[193] Edward Weston of Broughton, Nottinghamshire, used identical words, telling his minister Richard Colebrand: 'I am as good a man as yourself, and as true and as honest.'[194] These were levelling terms that undercut God's scheme, and were as offensive when applied to ministers as to magistrates. Edward Clench of Grantchester, Cambridgeshire, denounced his vicar as 'a knave', addressed him as 'sirrah', and said 'he kept . . . as good a man as him to wipe his shoes'.[195]

Verbal abuse by parishioners was so common that some clerics accepted it as the price of their calling. There were 'none more censured, none more neglected, none more vilified, none more slighted in many places than we of the clergy', lamented William Hardwick of Reigate in 1638. It was part of the burden of performing God's work to suffer the derision of 'every ignorant and profane wretch', a burden shared by puritans and ceremonialists alike.[196] 'Base speeches' arose from disputes over money, morality, or parochial relationships, as well as styles of churchmanship, and they threatened the social order by demeaning one of its central pillars.

Ordination and incumbency were supposed to elevate ministers above the common fray, but occasionally animosity turned violent. Richard Clind, a high-tempered gentleman in Shropshire, threatened the minister at Wellington with 'many railing and reviling speeches', and in the midst of the Palm Sunday sermon in 1639 drew his sword, 'to the terror of the minister and disturbance of the whole congregation'.[197] The Greenfield brothers of Whalley, Cheshire, beat their minister with fists and sticks, challenged him to fight, and threatened to kill him.[198] At Normanton, Rutland, the barber Thomas Bowyer not only abused the parson with vile language, but injured him physically by pulling his beard, elbowing his chest, 'flinging a glass of burnt wine into his eyes, beating him with his fist, kicking him with his feet, throwing a candlestick and stool at him, striking him with a crabtree cudgel, drawing blood of him in divers places', and 'other barbarous insolencies'.[199] Outbursts like these grew from disputes over worship, church decoration, seating, or tithes, as well as everyday social frictions. Clergymen could interpret them as signs of reprobation, symptoms of disorder, or predictable excesses of 'the worser sort'.

Behind many of these disputes, was the unspoken question, 'who owns the church?' The Church of England, as organization and institution, belonged to the nation and to God. The king was its head and defender, each bishop directed his diocese, and the clergy manned the offices and livings. But what of the physical church, the local landmark, the oldest and most substantial structure in most parishes? That too belonged to God, but it also belonged to the people (though the chancel was assigned to the incumbent and the nave to the congregation). Generations of parishioners had endowed their church, built it, and maintained its material fabric; they used it as their community centre as well as their house of worship. Patrons, impropriators, churchwardens, and parishioners shared responsibility with the clergy for its edification and upkeep. Few liked to be told by outsiders how their church should be arranged or arrayed, or how to behave in its precincts.

Many people experienced the church as a place to meet neighbours as much as a sanctum to address God. Then as now, it was a social venue as well as a setting for worship and instruction. Parish religion was flavoured by habit and duty as much as by contact with divinity. The church was formally a place of worship, an arena of sanctity, but it operated too as a contested space with a variety of secular and social functions.

Parishioners used churches to store fire-fighting equipment, ladders, and leather buckets, alongside the parish arms and armour, lumber, and other tackle. The parish chest, in the church tower or vestry, held muniments, deeds, and community archives, as well as parish registers and religious books. The church porch might be used as a schoolroom, a place of assignation, or the venue for settlement of debts. Parishioners gathered in church for parish business, for juries or vestries, for payment of dues, and even for plays and interludes.[200] It was where declarations were declared and royal proclamations proclaimed, where people learned the kingdom's business. Many parishioners treated the church as they would any other meeting place, behaving in ways that critics regarded as offensive, disorderly, or profane.[201]

Notions of 'comeliness', 'decorum', and 'order' were supposed to operate in church, just as they governed secular relations. Peace and conformity in worship were thought pleasing to God and essential for social cohesion. Nothing should be done there 'confusedly, according to every rash brain', but rather in conformity to the 'order which God hath established', preached Henry Paynter.[202] But, despite their best efforts, wrote the minister Robert Abbot, the church was too often 'a place of gazing, pride, contention, lustful thoughts', where parishioners succumbed to 'gadding eyes, wandering thoughts, high looks, and worse'.[203] Too many people behaved as if 'churches are none other than ordinary and common places', complained William Hardwick, who observed 'some laughing, others prating, some courting, others bargaining', when they should have been focused on God.[204] It was insufferable, preached Robert Skinner, in a sermon before King Charles, that the church should be made 'a talking place . . . a gazing place . . . a place of rude contentions and uncivil contestations'.[205] The royal chaplain Walter Balcanquall similarly castigated all who would treat God's house as 'a house of good-fellowship' and subject it to profane misuses.[206] Archbishop Laud himself took offence at parishioners who used the church 'like a common hall', and urged proceedings against anyone who used the communion table 'to write and receive monies'.[207]

Caroline ecclesiastical court records are filled with proceedings against lay men and women for 'joggling and shuffling', 'brabbling and scolding', 'brawling and striving', 'chiding and railing', and 'swearing and cursing' in church.[208] Churchwardens and ministers intervened to stop rising tempers, slapping of faces, boxing of ears, and 'laying on of violent hands', as everyday enmities carried over to the house of worship. Visitation courts reprimanded parishioners 'for brawling and fighting together in church', 'immoderate' noise-making, or blasphemous swearing, as they sought to impose order.[209] Though many of 'the better sort' were dutiful and well instructed, an untold number fell short of the standards that their ministers and governors demanded.

Churches became sites of contention when neighbours competed for intangible benefits associated with custom, honour, rank, and reputation. Obligated as they were to gather on Sundays and holy days, parishioners measured status by placement for worship. Much of the 'brawling and striving' that offended the authorities was sparked by disputes over seating. Whether they were grouped together as families or segregated by gender (the two principle arrangements in early modern churches), parishioners understood that their seating reflected 'the dignity and degree of the party'.[210] In parishes that reserved separate seats for men and women, married couples were sometimes presented 'for sitting promiscuously together'.[211] 'Broils about seats' occasioned 'much disorder' in parishes throughout England, with consequent 'wrangling', 'jangling', 'contending', and disturbance.[212] The periodic reassignment of seats by churchwardens caused as much trouble as it solved. 'Immodest thrusting' and 'striving in the church for a seat' continued at Puddletown, Dorset, notwithstanding the attempt in 1635 to place everyone 'according to their several ranks and degrees'.[213] The vice-chancellor's rearrangement of seats at Great St Mary's, Cambridge, in 1639 worsened relations between town and gown because it over-rode the 'ancient rights' of certain citizens and encroached on the area 'where some of the ancientest parishioners are placed'. The dispute concerned honour, custom, rights, and authority, with little bearing on the worship of God.[214]

Christmas services at Dodleston, Cheshire, were disrupted in 1625 when John Barlow took Robert ap Edwards 'by the arm and thrust him, saying, know thy place'. There was elbowing and shoving as well unseemly language, which caused a woman in the congregation to say 'she never saw a man so rude in church before'.[215] Similar disturbances at Stockport, Cheshire, in 1631 involved John and Elizabeth Cheetham sitting on Elizabeth Brookshaw's head, when they 'did hale and pull her violently that her clothes did crack', in order to dislodge her from their seat.[216] William Ridgeway of Stockport, Cheshire, went further in 1630 when he drew a knife 'in the church on the sabbath in time of divine service, attempting to stab Thomas Strethill because, as he alleged, he sat in his stall'.[217] Secular and ecclesiastical authorities were horrified by such disturbances.

More neighbours came to blows at Eccleston, Lancashire, in 1632, with much pulling of hair, bending of ears, and knocking of heads, over rights to prime seating. Thomas Broughton, esquire, manhandled Thomas Young, gentleman, telling him: 'thou art a proud coxcombly fool.' The occupant of the seat declared 'he had as good right to sit there' as his challenger, and the intruder 'pulled him by the ear and bended his head downward and knocked his head against the bench'.[218] Another fight over seats in church at Aldford, Cheshire, caused the minister to come down from his pulpit, and churchwardens had to pull the combatants apart.[219]

The desire of elite families to erect more comfortable and private pews, appropriate to their status, and for people in general to seek the most advantageous seating, occasioned endless disputes about honour and authority that interfered with devotional practice. In 1638, for example, the churchwardens of Leverington, Cambridgeshire, presented John Crosse 'for having set up a seat to the hindrance of many of the parishioners... he having twice made the seat lower and once narrower, yet still it hindereth the prospect of the people'.[220] Aggressive claims to seating disrupted parochial harmony and did nothing to advance God's service.

Women, according to St Paul, were allowed no voice in church, but that did not stop some women from pursuing loud quarrels. Brawling over church seats at Littleborough, Cheshire, in 1629, Grace Lightowler used a prayer book as a weapon to beat another parishioner.[221] Mary Lewis of Iver, Buckinghamshire, cemented her reputation as a scold on Advent Sunday 1634 by 'wishing fire and brimstone would descend from heaven and consume both houses and families'.[222] Priests and parishioners sought to quieten the noise and deflect it to more secular settings.

The variables of status, wealth, propriety, and gender were all engaged one Sunday in 1637 when Elizabeth Stevens, the wife of William Stevens of Brislington, Somerset, treated the parish to a display of indignation. She made her way to 'the upper part of the church, to the pew door of Mr Samuel Mogg's, and did use him in very unfitting terms and words there with scolding manner, saying that the said Mogg was a malicious carcass, and said, will your worship starve my husband?' Samuel Mogg was evidently a gentleman, perhaps related to the Richard Mogg who was under-sheriff of Somerset, and he may have been William Stevens's landlord or employer. Instead of remaining silent and subordinate, Elizabeth Stevens spoke her mind and stood up for her family. Her address to Mr Mogg as 'your worship' simultaneously emphasized and mocked his position as an honourable 'carcass'. An attack like this against a superior would be disorderly in any circumstances, but it was especially scandalous for being in church and the work of a woman.[223]

Other disturbances occurred when legal processes interrupted religious proceedings, because servers of writs knew that their targets would be at worship. A bailiff at Fulmer, Buckinghamshire, arrested William Allen for debt in church on Christmas Day 1634, 'when he purposed to have received the sacrament, and while yet the best part of God's service was in doing'.[224] Actions like these distracted the minister and congregation, and could lead some debtors to avoid coming to church, thereby breaking the law and thwarting its principle of commonality.

Church attendance was mandatory, but some people had trouble maintaining attention. Coming to church on their days of rest, hundreds of hard-working parishioners offended by dozing.[225] Daniel Scott of Littleport, Cambridgeshire, was cited before the bishop's court in 1638 'for making it his common practice to sleep in time of divine service and sermon'.[226] Thomas Fryer of North Hales, Suffolk, apologized for his disorderly snoring.[227] William Sotherby of Ludham, Norfolk, felt moved 'to awake one that was asleep' and was himself cited for 'walking and talking in the church in time of divine service'.[228] A sleeper's ears were closed to spiritual instruction, claimed the Suffolk minister Robert Shelford, so 'besides the contempt of God, sleep is to all holy duties an extinction'.[229]

Men were supposed to remove their hats in church, as inferiors did before superiors, but hundreds kept their heads covered, to the anger of the authorities and the apparent dishonour of God.[230] Thomas Tirell of St Peter's, Colchester, declared in 1639 'that he would be drawn in pieces by wild horses before he would keep off his hat in the church'.[231] For him it was a matter of principle, though others excused their behaviour by claiming a head cold. Jermyn Record of Belaugh, Norfolk, bared his head upon demand but caused worse consternation by 'laying his hat upon the communion table'.[232] Several young men at Beverley, Yorkshire, disturbed the congregation in 1637 by 'throwing up their hats in the church.'[233]

Women could keep their heads covered, and were supposed to exercise decorum. They were not supposed to pull and throw each other's hats and baskets, like the young women at Wing, Buckinghamshire, who disrupted services in 1633.[234] Young people too often engaged in socializing, flirting, and jesting in church, like John Clenton of Outwell, Norfolk, who offended in 1635 'by pulling off the hat of Margery Carter'.[235]

Laughter undermined religious solemnity, offending the guardians of gravitas.[236] Edmund Booth of Holton, Norfolk, not only laughed in church and called most of his neighbours cuckolds, but further profaned the sanctity of service in March 1633 when 'there was a fart let in the church in sermon time and he was vehemently suspected for the same'.[237] Another joker at Chesham, Buckinghamshire, broke 'an addle egg on the shoulder of William Wilkinson presently after service at morning prayer' in 1636.[238]

A woman in Cambridgeshire was cited in 1638 'for scoffing at an exhortation made by the minister in his sermon'.[239] A Norfolk man was examined 'for irreverently and profanely laughing at church' on a Sunday in 1639.[240] Richard Ferrer of Wheatacre Burgh, Norfolk, demeaned God's house by his 'unreverent jests and behaviour in the church in chewing of tobacco in time of divine service'. One of his jokes was that when the devil took Christ to the top of the Temple and offered him all the kingdoms of the world if he would worship him, 'then he reserved Burgh to himself'.[241] A Yorkshireman used 'profane and irreverent words in time of divine service' by jesting on the double meaning of the word 'office' (as in 'house of office' or privy). 'When the minister wished the churchwardens to look to their offices,' William Fowes of Woodkirk observed, 'it's sharp shitting in a frosty morning'. The minister and churchwardens were not amused, and cited the offender to diocesan officials.[242] Puritans and ceremonialists joined together in opposing this profanity, for, as St Gregory counselled, 'where laughing is in the church, there is the devil's work'.[243] The clerical estate closed ranks against profane parishioners who ignored or mocked their efforts.

Ecclesiastical officials could not see the humour when the layman Thomas Thorne delivered a mock sermon from a hogshead set up like a pulpit in an alehouse at Barrington, Somerset, during the Christmas holidays in 1636. Thorne allegedly took as his text the word 'Malt', divided into four parts: 'M: much, A: ale, L: little, T: thrift, and so went on making a large discourse or speech therein, to the great laughter of those present and disgrace of the clergy.'[244] A similar episode occurred at Hampstead, Buckinghamshire, in November 1639 when 'getting into a pulpit in a joiner's shop', where the fixture awaited installation in a church, a parishioner 'took a text out of Toby, which he divided into three parts: Toby, Toby's dog, and Toby's dog's tail'. Charged in High Commission with profanity, the offender argued that the pulpit was not yet consecrated, and in any case the text was apocryphal, but he was fined £500.[245]

Alcoholic excesses drew some parishioners deeper into trouble. They might come to church drunk, make disturbing noises, and then further defile God's house by urinating, vomiting, or 'easing their bodies' in the church or churchyard.[246] One offence quickly compounded another. When churchwardens at Stokesby, Norfolk, found Henry Martin making water 'very beastly against the church wall' one Sunday in 1634 he answered them 'with reproachful speeches, and said he would do it despite them and the law'. This was not the end of the matter, as the confrontation grew in intensity. Martin was charged with 'swearing and blaspheming the name of God' as he 'very villainously did persevere in his lewd behaviour', and was made to perform penance or face temporary excommunication.[247] Similar sanctions applied to those discovered in church with their breeches and hose down, or engaged in sex in sanctified porches, churchyards, or belfries.[248]

Parishioners commonly brought their dogs into church, causing pollution and disruption.[249] In an especially shocking episode at Tadlow, Cambridgeshire, on Christmas Day 1638, a parishioner's dog 'took of the bread which was provided for the celebration of the holy sacrament of the Lord's Supper, and which was set upon the holy table uncovered, and ran out of the church with it', so that communion had to be abandoned.[250] Some of the bishops who insisted on railing the altars justified their innovation as a guard against canine wanderers.[251]

Gross profanity was especially distressing to champions of the beauty of holiness. When parishioners at Knotting, Bedfordshire, used the chancel as a cockpit in 1637, and 'laughed and sported' at the newly installed communion rails, they were not just wagering on fighting cocks but commenting on the altar policy.[252] Ceremonialists were incensed when Thomas Easton of Loughton, Buckinghamshire, violated God's house by 'leading a horse into the church' one day in November 1636.[253] When another horse entered the church at Edwardstone, Suffolk, in 1637, the offender excused himself, 'because there was at that time a most terrible tempest', and he and his mount needed shelter.[254] New Year's Day revellers at Ely disrupted cathedral services in 1639 'by the roasting of a cat tied to a spit' in the yard outside the choir, causing 'great noise and disturbance' and annoyance to bishop Matthew Wren.[255] Casual profanity like this was hard to distinguish from deliberate provocation.

Ceremonialists were also affronted by the misuse of liturgical equipment and disrespect for the holy sacraments. William Williamson, a churchwarden and alehouse-keeper at Worlington, Norfolk, was cited before bishop Corbett in 1633 because he 'keepeth the communion cup in his house and drinketh in it there'.[256] In 1634 a chapel warden of Holt, Cheshire, took the communion table from the church to the alehouse and used it to play cards and dice.[257] Other offenders included William Rose of Prescot, Lancashire, cited 'for washing his hands in the baptistery or font very irreverently and undecently', and John Paynes of Tattenhall, Cheshire, who was censured for 'telling of his money . . . and making a noise' while others were taking communion.[258]

Profanity with regards to the altar was reprehensible because it showed a failure of Christian instruction. William Holme of Bugthorpe, Yorkshire, was cited 'in 1627 for unreverent behaviour in the church in time of divine service, taking the communion table cloth and putting it about him, in derision of the minister then having on the surplice'. Robert Raven of Blacktoft, Yorkshire, offended a few years later by 'wiping his face being sweaty with the cloth of the communion table'.[259] Henry Bugge, a parishioner at Plungar, Leicestershire, behaved

> unreverently . . . at the communion table presently after the communion was ended, leaning his back against the table and willing his neighbours to come and drink with him of the wine that was left, filling a cup himself and drinketh of it, saying that the wine did not belong to the minister but was his and the rest that were of the parish.[260]

Even more shocking, as bad as the dog that stole the communion bread, was the incident at St Sepulchre's church, London, involving 'a woman dandling and dancing her child upon the Lord's holy table', leaving behind 'a great deal of water', which one observer reckoned 'were not tears of devotion'.[261]

Sabbath Offences

The Act of Uniformity required everyone 'to resort to their parish church' on Sundays and holy days, at risk of a fine of 1*s*. for each absence.[262] But a minority of scofflaws skimped on attendance or habitually 'neglected to attend' their parish church.[263] A hard core of serial offenders preferred drinking in alehouses to dutiful church attendance. Teenagers, servants, transients, and ne'er-do-wells were among those who wondered why they had to go to church at all, and were sometimes found carousing when the rest of the parish was at worship. From their point of view their free time was their own, though moralists would argue that no time was 'free', and that every hour was accountable to one's family, one's employer, and God.

The task fell to churchwardens 'to search alehouses and other places for idle company on Sundays in service time', though sometimes on finding Sabbath drinkers they sat down to share their tipple.[264] Churchwardens at

Whitechapel, Middlesex, cited parishioners before the diocesan court in 1626 'for having company drinking in their houses' when they should have been in church on the Powder Plot anniversary of 5 November.[265] At Littleton, Somerset, when churchwardens discovered men 'drinking and roaring in most rude manner... on Sundays and holy days during the time of morning and evening prayer', the roisterers resisted attempts to restrain them.[266] Sunday drinkers often spoke ill of the church and churchwardens, in an escalating chain of confrontation. 'Shit on the church, what care I for the church?' said Nicholas Crisp of Foulness, Essex, in 1633, when told he should have been at service.[267]

Thomas Flatman of Pulham Market, Norfolk, was similarly cited in 1634, and told the churchwarden who rebuked him 'he was a busy fellow, that he had nothing to do with him'.[268] When churchwardens at Downham, Cambridgeshire, presented William Segrave in 1638 for being absent from church, he abused them, saying 'that they were all forsworn men'. Thomas Blake of Thetford, Norfolk, responded to a churchwarden's warning by swearing 'by God's blood' and calling the official a liar.[269] When similarly confronted in 1638, Thomas Lockwood of Rayleigh, Essex, asserted that 'he might choose whether he would go to church or no', transgressing both law and custom.[270]

The law reserved Sundays and holy days for the service of God, all labour prohibited, but petty violations were common. The godly Edward Moreton was pleased to hear in 1626 of more laws in the making, 'restraining of carriers, drovers, etc., from travelling on the Lord's Day'.[271] Ecclesiastical officials repeatedly cited parishioners who ploughed fields, tended cattle, sheared sheep, ground corn, made hay, dried malt, set hop-poles, cut hedges, dug ditches, sold pears, or carted goods on the Sabbath, as if the Lord's Day was no exception to the farming routine. Thomas Cootes of Tilney St Lawrence, Norfolk, was cited in 1633 'for going about his own business upon the sabbath'. William Hansell of Yarmouth made things worse for himself after 'profanely working on the feast day of St John Baptist', by using 'very bad, lewd and unreverent speeches, saying... shite on the [archdeacon's] court'.[272] Other parishioners were found serving beer, selling meat, shaving beards, mending shoes, making barrels, carrying wood, spreading muck, working cloth, or otherwise busy at their trades on Sundays, or using the day for angling or hunting with dogs in pursuit of pleasure. Most of these people believed they had met their obligations by coming once to church, as if the rest of God's day was their own.[273]

Sabbatarian offences were subject to both ecclesiastical and secular censure. Parliamentary legislation in 1627 acknowledged that 'the Lord's Day commonly called Sunday is much broken and profaned by carriers, waggoners, carters, wain-men, butchers and drivers of cattle, to the great dishonour of God and reproach of religion'. The law specifically banned commercial transport and the butchery of animals on Sundays, and empowered Justices of the Peace to levy fines on offenders.[274] In further pursuit of godly discipline, the Lord Mayor of London attempted in 1629 to curtail the 'rude and profane' violation of the sanctity of the Sabbath. There should be no 'buying, selling, uttering or venting' of wares or commodities on that day, no 'porters carrying of burdens', no tradesmen 'working in their ordinary callings'. The authorities also planned to crack down on 'vintners, alehouse keepers, tobacco and strong water sellers', who 'greatly profane the sabbath day by suffering company to sit drinking and bibbing in their houses'. The City was supposed to shut down on Sundays and holy days, except for churchgoing and religiously approved activities, though enforcement was slack and erratic. Church leaders might have been expected to welcome this effort by the secular powers, but William Laud, then bishop of London, considered it an encroachment on his jurisdiction.[275]

Preserving the sanctity of the Sabbath was never a priority of secular magistrates, but two shoemakers were cited at Worcester Quarter Sessions in 1631 for selling shoes and carrying on their trade on a Sunday.[276] Robert Webb of Wilburton, Cambridgeshire, was likewise presented before the Ely assizes in 1638, 'for drawing of beer in the time of divine service and suffering of divers persons in his house' on a Sunday.[277] Bishop Matthew Wren of Ely was a stickler for Sabbath observances, prosecuting, among others, Richard Page of Emneth 'for carrying a piece of wood in a wheelbarrow through the town on a Sunday after evening prayer'; Ralph Burnham of Whittelsea for 'unloading his cart and making up his cart before morning prayer', thereby profaning the Sunday; and Robert Norman of Ely not just for going about his business but 'for killing a hog on Sunday next after Michaelmas'. The archetypal 'busy' bishop, Wren also cited four female servants at Wisbech 'for being sporting at the bowling green in time of divine service'.[278]

The church courts were especially concerned with activities that interfered with obligatory worship. The consistory court at Chester, for example, took action against the Ingham brothers of Rostherne in 1633 'for coursing hares with greyhounds on Sundays in service time'.[279]

A London diocesan court cited the keeper of a Bedlam who 'profaned the sabbath by public showing of the poor distressed mad people for money in time of service'.[280] A convivial coffin-maker in the London parish of St Sepulchre, London, fell foul of the archdeacon in 1636 for selling drink and 'having company in his house on Candlemas day and St Mathias day last past'.[281] A musician at Brisley, Norfolk, was cited 'for fiddling to young people in service time' in 1627. Another Norfolk fiddler was charged in 1637 with 'fiddling at Acle on Ascension day last, and by that means drawing company to him and keeping them from church'.[282]

Sanctions against laymen were relatively mild, rarely more severe than admonishment or temporary excommunication. Some of the church courts were also willing to consider excuses. John Ball of Pickwell, Leicestershire, told Archbishop Laud's visitation court in 1634 'that he did dress a lamb that was eaten with maggots upon a Sunday, which lamb was ready to perish, but that he did not otherwise work upon the sabbath'. William Throne's excuse for ploughing on St Martin's day was 'that he was seven miles from home and had but one day's work to do and had no more hay for his oxen, so that he did it upon necessity'. John Glover acknowledged that his servant 'did carry a sack of corn to the mill on horseback' one Sunday after evening prayer, but it was done, he said, without his knowledge or consent.[283] John Benham of Winterbourne Earls, Wiltshire, explained to the archdeacon in 1640 that he unloaded a cart of corn on a Sunday morning 'which otherwise had been spoilt by the rain'.[284] 'Cases of urgent necessity' found relatively sympathetic hearings among some Caroline clerics, though hard-liners were not so accommodating.[285] Refractoriness was no more acceptable among parishioners than among subjects in this church protected and governed by the king.

Accumulated Tensions

Charles I wanted order and conformity in religion, but his programmes and preferments generated friction. Almost every area of Caroline religious policy sparked controversy. At the local level, the conversion of communion tables to altars, the high-church adoption of the word priest, and the priests' insistence on kneeling and bowing, all seemed setbacks to godliness. The decorative makeover of high-profile churches, with proliferation of saints and angels and gilded letters IHS, showed which way the wind was blowing. From the suppression of Calvinist preaching to the licensing of Sunday sports, from the promotion of ceremonialist bishops to the war with presbyterian Scotland, from the queen's catholic chapel to the presence of papal agents at court, an orthodox protestant monarch sent signals that seemed to indicate a reversal of the Reformation. The shifts in religious culture, blessed by the king, seemed to be tending towards Rome. It is no wonder that popular opinion could imagine Laud angling for a cardinal's hat, or King Charles secretly attending mass with his queen.

Parish worship had always harboured variant streams within a nominally uniform framework. Piety and profanity coexisted, alongside devotion and disgruntlement, slovenliness and decorum. Enmity, anger, envy, and suspicion had always soured relationships within the Christian community, for no less could be expected from sinful mankind. Recognizing this, the Jacobean religious polity had accommodated minor diversity and contained the most divisive tendencies. King James and his bishops exercised ecclesiastical leadership but they knew their limits and left well enough alone.[286]

The Caroline regime, by contrast, was interventionist and therein lay its flaw. True to his principles, King Charles sought renewal within his church to make it more honourable to God. But in doing so he disturbed the customary balance and re-energized a quietened opposition. The king's desire for order and discipline, and the pressure of his prelates for ceremonial uniformity, ended the era of broadly accommodating inclusiveness to which many parishioners had become accustomed. Even routine efforts to secure reverence and piety caused inconvenience and resentment. Resistance was piecemeal and uncoordinated, and often unsuccessful, but accumulated tensions sharpened into fractures. Though royal and episcopal policies were designed for harmony and regularity, they stirred up anxiety and resentment. Imposed by authority, with minimal room for negotiation, they changed the pulse of parish life. These developments help explain how a crisis concerning kingship, finance, law, liberty, and the constitution gave shape to a civil war about religion.

8

The King's Declaration and the People's Sports

Following the example of James I, but without the pragmatism or finesse of that monarch, King Charles issued his 'Declaration of Lawful Sports' on 19 October 1633. It was done, he said, 'for the service of God, and for suppressing of any humours that oppose truth, and for the ease, comfort, and recreation of our well-deserving people'. But instead of promoting harmony it led to bitter and unnecessary division. Siding with proponents of a merry England who valued fellowship and festivity, in harmony with God's service, the Declaration authorized 'honest recreations' such as dancing and athletics, and allowed parishioners to engage in them after church on Sundays.[1] It clashed, however, with devout protestants who stood firm for the sanctity of the Lord's day. 'Remember the sabbath day, to keep it holy,' read the fourth of the Ten Commandments. Puritans in particular argued that the king's Declaration encouraged sinners in their 'wicked and evil courses', and exposed the people of England to God's 'avenging justice, both general, national, and personal', for violation of his law.[2] King James had published his Book of Sports in 1618, originally with reference to Lancashire, but with little follow-up or fuss; King Charles's version, by contrast, mobilized royal and ecclesiastical authority to enjoin nationwide compliance. Ministers who refused to read the Declaration from their pulpits now faced suspension, and parishioners argued whether dancing, ball games, and other Sunday frolics were more pleasing to the devil than to God. This chapter considers how King Charles's Declaration pitted royal authority against godly conscience. It politicized the practices of popular recreation, exacerbated the cultural tensions of the 1630s, and drove resisters deeper into puritanism.[3]

The Discipline of the Sabbath

Sundays and holy days were set aside for religious observances. Nobody was supposed to work on the Lord's day, though in practice there was winking when some people went about their business. King Charles himself saw no obstacle to meeting in Council or attending masques on a Sunday, and tolerant churchmen recognized the claims of 'necessity'.[4]

Godly clerics, however, insisted that the Sabbath was reserved for 'pious contemplations, reading of the Scriptures or hearing them read, recollecting what hath been heard from the mouths of God's messengers, speaking of the things which belong to the kingdom of God, singing of psalms, visiting the sick, and the like holy helps and acts of piety proper for that time'. It was no time for profane activity or revelry, such as 'dancing, May games, Whitsun ales, and sports', whereby 'God's name is dishonoured' and 'God's spiritual kingdom is prejudiced'.[5] Followers of the Calvinist William Perkins acknowledged some value in 'refreshing of body and mind', but condemned 'idle recreations' that could be 'occasions of sin'.[6] Less demanding churchmen recognized the importance of mandatory worship, but left the time after services to local discretion. Some acknowledged the health benefits of holy day recreations, and saw 'mirth and merry company' as antidotes to melancholy.[7]

Before 1633 it was mostly a matter of local discretion whether music and dancing, drinking and merry-making, or sports like archery and wrestling were permissible Sabbath activities provided they did not clash with church attendance. Customary recreations included team sports like village football, bat and ball games like stoolball or cricket, chasing games such as barley-break, running, leaping, bowling, or fives (a hand-ball game), and social activities such as morris and maypole dancing. Football could be played year round, but many of these games flourished best on summer evenings. In some parishes the minister and churchwardens joined in.[8] Churchwardens occasionally cited parishioners for playing 'skill bones' (knucklebones) or loggits (a stick-throwing game) on the Lord's day, but rarely made such presentments after the 1633 Declaration.[9]

The very first statute passed in King Charles's first parliament had tightened the law against the profanation of the Sabbath. Recognizing that 'the holy keeping of the Lord's day is a principal part of the true service of God, which in very many places of this realm hath been and now is profaned and neglected by a disorderly sort of people', it forbade people from leaving their home parish on Sundays 'for any sports or pastimes whatsoever', and placed a general ban on 'bear-baiting, bull-baiting, interludes, common plays, or other unlawful exercises or pastimes' on the Lord's day. The quick passage of this bill may have resulted from an uncharacteristic attempt by Charles I to placate elements in parliament who had sought for some years to pass similar measures. The former royal chaplain Henry Burton called it 'the prime gem in his royal diadem'. Enforcement depended upon local constables, churchwardens and justices, so long as ecclesiastical jurisdiction 'shall not be abridged'. The legislation of 1625 outlawed the blood sports of baiting bears and bulls on Sundays (though not hunting), and forbade 'other unlawful exercises or pastimes', but was not incompatible with the Jacobean Declaration, which permitted 'lawful' games and sports.[10]

Many communities were divided between supporters of customary recreations and critics who found them offensive. There was no legal prohibition of parish wakes or dedication feasts, maypoles or May games, but some local figures frowned on their foolery and frolic. Puritan clergy and godly magistrates had long attempted to suppress them. Proponents of 'the reformation of manners' saw Sunday sports and holiday pastimes as affronts to good order, and strict interpreters of the fourth commandment saw them angering God. The stage was set for clashes and disagreements that imperilled magisterial authority, ecclesiastical discipline, and community cohesion, and the king had yet to show his hand. It was a common lament among puritans 'that Christ hath received of Christians more wounds on a Sunday then he did of the Jews'.[11] On the other hand, a champion of the annual Cotswold games complained that 'country wakes and whirlings', carnivals and rush-bearing, May games and Whitsun ales, were all 'so reproved, traduced, condemned... that now few dare set them afoot'.[12] The cultural stresses were deeply veined, but had yet to amount to a rupture.

Magistrates in some areas became enforcers of sabbatarian discipline. Armed with the statute of 1625, the Worcestershire Quarter Sessions proceeded in 1627 against seven offenders, including a parish constable, who 'contrary to his majesty's laws played bowls in Birlingham churchyard on the first day of May'.[13] Justices at the Staffordshire Quarter Sessions in 1631 pressed for action in the name of the king against anyone who played 'unlawful games' on the Sabbath or otherwise profaned the Lord's day.[14] Reforming justices cracked down on offenders involved in Sunday drinking and 'company keeping', 'unlawful gaming', loitering with cards, and shooting of arrows when they should have been in church.[15] Ignatius Jurdain, the godly mayor of Exeter, attacked 'bowling and cudgel-playing, and other profane pastimes then used', in his attempt at local reform of the sabbath.[16]

The most bitter disputes occurred in Somerset, where magistrates, clerics and parishioners disagreed about what was seemly, comely, or permissible on Sunday evenings, in sacred space, in sacred time, or under parish sponsorship. The controversy over the Somerset church ales has been much studied, and has generally been regarded as a precipitant for King Charles's Book of Sports. Cultural, factional, and jurisdictional rivalries divided community leaders, though not necessarily along puritan lines. The assize chief justice and his allies sought to suppress parish wakes and revels, while episcopal authorities maintained them as occasions of good fellowship and as fund-raising opportunities for good causes. Critics worried about the sale of alcohol and inducements to disorder, while supporters upheld the decency, value, and antiquity of parish feasts. Theologically grounded sabbatarian concerns were a minor component, though bishops Laud and Piers used the dispute to bring the 'preciser sort' to discipline. A series of meetings, orders, messages, reports, and instructions between March 1632 and October 1633 culminated in Charles I's reissue of his father's Book of Sports.[17]

The King's Declaration

Political historians have argued whether responsibility for the reissue of the Declaration of Sports should be assigned to Charles I or his new archbishop, who was consecrated at Canterbury just a month earlier. Many contemporaries identified the Declaration with archbishop Laud, whom the puritan Henry Burton included among its 'arch patrons'.[18] The current weight of opinion sees Charles as the instigator and Laud as his loyal coadjutor, although the archbishop may have prompted the king.[19] Publicly it was 'the king's book', backed by royal authority. It may have been a misuse of power. By taking sides in a cultural dispute, rather than seeking to ignore or disarm it, Charles turned a matter of local discretion into a national issue. By demanding conformity and compliance, he turned matters of leisure and custom into tests of obedience and discipline. The Caroline Declaration politicized the reformation of manners and inserted the king more controversially than ever into the social and religious life of every parish. The new policy identified the crown with the culture of licence rather than the culture of probity, and in some eyes more with darkness than with light.

Lacking the legal force of a statute or proclamation, the Declaration was an act of prerogative that expressed a shift of policy, framed by the royal will. It repeatedly referred to the king's 'pleasure' that these directions be followed. Printed in London by the 'printer to the king's most excellent majesty', with all the authority thereby denoted, it carried imposing visual symbols, a full-page royal coat of arms, and a decorative heading of three linked British crowns. The iconography of the Declaration announced its origin and its force. The central provision mandated

> that after the end of divine service, our good people be not disturbed, letted, or discouraged from any lawful recreation, such as dancing, either men or women, archery for men, leaping, vaulting, or any other such harmless recreation, nor from having of May games, Whitsun ales, and morris dances, and the setting up of maypoles and other sports therewith used . . . and that

¶ By the King.

OVr Deare Father of blessed Memory, in his returne from Scotland, comming through Lancashire, found that his Subiects were debarred from Lawful Recreations vpon Sundayes after Euening Prayers ended, and vpon Holy dayes: And Hee prudently considered, that if these times were taken

A 3 from

Figure 10. The King's Book of Sports, 1633. *The Kings Maiesties Declaration to his Subiects, Concerning Lawfull Sports to be used* (1633), sigs A2^{v} and A3.

women shall have leave to carry rushes to the church for the decoring of it, according to their old custom.[20]

Explaining this development to Lord Wentworth in Ireland, the Westminster observer George Garrard referred to 'the king's Declaration lately set out to give liberty to servants after evening prayer to use lawful exercises for refreshment'. Writing in December 1633, Garrard noted that the Declaration sparked 'much difference in opinion'. 'Though it be the same verbatim that was published in King James's time, yet it is commanded to be read in all the churches here and in the country,' and therein lay the difference. The Declaration was as much about power as religion. It forced people into choices and illuminated loyalties. Apologists could observe that King Charles's Declaration was nothing new, and therefore inoffensive, but the cultural, religious, and political circumstances of the 1630s were radically different. Referring to the dispute among Somerset magistrates over 'wakes and love feasts', Garrard noted, 'this new Declaration shuts their mouths for the future'.[21] Historians who minimize the effect of the Declaration by citing its Jacobean precedent should be similarly cautioned.

Thomas Crosfield at Oxford also observed that the Declaration was 'first published by King James', but was reissued now 'to the opposition of some doctrine taught by some of our divines' and to protect church dedication feasts, 'commonly called wakes', from puritan attack. It would also stop the mouths of Roman Catholics who claimed 'there is no tolerable recreation allowed in our religion', and would have the added benefit of encouraging 'the common people' in 'such exercises as may make their bodies more able for war'. Although he approved of it, Crosfield recognized that the king's book was 'much agitated by precise men . . . because as they pretend it opens a gap to much licentiousness'.[22]

The Declaration carried multiple messages, and would have various consequences. It directed attention to the law and theology of the Sabbath, and led many ministers to interrogate their consciences. Wrapped up as it was in the royal prerogative, the king's book called for public commitments of duty and subjection. It generated a stir of commentary and criticism in private conversations, in pulpits and the press, and sharpened divisions within English religious culture.

The eighteen-page booklet of 1633 would cost sixpence or more to buy and would take a good five minutes to read. It was backed by letters to the bishops to see the work published in every parish, with instructions that the names of incumbents who refused to read it aloud should be returned to London. Five hundred copies arrived at Wells at the end of November for distribution in the diocese where the trouble began.[23]

Churchwardens' accounts reveal not only the amount they paid and their alacrity of payment, but also the names by which the Declaration travelled. Most referred it as a 'book', although no such word appears in its text. The varying unofficial nomenclature suggests something between unease and uncertainty as parishes grappled with its implications. At Great St Mary's, Cambridge, the churchwardens paid *6d.* in 1634 'for a book of the king's Declaration'.[24] Holy Trinity, Cambridge, belatedly acquired 'the book reading of recreations' in 1635.[25] Churchwardens at Great Yarmouth, Norfolk, paid *8d.* for a book 'concerning sports and recreations of the Sunday'.[26] At Framlingham, Suffolk, they paid the same for a book 'touching liberty of sabbath days'.[27] In Essex at Saffron Walden it was 'a book for the publishing of recreation',[28] at Thaxted 'the book of recreations on Sundays'.[29] Churchwardens at Strood, Kent, referred to 'a book of sports'.[30]

Devonshire parishes identified the king's book in various ways. At Bere Ferrers it was simply 'a book to be read in the church' that cost the churchwardens *6d.*[31] At Clawton it was 'a book of recreations allowed by our king's majesty'.[32] Churchwardens at Hartland called it 'a book of toleration for pastimes'.[33] At Honiton it was 'the king's majesty's book of declarations' and here it cost 1*s.*[34] Woodbury paid 'for a book sent to be published concerning his majesty's liberty for certain recreations therein expressed'.[35] Sherborne, Dorset, recorded 'one book concerning the toleration of recreation upon the sabbath day'.[36] Cerne Abbas paid *8d.* 'for a book entitled the king's majesty's Declaration', only a short while after paying 3*s.* 10*d.* 'for taking down the maypole and making a tower ladder of it'.[37] At Long Burton, Dorset, it was 'the book of recreation and pastime'.[38] The parish of St Edmund, Salisbury, paid *6d.* for 'the book of toleration'.[39] Newark, Nottinghamshire, acquired 'a book of recreations sent by the bishop',[40] while at nearby Upton it was 'a book that came from the king's majesty'.[41] St Mary's Chester noted 'the book of toleration of lawful recreations'.[42] In Henry Burton's parish of St Matthew, Friday Street, London, it was simply, and perhaps ominously, 'the king's book'.[43] Referring scornfully to the declaration a few years later, Sir Benjamin Rudyard called it 'the morris book' that licensed games and dancing.[44] The most reckless and censorious puritans saw it as the work of the devil.[45]

The government insisted that ministers publish the Declaration in their parishes, and local ecclesiastical authorities set up systems to monitor compliance, with varying degrees of efficiency. Bishop Matthew Wren at Hereford, and later at Norwich, asked parish officers, 'hath the king's declaration concerning the lawfull sports and recreations been published among you, yea or no? If so, when was it done, in what manner, and by whom?'[46] Following instructions from bishop Davenant of Salisbury, the churchwardens at Long Burton, Dorset, exhibited a certificate 'that the book of recreation and pastime was read in church' in 1634.[47] A similar 'certificate of the toleration' cost the churchwardens of Sherborne *6d.*[48] At Hitchin, Hertfordshire, they certified that their curate had read the Declaration 'distinctly and treatably . . . after the reading of the first Lesson . . . most of the parishioners being present'.[49] The churchwardens of North Nibley, Gloucestershire, who had apparently slacked in this matter, paid fees and fines of two shillings and sixpence in 1635 when explaining their remissness to the archdeacon.[50] At Holy Trinity, Cambridge, late in compliance, they paid two shillings 'for a presentment for not reading the book of liberty' in 1635.[51] These pecuniary mulcts, however, were trivial compared to the loss of income and status for dissenting clerics who faced suspension from their ministry.

To Read or Not to Read

For radicalized puritans like Henry Burton, the king's book was a declaration of war on God. Its publication 'set open the floodgates to this presumptuous sin of sabbath breaking'. By encouraging sinners in their 'wicked and evil courses', and by rejecting 'the precepts and admonitions of God and his faithful ministers', the king's book exposed England to God's 'avenging justice'. The 'tragedy' lay not just in official encouragement of 'ethnic pastimes' but also in the evidence that the king was an apostate, reneging on his promise of 1625 to promote respect for the Lord's day.[52]

Burton declared in his London pulpit, and dared to repeat in print (from Amsterdam), that the book was 'a snare and engine to out good ministers . . . a most pernicious snare to all the ministers of England . . . to overturn the fourth commandment'. It encouraged 'unbridled, untaught and unseasoned youth' to engage, with the king's permission, in pastimes that godly masters, ministers and parents disapproved. The Book of Sports, thundered Burton, risked 'cutting in sunder the very sinews, not only of religion but of all civil society at one blow'.[53]

Nonsense, remonstrated the conformist Christopher Dow. The king's Declaration merely intended 'to take away that scandal, which some rigid sabbatarians had brought upon our religion, to the hindering of the conversion of catholic recusants'. It revealed his majesty's 'charitable intention' of allowing people to pursue 'such honest recreations as might serve for their refreshment, and better enabling them to go through with their hard labours on other days', and 'did not forget his wonted respect to piety and the service of God, or due sanctification of the Lord's day'.[54] From one perspective the Declaration was benign, from another malicious. Caught in the middle were anxious clerics, whose ministry depended upon their public compliance, and parishioners who needed guidance on how to spend their Sundays.

The requirement that ministers everywhere publish the king's Declaration in their parishes caused many of them anxiety. The so-called godly or puritan clergy were especially troubled. If they had preached conscientiously against the profanation of the Sabbath, how could they now in conscience support a programme that made the Lord's day an occasion for festive recreation? If they had campaigned against such customs as parish wakes, maypoles, garlands, and dancing as remnants of popery and superstition, and had denounced such practices as inducements to sin, how could they endorse their legitimation? The Declaration tore them in competing directions, pitting one vision of order against another.

'This Declaration for allowing such plays, feasts, banquets, church ales, drinkings, profane usages and pastimes on the Lord's day' risked making it instead 'the Devil's day', wrote one anonymous cleric. It was so 'point blank against the statutes of the realm, the homilies, articles, canons of the church . . . yea, against the constant doctrine of all godly and faithful ministers' that he wondered 'if the Declaration be his majesty's'.[55] Was it, perhaps, a sign that malignant advisors had gained control of the state? Puritans in Buckinghamshire thought the Declaration a device of the 'priests and bishops . . . to vex the godly'.[56] The very Sunday sports that the king now deemed 'lawful', meaning socially and legally acceptable, were 'unlawful' in godly eyes; they were dangerous to salvation and contrary to the commands of God. One conflicted minister struggled because it was 'sinful disobedience to his sacred majesty' not to publish the Declaration as ordered, but also a 'violation of God Almighty's laws' to endorse sinful sports on the Sabbath.[57] Other members of the godly community shared advice and support while trying to resolve their consciences. One of them, Nicholas Eastwick of Warkton, Northamptonshire, was not entirely decided 'whether recreations on the Lord's day be lawful or not', but he was distressed to find 'the supreme authority would... have quickened men to practice them'. 'His majesty's Declaration', he told Samuel Ward at Cambridge, 'hath caused much distraction and grief in many honest men's hearts'. With profound misgivings, he allowed the book to be published in his church on the basis not of its content but its authority.[58]

William Morton, a 'preacher of God's word' at Leicester, with ties to puritans at Newcastle-upon-Tyne, puzzled out the problem in a four-page memorandum on the question of 'whether it is lawful for a minister to publish the book of the lawfulness of sports to be used on the Lords day'. The very title of this disquisition evokes two systems of authority that were often in conflict: the law of God and the law of man. Was it possible, Morton asked, to thread a way between the lord of heaven and the lord of England? Could a godly minister's conscience be reconciled with his dutiful 'obedience to the king'? What if the king's course seemed contrary to God's? For ministers of the 'profane and dissolute' sort, meaning, so Morton thought, the majority of the conformist clerical profession, the king's book posed no problem. Some of them actively encouraged the culture of the ale bench and joined in Sunday sports. But for 'such as desire to walk by preaching and practice' in the way of God, like Morton and his brethren, the Declaration raised both practical and spiritual complications.[59]

One concern among more fearful members of the godly community was that this Declaration was merely the thin end of a Romanizing wedge. '[If] I publish this, thereby to obey authority, I may publish any other thing that shall be commanded. What if enjoined to publish that the mass is good, images not unlawful, the reading of Scriptures dangerous to lay people, to fill them with schism? Then shall our ministry be used to infect the people.' Should the line be drawn now against this profanation, Morton wondered, or should the godly community gird itself for future struggles?

Possible ways forward involved casuistical reinterpretation of the wording of the Declaration, and wilful misreading of instructions to publish it in the parishes. In its original Jacobean form, the Declaration invoked the king's 'loyal subjects', his 'loving subjects', and, at least four times, 'our good people'. Charles I's re-promulgation referred repeatedly to 'our good people', 'our well-deserving people', and 'our loyal and dutiful subjects'. It was clearly addressed to subjects who understood their obligations, to encourage them therein. But Morton turned this around by suggesting that 'dissolute people, the frequenters and adorers of these sports, in whom ministers find so much gross ignorance and opposition', could not possibly be styled 'the king's good people'. In which case, perhaps, the Declaration did not apply.

This did not resolve the very practical problem of whether or not to comply with the instruction to publish the Declaration in the parish. But what if a minister, convinced in his conscience that the book was dangerous, merely went through the motions while showing 'his dislike of it to the people'? After all, as Morton noted, 'approbation is not required, only publication commanded'. There was also room for some creative fudgery, for, 'though Sunday be the day appointed for it, the time of day, whether in service or before or after is not expressed'. Perhaps a minister could meet the requirements by publishing the Declaration to an empty church, or having someone read it in his stead.

Having set forth these possibilities, Morton immediately considered their consequences. Such deception, if reported, would mostly likely expose godly ministers to the 'rage' of episcopal authorities. 'For ministers to show opposition in this... will be interpreted to flow from a spirit of contradiction,' which could lead to their punishment and suspension. How did this help the godly cause, Morton asked, when 'the putting out of so many lights may be the thing aimed at by them who would bring in darkness?' What was the benefit in risking suspension? Perhaps it was better, in current circumstances, to comply with the Declaration and trust in the Lord. 'It is wisdom in evil times to gain time, who knows what the day may bring forth? The storm may blow over as in King James's time. Thus our liberty may be reserved for better times.' Morton's meditation came to no clear conclusion, but thoughts like these gave cover to those who decided to temporize by outward compliance. Conformity, after all, could be a strategy as well as an impulse or conviction. A similar dilemma faced some of those who considered moving to Massachusetts, but girded themselves instead for God's struggle in England.

Salves to Conscience

The requirement to read the king's Book of Sports posed moral and professional challenges to ministers who disagreed with it. A variety of strategies evolved to substitute avoidance and prevarication for wholehearted compliance. The need to employ these strategies varied from place to place, since different dioceses imposed varying degrees of disciplinary pressure.

One way to keep distance from the book was by having a substitute publish it to the congregation. Richard Clayton, the rector of Shawell, Leicestershire, thought to salve his conscience in this regard by having the village schoolmaster read 'his majesty's book' in the church at Christmas, at a time when the minister was absent.[60] At Brigstock, Northamptonshire, the parish clerk read the words while the vicar ostentatiously covered his ears.[61] Another strategy was to publish into the void. Threatened with suspension unless he followed orders to read the king's book, Edward Williams, the minister at Shaftesbury, Dorset, read it an hour before service one holy day morning, declaring 'it was the parishioners' fault' if they were not present.[62] Others mumbled the words so they could not be heard, or read the book when the service was over or before the congregation had settled.

A high-risk strategy was to read the book and then to teach against it, high risk because direct attacks were likely to provoke official retaliation. Several staunch puritans daringly contrasted the Book of Sports with the Bible, to suggest that the king of England had parted company from God. Stephen Dennison, the puritan minister of St Katherine Cree, London, was heard to read the book, then to read the Ten Commandments, and to address his congregation: 'Dearly beloved, you have heard now the commandments of God and man, obey which you please.' Another cleric at St Giles in the Fields reportedly fulfilled his duty by reading the book, 'and the same day preached upon the fourth commandment: Remember the sabbath day, to keep it holy'.[63] Others were more forthright in their condemnation. 'Whatsoever the king is pleased to have done . . . the king of heaven commands us to keep the sabbath,' preached vicar Bartholomew of Enmore, Somerset. How could King Charles 'allow of that which God did forbid?' asked William Treble of nearby Combe Florey.[64] Edward Williams, the minister of Shaftesbury, who had earlier read the book to an empty church, used his Easter sermon in 1634 to uphold the sanctity of the Sabbath. By this book, said parson Williams, perhaps holding aloft a copy of the Declaration, 'God was more dishonoured, and the devil better served, on the Sunday than all the week besides'. Were there not ten commandments, and should we now have nine? As Joshua said to the Israelites, he continued, 'choose ye whom ye will serve. But as for me and my house, we will serve the Lord.' Shocked parishioners informed archbishop Laud of this latest of their minister's provocations.[65]

A gentleman parishioner, Francis Thompson, smarting under accusations of adultery, reported Henry Page of Ledbury, Herefordshire, for pouring 'scorn and derision' on 'the king's most excellent majesty's Declaration concerning the lawfulness of recreation upon Sundays and holy days'. Vicar Page apparently asked his people:

> Is it not as lawful to pluck at a cart rope upon the sabbath day as at a bell rope? Is it not as lawful for a weaver to shoot his shuttle on the sabbath day as for a man to take his bow to shoot? And is it not as lawful for a woman to spin at her wheel or for a man to go to plough or cart as for a man on the sabbath day to dance that devilish round?

Compounding other failures to conform, like not making the sign of the cross in baptism and generally neglecting the surplice, these accusations brought Page before the court of High Commission. Facing deprivation, he decided to submit, 'not puritan-like . . . by shift and evasions to shuffle it, but . . . with an humble and ingenuous confession'. The vicar said he was sorry for the alleged words that 'slipped from him', and now he was ready 'to read the king's book'.[66]

In Buckinghamshire the Laudian toady John Andrews made it his business to denounce fellow-ministers who failed to read the Declaration. In April 1635 he informed Sir John Lambe, dean of the court of arches and Laud's commissary for the archdeaconry of Buckingham, that, in the deaneries of Burnham, Wycombe, and Wendover, 'very few incumbents' did their duty, 'and they for their obedience are slandered'. After Lambe had suspended the ministers of Chalfont St Giles and Chesham, Andrews reported, parishioners 'banned and cursed' diocesan officials 'to the pit of hell', and avowed that they 'suffer[ed] persecution for righteousness sake'. The women, he said, were especially vocal in support of their suspended priests.[67] A year later Andrews wrote directly to archbishop Laud to report refusals by 'the faction' to read 'his majesty's book touching lawful sports on holy days after divine service'. 'Indeed some there be', he continued, 'who in their Cartwrightian uncanonical prayers before sermons, do pasquil and libel a little against it . . . saying: we beseech thee good Lord, stand up and defend thy Sa-ba-oths from profanation, and vindicate thy holy word from contempt; as if his majesty did either desire God's holy days should be profaned, or his blessed word contemned'.[68] After repeated warnings the vicar of Olney 'equivocated and dissembled' when he read the book and then 'let the people see how ill it was'.[69]

The book had become a shibboleth, a test of orthodoxy and allegiance. Just as the regime sought constantly to distinguish 'factious spirits' from the king's 'loving subjects', so the king's book served to differentiate refractory from dutiful ministers, the bad from the good. As one newswriter remarked in September 1634, 'the state doth now take notice that the reading and the not reading this book is become a mark of distinction to know a good and bad minister'. If they refused to read the king's book, what other refusals might follow? 'The question will not be, whether it be lawful or not lawful to sport upon the Lord's day, but whether these ministers have all done ill to disobey the command of authority.'[70] Ministers who 'refuse to publish their sovereign's royal pleasure' by reading the Declaration were 'justly punished', said Christopher Dow, not for their views on the sabbath but for their sinful disobedience to the king's authority.[71]

Most of the ministers who baulked at the Book of Sports insisted that they were 'otherwise conformable'. They followed the prayer book, wore their surplices, and were not known as 'puritans'. A manuscript newsletter in March 1634 told how several such ministers in Surrey were suspended 'for not reading of the king's book for dancing and other recreations', and now faced loss of their livings. In July 1634 fourteen more in the diocese of Winchester were similarly suspended over 'the king's book . . . for liberty of recreations'.[72] The sixty or so ministers in the diocese of Peterborough who refused to read the Declaration were likewise 'orthodoxal diligent preachers', according to one of their colleagues.[73] If this is true, it points to the potential of the king's Declaration to antagonize moderate conformists and turn them against the regime.

Enforcement varied from jurisdiction to jurisdiction. Bishops Piers of Bath and Wells, Curle of Winchester, and Wren of Norwich were the most rigorous and demanding, the northern dioceses most accommodating. Archbishop Laud, surprisingly, was among the more flexible administrators, repeatedly allowing objectors time to explain and appeal.[74] Ministers who clashed with officials over the king's Book of Sports faced an escalating register of sanctions of admonishment, suspension, and deprivation. Suspension from ministry barred a cleric from performing his functions; suspension from benefice stopped his income; deprivation and ejection ended his career. One man's ouster was another's opportunity, and it was soon reported that 'some divines are making means to get into their livings'. There was never a shortage of ordinands and place-seekers angling for preferment. When several ministers in Surrey were suspended for not reading the king's book, commentators predicted that 'some others will be put into their livings, and they shall be thrust out'.[75] There were no mass expulsions, but several hundred ministers experienced suspension. The Suffolk gentleman Robert Reyce alarmed his friends in New England with news of 'many ministers suspended and put from their places for not conformity and reading the king's book for liberty and recreation on the Lord's day'.[76] Only the most conscience-stricken (or most obstinate, depending on point of view) resisted to the point of deprivation. One of them was Laurence Snelling, rector of Cray St Paul's, Kent, since Jacobean times, who could not bring himself to read the Declaration. He was first presented for his non-compliance in November 1633, and for four years held out against admonishment, suspension, and excommunication, until he was called before the Court of High Commission. Given one last chance in February 1638, Snelling still refused, and so continued excommunicate and was deprived of his rectory. The court could accommodate his failure to bow at the 'the blessed name of our saviour Jesus', and even wink at his laxity in wearing the surplice, but disobedience to his king and bishop was unforgiveable.[77]

Puritan memorialists exaggerated the suffering and disruption provoked by the Declaration, while apologists for the regime set it at a minimum. The Laudian Peter Heylyn chided Henry Burton for his 'false and unjust clamours' and discounted puritan claims of 'censure' and 'persecution'. Suspensions were by nature temporary, contrition secured absolution, and only the most obdurate nonconformists lost their posts. 'Call you this a persecution,' Heylyn asked, 'when a few refractory persons are justly punished in a legal way for their disobedience?'[78] The numbers might have been higher and the pastoral cost more damaging had not hundreds of ministers heeded counsels of casuistry, caution, moderation, and restraint.

Contested Sports

Historians usually treat the Declaration of Sports as a test for the ministry, as if it was primarily a clerical issue. But the laity were directly involved, as the immediate audience to whom the Declaration was to be declared and as subjects whose Sundays it affected. If, as seems likely, it was read in most parishes, either by the incumbent or by a surrogate, the king's book of 1633 may have been the most widely disseminated of all royal declarations. Parishioners almost everywhere had the chance to hear the royal words and to ponder their message. The king's book was a text to be discussed as much as an order to be observed.

Recreational enthusiasts cheered the Declaration and hurried to take advantage of it, while other parishioners displayed disapproval. Pockets of lay hostility are suggested by the newswriter Edward Rossingham's comment that 'the state is obliged to vindicate those that read this book, because they suffer for it among the people'.[79] Richard Wettnoll, a baker of the parish of St Anne Agnes, London, showed his contempt by 'putting his hat on in time of divine service and going out of the church when the king's book was read', and was excommunicated until he performed penance.[80] Raphael Britten, a silk buyer from Olney, Buckinghamshire, supported ministers who refused to read the Book of Sports, saying 'no good man will read it or cause it to be read'.[81] The painter James Priest declared somewhat drunkenly at Cambridge one Sunday that 'some scurvy popish bishop hath got a toleration . . . for these boys to play upon the sabbath day, which if the king did understand himself he would not suffer it'. Later, contrite and sober, Priest affected surprise to be told that he 'had spoken against the bishops, and against the book of recreation', and offered apology.[82]

Evidence from Berkshire shows that there too the king's Book of Sports became a topic for alehouse chatter. Late in 1633 a gathering of artisans (including a tanner, a shoemaker, a minstrel, and two tallow chandlers) 'fell into discourse about the bishops', and Edward Parsons of Aldermaston, tanner, jested to the minstrel Thomas Hellyer 'that now his roguish profession might go forward again', and called archbishop Laud 'an unsanctified rascal' for 'setting forth the book of recreations'. He also referred to bishop Bowle of Rochester as 'a sot', and was summoned a few months later to explain himself before the Privy Council.[83] In another overheard conversation, Arthur

Durvall of Ditcheat, Somerset, told a friend in 1634 'that it was as great a sin for a man to play bowls on a sabbath day as it was to lie with his neighbour's wife', notwithstanding the king's Book of Sports.[84] At Stony Stratford, Buckinghamshire, in 1635 John Boone and James Miller took direct action against licensed recreations by 'sawing down a maypole and drawing it away on the sabbath day'.[85]

Godly gentlemen expressed politer disapproval of the Book of Sports. Ignatius Jurdain, a Devonshire merchant and former member of parliament, wrote to the bishop of Exeter 'to desire the king to recall it', but succeeded only in drawing attention to himself as a puritan trouble-maker. According to a later account, Jurdain's opposition so angered King Charles that he threatened to hang him.[86] The melancholic Bedfordshire gentleman John Spencer sought several times to warn King Charles of the dangers posed by his 'book for the recreation upon the Lord's day'.[87] The Kentish gentleman Edward Boys, patron of the living at Goodnestone, also spoke disparagingly of 'the book of sabbath recreations' in 1634, saying 'that it was unfit such books should be sent for ministers to read in the church'. Later, however, he changed his mind and said 'it was a good book, and if it were read the sabbath would be better kept than ever it was'. His change of heart may have been associated with his scheme to secure the living for his cousin, and this may have been easier if the incumbent Richard Culmer was suspended for failing to read the king's book.[88]

One effect of the Declaration was to undercut godly ministers who had preached against pastimes that were now explicitly approved. At Shawell, Leicestershire, for example, where Richard Clayton had rebuked parishioners for their sabbath recreations, the rector's enemies turned the Book of Sports against him. He had several times prohibited 'running and dancing and... [had] forbidden musicians or fiddlers and pipers to play, saying it was profane and unlawful', and had set some offenders in the stocks. On one occasion he silenced the music by buying the piper's instrument (a set of Scottish pipes) and paying him to play no more on Sundays. Parishioners denounced Clayton's actions before archbishop Laud's visitation court in 1634 and claimed that they were 'thereby debarred of their lawful recreations graciously allowed them by his majesty'.[89] Another minister in Leicestershire could keep his congregation from flocking to their evening games only by extending his sermon with long extempore prayers until it was too dark for after-church amusements.[90]

Merry-makers charged with profanation of the Sabbath now claimed royal protection, even if their games took place during service time. The archdeacon of Berkshire heard in November 1633, soon after the promulgation of the king's book, that earlier in September 'there were divers of the parishioners of Compton were absent from evening prayer . . . and were dancing in a corn field or meadow called Priory Mead'. Though this was patently transgressive, the ecclesiastical authorities were disinclined to discover the names of the church-avoiders or 'what sport or recreation they then and there used'. An unofficial harvest festival gained retroactive cover from the king's Declaration of Sports.[91] In Leicestershire too, when parishioners of Hungarton and Keame were found 'playing at hand-ball on Sunday in time of divine service' in May 1634, they protested that evening prayer was ended and their activity was now permitted.[92] Participants in May games and morris dances at Donnington, Yorkshire, in 1634 also claimed they were licensed by the king's Book of Sports.[93] So too did one group of parishioners in Northamptonshire in 1635 who disputed whether 'ringing a peal or two, dancing, playing at football, barley-break, and other recreations on the Sunday after evening prayer' was lawful.[94] Sunday evening dancing at Olney, Buckinghamshire, deteriorated into a tumult in 1636 after the vicar brought out constables with halberds to halt the revels.[95]

Recreational activities were revitalized in Somerset, and a festive revival took hold in other parts of England.[96] Diocesan officials in Oxfordshire became more permissive of drinking at Rogationtide perambulations after the king's Declaration of Sports.[97] Bishop Montague of Norwich was untroubled by 'dancings, morrises, meetings at Easter, drinkings, Whitsun ales, midsummer merrimakes and the like, nor by stoolball, football, wrestlings, wasters' or boys' sports', so long as they steered clear of the consecrated churchyard. He none the less insisted that no parishioner 'profane any Sunday or holy day by any unlawful gaming, drinking or tippling' during time of service.[98] The churchwardens of Shipston-upon-Stour, Worcestershire, proudly recorded a surplus of £4 in accounts for 1635, 'being money gotten by the youth of the town of Shipston at a May game' to buy coal for the poor.[99] Traditionalists cited the Book of Sports to justify their practices, while protestors looked beyond it to what they thought to be the law of God.

At Woolston, Worcestershire, after the king's Declaration, 'many of the inhabitants the spring following were emboldened to set up maypoles, morris dance, and a Whitsun ale, continuing their rude revelling a week together, with many affronts to their ancient and reverend pastor'. In parishes nationwide, observed Henry Burton, 'when prayer and sermon were ended, the drum is struck up, the pieces discharged, the musicians play, and the rout fall a dancing till the evening'. Puritans like Burton were horrified by official encouragement to debauchery, and saw the providential hand of God when participants in such antics came to grief. Burton's compendium of tragedies that befell profaners of the Sabbath shows them brewing beer, engaging minstrels, erecting maypoles, dancing lasciviously, and generally running riot on the Lord's day, and then experiencing fatal or near fatal accidents. Time and again, in Burton's account, reprobate merry-makers excused their violation of the Sabbath by reference to the king's Declaration, as if 'the Book of Sports gave them full liberty'. The effect, he said, was like dry fuel to a flame, or like pent-up waters that wildly broke forth from the floodgates.[100]

Parish revellers found support from clerics like Alexander Clark, vicar of Bredfield, Suffolk, who encouraged everyone to 'play and follow their business on the Lord's day', and who 'publicly sported himself with his parishioners on the Lord's day at barley-break'; like Nicholas Wright, the rector of Theydon Garnon, Essex, who 'preached to maintain the lawfulness' of the king's book, and cheered on 'football-playing and other ungodly practices' on Sundays; and like Henry Hannington, vicar of Hougham, Kent, who, having read the Book of Sports, had 'beer laid into his bar, and dancing and drinking there that day; and to give them more time for it, he dismissed the congregation with a few prayers and let off preaching in the afternoon'. The godly termed these priests 'malignant', though such clerics thought of themselves as upholders of the rhythms and rituals of parish life.[101]

Though Maytide customs belonged to an ancient tradition, perhaps older than Christianity, they heightened tension along the cultural fault-lines of early Stuart England. May morning observances in Oxford in 1634 led to a confrontation between traditional celebrants who would decorate the church with floral garlands, and custodians of order and sanctity who sought to protect God's house from abuse. When John Eastbrook, a master of arts of New Inn Hall, arrived for service in the church of St Peter in the Bailey, he found a young man climbing a beam, trying to affix a garland to the chancel screen. Affronted by this unseemly behaviour, and outraged by the young man's dirty shoes, Eastwood pulled him down by the heels and began to berate him. Revellers, students, scholars, and citizens joined the fray. The resulting fight was 'violent and furious', leaving several people injured. The contest pitted age against youth, respectability against rambunctiousness, and, to a lesser degree, gown against town. The Oxford parishioners were divided, with Edward Mitchell the butcher supporting the erection of the garlands, and John Wildgoose and others trying to pull them down. The academics too were split between those like Christopher Rogers, the principal of New Inn Hall, who thought that the Book of Sports 'opens a gap to much licentiousness', and those more respectful of the royal will. When university authorities investigated the incident, they asked Eastbrook 'whether he doth allow of those sports and recreations which are allowed by the king's majesty's late Declaration', and whether he 'hath spoken words in contempt and dislike of the same?' Issues of royal authority were at stake, and Eastbrook was made to acknowledge his fault, performing penance, openly in the church. The garlands, presumably, stayed up for the duration of May, not only at St Peter's but in most of the churches of Oxford.[102] May Day passed more peaceably at nearby Woodstock, the king's manor, where officials purchased a maypole in 1634 at the township's expense.[103]

The Declaration of Sports did not end the reformation of manners, nor did it ease the cultural stresses that troubled early Stuart England. The king's initiative temporarily silenced some godly magistrates and their puritan clerical allies, but some of the 'preciser sort' still sought to curb Sunday revels. Gabriel Sangar, the rector of Sutton Mandeville, Wiltshire, still told parishioners 'that those that did take recreations upon the sabbath day were not the children of God, but rather to be termed reprobates'.[104] In Lincolnshire, Richard Northen, the curate of Hainton, declared it a theft from God to 'take any recreations on the sabbath day, and he was worse than a thief, for he was a villain and a sacrilegious thief that did allow them'. The curate and constable chased Sunday pipers and dancers with pitchforks and set some of them in the stocks. Northen had to answer for his offences in the court of High Commission.[105] Notwithstanding the king's Declaration, the churchwardens of Brislington, Somerset, 'inhibited the young people their lawful sport after evening prayer' on Whit Sunday 1636, 'and set the musicians by the heels'. The conformist minister Oliver Chiver complained of their hypocrisy, because 'they suffer unlawful gaming and tippling almost every Sunday and present not any for it'.[106] A Shropshire man said that year that, if the minister did not allow Sunday dancing, now permitted by the king's book, 'he should catechize and preach to the walls' of an empty church.[107] A justice

Cole in Suffolk in 1637 threatened to indict anyone 'who used on Sundays any of those sports permitted in the king's book, and against the statute' of 1625, although the momentum of the time was against him.[108]

Writing to the Laudian lawyer Sir John Lambe in April 1639, the arch-conformist Robert Sibthorpe denounced his puritan neighbour Francis Marston, the minister of Brackley, Northamptonshire, for trying to exclude musicians from the parish for fear 'that they would be a means that the people would make use of the liberty of his majesty's Declaration of Lawful Sports'. Two musicians had recently arrived in Brackley, and the community split over whether to label them as vagrants who should be punished and expelled, or lawful incomers to be allowed to settle. The puritan 'faction' wanted them gone, and persuaded a godly magistrate to proceed against them. Sibthorpe, and those he called 'the best of my parishioners', by contrast welcomed the musicians, who recruited three more, and arranged for the quintet to be 'licensed for the waits or music of our Brackley fair, which is upon St Andrew's day' (30 November). Here as elsewhere, cultural differences exacerbated by the Book of Sports grew into conflicts about a range of issues, including social policy and magisterial authority, with each group 'infinitely offended' by the other.[109]

Ecclesiastical courts continued to cite offenders against the Sabbath, but with a light and lenient touch. When Robert Lord and others were cited in 1634 'for playing at nine men's morris in the churchyard on Sunday' at Bitteswell, Leicestershire, they were simply admonished and dismissed. Their error was the misuse of consecrated ground, not the profanation of the Lord's day.[110] John Hutchinson of York was cited in 1636 'for playing at nine holes and ten bones several times upon the Sunday in times of divine service', but might have stayed out of trouble if he had chosen a better time of day.[111] Ten men of Stanhope, Durham, who were cited in 1636 'for playing at bowls in the evening prayer time' promised not to offend in the future.[112] Young men of Beverley, Yorkshire, could still face presentment 'for playing football on a Sunday about Christmas' 1635, though most likely, on this occasion, because their game turned violent.[113] When swarms of young college men played Sunday football in the castle yard at Cambridge in April 1640, the vice-chancellor John Cosin rebuked them not for violating the Sabbath but for fighting with townsmen.[114]

Critics of the king's Declaration had limited access to the press and were reduced to publishing, if they dared, in Amsterdam or Edinburgh. Episcopal licencers were said to have expunged 'wholesome doctrine' relating to the

Sabbath in William Jones, *A Commentary upon the Epistle of Saint Paul to Philemon* (1635), 'lest it should mar a ball, a wake, or a morris dance upon the Lord's Day, and to comply with the Book of Sports'.[115] Henry Burton's books, published illicitly in the Netherlands, brought him to Star Chamber, the pillory, disfigurement, and prison. The lawyer William Prynne shared similar punishment for 'seditious' writings including *Newes from Ipswich* (Edinburgh?, 1636), which claimed that the prelates had turned the Lord's day into 'the Devil's day . . . to advance his own kingdom and service on it'.[116]

Supporters, on the other hand, enjoyed both patronage and opportunity, and brought forth a series of licensed expositions. Their publications of the mid-1630s amplified the arguments permitting Sunday sports and upholding royal authority. Preaching before the king himself in 1635, the royal chaplain Thomas Turner railed against 'fault-finding Pharisees' who demanded over-strict observance of the Sabbath. Noting that 'God loves mercy better than sacrifice', Turner commended King Charles for declaring 'that the Lord's day be so sanctified as that harmless recreations be not denied to Christians'.[117] Francis White, the bishop of Ely, also published at length against 'the novel sabbath teachers', and insisted that 'honest and moderate recreation was not prohibited, either in the Law or the Prophets'.[118]

Robert Sanderson, a self-styled 'reverend, religious and judicious divine' who was later made bishop of Lincoln, answered the question 'whether it be lawful to use any bodily recreation on the Lord's day' affirmatively, saying that his majesty's Declaration 'put it past disputation'. The royal word extinguished every other argument. Sanderson particularly commended those recreations 'which give the best refreshment to the body and leave the least impression in the mind', preferring 'shooting, leaping, pitching the bar, stoolball, etc.' to such alehouse pursuits as 'dicing and carding'. He also recognized that 'walking and discoursing, which to men of liberal education is a pleasant recreation, is no way delightsome to the ruder sort of people, who scarce account anything a sport which is not loud and boisterous'.[119] *Plus ça change*. Most of the published endorsers of rustic Sunday sports would never themselves stoop to playing them.

Reversal

Supporters of the Book of Sports and the rest of the Laudian and ceremonialist programme suffered sharp reversals in the revolutionary turnabout of the early 1640s. With Laud and Wren in prison, and parliament flexing untested muscles, the opportunity arose again to embrace reformation. With the collapse of episcopal licensing, writings like Burton's *Divine Tragedie* and Prynne's *Newes from Ipswich* could be openly republished. New tracts and pamphlets expounded the doctrine of the Sabbath and excoriated Sunday sports.[120] Parliamentary authorities rehabilitated ministers who had earlier been censured, and subjected supporters of the king's book to scrutiny. Godly ministers and magistrates cracked down again on Sabbath disorders, and silently nullified the king's Declaration.[121]

In March 1641 the Justices of Shropshire decided 'that the meetings called wakes be suppressed and no more kept on the Lord's day of Sunday'.[122] A Staffordshire Grand Jury similarly decided that, because wakes were 'kept on the Lord's day, commonly called Sunday, and do then occasion by so great a concourse and resort of idle people many great quarrels and drunkenness and misdemeanours, and all other profanations of that day, and do also draw together a great company of vagrants and wanderers', they should henceforth be suppressed.[123] Preaching before the Exeter assize in August 1642, Thomas Trescot urged magistrates to purge the Sabbath of 'bacchanalian revellings and heathenish May games, with other like filth and ordure' that profaned it in recent years.[124] Local battle lines were drawn in a cultural contest that was not resolved by revolution or civil war.

As an act of atonement and purgation, in a war that was not going their way, parliament in May 1643 ordered 'that the book concerning the enjoining and toleration of sports upon the Lord's day be forthwith burned by the hand of the common hangman'. Described by the puritan memorialist John Vicars as 'that most mischievous and abominably profane and pernicious book', the Declaration of Sports was consumed by fire on 10 May 1643 'in the very place where the Romish cross in Cheapside formerly stood' before it was destroyed a week earlier.[125] The burning was a symbolic action, a ritual cleansing, and a dramatic announcement of godly policy.

As if that was not enough to propitiate an angry divinity, parliament followed in April 1644 with an ordinance to prevent the profanation of the Sabbath. The Lord's day was no longer an occasion to 'use, exercise, keep, maintain, or be present at any wrestlings, shooting, bowling, ringing of bells for pleasure or pastime, masque, wake otherwise called feasts, church ale, dancing, games, sport or pastime whatsoever'. Adult offenders were to be fined 5*s*., and children under fourteen 1*s*. All maypoles were to be taken down and no more erected. Identified now by its correct name, all copies of *The Kings Maiesties Declaration to his Subjects, Concerning Lawfull Sports* were to be 'seized, suppressed, and publicly burnt by the Justices of Peace', along with other books or pamphlets 'against the morality of the fourth commandment'. Like the now-defunct Declaration, this ordinance was ordered to be read in all parish churches, before the Lord's-day morning sermon.[126] Like the king's book it replaced, the parliamentary order attempted to impose one version of lawfulness on another. And, like the king's book, it foundered on local divisions and particularities. Its effectiveness was handicapped by the continuing civil war, but even more by the fractured nature of English religious culture, which remained unamenable to centralized control. The sanctity or sociability of the Sabbath remained a matter of contention, and not even Cromwell's Major Generals could effectively secure uniformity.[127] The revival of maypoles, popular festivities, and the rehabilitation of Sunday sports were among the most visible aspects of the Restoration.

9

Sacred Kingship Eclipsed

Well-intentioned folly cost England an unnecessary war with Scotland, with catastrophic consequences for the king and both kingdoms. A chain of errors ended Charles I's halcyon days and plunged his country into confusion. At huge financial and social cost, the largest land army mobilized since the days of Henry VIII deployed not against dynastic or confessional enemies on the Continent but against the king's own protestant subjects to the north. This was the most unprosperous war of all, from the king's point of view, for it forced him to call the parliament that would end in his destruction.

The compound crisis of 1637–42, in which royal authority foundered, press-censorship collapsed, the church split apart, and parliament over-ruled the royal prerogative, involved tens of thousands of people as actors, spectators, and alarmed citizens and subjects. The mobilization was more comprehensive and more intrusive, and its consequences more devastating, than the military crises of the 1620s. The cataclysm began with revolt in Scotland and spread to all three Stuart kingdoms. The civil war that followed, and the post-war stasis that compounded the conflict saw a massive mustering of energies on all sides. In-fighting among the victors, a purge of parliament, and a contentious radical Leveller movement shaped the environment for the trial and execution of Charles I in January 1649. Revolutionary England produced the ultimate trampling on majesty, a kingdom without a king.

This chapter shows how men and women articulated their allegiance in the course of the crisis, as all sides appealed for popular support. It seeks to capture demotic voices as well as the better-known commentary of the elite. The views of the gentry and clergy were better recorded, but they had always been accompanied by people speaking out of turn and violating the protocols of deference and respect. Although some subjects in all periods railed intemperately against the established order, and a few poured scorn on their monarch, expressions of hostility to the throne and its occupant quickened in the early 1640s. Critics may have been more willing to speak their minds as customary authority crumbled, and more such remarks might have been recorded if officials had not been more occupied with warfare than with examining offenders. Surviving fragments indicate a loss of respect for kingship and growing ambivalence towards King Charles, which made the demystification of majesty a central feature of the Revolution.

Political leaders maintained the fiction that the king could do no wrong, but ordinary people were less attached to that notion. The evidence is problematic, but it appears that seditious remarks grew more reckless as royal authority eroded. Newspapers and pamphlets provided new avenues of discourse, popular commentary left *arcana imperii* in shreds, while a new political theory located sovereignty not in the king but in the people.

Mutiny in Scotland

The Scottish crisis was the precipitant of England's troubles. Though Charles attended intermittently to Scottish business during the first dozen years of his reign, and travelled to Edinburgh in 1633 for his Scottish coronation, it was only after 1637 that north British affairs took centre-stage. Advised by archbishop Laud, with input from Scottish clerics, the king decided in 1637 that his northern kingdom should follow a standard religious liturgy. The result was *The booke of common prayer, and administration of the sacraments. And other parts of divine service for the use of the Church of Scotland.* A shrewd Italian observer remarked that King Charles 'resolved that all the ceremonies newly brought into the church should be punctually observed in that kingdom'. It was bound to cause trouble, he predicted, and 'the court expects the issue with curiosity, many being of opinion that the Scots will not easily submit'.[1] Accustomed to free forms of worship, the presbyterian Scots reacted angrily to this set text imposed from London, and resistance grew into revolt. The royal initiative was no more necessary but far more damaging than the king's Declaration of Sports.

Historians have examined the origins and precipitants of this crisis, seeing Jacobean roots and complexities on both sides of the border. Important studies probe Scottish politics and Covenanter ideology, and dealings

The Arch-Prelate of St Andrewes in Scotland
reading the new Service-booke in his pontificalibus
assaulted by men & women, with Crickets stooles
Stickes and Stones.

Figure 11. The Prayer Book Revolt in Scotland, 1637. John Vicars, *All the Memorable & Wonder-strikinge, Parlamentary Mercies effected & afforded unto this our English nation* (1642), first image.

between London and Edinburgh. A pan-British approach pays obvious dividends, but much remains to be learned about the domestic unfolding of the drama and its impact on King Charles's southern kingdom. It occurred while worsening weather brought 'such inundations and floods and winds, as no man living remembers the like', and may have inclined some in Scotland to more desperate measures.[2]

The English, for the most part, were ignorant about the Scots and many were prejudiced against them. The London businessman Francis Harris, for example, avowed that 'he could not abide Scotsmen, nor would have anything to do with them . . . and wished he had never known them'.[3] Sir Nicholas Stodderd gave his opinion 'that our kingdom of England never prospered since a Scot governed . . . and that the basest Englishman, even a hangman, was better than the best Scottishman'.[4] A character in the play *The Valiant Scot*, performed in London in 1637, declared the Scots 'a nation haughty and full of spleen'.[5] 'We here consider the Scottish affairs much after the case that country people do the moon', one observer commented in 1638; 'some think it now bigger than a bushel, and some too wise imagine it a vast world, and strange things undiscovered in it'.[6] The crisis unleashed by Charles I's imposition of a prayer book on his northern kingdom forced people everywhere to take note of Scottish affairs and their king's role in them.

The 'attempt to bring in our English church service into Scotland... made a great hubbub there, and was repelled with much violence by the common people', so George Garrard informed Lord Wentworth in Ireland.[7] When the new prayer book first appeared in Edinburgh's St Giles cathedral on 23 July 1637, the authorities and dignitaries 'were by the women beaten out of the church with their little stools... and in their return home in the streets saluted with so many stones as endangered their lives', another correspondent reported.[8] Subsequent attempts to introduce the prayer book 'sped worse... with greater violence than before', persuading Garrard 'that there is no hope that it will be effected'.[9] William Hawkins wrote similarly to the Earl of Leicester of the 'very ill success' in introducing the prayer book, and 'the people triumphing in their refusal of it'.[10] Scotland was on the edge of revolt, though not yet united in resolve.

The Scottish Covenant, signed in February 1638, committed subscribers to the maintenance of reformed religion, as perfected in the Kirk, while deferring in principle to the majesty and authority of the king. The Covenanters held King Charles to his coronation oath, to maintain Christ's true religion, and rejected 'foul aspersions' that their resistance to his policy constituted rebellion. Instead they claimed to be acting legally, reasonably, and in harmony with God's cause, to protect Kirk and country from popish contamination.[11] The king told the Marquess of Hamilton a few months later that the Scottish Covenanters would reduce him to the level of a duke of Venice, and 'I will rather die than yield to these impertinent and damnable demands'.[12] (The Duke or Doge of Venice was a figurehead monarch, 'merely titular and a cipher', of a state that some thought 'aristocratical, if not democratic'.[13])

Caroline authorities denied that the revolt had anything to do with religion. King Charles himself referred in January 1639 to

> the late disorder in our realm of Scotland, begun upon pretence of religion but now appearing to have been raised by factious spirits, and fomented by some few ill and traitorously affected particular persons, whose aim hath been by troubling the peace of that our kingdom, to work their own private ends, and indeed to shake off all monarchical government.[14]

It was typical of thc Caroline regime to see the worst in its subjects and critics. The Covenanters, by this analysis, were driven not by conscience or grievance but by ambition.

A rambling proclamation in February 1639, issued 'to inform our loving subjects of our kingdom of England of the seditious practices of some in Scotland, seeking to overthrow our regal power under false pretences of religion', vilified the Covenanters as 'turbulent', 'unquiet', and 'factious spirits', 'desperate hypocrites' driven by 'malice' and whipped up to 'rage and fury'. Their cause was 'odious', their proceedings 'froward and perverse', their dealings 'most cunning and subtle'. Under 'pretences of religion, the common cloak for all disobedience', the rebels intended 'to shake off all monarchical government, and to vilify our regal power', with words and actions that were 'dangerous', 'mutinous', 'seditious', 'rebellious', and 'traitorously affected'. The core of the matter, King Charles proclaimed, was not 'whether a service book [is] to be received or not, nor whether episcopal government shall be continued, or presbyterial admitted, but whether we are their king or not'. The whole declaration was supposed to be read aloud in every church during service time, 'that all our people to the meanest may see the notorious carriages of these men, and likewise the justice and mercy of our proceedings'.[15] Most English parishes complied, but when the proclamation was read at Exeter cathedral the mayor and aldermen sat 'with their hats on', and were later forced to apologize for 'their irreverent carriage' against the king's proceedings.[16]

The official line was that the Scots were rebels pure and simple. According to archbishop Neile of York, whose province abutted the Scottish border, 'it is not religion but sedition that stirs in them.'[17] Archbishop Laud was scornful that 'these impudent rebels pretend religion for their cloak, as if no man saw their cloak was made of other stuff'.[18] 'What they really want is to change the government of the church and commonwealth, and to get the power into their own hands,' declared a commentary distributed in Newcastle in May 1639.[19] Loyal pulpits repeated the message that the Scots were rebels, and some clergy went so far as to call them 'worse than papists or barbarians'.[20] One preacher at Canterbury compared the Scots 'to the Gunpowder traitors, because . . . they had blown the bishops and popery out of Scotland'.[21]

Determined to restore allegiance, as any monarch would, Charles assembled forces to fight the rebels. The king announced that he would head the army at York in person, 'wherein we nothing doubt but the affection, fidelity and courage of our people shall well appear'. This was bravado, but also determined kingship. It was grounded in Charles's confidence in his people's love and loyalty, and in the absolute righteousness of his cause. The nation would surely rally against 'the disloyal designs of ill-affected persons'.[22] The resulting conflict is known to history as 'the Bishops' Wars', but the military effort to crush the Scots might better be called 'King Charles's Scottish wars' or even 'the king's northern follies'.

Unfortunately for King Charles, a considerable number of his English subjects had doubts about the crown's presentation of the crisis. The Scots waged an effective propaganda war, flooding the southern kingdom with pamphlets, tracts, and manuscripts that found receptive readers.[23] Writings favourable to the Scots, such as *The Late Proceedings in Scotland* (circulated in manuscript from 1637) and *The Protestation of the Noblemen . . . and Subscribers of the Confession of Faith and Covenant* (printed at Edinburgh in 1638), spread surreptitiously and were occasionally intercepted.[24] One list of intended recipients of Scottish books included London merchants, a factor, a comfit maker, a linen draper, a glass seller, a printer, 'Mr Burnett in Norwich', and 'Mrs Eleanor Chapman in the Old Exchange'.[25] Authorities at Chester as well as the metropolis expressed concern at the 'scattering of seditious books', and sought with limited effect 'to apprehend the dispersers, and such as have received such books'. 'Seditious pamphlets . . . are spreading everywhere,' warned archbishop Laud in 1639.[26] The Covenanters had effective agents and friends in London who distributed 'libels and Scottish pamphlets', including one who lurked around the Inns of Court 'with a cloak bag full of books'.[27] Printed ballads in 1639 were mostly hostile to the covenanters, but by the end of 1640 their general refrain was 'grammercie good Scot'.[28]

Scottish propaganda alone does not explain English reactions, for many of the king's subjects were already inclined to think ill of him. Accumulated grievances, resentments, and anxieties predisposed some people to question their sovereign's intentions, as they had with the Book of Sports, the altar policy, and Ship Money. The northern crisis opened a new zone of contention, exposing and sharpening the kingdom's divisions amid an already chilled and pinched economy. News spread quickly about 'a great mutiny in Scotland at this present time about our form of prayer which they should use, and other matter concerning religion'.[29] Conversation tackled such topics as the merits of the Scottish cause and the authority of kings and bishops. Humble folk as well as gentlemen voiced opinions that could be construed as dissident or seditious, as the regime lost control of the discursive agenda.

Discussion ranged from wonder at the event to anxiety about its consequences. The Kentish gentleman Henry Oxinden believed the Scots to be 'as disobedient and insolent as ever', but he found 'variety of humours, discourse and opinions' in London.[30] 'This northern news fills every honest and loyal subject's heart full of grief,' wrote Richard Barrington in June 1639, 'and it is the cause that there is little trading in the city and less money stirring, for no man will lend, nor will any pay what they owe'.[31] Sir John Innis told house guests that year that King Charles was 'transported into much affright and passion' by news from the north, and that the Scots could count on support from France, Sweden, Holland, 'with several nations and states'.[32] On the king's dealings with Scotland, one widely distributed manuscript observed, 'not three men are of the same opinion in all, and then each family must have a war with itself'.[33] 'These are strange, strange spectacles', wrote Sir Henry Slingsby, 'that we should engage ourself in a war one with another, and with our own venom gnaw and consume ourself'.[34]

To express support for the Covenanters would identify the speaker as refractory and ill-affected, but scores of Charles I's subjects risked such censure. The Northumberland landowner John Alvred declared in July 1638 that the Scots were 'brave boys and would make us all quake . . . and that they did well . . . The king would get nobody to fight against them, for they were our own nation and our own blood.'[35] Another commentator in Cornwall acknowledged the king's right to crush rebellion, 'granting it be one', but was not convinced that the Scots 'profess any enmity to England'.[36] When a group of Tyneside businessmen 'fell into discourse of the Scottish business' in December 1638, the Newcastle merchant Ralph Fowler gave his opinion that 'the Scottish Covenanters were in no way to be accused, for they did nothing but in defence of their own right and maintenance of the gospel . . . and that for his part he thought he should not fight against them in that quarrel'. Asked by a companion, 'whether if the king should command him to fight against the Covenanters, he would refuse it or not', Fowler said that 'he would examine that cause himself, and if he thought in his own conscience the Scots were in the right, he would not fight against them for all the kings in the world'.[37] Dissident preachers fuelled the flames, like one in Norfolk who 'covertly insinuated to his auditors that they should pray for the good success of the Scotch rebels'.[38] Thomas Case at Manchester similarly preached in favour of the Scots to subjects with independent opinions.[39]

Tale-bearers brought more scandalous opinions to light. Holding forth in a lodging house near Temple Bar in February 1639, a slightly inebriated Captain Napier avowed 'that there are as wise men in the new Covenant of Scotland as any are in the world' and that Scottish soldiers were 'as able and as well-armed as any are in the world' and would soon invade England. The king, he declared, 'might have helped these things in time, but now it was too late', for 'the king is deluded, seduced, and made a baby'.[40] 'All things are base and scurvy,' John Davis told another assembly of drinkers in London in June, adding more pointedly that the king dealt 'both basely and scurvily'.[41]

These were shocking words, but no more disrespectful than those of the Cheshire minister John Girtam, who shared his opinion in July 1639 that 'if Prince Henry had been alive at this day, there had been no rebellion in Scotland, neither durst the Scots so much as open their mouths against him'.[42] In August 1639, in conversation with a returning veteran from the garrison at Berwick, the London wax-chandler Robert Wardner declared 'that what the Scots did was for the good of this land, for they stood for a parliament'. Wardner then complained, 'what a shame it was that our king should be so misinformed' and 'to proceed in a war against them that was so unjust'.[43]

This time there was no Duke of Buckingham to blame for the kingdom's troubles, but a virulent stream of opinion pinned responsibility on archbishop Laud. 'It was the little bishop' who was to blame, declared Francis Harris in a Westminster tavern in January 1639.[44] 'My lord of Canterbury . . . has been the occasion of this strife between the Scots and us,' said the Buckinghamshire gentleman James Machison.[45] It was Laud, 'the pope of Lambeth', said Godfrey Cade of Southwark, who sparked this 'mutiny' in Scotland, Laud who 'doth pluck the royal crown off his majesty's head and trample it under his feet, and did whip his majesty's ass with his own rod'.[46] 'What have we to do with these priests' wars?' asked the Leicestershire lawyer John Oneby in March 1639. A neighbour answered him, 'they are not the priests' wars, they are the king's'. Oneby responded by quoting from Jeremiah: 'A wonderful and horrible thing is committed in the land; the prophets prophesy falsely and the priests bear rule by their means.'[47] Comments like these indicate that the *arcana imperii* had cracked wide open, and that individual subjects were forming opinions in opposition to policies of the crown.

King Charles's Northern Wars

Charles I's wars to subdue Scotland tested his military, political, and managerial skills, all, sadly, found wanting.[48] Plans for the land campaign called for 20,000 foot soldiers and 2,000 horse, at a cost of £100,000 a month, but inevitably the complement was lower and the real cost higher.[49] County levies produced a larger army than in the 1620s, but with no improvement in quality. As usual, the mobilization bore heavily on artisan and labouring communities. 'Our business here is training of companies, making of wagons, wheelbarrows, and other necessaries for war. The drum beats and I must away,' wrote Sir William Saville in September 1638.[50]

Figure 12. King Charles at War. 1639 etching by Wenceslas Hollar (1644 state).

Unlike the navy, which had benefited from Ship Money, England's land forces were perilously under-prepared. Available soldiers were 'raw and inexpert', or 'defective in arms' and training.[51] Military equipment was missing or unserviceable. Hasty attempts to bring in 'armour, pikes, swords, belts, and bandoliers' from Germany and the Low Countries procured many shipments that were defective or 'naught'. Corruption was ingenious and endemic. Among weapons that Sir Thomas Roe obtained in Hamburg, 'thirty of the muskets at least brake at the very first trial'. Of 2,000 pikes imported in December 1638, almost 90 per cent were too short or otherwise 'unserviceable'. Forty per cent of one batch of swords were defective. 'Imperfections and frauds' made many of the bandoliers almost useless, including some lined with paper instead of leather. Unscrupulous dealers on both sides of the Channel profited at the expense of English troops, who paid the price when their equipment failed.[52]

King Charles was said to be 'very well pleased' with the cavalry he reviewed in April 1639, but the infantry were disordered and ineffective. Report spread of troops 'robbing and spoiling' as they went.[53] Thomas Davis, 'a poor aged man', told drinkers at an inn at Newgate in June that the new recruits 'are more fitter to use such weapons as these are, laying his hands upon the place of his members, than for weapons of war'.[54] The king's standard-bearer Sir Edmund Verney famously observed that he had never seen 'so raw, so unskilful, and so unwilling an army brought to fight'.[55] Miserable conditions sapped morale. A correspondent of the Earl of Northumberland lamented the sad state of the king's forces: 'many of them by reason of ill weather and hard travelling are sick and have died.'[56] The Earl of Rutland remarked on the contrasting vigour of the Scottish troops, and commented: 'I wish our camp had been so fortunate, for many were dead to our great shame through fault of their officers, who did not forecast for victuals and huts to lie dry in wet weather.'[57] The Nottinghamshire gentleman Gervaise Eyre blamed the common soldiers themselves, telling his brother that 'there are many dead in the quarters, and many weak; and I believe many have suffered with their own slothfulness, in that they would not be of the labour to fetch wood to build huts, which they might have had within three miles, but they chose gorse and bones to prick about them' in days of cold and rainy weather.[58] There were few complaints about billeting in these campaigns, though local families complained of pilferage and predation.

The king himself accompanied his forces as far as Berwick, where he made an inconclusive peace with the Scots. Both armies disbanded towards the end of 1639, only to prepare again for continuing war.

To gain support and subsidies for his next campaign, King Charles summoned parliament in April 1640, the first since 1629. He was shocked and disappointed when members preferred to debate grievances from the previous eleven years rather than fund his war. After the early collapse of this Short Parliament the king excoriated those members who thwarted his wishes by their 'undutiful and seditious carriage', their 'subtle and malignant courses', their 'malice and disaffections to the state'. He blamed the political failure entirely on 'the malicious cunning of some seditiously-affected men', with no sense that his policies could have contributed to the impasse.[59] The king's words were disturbingly similar to those used a decade earlier to denounce the commonwealth-men in the last parliament before the personal rule. They also echoed the language that the king and his advisors used to vilify the rebellious Scots. The war would go forward, but without the necessary resources and without the solid backing of the representatives of the realm.

Groans could be heard across the country at 'the worst news that could . . . befall this kingdom'.[60] Robert Woodford in Northamptonshire found 'the hearts of good people were much dejected' by the news from Westminster.[61] 'Lord fit us for the worst times,' wrote William Bisbey to a kinsman in New England, 'we are full of fears generally'.[62] Many blamed 'the prelate of Canturbury' as 'the prime cause on earth' of the kingdom's distempers,[63] but the Essex countrywoman Margaret Grigge knew where to direct her animus. She told her neighbour 'that the king would not hear any of the counsel of the parliament, but would undo all his poor subjects', and that she wished that the apprentices who were demonstrating at Lambeth 'would destroy the king'.[64] Vernacular opinion, as ever, was more radical and more visceral than the politer formulations of the elite.

Recruiters gathered a second royal army in the spring of 1640, designed to field 30,000 men, though neither its numbers nor quality met expectations. Ill-prepared troops straggled north to their rendezvous in Yorkshire, some disgracing themselves with well-publicized debaucheries, mutinies, and attacks on Laudian churches. They were surprised by the Scottish invasion on 20 August, and their leading edge was shattered by the decisive Covenanter victory at Newburn a week later.[65] Much of London was panicked by the news, but some in the city responded with feasts and celebration for the success of the Scots.[66]

As on previous occasions, the officers blamed their subordinates. King Charles had been let down by 'the worser sort' of subjects, the hastily recruited common soldiers who fled from the Scottish onslaught. 'Our gentlemen behaved themselves right valiantly, and if they had not been basely forsaken by the ordinary troopers in likelihood had won the day,' one correspondent of the cavalier class reported.[67] 'The commanders and gentlemen' did their part 'manfully', but 'our ordinary troopers' fled in disgrace, wrote another.[68] If it was God who determined military outcomes, he had turned his face against King Charles even more decisively than at Cadiz or the Isle of Rhé. Charles I had lost his war, and he lost control of the northern part of England. Defeated, dispirited, and devoid of financial resources, the king was forced to call another parliament controlled by his fiercest critics. Two years later, conceding terms to the Scots who had outmatched him, King Charles recognized the Covenant that he had previously determined to resist unto death.[69]

Trampling on Majesty

King Charles returned to London on 30 October 1640 to a warm reception, having made concessions to the Scots in the Treaty of Ripon. People were generally glad to have their king back, pleased that the fighting in the north was over, and delighted at the prospects of a parliament. The memoirist John Evelyn was among those who watched his majesty 'ride in pomp... with all the marks of a happy peace, restored to the affections of his people'.[70] Popular affections were fickle, however, fluctuating with hopes of political accommodation, fears of popish plotting, and alarm at a distressed economy.

Parliament's seizure of the political initiative, beginning in November 1640, led to further erosion of royal authority. Critics of the Caroline regime responded not just with satires and libels, of the sort that followed debacles at Cadiz and the Isle of Rhé, but with revolutionary politics that transformed the relationship between the king and his people. Parliament determined to purge the king's advisors, to reverse the policies of the previous eleven years, and to move the Church of England towards further reformation. In as far as they achieved these goals, they transformed both kingship and the kingdom.

The much-vaunted royal prerogative withered as the king proved unable to command force or protect his officers and friends. Archbishop Laud went to the Tower, the Earl of Strafford to the block, as controversial counsellors were impeached or fled abroad. Parliament attacked the policies of the king's personal rule, outlawing Ship Money, rescinding the Book of Sports, and rehabilitating the puritan 'martyrs' Burton, Bastwick, and Prynne. Ceremonial innovations were reversed, hundreds of parishes were in turmoil, and episcopacy itself was imperilled. Episcopal licencers lost control of the press, amid an explosion of unregulated print. The Triennial Act of 1641 ended the king's power to call or dissolve parliaments at pleasure, and parliament's Militia Ordinance of 1642 took away his control of the armed forces. The king himself was more obviously associated with policies and problems after his 'evil' advisors were removed and discredited. Parliamentary leaders claimed to be protecting King Charles from those advisors, and most of the elite still held that kingship was sacred, but even before the outbreak of civil war they had witnessed or experienced a revolution.

After 1640 it became harder for local officials to perform 'the king's service' and conduct their business 'in the name of the king'. Obstinate and refractory subjects were increasingly inclined to remark that they 'cared not for the king nor his laws'.[71] In one of the most theatrical performances of practical antinomianism in the summer of 1641, Thomas Probert of Radnorshire laughed 'in a scornful or disdainful manner' when officers served him documents 'in the name of the king'. He tore the papers into pieces, 'and threw or cast the same into the dirt and mire', saying that 'he would not give a turd for the Council's process'. And as if that was not defiance enough, he 'being on horseback did with his said horse tread or trample the said letters under the said horse's feet'.[72] Told in June 1641 that 'it was against his majesty's laws' not to turn in his accounts, a churchwarden at Horsted Parva, Sussex, answered his minister, 'what care we for his majesty's laws and statutes?'[73] When the magistrate Sir Francis Cooke told the Essex alehouse-keeper Joan Allen in September 1641 'that he was one of the king's justices of peace, and in authority to see good rule order to be kept by the king's authority', she answered to his face that 'she knew not the king, nor cared not for him, nor for the said Sir Francis, nor would not obey his authority'.[74] John Munday, another disorderly housekeeper of St Giles in the Fields, similarly 'uttered many base and scandalous words against his majesty's justices of the peace, saying that he does not care a fart nor turd for them all'.[75]

Scattered comments like these do not necessarily indicate an epidemic of recalcitrance, nor the beginnings of republicanism, but they show that royal authority no longer commanded awe. Few were as explicit as the Yorkshireman Thomas Stafford, who gave his opinion in January 1641 that King Charles was 'fitter to be hanged than to be king'.[76] Alarmed by such views, Sir Gilbert Talbot remarked in July 1641, 'it is a pity to hear how his majesty's honour is torn by every mouth'.[77] Clerics like William Tutty at South Mimms, Hertfordshire, fuelled the flames by praying publicly in the autumn of 1641 'that God would be pleased to begin the work of grace in the king's heart' and 'that God would give in the king's heart to the cause of Jesus Christ, before it was too late'. Tutty also 'prayed for the queen, that it would please God to turn her heart, for she goeth or went a whoring after her own inventions'.[78]

The king was away from his capital from August to November 1641, concluding peace with the Scottish Covenanters, while comments like these continued to fester. The Grand Remonstrance of the House of Commons passed narrowly just a few days before his return, in an atmosphere of alarm and division. The trauma of the Irish rebellion aggravated anxieties associated with popish conspiracy theories, as the crisis lurched out of control. Charles hoped to gain advantage from a staged ceremonial civic entry, and was indeed greeted by 'great acclamations and joy of the giddy people' when he rode through London on 25 November, 'upon his safe and happy return' from Scotland. He found few reserves of 'love and affection', however, in a metropolis rapidly turning against him.[79] Parliament and the city were deeply divided, mobs dominated the streets, and volunteer Cavaliers urged his majesty to desperate counter-measures. The king's failed attempt to arrest his leading parliamentary opponents further undermined his position. The popular cry was 'privileges of parliament', not 'God save the king', as he left London in panic on 10 January 1642, fearful that mobs might tear the royal family apart. In March that year, as his coach left Cambridge for the north, the king was trailed by stone-throwing townswomen, urging him to return to his parliament.[80]

The crisis of legitimation intensified as 'the binding force of sovereignty' was diminished, especially among the restless multitude. The keystone to the arch of order was out of kilter, according to the Oxford cleric Richard Gardyner, as 'men swollen with pride, mad with headiness, treacherous in spreading calumnies, turbulent in sowing seditions', railed against sacred kingship.[81] 'Poor king,' wrote Thomas Knyvett in May 1642, 'he grows still in more contempt and slight here every day.'[82] William Stampe, the vicar of Stepney, Middlesex, observed in August 1642 that 'men now prayed to turn the king's heart, as if he were an heathen or a pagan', rather than the lord's anointed.[83] The king was abused by mean and ignorant people who 'carry Babel about them wherever they go'.[84] Royalists responded vigorously to such traducing of their sovereign, and appealed to deep reservoirs of subject-like sentiment, even among the king's enemies. The papermaker Henry Wheatley loyally declared in June 1642 that 'they were a company of fools that would not hold with the king'.[85] Thomas Elliot, who had formerly served the royal household, went further and swore 'that he would kill any man whom his majesty should command or bid him without questioning the cause'.[86]

The old polarity of 'the king's loving subjects' and 'the worser sort of people' was replaced by more vicious and divisive appellations, such as 'court parasites and ambitious flatterers' versus 'lovers of their king, of the truth, and of their country',[87] or those 'whom a foolish zeal hath besotted with an unwarrantable devotion to their sovereign' versus those 'who seek nothing but the peace and happiness of him and his people'.[88] Parliament differentiated 'the honest and well-affected party of the kingdom' from the 'wicked' and 'malignant party' that opposed them.[89] From the other side, they were 'rebels' and 'traitors'.

The royalist preacher Robert Mossom argued in 1642 that one cause of the 'rebellion' against King Charles was that 'too many . . . have curiously pried into *arcana imperii*, the ark of sacred royalty'.[90] A year later the royalist James Howell blamed England's troubles on 'a pack of perverse people, composed for the most part of the scummy and simplest sort', who were hostile to kingship and hierarchy.[91] Vulgar discussion of the great affairs of the kingdom had undermined the monarch and his natural aristocratic advisors. Earlier defenders of monarchy had argued that 'God's anointed ones' should not 'be touched with any virulent tongue, nor invectives of a bitter pen',[92] but the proliferation of newspapers, tracts, and pamphlets, in an atmosphere of unrestrained argument, made sure that nobody's character was safe from scrutiny, and that *arcana imperii* barely existed.

Demotic commentary in the spring and summer of 1642, between the king's departure from London and the outbreak of civil war, reveals popular participation in the debates directed from Westminster and York. 'There was much ado in parliament concerning the king's prerogative and the privileges of the subject,' observed the tailor Matthew Williams of Porthkerry, Glamorganshire. Being asked by a neighbour 'what he had to do with state businesses', Williams replied 'that the king was but a private gentleman during the pleasure of the parliament' and 'that the parliament hath power to make another king if the king will not comply and agree with the parliament'.[93] When King Charles arrived in Yorkshire in March 1642, to be greeted by supporters, the tanner Thomas Godsey exhibited 'insolent and tumultuous behaviour' and declared: 'I care not for the king (meaning our lord King Charles) nor his laws.'[94] His fellow Yorkshireman John Troutbeck declared in June 'that he could live as well without a king as with a king' and that the present monarch 'might be deposed for aught he knew'.[95] Samuel Andrewes, a village tailor at Arlington, Sussex, asserted in July 1642 'that if a Christian king commanded laws contrary to God's laws he ought not to be obeyed'. When his pastor reminded the congregation of their obligation to honour the Lord's anointed, Andrewes retorted that King Charles 'was not God's anointed, for God did not anoint him'.[96] In a similar altercation at Hunsdon, Hertfordshire, in August 1642 a parishioner responded to the rector's instruction to speak reverently of the monarch by demanding, 'what speak you of the king, he is nothing but words'.[97] Views like these were constitutionally naive, though perhaps politically prescient. They had little in common with the more thoughtful formulations of theorists and politicians, who spoke not of replacing the king but of saving his honour.

Constitutional Contention

England's ordeal encouraged discussion of fundamental constitutional principles, the foundations of government, divine-right theory, and the limits of royal authority. Traditionalists derived the supreme magistrate's supreme power directly from God, but commonwealth-men devised a radical alternative that founded all power in the people. The polarization of positions in the 1640s hardened the formation of anti-monarchical sentiments, while at the same time fostering a reiteration of the principles of sacred kingship. Though protagonists conducted their arguments in the pulpit and in print, they spilled over into other arenas, the marketplace, the alehouse, and the battlefield. The people of England were exposed to a crash course in citizenship, with an intensity that is rarely matched.

One publication of 1642 reprinted extracts from James I's writings on 'the true glory of kings', with supporting biblical texts.[98] Others warned of the collapse of the social edifice, and the end of all that people held dear. The cleric Richard Gardyner reminded his audience in London in March 1642 that the king was

> the lord's anointed . . . It is by him that we move in our proper sphere, and are not jostled out of it . . . Were it not for the binding force of sovereignty, who durst raise a dam against the torrent of corruption? Our meetings would be mutinies, our pulpits cockpits, authority would lose its authority, no subordination, no subjection, the honourable would be levelled with the base, the prudent with the child, all would be amassed and huddled up in an unjust parity, and the land overrun with inflexible generations.[99]

'Without the king the commonwealth cannot be safe, no more than a ship without a pilot in a stormy ocean,' preached an Oxford royalist, 'the supporting of his state is that *unum necessarium* for our safety, and the safety of the whole kingdom.'[100] These were elaborations of familiar arguments from the 1620s, but tended to become untenable if the king in question proved a fool or a tyrant.

Offering a path to reconciliation in June 1642, albeit on their own terms, parliament tendered the king the Nineteen Propositions. These offered King Charles a limited kingship, to reign in partnership with parliament, 'your majesty's great and supreme council', newly defined as the proper place for 'such matters as concern the public'. Henceforth the king could appoint no councillors, command no forces, and make no arrangement for his children's education or marriage without parliamentary approbation. They committed the king to a reformation in religion 'as both Houses of Parliament shall advise', and the removal of innovations, superstitions, and scandalous ministers. Though promising to preserve 'the royal honour, greatness and safety of your majesty and your posterity', the propositions were an insulting ultimatum that no sacred monarch could approve. They amounted to the imposition of a parliamentary regency, a suspension of kingly authority, until political trust could be restored.[101]

The king's scathing point-by-point response (most likely written by Sir John Colepepper and Viscount Falkland) began with a disquisition on constitutional principles, derived from conventional teaching on divine right kingship. Regal authority, it said, was a trust from God, the king was the guardian of law, and without fully empowered kingship the entire social fabric of rights and properties risked collapse into 'a dark equal chaos of confusion'.[102] Multiple printed editions gave wide circulation to these battling political ideas.

Claiming to speak in the name of the king for 'the good' of the people of England, the *Answer to the Nineteen Propositions* turned parliamentary rhetoric against itself. It began with a recitation of grievances, a kind of royal remonstrance, that labelled parliament 'an upstart authority' exercising 'a pure arbitrary power'. Among other crimes, 'to render us odious to our people . . . they have filled the ears of the people with the noise of fears and jealousies'.[103] The men at Westminster, said the *Answer*, were driven by 'ambition and private interest' and were led by 'evil counsels of ambitious turbulent spirits disaffected to God's true religion', an echo of parliament's charge against the king's supporters and the king's characterization of the Scots.[104] There could be little accommodation between parties so inclined to disparage each other.

Invoking the royal honour and the authority 'transmitted to us from so many ancestors', King Charles would accept no alteration of 'our just, ancient regal power' that would 'in effect . . . depose both ourself and our posterity'. The honorific trifles that parliament deigned to permit would leave him 'but the picture, but the sign of a king'. Against those propositions, the king determined to relinquish no rights to 'the ancient equal, happy, well-poised and never-enough commended constitution of the government of this kingdom, nor to make ourself of a king of England a duke of Venice, and this of a kingdom a republic'.[105] There would be no yielding, no accommodation. If ever England limited the power of kings, the *Answer* warned, there would be 'division and faction', with 'tumults, violence, [and] licentiousness'. 'All rights and proprieties, all distinctions of families and merit', would perish 'in a dark equal chaos of confusion, and the long line of our many noble ancestors in a Jack Cade or a Wat Tyler', recalling the late medieval rebels and more recent remarks about the shattering arch of order.[106]

History, law, and custom lay with the king, who could invoke both scripture and precedent to support his constitutional position. It would take some creativity to give theoretical backing to parliament's assertion of authority, and this was supplied by Henry Parker in his anonymously published *Observations upon some of his Majesties late Answers and Expresses*, which was on the London bookstalls by 2 July 1642. Parker's radical argument was that God was not the author of royal power, for 'power is originally inherent in the people'. Royal power was 'secondary and derivative', he claimed, because 'the fountain and efficient cause is the people'. The king's dignity 'was erected to preserve the commonalty, the commonalty was not created for his service'. This undercut the entire basis of divine right kingship, and made the people, represented now in parliament, 'the fountain and efficient cause' of political sovereignty. The state, by this interpretation, rested on a contract, *salus populi* was its governing principle, and the power of the monarch was merely 'conditionate and fiduciary'.[107]

Parker's *Observations* touched a nerve and made people talk. They launched a cascade of paper and a cataract of political theorizing that occupied the public arena for several years. Spawned in the aftermath of the Militia Ordinance, which denied the king command of his armed forces, the *Observations* advanced ideas that respectable politicians had yet to espouse. Parliament could reasonably claim to be the kingdom's highest court, the king's supreme council, and the true representative of the people, but it was a revolutionary leap to 'raise subjects to a capacity of sovereignty, and reduce their sovereign to become their subjects'.[108] Echoing Parker, a parliamentary pamphlet in July 1642 asserted that 'all the power which princes have is but derivative and secondary; the foundation and efficient cause is the people'. Another in November affirmed that 'kings come lawfully in with the choice and consent of their people'.[109] Divine-right kingship was cast aside.

Various printed 'answers', 'caveats', 'animadversions', 'examinations', and 'replies' sought to crush Parker's arguments, thereby giving them publicity.[110] Sir John Spelman fretted that these *Observations* 'intoxicated the vulgar' and 'entangled the more understanding' in argument and response. Wrong, dangerous, and seditious, engaging matters of 'high concernment', their effect was 'to abuse and intoxicate the minds of the wavering multitude' with the false notion that 'the people . . . are above the king'. To the contrary, Spelman insisted, 'regal power' was 'determined by God himself', and the king was 'above all other jurisdictions'. Members of parliament were but subjects, and 'the king remain[ed] their sovereign and superior'. To think otherwise was to 'tend to anarchy and destruction'.[111]

Several commentators warned that the observer's ideas not only dishonoured God and disgraced the king but also threatened principles of rank and hierarchy that sustained the social fabric. Anarchy and confusion lay in that direction. Echoing the reference to Wat Tyler in the king's response to the Nineteen Propositions, one critic quoted the fifteenth-century rebel text—'When Adam delve and Eve span, | Who was there a gentleman?'—and warned the observer, it 'would shake his title to his inheritance, and the name of a gentleman'.[112] Another denounced 'the wicked multitude, that would maintain each base-born tailor 'gainst their sovereign'.[113]

Royalist propagandists drew on history, law, theology, and sarcasm to counter Parker's *Observations.* Printed responses provided arguments for sermons and conversations that became more urgent as the crisis worsened. It was 'absurd' and 'dangerous', conservatives argued, to deny that the 'supreme power... in the supreme magistrate' came directly from God.[114] Adorned with an engraving of his sacred majesty, the pamphlet *Christus Dei, the Lords Annoynted* (Oxford, 1643) employed 'a theological discourse' to prove 'that the regal or monarchical power of our sovereign lord King Charles is not of human, but of divine right, and that God is the sole efficient cause thereof, and not the people'. To claim otherwise, John Jones argued, was 'desperate and more than dangerous', and opposed to 'orthodox Christian doctrine'. Anyone who advanced this position could only have been moved 'to seduce the vulgar into a base and profane misconceiving and vilifying of the royal power of kings'.[115] Another Oxford pamphlet denounced the 'puritanical doctrine' among 'the giddy people' that 'the people are better than the king, and of greater authority'. The spread of this view was both a cause and symptom of England's miseries.[116]

Royalist authors reminded readers that 'the king is not the people's but God's minister... He is not liable to the people, but only to God.'[117] An Oxford publication entitled *Obedience Active and Passive Due to the Supream Power* reiterated the claim that the king's power was 'derived from God'. 'His sacred majesty' was 'called God's anointed, the Lord's anointed, but never the people's anointed'. Subjects were obliged to 'honour him... give thanks to God for him... fear him... obey him... not murmur against him... not withhold his due from him', and never to resist the authority of 'God's lieutenant on earth'.[118] Another Oxford author similarly asserted that 'the king is only and immediately dependant from God, and independent from the people'.[119] Venturing a more moderate position, Sir John Spelman cited almost fifty biblical texts and the histories of more than a dozen Old Testament monarchs to consider the proposition 'that the persons and fortunes of all subjects are absolutely at the will and command of the prince, to dispose according to his will and pleasure'. While supporting divine-right kingship, Spelman also argued that kings were obliged to preserve the laws.[120] Fundamental divisions were unbridgeable, for either kingship was divine or it was not.

Conservative preachers reminded congregations of their 'duty to submit . . . to the king as supreme' and 'to show our subjection with all readiness and cheerfulness'.[121] 'The king is the father of his country . . . cursed is he that despiseth him,' preached Robert Mossom at York in November 1642. The king, he repeated, is 'the defender of our faith . . . the preserver of our peace . . . the protector of our laws', and rebellion against him 'is the rankest poison'.[122] 'The king is the higher power according to St Paul, the supreme authority according to St Peter, the father of the commonwealth according to the fifth commandment,' repeated Henry Ferne, urging 'obedience, honour and subjection according to those places'. Obedience was paramount, these authors repeated, and resistance to the monarch was defiance of God.[123]

The likelihood of civil war stimulated intense debate on the old problem of whether it was lawful to resist a king who 'will not discharge his trust, but is bent or seduced to subvert religion, laws and liberties'.[124] Was it better to obey a king who was betrayed by 'wicked counsel' and bent on 'an arbitrary and tyrannical monarchy', or to adhere to 'the wise representative body of the whole kingdom' in parliament, asked one publication in July 1642.[125] The matter took on extra urgency once hostilities commenced in the autumn. Royalists repeated the familiar nostrum that obedience was unconditional and that subjects should endure whatever political conditions prevailed. The only remedy was prayer and patience, preached Robert Mossom.[126]

Parliamentarians, however, were now ready to re-pose the old question 'is there no remedy against the willfulness of evil kings?' and this time to answer affirmatively.[127] Champions of the 'commonwealth' recalled Sir John Fortescue's fifteenth-century claim that the people (through parliament) could lawfully resist royal commandments that were 'illegal or destructive to themselves or the public'.[128] Some drew on the sixteenth-century *Vindiciae Contra Tyrannos*, which was eventually published in English in 1648. This notorious pamphlet considered 'whether it be lawful to resist a prince that doth infringe the law of God' or 'a prince which doth oppress or ruin a public state', pressing problems for revolutionary England.[129]

The first step, of course, was to pray to God 'that he would incline the king's mind to those things which are worthy of a Christian prince'. But God helps those who help themselves, so that it might become permissible 'by authority of the senate, magistrates and citizens so to moderate his power, that he may not easily break forth into tyranny'.[130] Positing 'a mutual compact betwixt king and people', another pamphlet published early in the civil war argued that the king must adhere to rule, 'and if he swerve from that, this dissolves the contract and gives the people power to defend and preserve themselves'.[131] Answering the question 'what kind of government is this kingdom?', the parliamentary newspaper *Mercurius Britanicus* explained in March 1644 that England had 'a mixed government of monarchy, aristocracy, and democracy; for if the last two had no share or coordination in the government but consultative, it were purely tyrannical, and arbitrary in one who might do and undo at pleasure'. Parliamentary soldiers might read this to understand why they had to fight.[132]

Resistance theory was a dangerous brew, much easier to refute than promote. Royalist pamphleteers lost little time in arguing it down. 'Touch not mine anointed' became a touchstone text for authors who argued that the people 'ought to adhere to their kings, whether good or bad'.[133] Even if a king was 'carried away with malignant counsel' and steered the ship of state towards the rocks, there were no grounds for 'active resistance, by taking up arms against a lawful sovereign prince', insisted Sir John Spelman.[134] Subjects were obliged to obey their king, concurred Dudley Digges, even 'whilst they do suffer under some accidental abuses'. It was 'high sin', he wrote, to entrench upon authority that descended from God.[135] 'Earthly kingdoms are erected of God,' advised another Oxford author, so that even 'obstinate heretics or bloody tyrants' must be obeyed.[136] Redress lay with God, with divine providence, not with political or military action. Robert Grosse likewise insisted that even if kings broke 'all bonds of laws, which yet God forbid they should . . . yet the people must not rise up in rebellion against them'.[137] A variant reading of scripture, however, saw not the king but the parliament and people of England as the lord's anointed.[138]

Railing Venom

For the tens of thousands of Englishmen in arms against him, his sacred majesty had become the head of an opposing army. It became easier to rail against the king when his forces were killing your neighbours and kinsmen. Responsible magistrates in parliamentary areas sought to curb anti-monarchical excesses, but a scatter of reported comments indicates that royal majesty was irreparably tarnished.

Early in the war, about the time of the battle of Edgehill, the Kentish sawyer Matthew Haman was heard to disparage King Charles, saying 'he is as nothing, if he were a king he would not murder his subjects'.[139] Worse was to follow in 1643, when parliamentary fortunes were at their lowest. The London gunsmith Thomas Aldberry avowed in July 1643 that 'there is no king, and he would acknowledge no king'.[140] John Bassett of Stepney also let it be known 'that he did not care for the king, and that he was as good a man as the king'.[141] Some Londoners went further, and wished the king's head impaled. Saying that 'the king was an evil and an unlawful king, and better to be without a king than to have him king', the housewife Alice Jackson of the parish of St Andrew Holborn hoped to see Charles's head on a pole.[142] Lacking a king to torment in person, certain 'roundheads' in Nottinghamshire allegedly pulled down a 'sign of the crown' from a tavern and 'dragged it through the dirt, and kicked it about the streets' of Mansfield.[143]

Norfolk authorities also heard 'words of high concernment' about the king in the summer of 1643. Rachael Mercy of Fakenham was allegedly heard 'railing with the other women', saying 'there is no king, no law, nor no justice . . . because the king was not where he should be'.[144] When Miles Cushion, a knacker of Fincham, Norfolk, declared 'in his cups' the following year that 'the king is no king, he is a bastard and was crowned with a leaden crown', one neighbour told him 'those words were bloody words' and another reported them to local justices.[145] Back in London, Joan Sherrard of St Dunstan in the West declared in 1644 that 'his majesty is a stuttering fool' and wished him dead. 'Is there never a Felton yet living?' she asked, referring to Buckingham's assassin, 'if I were a man, as I am a woman, I would help to pull him to pieces'. Nor was she alone at this time in compassing the king's death or offering to 'kill the king of England'.[146] Using derisory gestures in 1645, in response to the enquiry 'what was the king?', the Yorkshire artisan Thomas Beevers clicked his fingers and answered: 'the king was thus and so.'[147] For these commoners, even before the king was defeated, he was worthless, evil, and deserving of death. Elite parliamentarians dissociated themselves from such vulgarities, but the stream of venom suggests that 'the desacralization of monarchy' was already well advanced.[148]

Parliamentary leaders were careful to maintain the fiction that the king was 'seduced by wicked counsel' and that they intended only to rescue and restore true monarchy. The kingdom's ills were to be blamed on 'delinquents, malignants and disaffected persons' rather than 'his sacred majesty'.[149] Parliamentary publications generally shielded King Charles from direct sniping, but as the civil war climaxed he too came in for hostile criticism.[150] The capture of the king's secret papers, after parliament's victory at Naseby in June 1645, allowed his own words to be turned against him. Marchamount Nedham, author and editor of *Mercurius Britanicus*, exploited the opening of 'the king's cabinet' to expose the 'tricks, devices and labyrinths of state policy' and the king's 'many deceitful windings'.[151] *Arcana imperii* were explicitly made public, and Charles's intimate correspondence with Henrietta Maria showed him to be 'ruled wholly by his wife . . . to the manifest prejudice and ruin of our religion and nation'.[152] By August 1645 Nedham was naming Charles as 'a wilful king', and accusing him of 'a guilty conscience, bloody hands, a heart full of broken vows and protestations'.[153] Notwithstanding a reprimand from the House of Lords and the brief imprisonment of their printer, such comments could not be withdrawn or extinguished.[154] By the spring of 1646 *Mercurius Britanicus* was accusing the king of tyranny, for attempting to deprive the people of England of their liberties.[155]

The crumbling of royal authority and the humiliation of the monarch provoked a vigorous reaction from loyal gentlemen and clerics. Conservative treatises flowed from royalist Oxford (and perhaps hugger-mugger from London), along with newspapers and sermons. Their message, echoing a ballad of the time, was that nothing would be well until 'the king enjoys his own again'.[156] Another rash of propaganda followed the king's defeat, as leaders puzzled how to accommodate a wounded but still sacred monarch. 'Although you, dear sovereign, are not able with your sword to defend us, yet we must and will with our pens, to the danger of our lives, defend you,' wrote Edward Symmons in May 1646.[157] 'Thou art our sovereign still,' proclaimed a poem 'Upon his Majesty's Restraint at Holmeby' [Holdenby] the following year: 'Thou so great a sovereign to our grief | must sue unto thy subjects for relief.' But loyal subjects could hope and pray 'that as thy cause was so betrayed by men, | it may by angels be restored again'.[158] No new texts or arguments were needed to assert the claims of sacred kingship 'in these miserably distracted times' because the king's prerogatives remained 'transcendant . . . unforfeitable . . . untransferable', wrote James Howell in 1648: ''tis all one to put the sword in a mad man's hand, as in the people's.'[159]

The 'tyranny' of Charles I was a rhetorical conceit, used cautiously by elite politicians but favoured by headstrong radicals.[160] Frustrated by the 'intolerable mischiefs' of King Charles and by the view long maintained in parliament that 'the king can do no wrong', the Leveller Richard Overton urged the House of Commons in July 1646 to 'set forth King Charles his wickedness openly before the world'.[161] John Wildman denounced the king's tyranny at the Putney debates in 1647, noting that 'the degrees, of oppression, injustice, and cruelty are the turning stairs by which he ascends to absolute stately majesty and greatness'.[162] Arbitrary government in earlier years exhibited legal tyranny, but 'his majesty's failings' more recently exposed his guilt for 'all the blood, vast expence of treasure, and ruin that hath been occasioned by these wars'.[163]

The Royal Touch

Almost to the end of his life, King Charles displayed and demonstrated his sacredness by touching for 'the king's evil'. Normal court routine crumbled in the face of military exigency, but the king and his subjects still met occasionally for thaumaturgic contact. Charles performed this ceremony several times while quartered at Oxford, and parliament sometimes granted passes for sufferers to go there to be touched. The king's apparent ability to heal 'subjects afflicted with that grievous infirmity called the king's evil' confirmed his status as ruler by divine right.[164]

Early in 1643 it was said that 'divers hundreds of the king's poor subjects' implored King Charles to continue the practice of touching. A printed pamphlet representing itself as the petition of his majesty's 'loving and faithful subjects', sufferers from this unique ailment, desired 'some way whereby we may be enabled to approach your royal presence'. The pamphlet extolled 'the contaction and imposition of your majesty's sacred hands' by 'supernatural means of cure which is inherent in your sacred majesty' and spoke of the 'happiness which the subject of England possesseth in their sovereign'. Though ostensibly seeking access to a ritual interrupted by wartime, the publication stressed its admiration for 'a prince of unpatterned piety and goodness', whose 'sacred presence' was the source of 'our only happiness'.[165] It represented conciliators on the parliamentary side who wanted their king back.

Charles made the most of this tradition when his fortunes were at their lowest. Swarms of people sought out the king after his defeat, to show affection as well as to be cured, and his majesty obliged with his royal touch. Though defeated in battle, the royalist cause upheld the sacred qualities of their still potent sovereign. Travelling south from his Scottish captivity at the beginning of 1647, the king touched 'many diseased persons . . . without any other ceremony' at Ripon, Leeds, and other halts on his way to Holdenby House in Northamptonshire.[166] During the king's imprisonment there in April 1647 parliament became alarmed at 'the resort of a great number of people thither to be touched for the evil', even without the customary distribution of coins. They had more cause at Caversham in July, when he again touched 'abundance for the king's evil'.[167]

The king's exercise of this curative power became even more defiant, almost triumphant, while he was imprisoned at Carisbrook on the Isle of Wight. Varied sufferers made their way to the island, where the royalist writer John Taylor witnessed several touched by the king in October 1648. Among them were a crippled woman, 'and her lameness ceased in three days'; a woman blind in one eye, 'and after the king had touched her, her eye opened and she saw immediately'; and another 'exceeding lame' when 'she came to his majesty, and he touched her, whereby (through God's blessing) she was presently cured'. Others recovered from soreness, blindness, lameness, and chronic disability, but regained ease, sight, and mobility after their encounter with the king. A monarch who made the blind see and the lame walk apparently had Christlike qualities, despite his present sufferings. Taylor saw this as proof that 'his majesty . . . is not to be ranked or filed with common men', but rather was blessed as 'the gracious, favourable, and preserving hand of God'.[168] It would be hard to reduce such a king to the level of a duke of Venice.

Reports from the Isle of Wight, that his majesty 'hath wrought a strange cure there . . . upon a child, whose left eye was closed up with the evil, by prayer and by stroking it with fasting spittle', spread through the news stream. Royalists could interpret such cures as the work of 'God undoubtedly, to manifest him to be his immediate deputy, working a miracle by him', but the radical *Mercurius Militaris* declared that 'every simple gull will know that this story intends only to foster an opinion amongst the people, that his majesty's person is sacred, or that he is God's vicegerent'. *Militaris* reported sarcastically that 'the king of late spits medicine', and wondered, 'whence thou thinkest the virtue of his majesty's touch proceeds; is't from the holiness of his father James's seed?', which some thought unnaturally scattered. Gloating that King Charles 'dare not now spit out his poison against the people', the author also accused the defeated king of fornication with laundry maids and pollution with the French pox.[169] This provoked a blast from the guilefully named *Mercurius Impartialis* against any who dared 'to blaspheme that sacred person, who is the very express sign and type of God'.[170] People could make up their own minds about the potency of royal bodily fluids, when after the regicide a month later some cherished handkerchiefs dipped in the martyr's blood.[171]

It was necessary to paint Charles as a tyrant in order to kill him. He was accused of acting 'against the public interest, common right, liberty, justice, and peace of the people of this nation' and with using his rule 'to erect and uphold in himself an unlimited and tyrannical power', a charge the king reflected back at his accusers. Despite protestations that 'no earthly power' could judge a king, he was condemned 'as a tyrant, traitor, murderer, and public enemy to the good people of this nation'. And, lest the inconveniences of royal government should recur, the residual parliament abolished the very institution of kingship.[172] Backed by the army, the House of Commons declared that 'the people are under God the original of all just power' and their representatives 'unkinged the king' in the name of the people of England.[173]

Among the victors, at least those who stayed at Westminster, the legitimization of revolution and regicide required fresh doses of commonwealth theory, especially after *Eikon Basilike* appeared as the emblem of revived royalism.[174] John Milton supplied a strong draught in *The Tenure of Kings and Magistrates*, taking it as axiomatic that 'all men naturally were born free'. In some ancient past, following Adam's fall, 'they agreed by common league to bind each other from mutual injury' and entrusted power to kings and magistrates 'to be their deputies and commissioners'. This power, Milton insisted, was 'only derivative, transferred and committed to them in trust from the people'. Public officials 'at their first instalment' took oaths to do justice, 'with express warning, that if the king or magistrate proved unfaithful to his trust, the people would be disengaged'. Any king who turned to tyranny 'may be as lawfully deposed and punished as they were at first elected', a convenient justification for recent actions.[175]

Milton's republicanism, like the divine-right theory of his opponents, rested on fiction. It required a blackening of the king's reputation, his depiction as a 'tyrant', as much as *Eikon Basilike* portrayed King Charles as a saint. Neither rhetoric nor erudition could win the argument, though the power of the sword proved temporarily persuasive. A deep groan and a shocked silence followed the fall of the axe, as people sought to comprehend what they had accomplished.

10

The Blindness of Charles I

Adulatory apologies for Charles I peaked in the decades following his death. To the generation of the Restoration, the martyred monarch became 'the sun of our firmament, the light of our eyes ... the greatest of kings', even 'the best of kings since Christ'.[1] To Thomas Forde, writing in 1660, he was the 'most perfect mixture and composition of majesty and sweetness', famous for 'his pious and paternal care over his people'. He was 'an universal gentleman ... the most accomplished king this nation ever had'.[2] To William Winstanley, publishing in 1665, the late king constituted 'the exact pattern of piety, patience, and prudence', whose virtues 'will be had in everlasting remembrance'.[3] Not even the most fawning of modern Stuart apologists are so fulsome or so blinkered.

Historians have been fascinated by the personality, predilections, and policies of England's second Stuart monarch, though assessments vary with the viewpoint of the author and the sources consulted. Most are critical, though a few judge Charles more sinned against than sinning.[4] The contentious political culture of Caroline England harboured extreme and competing opinions, though elite and respectable voices are more likely to be heard. Loyal supporters of the crown upheld not just the sanctity of kingship but the personal qualities of 'his now majesty'. 'The king's loving subjects' showed him loyal and dutiful deference, with expressions of praise and thanks. Others, while acknowledging divine-right theory and the obligations of subjection, voiced varying misgivings about the reliability and ability of their sovereign. Civil war royalists were not necessarily enamoured of Charles I, and adhered more to the principle than to the man.

Most people—devoted, begrudging, or indifferent—kept their opinions to themselves, or balanced dutiful deference with prayerful silence. The constraints of *arcana imperii* and the dangers of *lèse-majesté* dampened outright criticism, but, as we have seen, a number of individuals worried openly about their king's shortcomings. This concluding chapter returns to commentary on royal character and competence, and its consequences for governance, as the king's two bodies slid disturbingly apart.

Impaired Vision

Contemporaries who served Charles I knew their king to be the best of all monarchs. He was, declared William Laud, 'another Hezekiah, a wise and religious king...every way fitted to the state he bears'.[5] Courtiers and clerics praised their king as mild and magnanimous, and 'ever studious and careful of the weal of his people'.[6] Thomas Morton, the bishop of Durham, waxed barely hyperbolic in 1639 when he lauded King Charles as 'the mirror of moral virtuousness, the lamp of religiousness, and miracle of clemency and patience', with further commendations for 'his wisdom, temperance, charity, justice [and] conjugal fidelity'.[7] From the viewpoint of the crown and most of the aristocracy, divine providence and hereditary succession had brought the ideal occupant to the throne, showering England with the blessings of sacred kingship. If the reign eventuated in violence and division, bloodshed and tears, it was not the king's fault, but rather the machinations of malignants and refractories. 'How is it possible', asked the cavalier Sir Roger Manley, 'that the best of princes should meet with the worst of subjects?'[8]

Charles I's royal virtues found tests in routine government, the exercise of patronage and deployment of the prerogative, as well as in the crises of the reign. Observers, both close and distant, found repeated opportunities to experience and assess his rule. The unfolding of events confirmed many in their confidence, but some critics feared that England was in trouble, that God's blessings were stinted, and that the king himself was deficient. A repeated scandalous complaint held that King Charles, supposedly 'his island's eye of government', keeping 'perpetual watch over his people and kingdoms',[9] was in fact short-sighted or even blind.

Long before the Grand Remonstrance of 1641, a groundswell of grumbling registered the king's alleged mistakes and the undermining of reciprocity and trust. Though 'unprosperous' outcomes could be attributed to 'evil advisors' or the caprices of providence, the principal choices and policies of the reign were his majesty's, with problems of his own compounding.

Echoing the prayer of the Reformation martyr William Tyndale—'Lord, open the king of England's eyes'—a sequence of anxious suppliants urged King Charles to look to himself, to open his eyes, and to change his course 'before it be too late'.[10]

An underground stream of opinion prayed for the king to be more supportive of the liberties of the subject, more attentive to the needs of the commonwealth, more receptive to the protestant cause. The signs of God's anger were clear to those with eyes to see: astronomical marvels, plagues, bad weather, a faltering economy, reversals by land and sea, even the loss of the king's firstborn. The causes were growing and manifold: ill-managed and unsuccessful wars; failure to recover the Palatinate; abandonment of Europe's protestants; fiscal devices of dubious legality; erosion of the protections of Magna Carta; the advancement of idolatry and superstition; relaxation or profanation of the Sabbath; and the harbouring of a catholic queen whose entourage facilitated the agenda of popery. This was an oppositional perspective, at variance with mainstream court opinion, though perhaps reflecting anxieties within the nation at large.

As earlier chapters have shown, a series of determined subjects sought to gain the king's attention, to warn him of mounting problems. Some were deeply disturbed individuals who confused the nation's troubles with their own, but all believed that God had turned against England and that ill-directed policy needed to be rooted out. These were loyal subjects who cherished the king as pastor to his people and steersman of the ship of state. Their opinions were neither profound nor original, and cannot be shown to be widespread, but they were moved by misgivings about the state of the country, the direction of policy, and the conduct and capability of their king.

Lucy Martin feared that the queen's religion might 'bring a greater plague on us all' and offered to tell King Charles 'how this great judgment may be turned away'.[11] Thomas Jarvis felt similarly moved to explain to the king what 'causeth God to be angry with us', and claimed that 'the remedy is very easy if it please you to hearken unto it, according to your desire'.[12] In 1629 the brewer Robert Triplet saw 'black clouds' that threatened 'great afflictions if not total destruction to us all' and warned his majesty that 'the hearts of your people ... decline as fast from you as from the Duke'.[13] Andrew Humfrey had visions of 'weeping and gnashing of teeth' in 1633, and prayed that God might bring the queen 'to believe in his holy gospel'. His persistence brought him several months in prison for 'carrying strange news to the king'.[14] Thomas Harrison was another in 1639 with 'some things to signify unto his majesty', including news of 'a most horrible conspiracy, plotted here in England, against the king and state'.[15] Likewise, fearing that 'the king and kingdom is in danger of utter ruin', Grace Cary sought 'to notify' his majesty of 'plots and treacheries... idolatry [and] superstition'.[16]

More reckless and more damaging, though drawn from the same wells of frustration, a few individuals voiced seditious scorn for the king. The lawyer Hugh Pyne famously remarked of King Charles, 'he is to be carried any whither... before God, he is no more fit to be king than Hickwright (an old simple fellow who was then Mr Pyne's shepherd)'.[17] The schoolmaster Alexander Gill dismissed King Charles in 1628 as 'a fine wise king' with 'wit enough to be a shopkeeper to ask "what do you lack?" and that is all'.[18] Both suffered imprisonment, though nothing worse, when the authorities learned of their words. Coarser contemporaries called King Charles a fool, a bastard, a boy, a baby, and a knave, or spoke 'fearfully ill-advised words' or 'vile, impious, malicious and seditious speeches against his majesty', long before the crisis of the 1640s.[19] These subjects were not over-awed by obligations of duty and deference, showed minimal respect for *arcana imperii*, and judged Charles unfit to govern. Anyone who thinks that comments to that effect by historians are 'anachronistic' needs to reread the historical record.[20]

Anonymously produced manuscripts put dangerous ideas in circulation and gave some protection for seditious opinion. An earlier libel on 'the five senses' was revived in 1628 to criticize King Charles's dependence on the Duke of Buckingham. The verses rehearsed the motif of royal blindness and the king's need for better vision:

> And now just God I humbly pray
> That though wilt take that slime away
> That keeps my sovereign's eyes from viewing
> The things that will be our undoing.[21]

Another manuscript proclaiming itself 'no libel, but a private admonition', posted at Paul's Cross in May 1629, told the king directly, 'thou hast lost the hearts of thy subjects', so that the relation of authority and subjection 'now ceaseth, violated on thy part... For the first thing God doth when he determineth to dethrone a king... is to take from him the hearts of his subjects.' Warning of 'the accursed thing' that contaminated the kingdom—along with idolatry, the breaking of parliaments, and the distressed state of

Christendom—the message reached its peroration: 'The lord open thine eyes as he did David's eyes . . . before it be too late.'[22] In similar vein, a repurposed Jacobean 'letter of advice' warned the king that 'in taverns ten healths are drunk to [Elizabeth of Bohemia and her family] more than to you', a measure of his fallen favour.[23]

Anxious subjects who were troubled by King Charles's kingship had limited access to the press before the 1640s, and even then were cautious and circumspect when dealing with royalty. They had few other avenues to express their frustration. An illicit publication from Amsterdam complained in 1630 that those about the king lacked 'eyes to see the hand of God go out against us', but was unwilling to charge the king directly.[24] Some, like the Northamptonshire puritan Robert Woodford, prayed that the king would have a change of heart, and recorded such sentiments in their private writings. In 1640 Woodford prayed that God would give the king 'David's heart and Solomon's wisdom, that he may improve the talent betrusted to him to the good of this so great a people'.[25] The standard prayer 'for the king's majesty', that God should 'replenish him with the grace of thy holy spirit, that he may always incline to thy will, and walk in thy way', assumed an ever-increasing urgency.[26]

The Scottish crisis persuaded some subjects that King Charles was more blind than clear-sighted. Seditious verses claimed that the king's evil advisors, specifically archbishop Laud and the Earl of Strafford, had deprived him of his senses:

Laudless Will of Lambeth Strand
And Black Tom Tyrant of Ireland
Like fox and wolf did lurk
With many rooks and magpies
To pick out good King Charles his eyes,
And then be Pope and Turk.[27]

The illicitly printed treatise *Englands Complaint to Iesus Christ Against the Bishops Canons* prayed explicitly that 'God should be pleased . . . to open the eyes of the king, to let him see how he and the state is abused' by the bustling bishops, then prayed again, 'the Lord open the king's eyes, to see how both himself and his people are abused and his kingdoms embroiled and endangered by these his prelates and priests'. Though studiously unwilling 'to conceive the least sinister thought' of King Charles himself, the author allowed no remedy 'until . . . the king reform himself, and renew his covenant and conditions of the kingdom to the good and just satisfaction of the people'.[28]

Outspoken parliamentary supporters continued to describe the king as blind, as if his truly kingly qualities were masked by visual impairment. Stanley Gower prayed in a letter to Sir Robert Harley in January 1641: 'God open the eyes and turn the heart of our king, that he may be thorough for the reformation wished.'[29] A Hertfordshire preacher prayed aloud that autumn 'that God would be pleased to begin the work of grace in the king's heart... before it was too late'.[30] In August 1642, however, the king reversed the trope when he raised his standard and prayed that 'it please God to open the eyes of our people' to the rightness of his position.[31]

Continuing the metaphor of visual incapacity, the parliamentary newspaper editor Marchamount Nedham fancied in 1644 that King Charles might somehow improve his vision:

> I hope some divine beam hath enlightened him from above, and dispelled that mist which was cast before his eyes, whereby he may behold and loathe the turpitude and vanity of prelacy, the partiality and malice of self-interest, ruminating delinquents; the veil of whose sophistry being removed, he cannot but see the cordial and sincere endeavours of his parliament, for the establishing of his kingdom in the true profession of the gospel, and his throne in all princely prerogatives, due to him and his posterity.[32]

It was a prayer for a different kind of monarch, less dependent on sycophantic courtiers, more attentive to the needs of the commonwealth, more committed to the protestant reformation.

Commentators in this tradition did not ask for an alternative succession, still less an end to monarchy, but rather that 'his now majesty' would live up to his rhetoric of sagacity, service, reciprocity, and love. King Charles believed himself bound by his oath and his honour to maintain his prerogatives and the privileges of the church, but no sovereign could succeed without acknowledging the diversity, aspirations, and distresses of his people. He needed to command their hearts as well as their loyalty. Theorists sometimes wondered whether it was better for a ruler to be loved than feared, but Charles I, alas, was neither.

Patience wore thin when the realm appeared to be in peril, and much of that peril seemed homemade. The king's 'loving subjects' could turn into 'refractory spirits' when their religious or constitutional expectations were threatened. People who normally performed their duties with fortitude and endurance could baulk or even resist if they thought the king in the wrong. Such was the case with the forced loan and Ship Money, with altar conversions and the Book of Sports, and even more so with the crisis in Scotland. The king could be cast as the 'man of blood', even when his motives and mischiefs were unfathomable.[33]

It is hard not to conclude that King Charles was the author of his own troubles. His haughtiness did not preserve him. Like any other monarch he had choices, room for discretion. There was no need for him to adhere so devotedly to the Duke of Buckingham in the early years of his reign, nor to rely so heavily on a coterie of nobles or a particular faction of the church. He would have been better served by a statesman of the calibre of a William or Robert Cecil, if he could find one. There was no need to make war against Spain and France, sequentially and simultaneously, and to launch operations for which resources and preparations were lacking. There was no need to pack the episcopal bench with hard-liners, or to reissue the Declaration of Sports with demands for strict compliance. There was no need to disrupt parish culture with the demands of ceremonial uniformity, or to impose a new prayer book on Scotland. The king did not need to frame every initiative as a test of authority, or every objection as refractoriness or malignancy. These were King Charles's own choices, and his kingdom was saddled with their repercussions.

There was little benefit to England in the king's prickly defence of his honour or the artistic cultivation of his court. Royal rigidity did little to secure his people's affections. The ceremonial and disciplinary tilt of the Church of England produced friction in many parishes, and a hard-line insistence on duty and uniformity replaced the broader inclusiveness of earlier regimes. Public anxieties about the spread of 'popery' and threats to 'the liberty of the subject' were exaggerated, and perhaps avoidable, but a sequence of signals and policies allowed those anxieties to flourish. High-profile Star Chamber actions against so-called seditious libellers exhibited a vindictive over-reach that did nothing to strengthen the regime.

Though the king's apologists could justify every policy, their explanations increasingly appeared strident and shallow. Accumulations of doubts and worry left royal authority blemished when it was most under pressure. Frustrations became frictions and frictions became fractures when princely wisdom seemed wanting. Cracks in the arch of order disturbed England's calmness, and exposed a groundswell of distempers that eased the slippage from crisis to civil war. The king's character was not necessarily instrumental, but his policies made possible the collapse of his power. The monarchical polity relied on a balance between kingly and popular expectations.

Subjects needed to know not just what obligations were expected of them, but how in practice the people and the crown served each other.

Histories that focus on the nobility and gentry yield detailed accounts of high political dealings. Every historian is beholden to them. But traditional elite history sheds little light on the shadowed substructures of the arch of order. By 1640 Charles I had over seven million subjects (five million in England and Wales), and a growing number doubted his abilities and his intentions. Though we cannot calculate the demography of dissent, it seems clear that the reciprocities of monarchy and subjecthood were damaged. Landowning families, tenants, artisans, and labourers all had a stake in the kingdom, and many were manifestly troubled. King Charles's policies eroded the respect, affection, and trust on which successful English kingship depended. When commoners lost confidence in the ability, probity, and wisdom of the king the consequence could be revolution.

Notes

PROLOGUE

1. The Palm Sunday sermon at court was most likely preached by the archbishop of Canterbury, George Abbot. On the outdoor preaching place, see Peter E. McCullough, *Sermons at Court: Politics and Religion in Elizabethan and Jacobean Preaching* (Cambridge, 1998), 42–9.
2. TNA, SP 16/24/12, copy in SP 16/24/13.
3. Christopher Wordsworth (ed.), *The Coronation of King Charles I* (Henry Bradshaw Society, vol. 2, 1892), 28; Leopold G. Wickham Legg (ed.), *English Coronation Records* (Westminster, 1901), 255.
4. Sermons on the plague and sin include Thomas Fuller, *A Sermon Intended for Paul's Crosse, but Preached in the Church of St Paul's* (1626); Joseph Hall, *A Sermon of Publike Thanksgiving for the Wonderful Mitigation of the Late Mortalitie* (1626); Robert Horne, *A Caveat to Prevent Future Iudgements: Or, An Admonition to All England* (1626); John Pyne, *A Brief Meditation upon the Fifteenth Verse of the Twenty Fourth Chapter of the Second Booke of Samuel* (1626), bound with *The Heart of the King; and the King of the Heart* (1628). For the sin of Achan, see Joshua 7:1. *Lachrymae Londoniensis. Or, Londons Teares and Lamentations for Gods Heavie Visitation of the Plague of Pestilence* (1626), 12, 27, attributes the plague to the nation's sins, and prays that God might direct, guide, instruct, and sanctify King Charles's queen.
5. Marc Bloch, *The Royal Touch: Sacred Monarchy and Scrofula in England and France* (1973).
6. Gary W. Kronk, *Cometography: A Catalog of Comets*, 5 vols (Cambridge, 1999), i. 333–43; Jeffrey Wilson, *A New Almanacke or Prognostication* (1626), sig. A^{v}; Robert Salter, *Wonderfull Prophecies from the Beginning of the Monarchy of this Land . . . with an Essay touching the late Prodigious Comete* (1626), 44–6. *A Strange Wonder, or, The Cities Amazement* (1641), sigs A2^{v}, A3^{v}–4, also associated 'that blazing star of our time' with 'deaths of great princes and potentates . . . plague and pestilence', and remarked that the 'unusual, sudden, unnatural return of the tide hath in this kingdom been evermore followed with continual dismal heavy issues'. Only a few days before Lucy Martin threw her letter, on 27 March 1626, the anniversary of King Charles's accession, 'a terrible earthquake' rocked central England from Derbyshire to Northamptonshire: Thomas Birch (ed.),

The Court and Times of Charles the First, 2 vols (1848), i. 94. For responses to similar occurrences, see Alexandra Walsham, *Providence in Early Modern England* (Oxford, 1999).

7. Esther S. Cope, *Handmaid of the Holy Spirit: Dame Eleanor Davies, Never Soe Mad a Ladie* (Ann Arbor, 1992); *Writings of Lady Eleanor Davies*, ed. Esther S. Cope (New York, 1996). There may be a closer connection, since Great Marlow, where Lucy Martin visited her sister, was only 15 miles from Englefield, Berkshire, the home of Sir John and Lady Eleanor Davies. See Eleanor Davies, *A Warning to the Dragon and all Angels* (1625), for her first prophetic vision in the summer of 1625.
8. TNA, SP 16/24/73.
9. The most likely possibility is the Dr Edmund Wilson who practised in the London parish of St Mary le Bow from 1606 to his death in 1633. He may have been the same Edmund Wilson, 'doctor of physic', who obtained a Privy Council pass in 1616 to travel abroad for three years, provided he did not go to Rome: *APC 1615–16*, 672; Margaret Pelling and Francis White (eds), *Physicians and Irregular Medical Practitioners in London 1550–1640* (British History Online database, 2004). For the curative use of blood, see Lauren Kassell, *Medicine and Magic in Elizabethan London: Simon Forman: Astrologer, Alchemist, and Physician* (Oxford, 2005), 188. The future leveller John Lilburne wrote in 1638 of sealing his testimony 'with my dearest blood' (Bodleian Library, Oxford, MS Bankes 18/21, fo. 33).
10. *APC 1625–26*, 432; Bethlem Royal Hospital Archives, Court of Governors, BCB-06, fo. 423^{v}.

INTRODUCTION

1. Influential studies of Charles I's kingship include Charles Carlton, *Charles I: The Personal Monarch*, 2nd edn (1995); Richard Cust, *Charles I: A Political Life* (Harlow, 2005); Richard Cust, *Charles I and the Aristocracy, 1625–1642* (Cambridge, 2013); Mark Kishlansky, *A Monarchy Transformed: Britain 1603–1714* (1996); Mark Kishlansky, 'Charles I: A Case of Mistaken Identity', *Past & Present*, 189 (2005), 41–80; Judith Richards, '"His Nowe Majestie" and the English Monarchy: The Kingship of Charles I before 1640', *Past & Present*, 113 (1986), 70–96; Conrad Russell, *The Fall of the British Monarchies 1637–1642* (Oxford, 1991); Kevin Sharpe, *The Personal Rule of Charles I* (New Haven and London, 1992); Kevin Sharpe, *Image Wars: Promoting Kings and Commonwealths in England 1603–1660* (New Haven and London, 2010); Tim Harris, *Rebellion: Britain's First Stuart Kings, 1567–1742* (Oxford, 2014).
2. Socially inflected explorations of early modern political culture include Thomas Garden Barnes, *Somerset 1625–1640: A County's Government during the 'Personal Rule'* (Cambridge, MA, 1961); Michael J. Braddick, *State Formation in Early Modern England c.1550–1700* (Cambridge, 2000); Peter Clark, *English*

Provincial Society from the Reformation to the Revolution: Religion, Politics and Society in Kent 1500–1640 (Cranbury, NJ, 1977); Alan Everitt, *The Community of Kent and the Great Rebellion 1640–60* (Leicester, 1966); Anthony Fletcher, *A County Community in Peace and War: Sussex 1600–1660* (1975); Felicity Heal and Clive Holmes, *The Gentry in England and Wales, 1500–1700* (Stanford, 1994); Steve Hindle, *The State and Social Change in Early Modern England, 1550–1640* (Basingstoke, 2000); Ann Hughes, *Politics, Society, and Civil War in Warwickshire, 1620–1660* (Cambridge, 1987); William Hunt, *The Puritan Moment: The Coming of Revolution in an English County* (Cambridge, MA, 1983); John Morrill, *Revolt in the Provinces: The People of England and the Tragedies of War 1630–1648*, 2nd edn (Harlow, 1999); Buchanan Sharp, *In Contempt of All Authority: Rural Artisans and Riot in the West of England, 1586–1660* (Berkeley and Los Angeles, 1980); David Underdown, *Revel, Riot and Rebellion: Popular Politics and Culture in England 1603–1660* (Oxford, 1985); David Underdown, *A Freeborn People: Politics and the Nation in Seventeenth-Century England* (Oxford, 1996); John Walter, *Crowds and Popular Politics in Early Modern England* (Manchester, 2006); Andy Wood, *The Politics of Social Conflict: The Peak Country, 1520–1770* (Cambridge, 1999); Andy Wood, *Riot, Rebellion and Popular Politics in Early Modern England* (Basingstoke, 2002). See also David Cressy, 'Conflict, Consensus and the Willingness to Wink: The Erosion of Community in Charles I's England', *Huntington Library Quarterly*, 61 (2000), 131–49; David Cressy, *England on Edge: Crisis and Revolution 1640–1642* (Oxford, 2006); and David Cressy, *Dangerous Talk: Scandalous, Seditious and Treasonable Speech in Pre-Modern England* (Oxford, 2010).

CHAPTER I

1. John Gauden, *Three Sermons Preached Upon Severall Publike Occasions* (1642), 2.
2. E. A. Wrigley and R. S. Schofield, *The Population History of England 1541–1871* (Cambridge, MA, 1981), 532, estimate an English population of 4,751,559 in 1625 and 5,228,671 in 1649; R. A. Houston, *The Population History of Britain and Ireland, 1500–1750* (Basingstoke, 1992), 28–30.
3. Stephen Jerome, *Englands Iubilee, or Irelands Ioyes Io-Paen, for King Charles his Welcome* (Dublin, 1625), epistle dedicatory. Cf. John Pyne, *A Brief Meditation upon the Fifteenth Verse of the Twenty Fourth Chapter of the Second Booke of Samuel* (1626), 28, for whom 'Dan to Beersheba' in Israel is like saying 'from the Start Point on our southern seas, unto Straithy Head in Scotland'.
4. Joseph Hall, *A Sermon of Publike Thanksgiving for the Wonderful Mitigation of the Late Mortalitie* (1626), 42. See also Thomas Fuller, *A Sermon Intended for Paul's Crosse, but Preached in the Church of St Paul's* (1626), 32: 'We have had so long, so large, so flourishing a time of peace, as our Goshen hath been as it were the envy of all the nations of the world... Germany groaning under persecution, France encumbered with her fatal infelicity, civil wars, Italy burdened with the

tyranny of Antichrist, Spain ambitiously desiring to fathom all, like to keep nothing, the Hollanders continually at war, only we, by the blessing of God, and the happy means of our late sovereign of ever-blessed memory have sit under our vines and fig trees.'

5. Richard Brathwaite, *The English Gentleman* (1630), 298.
6. TNA, National Register of Archives, Bound Vol. 20594, 556, Dorchester to the Earl of Cork, 29 July 1630.
7. *The Works of the Most Reverend Father in God, William Laud, D.D.*, ed. William Scott and James Bliss, 9 vols (Oxford, 1847–60), i. 211.
8. Edward Reynolds, *The Shieldes of the Earth* (1636), 47.
9. *The Earl of Strafforde's Letters and Dispatches*, ed. William Knowler, 2 vols (1739), i. 177, 226. Sir Thomas Wentworth, ennobled 1628, became Earl of Strafford in 1640.
10. *The Hamilton Papers . . . 1638–1650*, ed. Samuel Rawson Gardiner (Camden Society, NS, vol. 27, 1880), 65, Goring to Hamilton, 4 December 1638.
11. TNA, C115/108, no. 8617.
12. *Mr Speakers Speech, Before the King, in the Lords House of Parliament, July the third, 1641* (1641), 2.
13. Thomas Carew, *Poems* (1640), 130, cited in Ian Atherton and Julie Sanders (eds), *The 1630s: Interdisciplinary Essays on Culture and Politics in the Caroline Era* (Manchester and New York, 2006), 19.
14. Charles I, *His Majesties Declaration: To All His Loving Subjects, Of the causes which moved him to dissolve the last Parliament* (1640), 50–1.
15. *The Oxinden Letters 1607–1642*, ed. Dorothy Gardiner (1933), 173.
16. J.L., *Englands Doxologie* (1641), 1–2.
17. Thomas Morton, *Englands Warning-Piece: Shewing the nature, danger, and Ill Effects of Civill-Warre* (1642), 1.
18. Edward Symmons, *A Vindication of King Charles: or, A Loyal Subjects Duty* (1648), 107.
19. David Cressy, 'Describing the Social Order of Elizabethan and Stuart England', *Literature and History*, 3 (1976), 29–44; Keith Wrightson, *English Society 1580–1680* (1982), 17–38; J. A. Sharpe, *Early Modern England: A Social History 1550–1760*, 2nd edn (1997), 157–213.
20. BL, Sloane MS 649, fos 52–5.
21. G. E. Aylmer, *The King's Servants: The Civil Service of Charles I, 1625–42* (1961), 331; Lawrence Stone, *The Crisis of the Aristocracy 1558–1641* (Oxford, 1965), 138–43; Richard Cust, 'Charles I and the Order of the Garter', *Journal of British Studies*, 52 (2013), 343–69.
22. TNA, SP 16/182/31, SP 16/375/2; Huntington Library, Hastings MS, HA Misc. Box 1/32.
23. *APC 1629–30*, pp. vii–viii.
24. Andy Wood, 'Deference, Paternalism and Popular Memory in Early Modern England', in Steve Hindle, Alexandra Shepard, and John Walter (eds),

Remaking English Society: Social Relations and Social Change in Early Modern England (Woodbridge, 2013), 233–53.

25. Austin Woolrych, *Britain in Revolution 1625–1660* (Oxford, 2002), 66. 'Fines for not taking the order of knighthood' yielded the crown more than £173,500 by 1634: TNA, SP 16/285/89.
26. *CSPD 1634–35*, 186; G. D. Squibb, *The High Court of Chivalry: A Study of the Civil Law of England* (Oxford, 1959); Richard P. Cust and Andrew J. Hopper (eds), *Cases in the High Court of Chivalry, 1634–1640* (Harleian Society, NS, vol. 18, 2006).
27. Mark Kishlansky, 'Charles I: A Case of Mistaken Identity', *Past & Present*, 189 (2005), 61.
28. Aylmer, *King's Servants*, 331; Felicity Heal and Clive Holmes, *The Gentry in England and Wales 1500–1700* (Stanford, 1994), 97–135; Robert Bucholz and Newton Key, *Early Modern England 1485–1714* (Oxford, 2004), 155.
29. The classic formulations are Sir Thomas Smith, *De Republica Anglorum, The Maner of Governement or Policie of the Realme of England* (1583), 18–34; William Harrison, *The Description of England*, ed. Georges Edelen (Ithaca, NY, 1968), 113–21; Thomas Wilson, 'The State of England Ann-dom. 1600', ed. F. J. Fisher (*Camden Miscellany*, no. 16, 1936), 19–39.
30. William Gouge, *The Dignitie of Chivalrie, set forth in a sermon preached before the Artillery Company* (1626), 5.
31. Keith Wrightson, *Earthly Necessities: Economic Lives in Early Modern England* (New Haven and London, 2000), 184.
32. Richard Brathwaite, *The English Gentleman* (1630), title page, 311, *passim*; John Gough ('Philomusus'), *The Academy of Complements* (1640), 'epistle'.
33. TNA, SP 16/71/65; Staffordshire Record Office, D.661/11/1, Notebook of Richard Dyott 5; Cambridge University Library, MS Mn. 1. 45 (Baker transcripts), 99.
34. G.A., *Pallas Armata: The Gentlemans Armorie* (1639), 'To the Reader'.
35. Michael Dalton, *The Country Iustice, Conteyning the Practice of the Iustices of the Peace* (1618), 30.
36. Bodleian Library, MS Clarendon 14, fo. 161^{v}.
37. HMC, *Twelfth Report*, 246–7.
38. BL, Add. MS 33,936, fo. 73.
39. TNA, SP 46/76.
40. *Trevelyan Papers, Part III*, ed. W. C. and C. E. Trevelyan (Camden Society, OS, vol. 105, 1872), 178.
41. TNA, SP 46/76.
42. HMC, *Twelfth Report*, 191, 284; TNA, SP 16/126/70.
43. HMC, *Salisbury*, xxii. 258.
44. Stone, *Crisis of the Aristocracy*, 562–5.
45. Henry Ellis (ed.), *Original Letters Illustrative of English History*, 2nd edn, 3 vols (1825), iii. 189.

46. TNA, SP 16/79/54; Conrad Russell, *The Crisis of Parliaments: English History 1509–1660* (New York, 1971), 174.
47. Laud, *Works*, iii. 205.
48. TNA, National Register of Archives, Bound Vol. 20594, 712, Lord Dungarvon to the Earl of Cork, 28 July 1634. See also Stone, *Crisis of the Aristocracy*, 562–5.
49. Huntington Library, Hastings MS, HA Misc. Box 12/2, fo. 147.
50. *APC 1627 Jan.–Aug.*, 98, 105, 194, 353; HMC, *Salisbury*, xxii. 227, 229, 232; Huntington Library, Hastings Correspondence, Box 11, HA 10614, HA 46117.
51. Francis Rogers, *A Visitation Sermon Preached at the Lord Archbishops Trienniall and Ordinary Visitation* (1633), sig. C4.
52. Edwin George and Stella George (eds), *Bristol Probate Inventories Part 1: 1542–1650* (Bristol Record Society, vol. 54, 2002), 59, 62, 94.
53. David H. Smith, 'A Seventeenth Century Tinker's Will and Inventory', *Journal of the Gypsy Lore Society*, 4th ser., 1 (1977), 177.
54. Adam Fox, 'Food, Drink and Social Distinction in Early Modern England', in Steve Hindle, Alexandra Shepard, and John Walter (eds), *Remaking English Society: Social Relations and Social Change in Early Modern England* (Woodbridge, 2013), 165–87.
55. *Calendar of the Correspondence of the Smyth Family of Ashton Court 1548–1647*, ed. J. H. Bettey (Bristol Record Society, vol. 35, 1982), 101, 109; *The Papers of Sir Richard Grosvenor, 1st Bart. (1585–1645)*, ed. Richard Cust (Record Society of Lancashire and Cheshire, vol. 134, 1996), 57; 'The Diary of John Greene (1635–57)', ed. E. M. Symonds, *English Historical Review*, 43 (1928), 388; *Letters from Redgrave Hall: The Bacon Family 1340–1744*, ed. Diarmaid MacCulloch (Suffolk Records Society, vol. 50, 2007), 127; BL, Add. MS 28,006, fos 37–8^{v}; Huntington Library, Ellesmere MSS 6671, 6674, 6683, 6684; Huntington Library, Hastings MS, HA Misc. Box 12 (3); TNA, SP 46/77.
56. TNA, SP 16/285/19, Conway accounts, 1634–5. For aristocratic expenditure on food, see Stone, *Crisis of the Aristocracy*, 555–61.
57. Helen Stocks and W. H. Stevenson (eds), *Records of the Borough of Leicester... 1603–1688* (Cambridge, 1923), 221.
58. *APC 1627 Jan.–Aug.*, 105; TNA, SP 16/3/5.
59. *CSPD 1638–39*, 273.
60. Craig Muldrew, *Food, Energy and the Creation of Industriousness: Work and Material Culture in Agrarian England, 1550–1780* (Cambridge, 2011), 84–132, gives calorific values for various kinds of food, and argues that labourers were better fed than has previously been assumed. The period before the civil war, however, was 'a very difficult period of high food prices', and improvements occurred mainly in the later Stuart era: Muldrew, *Food Energy and the Creation of Industiousness*, 319. For later anthropometric estimates, see Roderick Floud, Kenneth Wachter, and Annabel Gregory, *Height, Health and History: Nutritional Status in the United Kingdom, 1750–1980* (Cambridge, 1990); Roderick Floud,

Robert W. Fogel, Bernard Harris, and Sock Chul Hong, *The Changing Body: Health, Nutrition, and Human Development in the Western World since 1700* (Cambridge, 2011). For the persistence of these differentials, see P. H. Whincup, D. G. Cook, and A. G. Shaper, 'Social Class and Height', *British Medical Journal*, 297 (15 October 1988), 980–1.

61. John Swan, *Redde Debitum. Or, A Discourse in Defence of Three Chiefe Fatherhoods* (1640), 33.
62. Alexandra Shepard and Judith Spicksley, 'Worth, Age, and Social Status in Early Modern England', *Economic History Review*, 64 (2011), 493–530, tables at 517 and 520. See also Alexandra Shepard, 'Honesty, Worth and Gender in Early Modern England, 1560–1640', in Henry French and Jonathan Barry (eds), *Identity and Agency in England, 1500–1800* (Basingstoke and New York, 2004), 87–105.
63. David Cressy, *Literacy and the Social Order: Reading and Writing in Tudor and Stuart England* (Cambridge, 1980), 118–41.
64. Wilfrid Prest (ed.), *The Professions in Early Modern England* (1987).
65. Discussions of lay–clerical relations in early modern England include Christopher Hill, *The Economic Problems of the Church from Archbishop Whitgift to the Long Parliament* (Oxford, 1956); Rosemary O'Day, *The English Clergy: The Emergence and Consolidation of a Profession 1558–1642* (Leicester, 1979), esp. chs 13 and 14; Rosemary O' Day, 'The Anatomy of a Profession: The Clergy of the Church of England', in Wilfrid Prest (ed.), *The Professions in Early Modern England* (1987), 25–63; Eamon Duffy, 'The Godly and the Multitude in Stuart England', *Seventeenth Century*, 1 (1986), 31–55; Christopher Haigh, 'Anticlericalism and the English Reformation', in Christopher Haigh (ed.), *The English Reformation Revised* (Cambridge, 1987), 56–74; Patrick Collinson, '"Shepherds, Sheepdogs, and Hirelings": The Pastoral Ministry in Post-Reformation England', in W. J. Sheils and Diana Wood (eds), *The Ministry: Clerical and Lay. Studies in Church History*, 26 (Oxford, 1989), 185–220; Kevin Sharpe, *The Personal Rule of Charles I* (New Haven and London, 1992), 274–402.
66. David Cressy, 'A Drudgery of Schoolmasters: The Teaching Profession in Elizabethan and Stuart England', in Wilfrid Prest (ed.), *The Professions in Early Modern England* (1987), 146.
67. Hill, *Economic Problems of the Church*, 235.
68. J. Evans, 'The Vicar of Godalming and his Parishioners in 1640', *Surrey Archaeological Collections*, 2 (1884), 213.
69. Bodleian Library, MS Carte 103, fo. 60.
70. Hill, *Economic Problems of the Church*, 203–4.
71. Prest (ed.), *Professions in Early Modern England*; Rosemary O'Day, *The Professions in Early Modern England, 1450–1800* (Harlow, 2000).
72. Cressy, 'Drudgery of Schoolmasters', 144–7.
73. TNA, SP 16/89/24.
74. *CSPD 1631–33*, 484.

75. *Earl of Strafforde's Letters*, ii. 148.
76. Bodleian Library, MS Carte 123, fo. 93; *APC 1627 Jan.–Aug.*, 63.
77. Mildred Campbell, *The English Yeoman in the Tudor and Stuart Age* (1967); Wrightson, *Earthly Necessities*, 188.
78. Wrightson, *Earthly Necessities*, 195.
79. Wrightson, *Earthly Necessities*, 194; Wrigley and Schofield, *Population History*, 642.
80. Andy Wood, *The Memory of the People: Custom and Popular Senses of the Past in Early Modern England* (Cambridge, 2013), 41 and *passim*.
81. Violet M. Howse (ed.), *Stanford-in-the-Vale Churchwardens' Accounts 1552–1725* (Faringdon, 1987), 183, 187, 190.
82. Wrightson, *Earthly Necessities*, 195–6.
83. *Calendar of Wynn (of Gwydir) Papers 1515–1690* (Aberystwyth, 1926), 237.
84. Huntington Library, Hastings MS, HA Misc. Box 12 (3), fo. 7v.
85. T. N. Brushfield, 'The Financial Diary of a Citizen of Exeter, 1631–43', *Report and Transactions of the Devonshire Association*, 33 (1901), 251.
86. *CSPD 1635*, 101.
87. TNA, REQ 2/568, unsorted.
88. Henry James Fowle Swayne (ed.), *Churchwardens' Accounts of S. Edmund and S. Thomas, Sarum, 1443–1702* (Salisbury, 1896), 192.
89. Devon Record Office, 1060/PW86.
90. *The Farming and Memorandum Books of Henry Best of Elmswell, 1642*, ed. Donald Woodward (1984), 40, 146.
91. TNA, SP 46/77, fos 37v, 86.
92. BL, Add. MS 28,006, fo. 37.
93. *Barrington Family Letters 1628–1632*, ed. Arthur Searle (Camden Society, 4th ser., 28, 1983), 46.
94. *Farming and Memorandum Books of Henry Best*, 180, 184.
95. BL, Harley MS 454, fos 3, 8v.
96. TNA, SP 46/77.
97. *Calendar of the Correspondence of the Smyth Family*, 78.
98. Cheshire Record Office, QJF/71/1, fo. 27.
99. Cressy, *Literacy and the Social Order*, 177.
100. Romans 13:1.
101. Swan, *Redde Debitum*, 17–19, 32–3.
102. Thomas Foster, *Plouto-Mastix: The Scourge of Covetousnesse; or, An Apologie for the Publike Good, against Privacie* (1631), 15.
103. John Randol, *Noble Blastus: The Honor of a Lord Chamberlaine: and of a Good Bed-Chamber-Man* (1633), 6.
104. John Swan, *Profanomastix. Or, a Brief and Necessarie Direction concerning the respects which we Owe to God, and his House* (1639), 'To the reader', 1.
105. Francis Rogers, *A Sermon Preached on September the 20. 1632* (1633), sigs B2–B4.

106. Thomas Hurste, *The Descent of Authoritie: or, The Magistrates Patent from Heaven* (1637), 1–4.
107. Bob Machin, '"To take theire plases wheare they shall not offend others"—the 1635 Re-Seating of Puddletown Church, Dorset', *Transactions of the Ancient Monuments Society*, 53 (2009), 7–14; Cheshire Record Office, EDC 5/1640/60. For more examples, see Keith Wrightson, '"Sorts of People" in Tudor and Stuart England', in Jonathan Barry and Christopher Brooks (eds), *The Middling Sort of People: Society and Politics in England, 1550–1800* (1994), 30, 228; Amanda Flather, *Gender and Space in Early Modern England* (2007), 144–5.
108. John Ball, *A Short Catechisme: Containing the Principles of Religion*, 18th impression (1637), 34; William Gouge, *A Short Catechisme, wherein are briefly handled the fundamentall principles of Christian Religion*, 7th edn (1635); John Dod, *A Plaine and Familiar Exposition of the Ten Commandments*, 18th edn (1632), 171, 216.
109. Keith Wrightson, 'Mutualities and Obligations: Changing Relationships in Early Modern England', *Proceedings of the British Academy*, 139 (2006), 157–94.
110. *APC 1627 Jan.–Aug.*, 283, 326, 390; *APC 1629 May–1630 May*, 24, 25; Bodleian Library, MS Firth *c.* 4, fo. 502. On economic worth, see Shepard and Spicksley, 'Worth, Age, and Social Status', 493–530.
111. Wrightson, '"Sorts of People"', 28–51.
112. Huntington Library, Stowe–Temple Correspondence, Box 8, STT 1633, STT 2284.
113. Cambridge University Library, Ely Diocesan Records, D/2/51, fo. 43.
114. *Ovatio Carolina: The Triumph of King Charles* (1641), 26, 11.
115. *APC 1630 June–1631 June*, 227; Charles I, *By the King. A Proclamation for the establishing of the Peace and Quiet of the Church of England* (14 June 1626); Charles I, *By the King. A Declaration of His Maiesties cleare intention, in requiring the Ayde of His loving Subiects, in that way of Loane which is now intended by His Highnesse* (7 October 1626); Bodleian Library, MS Rawlinson C. 197, fo. 12[v]; Bodleian Library, MS Bankes 65/28c, fo. 59.
116. TNA, SP 16/363/42; Wrightson, '"Sorts of People"', 34, 38, 228.
117. Huntington Library, Stowe–Temple Correspondence, Box 11, STT 1880, 1889.
118. William Sclater, *The Right Character of a True Subject* (1642), sig. A[v].
119. Gouge, *Dignity of Chivalrie*, 4, 5, 14, 24.
120. Bodleian Library, MS Rawlinson B. 431.
121. Marchamont Nedham, *Certain Considerations Tendered in all Humility* (1649), 2.
122. *APC 1630 June–1631 June*, 227.
123. Symon Gunton, *The History of the Church of Peterburgh* (1686), 106, recalling events of 1641.
124. Thomas Birch (ed.), *The Court and Times of Charles the First*, 2 vols (1848), i. 226.
125. Robert Dallington, *Aphorisms Civill and Militarie* (1613), 107, 211. Dallington (1561–1638), tutor to Prince Henry and Prince Charles, was rewarded with a knighthood in 1624.

126. Sir Henry Wotton, *Reliquiae Wottonianae*, 4th edn (1685), 326.
127. 'Avaunt you giddie-headed Multitude', in *Early Stuart Libels: An Edition of Poetry from Manuscript Sources*, ed. Alastair Bellany and Andrew McRae, Early Modern Literary Studies Text Series I (2005) <http://www.earlystuartlibels.net/htdocs/index.html> (accessed 2 June 2014).
128. TNA, SP 16/36/49, Captain Marmaduke Nielson to Secretary Nicholas, 24 September 1626.
129. Hurste, *Descent of Authoritie*, 15, 16.
130. Henry King, *A Sermon Preached at St Pauls March 27. 1640*, in *The Sermons of Henry King (1592–1669)*, ed. Mary Hobbs (Cranbury, NJ, and Aldershot, 1992), 222–3, 228. These were deeply conservative views of long ancestry. Writing in 1536, for example, Thomas Starkey declared that 'the people in every common weal be rude and ignorant, having of themselves small light of judgement, but ever in simplicity, as sheep follow the herd'. Being of 'weak and vulgar minds' and given to 'foolish and corrupt judgement', the people needed the firm direction of a king (Thomas Starkey, *Exhortation to the People, Instructyng theym to Unitie and Obedience* (1536), fos 28, 34).
131. John Featley, *Obedience and Submission: A Sermon* (1636), 19.
132. Thomas Lawrence, *Two Sermons. The First Preached at St Maries in Oxford* (Oxford, 1635), 18.
133. John Yates, *A Treatise of the Honor of Gods House* (1637), sig. $*^{\mathrm{v}}$.
134. Swan, *Profanomastix*, epistle dedicatory, epistle to the reader, 1; Swan, *Redde Debitum*, sig. A2^{v}.
135. Thomas Trescot, *The Zealous Magistrate* (1642), 5, 6.
136. Thomas Morton, *A Sermon Preached Before the Kings most Excellent Majestie, in the Cathedrall Church of Durham* (1639), 13.
137. *Constitutions and Canons Ecclesiasticall; Treated upon by the Archbishops of Canterbury and York* (1640), 4.
138. *CSPD 1640*, 190.
139. *A Discourse discovering some mysteries of our new state . . . shewing the rise and progresse of Englands unhappiness, ab anno illo infortunato, 1641* (Oxford, 1645), 24–5.
140. Thomas Rotherham, *A Den of Theeves Discovered. Or, Certain Errours and False Doctrines . . . Confuted* (1643), 15.
141. *Mercurius Pragmaticus*, 36 (5–12 December 1648). Cf. the view of Thomas Hobbes, that 'the people in general were so ignorant of their duty, as that not one perhaps of ten thousand knew what right any man had to command him, or what necessity there was of a king or commonwealth' (Thomas Hobbes, *Behemoth* (1682), ed. William Molesworth (New York, 1963), 3, 6).
142. 'How is it possible to believe, that the best of princes should meet with the worst of subjects?' asked the Restoration writer Sir Roger Manley, *The History of the Rebellions in England, Scotland, and Ireland* (1691), 2.
143. Patricia Crawford, *Women and Religion in England 1500–1720* (1993); Sara Mendleson and Patricia Crawford, *Women in Early Modern England 1500–1720*

(Oxford, 1998); Bernard Capp, *When Gossips Meet: Women, the Family and Neighbourhood in Early Modern England* (Oxford, 2003); Eleanor Hubbard, *City Women: Money, Sex, and the Social Order in Early Modern London* (Oxford, 2012); Ann Hughes, *Gender and the English Revolution* (2012).

144. John Elborow, *Euodias and Syntyche: or, The Female Zelots of the Church of Philippi* (1637), 4, 6, 7.
145. Norfolk Record Office, DN/VIS 5/3/1.
146. Henry Paynter, *Saint Pauls Rule for Religious Performances* (1632), 6–8. The touchstone texts are 1 Corinthians 14:34–5 and 1 Timothy 2:9–15.
147. Cheshire Record Office, EDC 5/1628/1. For more examples, see Laura Gowing, *Domestic Dangers: Women, Words, and Sex in Early Modern London* (Oxford, 1996); Capp, *When Gossips Meet*.
148. Oxford University Archives, Chancellor's Court Papers, 1626/117.
149. Richard Zouch, *The Sophister* (1639), Act 1, Scene 2.
150. TNA, SP 16/174/17.
151. Bodleian Library, MS Rawlinson A. 128, fo. 27.
152. Randol, *Noble Blastus*, 32–3.
153. Richard Younge, *The Poores Advocate* (1654), 9.
154. Bodleian Library, MS Firth c. 4, fo. 498; *APC 1629 May–1630 May*, 23.
155. Thomas Barnes, *Vox Belli, or, An Alarum to Warre* (1626), 1; *The Two Books of Homilies Appointed to be Read in Churches* (Oxford, 1859), 516–24.
156. *Statutes of the Realm*, 39 Eliz. 1. *c.* 3 (1598); 43 Eliz. 1. *c.* 2 (1601). For the operation of the poor law, see A. L. Beier, *Masterless Men: The Vagrancy Problem in England 1560–1640* (1985); Steve Hindle, *On the Parish? The Micro-Politics of Poor Relief in Rural England, c.1550–1750* (Oxford, 2004).
157. TNA, SP 16/139/1. See SP 16/167/43 for Shropshire returns, May 1630.
158. J. Charles Cox (ed.), *Three Centuries of Derbyshire Annals: As Illustrated by the Records of the Quarter Sessions*, 2 vols (1890), 152–3.
159. TNA, SP 16/174/17.
160. Paul Griffiths, *Lost Londons: Change, Crime and Control in the Capital City, 1550–1660* (Cambridge, 2008).
161. TNA, National Register of Archives, Bound Vol. 20594, 565, Dorchester to the Earl of Cork, 21 April 1631.
162. TNA, SP 16/139/1.
163. TNA, SP 16/181/123.
164. Gráinne Henry, 'Ulster Exiles in Europe, 1605–1641', in Brian MacCuarta (ed.), *Ulster 1641: Aspects of the Rising* (Belfast, 1993), 39–40; TNA, SP 16/141/75, SP 16/234/57; Charles I, *Stuart Royal Proclamations: Volume II: Royal Proclamations of King Charles I 1625–1646*, ed. James F. Larkin (Oxford, 1983), 233–5, 412–14.
165. TNA, SP 16/194/32.
166. TNA, SP 16/238/32. See also *William Whiteway of Dorchester His Diary 1618 to 1635* (Dorset Record Society, Dorchester, vol. 12, 1991), 111, for 'puppet

players' at Dorchester in 1630; HMC, *Gawdy* (1885), 157, for travelling players at Norwich; and Norfolk Record Office, NCR/16a/20, fo. 327, for 'pupping plays' in Norfolk in 1641.

167. TNA, SP 16/240/25. The anti-theatrical tradition culminates in William Prynne, *Histrio-Mastix: The Players Scovrge, or Actors Tragædie* (1633). See Jonas Barish, *The Antitheatrical Prejudice* (Berkeley and Los Angeles, 1981); Jean E. Howard, *The Stage and Social Struggle in Early Modern England* (1994).
168. Cust and Hopper (eds), *Cases in the High Court of Chivalry*, 9, 30, 135, 155; John Walter, 'Gesturing at Authority: Deciphering the Gestural Code of Early Modern England', in Michael J. Braddick (ed.), *The Politics of Gesture* (Oxford: Past & Present Supplement, 4, 2009), 96–127.
169. Reynolds, *Shieldes of the Earth*, 8, 11.
170. Gauden, *Three Sermons*, 68.
171. Michael Wigmore, *The Meteors: A Sermon* (1633), sig. C3.
172. Rogers, *Visitation Sermon*, sig. C4.
173. Bodleian Library, MS Rawlinson C. 421, fo. 27.
174. Elborow, *Euodias and Syntyche*, 12.
175. Thomas Warmstry, *Pax Vobis or A Charme for Tumultuous Spirits* (1641), title page, 10–11, 17, 30; Ephraim Udall, *The Good of Peace and Ill of Warre* (1642), 28, 29.
176. Anthony Cade, *A Sermon Necessarie for these Times* (Cambridge, 1639), 42–3.
177. Somerset Archives, DD/PH/227/16, fo. 1. For the authorship, see Thomas Cogswell, *The Blessed Revolution: English Politics and the Coming of War, 1621–1624* (Cambridge, 1989), 157–8.
178. John Taylor, *Wit and Mirth* (1626), title page; Bernard Capp, *The World of John Taylor, the Water-Poet, 1578–1653* (Oxford, 1994).
179. BL, Egerton MS 2715, fo. 327.
180. David Cressy, *Dangerous Talk: Scandalous, Seditious and Treasonable Speech in Pre-Modern England* (Oxford, 2010), 132 and *passim*.
181. Fuller, *Sermon Intended for Paul's Crosse*, 21.
182. Cheshire Record Office, QJF 70/2, fo. 47, Ralph Massey, husbandman, defaming Philip Pritchard, gentleman.
183. London Metropolitan Archives, MJ/SR 895, fo. 172.
184. TNA, SP 16/118/84.
185. TNA, DL 4/79/51.
186. BL, Hargrave MS 489, 14^{v}.
187. BL, Hargrave MS 489, fo. 11^{v}. Laud was giving judgment in a suit in Star Chamber involving *scandalum magnatum*, the disgracing of peers.
188. National Library of Wales, Great Sessions, Flintshire Gaol Files, 983/2/5.
189. East Sussex Record Office, QR/E/55/82.
190. Staffordshire Record Office, Q/SR/250, fo. 33.
191. Cambridge University Library, University Archives, Comm. Ct. III/16, no. 39.

192. TNA, SP 16/251/31. The innkeeper Richard Butler also declared that Magna Carta limited the king's prerogative, so that he 'ought not to fetch up any man by a messenger'.
193. TNA, SP 16/75/31.
194. TNA, SP 16/71/3, SP 16/83/65, PC 2/36, fo. 145.
195. Cambridge University Library, Ely Diocesan Records, LA/5a, fo. 33.
196. Maurice Ashley, *Life in Stuart England* (1964), 21, 22.
197. J. C. Atkinson (ed.), *North Riding of the County of York. Quarter Sessions Records. Vol. III* (1885), 270, 275.
198. John Lister (ed.), *West Riding Sessions Records. Vol. II. Orders, 1611–1642. Indictments, 1637–1642* (Yorkshire Archaeological Society, vol. 53, 1915), 60, 160.
199. Oxford University Archives, Chancellor's Court Papers, 1630/75.
200. Oxford University Archives, Chancellor's Court Papers, 1626/136.
201. Oxford University Archives, Chancellor's Court Papers, 1634/110.
202. Cheshire Record Office, EDC 5/1638/55.
203. Shropshire Record Office, Ludlow Borough Quarter Sessions, LB 11/4/68/3.
204. R. C. Anderson (ed.), *The Book of Examinations and Depositions 1622–1644* (Southampton Record Society, 1936), 18.
205. Staffordshire Record Office, Q/SR/244/30.
206. Cust and Hopper (eds), *Cases in the High Court of Chivalry*, 85.
207. Cust and Hopper (eds), *Cases in the High Court of Chivalry*, 135.
208. Cust and Hopper (eds), *Cases in the High Court of Chivalry*, 269.
209. 'The wisest King did wonder when hee spy'd', in *Early Stuart Libels*, ed. Bellany and McRae, Oiii2.
210. Robert Mossom. *The King on his Throne: Or, A Discourse maintaining the Dignity of a King, the Duty of a Subject, and the unlawfulnesse of Rebellion* (York, 1642), 13.
211. Kent History and Library Centre, Sandwich Borough Muniments, Mayor's Letter Book 1639–44, Sa/C1, fos 38–8^{v}, 52^{v}. The winners had 179 and 100 voices, Lord Grandison only 87.
212. BL, Add. MS 26,785, fo. 11.
213. HMC, *Seventh Report*, appendix, 549; William Hunt, *The Puritan Moment: The Coming of Revolution in an English County* (Cambridge, MA, 1983), 281–2.
214. TNA, SP 16/78/53.
215. TNA, SP 16/79/38.
216. TNA, PC 2/36, fos 207–207^{v}. For more on John Kettle, see John T. Evans, *Seventeenth-Century Norwich* (Oxford, 1979), 73–5; Andy Wood, *The 1549 Rebellion and the Making of Early Modern England* (Cambridge, 2007), 247–8.
217. TNA, SP 16/188/20, SP 16/195/5.
218. TNA, SP 16/190/45. For more on the Forest of Dean riots, see SP 16/188/20, SP 16/195/5, SP 16/215/5; Buchanan Sharp, *In Contempt of All Authority: Rural Artisans and Riot in the West of England, 1586–1660* (Berkeley and Los Angeles, 1980).

219. TNA, SP 16/193/11 and 66, SP 16/195/5, SP 16/195/56, SP 16/203/7.
220. TNA, SP 16/194/60. Buchanan Sharp, 'Rural Discontent and the English Revolution', in R. C. Richardson (ed.), *Town and Countryside in the English Revolution* (Manchester, 1992), 259–61.
221. TNA, SP 16/203/36; Sharp, *In Contempt of All Authority*, 97–106. See also SP 16/243/25 for more night-time riots by 'loose and disorderly persons' in the Forest of Dean in July 1633, with 'private encouragement from some gentlemen of quality in those parts'.
222. John Walter, 'Grain Riots and Popular Attitudes to the Law: Maldon and the Crisis of 1629', in John Brewer and John Styles (eds), *An Ungovernable People: The English and their Law in the Seventeenth and Eighteenth Centuries* (New Brunswick, NJ, 1980), 47–84.
223. *William Whiteway of Dorchester His Diary*, 115.
224. TNA, SP 16/133/19.
225. TNA, National Register of Archives, Bound Vol. 20594, 551, William Lake to the Earl of Cork, 31 March 1630.
226. TNA, PC 2/40, 536.
227. *CSPD 1639*, 232; Charles to the Commissioners of Sewers, 1629, quoted in Mark E. Kennedy, 'Charles I and Local Government: The Draining of the East and West Fens', *Albion*, 15 (1983), 24. See also William Dugdale, *The History of Imbanking and Drayning of divers Fenns and Marshes* (1662); H. C. Darby, *The Draining of the Fens*, 2nd edn (Cambridge, 1956); Keith Lindley, *Fenland Riots and the English Revolution* (1982); Clive Holmes, 'Drainers and Fenmen: The Problem of Popular Political Consciousness in the Seventeenth Century', in Anthony Fletcher and John Stevenson (eds), *Order and Disorder in Early Modern England* (Cambridge, 1985), 166–95; Clive Holmes, *Seventeenth-Century Lincolnshire* (Lincoln, 1980), 121–30.
228. Samuel Rawson Gardiner (ed.), *Reports of Cases in the Courts of Star Chamber and High Commission* (Camden Society, NS, vol. 39, 1886), 59–65. Cf. similar incidents in Yorkshire, TNA, SP 16/113/38.
229. TNA, SP 16/392/45; *CSPD 1638–39*, 301–2.
230. TNA, SP 16/392/45; *CSPD 1638–39*, 301–2.
231. TNA, SP 16/402/18.
232. Birch (ed.), *Court and Times*, i. 6, Mead to Stuteville 9 April 1625; HMC, *Cowper*, i. 398.
233. TNA, SP 16/1/37 and 95, SP 39/29/88.
234. TNA, SP 16/14/33; *CSPD 1635–36*, 446; David Cressy, 'Early Modern Space Travel and the English Man in the Moon', *American Historical Review*, 111 (2006), 961–82.
235. TNA, SP 16/4/156.
236. *CSPD 1625–26*, 240; TNA, SP 16/24/20, SP 16/54/18.
237. TNA, SP 16/44/33, SP 16/58/56, SP 16/59/29.
238. TNA, SP 16/126/53.

239. TNA, SP 16/14/75.
240. Birch (ed.), *Court and Times*, i. 11; *Earl of Strafforde's Letters*, ii. 129.
241. Henry Lord, *A Display of Two Forraigne Sects in the East Indies* (1630), sig. A2; George Sandys, *A Relation of Journey Begin An. Dom. 1610* (1615), with editions in 1621, 1627, 1632, and 1637; Henry Timberlake, *A Relation of the Travels of two English Pilgrimes* (1603), with editions in 1608, 1609, 1611, 1612, 1616, 1620, and 1631.
242. Bodleian Library, MS Carte 77, fos 394–8; TNA, C115/109, no. 8853; *Earl of Strafforde's Letters*, i. 360.
243. *Earl of Strafforde's Letters*, i. 225.
244. HMC, *Fourth Report*, 291.
245. TNA, SP 16/43/46.
246. BL, Add. MS 72,419, fos 17–21; Dorset History Centre, Weymouth Borough Records, WM. AD 1/2, 292–3.
247. TNA, SP 16/306/85.
248. Dorset History Centre, D/BOC/Box 22, 48.
249. HMC, *Egmont*, i. 90.
250. Claire S. Schen, 'Breaching "Community" in Britain: Captives, Renegades, and the Redeemed', in Michael J. Halvorson and Karen E. Spierling (eds), *Defining Community in Early Modern Europe* (Burlington, VT, 2008), 229–46.
251. David Cressy, *Coming Over: Migration and Communication between England and New England in the Seventeenth Century* (Cambridge, 1987), 68–71; Carla Gardina Pestana, *The English Atlantic in an Age of Revolution, 1640–1661* (Cambridge, MA, 2004), 229–34.
252. Alison Games, *Migration and the Origins of the English Atlantic World* (Cambridge, MA, 1999), 13–25; Alison Games, *The Web of Empire: English Cosmopolitans in an Age of Expansion 1560–1660* (Oxford, 2008).
253. HMC, *Twelfth Report*, 38–9.
254. Bodleian Library, MS Additional C 259, fo. 49; TNA, C115/107, no. 8491.
255. Huntington Library, Hastings MS, HA Misc. Box 12/2.
256. Charles Edward Banks, *Topographical Dictionary of 2885 English Emigrants to New England 1620–1650* (Baltimore, 1969), 90–2.
257. BL, Harley MS 454, fos 6, 9^{v}, 25^{v}.
258. Bodleian Library, MS Ashmole 423.
259. Brian Fagan, *The Little Ice Age: How Climate Made History 1300–1850* (New York, 2000). See also J. N. L. Baker, 'The Climate of England in the Seventeenth Century', *Quarterly Journal of the Royal Meteorological Society*, 58 (1932), 421–38; Vladimir Janković, *Reading the Skies: A Cultural History of English Weather, 1650–1820* (Chicago and London, 2000); Bruce M. S. Campbell, 'Nature as Historical Protagonist: Environment and Society in Pre-industrial England', *Economic History Review*, 63 (2010), 281–314.
260. Baker, 'Climate of England in the Seventeenth Century', 431, quoting a later Stuart observer.

261. Geoffrey Parker, *Global Crisis: War, Climate Change and Catastrophe in the Seventeenth Century* (London and New Haven, 2013), esp. 3–25, 355.
262. Bodleian Library, MS Rawlinson B. 243, fo. 20.
263. 'The Letany', *The Booke of Common Prayer* (1633), sig. A5.
264. *The Letters of John Chamberlain*, ed. Norman Egbert McClure (American Philosophical Society Memoirs, vol. 12, Philadelphia, 1939), 609.
265. Huntington Library, Hastings Correspondence, Box 11, HA 4834.
266. Huntington Library, Hastings Correspondence, Box 11, HA 5501.
267. Bodleian Library, MS Jones 39, fo. 85; Laud, *Works*, iii. 100.
268. HMC, *Eleventh Report*, appendix, part I, 26.
269. *CSPD 1625–26*, 62.
270. Bodleian Library, MS Ashmole 423, fo. 22; HMC, *Cowper*, i. 197, 203.
271. *Calendar of Wynn (of Gwydir) Papers*, 219.
272. HMC, *Cowper*, i. 221.
273. Bodleian Library, MS Ashmole 423, fo. 22.
274. HMC, *Cowper*, i. 230.
275. HMC, *Buccleuch*, i. 261–2.
276. HMC, *Various*, i. 95.
277. *Letters of John Holles 1587–1637*, ed. P. R. Seddon, 3 vols (Thoroton Society Record Series, 1983–6), iii. 312.
278. HMC, *Montagu*, 110.
279. HMC, *Rutland*, 477, Henry Wicliffe to George Falcon, 15 June 1626; HMC, *Fourth Report*, 289; Birch (ed.), *Court and Times*, i. 113–14; anonymous diary of public events, in William B. Bidwell and Maija Jansson (eds), *Proceedings in Parliament 1626*, 4 vols (New Haven, 1991–6), 34; John Rushworth, *Historical Collections: The Second Part* (1680), 391.
280. TNA, C115/107, nos 8500, 8501.
281. Bidwell and Jansson (eds), *Proceedings in Parliament 1626*, iv. 345.
282. *The Diary of Thomas Crosfield*, ed. Frederick S. Boas (Oxford, 1935), 13.
283. Queen's College Oxford, MS 390, fo. 25.
284. *A Royalist Notebook: The Commonplace Book of Sir John Oglander*, ed. Francis Bamford (1936), 27.
285. *William Whiteway of Dorchester His Diary*, 88, 93.
286. TNA, SP 16/85/62 and 64.
287. *Diary of John Rous, Incumbent of Santon Downham, Suffolk, from 1625 to 1642*, ed. Margaret Anne Everett Green (Camden Society, OS, vol. 66, 1856), 14, 24.
288. HMC, *Cowper*, i. 362.
289. BL, MS Harley 7000, fo. 215.
290. Huntington Library, Stowe–Temple Correspondence, Box 7, STT 1746.
291. Bodleian Library, MS Ashmole 423, fo. 23^{v}.
292. Bodleian Library, MS Top. Oxon. C. 378 (diary of Thomas Wyatt), fo. 253.
293. *Diary of John Rous*, 44–5.
294. *Barrington Family Letters*, 90.

295. Bodleian Library, MS Ashmole 423, fo. 23.
296. *Royalist Notebook*, ed. Bamford, 54.
297. *Barrington Family Letters*, 91.
298. HMC, *Buccleuch*, i. 269, Manchester to Mountague, 4 January 1630.
299. Laud, *Works*, iii. 212.
300. TNA, C115/105, no. 8142.
301. *Barrington Family Letters*, 145–6.
302. *Barrington Family Letters*, 149.
303. *William Whiteway of Dorchester His Diary*, 110.
304. *William Whiteway of Dorchester His Diary*, 113.
305. *CSPD 1629–31*, 389.
306. *William Whiteway of Dorchester His Diary*, 112, 113.
307. John Walter, *Crowds and Popular Politics in Early Modern England* (Manchester, 2006), 70.
308. Bodleian Library, MS Top. Oxon. C. 378, fo. 255.
309. Randol, *Noble Blastus*, 32.
310. TNA, C115/105, no. 8130.
311. Laud, *Works*, iii. 215.
312. Bodleian Library, MS Top. Oxon. C. 378, fo. 257.
313. *Diary of Thomas Crosfield*, 58.
314. *William Whiteway of Dorchester His Diary*, 121.
315. Laud, *Works*, iii. 215, 216.
316. *Royalist Notebook*, ed. Bamford, 77.
317. Bodleian Library, MS Top. Oxon. C. 378, fo. 260.
318. HMC, *Cowper*, i. 479.
319. Somerset Archives, DD/PH/219, no. 42.
320. Bodleian Library, MS Top. Oxon. C. 378, fo. 263.
321. *The Knyvett Letters (1620–1644)*, ed. Bertram Schofield (Norfolk Record Society, vol. 20, 1949), 81.
322. Laud, *Works*, iii. 217; *Winthrop Papers*, iii. *1631–1637* (Massachusetts Historical Society, Boston, 1943), 127–8.
323. BL, Harley MS 454, fo. 3ᵛ.
324. Laud, *Works*, iii. 219.
325. BL, Harley MS 454, fo. 3ᵛ.
326. Bodleian Library, MS Top. Oxon. C. 378, fo. 267.
327. Bodleian Library, MS Top. Oxon. C. 378, fo. 269; *Knyvett Letters*, 87; *CSPD 1634–35*, 488, 490.
328. *Earl of Strafforde's Letters*, i. 177.
329. BL, Harley MS 454, fo. 5ᵛ.
330. HMC, *Salisbury*, xxii. 277–8.
331. BL, Harley MS 454, fo. 6.
332. *Letters of John Holles*, iii. 459.
333. BL, Harley MS 454, fos 8, 8ᵛ.

334. Laud, *Works*, iii. 222.
335. BL, Harley MS 454, fos 9, 9^v.
336. *William Whiteway of Dorchester His Diary*, 156–7.
337. Laud, *Works*, iii. 223.
338. *CSPD 1634–35*, 490.
339. *CSPD 1634–35*, 488.
340. Henry Burton, *A Divine Tragedie Lately Acted* (1641), 15.
341. Burton, *Divine Tragedie* (1641), 5. Burton writes not to commemorate the frost but to mark the providential drowning of errant Sabbath breakers.
342. TNA, REQ 2/800/8.
343. TNA, C115/106, no. 8451; Bodleian Library, MS Carte 77, fo. 402^v.
344. HMC, *Rutland*, 496.
345. BL, Harley MS 454, fo. 9^v.
346. TNA, SP 16/283/71.
347. Huntington Library, Hastings Correspondence, Box 15, HA 5540.
348. *Earl of Strafforde's Letters*, i. 372, 374.
349. BL, Harley MS 454, fo. 10.
350. *Records of the Borough of Nottingham, vol. v . . . 1625–1702* (1900), 172.
351. BL, Egerton MS 2716, fo. 197, Edward Moundesford to Framlingham Gawdy, 8 May 1635.
352. Bodleian Library, MS Carte 77, fo. 402^v.
353. Laud, *Works*, iii. 224, 225.
354. Laud, *Works*, iii. 225.
355. R. H. Silcock, 'Crime, Criminals and Catchers: Worcestershire Assizes Cases in the 1630s and the 1650s', *Parergon*, NS 6 (1988), 185.
356. Laud, *Works*, iii. 226; Baker, 'Climate of England in the Seventeenth Century', 423.
357. *CSP Venice, 1636–9*, 61.
358. *Diary of John Rous*, 81.
359. *CSPD 1637*, 259; TNA, SP 16/362/101.
360. BL, Harley MS 454, fo. 12.
361. Laud, *Works*, iii. 227.
362. *The Correspondence (c.1626–1659) of Dorothy Percy Sidney, Countess of Leicester*, ed. Michael G. Brennan, Noel J. Kinnaman, and Margaret P. Hanney (Farnham and Burlington, VT, 2010), 73.
363. TNA, SP 16/337/15.
364. Bodleian Library, MS Top. Oxon. C. 378, fo. 292.
365. BL, Harley MS 454, fos 15^v, 16^v, 17.
366. *The Diary and Correspondence of Dr John Worthington*, ed. James Crossley (Chetham Society Remains, vol. 13, 1847), 4.
367. BL, Harley MS 454, fo. 14.
368. *Diary of Thomas Crosfield*, 94.
369. BL, Harley MS 454, fo. 14.

370. *Earl of Strafforde's Letters*, ii. 75, 87.
371. *The Diary of Robert Woodford, 1637–1641*, ed. John Fielding (Camden Society, 5th ser., vol. 42, 2012), 98.
372. TNA, SP 16/365/87.
373. Laud, *Works*, iii. 229, 230.
374. *Diary of Robert Woodford*, 153, 154.
375. *Earl of Strafforde's Letters*, ii. 148.
376. *Letters of the Lady Brilliana Harley*, ed. Thomas Taylor Lewis (Camden Society, os, vol. 58, 1854), 23.
377. BL, Harley MS 454, fo. 20.
378. TNA, SP 16/540, Morton letters no. 31.
379. Laud, *Works*, iii. 231; *CSPD 1637–38*, 599.
380. Laud, *Works*, iii. 231.
381. *Diary of Robert Woodford*, 249, 250.
382. *A True Relation of Those Sad and Lamentable Accidents, which happened in and about the Parish Church of Withycome in the Dartmoores, in Devonshire, on Sunday the 21 of October last, 1638* (1638), title page, 1–5.
383. *The Diary of Sir Henry Slingsby*, ed. Daniel Parsons (1836), 1–2, 28.
384. Laud, *Works*, iii. 231.
385. *Diary of Robert Woodford*, 276.
386. TNA, National Register of Archives, Bound Vol. 20594, 775.
387. *CSPD 1638–39*, 361.
388. TNA, SP 16/420/157.
389. HMC, *Third Report*, 77.
390. HMC, *Rutland*, 516.
391. BL, Harley MS 454, fos 25, 25^{v}.
392. BL, Harley MS 454, fo. 28.
393. Laud, *Works*, iii. 233–4.
394. David Cressy, *England on Edge: Crisis and Revolution 1640–1642* (Oxford, 2006), 30, 74, 122; Parker, *Global Crisis*, 355, 374.
395. Alexandra Walsham, *Providence in Early Modern England* (Oxford, 1999), 121–4.

CHAPTER 2

1. David Cressy, *Bonfires and Bells: National Memory and the Protestant Calendar in Elizabethan and Stuart England* (1989), 5, 36, 39. Late in 1625 the Tuscan agent at court reported the queen and her ladies were 'preparing a ball to be given in London on Candlemas day', an entertainment that had to be set aside (HMC, *Eleventh Report*, appendix, part I, 41). John Cosin's ostentatious display of Candlemas candles at Durham cathedral in 1628 provoked opposition from Peter Smart, *The Vanitie & Downe-fall of Superstitious Popish Ceremonies* (Edinburgh, 1628). On the weather, *The Works of the Most Reverend Father in God,*

William Laud, D.D., ed. William Scott and James Bliss, 9 vols (Oxford, 1847–60), iii. 181: 'It was a very bright sunshining day.'

2. David Cressy, *Dangerous Talk: Scandalous, Seditious and Treasonable Speech in Pre-Modern England* (Oxford, 2010), 91, 93.
3. Percy Ernst Schramm, *A History of the English Coronation* (Oxford, 1937), 141–78; David Martin Jones, *Conscience and Allegiance in Seventeenth Century England: The Political Significance of Oaths and Engagements* (Rochester, NY, 1999), 18; Conal Condren, *Argument and Authority in Early Modern England: The Presupposition of Oaths and Offices* (Cambridge, 2006), 52.
4. *CSP Venice, 1625–1626*, 51.
5. *The Autobiography and Correspondence of Sir Simonds D'Ewes*, ed. James Orchard Halliwell, 2 vols (1845), i. 271–8; *Lachrymae Londoniensis. Or, Londons Teares and Lamentations for Gods Heavie Visitation of the Plague of Pestilence* (1626).
6. Huntington Library, Hastings MS, HA 1930.
7. *Calendar of Wynn (of Gwydir) Papers 1515–1690* (Aberystwyth, 1926), 216.
8. Henry Petow, *Englands Caesar: His Maiesties most Royall Coronation* (1603); sigs C, Ciii; John Nichols, *The Progresses... of King James the First*, 4 vols (1828), i. 202, 227–8.
9. TNA, SP 16/11/70, SP 16/12/39; John Rushworth, *Historical Collections... ending the Fifth Year of King Charles, Anno 1629* (1659), 203; Roger Finlay, *Population and Metropolis: The Demography of London 1580–1650* (Cambridge, 1981), 156.
10. Charles I, *By the King. A Proclamation to declare His Maiesties pleasure, touching His Royall Coronation, and the Solemnitie thereof* (17 January 1626); Charles I, *Stuart Royal Proclamations: Volume II: Royal Proclamations of King Charles I 1625–1646*, ed. James F. Larkin (Oxford, 1983), 84.
11. William B. Bidwell and Maija Jansson (eds), *Proceedings in Parliament 1626*, 4 vols (New Haven, 1991–6), iv. 260, Joseph Mead to Sir Martin Stuteville, 13 January 1626; Thomas Fuller, *The Church History of Britain: From the Birth of Jesus Christ, until the Year MDCXLVII* (1656), book XI, 124; HMC, *Eleventh Report*, appendix, part I, 12, 15, 44; W. H. Overall and H. C. Overall (eds), *Analytical Index to the Series of Records Known as the Remembrancia... 1579–1664* (1887), 116, 417.
12. *The Correspondence of Nathan Walworth and Peter Seddon of Outwood*, ed. John Samuel Fletcher (Chetham Society, vol. 109, 1880), 9.
13. Laud, *Works*, iii. 181–2.
14. Christopher Wordsworth (ed.), *The Coronation of King Charles I* (Henry Bradshaw Society, vol. 2, 1892), 86; William Sanderson, *A Compleat History of the Life and Raigne of King Charles* (1658), 25; Samuel Rawson Gardiner, *A History of England under the Duke of Buckingham and Charles I: 1624–1628*, 2 vols (1875), i. 356; Peter Heylyn, *Cyprianus Anglicus: or, the History of the Life and Death of the most Reverend and Renowned Prelate William* (1671), 148; Sir Thomas Herbert, *Memoirs of the Last Two Years of the Reign of King Charles I* (1813), 184.

15. Bidwell and Jansson (eds), *Proceedings in Parliament 1626*, i. 21.
16. Cf. Henry Petow, *Englands Caesar: His Maiesties most Royall Coronation* (1603); H. A. Grueber (ed.), *Medallic Illustrations of the History of Great Britain and Ireland*, 2 vols (1904–11; repr. Lawrence, MA, 1979), plate XX, 1–2.
17. HMC, *Eleventh Report*, appendix, part I, 44, Amerigo Salvetti to Grand Duke of Tuscany, 3/13 February 1626; Bidwell and Jansson (eds), *Proceedings in Parliament 1626*, iv. 260, Mead to Stuteville, 13 January 1626; Thomas Birch (ed.), *The Court and Times of Charles I*, 2 vols (1848), i. 77–9, Mead to Stuteville, 4 February 1626; Rushworth, *Historical Collections... ending the Fifth Year of King Charles*, 203.
18. Judith Richards, '"His Nowe Majestie" and the English Monarchy: The Kingship of Charles I before 1640', *Past & Present*, 113 (1986), 70–96, esp. 82 on 'surprise, disappointment, and even, perhaps, disapproval at the king's decision to have what several referred to as a "private" coronation'.
19. Kevin Sharpe, *The Personal Rule of Charles I* (New Haven and London, 1992), 105; Kevin Sharpe, *Image Wars: Promoting Kings and Commonwealths in England, 1603–1660* (New Haven and London, 2010), 234.
20. Mark Kishlansky, 'Charles I: A Case of Mistaken Identity', *Past & Present*, 189 (2005), 65.
21. D'Ewes, *Autobiography and Correspondence*, i. 291–3; ii. 173–7; Stuart Handley, 'Cotton, Sir Robert Bruce (1571–1631)', *ODNB*.
22. *The Knyvett Letters (1620–1644)*, ed. Bertram Schofield (Norfolk Record Society, vol. 20, 1949), 69; *William Whiteway of Dorchester His Diary 1618 to 1635* (Dorset Record Society, vol. 12, Dorchester, 1991), 79; Bidwell and Jansson (eds), *Proceedings in Parliament 1626*, iv. 306; Birch (ed.), *Court and Times*, i. 78–9; HMC, *Rutland*, 476. See also HMC, *Eleventh Report*, appendix, part I, 44, Salvetti to Tuscany.
23. Gardiner, *History of England*, i. 355.
24. Fuller, *Church History*, book XI, 109; *Cabala, Sive Scrinia Sacra: Mysteries of State* (1691), 285.
25. Laud, *Works*, iii. 177, 182.
26. Thomas N. Corns, 'Duke, Prince and King', in Corns (ed.), *The Royal Image: Representations of Charles I* (Cambridge, 1999), 15.
27. Laud, *Works*, iii. 179–81, iv. 211; Heylyn, *Cyprianus Anglicus*, 148. The inventory of coronation regalia taken in 1606 records 'a cross with crucifix set with stones', which had disappeared by 1649: Leopold G. Wickham Legg (ed.), *English Coronation Records* (Westminster, 1901), 244, 272–5.
28. Rushworth, *Historical Collections... ending the Fifth Year of King Charles*, 203–4. Rushworth, following Prynne, refers to Cosin as 'master of the ecclesiastical ceremonies', though this inflates his role.
29. Wordsworth (ed.), *Coronation of King Charles I*, pp. xlix–liii; *Calendar of the Correspondence of the Smyth Family of Ashton Court 1548–1647*, ed. J. H. Bettey (Bristol Record Society, vol. 35, 1982), 73; HMC, *Rutland*, 476.

30. Huntington Library, Hastings MS, HA 5508. On the earl's chronic shortage of money, see *ODNB*, sub 'Hastings, Henry, fifth Earl of Huntingdon (1586–1643)'.
31. *CSPD 1625–26*, 230.
32. Wordsworth (ed.), *Coronation of King Charles I*, pp. xlix–liii, 86.
33. Gardiner, *History of England*, i. 355; D'Ewes, *Autobiography and Correspondence*, i. 292–3; ii. 174.
34. TNA, SP 16/20/8–19; Wordsworth (ed.), *Coronation of King Charles I*, 14–15; Legg (ed.), *English Coronation Records*, 249–50; D'Ewes, *Autobiography and Correspondence*, ii. 176; Sanderson, *Compleat History*, 25; Fuller, *Church History*, book XI, 122–3.
35. Richard Senhouse, *Foure Sermons Preached at the Court upon several occasions* (1627), 24; D'Ewes, *Autobiography and Correspondence*, i. 293; Heylyn, *Cyprianus Anglicus*, 148. Heylyn also thought it significant that the king was clothed in white, the colour of saints and of virginal innocence, rather than imperial purple.
36. Fuller, *Church History*, book XI, 109.
37. Schramm, *History of the English Coronation*, 179–83; Thea Cervone, *Sworn Bond in Tudor England: Oaths, Vows and Covenants in Civil Life and Literature* (Jefferson, NC, and London, 2011), 19–37.
38. Wordsworth (ed.), *Coronation of King Charles I*, 18–23; Legg (ed.), *English Coronation Records*, 251–2. Another recitation of the oaths appears in BL, Stowe MS 159, fos 121ᵛ–122.
39. Jones, *Conscience and Allegiance*, 26; Condren, *Argument and Authority*, 260; Dudley Digges, *An Answer to a Printed Book, Intituled, Observations upon some of His Majesties Late Answers and Expresses* (Oxford, 1642), 12. Queen Elizabeth II at her coronation in 1953 swore to govern according to the respective laws and customs of her various territories, to cause law and justice to be executed with mercy, and to maintain the doctrine, worship, discipline, and government of the Church of England: *The Form and Order of the Service that is to be Performed and the Ceremonies that are to be Observed in the Coronation of Her Majesty Queen Elizabeth II* (Oxford, 1953), 10–11.
40. There was no contemporary publication of the coronation oath of Charles I or description of the ceremony. The earliest is Sanderson, *Compleat History*, 24–8. Laud later commented that 'no king can swear himself out of his native right' (*The History of the Troubles and Tryal of... William Laud*, comp. Henry Wharton (1695), 322).
41. Bidwell and Jansson (eds), *Proceedings in Parliament 1626*, i. 21–2. Rushworth, *Historical Collections... ending the Fifth Year of King Charles*, 207, refers to 'the sacred rites of that blessed marriage between his people and him'.
42. D'Ewes, *Autobiography and Correspondence*, ii. 176; Richards, '"His nowe maiesty"', 80; R. Malcolm Smuts, 'Public Ceremony and Royal Charisma: The English Royal Entry in London 1485–1642', in A. L. Beier, David Cannadine, and James M. Rosenheim (eds), *The First Modern Society: Essays*

in *English History in Honour of Lawrence Stone* (Cambridge, 1989), 68, 83, 93. For a contrary view, see Sharpe, *Image Wars*, 230–66.

43. 1 Chronicles 16:22; Psalms 105:16; Ronald G. Asch, 'Sacred Kingship in France and England in the Age of the Wars of Religion: From Disenchantment to Re-enchantment?', in Charles W. A. Prior and Glenn Burgess (eds), *England's Wars of Religion Revisited* (Farnham and Burlington, VT, 2011), 42–4.
44. Wordsworth (ed.), *Coronation of King Charles I*, 28; Legg (ed.), *English Coronation Records*, 255.
45. Wordsworth (ed.), *Coronation of King Charles I*, 37, 42; Legg (ed.), *English Coronation Records*, 260, 263.
46. Wordsworth (ed.), *Coronation of King Charles I*, 27, 33; Legg (ed.), *English Coronation Records*, 255, 258.
47. John Milton, 'Eikonoklastes' (1650), in *Complete Prose Works of John Milton*, ed. D. M. Wolfe et al., 8 vols (New Haven, 1953–82), iii. 593; Milton, 'Defence of the People of England', in *Complete Prose Works*, iv. 530.
48. *Records of the Borough of Nottingham vol. v . . . 1625–1702* (1900), 108. For the vocabulary of celebration, see Cressy, *Bonfires and Bells*, 67–92.
49. *The Charge Against the King Discharged* (1649), 9.
50. James I, *The Trew Law of Free Monarchie*, in *King James VI and I: Selected Writings*, ed. Neil Rhodes, Jennifer Richards, and Joseph Marshall (Aldershot, 2003), 262.
51. John Cowell, *The Interpreter* (Cambridge, 1607), sub 'king'.
52. Henry Burton, *For God, and the King: The Summe of Two Sermons Preached on the Fifth of November last in St Matthewes Friday-Streete* (Amsterdam, 1636), 38–9.
53. Lambeth Palace Library, MS 3391, fos 42–42ᵛ.
54. TNA, ASSI 45/1/4, fo. 57.
55. *Charge Against the King Discharged*, 7–8; *A Declaration of the House of Commons . . . And a Copy of the Covenant between the Kings of England and the People, at their Coronation* (1649), 3–5.
56. *A Remonstrance of the Lords and Commons Assembled in Parliament . . . November 2. 1642* (1642), 25, 35–6, 38; *A Remonstrance or the Declaration of the Lords and Commons now Assembled in Parliament . . . As also the Oath of the Kings of England at their Coronation* (1642), 24.
57. *King James His Opinion and Iudgement, concerning a Reall King and a Tyrant* (1646). The book collector George Thomason acquired his copy on 6 January 1647. According to Sir John Fortescue (d. 1476), 'the king of England cannot alter nor change the laws of his realm at his pleasure. For why, he governeth his people by power, not only royal but also politique.' The people of England, Fortescue asserted, were 'ruled by such laws as they themselves desire', and no king could take taxes or change laws 'without the express consent and agreement of his whole realm in his parliament'. Every king of England was obliged to study these legal principles; to transgress them was to yield to 'ambition, riot, and wanton lust'. A product of fifteenth-century constitutional crises, Fortescue's *De Laudibus Legum Angliae* was reprinted in 1567, 1573, 1599, and 1616 as

A Learned Commendation of the Politique Lawes of England. No new edition appeared in the reign of Charles I, but it was reprinted twice under Charles II and several times in the eighteenth century.

58. *History of the Troubles and Tryal of . . . William Laud*, 318–25; *Articles Exhibited in Parliament against William Laud* (1640), 1–2; *CSPD 1641–43*, 522–3; Laud, *Works*, iv. 211–19.
59. Fuller, *Church History*, book XI, 124.
60. *A Remonstrance . . . November 2. 1642*, 25, 26–8, 33, 39; *The Subjects Liberty set forth in the Royall and Politique Power of England* (1643), 20. See also Corine Comstock Weston and Janelle Renfrow Greenberg, *Subjects and Sovereigns: The Grand Controversy over Legal Sovereignty in Stuart England* (Cambridge, 1981), 36, 62–5, 79.
61. A. S. P. Woodhouse (ed.), *Puritanism and Liberty: Being the Army Debates (1647–9)* (1938; repr. 1966), 109; see also 89, 110–12, 119–22, for Henry Ireton on the coronation oath.
62. *The Free-Holders Grand Inquest Touching Our Soveraigne Lord the King and His Parliament* (1648), 45–7.
63. Proverbs 16:10; Charles I, *His Maiesties Royal Protestation To all His loving Subiects* (1642), 6.
64. Henry Parker, *Observations upon some of His Majesties late Answers and Expresses* (1642), 3; Michael Mendle, *Henry Parker and the English Civil War: The Political Thought of the Public's 'Privado'* (Cambridge, 1995).
65. See Chapter 9.
66. John Geree, *A Case of Conscience Resolved. Wherein it is Cleared, that the King may without impeachment to his Oath, touching the Clergy at Coronation, consent to the Abrogation of Episcopacy* (1646), 1, 7, ventriloquizing the views of his opponents.
67. Charles I, *The Kings Cabinet Opened: or, Certain Packets of Secret Letters & Papers, Written with the Kings own Hand* (1645), 26.
68. Geree, *Case of Conscience Resolved*; John Geree, *ΣΙΝΙΟΡΡΑΓΙΑ, or the Sifters Sieve Broken* (1648); Edward Boughen, *Master Geree's Case of Conscience Sifted* (1650).
69. Geree, *Case of Conscience*, 1, 2, 5, and *passim*.
70. Samuel Rawson Gardiner (ed.), *The Constitutional Documents of the Puritan Revolution 1625–1660* (Oxford, 1906), 371–2, 375.
71. Henry Burton, *Lord Bishops, None of the Lords Bishops* (1649), sig. K4.
72. Milton, 'Eikonoklastes' (1650), in *Complete Prose Works*, iii. 593; Milton, 'Defence of the People of England', in *Complete Prose Works*, iv. 530; John Milton, *The Tenure of Kings and Magistrates* (1650), 10, 12, 26.
73. Elias Ashmole, *A Briefe Narrative of the Solemn Rites and Ceremonies performed upon the day of the Coronation of our Sovereign Lord King Charles II* (1661), 176; Legg (ed.), *English Coronation Records*, 287. James II swore a similar oath, but left out 'laws' in the promise 'to hold and keep the [laws and] rightful customs,

which the commonalty of this kingdom have' (Legg (ed.), *English Coronation Records*, 297).

74. *Free-Holders Grand Inquest*, 45–6.

CHAPTER 3

1. Corinne Comstock Weston and Janelle Renfrow Greenberg, *Subjects and Sovereigns: The Grand Controversy over Legal Sovereignty in Stuart England* (Cambridge, 1981); J. P. Sommerville, *Politics and Ideology in England, 1603–1640* (1986); Glenn Burgess, *The Politics of the Ancient Constitution: An Introduction to English Political Thought, 1603–1642* (University Park, PA, 1993).
2. *Sir Matthew Hale's the Prerogatives of the King*, ed. D. E. C. Yale (Selden Society, vol. 92, 1976), 61.
3. Epigrams of John Owen, in R(obert) H(ayman), *Quodlibets, Lately Come Over from New Britaniola* (1628), 31.
4. Downing College, Cambridge, Bowtell MS, 'Liber Rationalis', fos 326^{v}–327.
5. Marjorie Masten (ed.), *Woodstock Chamberlains' Accounts, 1609–50* (Oxfordshire Record Society, vol. 58, 1993), 103.
6. Helen Stocks and W. H. Stevenson (eds), *Records of the Borough of Leicester . . . 1603–1688* (Cambridge 1923), 219, 227.
7. *William Whiteway of Dorchester His Diary 1618 to 1635* (Dorset Record Society, vol. 12, Dorchester, 1991), 70.
8. *Diary of John Rous, Incumbent of Santon Downham, Suffolk, from 1625 to 1642*, ed. Margaret Anne Everett Green (Camden Society, OS, vol. 66, 1856), 1.
9. Sir John Beaumont, *Bosworth-field: With a Taste of the Variety of Other Poems* (1629), 118.
10. Bodleian Library, MS Rawlinson Letters 89, fo. 42.
11. *A True Discourse of all the Royal Passages, Tryumphs and Ceremonies* (1625), 1–2.
12. Henry Ellis (ed.), *Original Letters Illustrative of English History*, 2nd ser., 4 vols (1827), iii. 246.
13. Charles I, *Stuart Royal Proclamations: Volume II: Royal Proclamations of King Charles I 1625–1646*, ed. James F. Larkin (Oxford, 1983), 1–2; Stocks and Stevenson (eds), *Records of the Borough of Leicester*, 218–19. See also the broadsheet *Whereas it hath pleased Almighty God to call to his mercie our late Sovereigne Lord, King Iames* (1625).
14. Thomas Birch (ed.), *The Court and Times of Charles the First*, 2 vols (1848), i. 6, Meade to Stuteville, 9 April 1625.
15. HMC, *Eleventh Report*, appendix, part I, 5.
16. *The Letters of John Chamberlain*, ed. Norman Egbert McClure (American Philosophical Society Memoirs, vol. 12, Philadelphia, 1939), 610.
17. Birch (ed.), *Court and Times*, i. 7.
18. Birch (ed.), *Court and Times*, i. 8; HMC, *Eleventh Report*, appendix, part I, 6.
19. Huntington Library, Hastings MS, HA 1930.

20. *Calendar of Wynn (of Gwydir) Papers 1515–1690* (Aberystwyth, 1926), 214.
21. *Letters of John Chamberlain*, ed. McClure, 609, Chamberlain to Sir Dudley Carleton, 9 April 1625.
22. TNA, SP 16/17A, fo. 34v.
23. Sir Francis Bacon, *Cases of Treason* (1641), 18–21.
24. James I and VI, *The Trew Law of Free Monarchie*, in *King James VI and I: Selected Writings*, ed. Neil Rhodes, Jennifer Richards, and Joseph Marshall (Aldershot, 2003), 261.
25. Christopher Wordsworth (ed.), *The Coronation of King Charles I* (Henry Bradshaw Society, vol. 2, 1892), 37, 42; Leopold G. Wickham Legg (ed.), *English Coronation Records* (Westminster, 1901), 260, 263.
26. BL, Lansdowne MS 211, fos 88v–89.
27. *Stuart Royal Proclamations*, ed. Larkin, 47, also 91–3.
28. Somerset Archives, DD/PH/227/16, 'A discourse by way of dialogue between a counsellor of state and a country gentleman'. Conrad Russell suggests that this 'intriguing' dialogue, found among the papers of Sir Robert Phelips, emanated from the circle of the Duke of Buckingham as part of his attempt to build a partnership with parliament in 1624: Conrad Russell, *Parliaments and English Politics 1621–1629* (Oxford, 1979), 149–50. For the authorship see Thomas Cogswell, *The Blessed Revolution: English Politics and the Coming of War, 1621–1624* (Cambridge, 1989), 157–8.
29. James I, *Trew Law of Free Monarchie*, in *James VI and I: Selected Writings*, 261–2; James I, *The Kings Maiesties Speache to the Lords and Commons* (1610), sig. A4v.
30. *The Doctrine of the Bible: Or, Rules of Discipline* (1604, 1641), fos 2, 19v–20; Robert Horne, *The Christian Gouernor, in the Common-wealth, and Priuate Families* (1614), sig. A2v.
31. John Pyne, *The Heart of the King; and the King of the Heart* (1628), 10.
32. *The Works of the Most Reverend Father in God, William Laud, D.D.*, ed. William Scott and James Bliss, 9 vols (Oxford, 1847–60), i. 94, 101, 106, 110, 115, 116.
33. Stephen Jerome, *Englands Iubilee, or Irelands Ioyes Io-Paen, for King Charles his Welcome* (Dublin, 1625), epistle dedicatory.
34. BL, Add. MS 34,324, fo. 238.
35. J. P. Kenyon (ed.), *The Stuart Constitution* (Cambridge, 1966), 16; Bodleian Library, MS Tanner 72, fo. 300v.
36. *True Discourse of all the Royal Passages*, 30, 32, 34, 43.
37. Kevin Sharpe, *Image Wars: Promoting Kings and Commonwealths in England, 1603–1660* (New Haven and London, 2010), 232–3.
38. Laud, *Works*, i. 99, 115.
39. James I, *Trew Law of Free Monarchie*, in *James VI and I: Selected Writings*, 262; *The Letters, Speeches and Proclamations of King Charles I*, ed. Sir Charles Petrie (1935), 46, 47, 49, 62.
40. Isaac Bargrave, *A Sermon Preached Before King Charles March 27 1627* (1627), 2–3.

41. *Sir Robert Filmer: Patriarcha and Other Writings*, ed. Johann P. Sommerville (Cambridge, 1991), 3, 5, 35, 37.
42. Laud, *Works*, i. 124.
43. Staffordshire Record Office, D.1287/18/2/48, Bridgeman correspondence.
44. Bodleian Library, MS Rawlinson B. 243, fos 17–17^{v}, speech to Assize judges, June 1638.
45. TNA, National Register of Archives, Bound Vol. 20594, 676, Dungarvon to the Earl of Cork, 17 August 1632.
46. Sir Henry Wotton, *A Panegyrick of King Charles* (1649), 1, 81 (reproducing his writing of 1633).
47. Henry Peacham, *The Duty of all True Subiects to their King* (1639), 22–3. See also Richard Brathwaite, *The English Gentleman* (1630), 298, and Thomas Carew, *Poems* (1640), 130, on 'our halcyon days'.
48. John Sadler, *Masquerade du Ciel* (1640), sig. A3.
49. Laud, *Works*, i. 101.
50. John Swan, *Redde Debitum. Or, A Discourse in Defence of Three Chiefe Fatherhoods* (1640), 11.
51. Henry King, *A Sermon Preached at St Pauls March 27. 1640*, in *The Sermons of Henry King*, ed. Mary Hobbs (Cranbury, NJ and Aldershot, 1992), 228.
52. Robert Mossom, *The King on his Throne: Or, A Discourse maintaining the Dignity of a King, the Duty of a Subject, and the Unlawfulnesse of Rebellion* (York, 1642), 3.
53. TNA, SP 16/204/72.
54. *CSPD 1633–34*, 437.
55. Queen's College, Oxford, MS 390, fo. 47^{v}.
56. Henry Valentine, *God Save the King. A Sermon Preached in St Pauls Church the 27th of March 1639* (1639), 18. See also Thomas Morton, *A Sermon Preached Before the Kings most Excellent Majestie, in the Cathedrall Church of Durham* (1639), on 'subjection to the higher powers'.
57. Swan, *Redde Debitum*, 7, also 9, 10, 11, 21.
58. *Sermons of Henry King*, ed. Hobbs, 222.
59. *Gods Good Servant, and the Kings Good Subject. A sermon preached at Andover, at a visitation. May 17. 1639* (1642), 6–8.
60. *Constitutions and Canons Ecclesiasticall; Treated upon by the Archbishops of Canterbury and York* (1640), Canon 1 'concerning the regal power'.
61. *Gods Good Servant*, 6–8. Cf. Peacham, *Duty of all True Subiects*, 4: 'know well how to obey.'
62. Reynolds, *Shieldes of the Earth*, 1, 8; John Featley, *Obedience and Submission. A Sermon* (1636), 6–7.
63. Matthew Griffith, *Bethel: or, a Forme for Families* (1633), 430, 444.
64. Bodleian Library, MS Carte 123, fo. 65, MS Firth *c.* 4, fos 321, 423, MS Rawlinson D. 353, fo. 87; Huntington Library, Hastings MS, HM 55603, fo. 33.
65. Bodleian Library, MS Firth *c.* 4, fos 236, 321.

66. Kenyon (ed.), *Stuart Constitution*, 16; Bodleian Library, MS Tanner 72, fo. 300ᵛ. See also Sharpe, *Image Wars*, 145–54, on the king as custodian and embodiment of 'the common good'.
67. *CSPD 1638–39*, 154–5.
68. Roger Mainwaring, *Religion and Alegiance: In Two Sermons Preached before the Kings Maiestie* (1627), 9.
69. Thomas Foster, *Plouto-Mastix: The Scourge of Covetousnesse; or, An Apologie for the Publike Good, against Privacie* (1631), 15, 16, 22.
70. *Letters, Speeches and Proclamations of King Charles I*, 47; Bodleian Library, MS Firth *c.* 4, fo. 241; Huntington Library, Hastings MS, HA 1340.
71. *Letters, Speeches and Proclamations of King Charles I*, 63, 65, 70, 76; Charles I, *Basilika. The Workes of King Charles the Martyr* (1662), 374.
72. Bodleian Library, MS Firth *c.* 4, fo. 241.
73. Bodleian Library, MS Firth *c.* 4, fos 451, 453.
74. BL, Add. MS 72,417, fo. 17; Bodleian Library, MS Carte 1, fo. 89.
75. The angel coin was used to reward subjects cured of the king's evil: TNA, SP 16/286/1.
76. *Letters of John Holles 1587–1637*, ed. P. R. Seddon, 3 vols (Thoroton Society Record Series, 1983–6), ii. 346–8, 360, 366, 375.
77. BL, Hargrave MS 489, fos 97–8.
78. BL, Hargrave MS 489, fo. 100ᵛ.
79. BL, Stowe MS 561, fos 25–8ᵛ.
80. TNA, SP 16/17A, fo. 35.
81. *Sir Robert Filmer*, ed. Sommerville, 3, 5, 35, 37.
82. Huntington Library, Hastings Correspondence, Box 11, HA 1337, Charles to the Earl of Huntingdon, 17 September 1625.
83. HMC, *Buccleuch*, i. 263.
84. Richard Cust, *The Forced Loan and English Politics, 1626–1628* (Oxford, 1987).
85. *APC 1626, June–Dec.*, 134, 202.
86. Huntington Library, Hastings MS, HA 4226, HA 1341.
87. TNA, SP 16/35/46, SP 16/36/82.
88. HMC, *Buccleuch*, i. 264; Stocks and Stevenson (eds), *Records of the Borough of Leicester*, 233.
89. *APC 1627 Jan.–Aug.*, 31, 45.
90. HMC, *Tenth Report*, appendix, part 6, 128.
91. Norfolk Record Office, WLS/XVII/2, fos 56–60.
92. G. L. Harriss, 'Medieval Doctrines in the Debates on Supply, 1610–1629', in Kevin Sharpe (ed.), *Faction and Parliament: Essays on Early Stuart History* (1978), 92.
93. Robert Sibthorpe, *Apostolike Obedience: Shewing the Duty of Subjects to pay Tribute and Taxes to their Princes, according to the Word of God* (1627), 2, 14, 23, 35.
94. *Letters of John Holles*, ii. 366.
95. Mainwaring, *Religion and Alegiance*, title page, 8, 17, 27, 28–9.

96. Robert C. Johnson et al.(ed.), *Commons Debates 1628*, 6 vols (New Haven, 1977), iv. 102.
97. HMC, *Buccleuch*, i. 267.
98. HMC, *Buccleuch*, i. 265.
99. G. W. E. Bernard, *War, Taxation and Rebellion in Early Tudor England: Henry VIII, Wolsey, and the Amicable Grant of 1525* (Brighton and New York, 1986).
100. See TNA, SP 16/71/15, for payers and refusers in Bread Street Ward, London.
101. Huntington Library, Hastings MS, HA 8536.
102. TNA, SP 16/57/1, SP 16/89/4; Stocks and Stevenson (ed.), *Records of the Borough of Leicester*, 223; A. Ar., *The Practise of Princes* (Amsterdam, 1630), 22.
103. TNA, SP 16/84/20.
104. Birch (ed.), *Court and Times*, i. 177, 198.
105. Thomas B. Howell (ed.), *Cobbett's Complete Collection of State Trials*, 33 vols (1809–1826), iii. 1–233.
106. Thomas Cogswell, 'The Human Comedy in Westminster: *The House of Commons, 1604–1629*', *Journal of British Studies*, 52 (2013), 384.
107. TNA, SP 16/102/67; BL, Stowe MS 561, fos 22–8^{v}. Cf. Mark Kishlansky, 'Tyranny Denied: Charles I, Attorney General Heath, and the Five Knights Case', *Historical Journal*, 42 (1999), 53–83; John Guy, 'The Origins of the Petition of Right Reconsidered', *Historical Journal*, 25 (1982), 289–312.
108. Somerset Archives, DD/PH 277/16, fo. 2.
109. BL, Hargrave MS 489, fos 94–6^{v}.
110. TNA, SP 16/54/82.
111. *Letters of John Holles*, ii. 348, 360.
112. *Letters from Redgrave Hall: The Bacon Family 1340–1744*, ed. Diarmaid MacCulloch (Suffolk Records Society, vol. 50, 2007), 121.
113. TNA, SP 16/102/15.
114. Birch (ed.), *Court and Times*, i. 346.
115. *The Petition of Right: Exhibited to his Maiestie, By the Lords and Commons assembled in Parliament, concerning divers Right and Liberties of the Subject* (1642), sigs A2–A2^{v}.
116. TNA, SP 16/102/57, SP16/103/5; *The Diary of Sir Henry Slingsby*, ed. Daniel Parsons (1836), 319.
117. Birch (ed.), *Court and Times*, i. 362; *Diary of John Rous*, 16.
118. Russell, *Parliaments and English Politics*, 323–89.
119. TNA, SP 16/136/65; also SP 16/141/80.
120. Howell (ed.), *Cobbett's Complete Collection of State Trials*, iii. 387–99; manuscripts include BL, Add. MS 72,421, fo. 140; BL, Hargrave MS 489, fos 17–57^{v}; BL, Harley MS 597, fos 178–84; BL, Stowe MS 159, fos 16–27^{v}; Bodleian Library, MS Additional C 259, fos 47–47^{v}; Cambridge University Library, MS Mm. 6. 63/4, fos 3–7; TNA, C115/105/8119. See also Noah Millstone, 'Evil Counsel: The *Propositions to Bridle the Impertinency of Parliament*

and the Critique of Caroline Government in the Late 1620s', *Journal of British Studies*, 50 (2011), 813–39.

121. *The Correspondence of Thomas Hobbes. Electronic Edition. Vol. I, 1622–1659*, ed. Noel Malcolm (Charlottesville, VA, 2002), 7–8; Howell (ed.), *Cobbett's Complete Collection of State Trials*, iii. 387–99.
122. TNA, SP 16/376/24; Cyndia Susan Clegg, *Press Censorship in Caroline England* (Cambridge, 2008).
123. TNA, SP 16/178/3 and 4; L. J. Reeve, 'Sir Robert Heath's Advice for Charles I in 1629', *Bulletin of the Institute for Historical Research*, 59 (1986), 215–25. Heath became Chief Justice of Common Pleas but was sidelined by William Laud.
124. *Constitutions and Canons Ecclesiasticall; Treated upon by the Archbishops*, Canon 1.
125. Andrew Thrush, 'Naval Finance and the Origins and Development of Ship Money', in Mark Charles Fissel (ed.), *War and Government in Britain, 1598–1650* (Manchester and New York, 1991), 133–62.
126. Peace with France was sealed in April 1629 by the Treaty of Susa, and hostilities with Spain ended in November 1630 with the Treaty of Madrid.
127. Brathwaite, *English Gentleman*, 298; Reynolds, *Shieldes of the Earth*, 47–8.
128. BL, Add. MS 33,935, fo. 319v; *The Earl of Strafforde's Letters and Dispatches*, ed. William Knowler, 2 vols (1739), i. 225.
129. *CSPD 1633–34*, 90.
130. John Rushworth, *Historical Collections: The Second Part* (1686), 257–60. Leicester aldermen learned that the king required Ship Money, not only for his honour 'and the ancient renown of this nation', but also for 'the safety of yourselves and all his subjects in these troublesome and warlike times' (Stocks and Stevenson (ed.), *Records of the Borough of Leicester*, 281).
131. Most recent accounts stress the effectiveness of Ship Money, at least in its initial years, though post-revisionist scholars are again finding evidence of opposition. M. D. Gordon, 'The Collection of Ship Money in the Reign of Charles I', *Transactions of the Royal Historical Society*, 3rd ser., 4 (1910), 141–62; Peter Lake, 'The Collection of Ship Money in Cheshire during the Sixteen-Thirties: A Case Study of Relations between Central and Local Government', *Northern History*, 17 (1981), 44–71; Kevin Sharpe, *The Personal Rule of Charles I* (New Haven and London, 1992), 553; Henrik Langelüddecke, '"I finde all men & my officers all soe unwilling": The Collection of Ship Money, 1635–1640', *Journal of British Studies*, 46 (2007), 509–42.
132. Rushworth, *Historical Collections: The Second Part* (1686), 263; TNA, SP 16/335/67.
133. *Ship Money Papers and Sir Richard Grenville's Note-Book*, ed. Carol G. Bonsey and J. G. Jenkins (Buckinghamshire Record Society, vol. 13, 1965), 38–43; Stocks and Stevenson (ed.), *Records of the Borough of Leicester*, 297; Lake, 'Collection of Ship Money in Cheshire', 68. See, however, Langelüddecke, '"I finde all men & my officers all soe unwilling"', 516 and *passim*, for 'real and widespread' opposition.

134. B. E. Howells, *A Calendar of Letters Relating to North Wales. 1533–circa 1700* (Cardiff, 1967), 43.
135. HMC, *Ninth Report*, 390. Assessments by county and borough are listed in TNA, SP 16/333/61 and 62.
136. HMC, *Fifth Report*, 402.
137. TNA, SP 16/355/14, SP 16/370/83.
138. T. N. Brushfield, 'The Financial Diary of a Citizen of Exeter, 1631–43', *Report and Transactions of the Devonshire Association*, 33 (1901), 264–5; Sharpe, *Personal Rule*, 569–75.
139. TNA, SP 16/302/27.
140. TNA, C115/106, no. 8443.
141. *CSPD 1635*, 301.
142. *Calendar of the Correspondence of the Smyth Family of Ashton Court 1548–1647*, ed. J. H. Bettey (Bristol Record Society, vol. 35, 1982), 127–8.
143. TNA, C115/108, no. 8615. For more on Chaloner, see *CSPD 1636–37*, 560; *CSPD 1637*, 44–5, 106, 109–10, 176.
144. *Winthrop Papers*, iii. *1631–1637* (Massachusetts Historical Society, Boston, 1943), 355–6.
145. TNA, SP 16/290/75, SP 16/291/57.
146. Langelüddecke, '"I finde all men & my officers all soe unwilling"', 518–19, 526, 529; TNA, SP 16/379/132.
147. HMC, *Fifth Report*, 402.
148. TNA, SP 16/363/11 (2).
149. HMC, *Third Report*, 74; TNA, PC 2/47/179.
150. *CSPD 1636–37*, 416–18; *A Complete Collection of State-Trials, and Proceedings for High-Treason*, 6 vols (1730), i. 485–7.
151. Kenneth Fincham, 'The Judges' Decision on Ship Money in February 1637: The Reaction of Kent', *Bulletin of the Institute of Historical Research*, 57 (1984), 230–7, quoting Sir Roger Twysden, 231.
152. Cambridge University Library, MS Mm. 6. 63/1, fos 1–10.
153. *Complete Collection of State-Trials*, i. 524–5, 569, 658.
154. Huntington Library, Ellesmere MS 7877a; *Complete Collection of State-Trials*, i. 494–6.
155. Bodleian Library, MS Bankes 19/3, 44/10 and 11; *Earl of Strafforde's Letters*, ii. 167. See *Complete Collection of State-Trials*, i. 646–50 for Hutton's opinion, and 699–701 for Harrison's case.
156. TNA, SP 16/390/116.
157. BL, Egerton MS 2716, fo. 294.
158. HMC, *Gawdy*, 164.
159. *The Knyvett Letters (1620–1644)*, ed. Bertram Schofield (Norfolk Record Society, vol. 20, 1949), 91.
160. Michael Mendle, 'The Ship Money Case, *The Case of Shipmony*, and the Development of Henry Parker's Parliamentary Absolutism', *Historical Journal*,

32 (1989), 513–36. See also forthcoming work by Noah Millstone on 'Scribal Publication and the Clerical Underworld of Early Stuart London'.

161. *Complete Collection of State-Trials*, i. 525, 569, 658.
162. *The Oxinden Letters 1607–1642*, ed. Dorothy Gardiner (1933), 173.
163. Bodleian Library, Nalson MS 13, fo. 208.
164. TNA, SP 16/386/88.
165. TNA, SP 16/387/64.
166. Contrast Sharpe, *Personal Rule*, 583–95; Langelüddecke, '"I finde all men & my officers all soe unwilling"', 509–42; Fincham, 'The Judges' Decision on Ship Money', 230–7.
167. TNA, SP 16/395/40.
168. *CSPD 1637–38*, 437.
169. Bodleian Library, MS Bankes 37/54, fo. 112.
170. Gordon, 'Collection of Ship-Money', 143, 154; Langelüddecke, '"I finde all men & my officers all soe unwilling"', 533–42.
171. *CSPD 1637–38*, 444.
172. TNA, SP 16/383/46.
173. TNA, SP 16/410/9.
174. TNA, SP 16/433/2. See also investigation of sermons by Giles Randall in Northamptonshire and Edward Sparhawk in Essex, discussed in Chapter 7.
175. Oliver St John, *Mr St John's Speech to the Lords . . . Concerning Ship-Money* (1641), 4, 5.
176. *A Remonstrance of the State of the Kingdom* (1641), 5, 13–14.
177. *Sir Matthew Hale's the Prerogatives of the King*, 272–4; Eric N. Lindquist, 'The King, the People, and the House of Commons: The Problem of Early Jacobean Purveyance', *Historical Journal*, 31 (1988), 549–70; G. E. Aylmer, 'The Last Years of Purveyance 1610–1660', *Economic History Review*, NS 10 (1957), 81–93.
178. *A Remonstrance of the State of the Kingdom*, 34.
179. Huntington Library, Hastings Correspondence, Box 11, HA 4134; Lindquist, 'The King, the People and the House of Commons', 554.
180. Aylmer, 'Last Years of Purveyance', 85; Sharpe, *Personal Rule*, 111. Cf. Lindquist, 'The King, the People and the House of Commons', 551.
181. Bodleian Library, MS Rawlinson D. 666, section 2, fo. 39; HMC, *Fifth Report*, 402.
182. HMC, *Fifth Report*, 402.
183. HMC, *Various*, i. 99, 105.
184. TNA, SP 16/406/6.
185. HMC, *Fifth Report*, 402; TNA, SP 46/77, fos 308, 347, 349, 356.
186. Huntington Library, Hastings Correspondence, Box 11, HA 5502.
187. Huntington Library, Hastings Correspondence, Box 11, HA 5502; J. W. Willis Bund (ed.), *Worcestershire County Records. Division I . . . Calendar of Quarter Sessions Papers . . . 1591–1643* (Worcester, 1900), 398, 402, 431. For

more complaints and refusal to pay, see E. H. Bates Harbin (ed.), *Quarter Sessions Records for the County of Somerset, Vol. II. Charles I, 1625–1639* (Somerset Record Society, 24, 1908), 2–3; J. S. W. Gibson and E. R. C. Brinkworth (ed.), *Banbury Corporation Records: Tudor and Stuart* (Banbury Historical Society, vol. 15, 1977), 140.

188. J. M. Guilding (ed.), *Reading Records. Diary of the Corporation . . . Vol. II* (1895), 268.
189. TNA, SP 16/153/5.
190. Bodleian Library, MS Firth *c.* 4, fo. 539.
191. Huntington Library, Hastings Correspondence, Box 15, HA 4135.
192. Sharpe, *Personal Rule*, 111.
193. *Calendar of the Correspondence of the Smyth Family*, 118.
194. *CSPD 1635–36*, 218.
195. Lindsay Boynton, 'Billeting: The Example of the Isle of Wight', *English Historical Review*, 74 (1959), 35.
196. TNA, SP 16/58/14.
197. HMC, *Cowper*, i. 220; HMC, *Various*, i. 101–2; *CSPD 1639*, 535.
198. TNA, SP 16/170/4, SP 16/178/18.
199. TNA, SP 16/190/23, SP 16/216/21.
200. TNA, SP 16/222/40.
201. TNA, SP 16/241/42.
202. TNA, SP 16/387/89.
203. TNA, SP 16/400/6.
204. TNA, SP 16/400/6.
205. HMC, *Fifth Report*, 402.
206. TNA, SP 16/92/25.
207. TNA, SP 16/75/31.
208. Richard P. Cust and Andrew J. Hopper (ed.), *Cases in the High Court of Chivalry, 1634–1640* (Harleian Society NS, vol. 18, 2006), 135.
209. TNA, SP 16/71/35.
210. TNA, SP 16/83/65, PC 2/36, fo. 145.
211. TNA, SP 16/400/127. See also the testimony of Anthony Spittle in '156 De la Ware v. Crutchman alias West', in 'The Court of Chivalry 1634–1640', ed. Steven Rea and Richard Cust <http://www.court-of-chivalry.bham.ac.uk/index.htm> (accessed 2 June 2014).
212. TNA, SP 16/190/29.
213. *CSPD 1639*, 138–9.
214. *CSPD 1639–40*, 201–2.
215. Cambridge University Library, Ely Diocesan Records, E 10/4 (Assize records).
216. *CSPD 1638–39*, 471.
217. TNA, SP 16/338/28. For the soap monopoly, which earned the crown some £30,000 a year, see Sharpe, *Personal Rule*, 121–3, 259–62.

218. BL, Sloane MS 1039, fo. 93; Johnson et al. (eds), *Commons Debates 1628*, ii. 46; iii. 623, 629; iv. 348, 350.
219. David Cressy, *Saltpeter: The Mother of Gunpowder* (Oxford, 2013), 88–120.
220. Charles I, *By the King. A Proclamation for the maintenance and encrease of the Mines of Saltpeter, and the true making of Gunpowder, and reforming abuses concerning the same* (13 April 1625); *Stuart Royal Proclamations*, ed. Larkin, 16–20; *APC 1628 July–1629 April*, 235–6, 241; *APC 1629 May–1630 May*, 19–20.
221. Charles I, *By the King. A Proclamation for preservation of Grounds for making of Saltpeter, and to restore such grounds as are now destroyed, and to command Assistance to be given to His Majesties Saltpeter-Makers* (14 March 1635); *Stuart Royal Proclamations*, ed. Larkin, 453–7.
222. TNA, PC 2/42, 19–20.
223. Johnson et al. (eds), *Commons Debates 1628*, iii. 629; iv. 347; *CSPD 1629–31*, 188; TNA, SP 16/161/1, SP 16/165/38.
224. TNA, SP 16/101/46.
225. *CSPD 1629–31*, 318; TNA, SP 16/171/79; BL, Harley MS 1576, fo. 186v.
226. *CSPD 1636–37*, 53, 449; TNA, SP 16/328/31.
227. *CSPD 1637*, 129, 222–3; TNA, SP 16/361/110 and 112, SP 16/320/40 and 41, SP 16/320/30, SP 17/D/19.
228. *CSPD 1637–38*, 159, 174, 180, 190, 344, 372, 375, 453, 513, 589; *CSPD 1639*, 262–3: *CSPD 1640*, 91–2, 348; TNA, SP 16/335/54 and 59 and SP 16/361/110 for more complaints.
229. *CSPD 1639–40*, 176, 473; TNA, SP 16/445/79.
230. *CSPD 1631–33*, 557–8, 573; *CSPD 1633–34*, 85, 98, 108, 120; TNA, SP 16/233/23, SP 16/240/21, SP 16/241/71–73.
231. TNA, SP 16/190/45.
232. *CSPD 1635*, 443, Viscount Wimbledon to the mayor of Portsmouth, 22 October 1635.
233. David Cressy, *Dangerous Talk: Scandalous, Seditious and Treasonable Speech in Pre-Modern England* (Oxford, 2010), 115–31.
234. TNA, SP 16/116/56; *Calendar of the Correspondence of the Smyth Family*, 93; Ellis (ed.), *Original Letters*, 2nd ser., iii. 276–7; Birch (ed.), *Court and Times*, i. 431.
235. Ecclesiastes 10:16; William B. Bidwell and Maija Jansson (eds), *Proceedings in Parliament 1626*, 4 vols (New Haven, 1991–6), iv. 348.
236. Clarendon, *The History of the Rebellion and Civil Wars in England*, ed. W. Dunn Macray, 6 vols (Oxford, 1888), i. 21.
237. Charles I, *Basilika. The Workes of King Charles*, 363.
238. Laud, *Works*, i. 64, 132, 191, 195.
239. *The Hamilton Papers . . . 1638–1650*, ed. Samuel Rawson Gardiner (Camden Society, NS, vol. 27, 1880), 65.
240. TNA, SP 16/39/41.
241. *Diary of John Rous*, 19.
242. TNA, SP 16/124/28.

243. Phineas Hodson, *The Kings Request; Or, David's Desire* (1628), 29–31, 34.
244. TNA, SP 16/147/27.
245. TNA, SP 16/142/92.
246. TNA, SP 16/166/43.
247. John Cordy Jeaffreson (ed.), *Middlesex County Records. Vol. III . . . 1 Charles I to 18 Charles II* (Clerkenwell, 1888), 43; TNA, SP 16/248/60; Cressy, *Dangerous Talk*, 132–88.
248. Jeaffreson (ed.), *Middlesex County Records. Vol. III*, 54–5; TNA, SP 16/231/24, SP 16/258/45, PC 2/43, 431; Bodleian Library, MS Carte 123, fo. 180; Bodleian Library, MS Bankes 18/1, 18/2.
249. Staffordshire Record Office, D.1287/18/2/108, Bridgeman correspondence.
250. 'The Court of Chivalry 1634–1640', ed. Steven Rea and Richard Cust <http://www.court-of-chivalry.bham.ac.uk/index.htm>, no. 35 *Bawde* v. *Dawson*; Staffordshire Record Office, Q/SO/5, fo. 16, Q/SR/243, fos 6–7, 11.
251. TNA, SP 16/222/48.
252. TNA, SP 16/258/50, SP 16/260/10, PC 2/43, 443.
253. Jeaffreson (ed.), *Middlesex County Records. Vol. III*, 174.
254. TNA, SP 16/369/25, SP 16/362/96.
255. Bodleian Library, MS Bankes 37/54, fo. 112; *CSPD 1638–39*, 596.
256. *CSPD 1639*, 236.
257. *CSPD 1639–40*, 211–12, Nicholas Darton to Secretary Windebank.
258. Valentine, *God Save the King*, 15.
259. Swan, *Redde Debitum*, 7, 21.
260. *Sermons of Henry King*, ed. Hobbs, 222.
261. House of Commons Library, Standard Note SN/PC/03861 'The Royal Prerogative' (2009). Prerogative powers of making treaties and declarations of war are exercised by crown ministers, but the queen still retains ancient rights regarding swans and hidden treasure.
262. Keith Wrightson, '"Sorts of People" in Tudor and Stuart England', in Jonathan Barry and Christopher Brooks (eds), *The Middling Sort of People: Society and Politics in England, 1550–1800* (1994), 28–51.

CHAPTER 4

1. See Richard W. Stewart, 'Arms and Expeditions: The Ordnance Office and the Assaults on Cadiz (1625) and the Isle of Rhé (1627)', in Mark Charles Fissel (ed.), *War and Government in Britain, 1598–1650* (Manchester and New York, 1991), 112–32; Mark Charles Fissel, *English Warfare, 1511–1642* (2001), esp. 105–13, 255–81.
2. H. A. Grueber (ed.), *Medallic Illustrations of the History of Great Britain and Ireland*, 2 vols (1904–11; repr. Lawrence, MA, 1979), plate XX, 1–2.
3. HMC, *Tenth Report*, appendix, part 6, 128; HMC, *Buccleuch*, i. 264.
4. Bodleian Library, MS Firth *c.* 4, fo. 451.

5. TNA, SP 16/7/54, revised from SP 16/7/48.
6. TNA, SP 16/9/12 and 30, SP 16/11/32. For more reports, see TNA, SP 16/9/38 and 39, SP 16/10/67, SP 16/11/22, 48, 49, 66 and 67.
7. Edward Cecil (Lord Wimbledon), *A Iournall, and Relation of the Action . . . upon the coast of Spaine* (1626), 29.
8. *De Jure Maiestatis, or, Political Treatise of Government (1628–30) and The Letter-Book of Sir John Eliot (1625–1632)*, ed. Alexander B. Grosart, 2 vols (1882), i. 155.
9. 'There was a great fleete, all they that did see't', in *Early Stuart Libels: An Edition of Poetry from Manuscript Sources*, in Alastair Bellany and Andrew McRae, Early Modern Literary Studies Text Series I (2005) <http://www.earlystuartlibels.net/htdocs/index.html> (accessed 2 June 2014). See also C. H. Firth, 'The Reign of Charles I', *Transactions of the Royal Historical Society*, 3rd ser. 6 (1912), 19–24.
10. Cambridge University Library, MS Ii. v.9, fos 176–85; A. Ar., *The Practise of Princes* (Amsterdam, 1630), 15.
11. *Calendar of the Correspondence of the Smyth Family of Ashton Court 1548–1647*, ed. J. H. Bettey (Bristol Record Society, vol. 35, 1982), 81.
12. TNA, SP 16/61/53, SP 16/67/34–7, SP 16/70/26.
13. TNA, SP 16/65/36, SP 16/78/56; James Orchard Halliwell (ed.), *Letters of the Kings of England*, 2 vols (1848), ii. 272.
14. TNA, SP 16/67/57.
15. Reports from the field include TNA, SP 16/71/60 and 65, SP 16/73/82, 87 and 98, SP 16/76/26, SP 16/78/71, SP 16/84/24.
16. TNA, SP 16/85/94 and 95.
17. Sir Francis Seymour spoke in parliament in March 1628 on these 'two unprosperous attempts against the two chiefest powers of Christendom' (Robert C. Johnson et al. (eds), *Commons Debates 1628*, 6 vols (New Haven, 1977), vi. 103); A. Ar., *Practise of Princes*, 8; *A Declaration of the Parliament of England, Expressing the Grounds of their Late Proceedings* (1649), 7.
18. *The Diary of Thomas Crosfield*, ed. Frederick S. Boas (Oxford, 1935), 15, 16; *Diary of John Rous, Incumbent of Santon Downham, Suffolk, from 1625 to 1642*, ed. Margaret Anne Everett Green (Camden Society, os, vol. 66, 1856), 10–13.
19. TNA, SP16/142/93.
20. TNA, SP 16/85/84. See also 'And art return'd againe with all thy Faults, Thou great commaunder of the All-goe-naughts?', in *Early Stuart Libels*, ed. Bellany and McRae, Oii12.
21. TNA, SP 16/84/75, SP 16/85/96–8; Halliwell (ed.), *Letters of the Kings of England*, ii. 281.
22. Bodleian Library, MS Firth *c.* 4, fo. 147.
23. *The Fairfax Correspondence: Memoirs of the Reign of Charles the First*, ed. George W. Johnson, 2 vols (1848), i. 27, 32; HMC, *Fourth Report*, 289; TNA, SP 16/27/41.
24. HMC, *Tenth Report*, appendix, part 6, 113; HMC, *Salisbury*, xxii. 212.

25. Bodleian Library, MS Firth *c.* 4, fos 236, 320; *APC 1627 Jan.–Aug.*, 390.
26. Phineas Hodson, *The Kings Request; Or, David's Desire* (1628), 10.
27. HMC, *Salisbury*, xxii. 217–21.
28. Huntington Library, Hastings MS, HA 1345.
29. Bodleian Library, MS Carte 123, fos 107, 113.
30. BL, Add. MS 33,935, fo. 319^{v}; *The Earl of Strafforde's Letters and Dispatches*, ed. William Knowler, 2 vols (1739), i. 225.
31. Bodleian Library, MS Carte 77, fo. 274^{v}; Bodleian Library, MS Firth *c.* 4, fo. 322; TNA, SP 16/1/96, SP 16/21/43, SP 16/43/57; *Fairfax Correspondence*, i. 25–6.
32. *APC 1626 June–Dec.*, 350; TNA, SP 16/87/35.
33. HMC, *Rutland*, 47; *Letters of John Holles 1587–1637*, ed. P. R. Seddon, 3 vols (Thoroton Society Record Series, 1983–6), ii. 309. See also Geoffrey Parker, *The Military Revolution: Military Innovation and the Rise of the West, 1500–1800*, 2nd edn (Cambridge, 1996); Clifford J. Rogers (ed.), *The Military Revolution Debate: Readings on the Military Transformation of Early Modern Europe* (Boulder, CO, 1995); Frank Tallett and D. J. B. Trim (eds), *European Warfare, 1350–1750* (Cambridge, 2010); Charles Carlton, *This Seat of Mars: War and the British Isles, 1485–1746* (New Haven, 2011).
34. For the politics of this period see Conrad Russell, *Parliaments and English Politics, 1621–1629* (Oxford, 1979); Richard Cust, *The Forced Loan and English Politics, 1626–1628* (Oxford, 1987).
35. London Metropolitan Archives, MJ/SB/B/4, 27.
36. Johnson et al. (eds), *Commons Debates 1628*, ii. 451 and *passim*.
37. Bodleian Library, MS Firth *c.* 4, fos 1–5, 'The estate of all the trayned bands in England as well horse as foot'.
38. Huntington Library, Stowe–Temple Correspondence, Box 6, STT 921; Cheshire Record Office, CR 63/2/6, fo. 189; TNA, SP 16/381/66.
39. HMC, *Salisbury*, xxii. 24, 211, 266.
40. Hodson, *Kings Request*, 11.
41. Henrik Langelüddecke, '"The chiefest strength and glory of this kingdom": Arming and Training the "Perfect Militia" in the 1630s', *English Historical Review*, 118 (2003), 1264–1303.
42. TNA, SP 16/13/49, SP 16/90/114; *APC 1625–26*, 374; *CSPD 1625–26*, 233; Huntington Library, Stowe–Temple Correspondence, Box 6, STT 921, Box 7, STT 2258, STT 2445; Norfolk Record Office, WLS/XVII/2, fos 53^{v}–57.
43. TNA, SP 16/13/43–5; Marjorie Masten (ed.), *Woodstock Chamberlains' Accounts, 1609–50* (Oxfordshire Record Society, vol. 58, 1993), 106; *Instructions for Musters and Armes, And the use thereof* (1631). See also HMC, *Salisbury*, xxii. 281, for the training and preparation of trained bands 'in these stirring and hostile times' in 1637.
44. Bodleian Library, MS Firth *c.* 4, fo. 125; HMC, *Salisbury*, xxii. 232.

45. J. M. Guilding (ed.), *Reading Records. Diary of the Corporation . . . Vol. II* (1895), 236.
46. *APC 1625–26*, 28–30, 54; HMC, *Salisbury*, xxii. 211; Huntington Library, Hastings Correspondence, Box 11, HA 1335, warrant dated 1 May 1625.
47. TNA, SP 16/2/104.
48. Stephen J. Stearns, 'Conscription and English Society in the 1620s', *Journal of British Studies*, 11 (1972), 4–5.
49. Bodleian Library, MS Carte 123, fo. 67; Helen Stocks and W. H. Stevenson (eds), *Records of the Borough of Leicester . . . 1603–1688* (Cambridge 1923), 222; TNA, SP 16/3/59.
50. HMC, *Fifth Report*, 401.
51. HMC, *Salisbury*, xxii. 232; TNA, SP 16/4/160.
52. TNA, SP 16/2/95.
53. TNA, SP 16/4/160; Stearns, 'Conscription and English Society', 11.
54. Huntington Library, Hastings Correspondence, Box 11, HA 1282, 2884, 6752, 10880, 10881, 10885.
55. Stocks and Stevenson (eds), *Records of the Borough of Leicester*, 223; TNA, SP 16/57/1.
56. TNA, SP 16/66/41; Huntington Library, Hastings MS, HA 8536. See also TNA, SP 16/6/131, for the petition of Elizabeth Carpenter, pregnant wife of an impressed soldier, who had no other means of support.
57. TNA, SP 16/3/59.
58. Cheshire Record Office, QJF 54/3, fo. 99.
59. HMC, *Cowper*, i. 282.
60. TNA, SP 16/60/10; *APC 1627 Jan.–Aug.*, 331.
61. TNA, SP 16/2/127; *APC 1625–26*, 54, 95; Huntington Library, Stowe–Temple Correspondence, Box 6, STT 2270.
62. TNA, SP 16/2/101. See also TNA, SP 16/46 for the occupations of men pressed in Leicestershire in 1626; SP 16/62/13 and SP 16/72/11 for Devonshire and Derbyshire men in 1627, where between 40% and 50% were labourers.
63. TNA, SP 16/4/160. See also the case of Robert Court of Canterbury, pressed veteran of the Isle of Rhé. After he was declared dead, his widow remarried, only to find Robert alive and well but late returning. Found guilty of bigamy, Susan Court declared it was through 'ignorance, and not with any lewd intent', and successfully secured a royal pardon: TNA, SP 16/120/49.
64. Bodleian Library, MS Carte 123, fo. 67.
65. *APC 1627 Jan.–Aug.*, 98; HMC, *Salisbury*, xxii. 227, 229, 232; Huntington Library, Hastings Correspondence, Box 11, HA 10614, 46117.
66. TNA, SP 16/62/20 and 21.
67. TNA, SP 16/2/85; Stearns, 'Conscription and English Society', 3.
68. TNA, SP 16/3/33. See also TNA, SP 16/58/43 for allowances for Buckingham's soldiers in 1627.

69. *APC 1627 Jan.–Aug.*, 63, 98; Bodleian Library, MS Carte 123, fo. 93.
70. *APC 1627 Jan.–Aug.*, 105, 194.
71. TNA, SP 16/3/5. Craig Muldrew, *Food, Energy and the Creation of Industriousness: Work and Material Culture in Agrarian England, 1550–1780* (Cambridge, 2011), 84–132, estimates the calorific value of workmen's diets.
72. Thomas Birch (ed.), *The Court and Times of Charles the First*, 2 vols (1848), i. 24; TNA, SP 16/2/104; Stearns, 'Conscription and English Society', 15.
73. TNA, SP 16/61/56; HMC, *Cowper*, i. 301.
74. TNA, SP 16/68/13.
75. *APC 1627 Jan.–Aug.*, 158, 185.
76. *Diary of Thomas Crosfield*, 11, 13.
77. Bodleian Library, MS Firth *c.* 4, fo. 297; TNA, SP 16/56/17, SP 16/58/35, SP 16/59/41.
78. Bodleian Library, MS Firth *c.* 4, fos 337–56; TNA, SP 16/61/56; HMC, *Cowper*, i. 300–3; *APC 1627 Jan.–Aug.*, 163–4.
79. Bodleian Library, MS Carte 123, fos 69, 81; HMC, *Tenth Report*, appendix, part 6, 115; HMC, *Cowper*, i. 360; Norfolk Record Office, WLS/XVII/2, fo. 49; Guilding (ed.), *Reading Records . . . Vol. II*, 327.
80. TNA, SP 16/2/65, PC 2/33, fo. 43.
81. TNA, SP 16/3/33.
82. Barbara Donagan, *War in England 1642–1649* (Oxford, 2008), 170.
83. A. Ar., *Practise of Princes*, 22.
84. Anthony Fletcher, *A County Community in Peace and War: Sussex 1600–1660* (1975), 175, 196.
85. *APC 1625–26*, 416, 465; *APC 1626 June–Dec.*, 36; TNA, SP 16/3/33, SP 16/6/3, SP 16/62/57; HMC, *Cowper*, i. 288, 297.
86. TNA, SP 16/88/54, SP 16/103/78; *A Royalist Notebook: The Commonplace Book of Sir John Oglander* (1936), ed. Francis Bamford, 46; Lindsay Boynton, 'Billeting: The Example of the Isle of Wight', *English Historical Review*, 74 (1959), 25–9, 32, 36.
87. TNA, SP 16/12/18, 35, 81.
88. *CSPD 1625–26*, 214; TNA, SP 16/23/51, SP 16/24/26 and 52.
89. HMC, *Cowper*, i. 29; Dorset History Centre, D/BOC/Box 22, 46; *APC 1626 June–Dec.*, 261, 315, 348; TNA, SP 16/25/72, SP 16/27/5, SP 16/30/67, SP 16/31/33.
90. HMC, *Tenth Report*, appendix, part 6, 112; Johnson et al. (eds), *Commons Debates 1628*, ii. 391.
91. TNA, SP 16/84/61, SP 16/86/27.
92. TNA, SP 16/92/69.
93. TNA, SP 16/92/69.
94. *Diary of Thomas Crosfield*, 18.
95. Norfolk Record Office, WLS/XVII/2, fos 49–51.

96. Norfolk Record Office, WLS/XVII/2, fos 49–51; TNA, SP 16/96/46. See also TNA, SP 16/52/3 for 'the desolate and distressed state of this city' of Norwich.
97. See Bodleian Library, MS Firth *c.* 4, fos 455–6, for a violent confrontation at Witham, Essex, between Irish catholic troops and local civilians.
98. TNA, SP 16/95/8.
99. HMC, *Cowper*, i. 359.
100. TNA, SP 16/101/29.
101. TNA, SP 16/110/56.
102. Johnson et al. (eds), *Commons Debates 1628*, ii. 73,170, 253–4, 364, 391, 451; vi. 104, 222; TNA, SP 16/101/1 and 4; Boynton, 'Billeting', 23–40.
103. TNA, SP 16/135/43.
104. TNA, SP 16/101/1.
105. Johnson et al. (eds), *Commons Debates 1628*, iii. 270.
106. Johnson et al. (eds), *Commons Debates 1628*, ii. 73, 170, 254, 364; vi. 103.
107. Johnson et al. (eds), *Commons Debates 1628*, ii. 451; TNA, SP 16/101/1 and 4.
108. *The Petition of Right: Exhibited to his Maiestie, By the Lords and Commons assembled in Parliament, concerning divers Right and Liberties of the Subject* (1642), sigs A2, A2^{v}. The 'Grand Remonstrance' of December 1641 also condemned 'the charging of the kingdom with billeted soldiers in all parts of it'.
109. TNA, SP 16/111/47. For later complaints against billeting, see TNA, SP 16/113/15, SP 16/116/80.
110. TNA, SP 16/120/30, SP 16/133/60.
111. *APC 1625–26*, 28–30; TNA, SP 16/1/76, SP 16/2/34.
112. TNA, SP 16/7/54.
113. *APC 1625–26*, 179–80, 409; *APC 1627 Jan.–Aug.*, 155, 160, 398.
114. HMC, *Cowper*, i. 201.
115. HMC, *Cowper*, i. 362.
116. HMC, *Cowper*, i. 196.
117. *APC 1625–26*, 179–80.
118. TNA, SP 16/22/104.
119. HMC, *Cowper*, i. 197, 204, 209, 211, 287.
120. See SP 16/119/69, 'Orders and Instructions for the Better Government of the Navy', October 1628, for the beginnings of post-Buckingham naval reform; Brian Quintrell, 'Charles I and his Navy in the 1630s', *Seventeenth Century*, 3 (1988), 159–79; Kenneth R. Andrews, *Ships, Money and Politics: Seafaring and Naval Enterprise in the Reign of Charles I* (Cambridge, 1991); Andrew Thrush, 'Naval Finance and the Origins and Development of Ship Money', in Fissel (ed.), *War and Government in Britain*, 133–62.
121. *CSPD 1625–26*, 215; TNA, SP 16/1/96, SP 16/22/45 and 82, SP 16/25/16, SP 16/33/28.
122. TNA, SP 16/1/96, SP 16/41/56.
123. TNA, PC 2/33, fo. 335.

124. TNA, SP 16/31/112; *APC 1626 June–Dec.*, 40.
125. *Diary of Thomas Crosfield*, 5.
126. Bodleian Library, Carte MS 77, fo. 439v; Henry Ellis (ed.), *Original Letters Illustrative of English History*, 2nd edn, 3 vols (1825), iii. 249, John Pory to Joseph Mead, 17August 1626.
127. William B. Bidwell and Maija Jansson (eds), *Proceedings in Parliament 1626*, 4 vols (New Haven, 1991–6), iv. 345, 348.
128. TNA, C115/107, no. 8493, SP 16/37/74; Ellis (ed.), *Original Letters* (1825), iii. 250.
129. *APC 1626 June–Dec.*, 306; Charles I, *Stuart Royal Proclamations: Volume II: Royal Proclamations of King Charles I 1625–1646*, ed. James F. Larkin (Oxford, 1983), 108–10.
130. TNA, C115/107, no. 8499.
131. HMC, *Cowper*, i, 288; *Calendar of the Correspondence of the Smyth Family*, 80.
132. TNA, SP 16/50/16.
133. BL, Egerton MS 2715, fo. 320.
134. TNA, C115/107, no. 8541.
135. Birch (ed.), *Court and Times*, i. 189, 194.
136. HMC, *Cowper*, i. 328; TNA, SP 16/53/37 and 66.
137. TNA, C115/107, no. 8541.
138. *APC 1627 Jan.–Aug.*, 139, 163.
139. TNA, SP 16/90/91.
140. TNA, SP 16/85/24, SP 16/86/86, SP 16/87/37.
141. Charles I, *By the King. A Proclamation to Prevent the Purloyning and Stealing of Armes, Powder, and other Munition, and Habilliments of Warre* (8 December 1627); *Stuart Royal Proclamations*, ed. Larkin, 174–6.
142. Charles I, *By the King. A Proclamation for the Repressing of Disorders of Marriners* (17 February 1628); *Stuart Royal Proclamations*, ed. Larkin, 188–90.
143. *APC 1627 Jan.–Aug.*, 159.
144. TNA, SP 16/113/7.
145. *Letters of John Holles*, iii. 376, 377.
146. *Diary of Walter Yonge, Esq.*, ed. George Roberts (Camden Society, os, vol. 41, 1848), 112.
147. In August 1628 the fleet totalled seventy ships, with some 5,134 sailors and 3,046 landsmen, but it was never effectively deployed: TNA, SP 16/113/27.
148. *Calendar of the Correspondence of the Smyth Family*, 92.
149. Bodleian Library, MS Tanner 276, 114.
150. TNA, SP 16/116/2 and 23.
151. BL, Add. MS 72,418, fo. 81; TNA, PC 2/40/119. The king's sailors received better treatment later in the 1630s, without the pressure of war and with Ship Money filling royal coffers. In 1636 a plan emerged to set aside funds for the 'discharge of sick seamen, and that there be allowed to sick seamen put ashore for recovery of their health, five shilling apiece above their wages and conduct money' (*CSPD 1635–36*, 236).

152. *CSPD 1633–34*, 82.
153. HMC, *Third Report*, 40.
154. TNA, SP 16/185/5, SP 16/194/32.
155. Huntington Library, Hastings Correspondence, Box 14, HA 5534.
156. TNA, SP 16/312/57.
157. *Earl of Strafforde's Letters*, i. 226.
158. BL, Add. MS 72,419, fo. 52.
159. *CSPD 1635*, 95.
160. TNA, ASSI 35/81/1/9.
161. Fissel, *English Warfare*, 270–1; Donagan, *War in England*, 49; Jane E. E. Boys, *London's News Press and the Thirty Years War* (Woodbridge, 2011), 224, estimates 10,000 British mercenaries in the Dutch army and 20,000 with the Swedes in 1631. Gráinne Henry, 'Ulster Exiles in Europe, 1605–1641', in Brain MacCuarta (ed.), *Ulster 1641: Aspects of the Rising* (Belfast, 1993), 42, counts 28,400 Irishmen levied for foreign service in the reign of Charles I.
162. *Diary of Thomas Crosfield*, 67.
163. See, e.g., *Barrington Family Letters 1628–1632*, ed. Arthur Searle (Camden Society, 4th ser., vol. 28, 1983), 101, 134.
164. *Barrington Family Letters*, 101.
165. Boys, *London's News Press*, 224–33; BL, Add. MS 33,936, fos 4, 23, 51; TNA, C115/105, no. 8201, C115/106, no. 8420.
166. BL, Harley MS 597, fos 143, 146.
167. *Complete Collection of State-Trials*, i. 483–5; BL, Harley MS 1576, fos 205–207v. For the claim that King Charles had title to the 'narrow seas' and all the waters bordering the British Isles, see John Selden, *Mare Clausum seu de Dominio Maris* (1635), later Englished by Marchamount Nedham as *Of the Dominion, or Ownership of the Sea* (1652).
168. HMC, *Ninth Report*, 390.
169. O. Ogle, W. H. Bliss, et al. (eds), *Calendar of the Clarendon State Papers Preserved in the Bodleian Library*, 5 vols (Oxford, 1872–1970), i.188.
170. BL, Add. MS 21,506, fo. 18.
171. Conrad Russell, *The Fall of the British Monarchies 1637–1642* (Oxford, 1991), 92; Esther S. Cope and Willson H. Coates (eds), *Proceedings of the Short Parliament of 1640* (Camden Society, 4th ser., vol. 19, 1977), 165, 207.
172. Russell, *Fall of the British Monarchies*, 55–89; Mark Charles Fissel, *The Bishops' Wars: Charles I's Campaigns against Scotland 1638–1640* (Cambridge, 1994), 3–39; Victor L. Stater, 'The Lord Lieutenancy on the Eve of the Civil Wars: The Impressment of George Plowright', *Historical Journal*, 29 (1986), 279–96; *Letters and Papers of the Verney Family*, ed. H. Verney (Camden Society, OS, vol. 56, 1853), 228.
173. David Cressy, *England on Edge: Crisis and Revolution 1640–1642* (Oxford, 2006), 68–109.

CHAPTER 5

1. TNA, SP 16/3/53.
2. Thomas Birch (ed.), *The Court and Times of Charles the First*, 2 vols (1848), i. 49.
3. TNA, SP 16/226/17 and 34, C115/107, no. 8555; Birch (ed.), *Court and Times*, ii. 202, 204.
4. *William Whiteway of Dorchester His Diary 1618 to 1635* (Dorset Record Society, Dorchester, vol. 12, 1991), 126.
5. TNA, C115/105, no. 8203.
6. TNA, C115/107, no. 8555; Somerset Archives, DD/PH/219, no. 44.
7. Bodleian Library, MS Carte 77, fo. 413^{v}.
8. TNA, National Register of Archives, Bound Vol. 20594, 830.
9. Corinne Comstock Weston and Janelle Renfrow Greenberg, *Subjects and Sovereigns: The Grand Controversy over Legal Sovereignty in Stuart England* (Cambridge, 1981), 35; Judith Richards, '"His Nowe Majestie" and the English Monarchy: The Kingship of Charles I before 1640', *Past & Present*, 113 (1986), 70–96.
10. R. W. Hoyle (ed.), *Heard before the King: Registers of Petitions to James I, 1603–1616* (List and Index Society, vol. 38, 2006), p. xiv.
11. Kevin Sharpe, 'The Image of Virtue: The Court and Household of Charles I, 1625–1642', in David Starkey et al. (eds), *The English Court: From the Wars of the Roses to the Civil War* (1987), 227, 242, 244. See also Brian Weiser, *Charles II and the Politics of Access* (Woodbridge, 2003), 14–15: 'Charles I, like Louis XIII, restricted access in the sense of physical proximity, the ability to interact, and the conduits by which his subjects could communicate with him.'
12. Mark Kishlansky, 'Charles I: A Case of Mistaken Identity,' *Past & Present*, 189 (2005), 41–80, esp. 49, 61, 79, and 'Debate', with Clive Holmes, Julian Goodare, and Richard Cust, *Past & Present*, 205 (2009), 175–237. Kevin Sharpe, *Image Wars: Promoting Kings and Commonwealths in England, 1603–1660* (New Haven and London, 2010), 230, 583, follows Kishlansky but notes that his article 'has largely met with a hostile reception'.
13. Sharpe, 'Image of Virtue', 260; Kevin Sharpe, *The Personal Rule of Charles I* (New Haven and London, 1992), 209.
14. HMC, *Cowper*, i. 291–2; TNA, SP 16/178/6.
15. *Letters of John Holles 1587–1637*, ed. P. R. Seddon, 3 vols (Thoroton Society Record Series, 1983–6), iii. 303, Earl of Clare to his brother Sir George Holles, 10 April 1625.
16. Caroline M. Hibbard, 'The Role of a Queen Consort: The Household and Court of Henrietta Maria, 1625–1642', in Ronald G. Asch and Adolf M. Birke (eds), *Princes, Patronage, and Nobility: The Court at the Beginning of the Modern Age c.1450–1650* (Oxford, 1991), 393–414.

17. Arthur MacGregor (ed.), *The Late King's Goods: Collections, Possessions and Patronage of Charles I in the Light of the Commonwealth Sale Inventories* (1989), 19–22; Simon Thurley, *Whitehall Palace: An Architectural History of the Royal Apartments, 1240–1698* (New Haven and London, 1999).
18. Huntington Library, Hastings Correspondence, Box 14, HA 5533.
19. TNA, LS 13/30, Lord Steward's establishment list 1627; TNA, LC 3/1, Lord Chamberlain's establishment list 1641. See also G. E. Aylmer, *The King's Servants: The Civil Service of Charles I, 1625–42* (1961), 26–33, 472–6.
20. HMC, *Eleventh Report*, appendix, part I, 6.
21. *The Letters of John Chamberlain*, ed. Norman Egbert McClure (American Philosophical Society Memoirs, vol. 12, Philadelphia, 1939), 609, Chamberlain to Sir Dudley Carleton, 9 April 1625; TNA, SP 16/1/67, Sir Toby Matthew to Carleton, 17 April 1625.
22. Birch (ed.), *Court and Times*, i. 12.
23. *Calendar of the Correspondence of the Smyth Family of Ashton Court 1548–1647*, ed. J. H. Bettey (Bristol Record Society, vol. 35, 1982), 74; HMC, *Cowper*, i. 209–10. Among other offences, Stuart had complained of Buckingham's naval administration.
24. Charles I, *By the King. A Proclamation for restraint of disorderly and unnecessary resort to the Court* (17 May 1625). See also Charles I, *By the King. A Proclamation for restraint of unnecessary resorts to the Court* (26 June 1625), which is more specifically concerned with plague; Charles I, *Stuart Royal Proclamations: Volume II: Royal Proclamations of King Charles I 1625–1646*, ed. James F. Larkin (Oxford, 1983), 34–7, 45–6.
25. HMC, *Cowper*, i. 382.
26. TNA, LC 5/180, SP 16/375/2.
27. Huntington Library, Hastings MS, HA Misc. Box 1/32.
28. TNA, LC 5/180, SP 16/375/2.
29. (Martin Parker), *The King, and a Poore Northerne Man* (1640), sig. B.
30. TNA, LC 5/180, SP 16/375/2.
31. TNA, SP 16/182/31, SP 16/375/2; Huntington Library, Hastings MS, HA Misc. Box 1/32.
32. BL, Stowe MS 561, fos 3, 4.
33. *The Diary of Robert Woodford, 1637–1641*, ed. John Fielding (Camden Society 5th series, vol. 42, 2012), 246.
34. TNA, SO 3/9.
35. *CSPD 1645–47*, 393.
36. *CSPD 1635*, 296–7; *To the Kings Most Excellent Majesty. The Humble Petition of Divers Hundreds of the Kings Poore Subjects, Afflicted with that Grievous Infirmities, called The Kings Evil* (1643), 4. According to Hamon L'Estrange, *The Alliance of Divine Offices* (1659), 250, Queen Elizabeth touched with the sign of the cross, a detail discontinued by the early Stuarts. See also Marc Bloch, *The Royal Touch: Sacred Monarchy and Scrofula in England and France* (1973); George MacDonald

Ross, 'The Royal Touch and the Book of Common Prayer', *Notes and Queries*, NS 30 (1983), 433–5; Richards, '"His Nowe Majestie"', 86–93.

37. *Stuart Royal Proclamations*, ed. Larkin, 44, 238, 257, 416, 467.
38. *CSPD 1625–26*, 22, 367; *CSPD 1628–29*, 165; *CSPD 1629–31*, 124, 229; *CSPD 1631–33*, 164, 179, 357; *CSPD 1633–34*, 560; *CSPD 1634–35*, 216, 357; *CSPD 1635*, 1; TNA, SP 16/286/1.
39. *The Correspondence of Nathan Walworth and Peter Seddon of Outwood*, ed. John Samuel Fletcher (Chetham Society, vol. 109, 1880), 42; *CSPD 1637*, 403; *Stuart Royal Proclamations*, ed. Larkin, 44, 95, 238–9, 256–7, 349–50, 416–17, 433–4, 446–7, 466–7, 504–5, 535, 552–3, 574–5, 621–2, 629, 693.
40. Bodleian Library, MS Bankes 9, fos 41–2, 77.
41. Peter E. McCullough, *Sermons at Court: Politics and Religion in Elizabethan and Jacobean Preaching* (Cambridge, 1998), 42–9; *The Earl of Strafforde's Letters and Dispatches*, ed. William Knowler, 2 vols (1739), i. 226.
42. BL, Egerton MS 2716, fo. 294; *Earl of Strafforde's Letters*, ii. 130, 140. Works and Buildings accounts for 1637 include payment for 'six new columns under the Terrace in the Preaching Place', suggesting adaptation rather than abandonment of the outdoor auditory (TNA, E 351/3270).
43. BL, Stowe MS 561, fo. 8ᵛ.
44. *Earl of Strafforde's Letters*, i. 207.
45. Somerset Archives, DD/PH/219, no. 42.
46. *The Knyvett Letters (1620–1644)*, ed. Bertram Schofield (Norfolk Record Society, vol. 20, 1949), 88.
47. HMC, *Eleventh Report*, appendix, part 7, 148.
48. TNA, SP 16/375/2. Another version is in Huntington Library, Hastings MS, HA Misc. Box 1/32.
49. *Earl of Strafforde's Letters*, i. 225, 335.
50. TNA, C115/108, no. 8686.
51. TNA, C115/108, no. 8613.
52. *Earl of Strafforde's Letters*, ii. 140–1.
53. *Earl of Strafforde's Letters*, ii. 130.
54. 'The king stirs not from London before Christmas; the smallpox at Newmarket hindered his going thither,' wrote George Garrard in November 1634 (*Earl of Strafforde's Letters*, i. 338). See *Stuart Royal Proclamations*, ed. Larkin, 1084, for the forty places where the king signed proclamations.
55. Somerset Archives, DD/PH/219, no. 44.
56. Bodleian Library, MS Firth *c.* 4, fo. 539. The grand jury at Chelmsford assize heard complaints against purveyance of this sort in July 1631.
57. Charles I, *By the King. A Proclamation for restraint of disorderly and unnecessary resort to the Court* (17 May 1625); *Stuart Royal Proclamations*, ed. Larkin, 34–7.
58. BL, Stowe MS 561, fo. 3; TNA, SP 16/20/38; Bodleian Library, MS Ashmole 837, fo. 129ᵛ.

59. Henry R. Plomer (ed.), *The Churchwardens's Accounts of St. Nichols, Strood* (Kent Archaeological Society, Kent Records, vol. 5, 1927), 165, 173, for ringing 'when the king came by' in 1631 and 1634; Guildhall Library, MS 3556/1, for 'ringing at the king and queen's coming through the city'; Hammersmith and Fulham Archives, PAF/22, 'for ringing at the king's passing by and other times appointed'; J. Charles Cox and R. M. Serjeantson, *A History of the Church of the Holy Sepulchre, Northampton* (Northampton, 1897), 179, for hearty ringing in 1634 'when the king came through the town'.
60. Henry Ellis (ed.), *Original Letters Illustrative of English History*, 2nd edn, 3 vols (1825), iii. 196.
61. Bodleian Library, MS Additional C 259, fo. 40, William Dyndley to Sir Richard Beaumont, 29 September 1628.
62. TNA, SP 16/232/119.
63. TNA, SP 16/380/19; *Earl of Strafforde's Letters*, ii. 148.
64. TNA, SP 16/380/18.
65. TNA, E 351/544, E 351/3270, SP 16/237/60. Middlesex authorities in 1639 attended to the highway between Hendon and Hampstead, 'through which his majesty doth usually pass', which had become 'very offensive and dangerous for his majesty's passage' (London Metropolitan Archives, MJ/SB/B/4, 28–9).
66. HMC, *Cowper*, i. 213.
67. Huntington Library, Hastings MS, 1931; TNA, E 351/544, fos 188–188^{v}.
68. Daniel Lysons, *Magna Britannia*, 6 vols (1806–22), vi. 566–7.
69. TNA, C115/108, no. 8632.
70. David Cressy, *Dangerous Talk: Scandalous, Seditious and Treasonable Speech in Pre-Modern England* (Oxford, 2010), 115–31.
71. *Calendar of the Correspondence of the Smyth Family*, 72.
72. *A Royalist Notebook: The Commonplace Book of Sir John Oglander*, ed. Francis Bamford (1936), 19–21, 43, 44, 46, 49.
73. C. S. Terry, 'The Visits of Charles I to Newcastle in 1633, 1639, 1641, 1646–47, with Some Notes on Contemporary Local History', *Archaeologia Aeliana*, 21 (1899), 83–4, 96.
74. Charles I, *By the King. A Proclamation for restraint of disorderly and unnecessary resort to the Court* (17 May 1625).
75. C. H. Cooper, *Annals of Cambridge*, iii (Cambridge, 1845), 251.
76. Cooper, *Annals of Cambridge*, iii. 250.
77. *Records of Early English Drama: Oxford*, ed. John R. Elliott et al., 2 vols (London and Toronto, 2004), i. 461–2, 527–8.
78. Marjorie Masten (ed.), *Woodstock Chamberlains' Accounts, 1609–50* (Oxfordshire Record Society, vol. 58, 1993), 112, 149.
79. *The Diary of Thomas Crosfield*, ed. Frederick S. Boas (Oxford, 1935), 35, 55.
80. Bodleian Library, MS Top. Oxon. C. 378, fo. 256.

81. Bodleian Library, MS Jones 17, fos 300–9; *The Works of the Most Reverend Father in God, William Laud, D.D.*, ed. William Scott and James Bliss, 9 vols (Oxford, 1847–60), v. 56–9.
82. BL, Add. MS 33,935, fo. 325.
83. BL, Add. MS 33,936, fo. 15.
84. TNA, C115/107, no. 8548, C115/105, no. 8191, C115/106, no. 8396. For more on this visit, see David Cressy, 'The Death of a Vice-Chancellor; Cambridge, 1632', *History of Universities*, 26 (2012), 92–112.
85. TNA, National Register of Archives, Bound Vol. 20594, 676.
86. TNA, SP 16/223/63.
87. Bodleian Library, MS Rawlinson D. 399, fo. 101, MS Carte 77, fos 444–444^{v}, MS Tanner 71, fo. 113; BL, Egerton MS 2716, fo. 123; *The Fairfax Correspondence: Memoirs of the Reign of Charles the First*, ed. George W. Johnson, 2 vols (1848), i. 275; Clarendon, *The History of the Rebellion and Civil Wars in England*, ed. W. Dunn Macray, 6 vols (Oxford, 1888), i. 102–4.
88. Howard J. Murray, *A King's Treasure Lost* (Kirkaldy, 1999), 38–9, 59; Howard J. Murray, 'The Great Royal Treasure Hunt', *Scottish Diver* (March/April 1999), 15.
89. Clarendon, *History*, i. 102–4; *Fairfax Correspondence*, i. 276.
90. Peter Heylyn, *Antidotum Lincolniense* (1637), 85.
91. *Fairfax Correspondence*, i. 280–1; John Rushworth, *Historical Collections: The Second Part* (1680), 17; Bodleian Library, MS Ashmole 800, fos 28–38. For a hostile account of devotional practice at Little Gidding, see *The Arminian Nunnery* (1641).
92. Sharpe, *Personal Rule*, 778–9.
93. Laud, *Works*, iii. 217.
94. *Winthrop Papers*, iii. *1631–1637* (Massachusetts Historical Society, Boston, 1943), 127–8.
95. TNA, SP 16/240/53.
96. TNA, C115/105, no. 8158; Laud, *Works*, iii. 218.
97. TNA, C115/105, no. 8124.
98. BL, Harley MS 454, fo. 3^{v}.
99. Guildhall Library, MS. 3556/1, for ringing 'on the king's return from Scotland'.
100. Huntington Library, Hastings MS, HA Misc. Box 1/15.
101. *Diary of Thomas Crosfield*, 65, 77.
102. *Earl of Strafforde's Letters*, i. 226, 244.
103. Huntington Library, Hastings Correspondence, Box 14, HA 5534.
104. Helen Stocks and W. H. Stevenson (eds), *Records of the Borough of Leicester . . . 1603–1688* (Cambridge 1923), 274–80.
105. TNA, SP 16/271/86; Bodleian Library, Carte MS 74, fo. 177.
106. TNA, C115/106, no. 8442; Bodleian Library, Carte MS 77, fo. 359.
107. TNA, C115/106, nos 8442, 8465, 8471.

108. *CSPD 1635*, 330.
109. *Earl of Strafforde's Letters*, i. 435.
110. *Earl of Strafforde's Letters*, i. 463; Huntington Library, Ellesmere MS 6540.
111. Huntington Library, Ellesmere MS 6547; *Earl of Strafforde's Letters*, i. 468; HMC, *Sixth Report*, 278; *CSPD 1636*, 558. The favour shown to Bradbourne may not be unrelated to the fact that the king owed him £1,800 for work supplied: TNA, SP 16/306/7.
112. *Earl of Strafforde's Letters*, i. 463.
113. Bodleian Library, MS Top. Oxon. C. 378, fo. 278.
114. HMC, *Sixth Report*, 280; HMC, *Fourth Report*, 291.
115. TNA, SP 16/329/2, E 351/3279, for repairs and alterations to 'divers noblemen's house and others in time of the king and queen's progress'.
116. HMC, *Fourth Report*, 291; Laud, *Works*, iii. 227; TNA, SP 16/331/14.
117. *Records of Early English Drama: Oxford*, i. 527–8.
118. *Winthrop Papers*, iii. 355–6; TNA, SP 16/329/2.
119. Huntington Library, Stowe–Temple Correspondence, Box 10, STT 1337.
120. *Earl of Strafforde's Letters*, ii. 75, 87, 88; HMC, *Fourth Report*, 293.
121. HMC, *Third Report*, 74.
122. *Earl of Strafforde's Letters*, ii. 114.
123. *Earl of Strafforde's Letters*, ii. 116, 117.
124. *Earl of Strafforde's Letters*, ii. 168, 181.
125. TNA, C115/109, no. 8854; *Earl of Strafforde's Letters*, ii. 148, 181.
126. TNA, SP 16/415/27 and 35.
127. HMC, *Rutland*, 502.
128. Laud, *Works*, iii. 232; HMC, *Third Report*, 76.
129. Laud, *Works*, vii. 523.
130. Bodleian Library, MS Ashmole 800, fo. 50, Fleetwood to his father Sir Giles, 5 April 1639.
131. Bodleian Library, MS Ashmole 800, fo. 50; HMC, *Rutland*, 504; *CSPD 1638–39*, 340.
132. *CSPD 1639*, 48; HMC, *Rutland*, 504; *Correspondence of Nathan Walworth and Peter Seddon*, 42.
133. HMC, *Rutland*, 504–9.
134. *CSPD 1639*, 85; Terry, 'Visits of Charles I to Newcastle', 98–103. TNA, SP 16/422/67, has a plan of the king's pavilion and camp at Berwick.
135. HMC, *Rutland*, 509–12; Laud, *Works*, iii. 233.
136. TNA, SP 16/414/57; HMC, *Salisbury*, xxii. 303.
137. *The Diary of John Evelyn*, ed. William Bray, 6 vols (1879), i. 10–12, 38.
138. Guildhall Library, MS 2088/1 (St Andrew by the Wardrobe), MS 3556/1 (St Mary Aldermanbury), MS 4457/2 (St Stephen Coleman Street), and others.
139. See Chapter 9.
140. Huntington Library, Ellesmere MS 7851.

141. BL, Add. MS 75,354, fo. 7, Cumberland to his daughter Elizabeth, Countess Burlington, 26 September 1640.
142. John Taylor, *Englands Comfort, and Londons Ioy: Expressed in the Royall, Triumphant, and Magnificent Entertainment of our Dread Soveraigne Lord, King Charles, at his blessed and safe returne from Scotland* (1641), title page, 2, 3, 5; *Ovatio Carolina. The Triumph of King Charles* (1641), 13–17.
143. David Cressy, *England on Edge: Crisis and Revolution 1640–1642* (Oxford, 2006), 401. Royal travels are itemized in Sir Edward Walker (attrib.), *Iter Carolinum. Being a Succinct Relation of the Necessitated Marches, Retreats, and Sufferings of His Majesty Charls the I* (1660).
144. Bodleian Library, MS Additional 15,257, fos 82–92, a copy of 'A relation of what in part happened at Little Gidding upon the king's coming thither', collected by the antiquarian Thomas Hearne in 1731.
145. *A Letter Sent by a Yorkshire Gentleman to a Friend in London* (1642), 2.
146. *A True Relation of His Majesties Reception and Royall Entertainment at Lincoln: by the Knights, Esquires, Gentlemen, and Freeholders of the said County* (1642); *A Diurnall and Particular of the Last Weekes Daily Occurrents* (16–26 July 1642), 1–2, 7–8.

CHAPTER 6

1. Robert C. Johnson et al. (eds), *Commons Debates 1628*, 6 vols (New Haven, 1977), vi. 222. See also David Zaret, 'Petitions and the "Invention" of Public Opinion in the English Revolution', *American Journal of Sociology*, 101 (1996), 1497–1555.
2. Henry VIII in 1536, quoted in R. W. Hoyle, 'Petitioning as Popular Politics in Early Sixteenth-Century England', *Historical Research*, 75 (2002), 365–6.
3. R. W. Hoyle (ed.), *Heard before the King: Registers of Petitions to James I, 1603–1616* (List and Index Society, 38 and 39, 2006).
4. John Spencer, *A Discourse of Divers Petitions of High Concernment* (1641), sig. A2v.
5. Richard Cust, *Charles I: A Political Life* (Harlow, 2005), 53.
6. Charles I, *His Majesties Declaration: To All His Loving Subjects, Of the causes which moved him to dissolve the last Parliament* (1640), 54.
7. Cambridge University Library, University Archives, Collect. Admin. 8, 518–22.
8. Spencer, *Discourse of Divers Petitions*, 2–5.
9. Bodleian Library, Tanner MS 68, fo. 147, William Allanson to Samuel Wrighte, 8 October 1636, and fos 160–1 for the text of the petition.
10. TNA, REQ 1, 2, 3, and 4. I am grateful to Dr Tim Wales for his help exploring these records. See also TNA, SP 16/403 and SP 16/519, for batches of petitions.
11. *CSPD 1627–28*, 240.
12. *CSPD 1627–28*, 108.

13. *CSPD 1635–36*, 15.
14. BL, Harley MS 7000, letter of Theophilus Landonoy, 1626.
15. BL, Lansdowne MS 211, fo. 92.
16. John Nichols, *The History and Antiquities of the County of Leicestershire*, 4 vols (1795–1815), iii. 160.
17. TNA, REQ 2/296/28.
18. *CSPD 1625–26*, 206; *CSPD 1635–36*, 34.
19. TNA, SP 39/18/35, SP 39/19/31.
20. David Cressy, *Saltpeter: The Mother of Gunpowder* (Oxford, 2013), 94–7.
21. BL, Harley MS 1012, fos 11^{v}, 13^{v}, 14^{v}.
22. D. M. Barratt, 'The Bankes Papers: A First Report', *Bodleian Library Record*, 4 (1952–3), 313–23.
23. T. Brugis, *The Discovery of a Proiector* (1641), sig. B2.
24. TNA, SP 39/19/24.
25. TNA, SP 16/95/17, SP 16/295/18; *CSPD 1635*, 330. William Laud complained that his business at court was held up and that 'little or nothing can be done' until the king returned from Newmarket or Bagshot: *The Works of the Most Reverend Father in God, William Laud, D.D.*, ed. William Scott and James Bliss, 9 vols (Oxford, 1847–60), vi. 271, 314.
26. *CSPD 1635*, 432–3; TNA, SP 16/299/78. Heydon recalled these details in 1635 to remind Heath of certain transactions.
27. BL, Stowe MS 561, fo. 7.
28. *CSPD 1627–28*, 247, 298, 308; TNA, SP 16/74/12.
29. TNA, SP 39/18–23 for warrants 1625–8, SO 1–4 for Signet Office grants, permits, letters, licences, warrants, etc., 1627–44.
30. *CSPD 1625–26*, 234.
31. *A Royalist Notebook: The Commonplace Book of Sir John Oglander* (1936), ed. Francis Bamford, 30–1; Lindsay Boynton, 'Billeting: The Example of the Isle of Wight', *English Historical Review*, 74 (1959), 38.
32. Bodleian Library, MS Carte 1, fo. 457, Sir Patrick Wemys in 1641.
33. *CSPD 1631–33*, 128, 129; TNA, SP 16/198/9.
34. *The Earl of Strafforde's Letters and Dispatches*, ed. William Knowler, 2 vols (1739), i. 359–60.
35. Bodleian Library, MS Firth *c.* 4, fo. 495.
36. TNA, SP 16/120/35.
37. Huntington Library, Hastings Correspondence, Box 14, HA 4846, 4648, 4850, 4852.
38. Huntington Library, Hastings Correspondence, Box 15, HA 5547.
39. *The Correspondence (c.1626–1659) of Dorothy Percy Sidney, Countess of Leicester*, ed. Michael G. Brennan, Noel J. Kinnaman, and Margaret P. Hanney (Farnham and Burlington, VT, 2010), 63, 66, 73.
40. *Correspondence . . . of Dorothy Percy Sidney*, 112.

41. Peter Lake, 'The Collection of Ship Money in Cheshire during the Sixteen-Thirties: A Case Study of Relations between Central and Local Government', *Northern History*, 17 (1981), 53, citing BL, MS Harley 2093, fo. 92.
42. *Earl of Strafforde's Letters*, ii. 164.
43. Martin Parker, *The King, and a Poore Northerne Man* (1640), sig. B.
44. Cambridge University Library, University Archives, Collect. Admin. 8, 518–22.
45. *The Autobiography and Correspondence of Sir Simonds D'Ewes*, ed. James Orchard Halliwell, 2 vols (1845), ii. 68; Bodleian Library, MS Rawlinson A. 128, fo. 1; TNA, C115/106, no. 8397; BL, MS Harley 646, fo. 149; TNA, SP 16/215/9; *The Notebooks of Nehemiah Wallington, 1618–1654*, David Booy (Aldershot and Burlington, VT, 2007), 93; David Cressy, 'The Death of a Vice-Chancellor: Cambridge 1632', *History of Universities*, 26 (2012), 92–112.
46. Huntington Library, Ellesmere MS 6513. John Egerton, first Earl of Bridgewater (1579–1649), was President of the Council of the Marches, and also patron of John Milton, whose masque *Comus* was first performed at Ludlow in September 1633. 'My lord of Salisbury' was William Cecil, the second earl (1591–1668), a courtier and Privy Councillor to Charles I.
47. Huntington Library, Ellesmere MSS 6515, 6516, 6520. See Delamain's list of 'Bookes to be drawne up', including 'the royal scale', 'a tractate of the prince's highness', 'the prince elector's exercise', and 'practical fortification' (*CSPD 1625–49*, 467).
48. Huntington Library, Ellesmere MS 6521.
49. Richard Delamain, *Gram[m]elogia or, The Mathematicall Ring* (1630), sig. A2. For analysis of this 'hasty, ill-prepared and frequently amended publication', which appeared in at least four states by 1633, see D. J. Bryden, 'A Patchery and Confusion of Disjointed Stuffe: Richard Delamain's *Grammelogia* of 1631/3', *Transactions of the Cambridge Bibliographic Society*, 6 (1974), 158–66.
50. *CSPD 1629–31*, 138, 457; TNA, SP 16/154/61, SP 16/181/56.
51. Richard Delamain, *Grammelogia or, the Mathematicall Ring. Extracted from the Logarythmes, and Projected Circular* (1633?), sig. A3.
52. *CSPD 1631–33*, xviii.
53. William Oughtred, *The Circles of Proportion and the Horizontal Instrument... Translated into English and set forth for the publique benefit by William Forster* (1632), including 'The just apologie of Wil. Oughtred against the slanderous insimulations of Richard Delamain', sigs A–B3. See also E. R. G. Taylor, *The Mathematical Practitioners of Tudor & Stuart England* (Cambridge, 1954), 201.
54. HMC, *Salisbury*, xxii. 270.
55. *CSPD 1631–33*, 230; TNA, SP 16/205/90.
56. Huntington Library, Ellesmere MS 6521; Huntington Library, copy of Delamain, *Grammelogia*, Rare Book 59007.
57. *CSPD 1631–33*, 556–7; TNA, SP 16/233/19 and 20.
58. *ODNB*, sub 'Delamain Richard, the elder (d. 1644?)'.

59. *CSPD 1638–39*, 243.
60. *CSPD 1637–38*, 121; SP 16/377/126 and 127. See also *CSPD 1635*, 467, for payment of £10 to Richard Delamain in November 1635.
61. *CSPD 1637*, 289, 392; TNA, SP 16/363/49.
62. *CSPD 1639–40*, 191.
63. *CSPD 1641–43*, 450; HMC, *Fifth Report*, 82; *Journal of the House of Commons*, 10 vols (1802), iv. 197.
64. Sir Thomas Herbert, *Memoirs of the Last Two Years of the Reign of King Charles I* (1813), 187.
65. TNA, SP 16/169/5, SP 16/175/123; Huntington Library, Ellesmere MS 7950; *ODNB*, sub 'Norton, Bonham (1565–1635)'.
66. *CSPD 1635*, 31; TNA, SP 16/311/40.
67. BL, MS Harley 7000, fo. 470, George Gresley to Sir Thomas Puckering, 23 January 1634; *ODNB*, sub 'Nethersole, Sir Francis (*bap.* 1587, *d.* 1659)'.
68. TNA, SP 16/44/61.
69. Bodleian Library, MS Rawlinson C. 421, fo. 27; Michael Wigmore, *The Meteors: A Sermon* (1633), sig. C3.
70. BL, Add. MS 72418, fo. 81; TNA, PC 2/40, fo. 119. A similar attempt by mariners to gain the king's attention in 1626 led only to 'his majesty's high indignation' (TNA, SP 16/31/112); *APC 1626 June–Dec.*, 40, 306.
71. Andy Wood, *The Politics of Social Conflict: The Peak Country, 1520–1770* (Cambridge, 1999), 236–7.
72. TNA, SP 16/409/50, SP 16/392/45. Powell was also known as Edward Anderson.
73. BL, MS Harley 7000, fo. 470.
74. Bodleian Library, MS Tanner 68, fos 147, 160–1.
75. *Earl of Strafforde's Letters*, ii. 57.
76. Sheffield Archives, Wentworth Woodhouse Muniments, 21/203.
77. Charles Carlton, *Charles I: The Personal Monarch*, 2nd edn (1995), 239; Cust, *Charles I: A Political Life*, 345.
78. Sir Thomas Aston, *A Collection of Sundry Petitions Presented to the King's Most Excellent Majestie* (1642), sigs A2–A2^{v} and *passim*.
79. BL, Add. MS 33,936, fo. 265, Thomas Webb to William Moreton, May 1642.
80. *Barrington Family Letters 1628–1632*, ed. Arthur Searle (Camden Society, 4th ser., 28, 1983), 37, 77; TNA, SP 16/142/92.
81. A. Ar., *The Practise of Princes* (Amsterdam, 1630), 9.
82. TNA, SP 16/19/46.
83. TNA, SP 16/100/3.
84. TNA, SP 16/7/69, SP 16/9/31; *CSPD 1625–26*, 115.
85. TNA, SP 16/39/35.
86. *APC 1626 June–Dec.*, 348, 350; TNA, SP 16/105/67.
87. Birch (ed.), *Court and Times*, ii. 250, Edward Rossingham to Sir Thomas Puckering.

88. Bodleian Library, MS Bankes 18/34.
89. TNA, SP 16/49/64. Thomas Jarvis appears in the records again in 1630, denouncing Dorset magistrates as 'hypocrites and dissemblers', and attacking emigrants to New England as 'idolators, captivates and separatists' (Dorset History Centre, B2/8/1).
90. TNA, SP 16/132/35. Thomas Triplet, a student of Christ Church, did indeed gain preferment. BA in 1622, MA in 1625, in 1630 he became vicar of Woodham, Northumberland, and in 1631 rector of Whitburn, County Durham.
91. TNA, SP 16/132/35.
92. TNA, SP 16/142/92.
93. TNA, SP 16/243/5. Humfrey had nineteen years military service, mostly in Ireland and Holland. In a 'confession' dated March 1632 he identified himself as a part-time geomancer, a finder of lost goods, paying £6 annual rent 'near Bunhill in Finsbury Fields'. He also possessed a copyhold in Hampshire worth £24 a year. One of his visions involved the loss of his rapier, cloak, and hat, which were accoutrements of gentle status, though perhaps also the stuff of dreams.
94. TNA, SP 16/214/50, SP 16/281/4, SP 16/223/17, SP 16/246/19, SP 16/277/5.
95. TNA, SP 16/277/5.
96. Esther Cope, *Handmade of the Holy Spirit: Dame Eleanor Davies, Never Soe Mad a Ladie* (Ann Arbor, 1992), 36–7.
97. TNA, C115/106, no. 8451.
98. Laud, *Works*, iii. 220.
99. *CSPD 1635*, 270; TNA, SP 16/293/97, SP16/296/45, SP 16/536/5.
100. TNA, SP 16/317/16.
101. Bodleian Library, MS Bankes 18/1 and 2.
102. Spencer, *Discourse of Divers Petitions*, title page, 1, 5.
103. Spencer, *Discourse of Divers Petitions*, 2–8.
104. TNA, SP 16/423/23 and 28. This was the same Thomas Harrison who protested Justice Hutton's remarks in Hampden's case as 'treason' because they challenged the king's right to collect Ship Money.
105. The account of Grace Cary's attempt to meet the king is based on BL, Egerton MS 1044, fos 1–15, Cambridge University Library, Additional MS 32, fos 1–12; [Grace Cary] (as 'Theophilus Philaleithes Toxander'), *Vox Coeli to England, or, Englands Fore-Warning from Heaven* (1646), title page, 1–10, and Lady Eleanor Douglas (i.e. Davis), *Given to the Elector Prince Charles of the Rhyne from the Lady Eleanor, anno 1633* (1648), 5. Grace Cary appears briefly in Phyllis Mack, *Visionary Women: Ecstatic Prophecy in Seventeenth-Century England* (Berkeley and Los Angeles, 1994), 94, 97, 413, where she is identified as a 'puritan royalist'.

106. O. Ogle, W. H. Bliss, et al. (eds), *Calendar of the Clarendon State Papers Preserved in the Bodleian Library*, 5 vols (Oxford, 1872–1970), i. 205.
107. [Cary], *Vox Coeli*, 8–9.
108. TNA, SP 16/402/18; *CSPD 1638–39*, 301.
109. Bodleian Library, MS Rawlinson C. 573, 27, MS Bankes 18/10, fo. 17, MS Bankes, 18/8, fos 13–14.
110. TNA, SP 16/408/127.
111. *CSPD 1638–39*, 89–90; TNA, SP 16/401/19.
112. TNA, SP 16/415/100; *CSPD Addenda 1625–49*, 603.
113. BL, Add. MS 69,886, fos 120–1.
114. *The Letters, Speeches and Proclamations of King Charles I*, ed. Sir Charles Petrie (1935), 63, 70; Charles I, *Stuart Royal Proclamations: Volume II: Royal Proclamations of King Charles I 1625–1646*, ed. James F. Larkin (Oxford, 1983), 223.
115. John Taylor, *The Whole Life and Progresse of Henry Walker the Ironmonger* (1642), 4; Ernest Sirluck, 'To your tents, O Israel: A Lost Pamphlet', *Huntington Library Quarterly*, 19 (1955–6), 301–5; 1 Kings 12:16. Walker had previously dedicated *The Churches Purity* (1641), a fifteen-page attack on the Church of England, to King Charles.
116. J. P. Kenyon (ed.), *The Stuart Constitution 1603–1688*, 2nd edn (Cambridge, 1986), 220, citing the king's declaration of 26 May 1642 concerning Hull.
117. Bodleian Library, MS Ashmole 800, fo. 50.
118. TNA, SP 16/422/65.
119. Alan Everitt, *The Community of Kent and the Great Rebellion 1640–60* (Leicester, 1966), 65–6; Conrad Russell, *The Fall of the British Monarchies 1637–1642* (Oxford, 1991), 83; Mark Charles Fissel, *The Bishops' Wars: Charles I's Campaigns against Scotland 1638–1640* (Cambridge, 1994), 22. I am grateful to Charles Carlson and Mark Kishlansky for correspondence on this matter, and to Jason Peacey for directing me to the History of Parliament file on Sir Thomas Wilsford.
120. *Journal of the House of Commons*, i. 799; *CSPD 1623–25*, 237, 245, 261; TNA, SP 14/164, fo. 125; *The Oxinden Letters 1607–1642*, ed. Dorothy Gardiner (1933), 175, 212.
121. TNA, National Register of Archives, Bound Vol. 20594, 792, 799, 809.
122. Cf. William Shakespeare, *Henry V*, Act 4, prologue.

CHAPTER 7

1. The contested historiography on the Caroline church includes Nicholas Tyacke, *Anti-Calvinists: The Rise of English Arminianism, c. 1590–1640* (Oxford, 1987); Andrew Foster, 'Church Policies of the 1630s', in Richard Cust and Ann Hughes (eds), *Conflict in Early Stuart England: Studies in Religion and Politics 1603–1642* (1989), 193–223; Julian Davies, *The Caroline Captivity of the Church: Charles I and the Remoulding of Anglicanism* (Oxford, 1992); Kevin Sharpe, *The*

Personal Rule of Charles I (New Haven and London, 1992), 275–402; Peter Lake, 'The Laudian Style: Order, Uniformity and the Pursuit of the Beauty of Holiness in the 1630s', in Kenneth Fincham (ed.), *The Early Stuart Church, 1603–1642* (1993), 161–85; Anthony Milton, *Catholic and Reformed: The Roman and Protestant Churches in English Protestant Thought, 1600–1640* (Cambridge, 1995); Tom Webster, *Godly Clergy in Early Stuart England: The Caroline Puritan Movement, c.1620–1643* (Cambridge, 1997); Alexandra Walsham, 'The Parochial Roots of Laudianism Revisited: Catholics, Anti-Calvinists and "Parish Anglicans" in Early Stuart England', *Journal of Ecclesiastical History*, 49 (1998), 620–51. See also David Cressy, 'Conflict, Consensus, and the Willingness to Wink: The Erosion of Community in Charles I's England', *Huntington Library Quarterly*, 61 (2000), 131–49, and David Cressy, 'The Laudian Ascendancy', in David Cressy, *England on Edge: Crisis and Revolution 1640–1642* (Oxford, 2006), 129–48.

2. TNA, SP 16/339/82, *High Commission* v. *John Hansley*, 1636.
3. *Statutes of the Realm*, 1. Eliz, *c.* 2 (1559).
4. TNA, SP 16/17A.
5. *Constitutions and Canons Ecclesiastical. Treated upon by the Bishop of London* (1604), no. 55.
6. Bodleian Library, MS Rawlinson C 421, fo. 27.
7. HMC, *Fourth Report*, appendix, 125; Cambridge University Library, Ely Diocesan Records, D/2/51, fos 3^{v}, 61^{v}; Norfolk Record Office, ANW 3/32, ANW 6/8.
8. *Constitutions and Canons Ecclesiasticall; Treated upon by the Archbishops of Canterbury and York* (1640), sig. C3.
9. BL, Stowe MS 561, fo. 25, citing 26 Henry VIII *c.* 1.
10. *The Diary of Thomas Crosfield*, ed. Frederick S. Boas (Oxford, 1935), 14.
11. Edward Reynolds, *The Shieldes of the Earth* (1636), 8.
12. J. W. F. Hill, 'The Royalist Clergy of Lincolnshire', *Lincolnshire Architectural and Archaeological Society Reports and Papers*, vol. 2, part 1, NS for 1938 (Lincoln, 1940), 110.
13. Peter Heylyn, *Antidotum Lincolniense* (1637), 84.
14. East Sussex Record Office, QR/E/56/18.
15. Lancelot Andrewes, *XCVI Sermon . . . Published by His Majesties special Command* (1629). See also Peter E. McCullough, *Sermons at Court: Politics and Religion in Elizabethan and Jacobean Preaching* (Cambridge, 1998), 194–204.
16. TNA, SP 16/5/28.
17. *CSPD 1635–36*, 293, Charles to Norwich magistrates, 14 March 1636.
18. *Constitutions and Canons Ecclesiasticall; Treated upon by the Archbishops*, sigs B^{v}, G3^{v}.
19. Christopher Wren, *Parentalia; or, Memoirs of the Family of the Wrens* (1750), 46.
20. *Cabala, Mysteries of State, in Letters of the Great Ministers of K. James and K. Charles* (1654), 215. This was supposedly written in 1623, but its printing in 1654 had extra resonance in the wake of the regicide.

21. Bodleian Library, MS Eng. Hist. E. 28, fos 549–67; Charles Carlton, *Charles I: The Personal Monarch*, 2nd edn (1995), 62; Sharpe, *Personal Rule*, 280 n.
22. Bodleian Library, MS Eng. Hist. E. 28, fos 552–5, 566–7.
23. Bodleian Library, MS Eng. Hist. E. 28, fos 555, 561. Cf. Christopher Haigh, *The Plain Man's Pathways to Heaven: Kinds of Christianity in Post-Reformation England* (Oxford, 2007).
24. Bodleian Library, MS Tanner 71, fos 41–41v. Little is known about the lay penetration of the theological and ecclesiological controversies discussed in Tyacke, *Anti-Calvinists*, Sarah Mortimer, *Reason and Religion in the English Revolution: The Challenge of Socinianism* (Cambridge, 2010), and Charles W. A. Prior, *A Confusion of Tongues: Britain's Wars of Reformation, 1625–1642* (Oxford, 2012).
25. Charles I, *By the King. A Proclamation for the establishing of the Peace and Quiet of the Church of England* (14 June 1626); Charles I, *Stuart Royal Proclamations: Volume II: Royal Proclamations of King Charles I 1625–1646*, ed. James F. Larkin (Oxford, 1983), 90–3.
26. Nehemiah Rogers, *A Sermon Preached at the Second Trienniall Visitation* (1632), 10.
27. Edward Reynolds, *A Sermon Touching the Peace and Edification of the Church* (1638), 2, 11.
28. *The Letters, Speeches and Proclamations of King Charles I*, ed. Sir Charles Petrie (1935), 69. See also *Articles Agreed Upon . . . Re-printed by His Majesties Commandment: with his royal declaration prefixed thereunto* (1630), 1, 3.
29. Staffordshire Record Office, D.1287/18/2/48, Bridgeman correspondence.
30. *Obedience Active and Passive Due to the Supream Power* (Oxford, 1643), 1, 2, 4–9, 16. See also Chapter 9.
31. *The Letters of John Chamberlain*, ed. Norman Egbert McClure (American Philosophical Society Memoirs, vol. 12, Philadelphia, 1939), 609, Chamberlain to Sir Dudley Carleton, 9 April 1625.
32. *The Works of the Most Reverend Father in God, William Laud, D.D.*, ed. William Scott and James Bliss, 9 vols (Oxford, 1847–60), i *passim*.
33. Davies, *Caroline Captivity*, 10–45, 131. See also *The Diary of Sir Henry Slingsby*, ed. Daniel Parsons (1836), 9, on 'the benefit of confession' in preparation for communion.
34. HMC, *De L'Isle*, vi. 99.
35. *The Diary of Robert Woodford, 1637–1641*, ed. John Fielding (Camden Society, 5th ser., vol. 42, 2012), 246.
36. TNA, SP 16/5/28.
37. Bodleian, MS Jones 17, fo. 304.
38. TNA, SP 16/193/69.
39. *Constitutions and Canons Ecclesiasticall: Treated upon by the Archbishops*, 6, 8, sig. Ev.
40. See Chapter 6.
41. *The Earl of Strafforde's Letters and Dispatches*, ed. William Knowler, 2 vols (1739), ii. 142.

42. John Cordy Jeaffreson (ed.), *Middlesex County Records. Vol. III . . . 1 Charles I to 18 Charles II* (Clerkenwell, 1888), 74, 81; J. S. Cockburn (ed.), *Calendar of Assize Records: Kent Indictments. Charles I* (1995), 424; Bodleian Library, MS Bankes 18/19.
43. Bodleian Library, MS Carte 77, fo. 370.
44. *CSPD 1635–36*, 362; *CSPD 1636–37*, 37; *CSPD 1640*, 174, 272, 522; TNA, SP 16/326/18; HMC, *Portland*, iii. 67.
45. Bodleian Library, MS Bankes 37/37, fo. 80; BL, Egerton MS 2716, fo. 302; TNA, SP 16/391/85, SP 16/406/82.
46. *CSPD 1628–29*, 347; TNA, SP 16/118/35 and 56.
47. Caroline Hibbard, *Charles I and the Popish* Plot (Chapel Hill, NC, 1983), 141.
48. Bodleian Library, MS Rawlinson B 243, fos 18^{v}–19.
49. *Constitutions and Canons Ecclesiasticall; Treated upon by the Archbishops*, 4–5.
50. Huntington Library, Stowe–Temple Correspondence, Box 11, STT 1876, 1880.
51. TNA, SP 16/457/4.
52. Devon Record Office, Exeter Sessions Book 64, fo. 6^{v}.
53. Bodleian Library, MS Nalson 12, fo. 46.
54. Norfolk Record Office, DN/VIS 6/1. See also Michael C. Questier, *Catholicism and Community in Early Modern England: Politics, Patronage and Religion, c.1550–1640* (Cambridge, 2006).
55. Austin Woolrych, *Britain in Revolution 1625–1660* (Oxford, 2002), 32.
56. O. Ogle, W. H. Bliss, et al. (eds), *Calendar of the Clarendon State Papers Preserved in the Bodleian Library*, 5 vols (Oxford, 1872), i. 57.
57. Alexandra Walsham, *The Reformation of the Landscape: Religion, Identity, and Memory in Early Modern Britain and Ireland* (Oxford, 2011); David Cressy, 'The Downfall of Cheapside Cross: Vandalism, Ridicule, and Iconoclasm', in Cressy, *Travesties and Transgressions in Tudor and Stuart England* (Oxford, 2000), 234–50.
58. Wallace Notestein, Frances Helen Relf, and Hartley Simpson (eds), *Commons Debates 1621*, 7 vols. (New Haven, 1935), iii. 121.
59. J. H. E. Bennett and J. C. Dewhurst (eds), *Quarter Sessions Records with other Records of the Justices of the Peace for the County Palatinate of Chester 1559–1760* (Record Society of Lancashire and Cheshire, vol. 94, 1940), 94.
60. K. J. Lindley, 'The Lay Catholics of England in the Reign of Charles I, *Journal of Ecclesiastical History*, 22 (1971), 204.
61. Bodleian Library, MS Carte 77, fo. 388^{v}.
62. TNA, SP 16/349/116.
63. *CSP Venice, 1636–39*, 217; Lindley, 'Lay Catholics', 203–4.
64. *CSPD 1625–26*, 16.
65. *Diary of John Rous, Incumbent of Santon Downham, Suffolk, from 1625 to 1642*, ed. Margaret Anne Everett Green (Camden Society, OS, vol. 66, 1856), 2.
66. Staffordshire Record Office, D 1287/18/2, 24, Bridgeman correspondence.

67. TNA, SO 3/9. Lindley, 'Lay Catholics', 210, observes that King Charles 'exercised this prerogative very rarely'.
68. Staffordshire Record Office, D.1287/18/2, 45, Bridgeman correspondence; G. E. Aylmer, *The King's Servants: The Civil Service of Charles I, 1625–42* (1961), 138–9.
69. Lindley, 'Lay Catholics', 212.
70. Oxfordshire Record Office, Diocesan Papers *c.* 2, fo. 31.
71. Cressy, *Travesties and Transgressions*, 125.
72. Borthwick Institute, Cause papers and visitation books, diocese of Chester, C/V/CB 2, fo 77^{v}.
73. TNA, SP 16/122/38, SP 16/122/54, SP 16/123/12, SP 16/530/37.
74. Lindley, 'Lay Catholics', 203–4.
75. John Bramhall, *The Serpent Salve, or, A Remedie for the Biting of an Aspe* (York?, 1643), sig. D.
76. Richard Montague, *Appello Caesarem. A Iust Appeale* (1625), 321.
77. *The Correspondence of John Cosin*, part 1, ed. George Ornsby (Surtees Society, vol. 52, 1869), 123, 125.
78. John Brinsley, *The Glorie of the Latter Temple* (1631), 16.
79. Edward Cardwell, *A History of Conferences* (Oxford, 1840), 198–9. See also George Yule, 'James VI and I: Furnishing the Churches in his Two Kingdoms', in Anthony Fletcher and Peter Roberts (eds), *Religion, Culture and Society in Early Modern Britain: Essays in Honor of Patrick Collinson* (Cambridge, 1994), 188; Kenneth Fincham and Peter Lake, 'The Ecclesiastical Policies of James I and Charles I', in Fincham (ed.), *Early Stuart Church*, 23–49; Peter White, 'The *Via Media* in the Early Stuart Church', in Fincham (ed.), *Early Stuart Church*, 211–30; and Cressy, 'Conflict, Consensus, and the Willingness to Wink'. Kevin Sharpe, 'Private Conscience and Public Duty in the Writings of Charles I', *Historical Journal*, 40 (1997), 644, notes that, 'for all his protestations of consistency between "theory" and "practice," what James wrote was quite other than how he behaved'. For a hostile history of Jacobean ecclesiastical laxity, written in the 1630s, see Christopher Dow, *Innovations Unjustly Charged upon the Present Church and State* (1637), 191–8.
80. On local implementation, see John Fielding, 'Arminianism in the Localities: Peterborough Diocese, 1603–1642', in Fincham (ed.), *Early Stuart Church*, 93–113; Andrew Cambers, 'Pastoral Laudianism? Religious Politics in the 1630s: A Leicestershire Rector's Annotations', *Midland History*, 27 (2002), 38–51; John Walter, '"Affronts & Insolences": The Voices of Radwinter and Popular Opposition to Laudianism', *English Historical Review*, 122 (2007), 25–60; Sylvia Watts, 'The Impact of Laudianism on the Parish: The Evidence of Staffordshire and North Shropshire', *Midland History*, 33 (2008), 21–42.
81. Walsham, 'Parochial Roots of Laudianism', 621, 628, 637–42.
82. See, e.g., Berkshire Record Office, D/P8/5/1, Ashampstead accounts; Lincolnshire Archives, Louth St James accounts, 7/5; William Salt Library,

Stafford, MS 236/27, Eccleshall accounts; Cambridge University Library, MS Mm. 4. 29, Tredington act book, fo. 112; Cambridge University Library, Ely Diocesan Records, B/2/52, fos 6, 9, 9v, 11, 21, 49v; Gloucestershire Archives, GDR 201, fos 29, 33v; Somerset Archives, D/D/Ca 331, fo. 12; Borthwick Institute, Cause papers and visitations books, province and diocese of York, V. 1637. See also Foster, 'Church Policies in the 1630s', 215–16; Graham Parry, *The Arts of the Anglican Counter-Reformation: Glory, Laud and Honour* (Woodbridge, 2006); Kenneth Fincham and Nicholas Tyacke, *Altars Restored: The Changing Face of English Religious Worship, 1547–c.1700* (Oxford, 2007).

83. *Diary of Thomas Crosfield*, 74.
84. Robert Skinner, *A Sermon Preached Before the King at White-Hall* (1634), 14–15, 29, 35. See also Thomas Fuller, *The Church History of Britain*, ed. J. S. Brewer, 6 vols (Oxford, 1845), vi. 303, dating 'the general mending, beautifying and adorning of all English churches' to the early 1630s.
85. Heylyn, *Antidotum Lincolniense*, 84, 86. See also R. T., *De Templis, a Treatise of Temples* (1638), 177, 183–4, 201; Edward Boughen, *A Sermon Concerning Decencie and Order in the Church* (1638), 3.
86. Skinner, *Sermon Preached Before the King*, 29. See also Anthony Cade, *A Sermon Necessarie for these Times* (1639), sig. ¶2v; Robert Abbot, *The Holinesse of Christian Churches* (1638), 32; Walter Balcanquall, *The Honour of Christian Churches* (1633), 8, 15; R. T., *De Templis*, 176–7, 183–4, 195–6, 198, 200–1; Alexander Ross, *Gods House, or the House of Prayer Vindicated from Prophaneness and Sacriledge* (1642), 10.
87. *The Last Will and Testament of Superstition, Eldest Daughter to Antichrist* (1642), sig. A3v; John Gauden, *The Love of Truth and Peace* (1641), 3; Edmund Gurnay, *An Appendix unto the Homily against Images in Churches* (1641), repr. as *Gurnay Redvivus* (1660), 2, 9–10, 40, 59; John Milton, *Of Reformation touching church-discipline in England* (1641), 2, 3, 4, 29, 63. See also Daniel Cawdrey, *Superstitio Superstes: or, the Reliques of Superstition Newly Revived* (1641), sig. *4; John Vicars, *The Sinfulness and Unlawfulness, of having or making the Picture of Christ's Humanity* (1641), 'to the readers', 35, 65; Henry Burton, *Englands Bondage and Hope of Deliverance* (1641), 28; Peter Smart, *A Catalogue of Superstitious Innovations* (1642), 9, 14, 16.
88. Huntington Library, Hastings MS, HA 5537.
89. TNA, SP 16/380/94; Thomas Birch (ed.), *The Court and Times of Charles the First*, 2 vols (1848), ii. 259, Edward Rossingham to Sir Thomas Puckering, 4 January 1637; Esther S. Cope, *Handmaid of the Holy Spirit: Dame Eleanor Davies, Never Soe Mad a Ladie* (Ann Arbor, 1992), 83–4.
90. Edward Boughen, *Two Sermons: The First, Preached at Canterbury* (1635), 20; Boughen, *Sermon Concerning Decencie and Order*, 11.
91. Boughen, *Sermon Concerning Decencie and Order*, 12.
92. Skinner, *Sermon Preached Before the King*, 9.

93. Samuel Hoard, *The Churches Authority Asserted: In a Sermon Preached at Chelmsford* (1638), 53.
94. William Hardwick, *Conformity with Piety, Requisite in Gods Service* (1638), 11.
95. Philippians 2:10; *The Acts of the High Commission Court within the Diocese of Durham*, ed. W. H. D. Longstaff (Surtees Society, vol. 34, 1857), 190. Lapthorne was cited before the High Commission for preaching these words at Barnard Castle in 1636.
96. Cheshire Record Office, EDC 5/1628/67.
97. *The Petition and Article Exhibited in Parliament against Doctor Heywood* (1641), 1, 5–7, 9.
98. Skinner, *Sermon Preached Before the King*, 6.
99. Peter Studley, *The Looking-Glasse of Schisme* (1635), 76–7.
100. Thomas Lawrence, *Two Sermons. The First Preached at St Maries in Oxford* (Oxford, 1635), 4.
101. Foulke Robarts, *God's Holy House and Service* (1639), 75. See also John Swan, *Profanomastix. Or, a Brief and Necessarie Direction concerning the respects which we Owe to God, and his House* (1639), 17, 47–9.
102. Robert Shelford, *Five Pious and Learned Discourses* (Cambridge, 1635), 14–16.
103. William Quelch, *Church Customs Vindicated* (1636), 32, 51.
104. John Taylor, *Differing Worships, or, The Oddes, between some Knights Service and God's* (1640), 6.
105. Paul Griffiths, *Lost Londons: Change, Crime and Control in the Capital City, 1550–1660* (Cambridge, 2008), 173.
106. A. Percival Moore (ed.), 'The Metropolitical Visitation of Archdeacon [*sic*] Laud', *Associated Architectural Societies Reports and Papers*, 29 (1907), 490, 510, 521. See also Somerset Archives, D/D/Ca. 313, fo. 86^{v}.
107. Moore (ed.), 'Metropolitical Visitation', 523.
108. *Acts of the High Commission Court within the Diocese of Durham*, 157–8, 165.
109. Northamptonshire Record Office, Archdeaconry Correction Book 65, fo. 31^{v}. See also Cambridge University Library, Ely Diocesan Records, B/2/52, fo. 9^{v}.
110. Durham Cathedral Archives, DCS/SJB/7, fo. 30.
111. *Correspondence of John Cosin*, part 1, 174.
112. Lambeth Palace Library, MS 943, fos 625, 631–2.
113. Cressy, *Travesties and Transgressions*, 186–212; Davies, *Caroline Captivity*, 205–50; Sharpe, *Personal Rule*, 333–45; Kenneth Fincham, 'The Restoration of Altars in the 1630s', *Historical Journal*, 44 (2001), 919–40; Fincham and Tyacke, *Altars Restored*.
114. TNA, SP 16/223/17.
115. Fincham, 'Restoration of Altars', 922–7, 940.
116. *Constitutions and Canons Ecclesiasticall: Treated upon by the Archbishops*, sigs E3^{v}–E4^{v}.
117. Charles Chauncy, *The Retraction of Mr Charles Chancy* (1641), 6.

118. *Winthrop Papers*, iii. *1631–1637* (Massachusetts Historical Society, Boston, 1943), 356.
119. BL, Add. MS 11,045, fo. 19^{v}, Rossingham newsletter.
120. *CSPD 1640–41*, 525.
121. Bodleian Library, MS Rawlinson D. 158, fos 46–46^{v}, 50^{v}.
122. R. F. B. Hodgkinson (ed.), 'Extracts from the Act Books of the Archdeacons of Nottingham', *Transactions of the Thoroton Society*, 31 (1928), 136–7.
123. Parliamentary Archives, House of Lords Main Papers, undated petition of 1640.
124. Guildhall Library, MS 9064/18, fo. 23^{v}.
125. Cambers, 'Pastoral Laudianism?', 46.
126. Patrick Collinson, *The Religion of Protestants: The Church in English Society 1559–1625* (Oxford, 1982); Nicholas Tyacke, *The Fortunes of English Puritanism, 1603–1640* (1990); Peter Lake, *The Boxmaker's Revenge: 'Orthodoxy', 'Heterodoxy', and the Politics of the Parish in Early Stuart London* (Stanford, 2001); David R. Como, *Blown by the Spirit: Puritanism and the Emergence of an Antinomian Underground in Pre-Civil-War England* (Stanford, 2004).
127. Laud, *Works*, iii. 159.
128. Huntington Library, Stowe–Temple Correspondence, Box 11, STT 1891.
129. TNA, SP 16/393/15, SP 16/393/75.
130. TNA, SP 16/540, Morton letters no. 22; Haigh, *Plain Man's Pathways*, 18.
131. Nehemiah Wallington, *Historical Notices of Events Occurring Chiefly in the Reign of Charles I*, 2 vols (1869), i. 8, 9, 20, 24, 25, 26, 61, 72, 130, 139, 148.
132. David Como, 'Radical Puritanism, *c.*1558–1660', in John Coffey and Paul C. H. Lim (eds), *The Cambridge Companion to Puritanism* (Cambridge, 2008), 241–58.
133. Helen Stocks and W. H. Stevenson (eds), *Records of the Borough of Leicester . . . 1603–1688* (Cambridge 1923), 268.
134. Moore (ed.), 'Metropolitical Visitation', 520.
135. TNA, SP 16/280/33.
136. Oxfordshire Record Office, Archdeaconry Papers *c.* 12, fos 344–344^{v}.
137. Borthwick Institute, Cause papers and visitations books, province and diocese of York, V. 1629–30, fo. 108^{v}; Cheshire Record Office, EDC 5/1636/62.
138. Moore (ed.), 'Metropolitical Visitation', 505.
139. Roger Quatermayne, *Quatermayns Conquest Over Canterburies Court* (1642), 28.
140. BL, Add. MS 22,084, reverse foliation, fo. 4.
141. *Letters of John Chamberlain*, ed. McClure, 626, Chamberlain to Sir Dudley Carleton, 25 June 1625; Birch (ed.), *Court and Times*, i. 36.
142. *Barrington Family Letters 1628–1632*, ed. Arthur Searle (Camden Society, 4th ser., 28, 1983), 37.
143. *Barrington Family Letters*, 49, 56, 60, 77.

144. Sir John Eliot, *De Jure Maiestatis, or, Political Treatise of Government (1628–30) and the Letter-Book of Sir John Eliot (1625–1632)*, ed. Alexander B. Grosart, 2 vols (1882), ii. 39.
145. *The Saltonstall Papers . . . Volume I: 1607–1789*, ed. Robert E. Moody (Boston, 1972), 119.
146. *Winthrop Papers*, iii. 127.
147. *Diary of Robert Woodford*, 104, 298, 306.
148. TNA, SP 16/355/8, SP 16/361/64.
149. TNA, SP 16/350/54; William Hunt, *The Puritan Moment: The Coming of Revolution in an English County* (Cambridge, MA, 1983), 274, 276.
150. TNA, SP 16/540/4, Morton letters no. 22. The document is unattributed, but is linked to Morton's correspondence and is apparently in his hand.
151. *Articles of Enquiry and Direction for the Diocese of Norwich, in the First Visitation of the Reverend Father in God, Richard Mountaigu* (1638), sig. C[v].
152. *Complaints Concerning Corruptions and Grievances in Church Government* (1641), 4.
153. John Elborow, *Euodias and Syntyche: or, The Female Zelots of the Church of Philippi* (1637), 6–18.
154. Wallington, *Historical Notices*, i. 61.
155. *CSPD 1641–43*, 131; BL, Add. MS 5,829, fo. 9; John Harris, *The Puritanes Impuritie: Or the Anatomie of a Puritane or Separatist* (1641), 1–5. These terms appear in Huntington Library, Hastings MS, HM 6066, 'A New Ballad Called the Northamptonshire High Constable', *c.*1638, which tells the story of a puritan minister hung for murder.
156. *Constitutions and Canons Ecclesiasticall: Treated upon by the Archbishops*, 3, sig. E.
157. Christopher Hill, *The Economic Problems of the Church from Archbishop Whitgift to the Long Parliament* (Oxford, 1956), 210; Laud, *Works*, v. 327.
158. Humphrey Sydenham, *Moses and Aaron, or The Affinitie of Civill and Ecclesiastick Power* (1636), 141.
159. Richard Bayly, *The Shepheards Starre, or the Ministers Guide* (1640), 4.
160. Hardwick, *Conformity with Piety*, 8; Francis Rogers, *A Visitation Sermon Preached at the Lord Archbishops Trienniall and Ordinary Visitation* (1633), sig. B2.
161. Reynolds, *Sermon Touching the Peace and Edification of the Church*, 43.
162. Haigh, *Plain Man's Pathways*, 102.
163. George Herbert, 'A Priest to the Temple or, The Country Parson' [*c.*1632], in *The Works of George Herbert*, ed. F. E. Hutchinson (Oxford, 1941), 233, 237, 265.
164. Richard Baxter, *Confirmation and Restauration, The Necessary Means of Reformation* (1658), 162.
165. *Correspondence of John Cosin*, part 1, 218.
166. Huntington Library, Stowe–Temple Correspondence, Box 10, STT 963, Nathaniel Gyles to Sir Peter Temple, 10 December 1635.
167. *The Correspondence of Isaac Basire, DD.*, ed. W. N. Darnell (1831), 31.
168. *A Remonstrance on the behalfe of Cumberland and Westmerland* (1641), 3.
169. Bodleian Library, MS Rawlinson D. 399, fo. 184.

170. Robert Bolton, *Some Generall Directions for a Comfortable Walking with God*, 5th edn (1638), 115–16; Hardwick, *Conformity with Piety*, 8.
171. Somerset Archives, D/D/Cd. 66, fo. 173.
172. *CSPD 1635–36*, 105.
173. Bodleian Library, MS Carte 77, fo. 375.
174. Cheshire Record Office, EDC 5/1625/12.
175. Cheshire Record Office, EDC 5/1628/59. See also Cheshire Record Office, EDC 5/1634/104, 119.
176. *Acts of the High Commission Court within the Diocese of Durham*, 5.
177. Bodleian Library, Rawlinson MS D 363, fos 270–322. Note also Thomas Peckstone, vicar of Weston, Somerset, from 1598 to 1639, who reportedly had two bastards by two sisters, yet 'he winked at it' and 'seemed to huddle up his filthy and beastly whoredom' (Somerset Archives, D/D/Cd. 66, fo. 173).
178. Cheshire Record Office, EDC 5/1631/24; Norfolk Record Office, ANW 3/32.
179. TNA, SP 16/383/46, SP 16/393/93.
180. Bodleian Library, MS J. Walker C 11, fo. 63.
181. Cheshire Record Office, EDC 5/1640/71.
182. Moore (ed.), 'Metropolitical Visitation', 524.
183. Cheshire Record Office, EDC 5/1634/24, 25, 81, EDC 5/1635/58, 59.
184. Huntington Library, Hastings MS, HM 6066, fo. 3.
185. Judith Maltby, *Prayer Book and People in Elizabethan and Early Stuart England* (Cambridge, 1998); Christopher Marsh, 'Common Prayer in England, 1560–1640: The View from the Pew', *Past & Present*, 171 (2001), 66–94; Christopher Marsh, 'Sacred Space in England, 1560–1640: The View from the Pew', *Journal of Ecclesiastical History*, 53 (2002), 286–311; Christopher Marsh, 'Order and Place in England, 1560–1640', *Journal of British Studies*, 49 (2005), 3–26.
186. *Stuart Royal Proclamations*, ed. Larkin, 47, 91–3; *Constitutions and Canons Ecclesiastical. Treated upon by the Bishop of London*, canon 18.
187. Haigh, *Plain Man's Pathways*, 17–56.
188. Baxter, *Confirmation and Restauration*, 157–65; Eamon Duffy, 'The Godly and the Multitude in Stuart England', *Seventeenth Century*, 1 (1986), 31–55.
189. Nottingham University Library, Manuscripts and Special Collections, AN/A 47/1, fo. 183^{v}.
190. Haigh, *Plain Man's Pathways*, 50–3; Centre for Buckinghamshire Studies, D/A/V4, fo. 53^{v}; Norfolk Record Office, DN/VIS 6/1, fo. 55, VIS 7/1.
191. Norfolk Record Office, ANF/1/4.
192. TNA, SP 16/322/32.
193. Centre for Buckinghamshire Studies, D/A/V4, fo. 53^{v}.
194. Borthwick Institute, Cause papers and visitations books, province and diocese of York, V. 1627/2.
195. *CSPD 1639*, 367.

196. Hardwick, *Conformity with Piety*, 6.
197. Lichfield Record Office, B/V/1/64.
198. Cheshire Record Office, EDC 5/1628/20.
199. TNA, SP 16/355/114. See also London Metropolitan Archives, DL/C/319, fo. 69.
200. Swan, *Profanomastix*, 60.
201. Haigh, *Plain Man's Pathways*, 171.
202. Henry Paynter, *Saint Pauls Rule for Religious Performances* (1632), 6–7.
203. Abbot, *Holinesse of Christian Churches*, 15, 27.
204. Hardwick, *Conformity with Piety*, 11, 12.
205. Skinner, *Sermon Preached Before the King*, 26.
206. Balcanquall, *Honour of Christian Churches*, 16.
207. TNA, SP 16/285/47, instructions to Sir Nathaniel Brent, March 1635. See also Boughen, *Sermon Concerning Decencie and Order*, 1.
208. Borthwick Institute, Cause papers and visitations books, province and diocese of York, V. 1627, V. 1629–30; Cambridge University Library, Ely Diocesan Records, B/2/53, D/2/51; Leicestershire Record Office, I D 41/13/61; Lichfield Record Office, B/V/1/55, 28, B/V/1/61, 25; Oxfordshire Record Office, Diocesan Papers *c.* 2; Norfolk Record Office, ANF/1/4; Somerset Archives, D.D. Ca. 333.
209. Centre for Buckinghamshire Studies, D/A/V3; Cambridge University Library, Ely Diocesan Records, B/2/5; Cheshire Record Office, EDC 5/1627/42, EDC 5/1632/34, EDC 5/1636/12; Durham Cathedral Archives, DCD/SJB 7; Hereford Record Office, Office Court Books, Box 27; Hertfordshire Record Office, ASA 7/32; Lichfield Record Office, B/V/1/66; Norfolk Record Office, ANW 3/32, DN/VIS 6/1, DN/VIS 7/1; Oxfordshire Record Office, Archdeaconry Papers *c.* 12, Diocesan Papers *c.* 2; Somerset Archives, D.D. Ca. 331.
210. Essex Record Office, D/AED/9, fo. 18.
211. Cambridge University Library, Ely Diocesan Records, B/2/52, fos 26, 27^{v}.
212. Bodleian Library, MS Rawlinson A 128, fos 12–13^{v}; Borthwick Institute, Cause papers and visitations books, province and diocese of York, V. 1627, fo. 382; Centre for Buckinghamshire Studies, D/A/V2, fo. 92; Cheshire Record Office, EDC 5/1627/12, EDC 5/1631/3 and 10, EDC 5/1636/83, EDC 5/1639/8; Norfolk Record Office, ANW 2/72, ANW 3/32.
213. Bob Machin, '"To take theire plases wheare they shall not offend others"—the 1635 Re-Seating of Puddletown Church, Dorset', *Transactions of the Ancient Monuments Society*, 53 (2009), 7–14.
214. Cambridgeshire Record Office, P 30/4/2, fo. 30.
215. Cheshire Record Office, QJF 54/4, fo. 153.
216. Cheshire Record Office, EDC 5/1631/5, EDC 5/1632/66.
217. Borthwick Institute, Cause papers and visitations books, province and diocese of York, V. 1629–30, fo. 145.
218. Bodleian Library, MS Rawlinson A. 128, fos 12–13^{v}.

219. Cheshire Record Office, QJF 70/4, fo. 24.
220. Cambridge University Library, Ely Diocesan Records, D/2/51, fo. 47.
221. Cheshire Record Office, EDC 5/1629/8.
222. Centre for Buckinghamshire Studies, D/A/V2, fo. 177. For 'fire and brimstone', see Psalms 11:6, Ezekiel 38:23, and Revelation 14:10.
223. Somerset Archives, D/D/Ca. 310.
224. TNA, SP 16/287/31. See similar in Cheshire Record Office, EDC 5/1630/92.
225. Borthwick Institute, Cause papers and visitations books, province and diocese of York, V. 1629–30, fos 5[v], 16[v], 139[v], 173, 191[v]; Lincolnshire Archives, Vj.21, fo. 39[v]; Norfolk Record Office, DN/VIS 6/4, DN/VIS 7/1; Northamptonshire Record Office, Archdeaconry Correction Books 1627–1630, 339; Nottingham University Library, Manuscripts and Special Collections, AN/A 47/1, fo. 86[v]; Moore (ed.), 'Metropolitical Visitation', 497–8.
226. Cambridge University Library, Ely Diocesan Records, D/2/51, fo. 19[v].
227. Norfolk Record Office, DN/VIS 6/1.
228. Norfolk Record Office, DN/VIS 7/1.
229. Robert Shelford, *Five Pious and Learned Discourses* (Cambridge, 1635), 55.
230. Borthwick Institute, Cause papers and visitation books, diocese of Chester, C/V/CB 2, fo. 25[v]; Centre for Buckinghamshire Studies, D/A/V2, fo. 93[v]; Cambridge University Library, Ely Diocesan Records, D/2/51, fo. 9[v]; Gloucestershire Archives, GDR 201, fos 2[v], 58[v], 60; London Metropolitan Archives, DL/C/319, fos 51[v], 118[v]; Norfolk Record Office, DN/VIS 6/4; Northamptonshire Record Office, Archdeaconry Correction Books, 1627–1630, 53; Oxfordshire Record Office, Diocesan Papers *c.* 2, fos 4, 172. See also TNA, SP 16/43/20, for Bishop George Mountaigne on 'this profane abuse, scandalous to our religion'.
231. Haigh, *Plain Man's Pathways*, 120, 138.
232. Norfolk Record Office, DN/VIS 6/1, fo. 89.
233. Borthwick Institute, Cause papers and visitations books, province and diocese of York, V. 1636, fo. 258.
234. Centre for Buckinghamshire Studies, D/A/V2, fo. 82.
235. Norfolk Record Office, DN/VIS 7/1.
236. Borthwick Institute, Cause papers and visitations books, province and diocese of York, V. 1636, fo. 25; Cause papers and visitation books, diocese of Chester, R VI.A 23, fo. 406[v]; Centre for Buckinghamshire Studies, D/A/C/6, fo. 2, D/A/V3, fo. 114; Cambridge University Library, MS Mm. 4. 29, fos 104[v], 105, 108; Guildhall Library, MS 9064/18, fo. 67[v]; Lichfield Record Office, B/V/1/66; London Metropolitan Archives, DL/C/319, fo. 69. See also Keith Thomas, 'The Place of Laughter in Tudor and Stuart England', *TLS* (21 January 1977), 77–81.
237. Norfolk Record Office, DN/VIS 6/4.
238. Centre for Buckinghamshire Studies, D/A/V4, fo. 4.
239. Cambridge University Library, Ely Diocesan Records, D/2/51, fo. 53[v].

240. Norfolk Record Office, ANW 6/8.
241. Norfolk Record Office, DN/VIS 6/4.
242. Borthwick Institute, Cause papers and visitations books, province and diocese of York, V. 1636, fo. 139^{v}.
243. Abbot, *Holinesse of Christian Churches*, 13.
244. *Records of Early English Drama: Somerset*, ed. James Stokes (London and Toronto, 1996), 6.
245. BL, Add. MS 11,045, fo. 75^{v}.
246. Borthwick Institute, Cause papers and visitations books, province and diocese of York, V. 1627; Centre for Buckinghamshire Studies, D/A/C/6; Cambridge University Library, Ely Diocesan Records, D/2/51; Hertfordshire Record Office, ASA 7/32; Lichfield Record Office, B/V/1/64; Norfolk Record Office, ANW 3/32, DN/VIS 6/4, DN/VIS 7/1; Oxfordshire Record Office, Archdeaconry Papers *c.* 155; Haigh, *Plain Man's Pathways*, 90.
247. Norfolk Record Office, ANW 2/7s, fos 7^{v}–8.
248. TNA, SP 16/357/174; Cheshire Record Office, EDC 5/1637/38.
249. Borthwick Institute, Cause papers and visitation books, diocese of Chester, R VI.A 23, fo. 493^{v}; Cambridge University Library, Ely Diocesan Records, B/2/52, fo. 60^{v}; Cheshire Record Office, EDC 5/1640/94; Norfolk Record Office, DN/VIS 7/1. See also John Craig, 'Psalms, Groans and Dog-Whippers: The Soundscape of Sacred Space in the English Parish Church, 1547–1642', in Will Coster and Andrew Spicer (eds), *Sacred Space in Early Modern Europe* (Cambridge, 2005), 104–23.
250. Bodleian Library, MS Rawlinson D 1480, fo. 118.
251. Kenneth Fincham (ed.), *Visitation Articles and Injunctions of the Early Stuart Church*, 2 vols (Woodbridge, 1994–8), ii. 108, 148, 195.
252. TNA, SP 16/370/90.
253. Centre for Buckinghamshire Studies, D/A/V4, fo. 111^{v}.
254. TNA, SP 16/357/174.
255. Cambridge University Library, Ely Diocesan Records, B/2/53, fo. 17^{v}.
256. Norfolk Record Office, DN/VIS 6/4.
257. Cheshire Record Office, EDC 5/1634/54.
258. Borthwick Institute, Cause papers and visitations books, province and diocese of York, V. 1629–30, fos 114^{v}, 184.
259. Borthwick Institute, Cause papers and visitations books, province and diocese of York, V. 1627, fo. 283^{v}, V. 1640, fo. 130.
260. Leicestershire Record Office, I D 41/21.
261. Thomas Cheshire, *A True Copy of that Sermon which was preached at S. Pauls the tenth day of October last* (1641), 12.
262. *Statutes of the Realm*, 1 Eliz. I, *c.* 2.
263. Guildhall Library, MS 9064/19, fo. 54.
264. Moore (ed.), 'Metropolitical Visitation', 487, 503.
265. Guildhall Library, MS 9064/18, fos 117^{v}–118.

266. Somerset Archives, D.D. Ca. 333; Borthwick Institute, Cause papers and visitations books, province and diocese of York, V. 1629–30, fos 128, 129, 145.
267. Haigh, *Plain Man's Pathways*, 85.
268. Norfolk Record Office, ANF/1/4.
269. Cambridge University Library, Ely Diocesan Records, D/2/51, fo. 6[v], B/2/53, fo. 44[v].
270. Haigh, *Plain Man's Pathways*, 81.
271. BL, Add. MS 33,935, fo. 108.
272. Norfolk Record Office, ANW 3/32, ANW 2/72.
273. Borthwick Institute, Cause papers and visitations books, province and diocese of York, V. 1627, fo. 319, V. 1629–30, fos 7[v], 8[v], 22[v], 24[v], 60, 160[v]; Centre for Buckinghamshire Studies, D/A/V2; Cambridge University Library, Ely Diocesan Records, D/2/51, fo. 44; Durham Cathedral Library, Raine MS 130 (2); Lichfield Record Office, B/V/1/55, 28; Norfolk Record Office, ANW 3/32, DN/VIS 5/3/1, DN/VIS 6/1 and 4, DN/VIS 7/1; Haigh, *Plain Man's Pathways*, 86–7, 94–5, 151.
274. *Statutes of the Realm*, 3 Chas. I. *c*. 2.
275. Lambeth Palace Library, MS 943, fo. 129, endorsed by Laud, fo. 129[v].
276. J. W. Willis Bund (ed.), *Worcestershire County Records. Division I . . . Calendar of Quarter Sessions Papers . . . 1591–1643* (Worcester, 1900), 481.
277. Cambridge University Library, Ely Diocesan Records, E 10, Assize records.
278. Cambridge University Library, Ely Diocesan Records, D/2/51, fos 14, 44, 58[v], 66.
279. Cheshire Record Office, EDC 5/1633/45.
280. Guildhall Library, MS 9064/19, fo. 73[v].
281. Guildhall Library, MS 9059/1, fo. 11[v].
282. Norfolk Record Office, DN/VIS 5/3/2, 84, ANW 2/72, fo. 19.
283. Moore (ed.), 'Metropolitical Visitation', 489, 497, 503, 505–6.
284. Wiltshire Record Office, D2/4/1/16, fo. 163. For more examples, see Kenneth L. Parker, *The English Sabbath: A Study of Doctrine and Discipline from the Reformation to the Civil War* (Cambridge, 1988), 106–14.
285. Francis White, *A Treatise of the Sabbath-Day*, 3rd edn (1635), 231.
286. Kenneth Fincham, *Prelate as Pastor: The Episcopate of James I* (Oxford, 1990), esp. 299–304.

CHAPTER 8

1. Charles I, *The Kings Maiesties Declaration to His Subiects, Concerning Lawfull Sports to be Used* (1633).
2. Henry Burton, *A Divine Tragedie Lately Acted* (Amsterdam?, 1636), sig. A2.
3. Modern investigations include Kenneth L. Parker, *The English Sabbath: A Study of Doctrine and Discipline from the Reformation to the Civil War* (Cambridge, 1988), 178–216; Julian Davies, *The Caroline Captivity of the Church:*

Charles I and the Remoulding of Anglicanism 1625–1641 (Oxford, 1992), 172–204; Kevin Sharpe, *The Personal Rule of Charles I* (New Haven and London, 1992), 351–63; Alistair Dougall, *The Devil's Book: Charles I, the Book of Sports and Puritanism in Tudor and Stuart England* (Exeter, 2011). See also Jeremy Goring, *Godly Exercises or the Devil's Dance? Puritanism and Popular Culture in Pre-Civil War England* (1983).

4. Parker, *English Sabbath*, 106–21.
5. Bodleian Library, MS Rawlinson A. 409, fos 4, 61^{v}, 69. Cf. Henry Burton, *A Tryall of Private Devotions. Or, A Diall for the Houres of Prayer* (1628), sig F3^{v}; Lewis Bayly, *The Practice of Pietie* (1613), 572; this Jacobean manual was in its thirty-fifth edition by 1635.
6. William Perkins, *The Whole Treatise of the Cases of Conscience* (Cambridge, 1608), book 3, 116–27.
7. Robert Burton, *The Anatomy of Melancholy*, ed. Nicolas K. Kiessling, Thomas C. Faulkner, and Rhonda L. Blair, 6 vols (Oxford, 1990), ii. 116–18.
8. *Francis Willoughby's Book of Games: A Seventeenth-Century Treatise on Sports, Games and Pastimes*, ed. David Cram, Jeffrey L. Forgeng, and Dorothy Johnston (Aldershot and Burlington, VT, 2003).
9. Norfolk Record Office, DN/VIS 6/1, ANW 3/32.
10. *Statutes of the Realm*, 1 Chas. I, *c.* 1; Henry Burton, *A Brief Answer to a late Treatise of the Sabbath Day* (Amsterdam, 1635), 28.
11. Bodleian Library, MS Tanner 71, fo. 186.
12. Robert Dover, *Annalia Dubrensia. Upon the yeerely celebration of Mr Robert Dovers Olimpick Games upon the Cotswold-Hills* (1636), sig. B2.
13. J. W. Willis Bund (ed.), *Worcestershire County Records. Division I... Calendar of Quarter Sessions Papers... 1591–1643* (Worcester, 1900), 429.
14. Staffordshire Record Office, Q/SO/4, fo. 4^{v}.
15. George Chandler, *Liverpool under Charles I* (Liverpool, 1965), 118, 144–5, 154–5; Bund (ed.), *Worcestershire County Records*, 481.
16. Ferdinand Nicolls, *The Life and Death of Mr Ignatius Jurdain* (1654), 13.
17. T. G. Barnes, 'County Politics and a Puritan Cause Célèbre: Somerset Church Ales, 1633', *Transactions of the Royal Historical Society*, 5th ser. 9 (1959), 103–22; Thomas Garden Barnes, *Somerset 1625–1640: A County's Government during the 'Personal Rule'* (Cambridge, MA, 1961), 16, 90, 288, 293, 348; Parker, *English Sabbath*, 182–91; *The Works of the Most Reverend Father in God, William Laud, D.D.*, ed. William Scott and James Bliss, 9 vols (Oxford, 1847–60), vi. 319. For the Somerset church ales, see TNA, SP 16/238/4, 247/24, 248/12–14, 250/20, and the extract in David Cressy and Lori Anne Ferrell (eds), *Religion and Society in Early Modern England: A Sourcebook*, 2nd edn (2005), 172–4. In March 1628 Somerset justices revived an Elizabethan order 'that no church ale be admitted to be kept within any part of this shire', thereby triggering resistance (TNA, SP 16/96/7 and 15).

18. Burton, *Brief Answer to a late Treatise*, title page; Dow, *Innovations Unjustly Charged*, 39; TNA, SP 16/260/48.
19. Davies, *Caroline Captivity*, 172–204; Sharpe, *Personal Rule*, 354–5; Dougall, *Devil's Book*, 116–25. See, however, Richard Cust, *Charles I: A Political Life* (Harlow, 2005), 138, for 'Laud giving the lead for his less astute royal master'. See also Laud's defence at his trial in 1644, that the king commanded that the Declaration be printed, and there was nothing in it to give offence: Laud, *Works*, iv. 251–6.
20. *The Kings Maiesties Declaration*, 1, 10–11, 15–16.
21. *The Earl of Strafforde's Letters and Dispatches*, ed. William Knowler, 2 vols (1739), i. 166–7.
22. *The Diary of Thomas Crosfield*, ed. Frederick S. Boas (Oxford, 1935), 65–6, 68.
23. Laud, *Works*, vi. 329–30; Davies, *Caroline Captivity*, 180–2.
24. J. E. Foster (ed.), *Churchwardens Accounts of Great St Mary 1504–1635* (Cambridge, 1905), 465.
25. Cambridgeshire Record Office, P 27/5/2.
26. Norfolk Record Office, Y. C.39/2.
27. Suffolk Record Office, FC 101/E2/23.
28. Essex Record Office, Microfilm, T/A599/1.
29. Essex Record Office, D/P16/5/5.
30. Henry R. Plomer (ed.), *The Churchwardens Accounts of St Nicholas, Strood* (Kent Archaeological Society, Kent Records, vol. 5, 1927), 170.
31. Devon Record Office, 2237 A/PW/31.
32. Devon Record Office, 1593 PW/1.
33. Ivon L. Gregory (ed.), *Hartland Church Accounts, 1597–1706* (Frome and London, 1950), 156.
34. Devon Record Office, 1639 A/PW/1.
35. Devon Record Office, 2785 A/PW/1.
36. Dorset History Centre, PE/SH/CW1/106.
37. Dorset History Centre, R/1014.
38. Dorset History Centre, PE/LOB/CW 1.
39. Henry James Fowle Swayne (ed.), *Churchwardens' Accounts of S. Edmund & S. Thomas, Sarum 1443–1702* (Salisbury, 1896), 200.
40. Nottinghamshire Archives, PR 24,810
41. Nottinghamshire Archives, PR 1709.
42. Cheshire Record Office, P20/13/1.
43. Guildhall Library, MS 1016/1.
44. *The Journal of Sir Simonds's D'Ewes, from the Beginning of the Long Parliament*, ed. Wallace Notestein (New Haven, 1923), 6.
45. Dougall, *Devil's Book*, illustration 1, 147.
46. Kenneth Fincham (ed.), *Visitation Articles and Injunctions of the Early Stuart Church*, 2 vols (Woodbridge, 1994–8), ii. 147.
47. Dorset History Centre, PE/LOB/CW 1.

48. Dorset History Centre, PE/SH/CW1/106.
49. John Rushworth, *Historical Collections: The Second Part* (1686), 459.
50. Gloucestershire Archives, P230 CW2/1.
51. Cambridgeshire Record Office, P 27/5/2.
52. Burton, *Divine Tragedie* (1636), sigs A2–A2^{v}, 31, 42, 43.
53. Henry Burton, *For God, and the King. The Summe of Two Sermons Preached on the Fifth of November last in St Matthewes Friday-Streete* (Amsterdam, 1636), 59–60, 61–3.
54. Dow, *Innovations Unjustly Charged*, 78.
55. Bodleian Library, MS Rawlinson C. 573, fos 27–9. See also William Prynne, *News from Ipswich: Discovering certain late detestable practices of some domineering Lordly Prelates* (Edinburgh?, 1636), sig. A2^{v}.
56. TNA, SP 16/287/31.
57. Bodleian Library, MS Rawlinson A. 409, fo. 71^{v}.
58. Bodleian Library, MS Tanner 71, fo. 186; Tom Webster, *Godly Clergy in Early Stuart England: The Caroline Puritan Movement, c.1620–1643* (Cambridge, 1997), 228–30.
59. TNA, SP 16/540/4, Morton letters no. 22.
60. A. Percival Moore (ed.), 'The Metropolitical Visitation of Archdeacon [*sic*] Laud', *Associated Architectural Societies Reports and Papers*, 29 (1907), 533.
61. TNA, SP 16/280/54.
62. TNA, SP 16/267/6.
63. *Earl of Strafforde's Letters*, i. 166.
64. Davies, *Caroline Captivity*, 174, citing Somerset Archives, D/D/Ca. 313/47 and D/D/Ca. 301/56.
65. TNA, SP 16/267/6. Williams, like many opponents of the Book of Sports, was a Jacobean appointee, and had been rector of Shaftesbury since 1617. A Laudian faction in the parish denounced his 'anabaptistical and puritanical' leanings.
66. TNA, SP 16/375/78, SP16/397/91.
67. *CSPD 1635*, 26; TNA, SP 16/286/86, SP 16/287/31. See also SP 16/269/36 for an earlier report by Andrews.
68. TNA, SP 16/326/18.
69. TNA, SP 16/335/19.
70. Bodleian Library, MS Carte 77, fo. 360^{v}; TNA, C115/106, no. 8432.
71. Dow, *Innovations Unjustly Charged*, 104–5.
72. Bodleian Library, Carte MS 77, fos 346^{v}, 350^{v}, 360^{v}.
73. Bodleian Library, MS Tanner 71, fo. 186.
74. Davies, *Caroline Captivity*, 186–95; Sharpe, *Personal Rule*, 356; Dougall, *Devil's Book*, 126–31.
75. TNA, C115/106, no. 8432; Bodleian Library, MS Carte 77, fos 346^{v}, 360^{v}.
76. *Winthrop Papers*, iii. *1631–1637* (Massachusetts Historical Society, Boston, 1943), 356.

77. *CSPD 1637–38*, 240; TNA, SP 16/381/63; Rushworth, *Historical Collections: The Second Part* (1686), 459–61.
78. Peter Heylyn, *A Briefe and Moderate Answer, to the Seditious and Scandalous Challenges of Henry Burton* (1637), 110–15.
79. TNA, C115/106, no. 8432.
80. Guildhall Library, MS 9059/1, fos 94, 115.
81. *CSPD 1636–37*, 37.
82. *CSPD 1635*, 270; TNA, SP 16/293/97, SP 16/296/45, SP 16/536/5.
83. TNA, SP 16/260/48, 79 and 90. John Bowle was an energetic enforcer of the Book of Sports.
84. Christopher Haigh, *The Plain Man's Pathways to Heaven: Kinds of Christianity in Post-Reformation England* (Oxford, 2007), 94
85. TNA, SP 16/296/6. For more lay disapproval of the king's declaration, see TNA, SP 16/280/33, SP 16/285/48.
86. *Earl of Strafforde's Letters*, i. 166; Nicolls, *Life and Death of Mr Ignatius Jurdain*, 'To the Reader'.
87. John Spencer, *A Discourse of Divers Petitions of High Concernment* (1641), 3, 5.
88. TNA, SP 16/294/68; *CSPD 1640–41*, 453–4. For the effectiveness of this strategy, see Richard Culmer, *Cathedrall Newes from Canterbury* (1644), 3–4.
89. Moore (ed.), 'Metropolitical Visitation', 524–34.
90. David Underdown, *Revel, Riot and Rebellion: Popular Politics and Culture in England 1603–1660* (Oxford, 1985), 67.
91. Berkshire Record Office, D/A2/c74, fo. 114.
92. Moore (ed.), 'Metropolitical Visitation', 501.
93. Borthwick Institute, Cause papers and visitation books, diocese of Chester, C/V/CB 2, fo. 122.
94. *CSPD 1634–35*, 410.
95. TNA, SP 16/335/19.
96. Underdown, *Revel, Riot and Rebellion*, 86.
97. Oxfordshire Record Office, Diocesan Papers *c.* 2, fos 186–187ᵛ, 197, 203ᵛ–204.
98. Fincham (ed.), *Visitation Articles and Injunctions*, ii. 193, 206, compared to Richard Montague, *Articles of Enquiry and Direction for the Diocese of Norwich* (1638).
99. Worcestershire Record Office, DR446/21.
100. Henry Burton, *A Divine Tragedie Lately Acted* (1641), 1, 4, 11, 13–14, and *passim*.
101. John White, *The First Century of Scandalous, Malignant Priests* (1643), 19, 48. See also Underdown, *Revel, Riot and Rebellion*, 67, for John Lothwaite of Rockland St Peter, Norfolk, who 'read the Book with enthusiasm and turned up to shout "well-played" at Sunday football matches'.
102. Oxford University Archives, Chancellor's Court Depositions, Hyp/B/6, fos 132ᵛ–153, Chancellor's Court Papers 1634/85–7; *Diary of Thomas Crosfield*,

68, 133; Queen's College, Oxford, MS 390, fo. 70; Haigh, *Plain Man's Pathways*, 66, 116, 128, 141.

103. Marjorie Masten (ed.), *Woodstock Chamberlains' Accounts, 1609–50* (Oxfordshire Record Society, vol. 58, 1993), 154.
104. TNA, SP 16/265/14.
105. TNA, SP 16/410/9.
106. TNA, SP 16/322/32.
107. Davies, *Caroline Captivity*, 201, citing Hereford diocesan records.
108. Birch (ed.), *Court and Times*, ii. 277, Rossingham to Sir Thomas Puckering, 14 February 1637.
109. Huntington Library, Stowe–Temple Correspondence, Box 11, STT 1880, 1884.
110. Moore (ed.), 'Metropolitical Visitation', 497.
111. Borthwick Institute, Cause papers and visitations books, province and diocese of York, V. 1636, fo. 12.
112. Durham Cathedral Archives, DCD/SJB/6, fo. 3v.
113. Borthwick Institute, Cause papers and visitations books, province and diocese of York, V. 1636, fo. 258. See also Cheshire Record Office, EDC 5/1640/71 for violence against football players at Crosthwaite, Cumberland.
114. Cambridge University Library, Peterborough Dean and Chapter MS 20, fo. 33.
115. Lambeth Palace Library, MS. 943, fo. 736.
116. Prynne, *News from Ipswich*, sig. A2v. Three editions appeared in 1636, some perhaps secretly printed in London.
117. Thomas Turner, *A Sermon Preached before the King at White-Hall, the tenth of March* (1635), 19–21.
118. Francis White, *A Treatise of the Sabbath-Day*, 3rd edn (1635), 232–3.
119. Robert Sanderson, *A Soveraigne Antidote Against Sabbatarian Errours* (1636), 23–5.
120. Dougall, *Devil's Book*, 146–9.
121. BL, Add. MS 26,786, fos 7v, 8, 8v, 9v; Lambeth Palace Library, MS 943, fos. 735–7; Maija Jansson (ed.), *Proceedings in the Opening Session of the Long Parliament*, 7 vols (Rochester, NY, 2000–7), i. 368, 372, 377, ii. 525.
122. Offley Wakeman (ed.), *Shropshire County Records: Abstracts of the Orders made by the Court of Quarter Sessions for Shropshire, January, 1638–May, 1660* (Shrewsbury, 1905), 3.
123. Staffordshire Record Office, Q/SO/5, fo. 48.
124. Thomas Trescot, *The Zealous Magistrate* (1642), 25.
125. *Die Veneris 5. Maii. 1643* (1643); John Vicars, *Jehovah-Jireh. God in the Mount. Or, Englands Parliamentarie-Chronicle* (1644), 328.
126. C. H. Firth and R. S. Rait (eds), *Acts and Ordinances of the Interregnum, 1642–1660*, 3 vols (1911), i. 420–1.
127. Bernard Capp, *England's Culture Wars: Puritan Reformation and its Enemies in the Interregnum 1649–1660* (Oxford, 2012), 100–9.

CHAPTER 9

1. *CSPD 1637*, 468; TNA, SP 16/369/41 and 42. The anonymous report was translated by under-secretary George Weckherlin.
2. David Stevenson, *The Scottish Revolution 1637–44: The Triumph of the Covenanters* (Newton Abbot, 1973); Peter Donald, *An Uncounselled King: Charles I and the Scottish Troubles, 1637–1641* (Cambridge, 1990); John Morrill, *The Scottish National Covenant in its British Context* (Edinburgh, 1990); Conrad Russell, *The Fall of the British Monarchies 1637–1642* (Oxford, 1991); Mark Charles Fissel, *The Bishops' Wars: Charles I's Campaigns against Scotland, 1638–1640* (Cambridge, 1994); Geoffrey Parker, *Global Crisis: War, Climate Change and Catastrophe in the Seventeenth Century* (London and New Haven, 2013), 332–58, quotation at 333. See also Julian Goodare, 'Debate. Charles I: A Case of Mistaken Identity', *Past & Present*, 205 (2009), 189–201.
3. Bodleian Library, MS Bankes 18/2.
4. *CSPD 1635–36*, 260; TNA, SP 16/314/109; Bodleian Library, MS Bankes 43/35. Stodderd's remarks at the Fleet prison in 1632 became a Star Chamber matter in 1635.
5. J.W., *The Valiant Scot* (1637), sig. A3.
6. Bodleian Library, MS Ashmole 826, fo. 103; Folger Shakespeare Library, MS G. a. 11, 65.
7. *The Earl of Strafforde's Letters and Dispatches*, ed. William Knowler, 2 vols (1739), ii. 117.
8. HMC, *Fourth Report*, appendix, 293.
9. *Earl of Strafforde's Letters*, ii. 117.
10. HMC, *De L'Isle*, vi. 127, 130.
11. 'The Scottish National Covenant', in Samuel Rawson Gardiner (ed.), *The Constitutional Documents of the Puritan Revolution 1625–1660* (Oxford, 1906), 124–34. See also George Gillespie, *A Dispute Against the English–Popish Ceremonies Obtruded Upon the Church of Scotland* (Leiden?, 1637); *Reasons for which the Service Booke urged upon Scotland ought to be Refused* (Edinburgh?, 1638).
12. Gilbert Burnet, *The Memoires of the Lives and Actions of James and William Dukes of Hamilton* (1677), 55–6, 60; James Orchard Halliwell (ed.), *Letters of the Kings of England*, 2 vols (1848), ii. 299, 302.
13. *Some Seasonable Animadversions upon the late Observator . . . Together with a vindication of the King* (1642); William Ball, *A Caveat for Subjects, Moderating the Observator* (1642), 4; Sir John Spelman, *A View of a Printed Book Intituled 'Observations upon His Majesties Late Answers and Expresses'* (1642), 35. See also Gilbert Talbot's observation about the king in July 1641: 'those that most favour him compare him to a Duke of Venice' (HMC, *Sixth Report*, appendix, 286).
14. Huntington Library, Hastings Correspondence, Box 15, HA 1349.

15. Charles I, *By the King. A Proclamation and Declaration to inform Our loving Subjects of our Kingdom of England of the seditious practices of some in Scotland, seeking to overthrow Our Regall Power under false pretences of Religion* (27 February 1639); Charles I, *Stuart Royal Proclamations: Volume II: Royal Proclamations of King Charles I 1625–1646*, ed. James F. Larkin (Oxford, 1983), 662–7.
16. *CSPD 1639*, 160; TNA, SP 16/420/157.
17. Staffordshire Record Office, D 1287/18/2, 178, Bridgeman correspondence.
18. *The Works of the Most Reverend Father in God, William Laud, D.D.*, ed. William Scott and James Bliss, 9 vols (Oxford, 1847–60), vii. 576.
19. TNA, National Register of Archives, Bound Vol. 20594, 793.
20. J. F. W. Hill, 'The Royalist Clergy of Lincolnshire', *Lincolnshire Architectural and Archaeological Society Reports and Papers*, vol. 2, part 1, NS for 1938 (Lincoln, 1940), 46.
21. Richard Culmer, *Cathedrall Newes from Canterbury* (1644), 9.
22. Huntington Library, Hastings Correspondence, Box 15, HA 1349, HA 1350; HMC, *Salisbury*, xxii. 22, 299, 307.
23. Joad Raymond, *Pamphlets and Pamphleteering in Early Modern Britain* (Cambridge, 2003), 172–20; Sarah Waurechen, 'Covenanter Propaganda and Conceptualizations of the Public during the Bishops' Wars', *Historical Journal*, 52 (2009), 63–86.
24. Bodleian Library, MS Bankes 65/2. See also Joseph Black, '"Pikes and Protestations": Scottish Texts in England, 1639–40', *Publishing History*, 42 (1997), 5–19; Waurechen, 'Covenanter Propaganda', 66–73.
25. TNA, SP 16/413/121.
26. Staffordshire Record Office, D,1287/18/2, 180, 182.
27. TNA, SP 16/467/9; *CSPD 1640–41*, 40.
28. C. H. Firth, 'The Reign of Charles I', *Transactions of the Royal Historical Society*, 3rd ser. 6 (1912), 40–2.
29. BL, Egerton MS 2716, fo. 294, William Davy in March 1638.
30. *The Oxinden Letters 1607–1642*, ed. Dorothy Gardiner (1933), 154–5.
31. TNA, National Register of Archives, Bound Vol. 20594, 810, Barrington to the Earl of Cork.
32. Bodleian Library, MS Bankes 65/28b.
33. Bodleian Library, MS Ashmole 826, fo. 103^{v}.
34. *The Diary of Sir Henry Slingsby*, ed. Daniel Parsons (1836), 11.
35. TNA, SP 16/395/29.
36. *The Buller Papers*, ed. R. N. Worth (1895), 27.
37. TNA, SP 16/413/42. Denying these words, Fowler later asserted his willingness 'to serve his majesty with his life and means, where he shall be commanded'.
38. Staffordshire Record Office, D.1287/18/2, 183.
39. Cheshire Record Office, EDC 5/1638/112.
40. Bodleian Library, MS Bankes 18/3, 18/38, 581/1 and 2.

41. TNA, SP 16/426/7.
42. Cheshire Record Office, QJF 68/2, fo. 30.
43. Bodleian Library, MS Bankes 18/8.
44. Bodleian Library, MS Bankes 18/2.
45. *CSPD 1639*, 260.
46. *CSPD 1639*, 300; TNA, SP 16/423/83.
47. TNA, SP 16/425/16, SP 16/430/10; Jeremiah 5:30 and 31.
48. David Cressy, *England on Edge: Crisis and Revolution 1640–1642* (Oxford, 2006), 68–109.
49. TNA, National Register of Archives, Bound Vol. 20594, 792; Russell, *Fall of the British Monarchies*, 92; Esther S. Cope and Willson H. Coates (eds), *Proceedings of the Short Parliament of 1640* (Camden Society, 4th ser., vol. 19, 1977), 165, 207.
50. HMC, *Rutland*, 501; HMC, *Salisbury*, xii. 296–9.
51. *CSPD 1638–39*, 370; *CSPD 1639*, 56–8.
52. Laud, *Works*, vii. 578; *CSPD 1638–39*, 183–4; *CSPD 1639*, 55–6; *CSPD 1639–40*, 137.
53. TNA, SP 16/418/8; Huntington Library, Stowe–Temple Correspondence, Box 11, STT 1893, Robert Sibthorpe to Sir John Lambe, 17 June 1639.
54. TNA, SP 16/426/7.
55. Russell, *Fall of the British Monarchies*, 55–89; Fissel, *Bishops' Wars*, 3–39; Victor L. Stater, 'The Lord Lieutenancy on the Eve of the Civil Wars: The Impressment of George Plowwright', *Historical Journal*, 29 (1986), 279–96; *Letters and Papers of the Verney Family*, ed. H. Verney (Camden Society, OS, vol. 56, 1853), 228.
56. HMC, *Third Report*, 77.
57. HMC, *Rutland*, 515.
58. HMC, *Rutland*, 516–17.
59. Charles I, *His Majesties Declaration: To All His Loving Subjects, Of the causes which moved him to dissolve the last Parliament* (1640), 2–3, 46.
60. HMC, *Portland*, iii. 63; *The Diary of John Evelyn*, ed. William Bray (ed.) 6 vols (1879), i. 10; *Oxinden Letters*, 172–3.
61. *The Diary of Robert Woodford, 1637–1641*, ed. John Fielding (Camden Society, 5th ser., vol. 42, 2012), 352.
62. *The Wyllys Papers* (Collections of the Connecticut Historical Society, vol. 21, Hartford, CT, 1924), 12.
63. Huntington Library, Ellesmere MS 7001; Bodleian Library, MS Carte 1, fo. 288[v].
64. Essex Record Office, D/Deb 94/20.
65. Cressy, *England on Edge*, 71–95.
66. O. Ogle, W. H. Bliss, et al. (eds), *Calendar of the Clarendon State Papers Preserved in the Bodleian Library*, 5 vols (Oxford, 1872–1970), v. 722; John Adamson, *The Noble Revolt: The Overthrow of Charles I* (2007), 71; Bodleian Library, MS

Radcliffe Trust c. 32, fos 2–2^{v} (I am grateful to Jason Peacey for transcribing this document).

67. Staffordshire Record Office, D.661/11/1/5, Notebook of Richard Dyott.
68. Cambridge University Library, MS Mn. 1. 45, 99, Baker transcripts.
69. Charles Carlton, *Charles I: The Personal Monarch*, 2nd edn (1995), 226; Richard Cust, *Charles I: A Political Life* (Harlow, 2005), 304.
70. *The Diary of John Evelyn*, ed. E. S. de Beer, 6 vols (Oxford, 1955), ii. 26.
71. Bristol Record Office, Quarter Sessions Minute Book, JQS/M/3, fos 171, 176^{v}; Lincolnshire Archives, LQS/A/10/81; Cheshire Record Office, QJT 54/1, QJF 69/4; Staffordshire Record Office, Q/SR/243, fos 7, 11; London Metropolitan Archives, MJ/SR 890, *passim*.
72. Huntington Library, Ellesmere MS 7563.
73. East Sussex Record Office, QR/E/56/18.
74. Essex Record Office, Q/SBa 2/44.
75. London Metropolitan Archives, MJ/SR 909, fo. 106.
76. James Raine (ed.), *Depositions from the Castle of York* (Surtees Society, vol. 40, 1861), 3.
77. HMC, *Sixth Report*, appendix, 286.
78. Bodleian Library, MS Nalson 12, fos 46–7.
79. *Ovatio Carolina. The Triumph of King Charles* (1641), title page, 16; John Taylor, *Englands Comfort, and Londons Ioy: Expressed in the Royall, Triumphant, and Magnificent Entertainment of our Dread Soveraigne Lord, King Charles, at his blessed and safe returne from Scotland* (1641), 5.
80. For the politics of this period, see Russell, *Fall of the British Monarchies*, 360–72, 400–38; Cust, *Charles I: A Political Life*, 310–17; Cressy, *England on Edge*, 379–95.
81. Richard Gardyner, *A Sermon Appointed . . . on the Day of His Maiesties Happy Inauguration* (1642), 9, 27.
82. *The Knyvett Letters (1620–1644)*, ed. Bertram Schofield (Norfolk Record Office, vol. 20, 1949), 103.
83. Bodleian Library, MS Tanner 62, fo. 212.
84. *The Sovereignty of Kings* (1642), Sig. A3^{v}.
85. Bodleian Library, MS Tanner 63, fo. 67.
86. Bodleian Library, MS Nalson 13, fo. 163.
87. *The Unlimited Prerogative of Kings Subverted* (1642), sigs A, B4.
88. J.M., *A Reply to the Answer . . . to a Printed Books Intituled Observations* (1642), 1, 46.
89. Joad Raymond, *Making the News: An Anthology of the Newsbooks of Revolutionary England 1641–1660* (Moreton-in-Marsh, 1993), 62–4.
90. Robert Mossom, *The King on his Throne: Or, A Discourse maintaining the Dignity of a King, the Duty of a Subject, and the Unlawfulnesse of Rebellion* (York, 1642), 3.
91. James Howell, *The True Informer . . . of the sad distempers in Great Britanny and Ireland* (1643), 5.

92. John Swan, *Redde Debitum. Or, A Discourse in Defence of Three Chiefe Fatherhoods* (1640), 21.
93. Essex Record Office, D/Deb/16/1–4, Bramston papers, certified copies from Glamorganshire Quarter Sessions.
94. John Lister (ed.), *West Riding Records. Vol. II, Orders, 1611–1642. Indictments, 1637–1642* (Yorkshire Archaeological Society Record Series, 53, 1915), 367.
95. TNA, ASSI 45/1/4, nos 55–8; Raine (ed.), *Depositions from the Castle of York*, 4–5.
96. East Sussex Record Office, QR/E/57/60–4.
97. Hertfordshire Archives, MS 46351, articles against Edward Jude.
98. James I, *The Dutie of a King in His Royal Office ... declaring the true glory of kings* (1642).
99. Gardyner, *Sermon Appointed*, 9.
100. Thomas Morton?, *The Necessity of Christian Subjection* (Oxford, 1643), 18, 20–1.
101. *Propositions Made by both Houses of Parliament to the Kings Maiesty for a reconciliation of the differences betweene His Majesty and the said Houses* (1642); *Nineteen Propositions Made By both Houses of Parliament, to the Kings most Excellent Majestie: With His Majesties Answer thereunto* (Cambridge, 1642).
102. Charles I, *His Majesties Answer to the Nineteen Propositions of both Houses of Parliament* (Cambridge, 1642), 1–14. For further exposition, see Michael Mendle, *Dangerous Positions: Mixed Government, the Estates of the Realm, and the Making of the Answer to the XIX Propositions* (Tuscaloosa, AL, 1985).
103. *His Majesties Answer to the Nineteen Propositions*, 1–3.
104. *His Majesties Answer to the Nineteen Propositions*, 3; *Propositions Made by both Houses of Parliament*, sig. A2.
105. *His Majesties Answer to the Nineteen Propositions*, 4–7, 11.
106. *His Majesties Answer to the Nineteen Propositions*, 12, 14; Bodleian Library, MS Tanner 72, fo. 300^v.
107. Henry Parker, *Observations upon some of his Majesties late Answers and Expresses* (1642), 1, 2, 3, 4, 8. For a full discussion of Parker's life and thought, see Michael Mendle, *Henry Parker and the English Civil War: The Political Thought of the Public's 'Privado'* (Cambridge, 1995). See also Thomas Ertman, *Birth of the Leviathan: Building States and Regimes in Medieval and Early Modern Europe* (Cambridge, 1997), on the transition from an absolutist 'patrimonial' state to a bureaucratic 'communitarian' constitutionalism.
108. *Animadversions upon those Notes Which the late Observator hath Published* (1642), 6.
109. *An Appeale to the World in these Times of Extreame Danger* (1642), 7. The collector George Thomason had his copy on 12 July 1642.
110. Responses to the *Observations* include *An Appendix to the Late Answer ... Or, Some Seasonable Animadversions upon the late Observator ... Together with a Vindication of the King* (1642); William Ball, *A Caveat for Subjects, Moderating*

the Observator (1642); Richard Burney, *An Answer or Necessary Animadversions, upon Some late Impostunate Observations Invective against his Sacred Maiesty* (1642); Dudley Digges, *An Answer to a Printed Book, Intituled, Observations upon some of His Majesties Late Answers and Expresses* (Oxford, 1642); John Jones, *An Examination of the Observations Upon His Majesties Answers* (1643); John Jones, *Christus Dei, The Lords Annoynted . . . written in answer to a late printed pamphlet* (Oxford, 1643); Sir John Spelman, *A View of a Printed Book Intituled 'Observations upon His Majesties Late Answers and Expresses'* (1642).

111. Spelman, *View of a Printed Book*, 3, 4, 7, 8, 12, 15, 18, 30.
112. *Animadversions upon those Notes Which the late Observator hath published*, 6.
113. Bodleian Library, MS Nalson 2, fo. 208.
114. Lambeth Palace Library, MS 3391, fos 42–42^{v}.
115. Jones, *Christus Dei*, title page, 2, 8. See also Morton?, *Necessity of Christian Subjection*.
116. *A Discourse discovering some mysteries of our new state . . . shewing the rise and progresse of Englands unhappiness, ab anno illo infortunato, 1641* (Oxford, 1645), 4, 6, 24.
117. Jones, *Christus Dei*, 11–12.
118. *Obedience Active and Passive Due to the Supream Power* (Oxford, 1643), 1, 2, 4–9, 16.
119. John Maxwell, *Sacro-sancta Regum Majestas: or, the Sacred and Royall Prerogative of Christian Kings* (Oxford, 1644), 6.
120. Sir John Spelman, *Certain Considerations Upon the Duties of both Prince and People* (Oxford, 1643), 1.
121. Edward Reynolds, *Eugenia's Teares* (1642), 40; Morton?, *Necessity of Christian Subjection*, 7.
122. Mossom, *King on his Throne*, 5, 39, 40.
123. Henry Ferne, *The Resolving of Conscience* (1642), title page, epistle to the reader. See also Thomas Swadlin, *The Soveraignes Desire Peace: The Subiects Dutie Obedience* (1643), 18, 25.
124. Ferne, *Resolving of Conscience*, title page, epistle to the reader.
125. *An Appeale to the World in these Times of Extreame Danger* (1642), 7.
126. Mossom, *King on his Throne*, 9–13.
127. *The Definition of a King, With the Cure of a King Wilfully Mad, and the Way to Prevent Tyranny* (1642), 2; Jermiah Burroughes, *The Glorious Name of God, The Lord of Hosts* (1643), 40–1.
128. *The Subjects Liberty set forth in the Royall and Politique Power of England* (1643), title page; Philip Hunton, *A Treatise of Monarchie* (1643), 52; Sir John Fortescue, *De Laudibus Legum Angliae: A Learned Commendation of the Politique Lawes of England* (1616), 26, 84.
129. *Vindiciae Contra Tyrannos: A Defence of Liberty Against Tyrants* (1648), title page. Recent scholarship includes Anne McLaren, 'Rethinking Republicanism: *Vindiciae Contra Tyrannos* in Context', *Historical Journal*, 49 (2006), 23–52, and Stefania Tutino, 'Huguenots, Jesuits and Tyrants: Notes on the *Vindiciae*

Contra Tyrannos in Early Modern England', *Journal of Early Modern History*, 11 (2007), 175–96.

130. *Definition of a King*, 3.
131. J. M., *A Reply to the Answer... to a Printed Books Intituled Observations* (1642), 2.
132. *Mercurius Britanicus*, 25 (26 February–6 March 1644); Jason Peacey, 'The Struggle for *Mercurius Britanicus*: Factional Politics and the Parliamentarian Press, 1643–1646', *Huntington Library Quarterly*, 68 (2005), 517–44.
133. I. I., *Reasons why this Kingdom, as all others... ought to adhere to their kings, whether good or bad* (1642), title page; John Doughty, *The King's Cause Rationally, Briefly, and Plainly Debated, as it Stands de facto. Against the Irrational, Groundless Misprisions of a Still Deceived Sort of People* (Oxford, 1644), 3.
134. Spelman, *View of a Printed Book*, 26.
135. Digges, *Answer to a Printed Book*, 1–2.
136. Morton?, *Necessity of Christian Subjection*, 1, 7, 12.
137. Robert Grosse, *Royalty and Loyalty or A Short Survey of the Power of Kings over their Subjects: and the Duty of Subjects to their Kings* (1647), 32–3.
138. Burroughes, *Glorious Name of God*, 36, 38. Cf. *A Declaration of the Parliament of England, Expressing the Grounds of their Late Proceedings* (1649), 14: 'the words Touch not mine anointed were spoken [not] of kings but unto kings, who were reproved and enjoined to do no harm to the prophets and saints of God, there understood to be his anointed.' See also Robert Zaller, 'Breaking the Vessels: The Desacralization of Monarchy in Early Modern England', *Sixteenth Century Journal*, 29 (1998), 765.
139. Bodleian Library, MS Nalson 13, fo. 303.
140. John Cordy Jeaffreson (ed.), *Middlesex County Records. Vol. III... 1 Charles I to 18 Charles II* (Clerkenwell, 1888), 88, 89.
141. Jeaffreson (ed.), *Middlesex County Records. Vol. III*, 174.
142. Jeaffreson (ed.), *Middlesex County Records. Vol. III*, 88.
143. John Taylor, *The Conversion, Confession, Contrition, Coming to Himself, & Advice of a Mis-led, Ill-bred, Rebellious Round-Head* (1643), sig. B2.
144. Norfolk Record Office, C/S3/34.
145. Norfolk Record Office, C/S3/34.
146. Jeaffreson (ed.), *Middlesex County Records. Vol. III*, 93, 94, 118.
147. TNA, ASSI 45/1/5, fo. 16.
148. Zaller, 'Breaking the Vessels', 757–78. Cf. Jeffery Merrick, *The Desacralization of the French Monarchy in the Eighteenth Century* (Baton Rouge, 1990).
149. Raymond, *Making the News*, 51, 63, 71.
150. Joseph Frank, *The Beginnings of the English Newspaper 1620–1660* (Cambridge, MA, 1961); Raymond, *Making the News*; Joad Raymond, *The Invention of the Newspaper: English Newsbooks 1641–1649* (Oxford, 1996, 2005). See also C. Nelson and M. Seccombe (eds), *British Newspapers and Periodicals, 1641–1700: A Short-Title Catalogue of Serials Printed in England, Scotland, Ireland, and British America* (1987); Jason Peacey, *Politicians and Pamphleteers: Propaganda*

and Politics during the English Civil Wars and Interregnum (Aldershot, 2004); Jason Peacey, *Print and Public Politics in the English Revolution* (Cambridge, 2013).

151. *Mercurius Britanicus*, 90 (14 July 1645); Charles I, *The Kings Cabinet Opened: or, Certain Packets of Secret Letters & Papers, Written with the Kings Own Hand* (1645).
152. *Mercurius Britanicus*, 91 (21 July 1645).
153. *Mercurius Britanicus*, 92 (4 August 1645). See also Joyce Macadam, '*Mercurius Britanicus* on Charles I: An Exercise in Civil War Journalism and High Politics, August 1643 to May 1646', *Historical Research*, 84 (2011), 470–92.
154. Raymond, *Invention of the Newspaper*, 42–3.
155. *Mercurius Britanicus*, 130 (18 May 1646).
156. Firth, 'Reign of Charles I', 58.
157. Edward Symmons, *A Vindication of King Charles: or, A Loyal Subjects Duty* (1648), sig. A.
158. Folger Shakespeare Library, MS V. b. 303, fo. 324.
159. James Howell, *The Instruments of a King: or, A Short Discourse of the Sword. The Scepter. The Crowne* (1648), 2, 5. See also Thomas Bayly, *The Royal Charter Granted unto Kings, by God Himself* (1649).
160. John Morrill, *The Nature of the English Revolution* (1993), 285–306.
161. [Richard Overton], *A Remonstrance of Many Thousand Citizens, and other Free-born People* (1646), 5–6.
162. A. S. P. Woodhouse (ed.), *Puritanism and Liberty; Being the Army Debates (1647–9)* (1938, repr. 1966), 427.
163. John Jubbes, *Several Proposals for Peace & Freedom, By an Agreement of the People* (1648), 3–4.
164. *Journal of the House of Lords*, 10 vols (1802), v. 605; *Journal of the House of Commons*, 10 vols (1802), iii. 208; M. R. Toynbee, 'Charles I and the Kings Evil', *Folk-Lore*, 61 (1950), 1–14.
165. *To the Kings Most Excellent Majesty. The Humble Petition of Divers Hundreds of the Kings Poore Subjects, Afflicted with that Grievous Infirmities, called The Kings Evil* (1643), 4, 6, 8.
166. Toynbee, 'Charles I and the Kings Evil', 3. 6.
167. *Journal of the House of Commons*, v. 151; *State Papers Collected by Edward, Earl of Clarendon*, 3 vols (Oxford, 1767), ii, appendix, p. xxxvii.
168. John Taylor, *Tailors Travels, from London to the Isle of Wight* (1648), 10–12; Matthew 11, 2:5.
169. *Mercurius Militaris*, 2 (10–17 October 1648); Raymond, *Making the News*, 178–9.
170. *Mercurius Impartialis*, 1 (5–12 December 1648); Raymond, *Invention of the Newspaper*, 68.
171. *Mercurius Pragmaticus*, 29 (10–17 October 1648); *Mercurius Militaris* (10–17 October 1648); *Mercurius Impartialis* (5–12 December 1648); Raymond, *Making the News*, 178–9; Toynbee, 'Charles I and the Kings Evil', 11–13.

172. Gardiner (ed.), *Constitutional Documents of the Puritan Revolution*, 372, 374, 380, 384–7.
173. *A Declaration of the House of Commons in Parliament Assembled . . . And a Copy of the Covenant between the Kings of England and the People, at their Coronation* (1649), title page, 2; John Milton, *The Tenure of Kings and Magistrates* (1650), 35.
174. Charles I, *Eikon Basilike: The Pourtraicture of His Sacred Majestie in His Solitudes and Sufferings* (1649).
175. Milton, *Tenure of Kings and Magistrates*, 8–11.

CHAPTER 10

1. *The Faithful, yet Imperfect, Character of a Glorious King, King Charles I, his Country's and Religion's Martyr* (1660), 1, 2, 8; *An Elegie and Epitaph On that glorious Saint, and blessed Martyr, King Charles I* (1661), title page.
2. Thomas Forde, *Virtus Rediviva: Or, A Panegyrick on the late K. Charls the I* (1660), 5, 7, 27.
3. William Winstanley, *The Loyal Martyrology* (1665), 16.
4. Contrast Conrad Russell, 'The Man Charles Stuart', in his *The Causes of the English Civil War* (Oxford, 1990), 185–211, with Mark Kishlansky, 'Charles I: A Case of Mistaken Identity', *Past & Present*, 189 (2005), 41–80.
5. *The Works of the Most Reverend Father in God, William Laud, D.D.*, ed. William Scott and James Bliss, 9 vols (Oxford, 1847–60), i., 110, 116, sermon before the king, 19 June 1625.
6. Bodleian Library, MS Rawlinson B. 243, fos 17–17^{v}.
7. Thomas Morton, *A Sermon Preached Before the Kings most Excellent Majestie, in the Cathedrall Church of Durham* (1639), 40.
8. Sir Roger Manley, *The History of the Rebellions in England, Scotland, and Ireland* (1691), 2.
9. *Fortunes Tennis-ball* (1640), 1; Bodleian Library, MS Firth *c.* 4, fo. 236.
10. John Foxe, *Acts and Monuments* (1583), book 8, 1103.
11. TNA, SP 16/24/12, 13, and 73.
12. TNA, SP 16/49/64.
13. TNA, SP 16/132/35.
14. TNA, SP 16/243/5, SP 16/277/5.
15. TNA, SP 16/423/23 and 28. Harrison was a Laudian loyalist who feared for King Charles's safety.
16. Eleanor Douglas [i.e. Davis], *Given to the Elector Prince Charles of the Rhyne from the Lady Eleanor, anno 1633* (1648), 5; [Grace Cary] (as 'Theophilus Philaleithes Toxander'), *Vox Coeli to England, or, Englands Fore-Warning from Heaven* (1646).
17. Thomas B. Howell (ed.), *Cobbett's Complete Collection of State Trials*, 33 vols (1809–26), iii. 359.
18. TNA, SP 16/116/56; *CSPD 1628–29*, 240; Thomas Birch (ed.), *The Court and Times of Charles the First*, 2 vols (1848), i. 431.

19. Bodleian Library, MS Bankes 18/1, 18/2, 18/3, 18/38, 58/1–2; BL, Add. MS 11045, fos 3v–4, 7; TNA, SP 16/163/61, SP 16/248/60, SP 16/258/45, SP 16/397/26–8, SP 16/427/115, SP 16/439/18, PC 2/43, 431, PC 2/50, fo. 67; Essex Record Office, T/A 418/99/114, T/A 418/107/90.
20. Kevin Sharpe, *Remapping Early Modern England: The Culture of Seventeenth-Century Politics* (Cambridge, 2000), 178; Kishlansky, 'Charles I: A Case of Mistaken Identity', 50.
21. *APC 1628 July–1629 April*, 134; TNA, SP 16/111/5; *Calendar of the Correspondence of the Smyth Family of Ashton Court 1548–1647*, ed. J. H. Bettey (Bristol Record Society, vol. 35, 1982), 93; Alastair Bellany and Andrew McRae (eds), *Early Stuart Libels: An Edition of Poetry from Manuscript Sources*, Early Modern Literary Studies Text Series I (2005) <http://www.earlystuartlibels.net/htdocs/index.html> (accessed 2 June 2014).
22. TNA, SP 16/142/92 and 93.
23. Cambridge University Library, MS Ii. v.9, fo. 116v; *Tom Tell Troath or A Free Discourse Touching the Manners of the Tyme* (Amsterdam?, 1630), 3; George Calvert, *The Answer to Tom-Tell-Troth* (1642), 4.
24. A. Ar., *The Practise of Princes* (Amsterdam, 1630), 2.
25. *The Diary of Robert Woodford, 1637–1641*, ed. John Fielding (Camden Society, 5th ser., vol. 42, 2012), 358.
26. 'The Letany', *The Booke of Common Prayer* (1633), sig. A5.
27. TNA, SP 16/477/48. Rooks and magpies referred to black-clad bishops and priests.
28. *Englands Complaint to Iesus Christ Against the Bishops Canons* (1640), sigs A3, B3v, C3v, F3.
29. BL, Add. MS 70,003, fo. 3.
30. Bodleian Library, MS Nalson 12, fos 46–7.
31. Charles I, *Basilika: The Workes of King Charles the Martyr* (1662), 205.
32. *Mercurius Britanicus*, 61 (9–16 December 1644).
33. Patricia Crawford, '"Charles Stuart, that Man of Blood"', *Journal of British Studies*, 16 (1971), 41–61.

Bibliography

All works cited were published in London unless otherwise indicated.

MANUSCRIPT SOURCES

Berkshire Record Office, Reading

D/A2/c74 Archdeaconry acts
D/P8/5/1 Ashampstead accounts

Bethlem Royal Hospital Archives, London

Court of Governors, BCB-06

Bodleian Library, Oxford

Add. C 259 Beaumont correspondence
Add. 15,257 Hearne papers
Ashmole 38 Verse miscellany
Ashmole 423 Napier diary
Ashmole 800 Newsletters
Ashmole 826 Scottish business
Bankes 9, 13, 18, 19, 37, 41, 42, 43, 58, 63, 65 Bankes papers
Carte 1, 2, 63, 74, 77, 78, 80, 103, 123, 130, 228 State papers
Cherry 2 Williams papers
Clarendon 6, 14, 251–7 Clarendon papers
Eng. Hist. E. 28 Miscellany
Firth *c.* 4 Lieutenancy papers
Jones 17, 39 State papers
Nalson 2, 12, 13 State papers
Radcliffe Trust c. 32 State papers
Rawlinson A. 127–8 Star Chamber
Rawlinson A. 409 Sabbath offences
Rawlinson B. 243 Star Chamber
Rawlinson B. 431 Legal precepts
Rawlinson C. 197 Council of the North
Rawlinson C. 368 Wren papers
Rawlinson C. 421 Clerical papers
Rawlinson C. 573 Clerical papers
Rawlinson C. 674 State papers
Rawlinson C. 827 Star Chamber

Rawlinson D. 141 'Memorable accidents'
Rawlinson D. 158 Radwinter affronts
Rawlinson D. 317B State papers
Rawlinson D. 353 State papers
Rawlinson D. 392 State papers
Rawlinson D. 399 State papers
Rawlinson Letters 89 Usher papers
Tanner 65–72 Clerical and state papers
Top. Oxon. C. 378 Wyatt diary
J. Walker C.11 Scandalous ministers
Oxford University Archives, Chancellor's Court Papers and Depositions

Borthwick Institute, York
Cause papers and visitation books, diocese of Chester
Cause papers and visitations books, province and diocese of York

Bristol Record Office, Bristol
JQS/M/3 Quarter Sessions minutes

British Library, London
Add. 5,829 Scandalous ministers
Add. 11,045 Rossingham newsletters
Add. 15,672 Scandalous ministers
Add. 22,084 Scandalous ministers
Add. 26,785–6 Dering notes
Add. 28,006 Oxinden accounts
Add. 33,935–6 Moreton letters
Add. 34,324 Caesar collections
Add. 35,331 Younge diary
Add. 48,057 Yelverton papers
Add. 69,885–6 Coke papers
Add. 72,417–9 Trumball papers
Add. 72,421 Trumball papers
Add. 75,354 Althorp papers
Egerton 1044 Grace Cary relation
Egerton 2646 Barrington papers
Egerton 2715–16 Gawdy papers
Hargrave 489 Star Chamber
Harley 454 Mildmay diary
Harley 597 Banks and Heath papers
Harley 646 D'Ewes autobiography
Harley 1012 Grants and licences
Harley 1026 Pagitt memoranda
Harley 1576 Law papers
Harley 4022 Star Chamber
Harley 7000 State papers

Lansdowne 211 State papers
Lansdowne 620 Star Chamber
Sloane 649 Dury papers
Sloane 922 Wallington papers
Sloane 1039 Hooke papers
Sloan 1457 Wallington notes
Stowe 159 Star Chamber
Stowe 561 Household ordinances

Cambridge University Library, Cambridge
Add. MS 32 'England's forewarning'
Ely Diocesan Records, B/2/48–55, D/2/49–51, E 10/4, LA/5a
Ii. v.9 Political papers
Mm.1.45 Brady collection
Mm. 4. 29 Tredington act book
Mm. 4. 57 Cambridge memoranda
Mm. 6. 63 Littleton papers
Mn. 1. 45 Baker transcripts
Peterborough Dean and Chapter MS 20
University Archives, Collect. Admin. 8 'Tabor's Book'
University Archives, Commissary and Vice-Chancellor's Court Records
University Archives, Comm. Ct. III/16, no. 39

Cambridgeshire Record Office, Cambridge
P 27/5/2 Holy Trinity accounts
P 30/4/2 Great St Mary accounts

Centre for Buckinghamshire Studies, Aylesbury
D/A/C4–6, D/A/V2–4 Archdeaconry papers

Cheshire Record Office, Chester
CR 63/2/6 Militia records
EDC 5 Consistory Court Papers
P20/13/1 St Mary, Chester accounts
QJF 54, 69, 70, 71 Quarter Sessions Rolls

Devon Record Office, Exeter
Exeter Sessions Book 64
1060/PW86 Crediton accounts
1593 PW/1 Clawton accounts
1639 A/PW/1 Honiton accounts
2237 A/PW/31 Bere Ferrers accounts
2785 A/PW/1 Woodbury accounts

Dorset History Centre, Dorchester
B2/8/1 Dorchester Borough Records
D/BOC/Box 22 Bond chronicle

PE/LOB/CW 1 Long Burton accounts
PE/SH/CW1/106 Sherborne accounts
R/1014 Cerne Abbas accounts
WM.AD 1 Weymouth Borough records

Downing College, Cambridge
Bowtell MS, 'Liber Rationalis'

Durham Cathedral Library and Archives, Durham
DCD/SJB/7 Diocesan records
Raine MS 130

Durham University Library, Durham
MSP 9 Mickelton manuscripts

East Sussex Record Office, Lewes
QR/E/55–7 Quarter Sessions

Essex Record Office, Chelmsford
D/AED/9 Archdeaconry records
D/Deb/16 and 94 Bramston papers
D/P16/5/5 Thaxted accounts
Q/SBa 2/44 Quarter Sessions
T/A 418/99, 418/107 Calendar of Assize Records
T/A599/1 Saffron Walden accounts (microfilm)

Folger Shakespeare Library, Washington
G. a. 11 Scottish business
MS V. b Political verses

Gloucestershire Archives, Gloucester
GDR 201 Diocesan records
P230 CW2/1 North Nibley accounts

Guildhall Library, London (transferred to London Metropolitan Archives)
1016/1 St Matthew Friday Street accounts
2088/1 St Andrew by the Wardrobe accounts
3556/1 St Mary Aldermanbury accounts
4457/2 St Stephen Coleman Street accounts
9059/1 Archdeaconry acts
9064/18 and 19 Commissary acts

Hammersmith and Fulham Archives, Hammersmith
PAF/22 Fulham accounts

Hampshire Record Office, Winchester
44M69/G4 Jervoise of Herriard Papers

Hereford Record Office, Hereford
Office Court Books, Box 27

Hertfordshire Archives, Hertford
ASA 7/32 Archdeaconry records
MS 46351 Articles against Edward Jude

Huntington Library, San Marino, California
Ellesmere MSS
Hastings MSS
Huntington MSS
Stowe–Temple MSS

Kent History and Library Centre, Maidstone (formerly East Kent Archives)
Sandwich Mayor's Letter Book 1639–44

Lambeth Palace Library, London
943 Laud papers
3391 Bramston papers

Leicestershire Record Office, Leicester
I D 41/13/61–5, I D 41/21 Archdeaconry records

Lichfield Record Office, Lichfield
B/V/1/55–66 Archdeaconry records

Lincolnshire Archives, Lincoln
Louth St James accounts
LQS/A/10/81 Quarter Sessions
Vj.21 Diocesan records

London Metropolitan Archives, London
DL/C/319 Diocesan records
MJ/SB/B/4 Sessions book
MJ/SR 890–909 Sessions rolls

The National Archives, Kew
ASSI 45 Northern Assize depositions
C115 Scudamore newsletters
DL 4/79/51 Duchy of Lancaster depositions
E/351 Household accounts
LC 3 and LC 5 Household accounts and orders
LS 1 and 13 Lord Steward's accounts
National Register of Archives, Bound Volumes
PC 2 Privy Council registers
REQ 2 Court of Requests

SO 1–4 Signet Office warrants
SP 16 State Papers
SP 17 State Papers
SP 39 State Papers
SP 46 State Papers

National Library of Wales, Aberystwyth
Great Sessions 983/2/5 Flintshire gaol files

New College, Oxford
MS 9502 Woodford diary

Norfolk Record Office, Norwich
ANF/1/4, ANW 2/72, ANW 3/32, ANW 6/8 Archdeaconry records
C/S1/6 Sessions book
C/S3/26–34 Sessions rolls
DN/VIS 5, 6, 7 Diocesan records
NCR/16a/20 Norwich court book
WLS/XVII/2 Walsingham of Merton papers
Y. C.39/2 Yarmouth accounts

Northamptonshire Record Office, Northampton
Archdeaconry Correction Books 1627–1630

Nottinghamshire Archives, Nottingham
PR 1709 Upton accounts
PR 24,810 Newark accounts

Nottingham University Library, Nottingham
AN/A 47/1 Archdeaconry Records
CL/C Clifton Letters

Oxfordshire Record Office, Oxford
Archdeaconry Papers *c.* 12
Diocesan Papers *c.* 2

Parliamentary Archives, London
House of Lords Main Papers

Queen's College Oxford
MS 390 Crosfield diary

Sheffield Archives, Sheffield
Wentworth Woodhouse Muniments

Shropshire Record Office, Shrewsbury
LB 11/4/68/3 Ludlow Sessions

Somerset Archives, Taunton
DD/PH/219–27 Phelips Manuscripts
D/D/Ca. 313–331 Diocesan records
D/D/Cd. 66 Diocesan records

Staffordshire Record Office, Stafford
D.661/11/1/5 Dyott notebook
D.1287/18/2 Bridgeman correspondence
Q/SO/4 and 5 Sessions orders
Q/SR/243–50 Sessions rolls

Suffolk Record Office, Ipswich
FC 101/E2/23 Framlingham accounts

William Salt Library, Stafford
236/27 Eccleshall accounts

Wiltshire Record Office, Trowbridge
D2/4/1/16 Archdeaconry records

Worcestershire Record Office, Worcester
DR446/21 Shipston-upon-Stour accounts

PRINTED PRIMARY SOURCES

A., G., *Pallas Armata. The Gentlemans Armorie* (1639).

Abbot, Robert, *The Holinesse of Christian Churches* (1638).

The Acts of the High Commission Court within the Diocese of Durham, ed. W. H. D. Longstaff (Surtees Society, vol. 34, 1857).

Acts of the Privy Council of England, 1542–1631, ed. J. R. Dasent et al., 45 vols (1890–1964).

Anderson, R. C. (ed.), *The Book of Examinations and Depositions 1622–1644* (Southampton Record Society, 1936).

Andrewes, Lancelot, *XCVI Sermons ... Published by His Majesties special Command* (1629).

Animadversions upon those Notes Which the late Observator hath published (1642).

An Appeale to the World in these Times of Extreame Danger (1642).

An Appendix to the Late Answer ... Or, Some Seasonable Animadversions upon the late Observator ... Together with a Vindication of the King (1642).

Ar., A., *The Practise of Princes* (Amsterdam, 1630).

The Arminian Nunnery (1641).

Articles Agreed Upon ... Re-printed by His Majesties Commandment: with his royal declaration prefixed thereunto (1630).

Articles Exhibited in Parliament against William Laud (1640).

Articles of Enquiry and Direction for the Diocese of Norwich, in the First Visitation of the Reverend Father in God, Richard Mountaigu (1638).

Ashmole, Elias, *A Briefe Narrative of the Solemn Rites and Ceremonies performed upon the day of the Coronation of our Sovereign Lord King Charles II* (1661).

Aston, Sir Thomas, *A Collection of Sundry Petitions Presented to the King's Most Excellent Majestie* (1642).

Atkinson, J. C. (ed.), *North Riding of the County of York. Quarter Sessions Records. Vol. III* (1885).

Bacon, *Letters from Redgrave Hall: The Bacon Family 1340–1744*, ed. Diarmaid MacCulloch (Suffolk Records Society, vol. 50, 2007).

Bacon, Sir Francis, *Cases of Treason* (1641).

Balcanquall, Walter, *The Honour of Christian Churches* (1633).

Ball, John, *A Short Catechisme: Containing the Principles of Religion*, 18th impression (1637).

Ball, William, *A Caveat for Subjects, Moderating the Observator* (1642).

Bargrave, Isaac, *A Sermon Preached Before King Charles March 27 1627* (1627).

Barnes, Thomas, *Vox Belli, or, An Alarum to Warre* (1626).

Barrington, *Barrington Family Letters 1628–1632*, ed. Arthur Searle (Camden Society, 4th ser., vol. 28, 1983).

Basire, *The Correspondence of Isaac Basire, DD.*, ed. W. N. Darnell (1831).

Baxter, Richard, *Confirmation and Restauration, The Necessary Means of Reformation* (1658).

Bayly, Lewis, *The Practice of Pietie* (1613).

Bayly, Richard, *The Shepheards Starre, or the Ministers Guide* (1640).

Bayly, Thomas, *The Royal Charter Granted unto Kings, by God Himself* (1649).

Beaumont, Sir John, *Bosworth-field: With a Taste of the Variety of Other Poems* (1629).

Bennett, J. H. E., and Dewhurst, J. C. (eds), *Quarter Sessions Records with other Records of the Justices of the Peace for the County Palatinate of Chester 1559–1760* (Record Society of Lancashire and Cheshire, vol. 94, 1940).

Best, *The Farming and Memorandum Books of Henry Best of Elmswell, 1642*, ed. Donald Woodward (1984).

Bidwell, William B., and Jansson, Maija (eds), *Proceedings in Parliament 1626*, 4 vols (New Haven, 1991–6).

Birch, Thomas (ed.), *The Court and Times of Charles the First*, 2 vols (1848).

Bolton, Robert, *Some Generall Directions for a Comfortable Walking with God*, 5th edn (1638).

The Booke of Common Prayer (1633).

Burroughes, Jermiah, *The Glorious Name of God, The Lord of Hosts* (1643).

Boughen, Edward, *Two Sermons: The First, Preached at Canterbury* (1635).

Boughen, Edward, *A Sermon Concerning Decencie and Order in the Church* (1638).

Boughen, Edward, *Master Geree's Case of Conscience Sifted* (1650).

Bramhall, John, *The Serpent Salve, or, A Remedie for the Biting of an Aspe* (York?, 1643).

Brathwaite, Richard, *The English Gentleman* (1630).

Brinsley, John, *The Glorie of the Latter Temple* (1631).
Brugis, T., *The Discovery of a Proiector* (1641).
Brushfield, T. N., 'The Financial Diary of a Citizen of Exeter, 1631–43', *Reports and Transactions of the Devonshire Association*, 33 (1901), 187–269.
Buller, *The Buller Papers*, ed. R. N. Worth (1895).
Burnet, Gilbert, *The Memoires of the Lives and Actions of James and William Dukes of Hamilton* (1677).
Burney, Richard, *An Answer or Necessary Animadversions, upon Some late Impostumate Observations Invective against his Sacred Maiesty* (1642).
Burton, Henry, *A Tryall of Private Devotions. Or, A Diall for the Houres of Prayer* (1628).
Burton, Henry, *A Brief Answer to a late Treatise of the Sabbath Day* (Amsterdam, 1635).
Burton, Henry, *For God, and the King: The Summe of Two Sermons Preached on the Fifth of November last in St Matthewes Friday-Streete* (Amsterdam, 1636).
Burton, Henry, *A Divine Tragedie Lately Acted* (Amsterdam?, 1636).
Burton, Henry, *A Divine Tragedie Lately Acted* (1641).
Burton, Henry, *Englands Bondage and Hope of Deliverance* (1641).
Burton, Henry, *Lord Bishops, None of the Lords Bishops* (1649).
Burton, Robert, *The Anatomy of Melancholy*, ed. Nicolas K. Kiessling, Thomas C. Faulkner, and Rhonda L. Blair, 6 vols (Oxford, 1990).
Cabala, Mysteries of State, in Letters of the Great Ministers of K. James and K. Charles (1654).
Cabala, Sive Scrinia Sacra: Mysteries of State (1691).
Cade, Anthony, *A Sermon Necessarie for these Times* (Cambridge, 1639).
Calendar of State Papers Domestic ... Charles I, ed. John Bruce et al., 23 vols (1858–97).
Calendar of State Papers ... Venice, ed. Rawdon Brown et al., 38 vols (1864–1947).
Calvert, George, *The Answer to Tom-Tell-Troth* (1642).
Carew, Thomas, *Poems* (1640).
[Cary, Grace] (as 'Theophilus Philaleithes Toxander'), *Vox Coeli to England, or, Englands Fore-Warning from Heaven* (1646).
Cawdrey, Daniel, *Superstitio Superstes: or, the Reliques of Superstition Newly Revived* (1641).
Cecil, Edward, *A Iournall, and Relation of the Action ... upon the coast of Spaine* (1626).
Chamberlain, *The Letters of John Chamberlain*, ed. Norman Egbert McClure (American Philosophical Society Memoirs, vol. 12, Philadelphia, 1939).
The Charge Against the King Discharged (1649).
Charles I, *By the King. A Proclamation for the maintenance and encrease of the Mines of Saltpeter, and the true making of Gunpowder, and reforming abuses concerning the same* (13 April 1625).
Charles I, *By the King. A Proclamation for restraint of disorderly and unnecessary resort to the Court* (17 May 1625).

Charles I, *By the King. A Proclamation for restraint of unnecessary resorts to the Court* (26 June 1625).

Charles I, *By the King. A Proclamation to declare His Maiesties pleasure, touching His Royall Coronation, and the Solemnitie thereof* (17 January 1626).

Charles I, *By the King. A Declaration of His Maiesties cleare intention, in requiring the Ayde of His loving Subiects, in that way of Loane which is now intended by His Highnesse* (7 October 1626).

Charles I, *By the King. A Proclamation for the establishing of the Peace and Quiet of the Church of England* (14 June 1626).

Charles I, *By the King. A Proclamation to Prevent the Purloyning and Stealing of Armes, Powder, and other Munition, and Habilliments of Warre* (8 December 1627).

Charles I, *By the King. A Proclamation for the Repressing of Disorders of Marriners* (17 February 1628).

Charles I, *The Kings Maiesties Declaration to His Subiects, Concerning Lawfull Sports to be used* (1633).

Charles I, *By the King. A Proclamation for preservation of Grounds for making of Saltpeter, and to restore such grounds as are now destroyed, and to command Assistance to be given to His Majesties Saltpeter-Makers* (14 March 1635).

Charles I, *By the King. A Proclamation and Declaration to inform Our loving Subjects of Our Kingdom of England of the seditious practices of some in Scotland, seeking to overthrow Our Regall Power under false pretences of Religion* (27 February 1639).

Charles I, *His Majesties Declaration: To All His Loving Subjects, Of the causes which moved him to dissolve the last Parliament* (1640).

Charles I, *His Majesties Answer to the Nineteen Propositions of both Houses of Parliament* (Cambridge, 1642).

Charles I, *His Maiesties Royal Protestation To all His loving Subiects* (1642).

Charles I, *The Kings Cabinet Opened: or, Certain Packets of Secret Letters & Papers, Written with the Kings own Hand* (1645).

Charles I, *Eikon Basilike: The Pourtraicture of His Sacred Majestie in His Solitudes and Sufferings* (1649).

Charles I, *Basilika. The Workes of King Charles the Martyr* (1662).

Charles I, *The Letters, Speeches and Proclamations of King Charles I*, ed. Sir Charles Petrie (1935).

Charles I, *Stuart Royal Proclamations: Volume II: Royal Proclamations of King Charles I 1625–1646*, ed. James F. Larkin (Oxford, 1983).

Chauncy, Charles, *The Retraction of Mr Charles Chancy* (1641).

Cheshire, Thomas, *A True Copy of that Sermon which was preached at S. Pauls the tenth day of October last* (1641).

Clarendon, *State Papers Collected by Edward, Earl of Clarendon*, 3 vols (Oxford, 1767).

Clarendon, *The History of the Rebellion and Civil Wars in England*, ed. W. Dunn Macray, 6 vols (Oxford, 1888).

Cockburn, J. S. (ed.), *Calendar of Assize Records: Kent Indictments. Charles I* (1995).

Complaints Concerning Corruptions and Grievances in Church Government (1641).

A Complete Collection of State-Trials, and Proceedings for High-Treason, 6 vols (1730).
Constitutions and Canons Ecclesiasticall; Treated upon by the Archbishops of Canterbury and York (1640).
Constitutions and Canons Ecclesiasticall. Treated upon by the Bishop of London (1604).
Cope, Esther S., and Willson, H. (eds), *Proceedings of the Short Parliament of 1640* (Camden Society, 4th ser., vol. 19, 1977).
Cosin, *The Correspondence of John Cosin*, part 1, ed. George Ornsby (Surtees Society, vol. 52, 1869).
'The Court of Chivalry 1634–1640', ed. Steven Rea and Richard Cust <http://www.court-of-chivalry.bham.ac.uk/index.htm>.
Cowell, John, *The Interpreter* (Cambridge, 1607).
Cox, J. Charles (ed.), *Three Centuries of Derbyshire Annals: As Illustrated by the Records of the Quarter Sessions*, 2 vols (1890).
Crosfield, *The Diary of Thomas Crosfield*, ed. Frederick S. Boas (Oxford, 1935).
Culmer, Richard, *Cathedrall Newes from Canterbury* (1644).
Cust, Richard P., and Hopper, Andrew J. (eds), *Cases in the High Court of Chivalry, 1634–1640* (Harleian Society, NS, vol. 18, 2006).
Dallington, Robert, *Aphorisms Civill and Militarie* (1613).
Dalton, Michael, *The Country Iustice, Conteyning the Practice of the Iustices of the Peace* (1618).
Davies, Eleanor, *A Warning to the Dragon and all Angels* (1625).
Douglas [i.e. Davies], Eleanor, *Given to the Elector Prince Charles of the Rhyne from the Lady Eleanor, anno 1633* (1648).
Davies, *Prophetic Writings of Lady Eleanor Davies*, ed. Esther S. Cope (New York, 1996).
A Declaration of the House of Commons in Parliament Assembled . . . And a Copy of the Covenant between the Kings of England and the People, at their Coronation (1649).
A Declaration of the Parliament of England, Expressing the Grounds of their Late Proceedings (1649).
The Definition of a King, With the Cure of a King Wilfully Mad, and the Way to Prevent Tyranny (1642).
Delamain, Richard, *Gram[m]elogia or, The Mathematicall Ring* (1630).
Delamain, Richard, *Grammelogia or, the Mathematicall Ring. Extracted from the Logarythmes, and Projected Circular* (1633?).
D'Ewes, *The Autobiography and Correspondence of Sir Simonds D'Ewes*, ed. James Orchard Halliwell, 2 vols (1845).
D'Ewes, *The Journal of Sir Simonds's D'Ewes, from the Beginning of the Long Parliament*, ed. Wallace Notestein (New Haven, 1923).
Die Veneris 5. Maii. 1643 (1643).
Digges, Dudley, *An Answer to a Printed Book, Intituled, Observations upon some of His Majesties Late Answers and Expresses* (Oxford, 1642).
A Discourse discovering some mysteries of our new state . . . shewing the rise and progresse of Englands unhappiness, ab anno illo infortunato, 1641 (Oxford, 1645).
A Diurnall and Particular of the Last Weekes Daily Occurrents (16–26 July 1642).

The Doctrine of the Bible: Or, Rules of Discipline (1604, 1641).

Dod, John, *A Plaine and Familiar Exposition of the Ten Commandments*, 18th edn (1632).

Doughty, John, *The King's Cause Rationally, Briefly, and Plainly Debated, as it Stands de facto. Against the Irrational, Groundless Misprisions of a Still Deceived Sort of People* (Oxford, 1644).

Dover, Robert, *Annalia Dubrensia. Upon the yeerely celebration of Mr Robert Dovers Olimpick Games upon the Cotswold-Hills* (1636).

Dow, Christopher, *Innovations Unjustly Charged upon the Present Church and State* (1637).

Dugdale, William, *The History of Imbanking and Drayning of divers Fenns and Marshes* (1662).

Early Stuart Libels: An Edition of Poetry from Manuscript Sources, ed. Alastair Bellany and Andrew McRae, Early Modern Literary Studies Text Series I (2005) <http://www.earlystuartlibels.net/htdocs/index.html>.

Elborow, John, *Euodias and Syntyche: or, The Female Zelots of the Church of Philippi* (1637).

An Elegie and Epitaph On that glorious Saint, and blessed Martyr, King Charles I (1661).

Eliot, *De Jure Maiestatis, or, Political Treatise of Government (1628–30) and The Letter-Book of Sir John Eliot (1625–1632)*, ed. Alexander B. Grosart, 2 vols (1882).

Ellis, Henry (ed.), *Original Letters Illustrative of English History*, 2nd edn, 3 vols (1825).

Ellis, Henry (ed.), *Original Letters Illustrative of English History*, 2nd ser., 4 vols (1827).

Englands Complaint to Iesus Christ Against the Bishops Canons (1640).

Evelyn, *The Diary of John Evelyn*, ed. William Bray, 6 vols (1879).

Evelyn, *The Diary of John Evelyn*, ed. E. S. de Beer, 6 vols. (Oxford, 1955).

Fairfax, *The Fairfax Correspondence: Memoirs of the Reign of Charles the First*, ed. George W. Johnson, 2 vols (1848).

The Faithful, yet Imperfect, Character of a Glorious King, King Charles I, his Country's and Religion's Martyr (1660).

Featley, John, *Obedience and Submission. A Sermon* (1636).

Ferne, Henry, *The Resolving of Conscience* (1642).

Filmer, *Sir Robert Filmer: Patriarcha and Other Writings*, ed. Johann P. Sommerville (Cambridge, 1991).

Fincham, Kenneth (ed.), *Visitation Articles and Injunctions of the Early Stuart Church*, 2 vols (Woodbridge, 1994–8).

Firth, C. H., and Rait, R. S. (eds), *Acts and Ordinances of the Interregnum, 1642–1660*, 3 vols (1911).

Forde, Thomas, *Virtus Rediviva: Or, A Panegyrick on the late K. Charls the I* (1660).

The Form and Order of the Service that is to be Performed and the Ceremonies that are to be Observed in the Coronation of Her Majesty Queen Elizabeth II (Oxford, 1953).

Fortescue, Sir John, *De Laudibus Legum Angliae: A Learned Commendation of the Politique Lawes of England* (1616).

Fortunes Tennis-ball (1640).

Foster, J. E. (ed.), *Churchwardens Accounts of Great St Mary 1504–1635* (Cambridge, 1905).

Foster, Thomas, *Plouto-Mastix: The Scourge of Covetousnesse; or, An Apologie for the Publike Good, against Privacie* (1631).

Foxe, John, *Acts and Monuments* (1583).

The Free-Holders Grand Inquest Touching Our Soveraigne Lord the King and His Parliament (1648).

Fuller, Thomas, *A Sermon Intended for Paul's Crosse, but Preached in the Church of St Paul's* (1626).

Fuller, Thomas, *The Church History of Britain: From the Birth of Jesus Christ, until the Year MDCXLVII* (1656).

Fuller, Thomas, *The Church History of Britain*, ed. J. S. Brewer, 6 vols (Oxford, 1845).

Gardiner, Samuel Rawson (ed.), *Reports of Cases in the Courts of Star Chamber and High Commission* (Camden Society, NS, vol. 39, 1886).

Gardiner, Samuel Rawson (ed.), *The Constitutional Documents of the Puritan Revolution 1625–1660* (Oxford, 1906).

Gardyner, Richard, *A Sermon Appointed... on the Day of His Maiesties Happy Inauguration* (1642).

Gauden, John, *The Love of Truth and Peace* (1641).

Gauden, John, *Three Sermons Preached Upon Severall Publike Occasions* (1642).

George, Edwin, and George, Stella (eds), *Bristol Probate Inventories Part 1: 1542–1650* (Bristol Record Society, vol. 54, 2002).

Geree, John, *A Case of Conscience Resolved. Wherein it is Cleared, that the King may without impeachment to his Oath, touching the Clergy at Coronation, consent to the Abrogation of Episcopacy* (1646).

Geree, John, *ΣΙΝΙΟΡΡΑΓΙΑ, or the Sifters Sieve Broken* (1648).

Gibson, J. S. W., and Brinkworth, E. R. C. (eds), *Banbury Corporation Records: Tudor and Stuart* (Banbury Historical Society, vol. 15, 1977).

Gillespie, George, *A Dispute Against the English–Popish Ceremonies Obtruded Upon the Church of Scotland* (Leiden?, 1637).

Gods Good Servant, and the Kings Good Subject. A sermon preached at Andover, at a visitation. May 17. 1639 (1642).

Gouge, William, *The Dignitie of Chivalrie, set forth in a sermon preached before the Artillery Company* (1626).

Gouge, William, *A Short Catechisme, wherein are briefly handled the fundamentall principles of Christian Religion*, 7th edn (1635).

Gough, John ('Philomusus'), *The Academy of Complements* (1640).

Greene, 'The Diary of John Greene (1635–57)', ed. E. M. Symonds, *English Historical Review*, 43 (1928), 385–94, 598–604.

Gregory, Ivon L. (ed.), *Hartland Church Accounts, 1597–1706* (Frome and London, 1950).

Grenville, *Ship Money Papers and Sir Richard Grenville's Note-Book*, ed. Carol G. Bonsey and J. G. Jenkins (Buckinghamshire Record Society, vol. 13, 1965).

Griffith, Matthew, *Bethel: or, a Forme for Families* (1633).

Grosse, Robert, *Royalty and Loyalty or A Short Survey of the Power of Kings over their Subjects: and the Duty of Subjects to their Kings* (1647).

Grosvenor, *The Papers of Sir Richard Grosvenor, 1st Bart. (1585–1645)*, ed. Richard Cust (Record Society of Lancashire and Cheshire, vol. 134, 1996).

Guilding, J. M. (ed.), *Reading Records. Diary of the Corporation ... Vol. II* (1895).

Gunton, Symon, *The History of the Church of Peterburgh* (1686).

Gurnay, Edmund, *An Appendix unto the Homily against Images in Churches* (1641).

Gurnay, Edmund, *Gurnay Redivivus* (1660).

Hale, *Sir Matthew Hale's the Prerogatives of the King*, ed. D. E. C. Yale (Selden Society, vol. 92, 1976).

Hall, Joseph, *A Sermon of Publike Thanksgiving for the Wonderful Mitigation of the Late Mortalitie* (1626).

Halliwell, James Orchard (ed.), *Letters of the Kings of England*, 2 vols (1848).

Hamilton, *The Hamilton Papers ... 1638–1650*, ed. Samuel Rawson Gardiner (Camden Society, NS, vol. 27, 1880).

Harbin, E. H. Bates, *Quarter Sessions Records for the County of Somerset, Vol. II. Charles I, 1625–1639* (Somerset Record Society, vol. 24, 1908).

Hardwick, William, *Conformity with Piety, Requisite in Gods Service* (1638).

Harley, *Letters of the Lady Brilliana Harley*, ed. Thomas Taylor Lewis (Camden Society, OS, vol. 58, 1854).

Harris, John, *The Puritanes Impuritie: Or the Anatomie of a Puritane or Separatist* (1641).

Harrison, William, *The Description of England*, ed. Georges Edelen (Ithaca, NY, 1968).

H(ayman), R(obert), *Quodlibets, Lately Come Over from New Britaniola* (1628).

Herbert, *The Works of George Herbert*, ed. F. E. Hutchinson (Oxford, 1941).

Herbert, Sir Thomas, *Memoirs of the Last Two Years of the Reign of King Charles I* (1813).

Heylyn, Peter, *Antidotum Lincolniense* (1637).

Heylyn, Peter, *A Briefe and Moderate Answer, to the Seditious and Scandalous Challenges of Henry Burton* (1637).

Heylyn, Peter, *Cyprianus Anglicus: or, the History of the Life and Death of the most Reverend and Renowned Prelate William* (1671).

Historical Manuscripts Commission, *Third Report* (1872).

Historical Manuscripts Commission, *Fourth Report* (1874).

Historical Manuscripts Commission, *Fifth Report* (1876).

Historical Manuscripts Commission, *Sixth Report* (1877).

Historical Manuscripts Commission, *Seventh Report* (1879).

Historical Manuscripts Commission, *Eighth Report* (1881).

Historical Manuscripts Commission, *Ninth Report* (1884).

Historical Manuscripts Commission, *Report on ... Gawdy* (1885).

Historical Manuscripts Commission, *Tenth Report* (1887).
Historical Manuscripts Commission, *Eleventh Report* (1887).
Historical Manuscripts Commission, *Manuscripts of... Rutland* (1888).
Historical Manuscripts Commission, *Twelfth Report* (1888).
Historical Manuscripts Commission, *Manuscripts of... Cowper*, 3 vols (1888–89).
Historical Manuscripts Commission, *Manuscripts of... Portland*, 4 vols (1891–97).
Historical Manuscripts Commission, *Report on... Buccleuch*, 3 vols (1899–1926).
Historical Manuscripts Commission, *Report on... Various*, 2 vols (1901–3).
Historical Manuscripts Commission, *Report on... Egmont* (1905).
Historical Manuscripts Commission, *Report on... Middleton* (1911).
Historical Manuscripts Commission, *Report on... De L'Isle*, 6 vols (1925–66).
Historical Manuscripts Commission, *Report on... Hastings*, 4 vols (1928–47).
Historical Manuscripts Commission, *Calendar of... Salisbury*, xii (1971).
Hoard, Samuel, *The Churches Authority Asserted: In a Sermon Preached at Chelmsford* (1638).
Hobbes, Thomas, *Behemoth* (1682), ed. William Molesworth (New York, 1963).
Hobbes, *The Correspondence of Thomas Hobbes. Electronic Edition. Vol. I, 1622–1659*, ed. Noel Malcolm (Charlottesville, VA, 2002).
Hodgkinson R. F. B. (ed.), 'Extracts from the Act Books of the Archdeacons of Nottingham', *Transactions of the Thoroton Society*, 31 (1928), 136–7.
Hodson, Phineas, *The Kings Request; Or, David's Desire* (1628).
Holles, *Letters of John Holles 1587–1637*, ed. P. R. Seddon, 3 vols (Thoroton Society Record Series, 1983–6).
Horne, Robert, *The Christian Gouernor, in the Common-wealth, and Priuate Families* (1614).
Horne, Robert, *A Caveat to Prevent Future Iudgements: Or, An Admonition to All England* (1626).
Howell, James, *The True Informer... of the sad distempers in Great Britanny and Ireland* (1643).
Howell, James, *The Instruments of a King: or, A Short Discourse of the Sword. The Scepter. The Crowne* (1648).
Howell, Thomas B. (ed.), *Cobbett's Complete Collection of State Trials*, 33 vols (1809–26).
Howells, B. E. (ed.), *A Calendar of Letters Relating to North Wales. 1533–*circa *1700* (Cardiff, 1967).
Howse, Violet M. (ed.), *Stanford-in-the-Vale Churchwardens' Accounts 1552–1725* (Faringdon, 1987).
Hoyle, R. W. (ed.), *Heard before the King: Registers of Petitions to James I, 1603–1616* (List and Index Society, vols 38 and 39, 2006).
Hunton, Philip, *A Treatise of Monarchie* (1643).
Hurste, Thomas, *The Descent of Authoritie: or, The Magistrates Patent from Heaven* (1637).
I., I., *Reasons why this Kingdom, as all others... ought to adhere to their kings, whether good or bad* (1642).

Instructions for Musters and Armes, And the use thereof (1631).

James I, *The Kings Maiesties Speache to the Lords and Commons* (1610).

James I, *The Dutie of a King in His Royal Office... declaring the true glory of kings* (1642).

James I, *King James VI and I: Selected Writings*, ed. Neil Rhodes, Jennifer Richards, and Joseph Marshall (Aldershot, 2003).

Jansson, Maija (ed.), *Proceedings in the Opening Session of the Long Parliament*, 7 vols (Rochester, NY, 2000–7).

Jeaffreson, John Cordy (ed.), *Middlesex County Records. Vol. III... 1 Charles I to 18 Charles II* (Clerkenwell, 1888).

Jerome, Stephen, *Englands Iubilee, or Irelands Ioyes Io-Paen, for King Charles his Welcome* (Dublin, 1625).

Johnson, Robert C. et al. (eds), *Commons Debates 1628*, 6 vols (New Haven, 1977).

Jones, John, *An Examination of the Observations Upon His Majesties Answers* (1643).

Jones, John, *Christus Dei, The Lords Annoynted... written in answer to a late printed pamphlet* (Oxford, 1643).

Jones, William, *A Commentary upon the Epistle of Saint Paul to Philemon* (1635).

Journal of the House of Commons, 10 vols (1802).

Journal of the House of Lords, 10 vols (1802).

Jubbes, John, *Several Proposals for Peace & Freedom, By an Agreement of the People* (1648).

King, *The Sermons of Henry King (1592–1669)*, ed. Mary Hobbs (Cranbury, NJ, and Aldershot, 1992).

King James His Opinion and Iudgement, concerning a Reall King and a Tyrant (1646).

Knyvett, *The Knyvett Letters (1620–1644)*, ed. Bertram Schofield (Norfolk Record Society, vol. 20, 1949).

L., J., *Englands Doxologie* (1641).

Lachrymae Londoniensis. Or, Londons Teares and Lamentations for Gods Heavie Visitation of the Plague of Pestilence (1626).

The Last Will and Testament of Superstition, Eldest Daughter to Antichrist (1642).

Laud, *The History of the Troubles and Tryal of... William Laud*, comp. Henry Wharton (1695).

Laud, *The Works of the Most Reverend Father in God, William Laud, D.D.*, ed. William Scott and James Bliss, 9 vols (Oxford, 1847–60).

Lawrence, Thomas, *Two Sermons. The First Preached at St Maries in Oxford* (Oxford, 1635).

Lawson, William, *A New Orchard and Garden* (1626).

Legg, Leopold G. Wickham (ed.), *English Coronation Records* (Westminster, 1901).

L'Estrange, Hamon, *The Alliance of Divine Offices* (1659).

A Letter Sent by a Yorkshire Gentleman to a Friend in London (1642).

Lister, John (ed.), *West Riding Sessions Records. Vol. II. Orders, 1611–1642. Indictments, 1637–1642* (Yorkshire Archaeological Society, vol. 53, 1915).

Lord, Henry, *A Display of Two Forraigne Sects in the East Indies* (1630).

M. J., *A Reply to the Answer . . . to a Printed Books Intituled Observations* (1642).

Mainwaring, Roger, *Religion and Alegiance: In Two Sermons Preached before the Kings Maiestie* (1627).

Manley, Sir Roger, *The History of the Rebellions in England, Scotland, and Ireland* (1691).

The Manner of the sitting of the Lords spirituall and temporall, as peeres of the realme in the higher house of Parliament (1628).

Masten, Marjorie (ed.), *Woodstock Chamberlains' Accounts, 1609–50* (Oxfordshire Record Society, vol. 58, 1993).

Maxwell, John, *Sacro-sancta Regum Majestas: or, the Sacred and Royall Prerogative of Christian Kings* (Oxford, 1644).

Mercurius Britanicus (1644–6).

Mercurius Impartialis (1648).

Mercurius Militaris (1648).

Mercurius Pragmaticus (1648).

Milton, John, *Of Reformation touching church-discipline in England* (1641).

Milton, John, *The Tenure of Kings and Magistrates* (1650).

Milton, John, *Complete Prose Works*, ed. D. M. Wolfe et al., 8 vols (New Haven, 1953–82).

Montague, Richard, *Appello Caesarem. A Iust Appeale* (1625).

Montague, Richard, *Articles of Enquiry and Direction for the Diocese of Norwich* (1638).

Mr Speakers Speech, Before the King, in the Lords House of Parliament, July the third, 1641 (1641).

Moore, Percival A. (ed.), 'The Metropolitical Visitation of Archdeacon [*sic*] Laud', *Associated Architectural Societies Reports and Papers*, 29 (1907), 479–534.

Morton, Thomas, *A Sermon Preached Before the Kings most Excellent Majestie, in the Cathedrall Church of Durham* (1639).

Morton, Thomas, *Englands Warning-Piece: Shewing the nature, danger, and Ill Effects of Civill-Warre* (1642).

Morton?, Thomas, *The Necessity of Christian Subjection* (Oxford, 1643).

Mossom, Robert, *The King on his Throne: Or, A Discourse maintaining the Dignity of a King, the Duty of a Subject, and the Unlawfulnesse of Rebellion* (York, 1642).

Nedham, Marchamont, *Certain Considerations Tendered in all Humility* (1649).

Nichols, John, *The Progresses . . . of King James the First*, 4 vols (1828).

Nicolls, Ferdinand, *The Life and Death of Mr Ignatius Jurdain* (1654).

Nineteen Propositions Made By both Houses of Parliament, to the Kings most Excellent Majestie: With His Majesties Answer thereunto (Cambridge, 1642).

Notestein, Wallace, Relf, Frances Helen, and Simpson, Hartley (eds), *Commons Debates 1621*, 7 vols (New Haven, 1935).

The Oath of the kings of England . . . likewise propositions made by both Houses of Parliament to the kings Majesty for a reconciliation of the differences betweene His Majesty and the said Houses (1642).

Obedience Active and Passive Due to the Supream Power (Oxford, 1643).

Oglander, *A Royalist Notebook: The Commonplace Book of Sir John Oglander*, ed. Francis Bamford (1936).

Ogle, O., Bliss, W. H., et al. (eds), *Calendar of the Clarendon State Papers Preserved in the Bodleian Library*, 5 vols (Oxford, 1872–1970).

Oughtred, William, *The Circles of Proportion and the Horizontal Instrument... Translated into English and set forth for the publique benefit by William Forster* (1632).

Ovatio Carolina: The Triumph of King Charles (1641).

Overall, W. H., and Overall, H. C. (eds), *Analytical Index to the Series of Records Known as the Remembrancia... 1579–1664* (1887).

Overton, Richard, *A Remonstrance of Many Thousand Citizens, and other Free-born People* (1646).

Oxinden, *The Oxinden Letters 1607–1642*, ed. Dorothy Gardiner (1933).

Parker, Henry, *Observations upon some of His Majesties late Answers and Expresses* (1642).

Parker, Martin, *An Exact Description of the manner how his Maiestie and his Nobles went to the Parliament* (1640).

Parker, Martin, *The King, and a Poore Northerne Man* (1640).

Paynter, Henry, *Saint Pauls Rule for Religious Performances* (1632).

Peacham, Henry, *The Duty of all True Subiects to their King* (1639).

Perkins, William, *The Whole Treatise of the Cases of Conscience* (Cambridge, 1608).

The Petition and Articles Exhibited in Parliament against Doctor Heywood (1641).

The Petition of Right: Exhibited to his Maiestie, By the Lords and Commons assembled in Parliament, concerning divers Rights and Liberties of the Subject (1642).

Petow, Henry, *Englands Caesar: His Maiesties most Royall Coronation* (1603).

Plomer, Henry R. (ed.), *The Churchwardens's Accounts of St Nicholas, Strood* (Kent Archaeological Society, Kent Records, vol. 5, 1927).

Privy Council Registers Preserved in the Public Record Office Reproduced in Facsimile, 12 vols (1967–8).

A Prophecie of the Life, Reigne, and Death of William Laud (1644).

Propositions Made by both Houses of Parliament to the Kings Maiesty for a reconciliation of the differences betweene His Majesty and the said Houses (1642).

Prynne, William, *Histrio-Mastix: The Players Scourge, or Actors Tragædie* (1633).

Prynne, William, *News from Ipswich: Discovering certain late detestable practices of some domineering Lordly Prelates* (Edinburgh?, 1636).

Pyne, John, *A Brief Meditation upon the Fifteenth Verse of the Twenty Fourth Chapter of the Second Booke of Samuel* (1626).

Pyne, John, *The Heart of the King; and the King of the Heart* (1628).

Quatermayne, Roger, *Quatermayns Conquest Over Canterburies Court* (1642).

Quelch, William, *Church Customs Vindicated* (1636).

Raine, James (ed.), *Depositions from the Castle of York* (Surtees Society, vol. 40, 1861).

Randol, John, *Noble Blastus: The Honor of a Lord Chamberlaine: and of a Good Bed-Chamber-Man* (1633).

Reasons for which the Service Booke urged upon Scotland ought to be Refused (Edinburgh?, 1638).

Records of Early English Drama: Oxford, ed. John R. Elliott et al., 2 vols (London and Toronto, 2004).

Records of Early English Drama: Somerset, ed. James Stokes (London and Toronto, 1996).

Records of the Borough of Nottingham, vol. v . . . 1625–1702 (1900).

A Remonstrance of the Lords and Commons Assembled in Parliament . . . November 2. 1642 (1642).

A Remonstrance of the State of the Kingdom (1641).

A Remonstrance on the behalfe of Cumberland and Westmerland (1641).

A Remonstrance or the Declaration of the Lords and Commons now Assembled in Parliament . . . As also the Oath of the Kings of England at their Coronation (1642).

Reynolds, Edward, *The Shieldes of the Earth* (1636).

Reynolds, Edward, *A Sermon Touching the Peace and Edification of the Church* (1638).

Reynolds, Edward, *Eugenia's Teares* (1642).

Robarts, Foulke, *God's Holy House and Service* (1639).

Rogers, Francis, *A Sermon Preached on September the 20. 1632* (1633).

Rogers, Francis, *A Visitation Sermon Preached at the Lord Archbishops Trienniall and Ordinary Visitation* (1633).

Rogers, Nehemiah, *A Sermon Preached at the Second Trienniall Visitation* (1632).

Ross, Alexander, *Gods House, or the House of Prayer Vindicated from Prophaneness and Sacriledge* (1642).

Rotherham, Thomas, *A Den of Theeves Discovered: Or, Certain Errours and False Doctrines . . . Confuted* (1643).

Rous, *Diary of John Rous, Incumbent of Santon Downham, Suffolk, from 1625 to 1642*, ed. Margaret Anne Everett Green (Camden Society, OS, vol. 66, 1856).

Routledge, F. J. (ed.), *Calendar of the Clarendon State Papers Preserved in the Bodleian Library*, 5 vols (Oxford, 1869–1970).

Rushworth, John, *Historical Collections . . . . ending the Fifth Year of King Charles, Anno 1629* (1659).

Rushworth, John, *Historical Collections: The Second Part* (1680, 1686).

Sadler, John, *Masquerade du Ciel* (1640).

Salter, Robert, *Wonderfull Prophecies from the Beginning of the Monarchy of this Land . . . with an Essay touching the late Prodigious Comete* (1626).

Saltonstall, *The Saltonstall Papers . . . Volume I: 1607–1789*, ed. Robert E. Moody (Boston, 1972).

Sanderson, Robert, *A Soveraigne Antidote Against Sabbatarian Errours* (1636).

Sanderson, William, *A Compleat History of the Life and Raigne of King Charles* (1658).

Sandys, George, *A Relation of a Journey Begin An. Dom. 1610* (1615).

Sclater, William, *The Right Character of a True Subject* (1642).

Selden, John, *Mare Clausum, seu, de Dominio Maris* (1635).

Selden, John, *Of the Dominion, or Ownership of the Sea*, trans. Marchamount Nedham (1652).

Senhouse, Richard, *Foure Sermons Preached at the Court upon several occasions* (1627).
Shelford, Robert, *Five Pious and Learned Discourses* (Cambridge, 1635).
Sibthorpe, Robert, *Apostolike Obedience: Shewing the Duty of Subjects to pay Tribute and Taxes to their Princes, according to the Word of God* (1627).
Sidney, *The Correspondence (c.1626–1659) of Dorothy Percy Sidney, Countess of Leicester*, ed. Michael G. Brennan, Noel J. Kinnaman, and Margaret P. Hanney (Farnham and Burlington, VT, 2010).
Skinner, Robert, *A Sermon Preached Before the King at White-Hall* (1634).
Slingsby, *The Diary of Sir Henry Slingsby*, ed. Daniel Parsons (1836).
Smart, Peter, *The Vanitie & Downe-fall of Superstitious Popish Ceremonies* (Edinburgh, 1628).
Smart, Peter, *A Catalogue of Superstitious Innovations* (1642).
Smith, Sir Thomas, *De Republica Anglorum, The Maner of Governement or Policie of the Realme of England* (1583).
Smyth, *Calendar of the Correspondence of the Smyth Family of Ashton Court 1548–1647*, ed. J. H. Bettey (Bristol Record Society, vol. 35, 1982).
Some Seasonable Animadversions upon the late Observator... Together with a Vindication of the King (1642).
The Sovereignty of Kings (1642).
Spelman, Sir John, *A View of a Printed Book Intituled 'Observations upon His Majesties Late Answers and Expresses'* (1642).
Spelman, Sir John, *Certain Considerations Upon the Duties of both Prince and People* (Oxford, 1643).
Spencer, John, *A Discourse of Divers Petitions of High Concernment* (1641).
Stanford, Sir William, *An Exposition of the Kings Prerogative* (1607).
Starkey, Thomas, *Exhortation to the People, Instructyng theym to Unitie and Obedience* (1536).
Statutes of the Realm, ed. T. E. Tomlins et al., 11 vols (1810–28).
Stocks, Helen, and Stevenson, W. H. (eds), *Records of the Borough of Leicester... 1603–1688* (Cambridge, 1923).
St John, Oliver, *Mr St John's Speech to the Lords... Concerning Ship-Money* (1641).
A Strange Wonder, or, The Cities Amazement (1641).
Studley, Peter, *The Looking-Glasse of Schisme* (1635).
The Subjects Liberty set forth in the Royall and Politique Power of England (1643).
Swadlin, Thomas, *The Soveraignes Desire Peace: The Subiects Dutie Obedience* (1643).
Swan, John, *Profanomastix. Or, a Brief and Necessarie Direction concerning the respects which we Owe to God, and his House* (1639).
Swan, John, *Redde Debitum. Or, A Discourse in Defence of Three Chiefe Fatherhoods* (1640).
Swayne, Henry James Fowle (ed.), *Churchwardens' Accounts of S. Edmund and S. Thomas, Sarum, 1443–1702* (Salisbury, 1896).
Sydenham, Humphrey, *Moses and Aaron, or The Affinitie of Civill and Ecclesiastick Power* (1636).

Symmons, Edward, *A Vindication of King Charles: or, A Loyal Subjects Duty* (1648).
T., R., *De Templis, a Treatise of Temples* (1638).
Taylor, John, *Wit and Mirth* (1626).
Taylor, John, *Differing Worships, or, The Oddes, between some Knights Service and God's* (1640).
Taylor, John, *Englands Comfort, and Londons Ioy: Expressed in the Royall, Triumphant, and Magnificent Entertainment of our Dread Soveraigne Lord, King Charles, at his blessed and safe returne from Scotland* (1641).
Taylor, John, *The Whole Life and Progresse of Henry Walker the Ironmonger* (1642).
Taylor, John, *The Conversion, Confession, Contrition, Coming to Himself, & Advice of a Mis-led, Ill-bred, Rebellious Round-Head* (1643).
Taylor, John, *Tailors Travels, from London to the Isle of Wight* (1648).
These Trades-men are Preachers in and about the City of London (1647).
Timberlake, Henry, *A Relation of the Travels of two English Pilgrimes* (1603).
To the Kings Most Excellent Majesty. The Humble Petition of Divers Hundreds of the Kings Poore Subjects, Afflicted with that Grievous Infirmities, called The Kings Evil (1643).
Tom Tell Troath or A Free Discourse Touching the Manners of the Tyme (Amsterdam?, 1630).
Trescot, Thomas, *The Zealous Magistrate* (1642).
Trevelyan, *Trevelyan Papers, Part III*, ed. W. C. and C. E. Trevelyan (Camden Society, OS, vol. 105, 1872).
A True Discourse of all the Royal Passages, Tryumphs and Ceremonies (1625).
A True Relation of His Majesties Reception and Royall Entertainment at Lincoln: by the Knights, Esquires, Gentlemen, and Freeholders of the said County (1642).
A True Relation of Those Sad and Lamentable Accidents, which happened in and about the Parish Church of Withycombe in the Dartmoores, in Devonshire, on Sunday the 21 of October last, 1638 (1638).
Turner, Thomas, *A Sermon Preached before the King at White-Hall, the tenth of March* (1635).
The Two Books of Homilies Appointed to be Read in Churches (Oxford, 1859).
Udall, Ephraim, *The Good of Peace and Ill of Warre* (1642).
The Unlimited Prerogative of Kings Subverted (1642).
Valentine, Henry, *God Save the King: A Sermon Preached in St Pauls Church the 27th of March 1639* (1639).
Verney, *Letters and Papers of the Verney Family*, ed. H. Verney (Camden Society, OS, vol. 56, 1853).
Vicars, John, *The Sinfulness and Unlawfulness, of having or making the Picture of Christ's Humanity* (1641).
Vicars, John, *All the Memorable & Wonder-strikinge, Parlamentary Mercies effected & afforded unto this our English nation* (1642).
Vicars, John, *Jehovah-Jireh: God in the Mount. Or, Englands Parliamentarie-Chronicle* (1644).

Vindiciae Contra Tyrannos: A Defence of Liberty Against Tyrants (1648).
W., J., *The Valiant Scot* (1637).
Wakeman, Offley (ed.), *Shropshire County Records: Abstracts of the Orders made by the Court of Quarter Sessions for Shropshire, January, 1638–May, 1660* (Shrewsbury, 1905).
Walker, Sir Edward (attrib.), *Iter Carolinum. Being a Succinct Relation of the Necessitated Marches, Retreats, and Sufferings of His Majesty Charls the I* (1660).
Walker, Henry, *The Churches Purity* (1641).
Wallington, Nehemiah, *Historical Notices of Events Occurring Chiefly in the Reign of Charles I*, 2 vols (1869).
Wallington, *The Notebooks of Nehemiah Wallington, 1618–1654*, ed. David Booy (Aldershot and Burlington, VT, 2007).
Walworth, *The Correspondence of Nathan Walworth and Peter Seddon of Outwood*, ed. John Samuel Fletcher (Chetham Society, vol. 109, 1880).
Warmstry, Thomas, *Pax Vobis or A Charme for Tumultuous Spirits* (1641).
Wentworth, *The Earl of Strafforde's Letters and Dispatches*, ed. William Knowler, 2 vols (1739).
Whereas it hath pleased Almighty God to call to his mercie our late Sovereigne Lord, King Iames (1625).
White, Francis, *A Treatise of the Sabbath-Day*, 3rd edn (1635).
White, John, *The First Century of Scandalous, Malignant Priests* (1643).
Whiteway, *William Whiteway of Dorchester His Diary 1618 to 1635* (Dorset Record Society, vol. 12, 1991).
Wigmore, Michael, *The Meteors: A Sermon* (1633).
Willis Bund, J. W. (ed.), *Worcestershire County Records. Division I... Calendar of Quarter Sessions Papers... 1591–1643* (Worcester, 1900).
Willoughby, *Francis Willoughby's Book of Games: A Seventeenth-Century Treatise on Sports, Games and Pastimes*, ed. David Cram, Jeffrey L. Forgeng, and Dorothy Johnston (Aldershot and Burlington, VT, 2003).
Wilson, Jeffrey, *A New Almanacke or Prognostication* (1626).
Wilson, Thomas, 'The State of England Ann-dom. 1600', ed. F. J. Fisher (*Camden Miscellany*, no. 16, 1936), 19–39.
Winstanley, William, *The Loyal Martyrology* (1665).
Winthrop, *Winthrop Papers*, iii. *1631–1637* (Massachusetts Historical Society, Boston, 1943).
Woodford, *The Diary of Robert Woodford, 1637–1641*, ed. John Fielding (Camden Society, 5th ser., vol. 42, 2012).
Woodhouse, A. S. P. (ed.), *Puritanism and Liberty: Being the Army Debates (1647–9)* (1938; repr. 1966).
Wordsworth, Christopher (ed.), *The Coronation of King Charles I* (Henry Bradshaw Society, vol. 2, 1892).
Worthington, *The Diary and Correspondence of Dr John Worthington*, ed. James Crossley (Chetham Society Remains, vol. 13, 1847).
Wotton, Sir Henry, *A Panegyrick of King Charles* (1649).

Wotton, Sir Henry, *Reliquiae Wottonianae*, 4th edn (1685).
Wren, Christopher, *Parentalia; or, Memoirs of the Family of the Wrens* (1750).
Wyllys, *The Wyllys Papers* (Collections of the Connecticut Historical Society, vol. 21; Hartford, CT, 1924).
Wynn, *Calendar of Wynn (of Gwydir) Papers 1515–1690* (Aberystwyth, 1926).
Yates, John, *A Treatise of the Honor of Gods House* (1637).
Yonge, *Diary of Walter Yonge, Esq.*, ed. George Roberts (Camden Society, OS, vol. 41, 1848).
Younge, Richard, *The Poores Advocate* (1654).
Zouch, Richard, *The Sophister* (1639).

SECONDARY SOURCES

Adamson, John, *The Noble Revolt: The Overthrow of Charles I* (2007).
Andrews, Kenneth R., *Ships, Money and Politics: Seafaring and Naval Enterprise in the Reign of Charles I* (Cambridge, 1991).
Asch, Ronald G., 'Sacred Kingship in France and England in the Age of the Wars of Religion: From Disenchantment to Re-Enchantment?', in Charles W. A. Prior and Glenn Burgess (eds), *England's Wars of Religion Revisited* (Farnham and Burlington, VT, 2011), 27–47.
Ashley, Maurice, *Life in Stuart England* (1964).
Atherton, Ian, and Sanders, Julie (eds), *The 1630s: Interdisciplinary Essays on Culture and Politics in the Caroline Era* (Manchester and New York, 2006).
Aylmer, G. E., 'The Last Years of Purveyance 1610–1660', *Economic History Review*, NS 10 (1957), 81–93.
Aylmer, G. E., *The King's Servants: The Civil Service of Charles I, 1625–42* (1961).
Baker, J. N. L., 'The Climate of England in the Seventeenth Century', *Quarterly Journal of the Royal Meteorological Society*, 58 (1932), 421–38.
Banks, Charles Edward, *Topographical Dictionary of 2885 English Emigrants to New England 1620–1650* (Baltimore, 1969).
Barish, Jonas, *The Antitheatrical Prejudice* (Berkeley and Los Angeles, 1981).
Barnes, T. G., 'County Politics and a Puritan Cause Célèbre: Somerset Church Ales, 1633', *Transactions of the Royal Historical Society*, 5th ser. (1959), 103–22.
Barnes, Thomas Garden, *Somerset 1625–1640: A County's Government during the 'Personal Rule'* (Cambridge, MA, 1961).
Barratt, D. M., 'The Bankes Papers: A First Report', *Bodleian Library Record*, 4 (1952–3), 313–23.
Beier, A. L., *Masterless Men: The Vagrancy Problem in England 1560–1640* (1985).
Bernard, G. W. E., *War, Taxation and Rebellion in Early Tudor England: Henry VIII, Wolsey, and the Amicable Grant of 1525* (Brighton and New York, 1986).
Black, Joseph, '"Pikes and Protestations": Scottish Texts in England, 1639–40', *Publishing History*, 42 (1997), 5–19.

Bloch, Marc, *The Royal Touch: Sacred Monarchy and Scrofula in England and France* (1973).

Boynton, Lindsay, 'Billeting: The Example of the Isle of Wight', *English Historical Review*, 74 (1959), 23–40.

Boys, Jane E. E., *London's News Press and the Thirty Years War* (Woodbridge, 2011).

Braddick, Michael, *God's Fury, England's Fire: A New History of the English Civil Wars* (2008).

Braddick, Michael J., *State Formation in Early Modern England* c.*1550–1700* (Cambridge, 2000).

Bryden, D. J., 'A Patchery and Confusion of Disjointed Stuffe: Richard Delamain's *Grammelogia* of 1631/3', *Transactions of the Cambridge Bibliographic Society*, 6 (1974), 158–66.

Bucholz, Robert, and Key, Newton, *Early Modern England 1485–1714* (Oxford, 2004).

Burgess, Glenn, *The Politics of the Ancient Constitution: An Introduction to English Political Thought, 1603–1642* (University Park, PA, 1993).

Cambers, Andrew, 'Pastoral Laudianism? Religious Politics in the 1630s: A Leicestershire Rector's Annotations', *Midland History*, 27 (2002), 38–51.

Campbell, Bruce M. S., 'Nature as Historical Protagonist: Environment and Society in Pre-industrial England', *Economic History Review*, 63 (2010), 281–314.

Campbell, Mildred, *The English Yeoman in the Tudor and Stuart Age* (1967).

Capp, Bernard, *The World of John Taylor, the Water-Poet, 1578–1653* (Oxford, 1994).

Capp, Bernard, *When Gossips Meet: Women, the Family and Neighbourhood in Early Modern England* (Oxford, 2003).

Capp, Bernard, *England's Culture Wars: Puritan Reformation and its Enemies in the Interregnum 1649–1660* (Oxford, 2012).

Cardwell, Edward, *A History of Conferences* (Oxford, 1840).

Carlton, Charles, *Charles I: The Personal Monarch*, 2nd edn (1995).

Carlton, Charles, *This Seat of Mars: War and the British Isles, 1485–1746* (New Haven, 2011).

Cervone, Thea, *Sworn Bond in Tudor England: Oaths, Vows and Covenants in Civil Life and Literature* (Jefferson, NC, and London, 2011).

Chandler, George, *Liverpool under Charles I* (Liverpool, 1965).

Clark, Peter, *English Provincial Society from the Reformation to the Revolution: Religion, Politics and Society in Kent 1500–1640* (Cranbury, NJ, 1977).

Clegg, Cyndia Susan, *Press Censorship in Caroline England* (Cambridge, 2008).

Cogswell, Thomas, *The Blessed Revolution: English Politics and the Coming of War, 1621–1624* (Cambridge, 1989).

Cogswell, Thomas, 'The Human Comedy in Westminster: *The House of Commons, 1604–1629*', *Journal of British Studies*, 52 (2013), 370–89.

Collinson, Patrick, *The Religion of Protestants: The Church in English Society 1559–1625* (Oxford, 1982).

Collinson, Patrick, '"Shepherds, Sheepdogs, and Hirelings": The Pastoral Ministry in Post-Reformation England', in W. J. Sheils and Diana Wood (eds), *The Ministry: Clerical and Lay. Studies in Church History*, 26 (Oxford, 1989), 185–220.

Como, David, 'Radical Puritanism, *c.*1558–1660', in John Coffey and Paul C. H. Lim (eds), *The Cambridge Companion to Puritanism* (Cambridge, 2008), 241–58.

Como, David R., *Blown by the Spirit: Puritanism and the Emergence of an Antinomian Underground in Pre-Civil-War England* (Stanford, 2004).

Condren, Conal, *Argument and Authority in Early Modern England: The Presupposition of Oaths and Offices* (Cambridge, 2006).

Cooper, C. H., *Annals of Cambridge*, iii (Cambridge, 1845).

Cope, Esther S., *Handmaid of the Holy Spirit: Dame Eleanor Davies, Never Soe Mad a Ladie* (Ann Arbor, 1992).

Corns, Thomas N. (ed.), *The Royal Image: Representations of Charles I* (Cambridge, 1999).

Cox, J. Charles, and Serjeantson, R. M., *A History of the Church of the Holy Sepulchre, Northampton* (Northampton, 1897).

Craig, John, 'Psalms, Groans and Dog-Whippers: The Soundscape of Sacred Space in the English Parish Church, 1547–1642', in Will Coster and Andrew Spicer (eds), *Sacred Space in Early Modern Europe* (Cambridge, 2005), 104–23.

Crawford, Patricia, '"Charles Stuart, that Man of Blood"', *Journal of British Studies*, 16 (1971), 41–61.

Crawford, Patricia, *Women and Religion in England 1500–1720* (1993).

Cressy, David, 'Describing the Social Order of Elizabethan and Stuart England', *Literature and History*, 3 (1976), 29–44.

Cressy, David, *Literacy and the Social Order: Reading and Writing in Tudor and Stuart England* (Cambridge, 1980).

Cressy, David, *Coming Over: Migration and Communication between England and New England in the Seventeenth Century* (Cambridge, 1987).

Cressy, David, 'A Drudgery of Schoolmasters: The Teaching Profession in Elizabethan and Stuart England', in Wilfrid Prest (ed.), *The Professions in Early Modern England* (1987), 129–53.

Cressy, David, *Bonfires and Bells: National Memory and the Protestant Calendar in Elizabethan and Stuart England* (1989).

Cressy, David, 'Conflict, Consensus and the Willingness to Wink: The Erosion of Community in Charles I's England', *Huntington Library Quarterly*, 61 (2000), 131–49.

Cressy, David, *Travesties and Transgressions in Tudor and Stuart England* (Oxford, 2000).

Cressy, David, 'Early Modern Space Travel and the English Man in the Moon', *American Historical Review*, 111 (2006), 961–82.

Cressy, David, *England on Edge: Crisis and Revolution 1640–1642* (Oxford, 2006).

Cressy, David, *Dangerous Talk: Scandalous, Seditious and Treasonable Speech in Pre-Modern England* (Oxford, 2010).

Cressy, David, 'The Death of a Vice-Chancellor; Cambridge, 1632', *History of Universities*, 26 (2012), 92–112.

Cressy, David, *Saltpeter: The Mother of Gunpowder* (Oxford, 2013).

Cressy, David, and Ferrell, Lori Anne (eds), *Religion and Society in Early Modern England: A Sourcebook*, 2nd edn (2005).

Cust, Richard, *The Forced Loan and English Politics, 1626–1628* (Oxford, 1987).

Cust, Richard, *Charles I: A Political Life* (Harlow, 2005).

Cust, Richard, *Charles I and the Aristocracy, 1625–1642* (Cambridge, 2013).

Cust, Richard, 'Charles I and the Order of the Garter', *Journal of British Studies*, 52 (2013), 343–69.

Cust, Richard, 'Debate. Charles I: A Case of Mistaken Identity', *Past & Present*, 205 (2009), 201–12.

Darby, H. C., *The Draining of the Fens*, 2nd edn (Cambridge, 1956).

Davies, Julian, *The Caroline Captivity of the Church: Charles I and the Remoulding of Anglicanism* (Oxford, 1992).

Donagan, Barbara, *War in England 1642–1649* (Oxford, 2008).

Donald, Peter, *An Uncounselled King: Charles I and the Scottish Troubles, 1637–1641* (Cambridge, 1990).

Dougall, Alistair, *The Devil's Book: Charles I, the Book of Sports and Puritanism in Tudor and Stuart England* (Exeter, 2011).

Duffy, Eamon, 'The Godly and the Multitude in Stuart England', *Seventeenth Century*, 1 (1986), 31–55.

Ertman, Thomas, *Birth of the Leviathan: Building States and Regimes in Medieval and Early Modern Europe* (Cambridge, 1997).

Evans, J., 'The Vicar of Godalming and his Parishioners in 1640', *Surrey Archaeological Collections*, 2 (1884), 210–23.

Evans, John T., *Seventeenth-Century Norwich* (Oxford, 1979).

Everitt, Alan, *The Community of Kent and the Great Rebellion 1640–60* (Leicester, 1966).

Fagan, Brian, *The Little Ice Age: How Climate Made History 1300–1850* (New York, 2000).

Fielding, John, 'Arminianism in the Localities: Peterborough Diocese, 1603–1642', in Kenneth Fincham (ed.), *The Early Stuart Church, 1603–1642* (1993), 93–113.

Fincham, Kenneth, 'The Judges' Decision on Ship Money in February 1637: The Reaction of Kent', *Bulletin of the Institute of Historical Research*, 57 (1984), 230–7.

Fincham, Kenneth, *Prelate as Pastor: The Episcopate of James I* (Oxford, 1990).

Fincham, Kenneth, 'The Restoration of Altars in the 1630s', *Historical Journal*, 44 (2001), 919–40.

Fincham, Kenneth, and Lake, Peter, 'The Ecclesiastical Policies of James I and Charles I', in Kenneth Fincham (ed.), *The Early Stuart Church, 1603–1642* (1993), 23–49.

Fincham, Kenneth, and Tyacke, Nicholas, *Altars Restored: The Changing Face of English Religious Worship, 1547–c.1700* (Oxford, 2007).

Finlay, Roger, *Population and Metropolis: The Demography of London 1580–1650* (Cambridge, 1981).

Firth, C. H., 'The Reign of Charles I', *Transactions of the Royal Historical Society*, 3rd ser. 6 (1912), 19–24.

Fissel, Mark Charles (ed.), *War and Government in Britain, 1598–1650* (Manchester and New York, 1991).

Fissel, Mark Charles, *The Bishops' Wars: Charles I's Campaigns against Scotland 1638–1640* (Cambridge, 1994).

Fissel, Mark Charles, *English Warfare, 1511–1642* (2001).

Flather, Amanda, *Gender and Space in Early Modern England* (2007).

Fletcher, Anthony, *A County Community in Peace and War: Sussex 1600–1660* (1975).

Floud, Roderick, Wachter, Kenneth, and Gregory, Annabel, *Height, Health and History: Nutritional Status in the United Kingdom, 1750–1980* (Cambridge, 1990).

Floud, Roderick, Fogel, Robert W., Harris, Bernard, and Hong, Sock Chul, *The Changing Body: Health, Nutrition, and Human Development in the Western World since 1700* (Cambridge, 2011).

Foster, Andrew, 'Church Policies of the 1630s', in Richard Cust and Ann Hughes (eds), *Conflict in Early Stuart England: Studies in Religion and Politics 1603–1642* (1989), 193–223.

Fox, Adam, 'Food, Drink and Social Distinction in Early Modern England', in Steve Hindle, Alexandra Shepard, and John Walter (eds), *Remaking English Society: Social Relations and Social Change in Early Modern England* (Woodbridge, 2013), 165–87.

Frank, Joseph, *The Beginnings of the English Newspaper 1620–1660* (Cambridge, MA, 1961).

Games, Alison, *Migration and the Origins of the English Atlantic World* (Cambridge, MA, 1999).

Games, Alison, *The Web of Empire: English Cosmopolitans in an Age of Expansion 1560–1660* (Oxford, 2008).

Gardiner, Samuel Rawson, *A History of England under the Duke of Buckingham and Charles I: 1624–1628*, 2 vols (1875).

Goodare, Julian, 'Debate. Charles I: A Case of Mistaken Identity', *Past & Present*, 205 (2009), 189–201.

Gordon, M. D., 'The Collection of Ship Money in the Reign of Charles I', *Transactions of the Royal Historical Society*, 3rd ser., 4 (1910), 141–62.

Goring, Jeremy, *Godly Exercises or the Devil's Dance? Puritanism and Popular Culture in Pre-Civil War England* (1983).

Gowing, Laura, *Domestic Dangers: Women, Words, and Sex in Early Modern London* (Oxford, 1996).

Griffiths, Paul, *Lost Londons: Change, Crime and Control in the Capital City, 1550–1660* (Cambridge, 2008).

Grueber, H. A. (ed.), *Medallic Illustrations of the History of Great Britain and Ireland*, 2 vols (1904–11; repr. Lawrence, MA, 1979).

Guy, John, 'The Origins of the Petition of Right Reconsidered', *Historical Journal*, 25 (1982), 289–312.

Haigh, Christopher, 'Anticlericalism and the English Reformation', in Christopher Haigh (ed.), *The English Reformation Revised* (Cambridge, 1987), 56–74.

Haigh, Christopher, *The Plain Man's Pathways to Heaven: Kinds of Christianity in Post-Reformation England* (Oxford, 2007).

Harris, Tim, *Rebellion: Britain's First Stuart Kings, 1567–1742* (Oxford, 2014).

Harriss, G. L., 'Medieval Doctrines in the Debates on Supply, 1610–1629', in Kevin Sharpe (ed.), *Faction and Parliament: Essays on Early Stuart History* (1978), 73–103.

Heal, Felicity, and Holmes, Clive, *The Gentry in England and Wales, 1500–1700* (Stanford, 1994).

Henry, Gráinne, 'Ulster Exiles in Europe, 1605–1641', in Brian MacCuarta (ed.), *Ulster 1641: Aspects of the Rising* (Belfast, 1993), 37–60, 195–200.

Hibbard, Caroline, *Charles I and the Popish Plot* (Chapel Hill, NC, 1983).

Hibbard, Caroline M., 'The Role of a Queen Consort: The Household and Court of Henrietta Maria, 1625–1642', in Ronald G. Asch and Adolf M. Birke (eds), *Princes, Patronage, and Nobility: The Court at the Beginning of the Modern Age c.1450–1650* (Oxford, 1991), 393–414.

Hill, Christopher, *The Economic Problems of the Church from Archbishop Whitgift to the Long Parliament* (Oxford, 1956).

Hill, J. F. W., 'The Royalist Clergy of Lincolnshire', *Lincolnshire Architectural and Archaeological Society Reports and Papers*, vol. 2, part 1, NS for 1938 (Lincoln, 1940).

Hindle, Steve, *The State and Social Change in Early Modern England, 1550–1640* (Basingstoke, 2000).

Hindle, Steve, *On the Parish? The Micro-Politics of Poor Relief in Rural England, c.1550–1750* (Oxford, 2004).

Hindle, Steve, Shepard, Alexandra, and Walter, John (eds), *Remaking English Society: Social Relations and Social Change in Early Modern England* (Woodbridge, 2013).

Holmes, Clive, *Seventeenth-Century Lincolnshire* (Lincoln, 1980).

Holmes, Clive, 'Drainers and Fenmen: The Problem of Popular Political Consciousness in the Seventeenth Century', in Anthony Fletcher and John Stevenson (eds), *Order and Disorder in Early Modern England* (Cambridge, 1985), 166–95.

Holmes, Clive, 'Debate. Charles I: A Case of Mistaken Identity', *Past & Present*, 205 (2009), 175–88.

House of Commons Library, Standard Note SN/PC/03861 'The Royal Prerogative' (2009).

Houston, R. A., *The Population History of Britain and Ireland, 1500–1750* (Basingstoke, 1992).

Howard, Jean E., *The Stage and Social Struggle in Early Modern England* (1994).

Hoyle, R. W., 'Petitioning as Popular Politics in Early Sixteenth-Century England', *Historical Research*, 75 (2002), 365–89.

Hubbard, Eleanor, *City Women: Money, Sex, and the Social Order in Early Modern London* (Oxford, 2012).

Hughes, Ann, *Politics, Society, and Civil War in Warwickshire, 1620–1660* (Cambridge, 1987).

Hughes, Ann, *Gender and the English Revolution* (2012).

Hunt, William, *The Puritan Moment: The Coming of Revolution in an English County* (Cambridge, MA, 1983).

Janković, Vladimir, *Reading the Skies: A Cultural History of English Weather, 1650–1820* (Chicago and London, 2000).

Jones, David Martin, *Conscience and Allegiance in Seventeenth Century England: The Political Significance of Oaths and Engagements* (Rochester, NY, 1999).

Kassell, Lauren, *Medicine and Magic in Elizabethan London: Simon Forman: Astrologer, Alchemist, and Physician* (Oxford, 2005).

Kennedy, Mark E., 'Charles I and Local Government: The Draining of the East and West Fens', *Albion*, 15 (1983), 19–31.

Kenyon, J. P. (ed.), *The Stuart Constitution* (Cambridge, 1966; 2nd edn, 1986).

Kishlansky, Mark, *A Monarchy Transformed: Britain 1603–1714* (1996).

Kishlansky, Mark, 'Tyranny Denied: Charles I, Attorney General Heath, and the Five Knights Case', *Historical Journal*, 42 (1999), 53–83.

Kishlansky, Mark, 'Charles I: A Case of Mistaken Identity', *Past & Present*, 189 (2005), 41–80.

Kishlansky, Mark, 'Debate: Charles I: A Case of Mistaken Identity. Reply', *Past & Present*, 205 (2009), 212–37.

Kishlansky, Mark, 'A Whipper Whipped: The Sedition of William Prynne', *Historical Journal*, 56 (2013), 603–27.

Kishlansky, Mark, 'Martyrs' Tales', *Journal of British Studies*, 53 (2014), 334–55.

Kronk, Gary W., *Cometography: A Catalog of Comets*, 5 vols (Cambridge, 1999).

Lake, Peter, 'The Collection of Ship Money in Cheshire during the Sixteen-Thirties: A Case Study of Relations between Central and Local Government', *Northern History*, 17 (1981), 44–71.

Lake, Peter, 'Anti-Popery: The Structure of a Prejudice', in Richard Cust and Ann Hughes (eds), *Conflict in Early Stuart England: Studies in Religion and Politics, 1603–1642* (1989), 72–106.

Lake, Peter, 'The Laudian Style: Order, Uniformity and the Pursuit of the Beauty of Holiness in the 1630s', in Kenneth Fincham (ed.), *Early Stuart Church, 1603–1642* (1993), 161–85.

Lake, Peter, *The Boxmaker's Revenge: 'Orthodoxy', 'Heterodoxy', and the Politics of the Parish in Early Stuart London* (Stanford, 2001).

Langelüddecke, Henrik, '"The chiefest strength and glory of this kingdom": Arming and Training the "Perfect Militia" in the 1630s', *English Historical Review*, 118 (2003), 1264–303.

Langelüddecke, Henrik, '"I finde all men & my officers all soe unwilling": The Collection of Ship Money, 1635–1640', *Journal of British Studies*, 46 (2007), 509–42.

Lindley, K. J., 'The Lay Catholics of England in the Reign of Charles I', *Journal of Ecclesiastical History*, 22 (1971), 199–221.

Lindley, Keith, *Fenland Riots and the English Revolution* (1982).

Lindquist, Eric N., 'The King, the People, and the House of Commons: The Problem of Early Jacobean Purveyance', *Historical Journal*, 31 (1988), 549–70.

Lysons, Daniel, *Magna Britannia*, 6 vols (1806–22).

Macadam, Joyce, '*Mercurius Britanicus* on Charles I: An Exercise in Civil War Journalism and High Politics, August 1643 to May 1646', *Historical Research*, 84 (2011), 470–92.

MacCuarta, Brian (ed.), *Ulster 1641: Aspects of the Rising* (Belfast, 1993).

McCullough, Peter E., *Sermons at Court: Politics and Religion in Elizabethan and Jacobean Preaching* (Cambridge, 1998).

MacGregor, Arthur (ed.), *The Late King's Goods: Collections, Possessions and Patronage of Charles I in the Light of the Commonwealth Sale Inventories* (1989).

Machin, Bob, '"To take theire plases wheare they shall not offend others"—the 1635 Re-Seating of Puddletown Church, Dorset', *Transactions of the Ancient Monuments Society*, 53 (2009), 7–14.

Mack, Phyllis, *Visionary Women: Ecstatic Prophecy in Seventeenth-Century England* (Berkeley and Los Angeles, 1994).

McLaren, Anne, 'Rethinking Republicanism: *Vindiciae Contra Tyrannos* in Context', *Historical Journal*, 49 (2006), 23–52.

Maltby, Judith, *Prayer Book and People in Elizabethan and Early Stuart England* (Cambridge, 1998).

Marsh, Christopher, 'Common Prayer in England, 1560–1640: The View from the Pew', *Past & Present*, 171 (2001), 66–94.

Marsh, Christopher, 'Sacred Space in England, 1560–1640: The View from the Pew', *Journal of Ecclesiastical History*, 53 (2002), 286–311.

Marsh, Christopher, 'Order and Place in England, 1560–1640', *Journal of British Studies*, 49 (2005), 3–26.

Mendle, Michael, *Dangerous Positions: Mixed Government, the Estates of the Realm, and the Making of the Answer to the XIX Propositions* (Tuscaloosa, AL, 1985).

Mendle, Michael, 'The Ship Money Case, *The Case of Shipmony*, and the Development of Henry Parker's Parliamentary Absolutism', *Historical Journal*, 32 (1989), 513–36.

Mendle, Michael, *Henry Parker and the English Civil War: The Political Thought of the Public's 'Privado'* (Cambridge, 1995).

Mendleson, Sara, and Crawford, Patricia, *Women in Early Modern England 1500–1720* (Oxford, 1998).

Merrick, Jeffery, *The Desacralization of the French Monarchy in the Eighteenth Century* (Baton Rouge, 1990).

Millstone, Noah, 'Evil Counsel: The *Propositions to Bridle the Impertinency of Parliament* and the Critique of Caroline Government in the Late 1620s', *Journal of British Studies*, 50 (2011), 813–39.

Milton, Anthony, *Catholic and Reformed: The Roman and Protestant Churches in English Protestant Thought, 1600–1640* (Cambridge, 1995).

Morrill, John, *The Scottish National Covenant in its British Context* (Edinburgh, 1990).

Morrill, John, *The Nature of the English Revolution* (1993).

Morrill, John, *Revolt in the Provinces: The People of England and the Tragedies of War 1630–1648*, 2nd edn (Harlow, 1999).

Mortimer, Sarah, *Reason and Religion in the English Revolution: The Challenge of Socinianism* (Cambridge, 2010).

Muldrew, Craig, *Food, Energy and the Creation of Industriousness: Work and Material Culture in Agrarian England, 1550–1780* (Cambridge, 2011).

Murray, Howard J., *A King's Treasure Lost* (Kirkcaldy, 1999).

Murray, Howard J., 'The Great Royal Treasure Hunt', *Scottish Diver* (March/April 1999), 15.

Nelson, C., and Seccombe, M. (eds), *British Newspapers and Periodicals, 1641–1700: A Short-Title Catalogue of Serials Printed in England, Scotland, Ireland, and British America* (1987).

Nichols, John, *The History and Antiquities of the County of Leicestershire*, 4 vols (1795–1815).

O'Day, Rosemary, *The English Clergy: The Emergence and Consolidation of a Profession 1558–1642* (Leicester, 1979).

O'Day, Rosemary, 'The Anatomy of a Profession: The Clergy of the Church of England', in Wilfrid Prest (ed.), *The Professions in Early Modern England* (1987), 25–63.

O'Day, Rosemary, *The Professions in Early Modern England, 1450–1800* (Harlow, 2000).

Parker, Geoffrey, *The Military Revolution: Military Innovation and the Rise of the West, 1500–1800*, 2nd edn (Cambridge, 1996).

Parker, Geoffrey, *Global Crisis: War, Climate Change and Catastrophe in the Seventeenth Century* (London and New Haven, 2013).

Parker, Kenneth L., *The English Sabbath: A Study of Doctrine and Discipline from the Reformation to the Civil War* (Cambridge, 1988).

Parry, Graham, *The Arts of the Anglican Counter-Reformation: Glory, Laud and Honour* (Woodbridge, 2006).

Peacey, Jason, *Politicians and Pamphleteers: Propaganda and Politics during the English Civil Wars and Interregnum* (Aldershot, 2004).

Peacey, Jason, 'The Struggle for *Mercurius Britanicus*: Factional Politics and the Parliamentarian Press, 1643–1646', *Huntington Library Quarterly*, 68 (2005), 517–44.

Peacey, Jason, *Print and Public Politic in the English Revolution* (Cambridge, 2013).

Pelling, Margaret, and White, Francis (eds), *Physicians and Irregular Medical Practitioners in London 1550–1640* (British History Online, 2004), http://www.british-history.ac.uk/report.aspx?compid=17981.

Pestana, Carla Gardina, *The English Atlantic in an Age of Revolution, 1640–1661* (Cambridge, MA, 2004).

Prest, Wilfrid (ed.), *The Professions in Early Modern England* (1987).

Prior, Charles W. A., *A Confusion of Tongues: Britain's Wars of Reformation, 1625–1642* (Oxford, 2012).

Questier, Michael C., *Catholicism and Community in Early Modern England: Politics, Patronage and Religion, c.1550–1640* (Cambridge, 2006).

Quintrell, Brian, 'Charles I and his Navy in the 1630s', *Seventeenth Century*, 3 (1988), 159–79.

Quintrell, Brian, *Charles I 1625–1640* (Harlow, 1993).

Raymond, Joad, *Making the News: An Anthology of the Newsbooks of Revolutionary England 1641–1660* (Moreton-in-Marsh, 1993).

Raymond, Joad, *The Invention of the Newspaper: English Newsbooks 1641–1649* (Oxford, 1996; 2005).

Raymond, Joad, *Pamphlets and Pamphleteering in Early Modern Britain* (Cambridge, 2003).

Reeve, L. J., 'Sir Robert Heath's Advice for Charles I in 1629', *Bulletin of the Institute for Historical Research*, 59 (1986), 215–24.

Reeve, L. J., *Charles I and the Road to Personal Rule* (Cambridge, 1989).

Richards, Judith, '"His Nowe Majestie" and the English Monarchy: The Kingship of Charles I before 1640', *Past & Present*, 113 (1986), 70–96.

Rogers, Clifford J. (ed.), *The Military Revolution Debate: Readings on the Military Transformation of Early Modern Europe* (Boulder, CO, 1995).

Ross, George MacDonald, 'The Royal Touch and the Book of Common Prayer', *Notes and Queries*, NS 30 (1983), 433–5.

Russell, Conrad, *The Crisis of Parliaments: English History 1509–1660* (New York, 1971).

Russell, Conrad, *Parliaments and English Politics, 1621–1629* (Oxford, 1979).

Russell, Conrad, 'The Man Charles Stuart', in Conrad Russell, *The Causes of the English Civil War* (Oxford, 1990), 185–211.

Russell, Conrad, *The Fall of the British Monarchies 1637–1642* (Oxford, 1991).

Schen, Claire S. 'Breaching "Community" in Britain: Captives, Renegades, and the Redeemed', in Michael J. Halvorson and Karen E. Spierling (eds), *Defining Community in Early Modern Europe* (Burlington, VT, 2008), 229–46.

Schramm, Percy Ernst, *A History of the English Coronation* (Oxford, 1937).

Sharp, Buchanan, *In Contempt of All Authority: Rural Artisans and Riot in the West of England, 1586–1660* (Berkeley and Los Angeles, 1980).

Sharp, Buchanan, 'Rural Discontent and the English Revolution', in R. C. Richardson (ed.), *Town and Countryside in the English Revolution* (Manchester, 1992), 259–61.

Sharpe, J. A., *Early Modern England: A Social History 1550–1760*, 2nd edn (1997).

Sharpe, Kevin, 'The Image of Virtue: The Court and Household of Charles I, 1625–1642', in David Starkey et al. (eds), *The English Court: From the Wars of the Roses to the Civil War* (1987), 226–60.

Sharpe, Kevin, *The Personal Rule of Charles I* (New Haven and London, 1992).

Sharpe, Kevin, 'Private Conscience and Public Duty in the Writings of Charles I', *Historical Journal*, 40 (1997), 643–65.

Sharpe, Kevin, *Remapping Early Modern England: The Culture of Seventeenth-Century Politics* (Cambridge, 2000).

Sharpe, Kevin, *Image Wars: Promoting Kings and Commonwealths in England 1603–1660* (New Haven and London, 2010).

Shepard, Alexandra, 'Honesty, Worth and Gender in Early Modern England, 1560–1640', in Henry French and Jonathan Barry (eds), *Identity and Agency in England, 1500–1800* (Basingstoke and New York, 2004), 87–105.

Shepard, Alexandra, and Spicksley, Judith, 'Worth, Age, and Social Status in Early Modern England', *Economic History Review*, 64 (2011), 493–530.

Silcock, R. H.,'Crime, Criminals and Catchers: Worcestershire Assizes Cases in the 1630s and the 1650s', *Parergon*, NS 6 (1988), 179–95.

Sirluck, Ernest,'To your Tents, O Israel: A Lost Pamphlet', *Huntington Library Quarterly*, 19 (1955–6), 301–5.

Smith, David H.,'A Seventeenth Century Tinker's Will and Inventory', *Journal of the Gypsy Lore Society*, 4th ser., 1 (1977), 177.

Smuts, R. Malcolm,'Public Ceremony and Royal Charisma: The English Royal Entry in London 1485–1642', in A. L. Beier, David Cannadine, and James M. Rosenheim (eds), *The First Modern Society: Essays in English History in Honour of Lawrence Stone* (Cambridge, 1989), 65–93.

Sommerville, J. P., *Politics and Ideology in England, 1603–1640* (1986).

Squibb, G. D., *The High Court of Chivalry: A Study of the Civil Law of England* (Oxford, 1959).

Stater, Victor L., 'The Lord Lieutenancy on the Eve of the Civil Wars: The Impressment of George Plowright', *Historical Journal*, 29 (1986), 279–96.

Stearns, Stephen J., 'Conscription and English Society in the 1620s', *Journal of British Studies*, 11 (1972), 1–23.

Stevenson, David, *The Scottish Revolution 1637–44: The Triumph of the Covenanters* (Newton Abbot, 1973).

Stewart, Richard W., 'Arms and Expeditions: The Ordnance Office and the Assaults on Cadiz (1625) and the Isle of Rhé (1627)', in Mark Charles Fissel (ed.), *War and Government in Britain, 1598–1650* (Manchester and New York, 1991), 112–32.

Stone, Lawrence, *The Crisis of the Aristocracy 1558–1641* (Oxford, 1965).

Tallett, Frank, and Trim, D. J. B. (eds), *European Warfare, 1350–1750* (Cambridge, 2010).

Taylor, E. R. G., *The Mathematical Practitioners of Tudor & Stuart England* (Cambridge, 1954).

Terry, C. S., 'The Visits of Charles I to Newcastle in 1633, 1639, 1641, 1646–47, with Some Notes on Contemporary Local History', *Archaeologia Aeliana*, 21 (1899), 83–145.

Thomas, Keith, 'The Place of Laughter in Tudor and Stuart England', *TLS* (21 January 1977), 77–81.

Thrush, Andrew, 'Naval Finance and the Origins and Development of Ship Money', in Mark Charles Fissel (ed.), *War and Government in Britain, 1598–1650* (Manchester and New York, 1991), 133–62.

Thurley, Simon, *Whitehall Palace: An Architectural History of the Royal Apartments, 1240–1698* (New Haven and London, 1999).

Toynbee, M. R., 'Charles I and the King's Evil', *Folk-Lore*, 61 (1950), 1–14.

Tutino, Stefania, 'Huguenots, Jesuits and Tyrants: Notes on the *Vindiciae Contra Tyrannos* in Early Modern England', *Journal of Early Modern History*, 11 (2007), 175–96.

Tyacke, Nicholas, *Anti-Calvinists: The Rise of English Arminianism,* c.*1590–1640* (Oxford, 1987).

Tyacke, Nicholas, *The Fortunes of English Puritanism, 1603–1640* (1990).

Underdown, David, *Revel, Riot and Rebellion: Popular Politics and Culture in England 1603–1660* (Oxford, 1985).

Underdown, David, *A Freeborn People: Politics and the Nation in Seventeenth-Century England* (Oxford, 1996).

Walsham, Alexandra, 'The Parochial Roots of Laudianism Revisited: Catholics, Anti-Calvinists and "Parish Anglicans" in Early Stuart England', *Journal of Ecclesiastical History*, 49 (1998), 620–51.

Walsham, Alexandra, *Providence in Early Modern England* (Oxford, 1999).

Walsham, Alexandra, *The Reformation of the Landscape: Religion, Identity, and Memory in Early Modern Britain and Ireland* (Oxford, 2011).

Walter, John, 'Grain Riots and Popular Attitudes to the Law: Maldon and the Crisis of 1629', in John Brewer and John Styles (eds), *An Ungovernable People: The English and their Law in the Seventeenth and Eighteenth Centuries* (New Brunswick, NJ, 1980), 47–84.

Walter, John, *Crowds and Popular Politics in Early Modern England* (Manchester, 2006).

Walter, John, '"Affronts & Insolences": The Voices of Radwinter and Popular Opposition to Laudianism', *English Historical Review*, 122 (2007), 25–60.

Walter, John, 'Gesturing at Authority: Deciphering the Gestural Code of Early Modern England', in Michael J. Braddick (ed.), *The Politics of Gesture* (Oxford: Past & Present Supplement, 4, 2009), 96–127.

Watts, Sylvia, 'The Impact of Laudianism on the Parish: The Evidence of Staffordshire and North Shropshire', *Midland History*, 33 (2008), 21–42.

Waurechen, Sarah, 'Covenanter Propaganda and Conceptualizations of the Public during the Bishops' Wars', *Historical Journal*, 52 (2009), 63–86.

Webster, Tom, *Godly Clergy in Early Stuart England: The Caroline Puritan Movement, c.1620–1643* (Cambridge, 1997).

Weiser, Brian, *Charles II and the Politics of Access* (Woodbridge, 2003).

Weston, Corine Comstock, and Greenberg, Janelle Renfrow, *Subjects and Sovereigns: The Grand Controversy over Legal Sovereignty in Stuart England* (Cambridge, 1981).

Whincup, P. H., Cook, D. G., and Shaper, A. G., 'Social Class and Height', *British Medical Journal*, 297 (15 October 1988), 980–1.

White, Peter, 'The *Via Media* in the Early Stuart Church', in Kenneth Fincham (ed.), *The Early Stuart Church, 1603–1642* (1993), 211–30.

Wood, Andy, *The Politics of Social Conflict: The Peak Country, 1520–1770* (Cambridge, 1999).

Wood, Andy, *Riot, Rebellion and Popular Politics in Early Modern England* (Basingstoke, 2002).

Wood, Andy, *The 1549 Rebellion and the Making of Early Modern England* (Cambridge, 2007).

Wood, Andy, 'Deference, Paternalism and Popular Memory in Early Modern England', in Steve Hindle, Alexandra Shepard, and John Walter (eds), *Remaking English Society: Social Relations and Social Change in Early Modern England* (Woodbridge, 2013), 233–53.

Wood, Andy, *The Memory of the People: Custom and Popular Senses of the Past in Early Modern England* (Cambridge, 2013).

Woolrych, Austin, *Britain in Revolution 1625–1660* (Oxford, 2002).

Wrightson, Keith, *English Society 1580–1680* (1982).

Wrightson, Keith, '"Sorts of People" in Tudor and Stuart England', in Jonathan Barry and Christopher Brooks (eds), *The Middling Sort of People: Society and Politics in England, 1550–1800* (1994), 28–51.

Wrightson, Keith, *Earthly Necessities: Economic Lives in Early Modern England* (New Haven and London, 2000).

Wrightson, Keith, 'Mutualities and Obligations: Changing Relationships in Early Modern England', *Proceedings of the British Academy*, 139 (2006), 157–94.

Wrigley, E. A., and Schofield, R. S., *The Population History of England 1541–1871* (Cambridge, MA, 1981).

Yule, George, 'James VI and I: Furnishing the Churches in his Two Kingdoms', in Anthony Fletcher and Peter Roberts (eds), *Religion, Culture and Society in Early Modern Britain: Essays in Honor of Patrick Collinson* (Cambridge, 1994), 182–208.

Zaller, Robert, 'Breaking the Vessels: The Desacralization of Monarchy in Early Modern England', *Sixteenth Century Journal*, 29 (1998), 757–78.

Zaret, David, 'Petitions and the "Invention" of Public Opinion in the English Revolution', *American Journal of Sociology*, 101 (1996), 1497–555.

Picture Acknowledgements

Bodleian Library, University of Oxford: **Figures 6** (Wood 401 (139)), **7** (C 13.13 (34) Linc.); © The British Library Board: **Figures 3** (c13143-30), **8** (STC 19248); Folger Shakespeare Library: **Figures 2, 9, 10**; The Huntington Library, San Marino, California: **Figures 4** (RB 63503), **5** (RB 59219), **11** (RB 60711); Society of Antiquaries: **Figure 1**; University of Toronto Wenceslaus Hollar Digital Collection/Wikimedia Commons: **Figure 12**.

Index